A Global History of History

A global history of historical writing, thought and the development of the historical discipline from the ancient world to the present. This is a definitive guide to human efforts to recover, understand and represent the past, bringing together different historical traditions and their social, economic, political and cultural contexts. Daniel Woolf offers clear definitions of different genres and forms of history and addresses key themes such as the interactions between West and East, the conflict of oral, pictographic and written accounts of the past and the place of history in society and in politics. Numerous textual extracts and illustrations in every chapter capture the historical cultures of past civilizations and demonstrate the different forms that historical consciousness has taken around the world. This book offers unique insights into the interconnections between different historical cultures over 3,000 years and relates the rise of history to key themes in world history. Special attention is paid to connections between the modern dominance of Western forms of historical consciousness and the impact of European empires on other parts of the world.

Daniel Woolf is Professor of History at Queen's University, Kingston, Ontario where he is currently also Principal and Vice-Chancellor. His previous publications include *Reading History in Early Modern England* (Cambridge, 2000) and the two-volume *Global Encyclopedia of Historical Writing* (1998). He is also general editor of the *Oxford History of Historical Writing* (2010–).

A Global History
of History

Daniel Woolf

QUEEN'S UNIVERSITY
KINGSTON, ONTARIO, CANADA

CAMBRIDGE
UNIVERSITY PRESS

CAMBRIDGE UNIVERSITY PRESS
Cambridge, New York, Melbourne, Madrid, Cape Town,
Singapore, São Paulo, Delhi, Tokyo, Mexico City

Cambridge University Press
The Edinburgh Building, Cambridge CB2 8RU, UK

Published in the United States of America by Cambridge University Press, New York

www.cambridge.org
Information on this title: www.cambridge.org/9780521699082

First published 2011

Printed in the United Kingdom at the University Press, Cambridge

A catalogue record for this publication is available from the British Library

ISBN 978-0-521-87575-2 Hardback
ISBN 978-0-521-69908-2 Paperback

For JAGW

CONTENTS

ILLUSTRATIONS

TEXT EXTRACTS

SUBJECT BOXES

PREFACE AND CONVENTIONS

The purpose of this book, in brief, is to provide a history of history, suitable for undergraduates, faculty members seeking a relatively concise introduction to the subject and the interested general reader. Many years of teaching courses on historiography, and the prescription of several different textbooks for the students in those courses, convinced me that a further work was needed, but most of all I have been struck for many years by the relative dearth of studies of 'historiography' (a term for discussion of which see below, in the introduction) which covered the entire span of human efforts to recover, understand and represent the past, from earliest known times to the present, and that did so in a geographically inclusive manner. There are several books covering very long time spans, and one or two with a global reach, but none in English, of which I am aware, that do both. A conviction that students ought to be exposed to the 'historical cultures' of other civilizations than their own has thus informed my choice of subject; a strong sense that there is a story to be told about the development of historical thought, historical writing and the modern historical discipline, and that it relates directly to some of the larger movements of world history (in particular the global engagement of different peoples and cultures over several millennia), provides the 'plot', if a work on historiography can be said to have a plot.

The years of teaching various aspects of the subject have also convinced me that students, especially those in compulsory courses on historiography, dislike most textbooks because they consist of a parade of names of great historians, most of whom the student has never heard of, and will in all likelihood never read, unless they go on to advanced study in the field. I have therefore tried to avoid creating such a parade, though the necessity of inclusiveness and breadth means that I may not always have succeeded. I have found that students unnecessarily fear historiography as 'difficult' or 'dull' (though it is not always clear what they mean by either word). Since the first time I heard the term 'historiography' as an undergraduate and began to write papers of various sorts (and ultimately a doctoral thesis) on historiographic topics, I have had a fascination with how we have, as a species, come to terms with the past. I find the great works of historiography as intellectually exciting and riveting as many great works of literature, though it is true that very few historians have written works that command a wide readership today. Many other past historical works, of lesser literary merit, can nonetheless provide us with windows into past cultures' ideas about their own pasts, and with traces of now-vanished notions about scholarship and truth. A broadening of my own horizons in the past fifteen years has not changed my attitude to the 'classic' histories, but it has led me to many non-Western works of historiography and thus to a different perspective on the more familiar 'canon' of great historians from Thucydides to the present. Many of these non-Western works are, happily, gradually becoming more readily available in English and other European languages.

While the chapters of this book are free-standing and can be assigned separately, the reader will derive more from the book if he or she reads them in order: there is, again, an argument and a story, and there is a continuity of themes between chapters.

In order to make the book more accessible, and allow it to serve multiple purposes, I have introduced a few features that are not normally found in texts on historiography. These are connected to, but can again, stand apart from, the main narrative. Four features in particular require explanation.

- The first is a series of 'Subject Boxes'. These provide additional detail on particular episodes or important points in the history of history, and sometimes on individual historians, approaches or 'schools'. They can be read on their own and are separated from the main narrative both in order to highlight them and not to distract from the account in the chapter itself.
- The second is a parallel series of offset 'Extracts', in addition to the quotations that appear in the main text. These are designed to provide illustrative examples, principally of lesser-known histories or historians, and often of non-European historical works (or works indicating historical consciousness even if they do not fit the normal expectations of what a history should look like). Quotations in the text proper routinely illustrate a point being made in the book; the offset extracts, while generally illustrative, can be detached and analysed separately. Instructors may, of course, find these too brief, and wish to prescribe separate, lengthier extracts from other works, or even the complete text by a particular historian, a Herodotus or Voltaire. In my experience, there is relatively little time in a twelve-week or even twenty-four-week course for students to read very many complete works, though it is certainly hoped that some will be sufficiently excited by the topic that they wish to pursue it on their own, or in further courses.
- The third is an annotated 'Further Reading' section for each chapter (rather than a single amalgamated bibliography), which can be found at the end of the book. On occasion, where two or more sections share several titles in common, their further reading sections have been combined; and in Chapter 8, an additional bibliographical appendix has been supplied, arranged by nation or region, reflecting

one important theme (the connection between history and modern nationalism) of that chapter. In the case of books for which there are multiple editions I have listed the edition which I have consulted, while sometimes noting for clarity the original year in which the work was published. This is especially necessary with some secondary works widely available in modern paperback editions but in fact authored many years or even decades ago and thus likely to have been superseded or at least modified by subsequent scholarship.

- The fourth feature is the inclusion of a number of pictures. With a few exceptions, these avoid the 'portrait gallery' (to go along with the textual 'parade') of famous historians. On rare occasions where images of individual historians are included it is typically in order to reveal something about contemporary (or later) perceptions of them. In several instances, the pictures are intended to help illustrate a particular point or to give the reader a clearer idea of the actual appearance of an object referred to, especially where dealing with physical forms of history other than the book (for instance, Inca quipus and Mesoamerican pictorial histories).

Diacriticals and transliteration

In a work such as this where many languages and scripts come into play, a balance needs to be struck between fidelity to the original and readability for the non-expert. I have thus in several instances adopted a 'minimal-diacritical' approach.

For Arabic the full standard system which I have followed in other works is unnecessarily elaborate in a book such as this which is intended for the relative novice. I have followed the usage and spellings in C. F. Robinson, *Islamic Historiography* (Cambridge, 2003), including dots above and below letters and bars above, but dispensing with underlined characters. With familiar proper or family names that are frequently used in English (such as 'Abbasid', 'Mamluk' or 'Muhammad'), diacriticals have been dispensed with.

In Arabic, the mark ' denotes a letter ('ayn) often transliterated as an inward facing single quotation mark; ' denotes a quite distinct character, hamza. Hamzas and 'ayns have generally been retained, using this form of transliteration.

Indian names and words are also heavily accented, especially those from earlier periods, but these marks have normally been discarded in sections on modern India and modern Indian historians, in keeping with current scholarly practice on the subcontinent.

Roman alphabet titles of books are not adjusted but appear as they would in normal bibliographical records.

Chinese names and words are rendered according to the pinyin system, which has supplanted the older Wade-Giles system as the standard protocol for transliteration: thus Mao Zedong not Mao Tse-tung. Certain exceptions to this rule apply for historians with established Western names, such as Confucius, whose Chinese name was either Kong Qiu or Kong Zi (Master Kong). The names of Chinese historians publishing in Western languages, and the titles of books originally issued in those languages, follow the actual spelling of the author or title, whether Wade-Giles or pinyin.

Korean words and names are more problematic, as no system has yet achieved dominance, including the long-standing McCune-Reischauer system, and romanization practices thus vary. I have therefore often provided alternative spellings of a word or name.

Chinese, Korean and Japanese names appear with the family name first followed *without a comma* by the given name. This is well-known and common practice for Chinese and Korean, but in the case of Japanese, Western journalistic practice has tended to invert the name order according to North American usage, a practice that we have not followed: thus a reference to Ienaga Saburō denotes a historian whose surname is Ienaga. Occasional exceptions, mainly historians whose names appear Western-style on their English-language publications, are indexed *with* commas to avoid confusion; a few Japanese historians (Motoori Norinaga and Hayashi Razan for instance) are by convention referred to by their given names, e.g. Norinaga. As with Arabic, where a word has become commonplace in English usage (for instance 'shogun'), the diacriticals are omitted.

Adjectives or adverbs constructed out of foreign terms, usually for the purpose of grouping a category of person or text, dispense with diacriticals. Thus we write on India about *purāṇa* (the noun), but about puranic texts.

Where the system of transliteration in a quoted or extracted text differs from my own usage (as for instance in the case of Chinese, where most translations until recently followed the Wade-Giles method, while I have used the now-standard pinyin system), I have maintained the spelling as it is in the source of the extract or quotation, and of course in actual titles of modern books and articles. Thus the historian referred to by me as 'Sima Qian' is the same individual referred to by earlier authors as 'Ssu-ma Ch'ien', which is simply the same name in Wade-Giles transliteration; Ban Gu is Pan Ku, and so on; the Qing dynasty is the same as the Ch'ing; and Mao Zedong is Mao Tse-tung. Occasionally where I have felt more explicit signposting is justified I have inserted the pinyin spelling in square brackets.

Citations and quotations

In an effort to maximize readability, footnotes have been kept to a minimum and are used to document very specific points and quotations or, on occasion, to add a detail of interest but not essential to the main narrative. Where a fact or point is uncontroversial, well known or contained in many other books, no footnote is provided. Bibliographic references for primary quotations and the longer extracts that accompany the main text are given in full. Not every item cited in a footnote is included in the 'Further reading' section.

Titles of historical works cited within the main text are routinely given in their original language (transliterated if in a non-Roman script) with an English translation of that title following in quotation marks, within parentheses; such translated titles are generally not italicized except where used subsequently in the main text or, naturally, if a particular edition of the work is cited, as in the footnotes and bibliography. The purpose of this somewhat cumbersome practice is to provide an understandable translation (typically one used in the secondary works on which I have relied) to English-speaking readers while also easing reference back to the work in its original language for those willing and able to read it. Where the meaning of a title seems reasonably obvious, or is cited fully in a note, no parenthetical translation is provided, and in some instances I have, for the sake of brevity, simply referred to a work by its most familiar English title. The foreign names of journals and periodicals are not normally translated, e.g. *Historische Zeitschrift*.

Dates

A multitude of calendars have been used by various peoples in the course of the past five thousand years. Full compliance with the non-Eurocentric principles of this book would suggest that dates be recorded as the authors being described recorded them, for instance using the Hijri year of the Muslim calendar. However, this would be far more confusing than helpful. While a compromise might have been to use dates in the format of Common Era (CE)/Before the Common Era (BCE), I have opted for familiarity and simplicity and used the more conventional 'BC' and 'AD'.

Vital dates (where known) for most historians (and many who were not historians but nonetheless figure in the narrative) are provided in the main text. Certain abbreviations for dates have been used:

b. = born, in the case of historians still living as of mid-2010.

c. = *circa*, approximate year where no firm year is known or agreed upon.

comp. = composed during or complete by.

d. = died. Used where a firm death year is known (or approximate, in which case noted as 'd. *c.*').

est. = established, for instance, a journal or historical society.

fl. = 'floruit', that is 'flourished': generally used in relation to authors for whom birth and death dates are entirely unknown or highly obscure; indicates active period.

r. = 'reigned'. When a monarch is noted, his or her regnal years, not years of birth and death, are noted in parentheses. The same applies to non-monarchical but significant officials, for instance popes.

In some cases alternative dates are used either because of lack of agreement in scholarship as to a single date, or in some instances because the date itself is tied to a particular chronological scheme which itself is ambiguous.

ACKNOWLEDGMENTS

The many historians mentioned in the next several hundred pages often acknowledged patrons, employers, monarchs and those who provided them with information or correction. It is both appropriate and a pleasure for me to do so in the case of this book.

My various undergraduate instructors (at Queen's University, to which I have recently returned) and graduate mentors at Oxford encouraged my early interest in historiography. They are too numerous to name individually, as are the dozens of colleagues in both early modern British/European history and, latterly, the broader history of historiography, whom I have met and profited from over several decades. Colleagues at the several other institutions in which I have worked generously provided references and suggestions. I have similarly learned a great deal from the many contributors to the *Global Encyclopedia of Historical Writing*, which I edited in the 1990s, and to its more recent successor, still in the process of appearing, *The Oxford History of Historical Writing*. I would, however, like to thank by name (though some of them have not always agreed with me on particular points or even approach), Michael Aung-Thwin, Michael Bentley, Stefan Berger, Peter Burke, William Connell, Antoon De Baets, Ewa Domańska, Georg Iggers, Donald R. Kelley, Ann Kumar, the late Joseph Levine, Fritz Levy, Chris Lorenz, Juan Maiguashca, Allan Megill, J. G. A. Pocock, Attila Pók, José Rabasa, Jörn Rüsen, Dominic Sachsenmaier, Masayuki Sato, Axel Schneider, Romila Thapar, Edoardo Tortarolo, Markus Völkel, Q. Edward Wang and Hayden White. Several institutions have invited me to lecture on historiography in the past few years and I have profited from questions and criticisms received on those occasions; in particular, a workshop on global historiography at the University of Vienna in April 2010, organized by Professor Deborah Klimburg-Salter, allowed me a dry run of the book's introduction. I must also acknowledge my debt to the work of two historiographers a generation senior to me (and whom I have corresponded with but regrettably never met in person), Ernst Breisach and the late John Burrow, both authors of surveys of Western historiography. If my book differs substantively from their own, especially in its geographic scope, it is the better for having obliged me to think carefully about the basis of that difference.

Maryanne Cline Horowitz, general editor of the *New Dictionary of the History of Ideas*, invited me in 2002 to write an essay on historiography for that publication.

The present book is an expansion of that essay, and I thank Michael Watson at Cambridge University Press both for encouraging me to write it and for his patience through many revisions. I thank Rosina di Marzo at the Press for having shepherded the book through production and Rose Bell for exemplary copyediting. I am grateful to the Board of Governors at my former institution, the University of Alberta, for providing me with a year's leave during which a (much longer) first draft of the book was written, and to the University of Alberta's Vice-President (Research) and Provost and Vice-President (Academic) for funding that allowed, among other things, the acquisition of the many illustrations and the hiring of graduate research assistance. Among my own graduate students at Alberta and (after 2009) Queen's, principally in the area of early modern England, who have put up with my digressions into global historiography, and often provided perceptive feedback, I thank Matthew Neufeld, Sarah Waurechen and Jane Wong Yeang-Chui. Other graduate students have assisted in other ways (including summarizing for me books in languages which I do not read), in particular Tanya Henderson, Carolyn Salomons, Tony Maan and Nina Paulovicova. The experience of teaching historiography to many students at all levels at Queen's (during an earlier, postdoctoral, stage of my career), Bishop's, Dalhousie, McMaster and the University of Alberta added immeasurably to my sense of what I liked in other textbooks and what I did not, which was of course not always the same as what the students liked.

Ian Hesketh, my research associate at Queen's, took time out from his other duties to provide a ruthlessly sharp critique and meticulous editing of the first version of the manuscript, shrinking it down from its previously unmanageable size. His ability to turn five words into two without loss of clarity is enviable. But for his assistance, the book would have been much later to appear, and unnecessarily long. He also provided invaluable assistance in the home stretch by compiling the timelines of key texts and events included in each chapter.

Several historians (including some already named above) provided extra assistance in the form of bibliographic references, clarification of particular points and readings of parts or whole of the manuscript. Apart from three anonymous referees for Cambridge University Press, all of whom provided commentary and suggestions for improvement, I thank for reading significant chunks of the book Donald Baker, John Bentley, Adam Budd (an exacting stylistic critique of the last four chapters), Fernando Cervantes, Tarif Khalidi and Baki Tezcan; and (again) Q. Edward Wang, José Rabasa, Juan Maiguashca, Romila Thapar, Dominic Sachsenmaier and Michael Aung-Thwin. Georg Iggers, who has been an ally for nearly twenty years in my conviction that historiography needed to be globalized, carefully read the entire manuscript. He alerted me very late in the process that my interpretation of twentieth-century trends, and my assessment of the current state of the discipline, had become more negative than I in fact intended.

As is customary, I preserve my greatest debts for last. My three children, Sarah, Samuel and David, have provided great joy and pride from their early childhood into adulthood; they have been among the rare class of pre-schoolers able to pronounce the word 'historiography'. My parents continue into their eighties to convey a convincing interest in and understanding of what I do for a living. Above all, my wife Julie Anne Gordon-Woolf, health administrator, part-time professional harpist and latterly spouse of a university vice-chancellor, has accompanied me on both my geographical and intellectual peregrinations, and has been a voice of encouragement, patience and reason throughout the project – a gift this tribute cannot remotely repay. It is to her that I dedicate this book.

And, as is also customary, none of the persons thanked here is responsible for the errors of fact or judgment that may remain.

DRW

Kingston, Ontario, April 2010

Introduction

> [T]he animal lives unhistorically ... Man, on the other hand, braces himself against the great and ever greater pressure of what is past: it pushes him down or bends him sideways, it encumbers his steps as a dark, invisible burden which he would like to disown, so as to excite their envy.[1]

'History' exists today because humans have the biological and neurological capacity to remember things and to frame relationships of a causal or symbolic nature around those things that have been remembered. It exists also because we are social creatures whose survival has been more or less dependent upon connections with other members of our species. We will never know the identity of the first human who, curious about his – or her – past, decided to inquire into the origins of his or her tribe, village or family, or what motivated that person to do so. This does not matter very much. The human inclination to unearth knowledge of one's past may well be natural rather than acquired (though no 'history gene' has yet been mapped). One modern scholar has even suggested that 'History is a human universal. Knowledge of the past is expressed by all human beings according to their different cultural and social systems. History is a generic form of consciousness in which the past experience of oneself or of others in an environment outside oneself is transformed into symbols that are exchanged.'[2]

However, the capacity to remember is not sufficient on its own to create the conditions for history to be made. Humans are the only species capable of *both* forming long-term memory (beyond the simple recollection of how to perform tasks or how to find a particular familiar location) *and* of communications. It is this latter function that permits the transmission of those memories, and other knowledge, to other members of the species. Written communication has been a significant technological enhancement to the preservation and communication of information over long distances or across long spans of time, but it is a relatively recent development, dating back at most five millennia to the earliest cuneiform tablets in Mesopotamia, to hieroglyphics in Egypt, and to bone inscriptions in China. Before then, humans relied on spoken language to communicate, and we know that very ancient cultures eventually learned to use speech, specifically in the form of poetry and song, to commemorate the deeds of the gods and heroes in their past. The oral beginnings of what we now call historical thinking and historical knowledge are long acknowledged; it will be repeated at points throughout this book that writing per se is not, as used to be thought, essential to their development, even in the modern era.

Distinguishing History from 'History'

What is now called 'history' in English goes by many different names in European languages alone: *histoire* in French, *Geschichte* in German, *storia* in Italian, *dzieje* in Polish, история in Russian. It has often been thought of in ways that we would now deem strange, even 'unhistorical'. Because this book is being written in English, I will use terms such as 'history', 'historical thought' and 'historical knowledge' frequently.

My choice of word usage requires a bit more elaboration. For the sake of clarity I have adopted the following practice. The word 'history', when used in English and not otherwise explained or clarified, should be taken as including the following meanings, depending upon the context of the discussion:

(a) a variety of forms (not all of which are written) in which the past is recovered, thought of, spoken of and written down, but *not* the evidence from the past used by the historian, speaker or thinker in constructing their text, speech, story, painting or monument;

(b) a particular *type* of historical writing, composed in continuous prose, as distinct from annals or chronicles arranged into discontinuous annual chunks (though we will see that this distinction is not always helpful, especially in pre-modern times, or in non-European contexts such as China);

(c) the 'discipline' of history as it has developed in the two centuries just passed.

All of these refer back in some way to accounts of the past or their manufacture rather than to the past itself. But 'history' has in the last quarter millennium acquired a fourth, and very different meaning, namely the 'accumulated events of the past' or even, when given qualities of personhood, intent, agency and moral preference, 'the manifest direction of the accumulated events of the past'. This is the sense in which the word has been used by certain philosophers of history and world historians from the time of G. W. F. Hegel in the early nineteenth century to that of Francis Fukuyama at the end of the twentieth and, with greater harm, by politicians, generals and ideologues of various persuasions who were convinced that 'History' was on their side – a crushing and merciless tsunami atop which they surfed as it obliterated those who stood in its way. This sense is a modern one, dating from the late eighteenth century, though there are certainly historians or historical thinkers, some of them discussed in this book, who well before Hegel treated the past as a collective and decodable pattern, worth speculating about. Because our subjects sometimes refer to 'History' in this sense, we must on occasion also do so when discussing their work. To make clear that I am referring to that usage (which E. H. Carr rejected along with providence, world spirit and manifest destiny)[3] and not any of those listed above as (a), (b) and (c), I have routinely capitalized the word 'History' when it is deployed in this way. Lower-case 'history', then, will denote variously the set of literary (and non-literary) forms that *contain* thought or statements about the past, *a mode of thinking about the past* as a set of events that occurred in real time and, in modern times, a professional *discipline*.

These small-h meanings, however, are also not entirely the same, nor do they relate to each other in identical ways across all cultures: it is possible to separate out the content, historical thinking, from the container and, conversely, to find various 'modes' of thinking, historical, poetic and mythical, within a single genre or a variety of genres, all of which are specific to time and place. '[H]istory can be, and is, composed in many genres', comment the three authors of a recent book on South Asian historical thought. 'The choice belongs with the historian, who aims at a particular audience and conforms to the preferences and exigencies of a given moment. A single story can also pass from one genre to another as it moves from one social milieu to another...' We would do well to remember the following: history is an act of communication (generally now verbal and graphic but, as we will see, sometimes through other means) between an author/speaker and a reader/ audience; and the truth value of any statement about the past is determined not only by *what* is contained in a text or recitation but in *how* the historian believes an audience will react to it, and how, in fact, that audience actually does so. South Asian audiences knew perfectly well, because of their sense of 'texture', when a work was being factual and when it was sliding into fiction, without it necessarily being signposted by the author.[4] This is not so very different from the kind of double-belief that Paul Veyne has ascribed to the ancient Greeks,[5] or which applied among the retellers of popular tales about the past in sixteenth- and seventeenth-century England. 'Truthful' and 'factual' are not identical and interchangeable terms, something which writers on poetics from Aristotle through Sidney, even working without a modern conception of the 'fact', recognized in asserting the truth value of poetry.

What Is Historiography?

Another word which will appear often is 'historiography'. Although this word has been used at various times to describe the writing of history, in the present book it will denote both 'history-writing' (its literal sense) and secondarily what we might call the 'meta' level of historical thinking, that is, the study of how history itself has been written, spoken or thought about over several millennia and in a wide variety of cultures. 'Historiography', like 'history', requires a bit more definition because, like 'history', it is fraught with different meanings. While it clearly (and *unlike* 'history/History') can never mean *the past*, and while in a strict sense it is almost by definition a written record of the past (the syllable 'graph' refers to written symbols), no two 'historiography' courses on a university curriculum will necessarily intend the same thing in using the word. In some modern history departments it would be possible, for instance, for a student to take a number of different courses called 'historiography', dealing with any of the following:

(a) a study of historical methods – essentially a 'how to do history' course; a variant of this is the study of historical errors and fallacies, or how *not* to do history;

(b) the review and study of the state of knowledge and key debates in one national area, sub-discipline or historical event, for instance 'recent trends in Sino-Japanese historiography' or (more clearly) 'the historiography of the Russian Revolution', where what is being referred to is past and current scholarship *about* the Russian Revolution, and not the writings of Pokrovskii, Pankratova and other historians active before and after 1917;

(c) the history of historical writing, as in 'Japanese historiography from the sixteenth to the nineteenth centuries', typically a review of the great historians and their texts, but sometimes expanding outward to consider non-canonical works, and even the wider social and cultural contexts within which such works were produced.

Among these three usages of the word 'historiography' we will not be using (a) very much if at all, even though we will have occasion to discuss the history of historical methods, and of what are sometimes called 'ancillary disciplines' to history, such as epigraphy (the study of inscriptions) and palaeography (the deciphering of old or unfamiliar handwriting); some celebrated historical errors and mis-steps will also be mentioned incidentally, in particular a number of infamous 'fakes'. Nor will usage (b) often appear. Where the word is used it will generally be as defined above by (c). In that sense, again, this entire book is an exercise in historiography, albeit of a more global range than the more traditional survey running from Herodotus through the nineteenth-century German Leopold von Ranke to today and invariably excluding anything outside the borders of Europe or North America. But two further qualifications must be added even here. First, the word 'historiography' in some past cultures has come to acquire a fourth possible meaning (d), now archaic in Western parlance, as something very close to or synonymous with 'history', that is, an account of the past. When authors of the Renaissance and seventeenth century, for instance, wished to refer to the authors of historical works (including often their own), they often indiscriminately blended the two. Thus the early sixteenth-century Florentine writer Francesco Guicciardini might be described as a 'historian' by one contemporary commentator and as a 'historiographer' by another. As late as the mid-eighteenth century, Voltaire used both terms, though in his case to draw an important distinction (see Chapter 6 below) between the *historiographe*, an officially sponsored compiler, and the *historien*, an independent writer of superior stylistic ability, answering only to his conscience and his public. This conflation of the two terms becomes even more complicated when dealing with the select group of authors who wrote not only about the past but about writing about the past. This is a smallish number, but it spans the world and goes back many hundred years to antiquity, including along the way notables from the Chinese critic Liu Zhiji in the eighth century to the French scholars Jean Bodin and Henri de la Popelinière in the late sixteenth century, to a modern-day writer such as the late classicist Arnaldo Momigliano. Most of these individuals thus wrote both history and historiography, the latter being understood as 'history of history' or 'consideration of the past and present practices and beliefs of historians'.

And that raises the second qualification. This book is an exercise in a particular type of historiography, the history of historical thought and writing. Its subjects are the many people, a majority but not all of them men until the twentieth century, who have recovered and/or represented the past either out of personal interest or with some wider social or political purpose in mind. And the book itself is also a *history* because it tells a story, in narrative form, of a particular subject over time, that subject being the genre or practice of which the book is a specimen. Yet the book is not, narrowly speaking, a history of *historiography* in senses (c) or (d), whether European or more global, if by that we limit ourselves to the modern conception of all history being written or printed and contained on paper or some similar material. Certainly, that will be a major topic. However, I have deliberately called this volume *A Global History of History* (and not *A Global History of Historiography*, or *A Global History of Historical Writing*) because I wish to include within its purview some other roads to the past which are often very different from written history. These would include, to provide two examples, the oral traditions from remote times or the direct testimony of eyewitnesses that, despite an overwhelming inclination towards the written word, historians and others have periodically used as an alternative access point into past events. They would also include non-scribal forms by which the past can be represented, some of which are simply writings in a different medium than paper or parchment (for instance ancient Mesopotamian stone chronicles, or Shang-era Chinese oracle bones), but others of which are strictly aural or visual rather than graphic. A good example of the latter is the quipu used, in conjunction with oral performance, by the pre-Columbian Andean peoples of Peru, who had no written language, to record their past.

Having said this, the book will not be concerned with *all* forms of representation of the past at *all* times and in *every* part of the world; much less is it intended as a comprehensive record of historiographical activity and its practitioners. To put it another way, this is a history of history *in* and *throughout* the world, but not a history of *all* the world's histories. Some countries feature quite often, others are drawn on for occasional illustration, and many will not be mentioned at all, a silence which should emphatically not be taken as implying that these are countries without historiography or, to borrow Eric R. Wolf's famous phrase, 'people without history'.[6] This is not a dictionary or encyclopedia (though several of these now do exist) of historians and historiography, and the curious reader should not look to this book for a concise account of Lithuanian or Sri Lankan historical writing, or for that matter British, American or Chinese historical writing, much less treat it as a reference source for biographical details on the 'great' historians of all countries.[7] So far as types of historical representation are concerned, several exclusions have been made, including historical fiction and history plays and, in more recent times, historical films and popular festivals. These retain an incidental place in the narrative, not least because many past eras did not make a firm distinction between a 'history' as contained in a play or poem and one contained in prose, nor even between a prose chronicle such as that published by the Elizabethan Englishman Raphael Holinshed and a history play as created by Shakespeare out of the materials contained in that chronicle. We cannot exclude an author such as Shakespeare entirely, any more than we should exclude Homer from a consideration of ancient Greek thought about the past, since the boundaries of the literally true and the imaginatively embellished have always been ambiguous. (We did not need a raft of late twentieth-century books on theory to tell us this, though perhaps the reminder was in order after a century or more of conceiving history as 'the true story of the past'.) Nor will we address, except in passing during the final chapter of the book, public manifestations of history such as monuments – the *lieux de mémoire* that Pierre Nora and others have drawn our attention to in recent years – or public celebrations (the 1989 bicentennial of the French Revolution for instance) or, the evolution of history curricula in school textbooks. All of these are worthy, important topics, but others are better qualified than I to write about them, and to include them all here would result in an unmanageably long, and hopelessly disparate, book that would not serve any constituency well.

Different Global Versions of History

Let us take up again the names by which history has been known. It is important to understand that translations are not always exact, and that many cultures do not have a single word that exactly corresponds to our 'history', for the very reason that they do not conceive of knowledge of the past in the same way, or classify its literary representations according to the same categories. The Chinese character 史, for example, which transliterates as 'shi', is often taken to mean either history or historian, but it originally meant 'scribe' or 'one who writes' (there is no usage of 'history' in Chinese that equates with 'the past', in contrast to the West). The meaning of *shi* changed in the sixteenth and seventeenth centuries whence it truly began to denote history rather than a scribe. Variants such as *guoshi* (national histories) and *tongshi* (general histories) eventually emerged.[8] Pre-Columbian American peoples had ways of preserving and recalling the past that did not in some cases involve writing at all – the above-mentioned quipus and Mesoamerican painted histories, for example. Many African peoples relied, until relatively recent times, on oral traditions, though in some places writing had developed either indigenously (as in Ethiopia) or through contact with Christianity and especially Islam.

This last point is essential to the conception of the current book. Because history comes in various forms and shapes, we must not confuse the vessel with its content – even though the vessel itself very clearly *shapes* the content, because the available forms of transmission and communication predetermine what can be known and how it is selected for preservation. A multitude of different civilizations that have inhabited this planet have conceived of the past in different ways, formulated different notions of its relationship to the present, and evolved different terms to denote its representation. These must be taken on their own merits and judged by their own standards, not by the fairly narrow standards of modern professional historians. On the other hand, they should not be studied entirely in isolation. Just as the history of the world is a story of encounters and conflicts between different peoples, so the history of history itself demonstrates that the different modes of knowing the past have often come into contact with and demonstrably influenced one another. With the advantage of hindsight, it looks now as if all the various streams of historical thinking that the world has seen have now flowed into the rather large lake of professional history built on European and especially nineteenth-century German academic practice. But this result was by no means inevitable, nor was it necessarily analogous to a conquest, since in many cases Western practices were willingly adopted, even zealously pursued by, social reformers in other countries seeking an alternative to long-standing and, to them, restrictive indigenous practices. Perhaps of even greater importance, the influences were not always in one direction. While Western history has certainly come to be the dominant model, it has in turn been profoundly influenced by its encounters with other forms of historical knowledge, even if only sharpening definitions of what history should and should not be by comparing it with an exotic but lesser 'other'. Spanish historical writing of the sixteenth century certainly had a huge impact on how the past of the newly discovered Americas was written, but the early modern missionaries who wrote those histories had to adapt their writings to the sources available in native oral and pictographic practices. I will argue further on that these contacts, and this growing awareness of alternative modes of historicity, obliged Europeans to make some decisions about what *they* deemed 'within-scope' for true history, and thereby prepared the ground for a hardening of European attitudes in the seventeenth and eighteenth centuries. This in turn set the table for the nineteenth-century achievement of Western hegemony over history – what I have termed in one chapter 'Clio's empire'. I have used the figure of Clio, the Greek muse supposed to have been daughter of Zeus and Mnemosyne (memory), frequently in this book as both a symbol and an image of the West's historical culture, and eventually the planet's. The book's cover features Clio in a striking iconographic representation of the link between history and empire. Its early nineteenth-century artist, who wanted to draw attention to Napoleon's 'historic' achievements, did so by having the classically garbed figure of the muse, a Roman-style bust of the emperor to her right (viewer's left), display a slate listing (in French) Napoleonic achievements to a number of figures representing the peoples of the world. The bust itself connects Napoleon with ancient Rome rather unsubtly via both the laurel and the inscription, 'Veni, Vidi, Vici' – the phrase 'I came, I saw, I conquered' ascribed by Plutarch and Suetonius to Julius Caesar. Clio gestures towards the bust with her left hand and holds the slate in her right (it is French, the modern language, not Latin, that is at the centre of the painting). Several of Clio's assembled audience raise their right hands in acknowledgment of, and apparent acquiescence to, France's hegemony. While some stand comfortably in the front row, others crowd in behind, and still others at the rear struggle to squeeze into the modest classical temple, including a few from regions where the Napoleonic armies would never march: in the full-size painting, the oriental figure of a Mongol or Chinese here visible at the right can be observed gripping a column with his left hand to balance himself as he leans in to hear, the implication being that even the unconquered ought to wish inclusion within this New World Order. Out of view here, a wigged figure, presumably Britain, crosses his right hand over his chest, also in deference. But within the view, immediately below the oriental observer, we can see another figure of ambiguous complexion and ethnicity, clasping his hands as he raises his eyes to the heavens – an invocation of thanks? Or, one wonders, a quiet prayer for deliverance?

The artist, Alexandre Veron-Bellecourt, was not making any kind of statement about the activity of studying or writing about the past; this was part of a series of paintings on various aspects of the Napoleonic successes to date. Veron-Bellecourt was, to use our parlance, focused on History, not history. Yet the painting is unintentionally prophetic of the developments of the next two centuries, during the course of which it would be Clio's empire, not Napoleon's, that would ultimately thrive. In a book aspiring to be global, why, one asks, do we allow a minor classical deity to stand for all the world's historiography? Does this not privilege a particular kind of history, a specific way of looking at the past? It does indeed, but not because I wish to suggest that the West is a synecdoche for the globe. My point is precisely the opposite: that the structures and practices of history in the Western world which we conventionally trace back to the classical era have *become* global over the course of the past several centuries, and with mixed consequences. The book attempts to explain how and why this occurred, while also exploring the ways in which the European approach to the study of the past, forged into the late nineteenth–early twentieth-century discipline, was syncretically adapted or altered better to mesh with radically different cultures.

This raises a further issue. As 'world history' and latterly 'global' history have gradually won both academic and curricular acceptance over the past few decades, it has become clear that the noblest plans for inclusiveness often run aground on the shoals of Eurocentrism. If on the one hand we simply 'add Asia (or Africa, or Latin America, or Polynesia) and stir', we wind up with a homogenized agglomerate vision of a single world historiography whose waters have magically converged in that large modern lake, itself seen only from its Western beaches. All the past traditions of historical writing, thinking, singing, painting and inscribing can be triumphantly sublimated into a victorious European project that looks something like the 'Borg' of *Star Trek* fame or, less ominously, one of the seventeenth-century philosopher Leibniz's monads, in which each small part reflects the whole. As Edward Said famously observed, the alleged universalism of various disciplinary fields, among which he includes historiography, is 'Eurocentric in the extreme, as if other literatures and societies had either an inferior or a transcended value', a loaded view which Said traced to Enlightenment thought.[9]

There are ways around this towards an inclusive historiography that borrows one principle attributed to Ranke and nineteenth-century historicism (a term defined at length in Chapter 7 below), and treats each historical culture as unique and of value. But, on the other hand, if we simply recount a number of parallel histories of history, West and East, we risk losing perspective; we will miss both the 'big picture', pointillist though it may be, *and* a sense of the relative scale, significance and magnitude of different types of history. We will also jeopardize any hope of making meaningful generalizations and of finding the red threads that may stretch, in a meandering fashion, from beginning to end. Here explicit comparison can help, together with attention to the ways in which historical cultures have been aware of one another for a very much longer time than they have interacted. R. G. Collingwood, as Eurocentric a historiographer as has ever lived, did not like comparison, and thought that it added nothing to our understanding of a particular event.[10] His mistake was lumping all comparative work with the drive towards general laws, not something any modern comparativist aspires to do. But Collingwood also wrote from the position not of an external observer but rather as an insider, dwelling at the heart of the dominant *régime d'historicité* (a useful phrase coined by the French classicist François Hartog).[11] This is a regime that has ruled over the study of the past since the nineteenth century, and has only rather recently been shaken by postmodern and postcolonial criticism.

Given the dominance of Western models, it would simply be stupid to claim that 'all forms of historicity have been equal and all can live in harmony' because that demonstrably hasn't happened. Micol Seigel suggests that the underlying contradiction in any narrative of world history is the project of narrative itself, 'an inescapable aspect of historical thinking' or, as the influential postmodern historiographer and literary theorist Hayden White has put it in one of his most important essays, that which bestows the illusion of reality on the past.[12] We can extend this further, to the meta-problem of narrating the past of the narration of the past. The challenge of the present book is thus to tell a coherent worldwide narrative of the history of history without creating either a kaleidoscope of different coloured histories, beautiful and dizzying, but ultimately momentary, transitory and meaningless, or its opposite, a Long March, a triumphalist narrative which leads *inevitably* to the modern academy. All histories are *not* the same, nor should they be measured in the same way. We do no service to Vedic era *purāṇas* or Mixtec painted histories to claim either that they are Western histories in embryo or to assert rosily that their truth claims should be taken as literally as their contemporary 'counterparts' in Europe; their creators would have been surprised at our taking them in that light. Similarly, we don't really know how the history of history will end, any more than we know with whom it began. It will only do so when that last man or woman writes or utters the last sentence about the past, and until then, any conclusion is provisional. (Let us hope that this person has time to reach a conclusion, and that anyone is there to hear it, though this seems unlikely.) The medieval chroniclers of the twelfth and thirteenth centuries could not have imagined the humanist historical writings of the fifteenth and sixteenth, much less the academic apparatus of the last century, or the Annales School. The progressive fragmentation of the discipline over the past half century, combined with the challenges of postmodernism, feminism and postcolonialism, examined here in Chapter 9, can suggest to the pessimist the impending doom of history; the house that we constructed over many generations, and in which we have been generally comfortable for over a century (though frequently redecorating and renovating it), may now be standing in the way of a number of intellectual bulldozers closing in from different directions. Or, perhaps that house is about to enter a new global golden age: the revolution in large databases, the internet and on-line research of the past decade alone has made it possible to conduct research in very different ways than we used to do, and doubtless will open up new channels of inquiry. So far as history is concerned, we do not know where current trends will eventually take our successors. To borrow a famous image from Hegel, the owl of Minerva continues, for now, to perch quietly on its branch.

'Rise' of the Discipline of History – a Tale too Triumphantly Told?

What is sometimes called the modern 'discipline' – an academic term beloved of professors and students rather than the public – of history has had for about 150 years a very clear set of professional codes and practices, generally understood by most, though of late challenged by alternative practices and differing senses of what is a proper subject for the historian. The 'profession' that adheres to this discipline is in some ways a very large and heterogeneous international craft guild, as fierce as any college of physicians or law society; and it has by and large policed and enforced its own codes and rules. Misdemeanours such as careless citation of sources lead to critical book reviews; capital crimes such as plagiarism or its opposite, the invention of sources (not an uncommon practice in earlier times) are dealt with most severely by the offender's own peers, leading to derision, condemnation, professional disgrace and even loss of employment. Somewhere in between lie felonies of various sorts ranging from shoddy research, failure to judge sources correctly, or credulous acceptance of facts without verification. The road the modern historian treads is a treacherous one, with hazards at every turn, and fiercely judgmental critics, observing from the shoulder, ever ready to pounce, often in packs, at the first scent of blood. The late Hugh Trevor-Roper, Lord Dacre (1914–2003), was a brilliant essayist and effective critic of what he saw as poor quality work by others. In the 'Gentry Controversy' of the 1950s (a controversy about upward social mobility in Tudor England and the evidence supporting it) he famously attacked the great British social historian R. H. Tawney (1880–1962) and a younger contemporary of Trevor-Roper himself, Lawrence Stone (1919–99) over some of their methods. But three decades later the hunter became the hunted. The now ennobled Lord Dacre, having throughout his career 'bet on red'[13] – that is, chosen a default position of scepticism – abruptly and unfortunately placed all his accumulated reputational winnings on black. He prematurely pronounced a set of forged diaries, concocted by a clever German trickster, as being in the genuine hand of Adolf Hitler. This single late-career lapse of judgment severely tarnished though it did not (and should not have) utterly destroy his reputation. 'Discipline' it would seem is a polite word for what has often been rough justice.

How historiography, taken as 'writing about the past', ended up at its modern point has been a tale oft told, beginning (at least in recent times) with Eduard Fueter's classic *Geschichte der Neueren Historiographie* (1911) published precisely a century before this book. Though Fueter began only with the early Renaissance, his book has proved paradigmatic for much 'history of history' in the century since. In the English-speaking world alone, a series of prominent historians have one-by-one presented their narratives of the discipline's past.[14] The Italian philosopher Benedetto Croce, in 1921, linked an overview of the history of history to an exposition of some of his ideas about how it worked, something his English counterpart R. G. Collingwood would also do two decades later. George Peabody Gooch (1873–1968), a journalist, thwarted politician and prolific non-academic historian, wrote an informative account of a much shorter period, the nineteenth century, during which the discipline had become professionalized and entered the custody of the academics. His early exposure to Lord Acton, the Cambridge historian, made Gooch a product of exactly the historiographical system that he described; and a very long life permitted him the luxury of a second edition two world wars later. Most recently, Donald R. Kelley has offered an intelligent and perceptive three-volume study of Western historical thinking, and the late John Burrow has written an elegant literary *History of Histories* which deliberately eschews comprehensiveness in pursuit of depth in the analysis of select master works. The stories in all these works differ in emphasis and selection of examples, but on the whole they are remarkably similar – different performances of the same play. The play itself, especially in surveys written before 1990, is cast in a comic tone, with a generally happy ending in the professional and academic historiography of the modern world. They feature a cast of familiar characters, nearly all 'pale and male' – they round up the usual suspects of the history of history from Thucydides to Toynbee, Herodotus to Hexter, ancient annals to modern Annales.

That this is so should not be at all surprising. Within our professionalized discipline we have depicted our journey to the historiographical present as an eighteenth-century morality tale, wherein the maiden Clio has survived various challenges to her honour, nearly taken some wrong turns, escaped seduction by wolfish ideology and rakish literature, and grown into the fine mature matron that she is today. The 'genealogy' of the West (those with history), whereby Greek led to Roman who led to Christian, and so on, is less a full genealogy than a fine pedigree of Old Testament-like qualities (complete with Mosaic lawgivers along the way, Egyptian slavery to be fled and intellectual wildernesses to be escaped). Herodotus (or Thucydides or Polybius) begat Livy and Tacitus who begat Eusebius and Augustine who begat a thousand years of chroniclers who begat Leonardo Bruni, Lorenzo Valla and Jean Bodin who begat Vico, Hume, F. A. Wolf and Gibbon, who begat Ranke, Mommsen and James Harvey Robinson, who begat the twentieth century. So far as being a story of Euro-American *historiography*, this is not entirely inaccurate, but it will not serve as a history of history. As a pedigree, it has purged the collateral and cadet lines, to say nothing of evidence of miscegenation – and unwanted progeny have been left quietly unacknowledged.

There are many problems with this kind of intellectual history. The most obvious of these is its teleological bent, its sheer 'whiggishness', to use the term first made famous by Sir Herbert Butterfield (1900–79) in the 1930s; in fact, there is probably no history so whiggish as history's history of itself. This is now being addressed by studies that focus on particular phases of historiography and resist situating them within the Great Story; they also attempt to situate historical writing within a social and cultural context, or they have turned away from the happy narrative of Clio's upbringing and education to interrogate the literary and rhetorical features of great historical texts much more deeply. To some extent, however, a narrative cannot be avoided, and there is a story to be told of how history got from then to now. We can, thanks to recent work, tell a much more complicated version of the story, complete with false starts, and with less hero-worship perhaps than before. To borrow from Hans Kellner, we are in a position to make the history of history less linear, and more 'crooked'.[15]

A second problem is the one already noted above: simply put, it is the assumption that only the West has produced a 'sound' historiography, while most other cultures have not.[16] Or, as J. H. Plumb put it, while acknowledging impressive Chinese achievements, only the acquisition of a critical attitude to sources and a sense of distance from the past can produce 'history in our sense'.[17] According to this line of thinking, other civilizations (China, Islam) have at best produced nice tries, also-rans. At worst (ancient India, Southeast Asia) they have produced myth with occasional nuggets of truth buried within. Or, they have been utterly devoid of historical writing (pre-colonial Africa, American indigenous populations) and even of historical consciousness – which is often seen as impossible without writing – till belatedly enlightened in modern times with Western historicity. Plumb was certainly correct that ancient Chinese historicity was not that of the modern West (or, as we will see, even of modern China), just as he was right to point to differences between the moral and didactic imperatives driving much Western historiography from antiquity to 1800, and the less explicitly moralizing academic history that succeeded it. But does that mean that only modernity, or only the West, have produced 'real' history? This is among the issues which this book explores.

West and East in Historiography

There is of course a fundamental problem even in using terms like West and East: they imply a central reference point in Europe. In directional terms, from the point of view of an eighteenth-century Japanese observer, 'west' would have included China and 'east' the horizonless void of the Pacific. More seriously, both terms are abstractions and lexical conveniences that group many disparate and unrelated cultures together under opposed binary categories. Calling the rest of the world the 'non-West' accentuates this problem unnecessarily by creating not only a binary pair but also a positive and negative polarity.[18] Nonetheless, part of the story of this book is precisely the achievement of global hegemony (perhaps impermanent, and on one level more tragic than comic) by western European historicity. That is, the book recounts over its nine chapters the following processes: a gradual reduction over the course of many centuries in possible pathways to the past; the establishment in a governing position of one broad set of codes and conventions to the exclusion of the different historical practices, alternative attitudes and countervailing beliefs that were in play elsewhere in the world at various points in the past; and the eradication of many of these not only from the modern enterprise of history but also from our very understanding of how that enterprise came into existence. Given this, I have (with some reluctance, and in full awareness of their relativity and limitations) employed collectivizing terms such as 'West' and 'Western', along with over-simple geographical terms such as 'East Asian' or even 'European', as convenient aggregations or modifications attached to systems of thinking about and representing the past – systems that in reality were much more variable, internally contested and impermanent. In short, terms such as these must be read throughout the book as if enclosed within permanent quotation marks.

We will return periodically to the problem of Eurocentrism in later chapters, but the weakness in most history of history (unlike, say, 'world history') hasn't really been *Eurocentrism* per se so much as something one might call *Eurosolipsism*. The placing of something at the centre of a map or a narrative at least acknowledges that there are peripheral parts, even if one can argue over what is centre and what periphery. But for the most part Western historiography, as represented in a century of surveys, has not placed its understanding of its past at the centre so much as made it the whole story. The periphery, the excluded, the marginal, the subordinate, the Other, whatever term one prefers, isn't simply a reducible supplement. It might as well not exist at all. In that respect, some of our early modern and Enlightenment predecessors, including favoured targets of postcolonialism like the eighteenth-century philologist William Jones and the nineteenth-century utilitarian James Mill, were streets ahead of us, often attuned to other approaches, and not always unremittingly hostile towards them. They at least acknowledged alternative roads to the past outside Europe, even if they were convinced that these roads led nowhere meaningful. This is a critical point: as suggested above, one of the arguments of this book will be that Western historiography has repeatedly and somewhat defensively fashioned itself, masking its internal insecurities and intellectual doubts, in response to other types of history that it encountered in the course of war, trade and other forms of contact. The great irony is that this occidental form of knowledge, having built itself into something unlike its oriental and 'ahistorical' counterparts, was by the nineteenth century sufficiently refined, confident in its methods and clear in its goals (themselves associated with Western success) that it could march with comparative ease – and sometimes by invitation – into those parts of the world that previously entertained different notions of what the past was and how and why it should be remembered. And there is a second irony: even with the most willing local admirers, European historical practices could not be grafted whole-sale on to foreign societies (any more than American democracy can be imposed today on countries with no democratic experience). In many instances they re-quired some modification in order to achieve broad acceptance. The rough fit and the compromises have been elided from the story of history as the twentieth century wrote it, along with most of the indigenous historical practices that they supplanted.

This elision occasioned in eminent twentieth-century historiographers such as Herbert Butterfield a kind of sympathetic tokenism (Butterfield respected some aspects of Chinese historiography and the odd Muslim such as Ibn Khaldūn); in others it reinforced a notion that history cannot be written for any period prior to contact with the West. In a now infamous utterance earlier in his career, Hugh Trevor-Roper dismissed the existence of any history in non-Muslim Africa prior to the arrival of Europeans:

Undergraduates, seduced, as always, by the changing breath of journalistic fashion, demand that they should be taught the history of black Africa. Perhaps, in the future, there will be some African history to teach. But at present there is none, or very little: there is only the history of the Europeans in Africa. The rest is largely darkness, like the history of pre-European, pre-Columbian America. And darkness is not a subject for history.[19]

Not only was there no history to study from preliterate societies; the very attempt to do so should be the pursuit of sociologists, archaeologists and anthropologists. For historians, it would be a distraction from the main event, the 'purposive move-ment' of History (here in the capital-H sense). In words that could easily have been written by an eighteenth-century philosophe, Trevor-Roper added a warning against such digressions, through which 'we may neglect our own history and amuse ourselves with the unrewarding gyrations of barbarous tribes in picturesque but irrelevant corners of the globe: tribes whose chief function in history, in my opinion, is to show to the present an image of the past from which, by history, it has escaped.'[20]

These quotations have been often repeated, and they are a great example of a provocatively and stunningly wrong generalization usefully producing the evi-dence for its own contradiction: its very wrongness became a rallying cry for forty years' worth of Africanists, and for others dealing with other parts of the non-European world, including American indigenous cultures (incidentally clobbered on the back-hand swing of Trevor-Roper's remarks). But Trevor-Roper is unfairly blamed for articulating clearly what in fact was a widely held position in his time and for much of the previous several hundred years. We will see early examples of this in the European encounters in the New World beginning in the sixteenth century, and they have continued to recent times. The early twentieth-century English fascist Houston Stewart Chamberlain had an even more derisory view of China and non-Christian society than Friedrich Nietzsche, and once again one without history, 'without' meaning both 'not possessing' (which was certainly mistaken) and 'outside', the position that Hegel had taken in the nineteenth century. When the eminent American historian Daniel J. Boorstin (1914–2004) returned from a visit to Puerto Rico in 1955, he made in the pages of the *Yale Review* the bizarre statement (at least to eyes half a century further on) that the island had no history worth telling, at least not before 1898 when it became an American protectorate; despite the vigorous protests of Puerto Rican historians, it would be nearly a quarter century before another American drove a spike through Boorstin's argument.[21]

At the opposite end of this denial of history to certain parts of the world, there has been a countervailing belief in historical consciousness as a rather unitary, coherent and culturally universal phenomenon. An American historian writing in 1987 took as virtually axiomatic the existence of a 'unifying theme that has given coherence to history', which she linked to a definition of man as 'a rational, political animal'.[22] Others have modulated this by asserting that historical thinking is indeed a common human feature but one that develops in different ways that are culturally specific. 'Man is a historical animal', commented two distinguished Africanists in the early 1980s, quickly qualifying this statement by observing that historical consciousness also 'reflects the society to which it belongs'.[23] One shrinks from universalizing historical-mindedness, or even interest in the past, as an innate feature of human nature. It is possible to acknowledge that there are people who have in fact lived quite happily without history, thank you very much. The anthropologist Marshall Sahlins, for instance, has proposed with reference to Hawaiian culture that a 'historylessness' was there induced by a continuous redistribution of land, preventing the formation of local lineages and thus any genealogical memories beyond living personal experience. The Maori of New Zealand, it has been suggested, live in a kind of 'eternal return' in which contemporaries appropriate to their own persons the acts of remote ancestors.[24] We should not seek ways of bestowing 'history' as a kind of badge of honour on every culture, much less trying to twist alternative modes of remembering or living with the past into Western categories. The historian of American native peoples, Calvin Martin, has made a similar observation. 'We historians ... quite deliberately insert an alarm clock in our posed scenes of Indians – and likewise furnish them with the wrong time. That is, we make them into a "people of history": assign them our terms and conception of living in time and space, our commitment to changing reality and changing humanity over the ages'.[25] Nor should one assume that a culture without history at one time necessarily lacks it at all times, as one ethnohistorian has recently argued in connection with the Inuit of Greenland and Canada.[26] The late anthropologist Claude Lévi-Strauss (1908–2009) long ago posited the notion of 'cold' and 'hot' societies as a preferable alternative to 'peoples without history', pointing out that any culture will have an attitude to the past, either rejecting its influence on the present in an effort to make their institutions timeless and permanent, or 'internalizing the historical process and making it the moving power of their development'.[27] We should be mindful that European cultures have at various times exhibited an equal ambivalence to change, even when they were commonly practising the writing of history.

Modern Historicity in Perspective

In a celebrated phrase, the postcolonial critic Dipesh Chakrabarty has called for the 'provincializing of Europe', noting that Europe has traditionally provided the scale against which the rest of the world is measured.[28] That being said, it is difficult to make European historiography simply one among several approaches. As most postcolonial scholars would concede, and as later chapters of this book will contend, the European-descended Western form of historiography, complete with its academic and professional institutions, *has* achieved dominance over other forms of writing or thinking about the past. This is paradoxically true even in circumstances where Western historical methods are seized and turned as a weapon on the very political or social structures that disseminated them (see Chapter 8). The more interesting questions are first, how this form of history came to be so influential, and second, whether it occurred without the 'victor' being affected in some ways by contact with the 'vanquished' (or in some cases, the 'vanished'). As Dominic Sachsenmaier has perceptively observed:

[I]t would be wrong to simply identify diffusion from the West to the rest as the only force behind the genesis of academic historiography as a worldwide phenomenon. Rather, the global spread of cultures of rationality, the modern academic system and university-based historiography occurred in an intricate *jeu d'échelles* of trans-local and local contexts, colonial power formations, liberation movements, transnational intellectual networks and other factors. In any case, many character traits of academic historiography – such as the strong presence of Eurocentric worldviews – need to be seen not merely as export products of an allegedly pristine European tradition but also as the result of the continent's expansion and many complex socio-political transformations resulting from it. Western historiography transformed at the same time as European academia began heavily influencing historical research elsewhere.[29]

My project in this book adopts a similar perspective, and attempts to meet Dipesh Chakrabarty at least part-way in recounting a somewhat different version of the history of history than has conventionally been told. The landscape thus takes in a variety of different historiographic traditions, running along parallel tracks for much of the time, but also criss-crossing and intersecting. These are embodied in different genres, transmitted in alternative forms of commemoration and communication (oral, pictorial, alphabetic), and created in widely varying social and political contexts. While the narrative necessarily proceeds in a sometimes non-linear manner, with rapid shifts from one part of the globe to another, I hope to convince the reader that a more pluralistic and complicated understanding of the history of history is both possible and necessary – and to demonstrate that there have been many avenues into the past, and differing beliefs about why the past matters at all.

Notes

1 Friedrich Nietzsche, 'On the Uses and Disadvantages of History for Life', *Untimely Meditations*, trans. R. J. Hollingdale (Cambridge, 1983), 61.

2 Greg Dening, 'A Poetic for Histories', in his *Performances* (Chicago, 1996), 36.

3 E. H. Carr, *What is History?* (New York, 1961), 60.

4 Velcheru Narayana Rao, David Shulman and Sanjay Subrahmanyam, *Textures of Time: Writing History in South India 1600–1800* (New York, 2003), 129.

5 Paul Veyne, *Did the Greeks Believe in their Myths? An Essay on the Constitutive Imagination*, trans. P. Wissing (Chicago, 1988).

6 Eric R. Wolf, *Europe and the People without History* (Berkeley, CA, 1982).

7 For which see 'Further reading', below.

8 These were themselves relatively late departures from a notion of history as the record of the deeds and words of emperors of successive ruling dynasties, rather than the cumulative record of all the peoples of the 'Middle Kingdom'. *Guoshi* actually appeared in the Han era (see ch. 1), but the term first began to refer to a written account of history in the Tang dynasty (see ch. 2) when there appeared several works bearing the title 'shi' denoting the written account of one or multiple dynasties. *Tongshi* is a much later arrival which refers to the writing of general history, ranging beyond the history of a single dynasty, though the word *tong* was used in the Tang period. The combined word *lishi*, which stands for 'history' in modern Chinese, first appears in the Ming era. I am grateful to Q. Edward Wang for assistance with the history of Chinese word usage.

9 Edward Said, *Orientalism* (London, 1978), 44.

10 R. G. Collingwood, *The Idea of History* (1946; Oxford, 1961), 223.

11 François Hartog, *Régimes d'historicité: présentisme et expériences du temps* (Paris, 2003). Hartog uses the phrase principally to describe changing attitudes to the relationship

between past, present and future rather than intellectual frameworks for the pursuit of knowledge of the past, but the two are not unrelated.

12 Micol Seigel, 'World History's Narrative Problem', *Hispanic American Historical Review* 84 (2004): 431–46, at 434; and Hayden White, 'The Value of Narrativity in the Representation of Reality', in *The Content of the Form: Narrative Discourse and Historical Representation* (Baltimore, 1987), 1–25.

13 A turn of phrase I owe to Peter Burke, in conversation with the author, 27 November 2007.

14 See below under 'Further reading' for the major English-language surveys of the past century.

15 Hans Kellner, *Language and Historical Representation: Getting the Story Crooked* (Madison, WI, 1989).

16 A phrase that runs through, and largely vitiates, the otherwise interesting comparative account in Donald E. Brown, *Hierarchy, History and Human Nature: The Social Origins of Historical Consciousness* (Tucson, CO, 1988).

17 J. H. Plumb, *The Death of the Past*, rev. edn (1969; Houndmills, Basingstoke, 2004), 13, 20–1 and this edition's new introduction by Niall Ferguson, xxxiff. Plumb attributed the failure of China to develop history (*sic*!) jointly to the absence of any great historical problem, any significant rupture in a unified past and to the dearth of conflicting pasts (such as Europe had to confront in Judaism and Islam) rather than supposed Chinese isolation (which as he knew, was myth rather than reality): ibid., 111–12.

18 The words 'West' and 'Western' when capitalized in this book denote not a geographic direction or region (for instance, western Europe) but the knowledge, culture and authority arising from the European sphere of influence, including its offspring (for instance, the United States, Australia), in contrast with Asian or indigenous American cultures. Certain geographical regions such as Southeast Asia, East Asia and the Near East have also been capitalized in keeping with convention.

19 H. R. Trevor-Roper, *The Rise of Christian Europe* (London, 1965), 9. Such is the outrage at these introductory remarks in what, originally, was a set of television lectures delivered in 1963, that the book's serious attempt to place Europe in its world context is generally overlooked.

20 Ibid., 9.

21 Allen Woll, *Puerto Rican Historiography* (New York, 1978), 1–2.

22 Gertrude Himmelfarb, *The New History and the Old* (Cambridge, MA, 1987), 25. It is doubtful that the author was including non-Western and pre-modern ideas of history in her analysis.

23 B. Hama and J. Ki-Zerbo, 'The Place of History in African Society', in Ki-Zerbo (ed.), *General History of Africa*, vol. 1: *Methodology and African Prehistory* (Paris and London, 1981), 43.

24 Marshall Sahlins, *Islands of History* (Chicago, 1985), 51, 59.

25 Calvin Martin (ed.), *The American Indian and the Problem of History* (New York, 1987), 16.

26 Yvon Csonka, 'Changing Inuit Historicities in West Greenland and Nunavut', *History and Anthropology* 6 (2005): 321–34.

27 Claude Lévi-Strauss, *The Savage Mind* (Chicago, 1966), 233–4.

28 Dipesh Chakrabarty, *Provincializing Europe: Postcolonial Thought and Historical Difference* (Princeton, NJ, 2000). See also Vinay Lal, *The History of History: Politics and Scholarship in Modern India* (Oxford and New Delhi, 2003), on 'the history of ahistoricity'.

29 Dominic Sachsenmaier, 'Global History, Pluralism, and the Question of Traditions', *New Global Studies* 3:3 (2009): article 3, at 3–4. See also Roxann Prazniak, 'Is World History Possible? An Inquiry', in Arif Dirlik, Vinay Bahl and Peter Gran (eds.), *History after the Three Worlds: Post-Eurocentric Historiographies* (Oxford, 2000), 221–39; Pamela Kyle Crossley, *What is Global History?* (Cambridge, 2008).

Twenty-fourth century BC	*Weidner Chronicle*
c. Twenty-second century BC	Sumerian King List
Tenth century to c. late seventh century BC	*Tanakh* (the Hebrew Bible)
Eighth century BC	*Synchronistic History*
704–681 BC	*Eponymous Chronicle*
Seventh to sixth century BC	Neo-Babylonian Chronicle series
c. 480 BC	*Chunqiu* ('Spring and Autumn Annals')
c. 420 BC	Herodotus' *Histories*
c. 400 BC	*Zuozhuan* ('Zuo Chronicle'); Thucydides' *History of the Peloponnesian War*
mid-second century BC	Polybius' *Histories*
c. 90 BC	Sima Qian's *Shiji* ('Records of the Grand Historian')
c. AD 90	Josephus' *Antiquities of the Jews, Jewish Wars* and *Against Apion*
c. AD 105–17	Tacitus' *Annals* and *Histories*
c. AD 111	Ban Gu's *Hanshu* ('History of the Former or Western Han')
c. AD 361	The *Dīpavaṃsa* ('Island Chronicle')
c. AD 391	Ammianus Marcellinus' *Res Gestae Libri XXXI* ('Thirty-one Books of Deeds')
c. Fifth century AD	The *Viṣnu Purāṇa*

1   Foundations[1]

Introduction

Our story commences over 4,000 years in the past, with the earliest known forms of historical record-keeping in the ancient Near East. This chapter, which will cover by far the longest span of centuries in the entire book, will begin with Mesopotamia, Egypt and the Israelites. We will then turn to the Greeks, who are responsible for the very word 'history', as well as for its personification in the muse, Clio (Fig. 1), and then to their classical successors, the Romans. Because we are concerned with the history of history as a global and not simply a European phenomenon, we will also have to track the parallel (and to our knowledge not, at this point, intersecting) historical culture emerging from the most ancient civilization of the East, the Chinese. There may well have been historical thinking and commemoration in the Americas and in Africa, perhaps even in Australasia, during these early millennia, but we will defer consideration of those places until later chapters and times for which there exists firmer evidence of historiographical practices. Finally, the very different historical culture of South Asia (extending chronologically well beyond the boundaries of European antiquity) is addressed here precisely because it can provide a sharp corrective to any notion that the various types of Western historicity were the only possible perspective that the present could take on the past.

The Ancient Near East

The Near East was a complex, multilingual region extending from Egypt and what became the land of the Israelites, through the Levant, embracing Mesopotamia proper and the land of the Hittites in Anatolia and northern Syria. Within this

Figure 1 | Clio, the Muse of History. Roman marble figure, c. AD 130–40, here depicted as a Roman lady; the missing left hand may have held a scroll.

region dwelled a number of very long-lived civilizations, and they did not recall or preserve their pasts in the same ways or consistently in the same types of record. The evidence is literally fragmentary, deriving as it does from inscriptions on steles, stone tablets or rocks, and writings on papyrus; a majority of these objects have not survived entirely intact. One looks in vain for 'history' as a concept, much less for works devoted to it. There is no lexical equivalent for either 'history' or 'historiography' in any language of the region, though the Hebrew words *tôledôt* ('genealogies') and *divrê hāyyāmîm* ('words of those days') might be considered approximate equivalents.[2] Terminology is important, especially when sorting out what peoples in the past thought, and so is the nomenclature of categories – the Greeks in particular took the generic divisions of history seriously, as would

Figure 2 | The Palermo stone, one of five fragments of a stele known as the Royal Annals of the Old Kingdom, other parts of which are kept in Cairo and London. All are part of a rectangular stele of black amphibole diorite with names of pre-dynastic rulers, levels of Nile floods and royal protocols. Engraved in the twenty-fifth century BC.

Renaissance humanists two millennia later. But it would be unwise to leap from the lack of linguistic terms, or of a literary genre, to the conclusion that 'there was no history back then'.

Arguments can certainly be made for a sense of the past in ancient Egypt, and in particular an effort to memorialize the successive dynasties of the Old, Middle and New Kingdoms. Very few of the 'annals' recorded by the first pharaohs remain extant: an early specimen is the 'Palermo stone' (twenty-fifth century BC, Fig. 2), a fragmentary stele (so named for one of its portions, in Palermo, Sicily) inscribed with king lists from pre-dynastic times down to the Fifth Dynasty in the mid-third millennium. This was probably used much later by the Hellenized Egyptian Manetho in his own *Aegyptiaca*, very little of which has survived. We know that the annals of the wars of Thutmose III (r. c. 1479–25) were extracted and copied on to a temple wall by a scribe, thereby preserving them. Elsewhere in the ancient Near East, various historical inscriptions and texts are attributable to the Hittites, Syrians and Phoenicians. A 'Tablet of Manly Deeds' was written in the seventeenth century BC during the reign of the Old Hittite king Hattusili I, and royal annals organizing the past by years continued for several centuries. The Hittites appear also to be the earliest people to have focused on the didactic and especially political uses of history, either justifying a particular situation by appeal to the past or by using its episodes to advise and admonish. It is in Mesopotamia proper, however, that one first finds unmistakable evidence of a deliberate human intention to write about the past, especially among the Babylonians and Assyrians. The successive peoples that inhabited the land between the Tigris and Euphrates, who developed proto-alphabetic writing in cuneiform, also created the elementary forms for the representation of the past, such as king lists, annals and chronicles, and the vessels for preserving their own records, the library and the archive.

Many of the stories eventually captured in writing preceded its development and had previously been preserved orally. 'Epic', a genre that relates the martial deeds and adventures of heroes and kings, often in interaction with the gods, was the oldest form of historical narrative. That many of the episodes which epics recount are legendary and that their heroes were either exaggerated or may never have existed at all is not in itself evidence of a lack of history or historical thinking: the singers of and listeners to these stories almost certainly believed at some level either in their literal truth or at least in the moral principles that they embodied. Though it recounts largely legendary episodes, the oldest extant epic, that of *Gilgamesh*, so-named for its eponymous hero, the king of Uruk, thus has some connection to history, as did later Babylonian epics of the second and first millennium. Further afield, the great Greek epics, the *Iliad* and the *Odyssey*, ascribed to the bard Homer, portray what Greeks of the eighth to fifth centuries BC believed to be their own ancient past. The border between epic and something that looks to us more like history – the listing of undeniably 'real' figures – is often blurred. The same Babylonian term 'tablet-box' that featured in the beginning of *Gilgamesh* also describes the pseudo-historical monumental inscription, supposedly written by the Akkadian king Naram-Sin in the late third millennium known as the 'Cuthean Legend'.

Closer to a recognizably historical document are a class of text that can broadly be called 'chronographic' – ascribing particular events to a specific date within a sequence – and which include sub-genres such as 'king lists', 'annals' and 'chronicles' (see Box 1). Among the earliest of these is the Sumerian king list, probably initiated in the twenty-second century, and existing in several recensions of considerably later date. It stretches back into mythical antiquity but goes beyond a mere list in later times to indicate inquisitive uncertainty about the historicity of some rulers expressed in the utterance 'Who was king? Who was not king?' It is also a deliberate attempt to present the historical record in a particular light, necessitated by the circumstances of the author's own time. Various other forms of

Box 1   King Lists, Annals and Chronicles

There is a distinction between these kinds of 'chronographic' historical documents
but it is often an ambiguous one. 'King lists' are exactly what the term suggests,
largely unadorned lists of rulers in succession (though they can be historical if
they are constructed retroactively, as appears to be the case with the Sumerian
King List). Annals and chronicles are more complex and the distinctions are slightly
artificial and they both contain multiple associations. Simply put, a set of 'annals' is
a simple series of annual records of events without much additional information or
commentary while a 'chronicle' is annalistically organized, but with some commentary and a narrative, albeit one self-contained within the year (often as an anecdote
or digression). The matter is further confused by the fact that even a chronicle
which includes relatively elaborate narratives is divided into discrete yearly units
that are also called annals. In short, an annal can be *either* a component unit within
a longer work that may be either a literary *form* called 'annals' or one called a
'chronicle' or a third which is a continuous history but organized on a yearly basis.

Sumero-Babylonian historical record exist, including building inscriptions, steles
and other durable media. Chronicles, written in the third person, begin as early
as a text called the *Chronicle of the Single Monarchy* which may date from the
Akkadian period (twenty-fourth to twenty-second century BC). Other genres, such
as astronomical diaries, played a part in establishing a precise chronological grid
against which to record events, and both the Babylonians of the second millennium and their neo-Babylonian or Chaldaean successors of the mid-first millennium were keen astronomers and devoted list-makers.

The neighbouring Assyrians, who shared with their Babylonian rivals a common
Sumerian culture and spoke a dialect of the Akkadian language, also authored
historiographic documents. The Assyrian King List, beginning with a series of
'17 kings who dwelt in tents', continues down to the late eighth century, its range
and structure suggesting that it was compiled from other documents requiring
elementary 'research'. Assyrian royal inscriptions include annals, commencing in
the early thirteenth century and composed in the first person; these recount the
history of particular campaigns, and do not have a Babylonian or Sumerian counterpart. The Assyrians also produced third-person chronicles such as the *Eponymous Chronicle*, which relays the annual military campaigns of its kings down

1: Assyrian Historical Propaganda: the *Synchronistic History*

Karaindash, king of Karduniash
and Ashur-bel-nisheshu, king of Assyria,
between them made a
treaty
and took an oath together concerning this very boundary.
Puzur-Ashur III, king of Assyria, and Burnaburiash I,
king of Karduniash, took an oath and
fixed this very boundary-line.

At the time of Ashur-uballit I, king of Assyria,
the Kassite troops
rebelled against
Karahardash,
king of Karduniash, son of Muballitat-Sherua –
daughter of Ashur-uballit I –
and killed him.
They appointed
Nasibugash,
a Kassite, son of a nobody, as sovereign over them.

Ashur-uballit I
marched to Karduniash
to avenge
Karjaindash, his grandson.
He killed Nazibugash, king of Karduniash.
He appointed
Kurigalzu II, the younger, son of Burnaburiash II,
as sovereign and put him on his father's throne.

At the time of Enlil-narari, king of Assyria, Kurigalzu II, the younger, was the king of Karduniash.

From A. K. Grayson (ed.), *Assyrian and Babylonian Chronicles* (Locust Valley, NY: J. J. Augustin, 1975), 158–9. Editor's interpolations have been added here without bracketing; however, line breaks are maintained as in Grayson's text.

---

to Sennacherib (r. 704–681). Finally, the Assyrians authored a number of 'omen-texts', allegedly prognosticating on future events.

Subtle differences in approach have been noted between Assyrian and Babylonian attitudes to the past. Assyrian royal annals are largely written in first-person bombastic prose, in the voice of the kings themselves. The Assyrian *Synchronistic History* (an eighth-century text which is unusual for having included an introduction and a conclusion), in describing boundary disputes from the fifteenth to early eighth centuries, invariably blames the Babylonians and never records Assyrian setbacks (Extract 1). The

Figure 3 | Cuneiform tablet with part of the Babylonian Chronicle (605–594 BC), obverse of tablet. Neo-Babylonian, c. 550–400 BC.

Chronicle of Tiglath-pileser, a tablet describing Assyro-Babylonian relations in the twelfth to eleventh centuries, and the *Esarhaddon Chronicle* from the period of Assyrian dominance during the early seventh century, are similarly tilted towards a pro-Assyrian perspective. In contrast, those accounts written by the Babylonians themselves are often more neutral, mentioning Babylonian defeats as well as victories.

The seventh and sixth centuries produced further works such as the Neo-Babylonian Chronicle series (Fig. 3), running from 747 to the Persian capture of Babylon in 539, and the Late Babylonian Chronicle series that continued this down to the third century, by which time contact with the Greeks had broadened the outlook of the authors. Variants of earlier texts also appeared: the 'Dynastic Chronicle', really a king list, is a late version of the much older Sumerian king list. The latest Babylonian work is that of Berossus, a contemporary of the Egyptian Manetho in the third century. Nothing of Berossus' original work (written in Greek rather than Akkadian) has survived though it was well known in Hellenistic and Roman times, though even then it had already doubtless been altered and edited; it is one of the long list of ancient texts of which we possess indirect or partial knowledge because later writers quoted from it.

The Persians, successors to Babylonian power in the sixth century, would continue this historiographical activity rather more modestly. There is little evidence of it from the reigns of the first two Achaemenid kings, Cyrus the Great

Figure 4 | The Cyrus cylinder, 530s BC. An account by Cyrus of Persia of his conquest of Babylon and the capture of Nabonidus, the last Babylonian king.

(r. mid-sixth century) and his son Cambyses: the clay record in the British Museum, known as the 'Cyrus cylinder' (Fig. 4), on which is inscribed in Babylonian cuneiform an account of Cyrus' conquest of Babylon, appears to be of Mesopotamian rather than Persian origin. But with the multilingual Behistun Inscription, Darius I (r. 521–486) became the first Persian king to have composed history. The inscription, whose paragraphs generally begin 'Darius the king says', is also the longest text produced by a Persian ruler, and the only one commonly taken to have been conceived as historical, insofar as it recalls events in the first few years of Darius' reign.

R. G. Collingwood (1889–1943), a respectable archaeologist and later an important philosopher of history, was reluctant to consider any Near Eastern or biblical text as legitimately historical. Like many of Collingwood's quotable utterances and blanket statements, this seems unduly restrictive.[3] There is evidence that, unlike straightforward king lists or chronicles that simply recorded events progressively as they happened, some of these authors sought to write about past occurrences. Since there is little evidence of a continuous tradition of record-keeping or chronicle-writing, wherein one author simply added to a work begun by his pre-decessors, then many of the works must have been the result of what we would now call 'research' – the examination, selection from and collation of multiple earlier sources. Many went beyond simply relating former events, aspiring to provide advice, counsel or cautionary tales, a recurring theme through much of the global history of historical writing. A didactic purpose emerges from one of the best-known examples of early Mesopotamian historical writing, the Old Babylonian *Weidner Chronicle*, a propagandistic composition reaching back to the early third millennium but largely devoted to the Sargonic dynasty of Akkad in the twenty-fourth and twenty-third centuries. Surviving only in much later copies, this is one of the first historical works clearly designed to recover and preserve the past for the edification of present and future, with a lesson attached, in this case the propagation of the cult of the god Marduk. Framed as a dialogue among divine beings, the account in the *Weidner Chronicle* of Sargon of Akkad and his grandson Naram-Sin contrasts the godliness of the former with the disobedience to Marduk of the latter, with the consequence of the downfall of Akkad at the hands of Gutian barbarians. The long-standing explanation of events through an alternating current of divine favour and punishment, a recurrent theme for many centuries, thus had an early start. It turned up again in the early seventh century when the later Assyrian defeat of Babylon was ascribed to Marduk's displeasure at recent kings, and it appears frequently throughout the travails of the children of Israel at the hands of foreign hosts depicted in the Hebrew Bible.

The Beginnings of Jewish Historical Thought

No other Western civilization has proved as difficult to explain, historiographically, as the Israelites, or Jews as they later became. Like most Near Eastern cultures they had a term for neither 'history' nor 'myth', and appear not to have held any strong belief about a distinction between the two. Somewhat exaggerated claims have been made for the uniqueness of the historical sense in the *Tanakh* (the Hebrew Bible), to the point of viewing the Hebrews, even more than the Greeks, as the inventors of history, or at least of History, in the sense of a cumulative flow of events towards a divinely ordained conclusion. All of this has been complicated by the modern and considerably more sophisticated understanding of the sequence and chronology of sections in the *Tanakh*, now known to have been the work of several hands, and to have been written in periods from the Davidic kingship (tenth century) to the Babylonian Exile (sixth century).

Another generalization, beloved of modern theologians and Christian religious historians, runs like this: the monotheistic religion of the Hebrews, and their belief in a covenant with a single God gave them a distinctive and unrivalled sense of past, present and future, and of a linear direction to time that differs sharply from the cyclical vision in other parts of the world, including the classical civilizations. Apart from the fact that one finds both a linear and cyclical sense of time in Greek and Roman writers (as we will see below), this argument has been discredited by the unmistakable evidence in Hebrew writings of historical cycles, the most obvious one being that of alternating divine pleasure and displeasure with the chosen people, leading in this world to the repeated experience of slavery and liberation, captivity and freedom. Certainly the use of typology and prefiguration which is an important part of the Jewish canon is hard to imagine on a strictly linear and eschatological vision of time, though the fulfilment of earlier events by later ones implies a progression rather than mere repetition. Contextually, it is also difficult to see the Israelite/Jewish sense of history as entirely extractable and insulated from its geographic setting, given the early contacts between the Israelites and the other peoples of the region.

All this aside, there is something going on in the *Tanakh* that is harder to find in the more fractured evidence from Mesopotamia. Biblical scholars of the past century, faced with the fact that a literal reading of the Hebrew Bible is difficult to sustain – and holding to the then widely held attitude that judged a history's value almost wholly by its reliability as a source – have sometimes distinguished between oral and ahistorical tales or *Sagen* and the more reliable written *Geschichte* (the terms are German because much of the modern scholarship has been conducted in that language). The most unarguably 'historical' section of the *Tanakh*, in that it describes times, persons and events of whose existence we are reasonably confident because there is evidence for them in external sources, was possibly the work of a single writer, the so-called Deuteronomistic Historian, and stretches from Deuteronomy (the last of the 'Five Books of Moses' or Torah) through 2 Kings, but even its reliability has been challenged. Recent scholarship has therefore cast doubt on the *historicity* of the *Tanakh* (that is, its basis in fact), without necessarily jettisoning the idea that one can find *historiography* (a deliberate effort to represent the past) within it, albeit a historiography never intended to capture literal, as opposed to religious, truth. In the early genealogies of Genesis and in the more chronological accounts of the Books of Samuel, Kings and Chronicles, one finds both an effort to memorialize events accurately as a written record and a strong sense of the divine destiny of the Israelites as a chosen people, a linear progress through which oscillates a recurrent cycle of triumph and misery as God first rescues his children from Egyptian slavery and then alternately chastises the erring Israelites for disobedience, sin or idolatry, and delivers them from successive oppressors. This achievement is striking – all the more so when one contrasts it with the dearth of Jewish secular historical writing during the millennium-and-a-half of Diaspora between Flavius Josephus (c. AD 37 to c. 100) and the sixteenth century when Jews, still scattered across Eurasia, began to rediscover the formal study of the past.

Of all the Jews, it is Josephus, who lived near the end of antiquity, who has given us the closest thing to a history in the classical sense. Josephus wrote several centuries after the authors of the *Tanakh*, and with a foot in both the Jewish and the Roman-Hellenistic worlds. This has made him an early example of a phenomenon we will see repeatedly, a historian from one culture writing in the milieu and style of another. He became a Roman citizen and adopted the name Flavius from the family name of his patrons, the Emperors Vespasian and Titus. All of this, plus his failure to die with his colleagues in Galilee during the rebellion against Rome, has led to the vilification of his character for two millennia. But of the value of his historical works, surviving versions of which were composed in Greek, there seems little doubt: his *Antiquities of the Jews* has proved an invaluable source for the social, legal and religious customs of the Jews; and his *Jewish Wars* is useful for the conflicts between the Jews and their enemies from the Seleucid capture of Jerusalem in 164 BC through to the sacking of the city and the destruction of its temple in Josephus' own time. Both works make a case for the antiquity of the Jews, and for their capacity to live peaceably within Roman rule, the rebellions having been in his eyes the work of successive generations of fanatics. In a further work, *Against Apion*, Josephus had occasion to criticize some of his Greek predecessors by way of defending the greater antiquity of Jewish tradition, announcing a feature which recurs in later ages, arguments over the relative age of institutions, nations, religions and even families.

Greek Historiography

Josephus wrote at the end of five centuries of Greek historiography. The Greeks have figured prominently in histories of history with good reason, even if this has often occurred to the neglect of achievements of greater antiquity further east. Why so much attention? For one thing, the very word 'history' itself is of Greek origin, first used in connection with the study of the past by Herodotus of Halicarnassus (see below). Second, it is with the Greeks that Europe began routinely to associate histories and their authors. While there are some anonymous Greek writings, we by and large know the names, or at least the supposed names, of the authors of most extant works, even the many that are fragmentary. Indeed, in some cases, *all* we have is the name and the knowledge that the person at some point wrote a history, once familiar to contemporary or subsequent writers but since lost. Third, with the Greeks we also leave behind – albeit only temporarily – the rather confining format of annals and chronicles, without abandoning chronological writing.

The origins of Greek historical thinking lay in epic poetry, in particular Homer's *Iliad* and *Odyssey*, which portrayed the heroic Bronze Age deeds of the Achaeans in and following the Trojan War. They ascribed much of the action alternately to human emotion or to divine whim. With the earliest Greek prose historians, a few centuries further on, we have moved more fully into the realm of human actions, albeit punctuated by divine involvement and especially by the influence of an ineffable and unpredictable force that later ages have called 'fortune' but the Greeks referred to as *Tyche* (*Τύχη*). Greek contact with the Phoenicians, who in turn had had dealings with Mesopotamia and Egypt, probably resulted in the acquisition of alphabetic writing, and the Homeric epics, previously transmitted orally, were finally written down several centuries after they first were performed. The oldest prose historical writings are those that are known by the collective name of 'logographers' (the Greek *λογογράφος* refers strictly to a writer of prose), most of whom were from Ionia, which lay in the eastern-most reaches of the Greek 'known world' or *oecumene*. Their works were often a combination of what we would now distinguish as the mythical and the historical, drawing on epic as well as the annals of particular cities about which they wrote.

Over a relatively short span of two or three centuries, the Greeks explored the past through several different genres of writing. These included, in the order in which they are now thought to have developed, genealogy or mythography; ethnography (the study of particular foreign lands and their people's customs); contemporary history/history 'proper' or a continuous narrative of sequential events with their causal connections; chronography (a system of time-reckoning, principally according to years of officials); and horography (the year-by-year history of a particular city). But it is in fifth-century Athens that one first encounters both the word *history* and the two historians whose works have survived largely intact and who are also known to us by name.

Herodotus (*c.* 484 to *c.* 420), the first of these, certainly had predecessors in the investigation of the past. Apart from Homer, these included the mythographer Hesiod (*fl. c.* 700), whose *Works and Days* had introduced the notion of a succession of declining ages (Golden, Silver, Bronze, Heroic and Iron); and Hellanicus of Lesbos (*c.* 490–405), the founder of Greek chronographic writing and notable for his attention to the problem of reconciling multiple chronologies. The Ionian writer Hecataeus of Miletus (*fl. c.* 500), sometimes included among the logographers, is important first because in his *Periodos Ges* ('Circuit of the Earth') he established the ethnographic genre built on personal travel and eyewitness reports, and second, because in his *Genealogiae* he set a precedent for later writers by establishing a serious distinction between the fictional and the factual.

While it is wrong to credit Herodotus, a wandering exile from his native Halicarnassus, with 'inventing' history, he was the first to use the word *ἱστορία* in connection with the past, though unintentionally. The Greek verb which transliterates

Figure 5 | Double-headed herm of the Greek historians Herodotus and Thucydides, from the Farnese Collection. Hellenistic sculpture.

as *historein* actually means 'to investigate'; Herodotus used the related noun ἱστορια (*historia* or, in Ionic, *historiê*) to mean something like 'inquiries' or perhaps 'discoveries', without specific reference to past or present. Herodotus was at least as interested in place as in time, his curiosity about the world owing much to Greek geographers and the genre of *Periegesis*, geographic guidebooks of the sixth century. It may also be said that Herodotus invented the historian as a distinctive personality that can be read out of his own prose. His Greek predecessors, though not anonymous, remain obscure figures, but with Herodotus we have the first real example of a historian self-identifying, sometimes giving personal details and at other times intruding with his thoughts or judgments on particular events. This trend would continue with Thucydides and the later Greek historians and by the time we get to Dionysius of Halicarnassus in the late first century BC, it is virtually an obligation of the historian to declare up-front his preferences, methods and biases – even his position with respect to previous historians.

Over the centuries, Herodotus' stock has risen, fallen and risen again several times over, but it is now commonplace to regard him and Thucydides as the twin founders of two very different approaches to the past; as early as the Hellenistic era the two were portrayed together in a double-headed bust (Fig. 5). This is by no means a useless division, so long as one remembers that it falls entirely within the Western tradition and cannot be generalized globally. Borrowing from Hecataeus,

Herodotus did not limit his scope to events themselves, though they remain at the core of his story; he paid attention to ethnographic issues, recording the customs and traditions of the Persians and other, non-Greek peoples. If he is the 'father' of history, it is of history in its more inclusive sense, which in our own day has swung heavily back into vogue with the rise of interest in the social and cultural past.

Herodotus began his *Histories* with perhaps the most succinct and naively unpretentious statement of purpose imaginable:

These are the researches of Herodotus of Halicarnassus, which he publishes, in the hope of thereby preserving from decay the remembrance of what men have done, and of preventing the great and wonderful actions of the Greeks and the Barbarians from losing their due meed of glory; and withal to put on record what were their grounds of feuds.[4]

He wished to inquire as to why, in the decades just previous to his birth, the Greeks and the βάρβαρος ('Barbarians', originally a Greek term for non-Greek-speaking peoples and which in his time had only just begun to acquire its derogatory associations) fought each other; and, following the epics from which he drew inspiration, he wanted to celebrate their achievements. The barbarians in question were the Persians under first Darius I and then his son Xerxes, and as it happens it is to Herodotus' story that we owe much of our knowledge of the rise of the Achaemenid dynasty, of the failed Persian invasions of Hellas (Greece) in the early fifth century, and of their defeats at the celebrated battles of Marathon in 490 and then Thermopylae, Plataea and the naval engagement of Salamis a decade later. The Greece of Herodotus' own time – dominated by an Athens increasingly resented by its own empire and feared by its rival Sparta – had been built on the outcome of the Persian conflict. But to explain the early fifth-century struggles, Herodotus realized that he had to look back further in time, and after an almost pro forma summary of legendary and epic episodes he begins his fascinating story with the wealthy Croesus of Lydia, conquered by Cyrus the Great of Persia, and with the rather vicious Medean king Astyages, Cyrus' own grandfather, whom he would depose.

Although far too young to have witnessed any of these sixth-century events, or even the Perso-Greek conflicts earlier in his own century, Herodotus travelled widely, spoke to many witnesses or those who had information from witnesses, and set down the truth as he believed it. While he was defended by later writers, Herodotus' reputation in subsequent centuries was not a positive one, as he was accused of credulity or even outright falsehood. The 'father of history' was often called the 'father of lies', the author of a history that lay on the foggy borderland between fact and fiction, its assertions not to be trusted. The sniping started almost immediately with an assault by Ctesias, a Persophile with access to Achaemenid records whose assault on his predecessor was so intemperate as to be self-undermining. Greeks were on the whole disinclined to theorize about the

2: Thucydides on His Own Historical Methods

With reference to the speeches in this history, some were delivered before the war began, others while it was going on; some I heard myself, others I got from various quarters; it was in all cases difficult to carry them word for word in one's memory, so my habit has been to make the speakers say what was in my opinion demanded of them by the various occasions, of course adhering as closely as possible to the general sense of what they really said. And with reference to the narrative of events, far from permitting myself to derive it from the first source that came to hand, I did not even trust my own impressions, but it rests partly on what I saw myself, partly on what others saw for me, the accuracy of the report being always tried by the most severe and detailed tests possible. My conclusions have cost me some labour from the want of coincidence between accounts of the same occurrences by different eye-witnesses, arising sometimes from imperfect memory, sometimes from undue partiality for one side or the other. The absence of romance in my history will, I fear, detract somewhat from its interest; but if it be judged useful by those inquirers who desire an exact knowledge of the past as an aid to the interpretation of the future, which in the course of human things must resemble if it does not reflect it, I shall be content. In fine, I have written my work, not as an essay which is to win the applause of the moment, but as a possession for all time.

From Thucydides, *The Peloponnesian War*, 1.1.22–23, trans. R. Crawley (1910; New York: Modern Library, 1951).

writing of history, but the first-century AD biographer Plutarch would go to the trouble of cataloguing Herodotus' alleged crimes in a treatise 'On the Malice of Herodotus'. The great Italian historiographer Arnaldo Momigliano (1908–87) once noted that Herodotus' critics put him between the rock of accusations that he plagiarized from his predecessors and the hard place of being charged with outright invention. He came out either thief or liar.[5]

His immediate successor, Thucydides, did not attack Herodotus by name but almost certainly had him in mind among the retailers of a history 'attractive at truth's expense' (*Pelop. War* 1.1.21). Thucydides (d. *c.* 401 BC) may be the most widely revered past historian in the entire European tradition, though he too was not without his critics even in antiquity. In the eighteenth century, when Thucydides' reputation was especially high, the philosopher-historian David Hume would declare the first page of the *Peloponnesian War* to be the commencement of 'real' history. Whether or not this is justified, it is true that Thucydides was father to a very different sort of history than his predecessor. It is quite likely that he heard an oral public reading of Herodotus some time in the 420s, when the latter's work first appeared in Athens (it may have been the subject of a parody in the comedian Aristophanes' play the *Acharnians* in 425) and this may have inspired Thucydides' own later efforts, despite their differences in approach (Extract 2). Where Herodotus was a perennial traveller, Thucydides was an Athenian through and through, a politician and unsuccessful general who found himself out of favour at a critical juncture in the Peloponnesian War. That conflict between Athens and Sparta (and their respective colonies and allies) endured for three decades and ultimately proved the ruin of Athens and the start of a rather short-lived period of Spartan hegemony. It is likely that Thucydides did not live to see the eventual outcome of this process, probably surviving the end of the war by only a few years, and his history breaks off at 411 without the war resolved, but it is a masterful account of the precipitous and unexpected defeat of the once-mighty *polis* that only decades before had humiliated Xerxes.

Like Herodotus, Thucydides relied on the spoken much more than the written word, though in a very different way. Herodotus had built much of his *Histories* on the foundation of oral tradition rather than written authority. Thucydides similarly did not practise very often that most basic form of research to all modern historians, study of older documents and their criticism and comparison, something often forgotten by those wishing to enthrone him as the visionary forefather of modern method. In fact, he relied on written sources only where he could not find a living witness, as for example in his account of the early history of Sicily. However, there the similarities end, and we observe Thucydides eschewing entirely several practices that were characteristic of Herodotus. For one thing, Thucydides was reluctant to look very far back for the causes of events. For another, he implied that only those who were 'insiders' to events such as himself could accurately recount those events: the belief that the historian should be a 'man of affairs' if not necessarily a general or a statesman was essentially born with his work. Privileged knowledge thus replaced an inferior form of hearsay: though Thucydides says rather little about his precise methods and sources, there would be no wandering interviews of possible eyewitnesses, and little reliance on oral evidence beyond the near-contemporary.

There is scant reference in Thucydides to the marvellous and unusual, a feature that enlivens Herodotus and which has remained a commonplace of ethnographically focused history throughout the centuries as one culture has discovered others. Where Herodotus, who had inherited some of the genealogical interests of his predecessors, populates his history with hundreds of named individuals there is a much more modest cast to the drama Thucydides stages. Where Herodotus painstakingly intervened in his own narrative to ensure that readers understood the problem of conflicting versions and incomplete sources, Thucydides tended to present a picture of seamless confidence, the complexities of evidence swept under a brilliant narrative rug. There is apparent certitude in his assertion that the cause of the Peloponnesian conflict lay not in the public reasons or triggers (disputes over colonies of Athens and Sparta) but in the wider phenomenon of Athens' rise to power and Sparta's rising fear of that power. Finally, Thucydides is also perhaps the first historian in the West to state very clearly the target audience for his work. If Herodotus sought to explain to his contemporaries the events of the previous decades, Thucydides openly admitted that he wrote his work not for 'the applause of the moment, but as a possession for all time' (*Pelop. War* 1.1.23), asserting, too, that the human condition was such as to make the future sufficiently like the present, and thus make his history a benefit and not merely an amusement for subsequent ages.

Thucydides' reputation for strict accuracy and truthfulness has not passed un-challenged. The classicist F. M. Cornford (1874–1943) argued that Thucydides had twisted his materials to fit the dramatic conventions of tragedy and that he had entirely overlooked the commercial causes of the war. Cornford's younger con-temporary, R. G. Collingwood, was deeply sceptical of Thucydides' veracity and even his claim to the title of historian.[6] Nor have readers always preferred the Athenian's austere, matter-of-fact narrative to the warmer and more colourful tapestry woven by Herodotus. As early as the first century BC, the Greek his-torian of Rome, Dionysius of Halicarnassus, who adhered to the general opin-ion that Thucydides 'has been most careful of the truth, the high-priestess of which we desire history to be',[7] was nonetheless critical of the Athenian and rather laudatory of Herodotus, whose subject of the Persian Wars seemed more noble and less distasteful than Thucydides' tale of calamity and folly. But no feature of Thucydides' history has caused his defenders so much trouble as his practice of including supposedly genuine speeches at critical points in his narrative. This concern of scholars derives from a long-standing fixation on what is best called by its German term, *Quellenkritik* ('source criticism'), the separation of tiny kernels of knowable and authentic wheat from baskets of supposititious, legendary or even outrightly mendacious chaff.

Recent scholarship has been more forgiving. We know, and Thucydides openly admits, that he did not personally hear all of the speeches that he relates, and that his memory of those that he did hear is imperfect – he did not record them word for word. On the other hand, one recent scholar has asserted that there is no single speech in Thucydides of which it can be said that it could *not* have been given in the manner and form in which he represents it.[8] The practice of including such speeches, possibly influenced by Greek tragedy, would not be short-lived, and it fulfilled an important role within a history, since words were deemed as significant and influential as deeds – in a sense, a famous and effective speech *was* a deed. The speech also provided an important narrative linkage between events, a device which the talented historian could use to enrich his account and transcend the boundaries of calendrical years. 'Speeches, so to speak, sum up events and hold the history together', Polybius would comment in the second century.[9] In the end, the only ancient historian known to have avoided speeches entirely is Pompeius

Box 2   Xenophon

An early heir to Thucydides' mantle as 'historian as soldier/statesman', Xenophon was born about the beginning of the Peloponnesian war (c. 431). He wrote his *Anabasis* (or 'march up-country') as an account of his own leadership of a group of Greek mercenaries after the defeat of their employer, Cyrus the Younger of Persia, who was challenging the authority of his older brother, the Persian king Artaxerxes II. While this text, and the *Cyropaedia* ('The Education of Cyrus'), about the upbringing and career of the same-named sixth-century Persian king, have been widely read by students of Greek language, Xenophon's major historical achievement rested with his *Hellenica*, covering Greek affairs from 411, where Thucydides broke off, to 362. In some ways this was the first example of a genre later known as 'the History of my own Life and Times'. It is a work that leaves out many important facts, but it illustrates better than most the fine line that historians were now treading between recounting the strict and unadorned truth and serving the higher purpose of lesson-provision, which sometimes required a deliberate distortion of chronology or exaggeration of events.

Trogus (*fl.* first century BC), and the practice would be revived by the classicizing humanist historians of the Renaissance.

With the declining autonomy and power of the *polis*, the independent Greek city state, and the failure of Athenian democracy, the fourth and third centuries saw increasing numbers of prominent and colourful tyrants, mercenaries, warlords and monarchs, culminating in Alexander the Great. There was unsurprisingly a refocusing of historical writing towards individuals and their achievements, as well as more direct authorial commentary on their characters. The beginnings of another long tradition, the role of the historian as not only the reporter but also the 'judge' of past misdeeds, can be found in what remains of the highly oratorical work of Ephorus and especially Theopompus, a severe critic of historical figures. In terms of surviving texts, we have fared rather better with a third major fourth-century historian, Xenophon (c. 431 to c. 352), who has enjoyed a generally high reputation (see Box 2).

Of the Greek historians after Thucydides, perhaps none has won as high praise as Polybius (c. 200–118), though this admiration was rather slow in coming and did not really peak until the Renaissance, which admired his sober tone, his keen attention to identifying the causes of events and his emphasis on the practical lessons of the past. Polybius influenced the Roman historian Livy, for whom he was a major source, but his reputation fell off in late antiquity and much of his work then virtually disappeared for a millennium. His fame never rested on the literary quality of his writing, which is rather dull compared with his fifth-century precursors, though Polybius cannot have been insensitive to style since he clearly understood the function of the historian as persuader and educator. He wrote, as he put it – coining a phrase later ages would borrow – a 'pragmatic history'. It is he who first framed the convention that the ideal historian would be a man of experience, a *topos* repeated periodically from his time to the nineteenth century AD. More than any other extant Greek historian, he also interrupted his account in places to provide the reader with explicit statements on methodology, discussing the need for historians to weigh different accounts, criticizing his predecessors by name; he paid greater attention than Thucydides to what we would now call the 'primary' sources of history, especially archives and inscriptions.

Polybius was at first a captive and then a guest of the Romans who had defeated the Achaean League of which he had been a functionary; like the Jew Josephus later on, he adapted enthusiastically to a Roman world. Sheer good luck brought him into contact with the Aemilii, architects of the Roman triumph over Carthage. Polybius admired what he saw, and it led him to think carefully about how world powers rise and fall. He articulated in the sixth book of his *Histories* a theory of predictable constitutional cycles (generally referred to as the *anakuklosis politeion*) among three pure and three corresponding perverted forms of government previously delineated by Aristotle, and postulated the stability of 'mixed' regimes consisting of all three pure forms. This was to prove a powerful tool of historical analysis in later centuries: according to Polybius, Rome owed its greatness to its balancing of monarchical, aristocratic and democratic elements, though even he evinced doubt that this balance could be maintained in perpetuity, worried by the democratic reforms that followed the final destruction of Carthage, the great external enemy, in 146. Apart from Tacitus two centuries later, it is difficult to think of an ancient historian who has had as profound an influence on the course of later *political* thought – Polybius' ideas would be taken up by Machiavelli in the sixteenth century, by English republicans in the seventeenth and by Montesquieu and the framers of the American constitution in the eighteenth.

Like Thucydides, Polybius believed in first-hand interrogation of witnesses; unlike Thucydides (and rather more like Herodotus) he asserted that much of this should be conducted through wide travels. This was a necessity since he sought to write a history of very different scope than the *Peloponnesian War*, a 'universal' history (that is, of the known world) such as Ephorus had attempted in the fourth century. But whereas in Ephorus the histories of different states and countries had been recounted side-by-side and separately, Polybius ensured that his parts formed a bigger whole. His *Histories* recounted a cumulative process throughout the *oecumene*, leading to a particular destiny, the hegemony of the Roman republic. Polybius' account was in part comparative, and – crucially – it was also interconnected. His term, συμπλοκή (*symploke*), for the connections between different states, allowed him to resolve the various threads of individual histories, increasingly merged after the key historical moment of the Conference of Naupactus in 217. This was not an easy task: Greek historians had traditionally dated events by years of civic officials; attention to precise chronology was of little interest to the vast majority – even Thucydides was normally content to describe an event as occurring within a particular season. The problem of multiple calendars and differing chronologies has from that day to this been among the things that the international historian has had to sort out before ever putting pen to paper. Polybius borrowed from Ephorus in organizing his material around Olympiads (the series of four-year cycles, commencing in 776, between Olympic games), in every book beginning with Italy and then branching out to other regions such as Sicily, Greece, Africa and even Asia and Egypt.

It is not simply the interconnectedness of his *Histories* that would give Polybius weight; his stress on the process of history towards the single goal or telos of Roman supremacy – driven there by a *Tyche* who assumes a role much less like random fortune than like a kind of deliberate fate – provided a model for much later Roman history. Ultimately it would feature prominently in the combination of Greek, Roman and Judaic views of the past that would characterize two millennia of Christian historical writing and, in its more secular variation, the liberal progressivist strand within modern historiography that sometimes goes by the name of 'the Whig interpretation of history'.[10] This is a formidable set of influences for a relatively minor Greek political figure who spent much of his life in exile.

Roman Historians to the Second Century AD

By Polybius' time, the centre of power around the Mediterranean had shifted westward to Rome, which had by the mid-second century subdued virtually every enemy its legions had encountered and was rapidly expanding across Europe and the Near East. By the early first century, it was not very difficult to predict where all this was heading and to spin accounts of history in the same direction, as Polybius had already done. Thus a Greek Stoic philosopher named Poseidonius of Apameia who saw Rome as the embodiment of Stoic values, set out to write yet another universal history which, like Polybius' work, would also influence subsequent Roman historians. Very little of Poseidonius remains, as we have seen with many of the Greek historians. The survival rate among known texts of Roman historians has been even worse. The work of Vergil's friend Gaius Asinius Pollio (d. AD 4) has vanished without a trace. Scant fragments remain of Aulus Cremutius Cordus, famous for being forced to commit suicide in AD 25 during the reign of the Emperor Tiberius, perhaps for having treated Julius Caesar's assassins too even-handedly. Of others such as Sallust we have their relatively minor works but not their major ones, or, as with Livy and Tacitus, what we have is a body of work missing several limbs and a good chunk of the torso. And, as with the Greeks, there are undoubtedly others whose very names have been lost along with their writings.

Historiography started slowly in Rome: whereas in Greece it had followed epic, the greatest Latin epic, the *Aeneid*, was a late arrival, composed by Vergil in the first century BC, and thus at virtually the same time that Livy, the great historian of the republic, was writing his prose history. There were early verse efforts at a narrative of the city's early history, in particular Gnaeus Naevius' (270–201) poem on the first Punic war, and Quintus Ennius' (239–169) *Annales*, an account of history from Aeneas to the early second century; barely sixty lines of Naevius and six hundred of Ennius now remain. Apart from these, two major families or groups of history-writing survive from early Rome, both of which had Greek influences. The first, perhaps derived from Greek horography, consisted of records maintained by a civic and religious official, the *pontifex maximus*, and annually transferred to bronze inscriptions in the Forum. These *Annales maximi* were little more than records of the sequence of annually appointed major officials – consuls, praetors, etc. The recurrent complaint by narrative historians of the triviality of the annalistic method, a commonplace during the Renaissance, would receive an early start in Cato's declaration that the records of the pontifex should not be imitated since they often amounted to 'how often grain was costly, how often darkness or something else blocked the light of the moon or the sun'.[11] Apart from the pontifical records, funeral orations, public inscriptions, family records and accounts by other magistrates of their periods in office (*commentarii*) would also provide material for historians. The second major family includes Roman writers who may have written continuous prose and, at least at first, composed their works in Greek. This included Quintus Fabius Pictor (*fl.* 225 BC), little of whose history has survived, though again he is known through later authors (he is one of Polybius' targets). Fabius is believed to have used a variety of sources ranging from earlier Greek writers to the *Annales maximi*, oral tradition, magistrate lists and chronicles kept by his own and other families. His work, which established the shape of early Roman history, would be complemented and revised by later historians.

The earliest-known prose history written in Latin, which has not survived, was the *Origines*, by the fiercely xenophobic politician and protector of Roman virtue, Cato the Censor (234–149), whose very choice of Latin was a protest against the

Greek influences which he saw as dangerously corrupting. Even he, however, followed the Greek model of continuous prose, and borrowed other aspects of Greek historiography such as the inclusion of what might be called 'remarkable facts'.[12] Later annalists such as C. Licinius Macer expanded the somewhat cursory account of early Roman history in their predecessors; interestingly, they have often been dismissed in subsequent ages as men of humble origins, with narrowly pro-Roman views and fertile imaginations, writers of entertainment quite without the senatorial seriousness and experience, much less the first-hand knowledge, of a Cato. This would not be the last time that high birth was seen as a necessary condition of historiographic talent.

Non-annalistic history remained for some time largely in Greek hands. The first-century works of Diodorus Siculus (c. 90–30) and Dionysius of Halicarnassus (c. 60 to after 7 BC) have survived rather more completely than most. Diodorus was a Sicilian Greek who, like Herodotus four centuries earlier, had travelled widely prior to writing his *Bibliotheca historica*. Another universal history in the manner of Polybius, it originally consisted of forty books, of which we have about a third intact. The title of 'Historical Library' was a reference to the number of earlier sources from which Diodorus drew his materials, which has often been a reason for dismissing this author as an unoriginal hack, though he would have understood himself instead as the culmination of a long stream of predecessors; 'tradition', a critical aspect of the historical enterprise, was beginning to weigh more heavily upon historians' choice of subjects and their arrangement of materials. Diodorus began with several books of geography and ethnography before launching into his narrative of events from the Trojan War to c. 60; as the ending has been lost, we do not know how far he got. The work is notable among other things for its practice of 'euhemerism' – the rationalization of reputed divine and semi-divine figures into human heroes and inventors in an attempt to historicize myth.

Dionysius of Halicarnassus focused more exclusively on Rome, and the main point of his *Roman Antiquities* was to defend Roman influence over the Greek world. In it we see the triumph of the rhetorical and hortatory strain of history-writing first seen in the time of Ephorus and Theopompus. It is Dionysius who coined the oft-repeated definition of history as 'philosophy teaching by example', and he continued the tradition of declaring, up-front, his own methods and preferences. Thus Dionysius would begin his *Roman Antiquities* with the following remarks:

Although it is much against my will to indulge in the explanatory statements usually given in the prefaces to histories, yet I am obliged to prefix to this work some remarks concerning myself. In doing this it is neither my intention to dwell too long on my own praise, which I know would be distasteful to the reader, nor have I the purpose of censuring other historians, as Anaximenes and Theopompus did in the prefaces to their histories; but I shall only show the reasons that induced me to undertake this work and give an accounting of the sources from which I gained the knowledge of the things I am going to relate.[13]

It should be clear by now that *historia* in its Latin or Graeco-Latin form had moved a great distance from the senses in either Herodotus or Thucydides. Where Herodotus had intended the word to mean 'inquiry', and had not linked it specifically to the past, and Thucydides had defined it more narrowly as the re-counting of recent or contemporary events, history had by the time of Diodorus and Dionysius become firmly associated with a *narrative of the past*, remote or recent, and increasingly with a focus on the political and military, despite the inclination of several authors to begin their works with geographic sections. Similarly, history was now quite definitively a branch of literature and spe-cifically of rhetoric. Persuasion had triumphed over research, or at least taken primacy, with the praise of the virtuous and successful, and condemnation of the corrupt, wicked or weak, a key motivation for any historian. If 'renown' was a feature of Greek historical writing and epic, its Latin counterpart *fama* now became inextricably linked to history, not only because historians saw it as their duty to praise and blame, but because the very fact that they did so provided an inducement to historical actors to do good.

The Romans were not much interested in knowledge of the past for its own sake and they produced very little of what we would call 'antiquarian' erudition since there was little hortatory value to be derived from it. Apart from the *Noctes Atticae* of Aulus Gellius (AD 125–180), which has antiquarian content, the sole excep-tion is the fragmentarily surviving *Antiquitates* by the prolific M. Terentius Varro (116–27). Roman authors, in contrast to the Greeks, also spent very little time thinking about *how* to write about the past and in what sub-genres. It is thus no accident whatever that the first really clear theorizing about history by a Roman was the product of a powerful orator, Marcus Tullius Cicero (106–43), whose discus-sion of history would be found principally in a dialogue entitled *De oratore* ('On the Orator'). For Cicero (*De Orat.* 2.36), history was *testis temporum, lux veritatis, nuncia vetustatis* – the witness of times, the light of truth and herald of antiquity. He articulated certain principles that would become axiomatic in later times, such as the obligation of the historian to tell nothing but the truth, without partiality (*De Orat.* 2.62), and he emphasized its connection with rhetoric by promoting an ornate style. Cicero's definition was scarcely profound, but it had the benefit of conciseness, and the weight of his great reputation, especially fifteen centuries after Cicero during the European Renaissance when his star was at its apogee. The rhetorical emphasis would be maintained two centuries later in the first work

Box 3   Julius Caesar

If Livy personified the historian as professional literary man, Gaius Julius Caesar was his opposite, an embodiment of the notion that generals are their own best historians, and together with one or two medieval Spanish kings and the sixteenth-century Mughal Emperor Babur, a member of that select group of rulers who have written their own histories. Caesar's two *Commentaries*, as he called them, relayed the stories respectively of his Gallic wars and expedition into Britain, and of the subsequent civil war he fought with his former colleague, Pompey the Great. Unsurprisingly self-laudatory (though he wrote in the third person), Caesar is not unfair to his opponents, and the *Commentaries*, allowing for their perspective, are a useful source for the last years of the republic. To the displeasure of several centuries of schoolboys, they would eventually prove even more popular as a Latin teaching-text.

devoted entirely to the proper writing of history, Lucian of Samosata's (c. AD 129 to after 180), *How to Write History*.

The major Roman innovation in historiography was a shaping of history into the cumulative story of world events. This was not, of course, strictly their invention – Polybius deserves much of the credit or blame for making Roman history move towards a goal. But the Romans had a strong sense of the divine destiny of their city and its expanding empire, and this provided both a horizon and an occasion for their history-writing in the way that curiosity about the known world as a whole had done for the Greeks. The Romans, however, also injected a teleological and progressive element that was absent in Greek historians before Polybius. Where cycles of rise and fall and the random hand of *Tyche* (fortune) appear in many of the Greek historians, history becomes more purposeful and almost providential among the Romans. When linked eventually with the eschatological elements of Jewish thought (Josephus providing an important bridge between these two worlds), this would provide a powerful basis for Christian historiography.

The first century BC produced two great Latin historians (three if we include Julius Caesar (see Box 3)) who composed rather different works. Easily the most influential was Titus Livius or Livy (59 BC to AD 17), who stands at the end of that line of republican annalists which began with Pictor. Most of Livy's long and ambitious work has been lost, but we have enough to know its shape and scope. (Of 142 books, 35 now survive and there are extant summaries of most of the lost ones.)

Organized into a set of 'decades' and 'pentads' (units of ten or five books), and within these as annals, Livy's first book – a self-contained text that he published in order to test the market for a history by a private citizen who held no major office or military command – begins with the Trojan arrival in Italy before moving to the establishment of Rome by Romulus (traditionally placed at 753 BC) and the period of the seven kings. Entitled *Ab Urbe Condita* ('from the foundation of the city') Livy's history was, for its time, the definitive account of the Roman republic which he, a provincial observer from Padua, had witnessed collapse after a half century of civil war, ending in the principate of Octavian or Augustus Caesar. Written in a Latin that later ages regarded either as impeccably pure or overly florid, the history combined the annalistic approach, with its recording of the year's officers, and a continuous prose narrative. In a way, it turned the genre of local history almost by accident into a variant of universal history, since Rome, at its peak of international influence and on the verge of becoming an empire in governance as well as influence, now controlled most of the Mediterranean world.

The other, and perhaps more interesting, major first-century historian was the politician and soldier known to us as Sallust (Caius Sallustius Crispus, 86–34 BC). Of plebeian origins, he was initially associated with Julius Caesar's 'popular' party and his official career climaxed with an undistinguished spell as governor of the province of Africa Nova. On his return to Rome Sallust turned to historical writing, penning histories first of the notorious conspiracy of the patrician Catiline in the year 63 and then of the war against the African king Jugurtha in the late second century. Sallust was widely respected in subsequent centuries, his works providing a template for writing the history of a particular event such as Catiline's conspiracy. More than any other Roman historian, Sallust was (and declared himself to be) the disciple of Thucydides, though he adopted a far more judgmental tone than had the Athenian. Sallust created the enduring theme – a favourite of historians from his own time through St Augustine and down to modernity – that Roman decline could be traced directly to the destruction of Carthage, which had left the Romans masters of their universe, but prey to the twin corruptors avarice and ambition, their growing empire the playground for internecine strife. Sallust also took Polybius' semi-rational *Tyche* and turned it into the feminine, capricious *Fortuna*, thereby handing on this all-purpose explanatory mechanism to late antiquity and beyond.

Imperial Rome, commencing with the rule of Augustus Caesar following the Battle of Actium in 31 BC, also had its historians, among whom the most highly regarded was, and remains, Publius (or Gaius) Cornelius Tacitus (c. AD 56 to c. 117). Where Livy had written in a flowing rhetorical style, Tacitus seems closer to Sallust, whom he admired, or, more remotely Polybius. Where Livy's work had been written with oral recitation in mind, Tacitus' was directed at the private reader. Long rhetorical flourishes were replaced in his writing by a terse, epigrammatic narrative, into which Tacitus intruded political *sententiae* that readers in a later age would find irresistible. His very name means 'silent', but Tacitus was in life a very skilful orator, a pupil of the rhetorician Quintilian, and eventually author himself of a treatise on rhetoric. His fame, however, has been built on a combination of apparently shrewd character judgment and an ability to say much in few words: 'Tacitean' has even become an adjective to describe an entire style of writing.

What made Tacitus such a success? In part, fortune was kind to his works, permitting the survival of most of his *Annals* and *Histories* through the Middle Ages (each in a single manuscript) during which time they were virtually unused; such was Christian antipathy to a writer regarded as both pagan and hostile. Like Sallust, Xenophon and Thucydides, Tacitus was a man of political and military experience, a senator who had advanced through the standard Roman *cursus honorum* leading to the consulship, which Tacitus held in AD 97, serving as provincial governor of the province of Asia (AD 112/113). In contrast to a much more prominent politician–historian, Caesar, he was able to effect an air of restrained neutrality, famously declaring that he wrote his works *sine ira et studio* (without anger or what we would now call an 'axe to grind'). And yet of Tacitus' political views there can be little doubt. For instance, his *Germania*, one of the most influential of ancient texts, praised the rough, uncultured but unspoiled virtue of the German tribes, and later became a literary source and justification for German Protestants' revolt against Roman Catholicism in the sixteenth century, and for German nationalism in the nineteenth and twentieth centuries.

Of Tacitus' two major works, both written rather later in his career, the *Histories* recount the turmoil leading from the fall of Nero through the 'Year of Five Emperors' (AD 68–9) and the accession of the Flavian line, ending with its disastrous last representative, Domitian. Tacitus' distaste for Domitian, to whom he admits he owed in part his own advancement, is evident, and *Agricola* ends with the emperor being compared unfavourably to so notorious a tyrant as Nero, on the grounds that Domitian took delight in personally witnessing the atrocities he had ordered (*Agricola*, cap. 45). Tacitus' treatment of the earlier emperors was somewhat more subdued in his subsequent masterpiece, the *Annals* (or *ab excessu Divi Augusti*) which covers the principate from the death of Augustus through Claudius, and which is perhaps the most remarkable example from classical antiquity of exhaustive research in both public and private sources as well as earlier historians. We have lost much of its middle section dealing with the mad emperor Caligula and the reputed fool Claudius, but most of what Tacitus wrote about Tiberius and Nero survives; both owe their subsequent infamy to Tacitus' relatively low-key but jugular-slicing references to Nero's credulity, lascivious depravity and spiteful jealousy or to Tiberius' obsessive paranoia. The historian's words of political wisdom – or 'prudence' as later ages would call it – were sometimes inserted indirectly, vocalized or even silently thought by his characters, often ironically. Tacitus' chronic understatement made it hard for readers in the Renaissance, when he was rediscovered with enormous enthusiasm, to decide whether he was an opponent of tyranny, providing advice on how to endure and survive under its sway, or really a Machiavellian exponent of strong rule whose *sententiae* should be carefully heeded by modern despots.

The Pagan Historians of Late Antiquity

The eighteenth-century French philosopher Montesquieu is supposed to have remarked 'Happy the people whose annals are tiresome', an observation of the fact that history by its very nature tends to record unpleasant things: crisis, war, rebellion and violence. It sometimes does seem that great history is mainly written during or after political crises rather than during prolonged periods of peace: there is simply more of interest to write about when things are going badly, or when there is a victory over adversity that must be commemorated. The western Roman Empire lingered on three full centuries after the death of Tacitus before a combination of 'barbarism and religion' (to quote another famed eighteenth-century figure, Edward Gibbon, the British historian of Roman decline) laid it low. So far as the evolution of Western historical writing is concerned, the most important developments of the late antique period were the advent of Christianity and, from the reign of Constantine in the early fourth century, its establishment as the official religion of the empire; the increasing instability, as Tacitus had observed, of an empire whose leaders ruled only so long as they had the support of the army; and the splitting of the increasingly unwieldy empire in the late third century into a western half (based at Rome) and an eastern (based at Byzantium, later renamed Constantinople), whence sprang the Greek-speaking Byzantine Empire. Just as significant as any of these internal developments, however, was an external threat: the looming presence of a number of barbarian peoples to both east and west. These were no longer traditional foes such as the forest-dwelling Germans of Tacitus' day, or the Parthians who had been a thorn in the Roman side since the late second century BC, but migratory tribes of Celts, Goths and Huns whose collective movements around Europe and Central Asia, known as the *Völkerwanderung*, would over the next several centuries encircle and infiltrate the empire. The Visigoths, one of these tribes, sacked Rome in AD 410 (precisely eight centuries after it had last been overrun, by the Gauls), and the last western Roman emperor was deposed by another Gothic general in 476. The Visigoths, Ostrogoths and other peoples such as the Franks, Saxons, Jutes and Lombards would eventually set up a series of independent monarchies in what remained of the former Roman dominions in Europe.

These internal and external phenomena were obviously not unrelated, but we should treat their historiographic consequences in turn. Deferring the Christian historians of late antiquity to our next chapter, this section will be devoted to the last of the pagan historians of Rome, who were variously Greeks, Romans or inhabitants of the wider empire. Most of these have enjoyed nothing like the attention meted out to the likes of Livy and Tacitus, a neglect not always fair. Cassius Dio (c. 155 to after 229), for example, authored a respectable history of Rome from Aeneas to 229, a period of nearly a millennium. Lucius Florus (*fl.* early second century AD), who would be briefly popular in the seventeenth century, is conventionally dismissed as a prosaic and unimaginative epitomizer of Livy, but it is through his work that we know something about those sections of Livy which have vanished; moreover, the epitomizer also developed a rather clever metaphor for the decline of Rome according to the human aging process in seven stages from infancy through senility and death. A more problematic work, the authenticity of which has remained a matter of dispute, is the collection of biographies known since the Renaissance as the *Historia Augusta*. This work, supposedly written by six different *scriptores* (authors) under the names Aelius Spartianus, Julius Capitolinus, Vulcacius Gallicanus, Aelius Lampridius, Trebellius Pollio and Flavius Vopiscus at the end of the third and beginning of the fourth century, purports to recount the rather sorry spectacle of a number of emperors and usurpers from Hadrian in the early second century to Numerian in the late third.

It is hard to dispute the suggestion, based on works like the *Historia Augusta*, that most of the late ancients are less interesting and innovative as historians than their illustrious predecessors, and most can be omitted in a survey such as this. But it is also true that several centuries of historiographers have seen the late antique pagan historians as small fish struggling in a rising Christian tide. In many cases we know very little about these authors and have only traces of their original works. Thus the reputation of the virulently anti-Christian Eunapius of Sardis (349–404), who had the dual misfortune of having his works lost and backing the wrong religious horse, has not flourished, though by all accounts he was a learned man, authoring a set of *Lives of Sophists* and a *Universal History*. At the outer end of the period, the late fifth-century author Zosimus was a minor official who wrote a *Historia Nova* (New History) of Rome describing its decline in the context of earlier empires like Persia and Macedonia – in some ways his was the 'downhill' slope intended to complete the 'uphill' story once related by Polybius, to whom Zosimus refers at the very outset of his own work.[14]

The most notable exception to this underwhelming group is the *Res Gestae Libri XXXI* ('Thirty-one Books of Deeds') by a Greek soldier from Antioch named Ammianus Marcellinus (c. 325 to after 391). The first thirteen books of Ammianus' thirty-one-book history have not survived, though we know from his own comments that he began it where Tacitus' *Histories* had left off, with the Emperor Nerva (r. 96–8). Ammianus is almost universally considered to be the last of the great ancient historians of Rome, and one of the last European historians for some centuries to compose his history in the grand rhetorical style, complete with speeches and a dearth of dates beyond those indicated by his annalistic framework. Ammianus' reputation has not been especially sullied by his unapologetic nostalgia for the glory days of pagan Rome or his enthusiasm for the Emperor Julian 'the Apostate' (r. 361–3), who briefly restored the old gods following Constantine's promotion of Christianity as the empire's favoured religion. Though a Greek, Ammianus wrote in Latin, the last in a series of citizens of the empire like Polybius and Josephus who had fallen in love with Rome. Unlike them, Ammianus also adopted the rulers' vocabulary, borrowing turns of phrase from the likes of Ovid, Lucan, Aulus Gellius and especially Cicero. Ammianus saw himself in relation to the Emperor Julian much as Polybius had stood in relation to Scipio Aemilianus, and he substituted the notion of a vengeful godlike 'Justice' for Polybian *Tyche*. It is Ammianus who first gave us, or at least popularized, the familiar designation of Rome herself as *urbs aeterna* (the eternal city). Later historians have valued his eyewitness account of the decline of the once-mighty Rome and his attention to economic and social as well as political causes of these drawn-out death throes. Ammianus' history is full of interesting information on the various parts of the empire and its peoples, and he is rather less unsympathetic to most of them than Tacitus, for example, had been to the Jews. He even includes scientific topics such as earthquakes and eclipses. Ammianus' attention to such matters is all the more remarkable and perhaps even unintended since he himself proclaimed that history should concentrate on the important and prominent events and ignore the trivial or commonplace (Ammianus 26.1.1–2), which should warn us that the announced intentions of historians, and the theories or protocols to which they purportedly subscribe, are as often as not violated in practice.

Chinese Historiography from Earliest Times to the Han Dynasty

The Romans' conquests took them to the Near East, Syria and Egypt, but no further; it would fall to Italians of a millennium later to visit China, an empire of equivalent size and greater longevity. No civilization in the world has consistently and continuously placed as high a priority on the recording and understanding

Figure 6 | Chinese oracle bone. Shang dynasty (1650–1066 BC).

of its past as the Chinese. Convention and their invention of the word 'history' has put the Greeks first in the present narrative, but we could just as easily have begun much farther east. As in Mesopotamia, the earliest forms of what became historical writing started as record-keeping, but with a much clearer tie to the past. The 'oracle bones' (inscribed fragments of bone or shell first unearthed in the late nineteenth century) which are the earliest extant source for the first definitively historical dynasty, the Shang (c. 1600 to c. 1046 BC), appear to have been created in direct response to the royal family's veneration of ancestors, and contain direct petitions to or communications with them (Fig. 6); their closest analogue may be the omen-texts of the contemporary Assyrians.

Exact analogies between Chinese and classical European historiography should be drawn within an awareness of their fundamental differences. For a start, the differences between an alphabetic and a logogrammatic mode of writing are significant. Though, as already noted, it changed its meaning after Herodotus' initial use, there is relatively little ambiguity about what the Greek word ἱστορια denotes. In Chinese, an uninflected and tonal language in which individual characters represent single syllables (a very small number of which are pictographic), and character-combinations represent multi-syllabic words, the same term can mean very different things depending on its context. *Shi* is not unambiguously the word for defining either history or its author. One should also not underestimate the profound differences posed by the complexities of *writing* in a logogrammatic system such as Chinese. Apart from their enormous reverence for tradition, one reason that scholars, from a very early stage, paid tireless attention to the verification of sources (and often deliberately eliminated inferior versions) is that the opportunities for a scribe to misunderstand what he was copying were incomparably greater given the ambiguity of particular logograms. The famous Chinese 'block printing' that was used beginning in the tenth century AD for reproducing manuscripts, well before the arrival of moveable type in Europe, did not necessarily reduce the risk of corruption as damaged blocks could produce distorted characters and bizarre meanings.

Moreover, certain fundamental mental assumptions were quite different. Most European thought until relatively recent times has seen time as corrosive, and change as an inevitable but overwhelmingly bad thing. The earliest Chinese philosophers, for all their intense reverence of tradition, saw time, rather like the Polybian *Tyche*, as an agent of change rather than a vessel in which change occurred, and they valued change as progressive and maturing rather than chaotic or regressive. The upheavals attending the transitions from one dynasty to the next were not so much the mark of failure as of the loss of the prime justification for rule, the 'Mandate of Heaven' (*tianming*). This was a much more deliberate and less wilful concept than the divine displeasure of the Greeks and Babylonians, though not the righteous and absolute deity of Judeo-Christianity. The Grand Historian Sima Qian (see below) would point out examples of good and wise men suffering hard lives and miserable deaths while villains prospered and died in their beds. Chronology, to which Chinese historians paid careful attention, was also conceived of very differently, based on frequently changed era names (the practice used in many Asian countries until the twentieth century) rather than the single chronology *ab orbe condita* (from the creation of the world), *ab urbe condita* (from the founding of the city) or (especially since the seventeenth century) BC and AD – this accounts for the much earlier development in China than in Europe of synchronous chronological tables. The Chinese also conceived of the various genres of history in ways we would find surprising: where 'annals' in the European tradition have usually been regarded as the most rudimentary form of historical record, traditional Chinese historiography regarded the annal as the highest form, the distillation of knowledge from other sources. Grant Hardy has argued that the modern preference since the Renaissance for the single-voiced omniscient narrator and an internally self-consistent story fits ill with the multiple voices and often competing accounts of a single event included by the greatest of ancient Chinese historians, Sima Qian, in his *Shiji*.[15]

Western historiography places a high value upon the independence of the historian from outside interference, though that arm's-length relationship has been ideal rather than fact in most circumstances. Official history, courtly history and other variants have traditionally not fared well in the estimation of modern Euro-American historiographers, for whom autonomy and freedom from influence is highly valued. In China, history was almost from the beginning connected with governance and eventually with the ruling dynasty of the day – yet Chinese historians saw no fundamental contradiction between this and their duty to record the truth, often at great personal risk. Indeed, it has been plausibly argued that the lack of a counterpart to the absolute truth of revealed religion in Christian Europe permitted the Chinese to invest the past with the equivalent quality of certainty. Finally, the historians of imperial China saw historical writing as a process of compilation from earlier sources, including verbatim inclusion of another historian's work. This is relatively foreign to Westerners who virtually since Herodotus have reacted rather sharply to plagiarism, and generally sought to proclaim their independence from previous authors. Confucius declared himself not a maker but a transmitter of wisdom, and the earliest historians similarly envisaged their work as primarily vehicles for the handing down of past knowledge. In practice they did much more, not uncommonly adding the value of moral judgments to bring out the normative aspects of the past and its clues to the meaning of the universe. Truth to an ancient Chinese historian was not the conformity of the history to *actual* reality, but its fidelity to its *sources*: the word *xin* does not mean truth in the modern sense but something more like 'trustworthiness' or reliability. Consequently, compared to the fragmentary survival of classical histories, many Chinese texts of similar antiquity have come down to us virtually wholesale, though modern scholars are rightly sceptical of the notion that Chinese historians added nothing of their own to their inherited materials.

Sir Geoffrey Lloyd, one of the few modern scholars equally at home in classical antiquity and early China, has written extensively comparing the two cultures. Lloyd repeats a well-known episode, taken from the celebrated commentary known as the *Zuozhuan*, concerning the assassination of Duke Zhuang of Qi by his minister, Cui Shu.[16] The story was repeated by Sima Qian, and periodically thereafter. It is famous principally because it epitomizes the Chinese historians' image of themselves as selfless defenders of the truth and of virtue. Three successive brothers, all historians (*dashi*), are put to death by Cui Shu after recording his treachery. Only when the entry, erased every time previously, is finally allowed to stand is a fourth brother satisfied, and even then a historian from the south was prepared to take his place in turn. This vigorous demonstration of the duty of the historian to report the truth, even to the point of death, is undercut by the fact that documents at other times are known to have been altered or even falsified, while the brothers' strident assertion of their devotion to the unadorned record is belied by the obvious dramatic embellishment that the *Zuozhuan* author was pursuing to make his point. It is hard to imagine such an anecdote in Greek or Roman history-writing, even in Thucydides or Tacitus.

Chinese historians consolidated much earlier than their European counterparts a clear and consistent set of rules and practices for the recovery and represen-tation of the past. They also acquired a progressively more official status for the historian that has no counterpart in Greece or even Rome. At first connect-ed with shamanistic divination of the universe's meaning, the word *shi* seems originally to have referred to a ritual official. It subsequently came to denote the ruler's secretary or an official responsible for keeping records; the related tradition of having the ruler flanked at all times by two Recorders of the Left and Right who took down his words and deeds separately was established quite early. Virtually never used by the Chinese, then or since, as a synonym for 'the past' (that is, the actual events that occurred in reality), history was, rather, the accumulated and arrayed *records* of that past (much later denoted as *li shi xue*). As such, it had become a major category of knowledge (along with philosophy, literature and the 'classics') as early as the fourth century BC. This was a status it never held in European antiquity and would not acquire in the West before the late seventeenth century. History in China was also, far more than in Greece, the exemplar *par excellence* of an imperializing or 'hegemonic' practice, one which achieved influence far outside its nominal political domain and eventually gov-erned the historiographical development of Mongolia, Japan, Korea and much of Southeast Asia.

Significant Chinese thinking about the past can be traced back to ancient ca-nonical texts such as the *Yijing* (or *I Ching*, 'Book of Changes'), which reached a definitive form about the end of the second millennium BC. 'History', taken as the authority of the past, had equivalent status with philosophy and poetry. It was represented among the original 'Six Classics' (only five of which, collectively called the *Wujing*, remained extant by the late third century) in two works, the *Shujing* (variously translated as 'Classic of History' or 'Classic of Documents'), one of the earliest collections of official documents, and in the *Chunqiu* ('Spring and Autumn Annals') once attributed to Confucius (see below). The *Shujing*, much of which may predate Herodotus by several decades, is a collection of decrees, dec-larations, public announcements and other texts by the kings of the Shang and especially Zhou dynasties. Deliberate writing *about* the past came somewhat later, and authorship in Chinese historiography prior to the Han is hard to establish, since with the exception of great sages such as Confucius, establishing the per-sona and identity of an author was not a priority either for writers or early read-ers. In some cases, the 'author' associated with a Chinese text is the politician or courtier who authorized its writing. In this manner, for example, the pre-Qin era politician Lü Buwei caused a massive text called the *Lüshi chunqiu* ('Master Lu's Spring and Autumn Annals') to be compiled in the 240s BC, perhaps by hundreds of authors.

For all these differences in practice and context, the reasons for turning to the past, in China, were not remarkably different from those that drove such pursuits in ancient Europe, especially the urge to find in the past a source of stability in troubled times, and to identify in it models of correct behaviour. Earliest Chinese thought articulated the notion that there were discernible patterns in the flow of human affairs from which one could learn to govern oneself and navigate a world of continuous change. As this suggests, Chinese thought about the past was very quickly linked to philosophy and the search for the *Dao* (the 'path' or moral order). The first significant independent work of history, the *Chunqiu* or *Spring and Autumn Annals*, essentially a chronicle of the state of Lu (not to be confused with the later *Lüshi chunqiu*), is an account of events from 722 to about 480 BC. It is generally associated with the influential philosopher Confucius or Master Kong (551–479), though what survives is probably a commentary on or revision by Confucius of an earlier work, now lost. In addition, Confucius' *Analects* convey some of the earliest statements about the proper role of a *shi*. 'I transmit but do not create. Being fond of the truth, I am an admirer of antiquity.'[17] Confucius also repudiated the recording of miracles and prodigies, thereby rejecting the shamanistic origins of the *shi* for something closer to divination, in which the historian brings his powers of reason to bear on the past to reveal the workings of the world.

The *Chunqiu* is in itself a spare text that lists little more than the skeleton of events; we depend for its meaning on the Chinese tradition of providing commentaries on earlier works. Several of these appeared in ensuing centuries, such as the above-mentioned the *Zuozhuan* and its near-contemporary text, the *Guoyu*. The earliest readers of these, such as the Warring States era (475–221) thinker, Mozi, tended to include the commentaries together with the original chronicle under the combined title of *Chunqiu*. These commentaries are difficult to date with any accuracy; both *Zuozhuan* and *Guoyu* are sometimes attributed to an obscure Confucian contemporary called Zuo Qiuming, but they have also been placed chronologically much later, and portions of both were undoubtedly additions by later scholars up to the early Han era. Their veracity – the degree to which they accurately recount events of the past – remains a matter of dispute.

The narratives in the *Zuozhuan* ('Zuo Commentary'), which is sometimes called the Zuo Chronicle because of its annalistic linkage to sections of the *Chunqiu*, deal with political struggles over succession or usurpation. The following quotation from the fourth year of Duke Yin (719 BC) gives some flavour of the work, including the use of direct quotation and the pointed moral at the end:

In the spring Chou-hsü of Wei assassinated Duke Huan and set himself up as ruler.

The ruler of Lu and the ruler of Sung were planning to meet, intending to renew their former alliance, but before the date of the meeting arrived, men from Wei came to Lu to report the rebellion in Wei .... [the writer goes on to describe Chou-hsü's own weaknesses as ruler and his failure to practise 'true virtue']

Shih Hou thereupon accompanied Chou-hsü on a visit to Ch'en. Shih Ch'üeh meanwhile sent an envoy to Ch'en to report, saying: 'Wei is a small and insignificant state, and I am an old man – the fact is that these two men have assassinated my lord, the ruler of Wei. May I ask you to take care of them for me?'

The men of Ch'en seized Chou-hsü and Shih Hou and requested Wei to supervise the matter.

In the ninth month the men of Wei dispatched Ch'ou, superintendent of the right, to supervise the execution of Chou-hsü at P'u. Shih Ch'üeh dispatched his house steward Nou Yang-chien to supervise the execution of his son Shih Hou in Ch'en.

The gentleman remarks: Shih Ch'üeh was a minister of utmost fidelity. He hated Chou-hsü, and his son Hou was allied with Chou-hsü. Is this not what is meant by the saying, a larger duty cancels out the bonds of kinship?[18]

Although the shape and tone of this extract seems very different from something we might read in Herodotus or Tacitus, there are many elements in common. Themes such as revenge and ambition, and a stock virtuous character such as the loyal servant, could just as easily be found in Greek writing of about the same time, while Shi Que's (= Shih Ch'üeh) rather ruthless execution of his own son may remind some readers of a celebrated episode in Livy, the condemnation of his own sons for treason by the famous deposer of tyrants, Lucius Junius Brutus. The punch-line to these episodes, delivered by 'The gentleman' (the author himself) is a slightly more intrusive and less subtle counterpart to Tacitus' sentences – though the intrusion is itself much more explicitly signalled. As with Tacitus, the wise utterances are just as often placed in the mouths of the protagonists during the main part of the account, and in a similarly dense and terse style.

The commentators drew on the *Chunqiu* and other early chronicles to present historical anecdotes and speeches in support of a Confucian outlook which, like the Buddhist, tended to a cyclical view of time that dominated Chinese historical thought until the nineteenth century. The *Zuozhuan* (Extract 3) has been identified by one scholar as the first Chinese historical text to bring together two previously distinct Chinese concerns in a single narrative, namely the traditional concern for remembrance and the wish to find meaning in historical events. Its authors followed chronology relentlessly, to the point that a reader would be required to

3: Early Chinese Historical Writing: the *Zuozhuan*

On the day *i-ch'ou*, Chao Ch'uan attacked and killed Duke Ling in the peach orchard.

Chao Tun, who had not yet crossed the mountains [on the border of the state], returned to the capital.

The grand historian [Tung Hu] wrote: 'Chao Tun assassinated his ruler' and showed the document to the court.

Chao Tun said, 'That is not true!'

The historian replied, 'You are the chief minister. When you fled you did not cross the border. Now you have returned you do not punish the culprit. If you are not responsible, who is?'

Chao Tun said, 'Alas! The words:

These longings of mine,

they've brought this grief on me!

apply to me.'

Confucius said: 'Tung Hu was a good historian of ancient times. In recording principles he did not conceal anything. Chao Tun was a good official of ancient times. For the sake of the principle he was willing to receive a bad name. What a pity! If he had crossed the border he might have escaped the charge.'

Selected from *The Tso Chuan: Selections from China's Oldest Narrative History*, trans. Burton Watson (New York: Columbia University Press, 1989). Reprinted with permission from the publisher. Watson's notes have been omitted but his bracketed interpolations allowed to stand; Wade-Giles transliteration is here retained. This selection from the *Zuozhuan*, recounting events from the year 607 BC, illustrates the early importance of historians in China and their close relation with rulers. The selection quotes Confucius' own commentary on the earlier historian Tung Hu.

move around the text in order to find the outcomes of events, creating 'a feeling that multifarious events have no definite beginnings and endings, that everything is indeed connected to everything else'.[19] The notion of cycles is raised here to a level beyond that which a Greek like Polybius could embrace: specific events, not just general patterns, were so likely to recur that the properly prepared reader could divine their signs in earlier events through complete knowledge and attendance to ritual propriety.

Given this conception of the orderly movement of events, Chinese historians acquired very early the understanding that history could provide a pool of examples with which to guide moral and especially political life. According to Sima Qian, who discussed Confucius' supposed compilation of the *Chunqiu*, the great sage believed that his own reputation would rest on his success as a historian. Sima also quoted one of his own contemporaries, Dong Zhongshu, to the effect that Confucius had 'judged the rights and wrongs of a period of 242 years and made a standard for an empire'.[20] Confucius' reported declaration that his political creed was better demonstrated by the examples of 'actual affairs' than in 'theoretical words' may be the first articulation of that superior exemplarity of history advocated by European historians from Dionysius of Halicarnassus through to Lord Bolingbroke in the eighteenth century, and disputed by philosophers and poets from Aristotle onward.

The Chinese worked anecdotal digressions into their accounts, making frequent use of flashbacks when a story, though chronologically out of place, could be adduced to deliver a moral message. They also included speeches and even conversations in their histories just as contemporary Greek authors had done. They also sometimes shifted events around either for aesthetic or rhetorical reasons. The Zuo commentators recount the story of one King Ling, brought down by his frivolous and spendthrift love of luxury and lack of respect for tradition. Ling was eventually deposed by his younger brother and obliged to commit suicide in 529, but the historiographers had his story climax a year earlier. Their narrative of the king's ruin, and the lessons drawn from it, occurs while the ruler, on one of his winter travels, is grief-stricken at the realization of his folly. The lessons are pointed much more sharply than following any European historian prior to Tacitus:

Confucius said, 'There is a maxim from times long past: "To control oneself and to restore rites is benevolence." Fine Indeed! If King Ling of Chu had been able to do this, how could he ever have been shamed at Ganxi.'[21]

Other philosophical schools departed from the dominant Confucianism, and the range of opinions on the process of historical change is considerably more varied than anything in the West during antiquity or the Middle Ages. The Daoists, pursuing harmony with nature and retreat from a world of cyclical but unpredictable change, did not accept that history had any discernible pattern or didactic value. Zou Yan (305–249), the putative founder of the 'Yin-Yang and Five Phases' school, postulated a comprehensive theory of historical change whereby each of five ages was characterized by a particular element – the legendary Yellow Emperor by earth, for instance, and the ensuing Xia dynasty by wood. These five phases, which Zou borrowed from the *Classic of History*, resemble Hesiod's five ages of gold through iron, but go much further. For Hesiod those terms were largely descriptive of a declining state of being and happiness. In Zou Yan's hands, the virtues of each age became determinative and explanatory as one element naturally triumphed over another and was in turn prevailed upon by the next, forcing a series of era-changes. The Mohists (followers of Mozi) and the Legalists also saw discernible patterns of progress, though the latter, adherents of a totalitarian philosophy

Figure 7 | The Qin book-burning under the Emperor Shi Huangdi, late third century BC, depicted in a seventeenth-century history of the lives of Chinese emperors.

adopted by the brutal Qin dynasty (221–206 BC), asserted that such progress, enforced by state control over naturally evil individuals, made the past largely irrelevant. After the Qin unification of various 'Warring States' into a single empire, their first emperor ordered an infamous book-burning and mass execution of scholars (Fig. 7), virtually eliminating records of the subordinated kingdoms.

There is a troubling similarity between the Legalists' view of history (and that of Zou Yan, which the Qin also found appealing) and much later versions emanating from twentieth-century totalitarianism.

The succeeding Han dynasty took power for most of the next four centuries, in the course of which Confucianism became the official creed. The most important early figure in Chinese historical thought and writing emerged in this world of a consolidated *Zhongguo* (literally, the 'Middle Kingdom', the Chinese name for their own country). Sima Qian (145–86 BC) is the first Chinese historian about whom we know a considerable amount, both because he himself made no pretence at anonymity and included a detailed genealogy of his own family back to legendary times, and because a first-century AD historian, Ban Gu, wrote a biography of his famous predecessor. Sima Qian did not originally intend to take up scholarship but felt an obligation to continue a work already begun by his father, Sima Tan, who had himself occupied the apparently hereditary office of *taishi* (variously translated as grand astrologer, grand scribe or sometimes grand historian) held by his family since the Zhou dynasty. So strongly did the younger Sima feel this imperative that when he fell out of favour with the emperor for defending a defeated general, he submitted to the disgraceful punishment of castration rather than commit suicide with honour but thereby fail in the completion of his father's work. By about 90 BC, he had composed the *Shiji* ('Records of the Grand Historian').[22]

The *Shiji* was arranged in five major sections, each of which proved a foundational model for future Chinese historical writing. The first section of twelve chapters, 'Basic Annals' (*benji*), provided an account of the major dynasties in series, from rise to fall; the second was a set of ten chapters of chronological tables (*biao*); the third held eight chapters of 'treatises' (*shu*) on branches of knowledge from astronomy and the calendar through agriculture, literature and music; the fourth includes thirty chapters on the great 'hereditary houses' (*shijia*) along with biographies of famed sages like Confucius; and finally, the fifth section contains seventy biographical 'arrayed traditions' or 'transmissions' (*liezhuan*) on statesmen, scholars and other categories, often paired (as the Greek biographer Plutarch would later do) to illustrate a character type. At the end of most of his chapters, rather like the author of the *Zuozhuan*, Sima would offer up a moral or comment upon the history just recounted. This, too, is not unlike classical European practice with the exception that the Chinese signal their authorial interventions much more clearly: Sima Qian's little excursuses are prefaced 'The Grand Historian says...', but as with most Chinese historians and the Greeks he makes free use of invented speeches, some of them admittedly copied from earlier works. The chronological tables, where some of Sima's most original writing occurs, were a particularly brilliant innovation, presenting a great deal of disparate data in grid format, and with synchronous dating – no mean feat given the earlier Qin destruction of the chronicles of rival kingdoms – and signifying a recognition that there could, indeed, be a universal set of dates shared between different realms and transcending particular dynasties.

This unusual and original organization had advantages and disadvantages. On the one hand, Sima did not need to interrupt the narrative of an event in one section to explain who a particular person was, since they were probably discussed elsewhere in one of the other principal sections – there are no Herodotean digressions to provide needed background or to explicate an event's longer-term significance. He could also escape strict chronology in the fifth, biographical section, allowing him to give precedence to the character types and patterns which he believed were played out in individual lives at various times. On the other hand, there being no index, the reader would be faced with looking for materials on a particular topic in several different places. And in some places the accounts may mutually contradict one another though it has been argued that this was either a deliberate pluralism of interpretation on Sima's part, or that, like Herodotus, he felt compelled to repeat even conflicting sources verbatim. The goal of the *Shiji* was not to impart a particular account of the past as unchallengeable or definitive – this is no Thucydidean 'last word' – but to promote the wisdom that will allow the intelligent reader to judge well. Sima is rather like the modern professor who tells his students that he is not interested in their ultimate recollection of the facts that have been imparted, but in their development of critical thinking skills. Not that this meant he believed any story should be accepted as given: at the beginning of the *Liezhuan* section, he outlines his own approach to testing the truth of his own sources, including the classics. This is a method that included Herodotean-style travels and queries to the elderly, but which on balance preferred the relative certainty of pre-Qin or 'Old Script' textual authority to the vagaries of oral tradition, at least as far as ancient history was concerned.

Sima Qian did far more in the *Shiji*, a work four times the length of Thucydides' *Peloponnesian War*, than to write a comprehensive account of Chinese history: he provided a history of what for the Chinese was the known world. The *Shiji* was also a literary collection, and an encyclopedia of chronology and biography, replete with collected wisdom for the use of his own and future rulers. According to a letter included in a later history, Sima had as clear an idea as Thucydides that he wanted later generations to profit from his work, telling his friend Ren An of his intent to deposit the work in the Archives so it 'may be handed down to men who will appreciate it'. The *Shiji* also included an ethnographic element, and his treatment of the Chinese enemy, the barbarian Xiongnu (a Turkic people who may have been the future Huns), provides an admiring rumination on their simple form of government which is redolent of Tacitus' much later *Germania*.[23]

Although it was not just a history, Sima Qian did evince in the *Shiji* a clear sense of the historian's purpose: to record major and minor occurrences accurately in order to counsel the present and to bestow fame on the good and infamy on evildoers. In ignoring some of the doubtful lore inherited from the *Chunqiu*, Sima was, in Confucius' terms, a 'maker' as much as he was a 'transmitter'. Among other things, he adapted the acceptance of change into a system of political cycles somewhat comparable to Polybius two generations previously. Sima rejected the Daoist view that there had been a golden age in the mythical past since destroyed by civilization. In his account of the dynasties, a great or wise founding emperor would establish a new dynasty with the Mandate of Heaven; the dynasty would close with a wicked or depraved emperor, though it is interesting to note that Sima did not see this as exactly inevitable since wise rule by an individual could override any fatalism – a view that runs counter to every imperial dynasty's sense that its own succession was predestined. However, change itself and deterioration were inescapable in the natural and the human world. Each of the dynasties had a defining virtue such as good faith or sincerity (the Xia), piety or reverence (the Shang) or refinement (the Zhou), and it was the deterioration of these virtues into flaws (good faith into rusticity, piety into superstition, refinement into empty display) that led inevitably to transfer of the Mandate. Just as Polybius' bad forms of government found correction with the next 'good' form in the *anakuklosis*, so the fault that brought one dynasty low would need correction with the next 'virtue' in the cycle: the Qin sealed their own doom by instituting excessively harsh laws when what was required (following the 'hollow show' of the late Zhou) was a return to good faith.[24]

Sima Qian's model for the compilation of facts about the past with its clearly worked-out format, a combination of year-by-year annals and individual biographical treatments, governed the next two millennia of Chinese historical writing, though it did not provide an exact model for it. It would be difficult to over-state the degree of Sima Qian's impact, which in the world of history-writing would come to exceed even that of Confucius and the post-Confucian commentaries. No ancient European historian, not Polybius or Tacitus, not even Herodotus or Thucydides, can claim that kind of influence, nor does European historical writing display the continuity of a systematic and eventually (under the Tang dynasty) bureaucratized study of the past that is exemplified by China. Sima consistently details his sources, presents alternative opinions and generally lets the reader know why he has written an account of an event or person in a particular way. Consequently the *Shiji* is also the first work of Chinese historiography to raise that question which has gnawed at us from antiquity to yesterday afternoon's senior undergraduate seminar: how is the past knowable? Again, a comparison with the Greeks is salutary: Sima Qian begins his story with the legendary, pre-dynastic Five

Emperors, and he nowhere crisply dismisses myth in the manner of a Hecataeus or even firmly separates it from history. In fact, he completely lacked, because it did not exist in Chinese, an equivalent term to the Greek *muthos* meaning fiction.

Reference to the lessons that the past can provide occur frequently, and speakers in Sima's narrative routinely appeal to history to provide advice for rulers. Sima adopts a common metaphor for history – one which we will see turn up periodically throughout the globe – that of the mirror, wherein we can see ourselves reflected.

Those living in the present age who wish to follow the ways of the ancients have (history as) a mirror, but the two time periods are not exactly the same. Since emperors and kings each had their distinctive rituals and their different tasks, if one wished to take their accomplishments as a guiding thread, how could one sew? If we want to see what brings honor and favor and what brings neglect and disgrace, our own age offers a multitude of examples of success and failure. Why is it necessary to learn from the ancient past?[25]

What is most striking about this comment is not the commonplace view that the past is rather like the present – so much so that it provides grounds for easy emulation and predictability. For Sima's mirror is not of the closet but of the carnival: what is seen on closer inspection is not exactly identical to that which stands before it. A ruler would be unwise to adopt the successful actions and wisdom of the past without alteration to current circumstances. This recognition that the past, while having many similar features to the present, also has important differences that must be grasped is something we will see again, periodically, for instance in the Renaissance Florentine historian Francesco Guicciardini. The further point, that recent history is not necessarily inferior as a pool of examples to antiquity, would also recur in subsequent writers.

In later centuries the *Shiji* would retroactively be counted as the first in a long series of twenty-four 'Standard Histories' (*zhengshi*), the official history of a dynasty written under its successor dynasty. In fact, no subsequent work emulated its scope for a millennium, till the Song dynasty. Most did not use all five of Sima's sections, though they invariably contained at least the annals and biographies. Unlike the *Shiji*, which covered both the Han and their predecessors, subsequent Standard Histories typically covered only one dynasty and were written after its fall, their conclusion providing the justification for the succession of the new dynasty. Sima Qian would most immediately be followed by the historian of the Former or Western Han dynasty (which ended in AD 9), Ban Gu (*fl.* AD 32–92) and, following his imprisonment and death, his sister Ban Zhao. As Sima Qian had followed his father, so the Bans were also taking up their own father's plan to continue the *Shiji*, of which nonetheless both had serious criticisms, including the manner in which Sima had extracted and paraphrased from the classics, and their predecessor's suspected allegiance to Daoism, which ran counter to what was by now a Confucian orthodoxy. The Bans' *Hanshu* ('History of the Former or Western Han') was the work of private citizens rather than an organized imperial office but there is no doubt that Ban Gu wrote under the command of the emperor. The *Hanshu* took on a more explicitly moralizing tone than its predecessor, for example in condemning the usurpation of Wang Mang (AD 9–23) that preceded the return of the Han; it even includes an enormous table listing 2,000 personalities from antiquity to the Han, arranged into categories such as 'sage' and 'fool'. Both in style and in scope it, rather than the *Shiji*, would set the pattern for subsequent histories to cover only a single dynasty. When we pick up the story of Chinese historiography in our next chapter, we will see, too, that the connection between historians and governance which began with Confucius would become much closer, as later emperors moved to institutionalize the writing of history.

Southern Asia from Antiquity to the Mid-First Millennium

The values and style of Chinese historiography were not those of its European counterparts, but their products are nonetheless clearly recognizable as histories, and they share common concerns with matters such as chronology, a normative function, a declared allegiance to representing 'the truth' and a commitment to the memorialization of particular facts about the past. For this reason, even the respect accorded to Chinese historical traditions in most Western histories of history (if mentioned at all) has usually been withheld entirely from other modes of apprehending the past that seem much more distant. Early Indian historical writing is among these. India's very capacity to generate thought and writing about the past has often been rejected – the Muslim al-Bīrūnī commented on the Hindu lack of interest in 'the historical order of things' as early as the 1020s; Edward Gibbon commented on a general 'Asiatic' lack of history in the eighteenth century; and the indictment was echoed by James Mill and by Georg Wilhelm Friedrich Hegel in the nineteenth century. The British officer and Rajput enthusiast Sir James Tod was similarly damning; while ancient Hindu texts might have 'much valuable historical information', it was difficult to sift this out. 'Plain historical truths have long ceased to interest this artificially fed people.'[26]

   This is a view that modern scholars of pre-colonial India have struggled to dispel, though from two very different directions. Some have argued that there is a historicity or at least historical consciousness in early Indian texts, even if it is not one that corresponds with modern notions of historical truth and factuality. More recently, postcolonial scholars have tackled the invidious comparison with European historiography in another way, by arguing that the very notion of scientific, positivist, chronological history, in the form bequeathed by the nineteenth century, is not a laurel to be worn by some and denied others, but rather a Western imposition of Enlightenment notions of truth upon a conquered South Asia, a privileging of a particular epistemological approach to the past and set of disciplinary rules that should *not* be applied to (and considered wanting in) other cultures such as the Indian, and which has actually disrupted a more legitimate and genuinely Indian sense of the past. Even Ranajit Guha, whose 'Subaltern' school articulates a more moderate form of this position, accepts the very Hegelian notion that he wishes to argue against when he suggests that there was no legitimately 'historical' work *by* an Indian until the early nineteenth century.[27]

Certainly the multiplicity of ethnic groups and languages, and the complexities within and between religions, did not permit anything like Western historiography to develop, whether or not it should have, if by that we mean a canonical set of historians in the style of Thucydides. Nor was there anything like the central government apparatus that had stimulated and would soon bureaucratize Chinese historiography. It is possible that Indian philosophy paid no special heed to history because the Hindu outlook denied the significance of short-term events in favour of much longer epochs or periods. The very notion of time in India was connected to a worldview that envisaged reality in numbers of very large magnitude – virtually the opposite of the Judeo-Christian idea, dominant till the nineteenth century, that Creation was only a few millennia old. What we have earlier referred to as 'cycles' in some forms of Western historical thought are a key feature of the Hindu 'yuga/kalpa' system. This is a theory of world ages, connected with astronomical calculations of the era, wherein one cycle of human years (or divine days) occurs within a larger cycle, and that within another; it generated time spans that run well beyond the billions of years in modern geological thought. According to this temporal scheme, four world ages or *yuga*s would follow each other continuously, during which cycle all things will decline. But these spiralling gyres of time are themselves mathematically diminished: each *yuga* is less long than its predecessor on a proportion of 4:3:2:1. The total of four *yuga*s is a *caturyuga* or *mahāyuga* of 4,320,000 human years, of which the last *yuga*, the Kali (within which human history has unfolded), is thought to have begun in the equivalent of 3102 BC. The cycle will repeat itself, punctuated by periods of destruction, and 1,000 of these *caturyuga*s constitutes a single *kalpa* or 'day of Brahma', which in turn fits into the 100-year duration of Brahma's life. With so long a duration imagined, and a concept of potentially endless reincarnation (and the same events with the same characters repeating themselves over and over), it is no wonder that both Hinduism and Buddhism have no notion of 'conquering' time; the effect of numbers in such magnitude is rather to create a sense of distance from it.[28]

But a dramatically different view of time does not *ipso facto* necessitate an absence of either thought about the past or oral and literate communication regarding its course and nature, or speculation about the meaning of its events. Historical forms *of some sort* assuredly did exist in ancient India, indicating a sense of the past quite different from that in the West, but scarcely the happy ignorance suggested by James Mill in his famous and extraordinarily influential *History of British India* (1817). The most well known, originating in the Vedic period, is the combined tradition known as *itihāsa-purāṇa*, which by the mid-first millennium AD had become an authoritative source for the ruling Brahman caste. *Itihāsa* translates as 'thus it was' and has come in more recent times to mean 'history', though it had no such association in ancient times. *Purāṇa* (in Sanskrit पुराण) refers to 'that which pertains to ancient times' or 'old lore'. As with many of the earliest forms of historical thought, they were at first conveyed orally, and since the nineteenth century it has been common practice to distinguish in Hinduism between two categories of knowledge. The higher of these is *Śruti* ('the heard'), which consists of the revealed tradition of the Vedas; the inferior form, called *Smṛti* ('that which is remembered'), includes human-created texts. *Itihāsa-purāṇa*, though it is sometimes considered a 'Fifth Veda', belongs among *smṛti* along with the great Sanskrit epics the *Rāmāyaṇa* and *Mahābhārata*, whose redactors refer to the *purāṇa*s. The *purāṇa*s, each dedicated to a Hindu deity and related to particular sects, often include sections comprising genealogies from earlier times and dynastic lists (the latter written in the future tense). They would be replicated well into the modern period (Figs. 8 and 9). In later times, rulers would attach themselves to these genealogies to support their authority and status.

Indian historical literature bifurcates somewhat with the establishment of Brahmanic authority, and a parallel tradition of works associated with bards and poets continued to evolve independently up to the present day, preserving the genealogies of tribal chiefs and nobles. The *Viṣnu Purāṇa* dated to the mid-first millennium AD contains a 'succession' chapter which illustrates both its outlook and the emergence of history from myth. It begins in remote mythical antiquity and continues generationally through a great flood and a major war which marks the end of a heroic age. Following this there is a shift to the future tense as events that have occurred are presented in the form of prophecy, and generational succession evolves into regnal periods consisting of real dynasties (of which the historical chronology is thought to be more accurate than in the genealogical narratives) and kings that are known from other sources to have ruled between the fourth century BC and fourth century AD. The texts are digressive and paratactic (that is, literally, 'side-by-side' where one sentence follows another without conjunction or linkage), and the tenses sometimes shift, which gives a further indication of the very different concept of the connection

Figure 8 | Rajput school (sixteenth to nineteenth centuries). Hanuman, King of the Monkeys, goes to Ceylon. Episode from the *Bhāgavata Purāṇa*, Hindu miniature, seventeenth century, from the court of Malwa.

between past and future within which the works were written. Thus an early section of a puranic text runs as follows:

Abhimanyu's son by Virāṭa's daughter Uttarā as Parīkṣit. Parīkṣit's son was king Janamejaya who was very righteous. From Janamejaya was born valiant Śatānīka. Śatānīka's son was valiant Aśvamedhadatta.

   From Aśvamedhadatta was born a victorious son, righteous Adhisīmakrṣṇa, who now reigns great in fame.

   Adhisīmakrṣṇa's son will be king Nicakṣu. When the city Hastināpura is carried away by the Ganges, Nicakṣu will abandon it and will dwell in Kauśāmbī. He will have eight sons of great might and valour.[29]

Early Indian historical tradition contains origin myths and extensive genealogical material on the descents of major families; these generally do not place the figures chronologically. The *ākhyāna*s were narratives of ancient heroes often recited in the context of religious rituals. *Gāthā*s, a term that literally means 'songs', has come to refer specifically to a class of ancient Indian songs celebrating the heroic

Figure 9 | Section of the *Sri Bhāgavata Purāṇa*, c. 1880–1900. Scroll of a Sanskrit text written in Devanagari script, with illustrations of Hindu stories; border of floral designs on a gold background.

acts of rulers and sages. *Narāśaṃsī* are a particular subset of these consisting of eulogies of warriors and rulers. *Charitas* (biographies, especially of kings) were a later addition to Indian literature, probably inaugurated in the seventh-century AD *Harshacharita* by Bāṇabhaṭṭa. There are also some biographies of individual rulers, beginning in the seventh century AD and peaking from the tenth to thirteenth centuries, as well as chronicles of ruling families (*vaṃśāvalis*, literally, 'path to succession'), generally the work of court poets or bards. An additional category is the collection of historical narratives or *Prabandha*, which again have a biographical orientation. These other sources, combined with archaeological and epigraphic evidence, have helped to confirm that there is accurate historical accounting to be found in the puranic texts. The puranic account of the death of the last of the Buddhist Maurya kings, Br̥adratha, in 185 BC, for instance, is verified in the *Harshacharita*.

Pre-Islamic India also developed other traditions of writing about the past distinct from *itihāsa-purāṇa*, mainly centred in monastic institutions. The Jainas, practitioners of a very ancient but non-Vedic religion, developed an independent historical tradition including *Rājāvalīs*, or chronicles of kings. Much of Jaina historical literature was produced after AD 900, though some early specimens go back to the fourth century BC. *Paṭṭāvalīs*, Jaina dynastic or succession lists, appear from *c.* 500 to 900 AD but most are of much later origin (1500–1700). The other major religion in the region, Buddhism, also showed an early commitment both to written history and to chronology. Apart from language variations (Pāli and Tibetan as well as Sanskrit), South Asian Buddhist historical writing diverged from the Brahmanic in at least one important respect, its conventional dating of events from a single point, the death of the Buddha *c.* 483 BC (a controverted date also used by some, but not all, Buddhist-influenced countries). The Pāli-language chronicles from Sri Lanka, for instance, focus on the history of a particular Buddhist order or monastery but also stray into secular history and the history of earlier times. Sri Lankan Buddhist historical works date from the fourth to as late as the nineteenth centuries, and are written predominantly in the learned tongue of some sects of South Asian Buddhism, Pāli. The most prominent of these are the *vaṃsa*s, of which examples include the *Dīpavaṃsa* ('Island Chronicle'), composed probably after the reign of King Mahāsena (r. *c.* 334 to 361) and the oldest extant *vaṃsa*; the *Mahāvaṃsa* ('Great Chronicle of Sinhalese Kings'), covering from the sixth century BC to the fourth century AD (compiled in the fifth century); and the *Vaṃsatthappakāsinī* ('Illumination of the Purpose of History'), a commentary on the *Mahāvaṃsa* composed during the tenth century. The tradition continued for many hundreds of years before reaching the *Cūḷavaṃsa* ('Lesser Chronicle'), a tripartite work first compiled in the twelfth century and continued periodically over the next 700 years (Extract 4). Together, these texts appear to preserve a cumulative history of nearly two millennia, and European orientalists of the nineteenth and twentieth centuries such as the Ceylon-based civil servant George Turnour and the German philologist Wilhelm Geiger trumpeted their reliability with increasing enthusiasm, often offering them up as exceptions to the by-then orthodox opinion of the weaknesses of Brahmanic 'history'. This optimistic view has certainly been challenged in recent years. However, regardless of their historicity, the durability of the *vaṃsa*s is remarkable and compares only with Chinese Standard Histories. To put it in perspective, consider what European historiography might look like if the kinds of chronicles written in Europe's Middle Ages had remained the main stream of historical writing until the time of Napoleon.

4: Annalistic Writing in the Vamsas: the Reign of Vijayabahu I (r. AD 1056–1111)

With the protection of Lanka in the vicinity of the sea the King charged powerful followers, acknowledged warriors, in regular turn. Since for the festival of the royal consecration a pasada and many other things had to be prepared, he (likewise) charged one of his followers with this and after he had there done reverence to the various places deserving of honour, he returned, after a sojourn of three months, to Pulatthinagara.

A troop leader known by the name of Adimalaya rebelled quite openly against the Monarch and came, the deluded one, hither with all his troops to fight, as far as the village known by the name of Andu, in the vicinity of the town. The Ruler of Lanka marched thither, destroyed the haughty one and returned to Pulatthinagara after bringing his troops into his power.

From the time that he was yuvaraja [ie, Crown Prince], the wise Prince, that best of men, had seventeen years chronicled in writing. Having betaken himself hereupon to Anuradhapura and well versed in custom, had enjoyed the high festival of the coronation after the manner of tradition, keeping not to evil but keeping firmly to pious action, he, secure (in the royal dignity), had the eighteenth year chronicled.

From *Cūlavaṃsa, being the more Recent Part of the Mahāvaṃsa*, trans. W. Geiger (into German) and by C. M. Rickmers into English, 2 vols. (1929; New Delhi and Chennai, Asian Educational Services, 2003), 209–10. Reproduced with permission from the Pali Text Society. Notes have been eliminated in this selection and diacriticals omitted. The passage is significant, as the translator comments, since it suggests that annals were being regularly maintained at court.

CONCLUSION

Our brief survey of the foundations of history across three millennia has revealed a number of themes that will recur throughout most of this book: the relation (or lack thereof) of history to actual events in the past; the duty of the historian to be truthful (though truth itself is a slippery target); the educative role of the historian; the belief that the past was, more or less, an exemplary mirror from which the present could learn; the relative value of written sources versus oral information; and the emerging ties between control over the writing of the past and political power. A further, significant point is the impact of contact with an 'other', with alien races, on the perception of representation of the past, either through providing a perspective on a past previously seen as special or unique or through outright adoption of a ruling power's forms of historical representation and endorsement of its hegemony. It is striking how, in different ways, most of these features can be found in both ancient Europe and in pre- and early imperial China. The next several centuries would see many of these threads further developed, refined and spread outside their homelands.

Notes

1 In this chapter most dates, except where otherwise noted, are BC.

2 Piotr Michalowski, 'Commemoration, Writing, and Genre in Ancient Mesopotamia', in Christina Shuttleworth Kraus (ed.), *The Limits of Historiography: Genre and Narrative in Ancient Historical Texts* (Leiden, 1999), 69–90, at 70.

3 R. G. Collingwood, *The Idea of History* (1946; Oxford, 1961).

4 From the opening passage of Herodotus, *Histories*, Book I, trans. G. Rawlinson (London, 1930).

5 Arnaldo Momigliano, *Studies in Historiography* (New York and Evanston, IL, 1966).

6 F. M. Cornford, *Thucydides Mythistoricus* (London, 1907); and Collingwood, *The Idea of History*, 30.

7 Dionysius of Halicarnassus, *On Thucydides*, trans. W. Kendrick Pritchett (Berkeley, CA, 1975), chapter 8, 5.

8 Donald Kagan, 'The Speeches in Thucydides and the Mytilene Debate', in Kagan (ed.), *Studies in the Greek Historians in Memory of Adam Parry* (Cambridge, 1975), 71–94, at 77.

9 Polybius, *Histories*, 12.25a3.

10 A phrase made famous in the same-named book by the Cambridge historian Herbert Butterfield, first published in 1931.

11 Charles W. Fornara, *The Nature of History in Ancient Greece and Rome* (Berkeley, CA, 1983), 24.

12 Ronald Mellor, *The Roman Historians* (London, 1999), 19.

13 *Roman Antiquities*, 1.1, trans. E. Cary, 7 vols. (Cambridge, MA, 1937–50), vol. I, 3.

14 Zosimus, *New History*, 1.1, trans. R. T. Ridley (Sydney, 1982), unpaginated.

15 Grant Hardy, *Worlds of Bronze and Bamboo: Sima Qian's Conquest of History* (New York, 1999).

16 G. E. R. Lloyd, *The Ambitions of Curiosity: Understanding the World in Ancient Greece and China* (Cambridge, 2002), 1–20.

17 *Analects* 7.1, quoted in Masayuki Sato, 'The Archetype of History in the Confucian Ecumene', *History and Theory* 46 (2007): 218–32, at 218.

18 From *The Tso Chuan [Zuozhuan]: Selections from China's Oldest Narrative History*, trans. Burton Watson (New York, 1989), 7–8. Wade-Giles transliteration retained.

19 Wai-yee Li, 'Knowledge and Scepticism in Ancient Chinese Historiography', in Kraus (ed.), *The Limits of Historiography*, 27–54, at 27, 30.

20 Steven W. Durrant, *The Cloudy Mirror: Tension and Conflict in the Writings of Sima Qian* (Albany, NY, 1995), 62–3.

21 Quoted by David Schaberg, 'Social Pleasures in Early Chinese Historiography and Philosophy', in Kraus (ed.), *The Limits of Historiography*, 1–26, at 12–14.

22 The most accessible English translation remains for the moment that by Burton Watson, *Records of the Grand Historian*, rev. edn, 2 vols. (New York, 1993). A modern multivolume translation by W. H. Nienhauser, Jr., et al., entitled *The Grand Scribe's Records* (Bloomington, IN, 1994) is in progress.

23 *Shiji*, trans. Watson, vol. I, xiii.

24 Burton Watson, *Ssu-ma Ch'ien: Grand Historian of China* (New York, 1958), 6, 142.

25 Quoted in Hardy, *Worlds of Bronze and Bamboo*, 203.

26 James Tod, *Annals and Antiquities of Rajas'than*, 2 vols. (London, 1829–32), vol. I, 22.

27 Ranajit Guha, *An Indian Historiography of India: A Nineteenth-Century Agenda and its Implications* (Calcutta and New Delhi, 1988).

28 I thank Professor Romila Thapar for this suggestion.

29 Quoted in F. E. Pargiter, *The Purāṇa Text of the Kali Age* (London, 1913), 65–6.

2 | History during the First Millennium AD

Introduction

By the late fifth century AD historical inquiry had been established in the classical world for nearly a millennium, and in China for rather longer. This chapter will trace the further development of Greco-Roman historiography through its late antique and early medieval period, introducing a significant new element, Christianity, into the mix and overlaying classical conventions of history-writing with attitudes and beliefs drawn from Judaism. The development of ecclesiastical historiography, which followed a different model than the narratives of classical antiquity would mark a significant departure. Meanwhile, the appearance of several 'barbarian' kingdoms across Europe ruptured the continuity of western European history and forced historians and monarchs alike to reconceive their relationship with the Roman past; in southeastern Europe the Byzantine emperors and their historians asserted their own claim on the Roman imperial past while preserving much of the Greek heritage. We will also here introduce the last of the major world historiographical traditions, Islam, which erupted on to the global stage with great speed in the early seventh century. Finally, on the other side of Eurasia, we will examine the 'bureaucratizing' of history-writing in China under the Tang dynasty and the beginnings of an East Asian offshoot of Chinese historical writing in neighbouring Japan.

Historical Writing in Christian and Barbarian Europe

A new religion, like a new state, will cement its triumph over the old through its control of the past, writing history into a new 'master-narrative' with itself as the inevitable and logical outcome of events. By Ammianus Marcellinus' time,

Christianity had been a reality for three centuries and the officially sanctioned religion of the empire for several decades. Christianity established itself in part by writing its own history and in part by recasting the history of the known world into a form that rendered the ancient past a prologue to the incarnation, ministry and resurrection of Christ, and saw in subsequent history a modern cosmic drama to be ended in human time by Christ's return. The roots of the Christian historical outlook, like the religion itself, lay in both Judaism and Greco-Roman culture, with Hellenized Jews such as Josephus and Philo of Alexandria (c. 20 BC to AD 50) providing a bridge between the two through their accounts of Jewish antiquity. Christianity repudiated the legal framework of Judaism but kept much else, including a vision of the past marked by the direct and frequent intervention of God, the punishment of the wicked and earthly triumph of the righteous, and a messianic conviction – stressed more by some writers than others – that the world had been created at a particular date and would ultimately expire. What eventually became known as the Old Testament proved indispensable in two ways for the development of Christian historical thought. First, operating lineally, it provided a ready-made history from the Creation, including a detailed account of the kings of David's line, into which Jesus had supposedly been born. Second, operating analogically, it generated in the persons of the Patriarchs, the Kings and the Prophets examples of pious behaviour and 'types' (that is, early anticipations) of Christ and his followers and, importantly, of Christian monarchs. It is useful to note here these two very different ways of thinking about the past: as direct antecedent and lineal 'cause' of the present – a flowing river of successive events – or as something more like a lake, a distinct temporal realm with only an unclear connection to what came after, but filled with examples, types and models from different periods. The tension between these two modes of thought runs through Western historiography up to the nineteenth century.

The influence of Greek and Roman historiography is less obvious but equally important. Chronography, which the Greeks had developed, was a crucial element in the Christian search for a usable past. Some of this had an expressly millenarian or apocalyptic purpose, as it attempted to calculate time not only backward to Creation but forward to the end of days, borrowing dates from pagan writers and prophesies from the Bible. But though the apocalyptic strain in historical writing is an important one, and would remain so for centuries, it was neither the critical impulse behind nor the dominant thread within chronography. Roman historical writing proved useful in a different way: once the empire itself turned Christian, it became the secular arm of God's will and a major force in the spread of Christianity throughout Europe. The Roman past, and with it the collected pasts of all the great empires of more remote antiquity from the Babylonians through the Persians and the Macedonians, formed another river of successions and events, parallel with Jewish history, and leading to a Christianized world – the world then being taken to include Europe, the Near East and Northern Africa.

The first major attempt at a Christian chronology had come in the early third century. The Libyan-born Christian and former soldier Sextus Julius Africanus (c. 160 to c. 240) composed in his *Chronografiai* a history of the world from the Creation to AD 221. Although the work itself has not survived, it was used extensively and quoted by patristic-age chronographers such as Eusebius and by later writers such as the Byzantine monk, George Syncellus (d. after 810). All the elements common to Christian chronographies for the next seventeen centuries were apparently to be found in Africanus' work: a wish to include the human past entire from various kingdoms and peoples within a single world history and chronology, regardless of the temporal gymnastics that had to be performed; speculation about the timing of the *Eschaton* or end of the world; and that other favourite occupation of historians and mathematicians up to the seventeenth century, finding an accurate date for the Creation, which Africanus placed in 5500 BC. Written in Latin, Africanus' book would paradoxically have more influence in the Greek-speaking east. The most influential work of early Christian chronography by far, however, was that of the Greek-speaking Eusebius of Caesarea (c. 260 or 275 to c. 339), who lived during the transition from an era of persecution by a succession of anti-Christian emperors, to the toleration of the religion under Constantine – of whom he would write a biography – and the convening of one of its most important doctrinal councils at Nicaea in 325. Eusebius' earliest work was a world chronicle, arranged by nations, which he began as a young man; much of the original Greek work has been lost, but its text has survived through subsequent writers and in other languages. The *Chronicle* included a section made up of *Chronological Canons*, or tables, beginning with the birth of Abraham which he placed at a year corresponding with 2016 BC. A typical entry for a year would list several corresponding dates and usually include information on persons or events, looking something like this:

Olympiad	Persian King	Macedonian King
78, year 4	Xerxes, year 17	Alexander, year 35

Sophocles and Euripides became famous; Socrates was born.[1]

Eusebius' *Chronicle* was translated into Latin and continued by St Jerome half a century later, in which form it became familiar to Western Christendom. Subsequent writers on both chronology and church history, such as England's Venerable Bede (see below) depended upon Eusebius' work, even where they suggested improvements. But his impact reached further than chronology, a genre prone to periodic flurries of intense activity followed by long lapses of interest. Eusebius' chronological entries borrowed extensively from Roman civic history and often included mentions of interesting phenomena such as comets or eclipses. Although it would not happen for some centuries yet, a fierce allegiance to annals as the easiest way in which to organize a history (owing in part to the endlessly elastic capacity of an individual annal to absorb multiple and often unrelated facts) would become a hallmark of western European historical writing in the later Middle Ages. Apart from biography and hagiography, continuous narrative in a classical vein would be rare for a millennium.

Eusebius not only realized Africanus' aspiration of a single world chronology; he solved other problems such as the reconciliation of apparent disparities among the Four Gospels, and through a later work, his *Church History*, the writing of which Eusebius commenced just before Diocletian's persecutions of 303–13, he bequeathed ecclesiastical history as a major grand category in European literature. The separation of ecclesiastical from secular history, though far from absolute, proved fundamental to medieval and early modern historical writing and to later Renaissance divisions among historical genres. The work is also interesting in its integration of biographies within a generally chronological account that followed the scheme Eusebius had already laid out in his earlier *Chronicle*.

The early Christian historians adopted much of what they found in Greek and Roman chronography, including the use of the first Olympiad and the rule of Ninus of Assyria as firm starting dates, though they were reluctant to follow the Greeks entirely and exclude as myth all events prior to that time. Apart from the fact that they wished to provide Christianity with antecedents independent of and prior to the Greeks, they could not jettison the early millennia that included much of Jewish history, including the Creation, the Flood, the Exodus and the Davidic Kingdom. An easier solution, derived from Josephus, was simply to treat all Greek sources as fundamentally flawed: the fact that the Greeks had been sceptical about the remote past was ironically turned into a reason not to trust them since they had plainly not cared much about it; that they had not even noted the existence of the Jews made Greek 'carelessness' even more palpable while raising in estimation Christian opinion of those Near Eastern peoples who had.

In the fourth century, following the foundation of the eastern Roman Empire at Constantinople (the former Byzantium) and the establishment of Christianity as the official religion of the empire, western and eastern European historical writing evolved in rather different directions. The continuity of the Byzantine Empire for another millennium facilitated the further development of classical historiography written to a high standard of accuracy, primarily in Greek, by historians such as John Malalas (c. 491–578). It should be remembered that for some time historians of differing religious inclinations were writing history virtually alongside one another – in a few cases, such as Priscus (*fl.* late fifth century), it is not even possible from their texts to be sure whether they were Christian fish or pagan fowl. Unlike most of the Roman and Hellenistic historians, who had mainly written about periods before their own time, most chose the Thucydidean path, writing about their own times or the very recent past, even though they were generally men of little influence – in contrast with a number of later Byzantine historians.

The most notable secular historian of this period, and the most obvious imitator of Thucydides' focus on military affairs, was Procopius of Caesarea (c. 500 to c. 554) who is an amphibian of sorts, not easily pigeonholed. His religious views have long been a matter of controversy, seeming as they do to tie him to a variety of Christian heresies or even Judaism. An astute reader of the thousand years of Greek history and philosophy that had preceded him, Procopius chronicled the campaigns of the Emperor Justinian (r. 527–65), for whose reign his *Wars* is the principal authority. It is a narrative after the fashion of Thucydides and has generally enjoyed a positive reputation. Perhaps unfortunately, Procopius has become more famous for a minor work, rediscovered in the Renaissance, initially called the *Anekdota* (literally 'unpublished work') but more popularly known as the *Secret History*, in which the author sought to emulate Suetonius' *Lives of the Caesars*. The *Secret History*, completed around 551, borrows the old Herodotean method of narrating through revealing but often hard-to-verify stories or episodes, but without Herodotus' measured judgments and sympathetic voice. In contrast to the earlier *Wars*, it is unrelentingly hostile to 'the demon in human flesh', Justinian, and includes scurrilous information about the court and the private lives of the emperor and his rampantly promiscuous empress, Theodora. He unwittingly spawned a new genre that eventually embraced a number of seventeenth- and eighteenth-century exposés offering lascivious details about royalty and other worthies, and their modern journalistic descendants the 'tell-all' memoir and celebrity tabloid.

Procopius had explicitly avoided dealing with ecclesiastical matters, though stating in the *Secret History* his intent (apparently unfulfilled) to write a separate history of the Church. Two points are to be gleaned from this: the first is a reminder of the importance of such generic distinctions, and in particular that between sacred and profane history, to which several centuries of future historians would adhere; the second is that despite such distinctions the same historian was perfectly capable of changing hats and writing in more than one genre. If Procopius failed to produce his own history of the Church, it may be because such works were by then not hard to find in the wake of Eusebius. Most early Byzantine historiography discussed secular events – nearly every historian, pagan or Christian, had something to say about one barbarian threat or another, and interest in church history per se seems for a time to have fallen off after the mid-fifth century. Byzantine church historians such as Socrates of Constantinople, Sozomen, Rufinus (a translator and continuator of Eusebius), Theodoret and, somewhat later, Evagrius Scholasticus were often, as one might expect given the religious agenda, highly polemical. But the fixation of ecclesiastical history on the foundation, survival, sorting out of doctrines within and then triumph of the Christian religion, accompanied by a steady eye towards the eventual return of Christ and the ultimate end of history had a positive impact on chronicity, as its writers generally maintained the attention to precise dating and periodization characteristic of Eusebius.

A further stylistic issue can be noted, itself a direct consequence of the overtly polemical and proselytizing quality of much of this work. In contrast to their secular counterparts and the entire classical tradition on which they rested, and despite their frequent appeal to oral sources, the authors of ecclesiastical history, though they often quoted dialogue, were generally averse to the practice of extended fictional speeches. Eusebius seems to have recognized at the outset that documents would serve his purpose better than rhetorical set-pieces, and his successors followed suit. They chose to buttress their arguments in a different way, by inserting original documents and letters, either verbatim or summarized, which had not been a characteristic of most classical histories, in part because it made for tedious reading and interrupted the textual flow. Socrates actually made of his simple style and inclusion of documents a virtue, supposing his interest in truth to be manifestly superior to that of ancients only interested in displaying their literary talents. Sozomen (c. 400 to c. 450) boasted of his careful attention to eyewitness testimony, which the Greek historians had taught him, but he was equally proud of his widespread travels to gather firewood-like armloads of documents, 'some of which are preserved to this day in the archives of the imperial palace and in churches, while others are kept scattered about in the files of learned men'.[2] Some he would summarize while others, following Eusebius' example, were presented in full. This documentary practice, and the absence of the invented speech, a key component of classical histories, would continue through early modern times. A clear ancestry for Reformation-era historians a thousand years on lies in both the oral and documentary practices of their late antique and Byzantine precursors.

The gap between Greek east and Latin west would widen over ensuing centuries, as would the divergence of the Orthodox and Catholic churches. Byzantine historiography would also evolve very differently from that in the Latin world, but apart from a number of chronographers, its high point would begin in the eleventh century, beyond the scope of the current chapter. We must also remember, however, that the Byzantine Empire of the sixth through tenth centuries did not experience either the turbulence of the Roman west, nor did it suffer to anything like the same degree the loss of its classical heritage. While Byzantium had its own enemies, inside and outside, it is easier to see political continuity from the perspective of Constantinople than from the vantage point of Rome, much less Paris. That continuity applies to cultural matters also: we now have the names and fragments of a good number of ancient Greek historians primarily through the efforts of Byzantine scholars, and a combination of Byzantine and Arabic learning would deliver much of the 'lost' Greek corpus back to the rest of Europe after 1400.

In Latin Christendom, religion provided the closest thing to a unifying force in the development of a common vocabulary and a shared set of standard themes for history-writing. Eusebius had been translated into Latin and beginning with St Augustine of Hippo, mainstream Christian thought embraced a Neoplatonic juxtaposition of two 'cities', a heavenly and an earthly, according to which events that unfolded in the human and natural world were inferior shadows or reflections of a higher reality in the divine sphere. These spheres were interlocking rather than separate. The divine will, under the rubric of 'Providence' lay behind major cataclysms such as the sack of Rome, and it inscrutably micromanaged the punishment of wrongdoing down to the level of the individual, though Augustine explicitly avoided discerning any overarching pattern to a rather wild sea of historical events. 'In general, the bad come to bad ends and the good enjoy eventual success', Augustine observed, though he had to concede that some times Bad Things happened to Good People, just as China's Sima Qian, five centuries earlier, had pointed out in analysing the seemingly unmerited fates of the worthy and the wicked. Borrowing from Genesis and the Gospels, Augustine also articulated the first comprehensive periodization scheme since Livy's epitomizer, Lucius Florus' analogy between Rome and a human life-span. History, suggested Augustine, was like a 'Great Week', corresponding with the Six Days of Creation. One is tempted to compare this with the Vedic 'Days of Brahma', but Augustine's scheme lacked both the huge numbers and almost infinite duration of Hindu time, and its progression was one of spiritual improvement rather than decline, since his own age, the Sixth Day, was also the age of Christ.

Augustine's disciple Orosius (fl. 414–18) gave his mentor's vision more concrete definition in a work which subsequent historical writers would find more serviceable than Augustine's *City of God* itself. It is not a great piece of historical writing, and the balloon of its medieval popularity was popped in the fifteenth century by a number of Renaissance humanists who found it wanting in both style and substance. Orosius' *Seven Books of History against the Pagans*, as he called it, was intended to put some meat on the Augustinian skeleton, in the form of historical examples of misfortunes and disasters, of the Latin doctor's defence of Christianity against culpability for the decline of the Roman Empire. But Orosius exceeded his brief: where Augustine had wished to show simply that suffering was a perennial aspect of the human condition, Orosius attacked pagan culture, in particular republican Rome, to demonstrate that the outlook for humanity was considerably rosier under Christianity, even in this world. The *Seven Books*, ending in AD 417, is the first universal history to narrate the unfolding of the divine will through all recorded time. It proved highly influential beyond Christendom, too: translated into Arabic in the tenth century, the *Seven Books* would eventually become a significant conduit for the transfer of Christian historical thought into the work of Islamic historians such as Ibn Khaldūn.

Orosius heightened the apocalyptic element in universal history by substituting for Augustine's 'Six Ages' the biblical notion of 'Four Monarchies' or world empires, lifted from the Book of Daniel, thereby investing human time with a deeper meaning than Augustine had contemplated. The 'two cities' theme itself would be reshaped and revisited many times, most explicitly in the twelfth century by the pro-imperial Otto, bishop of Freising (c. 1111–58), who used it as the title of his major historical work, entitled *The Chronicle of the Two Cities*, and expanded the Heavenly City to include the empire itself, drawing a distinction between the rather depressing circularity of earthly events and the *progressus* (edging towards modern 'progress') in sacred history towards a redemptive end. It was Otto who would provide the classic formulation of a historical continuity argument in the *translatio imperii*, the thesis that the Roman Empire, Christianity's secular arm, had not in fact fallen, but merely been 'translated' from Rome to the Franks and eventually to their emperor Charlemagne, the latest step in a process whereby each world empire of antiquity had been succeeded by another; on this view, the Carolingian was not a new empire but rather a continuation of that of Rome. The ultimate heirs of this process were the German Hohenstaufen emperors such as Otto's own nephew Frederick I, called Barbarossa (r. 1156–90). So durable and pliable an explanation was the *translatio* that it could be used and reused, and the chronology and identities of both earlier and successor empires revised to suit a writer's present circumstances. It was sufficiently commonplace that Charlemagne's capital Aix-la-Chapelle and several other European towns were described by chroniclers as 'Second Romes' in the course of the Middle Ages, while the Milanese maintained this fiction into the early eighteenth century. The conceit did not even need to be Christian: the Muslim Ottoman conquerors of Constantinople would appropriate the *translatio* in the fifteenth century to justify their own claims to be heirs of Rome, and a parallel to it was employed by Cortés in the sixteenth to justify the transfer of authority from the Aztec ruler to the Emperor Charles V.

Historical writing during the so-called Dark Ages from the fifth to the ninth centuries is a much more heterogeneous affair than in the Greek east. The collapse of the western Roman Empire and its displacement by various barbarian kingdoms obscured, but did not wholly break, the continuity with ancient models: a writer like the Briton Gildas (*fl.* early sixth century), whose *De Excidio Britanniae* ('On the Ruin of Britain') recounts the last days of pre-Saxon invasion Britain, sounds like an Old Testament prophet or a latter-day Tacitus in his moralizing criticism of the British and their kings. Yet the period was more shadowy than dark, for historians wrote significant accounts about the various Germanic peoples. Each

was quite different in scope and content and each transcended the limits of annals, variously drawing on Eusebius and certain Roman and Byzantine historians.
The challenge facing their authors was to integrate peoples of obscure origin, who
had until recently fallen outside the 'universal' empire, into the emerging Christian
meta-story. Throughout the world, contact with alien societies would provide in
later centuries a critical agent of historiographical change as well as a problem
for historians. Augustine's explanation for the appearance of the Huns and Goths
on the scene – that they were destined to enter the Church through contact with
a Christian Roman Empire – would be replicated over a millennium later in the
histories of Dominican, Franciscan and Jesuit missionaries in the Americas and the
Far East (see Chapter 5).

By AD 500 the Visigoths had established an independent monarchy in Spain, the
Ostrogoths in Italy and the Franks in what is now France and northern Germany;
the next century would see the Anglo-Saxons similarly entrenched in the southern
part of Britain. The Christianization of these peoples proceeded haltingly up to the
seventh century. Early historians such as the Visigothic John of Biclar (c. 540 to
after 621) tried valiantly to portray their kingdoms as a new Byzantium or new
Rome, and their Clovises and Recareds, Christian kings, as latter-day Constantines.
But to do so historians had to wrestle with several inescapable questions. Whence
came these Germanic tribes, with their warrior values, oral culture and (initially)
pagan beliefs? How could they be integrated into the converging Roman and
Judeo-Christian 'back stories'? Perhaps more urgently, how could the barbarian
kings, would-be successors to the western Roman emperors, write themselves into
that story in ways that made them look like legitimate emperors and justified their
hegemony?

There now began what would become a core activity of historians, and a major
interest of their powerful patrons, until the era of nineteenth-century nationalism:
the tracing of ethnic, linguistic and even familial history back to its origins. In
this activity it was useful to have allies, and the monarchs could turn to churchmen who had a vested interest in the political stability of their newly won flocks.
Certain rules applied in the game of identifying progenitors. Earlier ones were
better than later. Unconquered ancestors were on the whole preferable to subjugated ones. Cataclysmic, path-altering change should generally be suppressed or
explained away as a temporary aberration in favour of continuity. And almost any
sort of evidence was within bounds, including ingenious etymological speculation,
allegorical readings of scripture and other sources, the outright fabrication of entire lines of monarchs stemming from a legendary founder or even one invented
de novo and citation of 'authorities' who should be believed simply because they
were righteous and trustworthy informants of good repute. All this may sound
like a dismal condemnation of medieval and early modern historical methods,

but it should not. The kinds of philological and archaeological research that very gradually pushed these tactics out emerged from concern with precisely the same questions that concerned historians of the sixth to tenth centuries and their later medieval successors.

The most important variant of the early medieval quest for exalted ancient forebears, and the one that did the most intellectual damage in the long run (Nazi racial theory is its remote descendant), is that known by the Latin term *origo gentis* (pl. *origines gentium*, literally 'the origins of peoples'). This was especially prominent during and immediately after the *Völkerwanderung*, but it steamed on right through the Middle Ages, then through the Renaissance and Reformation, and acquired a new lease on life in the early nineteenth century (when, however, attention would shift away from remote ancestors and towards the identification of national character, cultural continuity and 'racial' attributes). The historians and other writers in search of a worthy ancestry had no difficulty finding such parentage. There were various fine candidates at hand, from ancient Greeks or Egyptians to a mysterious people known as the 'Scythians'. The latter were based on an actual Central Asian tribe mentioned by Herodotus but eventually and unhelpfully turned into a conglomeration of several distinct groups: Bede, for instance, would assign the Picts of northern Britain a Scythian origin. There were, too, those who stuck to biblical lineage and traced all peoples, Christian and pagan, back to one of the three sons of Noah, who had repopulated the earth through seventy-two tribes which, according to Josephus, had all spoken Hebrew until the multiplication of tongues at Shinar. Europeans according to this scheme sprang from the line of Japhet, Jews and Arabs from Shem (hence the word 'Semitic') and black Africans from Ham. Individual peoples sprang from sub-branches of this Noachic tree, for instance the Goths from Magog or the English from Gomer, both sons of Japhet. The more creative minds often tried to blend multiple schemes or cross-identify biblical figures with classical or historical ones (or even with gods, following the classical practice of euhemerism), and since, of course, different levels of antiquity were involved, it was possible to reconcile multiple 'families', biblical, classical and geographical, Noachidae with Germans and Trojans.

The Trojans were by far the most popular and flexible ancestral people, already deployed in Vergil's *Aeneid* to explain the remote origins of Roman civilization in Italy. They were first hauled on to the stage of post-Roman Europe by the authors of a seventh-century chronicle (ascribed to a fictitious author, one Fredegar) which reconciled pagan and Christian chronology by making the Trojans and Greeks descendants of Noah. The Trojans performed so well that they were invited back frequently by historians as well as by others – kings and the nobility were especially tempted by this ruse – in search of a spectacular ancestry. By the end of the Middle Ages the Abbot Johannes Trithemius (1462–1516), himself no stranger to myth-making, puzzled over the Trojans' popularity as forebears, 'as if there were no peoples in Europe before the fall of Troy, and as if the Trojans included no rascals'.[3] What worked for the Franks could be adapted for others, and in the tenth century the Normans and Saxons acquired a Trojan origin from the likes of Widukind of Corvey (925 to after 973) and Dudo of St Quentin (c. 986 to c. 1043). The Trojans under Aeneas had supposedly arrived in Italy well before the establishment of Rome. Offshoots of these refugees had also colonized other parts of the globe, which made the Trojans especially useful to those challenging Roman secular authority, since their independence could thereby be argued to have *preceded* Rome's in time by several centuries. The occasional wit would observe that the Trojans were in fact the great losers of the epic past, but their popularity as all-purpose ancestors remained intact well into the sixteenth century.

It was not enough, however, to identify the origins of a people. There were some serious second-order issues to be worked through, such as the relation of barbarian kings to the vestiges of the Roman Empire on the one hand and to a supposedly universal Christian church on the other. The former was easier than the latter: many historical thinkers simply viewed the Roman Empire of the west as terminated: 'Rome' now meant both a decaying city in central Italy that was also the seat of the papacy and the Byzantine Empire of the east whose authority the western tribes did not acknowledge. Eventually, some merit was seen in creating the fiction that the western empire had itself not ceased in the fifth century but merely been passed on to other peoples and their kings – the above-noted concept of the *translatio imperii*. Thus on Christmas Day 800, when the Frankish king Charlemagne was crowned Emperor of Rome, the empire was 'translated' to the Franks. The providential aspect of these changes – that various lines acquired and lost the empire – is different in detail and scope but not fundamentally in conception from the periodically bestowed and withdrawn Chinese 'mandate of heaven'. The relation of the new kings (who saw themselves as the heirs of Ancient Israel as much as of Old Rome) to the Church proved a thornier issue by far, and the chronicles of the Middle Ages are littered with famous tales of disputes between kings and clergy, and eventually between emperors and popes.

The most important quartet among the 'barbarian' historians produced remarkable works. Written in Latin, still the international language of western Europe, they included histories of the Goths (Jordanes' (d. 554) *Getica*, in part summarizing a lost history by a sixth-century writer named Cassiodorus), the Franks (Gregory of Tours (538–93/4), whose work might more accurately be described as a history of his own times, though it is framed as a Eusebian-style universal history), the Lombards (Paul the Deacon (d. 799?)), and the Anglo-Saxons (by Bede (d. 753)). In

Figure 10 | Opening leaf of Book I of a ninth-century manuscript of Bede's *Historia ecclesiastica gentis Anglorum*.

the present context, we must limit ourselves to the last-mentioned, a Benedictine monk who may have been the greatest Christian historian of the first millennium AD. He was certainly among the most imaginative and scholarly. The author of several historical and bibliographical works, Bede is credited with first introducing into historical writing the Christian calendar or *computus* whereby events were dated *anno domini*, from the birth of Jesus Christ, a system previously developed in the form of 'Easter Tables' by scholars such as the sixth-century monk Dionysius Exiguus, and more or less in common use by Carolingian times. Bede's longer work on time includes a 'World Chronicle', broadly following Augustine's Six Ages scheme.[4] His greatest achievement, however, was unquestionably the *Historia ecclesiastica gentis Anglorum* ('Ecclesiastical History of the English People'). The *Ecclesiastical History*, despite its title a wonderful blend of sacred and secular, tells the story of Britain from pre-Roman times to the year 731 (Fig. 10). After an introductory geographical and ethnographic description of Britain and its constituent peoples and several narrative chapters on the Romano-British era, Bede proceeds to the main body of his work: the settling of the Anglo-Saxons, their subjugation of the indigenous Britons and their conversion by Augustine of Canterbury, emissary of Pope Gregory 'the Great'. The work covers the several different English kingdoms, still very much in formation and disunited, with the Church providing the common spiritual centre and the connection of the island as a whole to wider Christendom.

Bede is no more dispassionate and neutral a commentator than any other historian of his time: his Christianity is both fervent and clear, as is his adherence to the Roman rite on which the English had settled. The account of the first conversion of the Britons under a mythical King Lucius and a sketchy Pope Eleutherius popularized a historical phantom that would not be exiled from history till the nineteenth century; Bede's rather arbitrary preference of the term *Angli* for the newly converted Saxons (quoting Pope Gregory the Great's famous pun on Angles and Angels) ensured that the entire *gens* of southern Britain, and their language, would be called 'English'. The *Ecclesiastical History* was also replete with the miraculous events and saintly lives that enlivened monastic historiography throughout the Middle Ages. To see in Bede a proto-modern, hard-edged archival scholar and ignore the literary and rhetorical aspects of his work would be seriously misguided. Nevertheless, his is a history of discrimination among sources, intelligent balancing of the oral and the written, shrewd interpolation of biographical and hagiographical anecdotes on particular individuals at various points, and a well thought-out, thematic vision of the whole. It is a creative and a critical work, not simply a transmitter of tradition.

Bede dedicated his *Ecclesiastical History* to Ceolwulf (r. 729–37), king of the northern Anglo-Saxon kingdom of Northumbria, where Bede's monastery was located. Bede's preface (Extract 5) illustrates both his motives and his methods, which depended on a combination of written evidence, his own knowledge and oral testimony. In it we see a variety of elements of medieval historical writing, some of which are not remarkably different from what we have seen either in antiquity or in other parts of the world: a firm belief in the 'praise-and-blame' aspect of history; its role as an educator of the powerful; the reliance on spoken as well as written sources and an indifference to the distinction (a more meaningful differentiation being that between trustworthy and untrustworthy accounts, whether oral or written); and the design of the book not just for private reading but for performance, through oral recitation, in a society only marginally literate – a noteworthy contrast with Isidore of Seville's (c. 560–636) grammatical conceptualization of history a century earlier (see Box 4 and Extract 6). Bede was also diligent in telling his readers not just where and from whom he got his information, but often how his informants in turn acquired theirs, establishing a chain of information back to proximity with events. In this last aspect he shared something with the historians produced by the new religion that had recently emerged in the Middle East, Islam.

5: Bede's *Ecclesiastical History*

I formerly at your request, most readily transmitted to you the Ecclesiastical History of the English Nation, which I had newly published, for you to read, and give it your approbation; and I now send it again to be transcribed, and more fully considered at your leisure. And I cannot but commend the sincerity and zeal, with which you not only diligently give ear to hear the words of the Holy Scripture, but also industriously take care to become acquainted with the actions and sayings of former men of renown, especially of our own nation. For if history relates good things of good men, the attentive hearer is excited to imitate that which is good; or if it mentions evil things of wicked persons, nevertheless the religious and pious hearer or reader, shunning that which is hurtful and perverse, is the more earnestly excited to perform those things which he knows to be good, and worthy of God. Of which you also being deeply sensible, are desirous that the said history should be more fully made familiar to yourself, and to those over whom the Divine Authority has appointed you governor, from your great regard to their general welfare. But to the end that I may remove all occasion of doubting what I have written, both from yourself and other readers or hearers of this history, I will take care briefly to intimate from what authors I chiefly learned the same.

My principal authority and aid in this work was the learned and reverend Abbot Albinus; who, educated in the Church of Canterbury by those venerable and learned men, Archbishop Theodore of blessed memory, and the Abbot Adrian, transmitted to me by Nothelm, the pious priest of the Church of London, either in writing, or by word of mouth of the same Nothelm, all that he thought worthy of memory, that had been done in the province of Kent, or the adjacent parts, by the disciples of the blessed Pope Gregory, as he had learned the same either from written records, or the traditions of his ancestors. The same Nothelm, afterwards going to Rome, searched into the archives of the holy Roman Church, found there some epistles of the blessed Pope Gregory, and other popes; and returning home, by the advice of the aforesaid most reverend father Albinus, brought them to me, to be inserted in my history. Thus, from the beginning of this volume to the time when the English nation received the faith of Christ, have we collected the writings of our predecessors, and from them gathered matter for our history; but from that time till the present, what was transacted in the Church of Canterbury, by the disciples of St Gregory or their successors, and under what kings the same happened, has been conveyed to us by Nothelm through the industry of the aforesaid Abbot Albinus…. [Bede lists his informants on the various other English kingdoms.] But what was done in the Church throughout the province of the Northumbrians, from the time when they received the faith of Christ till this present, I received not from any particular author, but by the faithful testimony of innumerable witnesses, who might know or remember the same; besides what I had of my own knowledge.

Selected from the author's preface to *The Venerable Bede, The Ecclesiastical History of the English Nation* (London: J. M. Dent, 1910), 1–3; bracketed phrasing added by the present author and translator's notes omitted.

extract

Box 4   Isidore of Seville

The Spanish bishop, Isidore, was one of the last great Christian Church Fathers and certainly among the most widely read in the Middle Ages. He was also a historian in his own right. He authored both a universal history (the first to adopt Augustine's 'Six Ages' scheme) and a shorter *History of the Goths* with appended histories of the Vandals and Suevi, and his thesis that the Goths were a divinely chosen people set to bring Christianity to Iberia – independent of external interference from debased imperial centres to the east – proved enormously influential on the future direction of Spanish historiography. But he is best known as a keen etymologist and encyclopedist who digested a wealth of classical and Christian learning for a Dark Age audience. His comments on history supply a definition which would be much-read throughout the Middle Ages, not least because of Isidore's firm conviction that history belonged to the realm of the written rather than the spoken word. Isidore was convinced (in contrast to Cicero) that history belonged to grammar – and medieval libraries would classify it accordingly – rather than rhetoric, that it was a text for writing and reading, not for speaking, and that it was about true events, not fictional ones, with the middle term of 'plausible narrations', those things that have not happened but could have, lying somewhere in between.

The Beginnings of Islamic Historiography

If East Asian historical writing differs from Western, and ancient Indian appears almost incommensurable with it, the historical writing of Islam can seem on the whole much less alien, its authors much more 'like us'. The Islamic is the youngest of the great world historiographical traditions, and three points about it need to be clearly understood at the outset. The first is that unlike the Chinese or Indian traditions, which had relatively little contact with the West until a much later period, the Islamic historiographical tradition had access relatively early to both classical and Judeo-Christian works, just as Islam itself was conceived within a broader Abrahamic family of religions. It thus lies at a somewhat lesser degree of 'independence' from classical/Judeo-Christian historiography than do the Chinese or Indian traditions, which of course helps to explain its similarities. The second is that Islamic historiography, like the religion it was developed expressly to support, had a very quick birth and a rather short formative period of two to three centuries

6: Isidore of Seville on history

xli. History (De historia). 1. A history (*historia*) is a narration of deeds accomplished; through it what occurred in the past is sorted out. History is so called from the Greek term ἰστορεῖν ('inquire', 'observe') that is, from 'seeing' or from 'knowing'. Indeed, among the ancients no one would write a history unless he had been present and had seen what was to be written down, for we grasp with our eyes things that occur better than what we gather with our hearing, 2. since what is seen is revealed without falsehood. This discipline has to do with Grammar, because whatever is worthy of remembrance is committed to writing. And for this reason, histories are called 'monuments' (*monumentum*), because they grant a remembrance (*memoria*) of deeds that have been done. A series (*series*) is so called by an analogy with a garland (*serta*) of flowers tied together one after the other.

 xlii. The first authors of histories (De primis auctoribus historiarum). 1. Among us Christians Moses was the first to write a history, on creation. But among the pagans, Dares the Phrygian was first to publish a history, on the Greeks and Trojans, which they say he wrote on palm leaves. 2. After Dares, Herodotus is held as the first to write history in Greece. After him Pherecydes was renowned, at the time when Ezra wrote the law.

 xliii. The utility of history (De utilitate historiae). Histories of peoples are no impediment to those who wish to read useful works, for many wise people have imparted the past deeds of humankind in histories for the instruction of the living. Through history they handle a final reckoning back through seasons and years, and they investigate many indispensable matters through the succession of consuls and kings.

 xliv. The kinds of history (De generibus historiae). 1. There are three kinds of history. The events of a single day are called an 'ephemeris' (*ephemeris*); we call this a 'diary' (*diarium*). What the Romans call 'daily' (*diurnus*), the Greeks call *ephemeris.* 2. Histories that are distributed into individual months are called 'calendars' (*kalendarium*). 3. Annals (*annales*) are the actions of individual years (*annus*), for whatever domestic or military matters, on sea or land, worthy of memory are treated year by year in records they called 'annals' from yearly (*anniversarius*) deeds. 4. But history (*historia*) concerns itself with many years or ages, and through the diligence of history annual records are reported in books. There is this difference between history and annals, namely, that history is of those times that we have seen, but annals are of those years that our age has not known. Whence Sallust consists of history, and Livy, Eusebius, and Jerome of annals and history. 5. And history, 'plausible narration' (*argumentum*), and fable differ from one other. Histories are true deeds that have happened, plausible narrations are things that, even if they have not happened, nevertheless could happen, and fables are things that have not happened and cannot happen, because they are contrary to nature.

Selected from *The Etymologies of Isidore of Seville*, I.xli–xliv.5, ed. Stephen A. Barney et al. (Cambridge University Press, 2006), 67, quoted here with minor changes to punctuation, and editors' Latin interpolations intact.

before it settled into a clear pattern with distinctive genres and rules of practice. The third, and most important, is that Islamic historiography is not synonymous with 'Arab' or 'Arabic' historiography. Throughout its history, and in spite of Arabic being the language of Islam's holy book the *Qur'an*, the religion has formed an *umma* or community of believers which, allowing for major divisions such as Sunni and Shiite, transcends ethnic and national categories. From fairly early in Islam's history, ethnic Arabs supplied a minority of the world's Muslims, and the very rapid expansion of Islam outside its initial Arabic base quickly ensured that Islamic historiography would eventually be practised by Persians, Egyptians, Turks and others, frequently writing in other languages than Arabic (though this remained the preferred language of those aspiring to a pan-Islamic readership up to the nineteenth century). This distinction between Arabic and Islamic is especially important to grasp since religious-based historical writing would in later times conflict with ethnic and nationalist sentiments.

Islamic historiography expressed a sense of temporal progress from Creation through the prophets (culminating with Muhammad) and leading eventually to the world's end. Both Muhammad and subsequent Muslim historians took Judeo-Christian biblical history as a point of departure, a back-story, rather than as an alternative to be discredited. For Islam the world was indeed finite and had been created at a particular point; Adam and Eve were the first humans (though they spoke Arabic, not Hebrew or Aramaic, and, according to some accounts, spent their exile from Eden in South Asia); and Muhammad was not the only prophet in history, but rather the last and greatest of a line stretching back to Abraham and sometimes Adam.

The determination of Muslim scholars to provide justification for their statements by establishing chains of authority reaching back to the Prophet makes them seem in some ways very modern. We should not succumb to the temptation of assuming that because Islam developed scholarly protocols for the establishment of truth and the preservation of tradition, that it should be unquestioningly praised for its accuracy – modern criticism has been just as effective in raising doubts about the literal accuracy of Muslim historical works as about Jewish or Latin ones. Moreover, though it appears to have been a very popular genre among the literate, and though there is a vast output of historical writing from medieval Islam, history was no more a full-time profession among its Muslim practitioners than it was elsewhere in the world, and indeed considerably less so than among the contemporary Chinese (see below). Virtually every Muslim who wrote a history or biography did so as an avocation, jurists and bureaucrats being especially often drawn to study of the past. Yet despite history's status as a second-tier profession, it nevertheless managed, a recent scholar has commented, to attract a number of first-rate minds.[5]

Though Islamic historiography was very new, it thrived in a region with a pre-existing interest in the past. There are indigenous examples of historiography, genealogy, semi-legendary stories and oral traditions among both Arabs and Persians, such as popular stories about battles (*Ayyām*), or about the history of particular regions such as Yemen. Pre-Islamic Arabs were certainly not indifferent to the past, and poetry or song, as had been the case with the early Greeks, provided a venue for recounting this. They also had a strong interest in tribal genealogy and a system for the assembly and transmission of poems, a *rawiya* being the guarantor of a poem's authenticity. Oral tradition would continue after the coming of Islam, as storytellers or *quṣṣāṣ* recounted tales of the life of the Prophet, forming a folklore that inevitably became intermixed with the scholarly traditions about Muhammad's life, and with the *Qur'anic* account of prehistory as a succession of forerunners to the Prophet. There was also a Christian and classical historiographic presence in the region, written in late antique Syriac, an Aramaic dialect widely used during the Christian patristic era in the Near East.

These precursors aside, Islamic historiography proper began in the mid-seventh century, its first subject being the life and deeds or expeditions (*maghāzī*) of Muhammad himself, whose *Hijra* to Medina in AD 622 provided a firm date on which to anchor an Islamic chronology. Both an attentiveness to dating and an interest in narrating the past developed within a generation or so of the death of Muhammad. The nearly immediate establishment of the caliphs as rulers and direct heirs of the Prophet, and the patronage of the historically minded Abbasid line that had seized power by 750, ensured a congenial environment for the development of various types of writing about the past. The efflorescence of texts is staggering: the historians of ninth-century Baghdad alone 'probably produced more narrative history in a week than all of contemporaneous France or Germany could produce in a year'.[6] Some of this history-writing would be official, in the sense that it was directly sponsored by the caliphs or other magnates, but it was not always so, and many of the great texts of the first three centuries were the labour of independent scholars, often jurists, sometimes writing chronographic accounts which provided a gloomy record of wars and political crises, thereby implicitly critical of caliphal rule since the time of Muhammad.

From virtually the beginning, a zealous effort to record only true statements about or by the Prophet, derived ultimately from the testimony of eyewitnesses (themselves evaluated as trustworthy and reliable or not), led to careful attention to the chain of transmission (*isnād*) whereby one successive authority passed information, often orally, down to the next: a *ḥadīth* or report of the words of the Prophet generally consisted of an *isnād* followed by a *matn* (the actual text). By the ninth century a virtual 'science of traditions' had evolved with rules for evaluating particular texts or testimonies and the capacity to expunge false or

corrupt *ḥadīth*s. This did not stand in the way of literary creativity – Muslim authors shared with their Byzantine, Chinese and classical counterparts a fondness
for using the fictitious speech to convey a message or lesson, and they loved to
include lists of various sorts – but it does signal a rather different predisposition
than applied elsewhere in Eurasia. The degree to which the standards of *ḥadīth*
were successfully exported to historical writing as a whole – whether, in effect,
the account of one historian writing contemporaneously with events was distorted
through transmission as successive authors added materials or elided others – is a
matter of debate for specialists.

What is most striking for our purposes is that whereas with most historians
up to this point, we are left to guess as to the basis of their statements, except
where they generously name their sources, or we are required to work them
out through the complex process of *Quellenforschung*, the chain of authority
here is explicit. *Ḥadīth* scholars were scrupulous in giving their readers and
hearers what we would now call the 'provenance' of any saying or deed, right
back to the time of Muhammad himself. The oral/aural nature of this discourse
is worth highlighting. Many early scholars were suspicious of writing since it
threatened to subvert the pure tradition of the *Qur'an* and the *Sunna* or the
'model way' of Muhammad himself, and students of Islam continued to study
for a very long time at the feet of master scholars, whose works were often
first written down in the form of lecture notes by the acolytes and read back to
the speaker. Finally, it has also been observed that medieval Islamic historians
were remarkably good about not excising inconvenient or contradictory facts.
In Bernard Lewis' words, they 'tell it like it was' and confess on those exceptional occasions when they do not, as when al-Ṭabarī, an important historian
of the ninth and tenth centuries, suppresses information he deems contrary to
public interest.[7]

The principal disadvantage of a historiography built on the *isnād* is that little
room is left for the testimony of non-believers. What was one to do with the evidence provided by a Christian or Jew? Conversely, how did one judge the truth of
evidence about foreign lands where no *isnād* equivalent existed? An early writer
such as Ibn Isḥāq, active before the rules for the system had really settled, had
no difficulty conferring with non-Muslims on pre-Islamic history. The problem
would become more severe for later historians – al-Ṭabarī regularly had to resort,
as his history approached modern times, to vague phrases such as 'I have heard'
or 'it was said', and it would especially affect those who travelled far afield, such
as al-Bīrūnī. But the willingness of historians to depart from the stricter observ-
ance of *isnād* practised by *ḥadīth* scholars ultimately provided some distance between history and *ḥadīth*, historians increasingly affiliating with the practice of
adab, what we might call philology or 'belles-lettres'. This proved liberating in the

sense that it permitted departure from the narrow track of the *isnād*; and histories written under the influence of *adab* provide more information as to the author's intentions in writing them. Historical thought was also influenced by philosophical concerns derived from the notion of *hikmah* (judgment or wisdom) and by a concept of research or inquiry (*bahth*). One remarkable work, the tenth-century *Murūj adh-dhahab wa ma'adin al-jawahir* ('The Meadows of Gold and Mines of Gems') exemplifies this broadening of perspective: a geographically and temporally wide-ranging work that begins with the descent of man from Adam and includes discussion of the contributions of various nations both ancient and modern to the arts and sciences. Its author, the Iraqi historian Abu'l Hasan al-Masūdī, reflects these humanistic tendencies and his book is notable both for its critical apparatus (he was among the tiny minority of Muslim historians who discounted the *isnād*s and distrusted tradition in general) and his bald assertion that 'for any science to exist it must be derived from history ... The superiority of history over all other sciences is obvious.' For al-Masūdī, history was both entertainment and science (*'ilm*), it was accessible to both the learned and the ignorant, and its practice transcended the differences between Arab and non-Arab.[8] There is here an unambiguous link back to the Greeks, with whom al-Masūdī and other Arabic writers were familiar (and, incidentally, responsible in large measure for preserving), in the conception of history as the fount of all experience – a source of knowledge of nature as well as that of the past.

As with other historiographies, it is useful to break down Islamic writings on the past into genres. Chase F. Robinson has suggested a threefold division, more or less settled by the first few decades of the ninth century (by which time an early genre of heroic but unchronological 'Conquest narratives' had been largely discarded) that includes the following:

(1) Chronographic works, in which the past is recounted in chronological order; these subdivide into ones organized annalistically (and sometimes within that by months or other sub-periods), and others organized by caliphal reign, and may originate in early contact by Muslims with Byzantine and Syriac historiographical genres.

(2) Biographical works relating the life of a single person; these are often known as *sīra* ('way of acting') because of the model for behaviour that they provide; contemporaries regarded this, especially the subvariant devoted to the life of Muhammad, as the highest form of historical writing.

(3) Prosopographic works about a particular social group, often composed of individual entries called *tarjama*, on individuals, wherein this class of writings overlaps with biography proper. The name for this type of collective work, which developed somewhat later than the other categories, is *ṭabaqa* (plural

ṭabaqāt) and for the most part it was devoted to men of learning; it is known to have been exported early, for instance to the Jews.

This is a very broad categorization; within it we find many subdivisions, including forms of history with long-standing European or even Chinese counterparts, such as universal history or even local history, typically focused on a particular city.[9]

Among the earliest Muslim historians in what is commonly called the 'formative' period (roughly to the mid-tenth century), many writings are only known to us fragmentarily or as part of subsequent works. These include 'Urwa ibn al-Zubayr (d. 712) and his successor, al-Zuhrī (d. 742), who was probably the first to sort through conflicts between written and oral traditions about the Prophet and to combine several accounts into one continuous written narrative. They were quickly followed by the first great and fully intact biography (*sīra*) of the Prophet, by Ibn Isḥāq (c. 704–67), known to us through his later editor, Ibn Hishām (d. c. 833); and then by the more critically and chronologically rigorous treatment of al-Wāqidī (747–823), who also wrote several further works on Islamic history. Ibn Isḥāq's *sīra* in particular became the model for all subsequent biographies of the Prophet.

The expansion of both Islam and caliphal authority in Iraq and then through the larger region of the Near and Middle East proved extremely rapid, and the rule of Muslims over non-Muslims was in itself the occasion of much historical writing on the *futūḥ* or wars of conquest. With this expansion went the spread of a literate culture, the creation of libraries and the development of what may loosely be called particular historical 'schools' based at cities such as Medina and Baghdad. If history was not quite a science at the level of *ḥadīth*, it was quickly turned into a junior branch of formal learning or *'ilm*.[10] Yet its real influence ran well beyond the tables of the scholars. Rulers and administrators realized early that history offered an excellent source of practical wisdom: the kind of advice book that recommends history, a feature of early modern Europe, was already well known in the Islamic world by the tenth century. Al-Masūdī remarks of the Umayyad caliph Mu'awiya, that he spent the first third of every night in study of the 'history and the *Ayyām* of the Arabs', and the last third having servants read aloud or recite from memory 'tales of the past and all kinds of political precepts' drawn from 'volumes containing the lives and histories of kings and their wars and stratagems'.[11] Those who wrote history were generally drawn from the social elite, and focused their accounts on figures of similar rank. Many were either professional jurists or (increasingly) bureaucrats and officials of some kind. The ninth-century historian al-Balādhurī (d. 892), for instance, spent much of his life as a mid-level servant of the Abbasid state.

Box 5   Ta'rīkh al-rusul wa'l-mulūk

Abū Ja'far al-Ṭabarī's *Ta'rīkh al-rusul wa'l-mulūk* was a vast work of 8,000 pages covering time since the Creation. Translated into Persian (by then the *lingua franca* in much of the region) during the mid-tenth century, it exemplifies the strong theological content and pronounced teleology of Islamic history at this stage, whereby all events were seen as leading to or presaging Islamic rule by the Prophet and then the Abbasids: its linear succession of monarchies from antiquity to modernity is remarkably similar to the European historians' theme of the *translatio imperii.*

Various geographic sub-branches of Islamic historiography had emerged by the end of the ninth century, respectively associated with the Western Arabian, Syrian and Iraqi regions. The outstanding works of this period include the genealogical histories of al-Balādhurī, the historical geography or world history of al-Ya'qubī (d. 897) and especially the universal chronicle of Abū Ja'far al-Ṭabarī (c. 839–923), *Ta'rīkh al-rusul wa'l-mulūk* ('History of Prophets and Kings') (see Box 5 and Extract 7). The scope of some of these works was very wide, including Christian history to the west and China to the east. Their authors speculated on a wide variety of issues. In Abū Nasr Muhammad ibn al-Farakh al-Fārābi (Alpharabius, c. 872–950), we find thoughts on the origins of civilization and the role of language which would be echoed nine centuries later in Italy by the Neapolitan historian–philosopher Giambattista Vico. In his *Kitab al-Huruf* ('Book of Letters') al-Fārābi wrote:

It is evident that the commoners and the masses precede the elite ... in time and that the body of common knowledge ..., which constitutes the basis of all popular opinions, precedes in time the practical crafts ... and the kinds of knowledge peculiar to each single craft. In their aggregate, these constitute the body of popular knowledge, the first to be produced and maintained by mankind ... at a time when their souls are readied and directed towards certain types of knowledge, opinions and perceptions in limited degrees ... Then, once words have stabilized in their meaning ... similes and metaphors emerge .... Hence the craft of rhetoric is always the first to arise ... it being the first of the analogical crafts .... At that point in time, the words of that nation become more eloquent than before and their language and speech are perfected .... The art of writing is then deduced ... by which they record in books what was difficult for them to preserve in memory ... Five crafts are then found among them: the craft of rhetoric, the craft of poetry, the ability to preserve their history, ... the craft of the science of their language and the craft of writing.[12]

7: Islamic Historical Writing in the Tenth Century: al-Ṭabarī

The Events of the Year
7
(MAY 11, 628 – APRIL 30, 629)
The Expedition to Khaybar

Then the year 7 began. The Messenger of God set out for Khaybar in the remainder of al-Muḥarram, leaving Sibā' b. 'Urfuṭah al-Ghifārī in charge of Medina. He traveled and halted with his army at a valley called al-Rajī', encamping between the people of Khaybar and [the tribe of] Ghaṭafān (according to the account from Ibn Ḥumayd – Salamah – Ibn Isḥāq) to prevent the latter from aiding the people of Khaybar, for they were going to back them against the Messenger of God.

It has been reported to me that, when Ghaṭafān heard that the Messenger of God had encamped near Khaybar, they assembled because of him and set out to aid the Jews against him. Having traveled a day's journey, they heard a sound behind them in their possessions and families. Thinking that the enemy had come at them from behind, they turned back and stayed with their families and possessions, leaving the way to Khaybar open to the Messenger of God. The Messenger of God began taking herds and property bit by bit and conquering Khaybar fortress by fortress. The first of their fortresses that he conquered was the fortress of Nā'im. Maḥmūd b. Maslamah was killed at it – a millstone was hurled on him from it and killed him. Next was al-Qamūṣ, the fortress of Ibn Abī al-Ḥuqayq. The Messenger of God took some of its people captive, including Ṣafiyyah bt. Huyayy b. Akhṭab (the wife of Kinānah b. al-Rabī' b. Abī al-Ḥuqayq) and two daughters of her paternal uncle. The Messenger of God chose Ṣafiyyah for himself. Diḥyah al-Kalbī had asked the Messenger of God for Ṣafiyyah; when the latter chose her for himself, he gave Diḥyah her two cousins. The captives of Khaybar were divided among the Muslims. Then the Messenger of God began taking the fortresses and property that were closest to him.

According to Ibn Ḥumayd – Salamah – Muḥammad b. Isḥāq – 'Abdallāh b. Abī Bakr – a member of the Aslam: The Banū Sahm, who were a part of Aslam, came to the Messenger of God and said, 'Messenger of God, by God we have been struck by drought and possess nothing.' But they found that the Messenger of God had nothing to give them. So the Prophet said: 'O God, Thou knowest their condition – that they have no strength and that I have nothing to give them. Open to them [for conquest] the greatest of the fortresses of Khaybar, the one most abounding in food and fat meat.' The next morning God opened the fortress of al-Ṣa'b b. Mu'ādh for them [to conquer]. There was no fortress in Khaybar more abounding in food and fat meat than it.

After the Messenger of God had conquered some of their fortresses and taken some of the property, they reached their fortress of al-Waṭīḥ and al-Sulālim, which was the last of

extract

the fortresses of Khaybar to be conquered. The Messenger of God besieged the inhabitants between thirteen and nineteen nights.

Selection from *The History of al-Ṭabarī (Ta'rīkh al-rusul wa'l-mulūk)*, vol. VIII, *The Victory of Islam*, translated and annotated by Michael Fishbein (Albany, NY: SUNY Press, 1997), 116–17. The editor's notes have been omitted. The 'Messenger of God' is the Prophet, i.e. Muhammad.

By the advent of the Baghdad-based Abbasids in the mid-eighth century, terminology to express the idea of an account of the past had also developed. The modern Arabic term for history, variants of which are in use in most Muslim countries, is *ta'rīkh* (or *tārīkh*), which first appeared about 644. Another word, *khabar*, denoted a report of the past (sometimes no longer than a paragraph) composed for historical interest rather than to shed light on Islamic law, and often devoted to the relation of a single event. Within another hundred years, by 900, another phenomenon we have seen elsewhere was also occurring within Islamic writing, namely the self-identification of historians as creative authors and not merely silent 'transmitters' or compilers of earlier materials. Unlike Western historians since Thucydides, however, it is also clear that many of them did not see an obligation to provide a definitive verdict on the past where sources disagreed, but rather to provide multiple accounts from which the reader could choose (an interesting if accidental replication of Sima Qian's approach in Han China). Genres of writing demand different things from their authors, even when the same author practises more than one kind. Thus al-Ṭabarī, who as a jurist was precise in pronouncing the correct interpretation of a passage of the *Qur'an* or a point of law, took an entirely different approach when writing his histories, relaying 'disagreement after disagreement'. In presenting contradictory and possibly false statements, he fell back in his *Ta'rīkh al-rusul wa'l-mulūk* on the argument that he was but a transmitter of past views, and that all knowledge of the past was dependent not on reason or deduction but on transmission:

Let him who examines this book of mine know that I have relied, as regards everything I mention therein which I stipulate to be described by me, solely upon what has been transmitted to me by way of reports which I cite therein and traditions which I ascribe to their narrators .... This is because knowledge of the reports of men of the past and of contemporaneous news of men of the present do not reach the one who has not witnessed them nor lived in their times except through the accounts of reports and the transmission of transmitters, to the exclusion of rational deduction and mental inference. Hence, if I mention in this book a report about some men of the past which the reader finds objectionable or worthy of censure because he can see no aspect of truth nor any factual substance therein, let him know that this is not to be attributed to us but to those who transmitted it to us and we have merely passed this on as it had been passed on to us.[13]

A peculiarity of early Islamic historiography is its orientation towards remote rather than more recent times. Whereas a Herodotus asked questions about the past of a generation or so before his time, and Thucydides virtually repudiated any past not contemporary, the first few generations of Muslim historians had a seeming aversion to contemporary or recent history, albeit one that did not last. To put it another way, if the early Greek historians privileged modernity in their accounts, Islamic historians, working within a scholarly tradition that valued not the past in general but that slice of the past which was foundational to Islam, gave priority to the time of the Prophet and then of the civil wars, reserving little attention for their own day. In this respect, they also differed from contemporary Chinese historians, for whom the past, both ancient and recent, was a worthy subject of study, its preservation and correct interpretation the business of government.

The Bureaucratization of History: Chinese Historiography to the End of the Tang Dynasty

The turmoil and disorder of the centuries around the collapse of the western Roman Empire have a close Chinese counterpart in the disunity that followed the end of the Eastern Han dynasty in 220. Just as both the idea and spectre of Rome haunted the Middle Ages, so memories of the glory days of Han power long outlived the dynasty itself. And just as Gnosticism, Christianity and Neo-Platonism flourished together in the late antique period, so Buddhism and a resurgent Daoism took hold in a China governed by short-lived and sometimes rival dynasties claiming suzerainty over all the empire – by the early fifth century a Buddhist named He Chingtian (370–447) even found himself in the position of official historian to Emperor Wen of Liu. Chinese intellectuals increasingly sought refuge in the past through renewed attention to the Confucian tradition. Many of these emperors encouraged historical writing: the Northern Wei ruler Xiaowen even remarked that historians were necessary because if they didn't record evil behaviour, what else would a bad ruler fear? A significant quantity of history was written by private scholars in both the northern and southern parts of the empire, including a number of contemporary histories of the mid-third-century 'Three Kingdoms' of Wei, Shu and Wu. Such was the proliferation of history-writing that by the end of the period the very word *shi*, which till then had meant the *writer* of a history, began increasingly to be used to denote the textual product itself. History was also now a distinctive category in the minds of bibliographers – second after the five surviving classics (*Wujing*) among the four classes (the other two being philosophy and literature) into which written documents had been organized since about the third century AD. Written history was divided formally into thirteen different subcategories, and historical learning or *shixue* itself became a recognized category of knowledge, with the three great histories of the Han and post-Han era, the *Shiji, Hanshu* and its successor, *Hou Hanshu,* becoming important texts in the education of future civil servants; by 822 a regular examination on all three was instituted.

This activity in the face of trouble should not surprise; there is no necessary correlation between political stability or social order and historical writing, and indeed there often occurs a greater impulse to capture the past during 'interesting' times. The successor states to the Han Empire each produced during the next four centuries a significant stock of histories. Dynastic history flourished where dynasties came and went with depressing frequency up until the reunification by the short-lived Sui dynasty (581–618). Ban Gu's *Hanshu* was followed first by Chen Shou's (233–97) *San'guozhi* ('Records of the Three Kingdoms') and eventually by Fan Ye's *Hou Hanshu* ('History of the Later or Eastern Han'), left unfinished at its author's beheading for political conspiracy in 445. In all, as many as 140 dynastic histories may have appeared between the end of the Han and the advent of the Tang; whereas Ban Gu had been able to list only a dozen historical works in the first century AD, by 656 the author of the *Suishu,* the dynastic history of the Sui, counted nearly 900. In addition to the traditional media of silk or bamboo, scholars were also beginning to use paper with increasing frequency. It is during this period that the later Han innovation of keeping *qijuzhu* or court diaries of 'activity and repose' became standard practice, providing material for later historians. Some of these diaries were maintained by female recorders, and the diarists themselves were active advisors on royal policy and protocol, not silent stenographers. The Emperor Wen of Liu (r. 424–53) became the first to order his own officials to compose a history of the previous dynasty, and by the mid-sixth century, in an effort to weed out unauthoritative histories, the Emperor Yuan of Liang (r. 552–5) declared some to be *Zhengshi* ('Standard Histories'), thereby giving birth to that term.

Genres were also evolving, as some historians opted for an annals–biography format and others for one combining annals and chronicles: gradually, the former swallowed the latter. The temporary weakening of Confucianism's hold combined with the neo-Daoist focus on the self to stimulate biographical writing outside the dynastic history framework; this often concerned individuals or categories of person who would previously have been 'out of scope' in this genre, including women and Buddhist monks. Finally, a variety of miscellaneous genres also appeared, including regional histories and local gazetteers, for instance Chang Qu's (c. 291–361) *Huayang guozhi* ('History of the Land of Huayang') (Box 6).

The abrupt downfall of the Sui after a disastrous invasion of Korea eventually produced the Tang dynasty and with it a significant change in both the status and practice of historiography. The Tang saw themselves in the same position with

Box 6   *Huayang guozhi*

Chang Qu's *Huayang guozhi* may stand as an example of the mixing and blurring of genres that occurred in Chinese history-writing at the end of the Han dynasty: it combined monographs on the geography, agriculture, transportation and history of this part of southwestern and western China from antiquity to the author's own time, with exemplary biographies in which the moral didacticism of the Han historians continued. This creativity with genre and ability to combine different formats and purposes is worth remembering; in comparison, adherence to genre boundaries would eventually prove a significant delimiter of potential subjects, and an obstacle to innovation, for Western historians.

respect to the Sui as the Han long before had been with respect to the Qin: the benevolent and wise dynasty that succeeded a unifying but ruthless and hence transitional predecessor. With respect to scholarship and history, it is hard to argue against their own positive self-image: in addition to creating the system of civil service exams (AD 622) that would endure for centuries, the Tang wove history-making into the operations of government. The second Tang emperor, Taizong (r. 626–49), a rather cutthroat figure who forced his own father into an early retirement, inaugurated a systematic 'bureaucratization' of history, building on the imperial sponsorship of histories under previous dynasties. There had been for some time a Bureau or Office of Literary Composition, a branch of the Imperial Library out of which earlier historians such as Fan Ye had operated. In 629, a new Bureau for the writing of history (*shiguan*) was created, attached initially to the Chancellery and a little over a century later moved to the Secretariat; the Bureau also had a branch office in the eastern capital of Luoyang. The charge to the Bureau was simple and succinct, even if its execution proved enormously complex:

The historiographers are responsible for the compilation of the National History. They may not give false praise, or conceal evil, but must write a straight account of events. The portents of heaven, earth, sun and moon, the distribution of mountains and rivers, fiefs and cities, the precedence between junior and senior lines of descent, ritual and military affairs, changes of reward and punishment, between prosperity and decline, all should be recorded. The historians should base themselves on the Court Diary and the Record of Administrative Affairs to make a Veritable Record, setting this out in chronological form and incorporating the principles of praise and blame. When this is completed it is to be stored in the official storehouse.[14]

The whole enterprise was also conceived not merely from a narrowly dynastic perspective (though the Tang viewed literary innovation as a key part of their own legacy) but with the intent of creating a reliable set of records, or national history (*guoshi*) of recent times, which would eventually be used for the future construction of a dynastic history. The Bureau also produced new histories of several post-Han dynasties, taking the orthodox Confucian Ban Gu's *Hanshu* rather than the rather more eclectic *Shiji* as its model. As institutionalized in the Bureau, the process thus clearly distinguished between the *recording* of historical events as they occurred and the *writing* of histories which later commemorated them in the form of a narrative. We will find no such clear conceptualization of this distinction elsewhere in the world at this time, or anything remotely approaching this assembly-line approach to production, with its ascending stages of composition from the daily event to the dynastic summary. The process began with the court diaries kept during the reign of an incumbent emperor, a memento of his sayings and actions to which the emperor himself was theoretically not supposed to have access – Taizong himself was famously denied a look at what his own diarists were recording. This, together with a more patchily maintained administrative record (no example of which survives), would be integrated starting in the early ninth century into a 'daily calendar' for each year. From this (or, prior to the advent of the Calendar, directly from the diaries and administrative records) and other, external materials, including privately authored biographies and histories, a set of 'Veritable Records' (*shilu*) would be developed at the end of each reign and, sometimes, a 'national history' of the reign itself usually emulating the annals–biography format of the Standard Histories; only one of these survived the end of the Tang dynasty.

The *shilu* were an innovation of the Tang for which there is no earlier precedent and they formed an essential part of all later dynasties' official historiography. They were particularly important as the first stage at which mere recording became actual composition and interpretation and at least initially they appear to have circulated around court, some even being sent abroad, notably to Japan. The *shilu* in turn, after the final eclipse of a dynasty and ascension of its successor, would provide the basis of the Standard History of that dynasty, a work which invariably included the two essential elements of basic annals and biographies of individual notables and sometimes foreign peoples. The Standard History might or might not include some of the other elements of Sima Qian's *Shiji* such as monographs and chronological tables – five histories completed in 636 contained basic annals and biographies only, though a monographs section was added subsequently. The Standard History was intended, at least in theory, to be the official and unchallengeable truth, not subject to rival versions or interpretations, and it was supposed to be a dynastic history of the nation as a whole, not merely the emperor

Box 7   Historical Encyclopedias

The invention of the Chinese historical encyclopedia is usually credited to Du
You (735–812), a Buddhist-influenced scholar whose *Tongdian* ('Comprehensive
Compendium' or 'Comprehensive Institutions') was compiled over three decades, at
a time when the Tang had recently been rattled by a major rebellion (755–63), in
order to convert knowledge of the past into a tool for present governance. The work
is notable for its sense of China's historical progress from barbarism to sophisticated
bureaucratic state.

and the court. Under the Tang, seven new *guoshi* were to be produced and seven
Standard Histories of previous dynasties, some of these being the work of individuals and others executed by teams.

Not all history that was written was dynastic history, nor was it all controlled
by the Bureau. There were also spinoffs, including institutional histories, historical encyclopedias (see Box 7) and privately authored histories, some of which
were the work of Bureau members writing on their own initiative. Many private
writers eschewed the complexities of the annals–biography format for a straightforward year-by-year chronicle. Towards the end of the dynasty, private histories
began to proliferate as the Bureau lost some of its control; unofficial histories
written in the chronicle format appeared as a few scholars sought to rewrite or
condense the often lengthy dynastic histories. Nevertheless, the overall trend by
the end of the Tang in the tenth century is unmistakable. History, once loosely
allied to government, was now virtually inseparable from it, with all the attend-
ant risks of censorship and limited freedom of thought that such alliances have
invariably posed to be weighed against the benefits of considerable financial and
institutional support. And there seems little doubt that the Bureau, like any institution, was structurally disposed to discourage further innovation and preserve
established practice.

Yet the Tang historiographical achievement is all the more admirable because
it *did*, in spite of the Bureau's power and influence, generate its own critics,
including a number of scholars suspicious of the integrity of the *shilu* for various reigns; in particular the dynasty produced in Liu Zhiji's *Shitong* ('Comprehensive Perspectives on Historiography') an especially perceptive commentary
on history-writing. Liu (661–721) had been bred to history from an early age.
He had heard his father expounding on the *Chunqiu* and the *Zuozhuan*, which

he found easier to master than the *Shujing* or Classic of History. His career as an official historian, however, was to prove short. He was deeply disillusioned with the Bureau, a 'refuge for idlers' and 'den for time-servers' from which he resigned. He despised the comfortable and easily corruptible life-style of its members ('hatted apes') and the vulnerability of the compilation process to political interference, whether by the emperor or by overly controlling chief ministers.[15] Liu was also sceptical about the literary merits of collectively com-posed histories: too many cooks made for a tasteless and indigestible broth. He waxed nostalgic for the era of the great single-authored works of pre-Tang days:

Among the excellent histories of states, it is their narration of events which makes them well-formed, and skill in the narration of events lies chiefly in succinctness. Great is the timely significance of succinctness! If we look successively at the historians from of old, we find that the work began with the *Book of Documents*. In what the pathfinders recorded, they aimed at keeping the events to a few. The *Spring and Autumn* changed the form, placing a premium on cutting down on words. Here we see the distinct stylistic effects of thinness and amplitude [in recording events], the different deeds of earlier and later histo-rians. It is when the text is concise while the events are rich that we have narrative writing at its best.

From the time of the Two Hans until the Three Kingdoms, the texts of state histories have suffered from increasing prolixity. In the Chin and after, they drift aimlessly ever farther; if one looks for extraneous sentences and picks out excess verbage, in a single line there are sure to be several words added without reason and on a foot of paper there will always be several lines expended needlessly. It is said that 'gathered mosquitoes make a thunder,' and 'enough down will break a carriage shaft.' If one is not sparing in paragraphs and sentences and his words and expressions are unlimited, so that it takes two carts to carry what he has written, what is there that is worth speaking of in such a work?[16]

Liu identified talent, knowledge and insight as the essential ingredients of the good historian, with truth and factuality being the highest goals to which that his-torian should aspire in writing; he also categorized historical genres more formally and organized all previous histories according to six 'schools'. Openly sceptical of elements of even the most revered ancient texts, Liu suggested improvements that future historians could make (and also produced several sons who became private historians). In the later eighth century, the writing of unofficial histories in chronicle form would increase, though few specimens of it survive. By the time the dynasty ended, the Tang could bequeath not only a state machine for the produc-tion of history, but a good deal of writing generated within and outside it, and a critical apparatus to evaluate the product and theorize about its improvement. All of this boded well for the later development of historiography under their eventual successors, the Song.

Early Japanese Histories to the End of the Tenth Century

History developed much later in Japan (which became a recognizable nation only in the fifth century AD) than in China, and then not in the same forms, despite the adoption of Chinese script, the mass importation of Chinese learning, the influence of Confucianism and then Buddhism, and the frequent use of Chinese as the language of composition. The differences are not trivial. It has sometimes been observed that while Confucian principles and Chinese historiographical models were adopted by the Japanese, none of the critical attitude to sources and to unverified traditions accompanied this importation and that to the contrary, Japanese historians regarded it virtually as a duty to accept ancient traditions: the eighteenth-century historian and nationalist, Motoori Norinaga, who disliked the Chinese influences on his country and explicitly rejected Confucian source criticism, would advise his readers not to approach old books with a sceptical 'Chinese heart' (*karagokoro*).[17] Moreover, where official history took some time to evolve in China, the Japanese connected history-writing with the imperial household right out of the starting gate, as a means of buttressing the relatively young Yamato dynasty. Private historical writing emerged rather later, when the tradition of official histories came to an abrupt halt in the early tenth century rather than, as in China, in parallel with them.

Chinese historical texts refer to the Japanese islands from as early as Sima Qian's time, and some of these texts are known to have circulated in Japan from the third century. Relatively low literacy would limit the writing of history for a very long time. Oral traditions are thought to have been recorded when the Japanese adopted Chinese script, and indigenous historical writing is known to have occurred in the Japanese archipelago from the early seventh century AD. Given the lack of a long tradition of written literature, the early monarchs and their families had rather the opposite problem than that which occasioned the great book burning by the Qin emperor nearly a millennium earlier: the urgent necessity was not the destruction of knowledge of the past but its rapid creation. The imperial prince Shōtoku is alleged to have commissioned at least three works, now lost, called respectively the *Tennōki* ('Record of the Emperors'), the *Hongi* ('Fundamental Records') and *Kokki* ('National Records'). Temmu (or Tenmu, r. 672–86), by tradition the fortieth emperor of Japan, ordered the compilation of a 'chronicle of the emperors and also of matters of high antiquity' in 681 in order to correct errors in and conflicts between imperial genealogies and the traditional origin tales of various great families. Though there was for now no contact between Japan and Europe, the coincidence of genealogical interest is worth noting, as is the determination to establish an anchor in the remote past for the nascent imperial regime. The main difference was the conspicuous absence of foreign immigrants such as the Trojans – medieval Japanese historians were reluctant to accept the story that Go Taihaku (equated with Wu Taibo, a Chinese prince mentioned by Sima Qian) had founded their imperial line.

The earliest extant historical texts date from the beginning of the Nara period (710–94), the *Kojiki* ('Record of Ancient Matters', completed AD 712) and *Nihon Shoki* ('Chronicles of Japan', otherwise known as *Nihongi*, comp. 720). The *Kojiki* was commissioned in 711,[18] ostensibly by the Empress Gemmei, while the *Nihon Shoki* may have been the result (or a later version of that result) of the work that her father-in-law, Temmu, had ordered. Both texts relayed a powerful mythology of the creation of the world and the subsequent foundation of the empire by the first human monarch, Jimmu (Jinmu), a direct descendant of the sun goddess. A more or less consistent theme of Japanese perceptions of the past, belief in the *Tennō* or emperor's divine ancestry would continue to be taught in twentieth-century Japanese schools. Both the *Kojiki* and *Nihon Shoki* begin their accounts from the creation of the world, drawing on legend, myth and oral tradition as well as on earlier documents that they purport to correct. The *Kojiki*, which has no clear chronology, ends about 628 while the *Nihon Shoki* concludes in 697.[19] There are important differences between the two works. The *Kojiki*, which celebrates Japanese origins and the divine descent of the emperors, was written in a commonly used mixture of Chinese and Japanese that grew unfamiliar to readers in later centuries. This led to the work's being neglected until the 1700s, though it proceeds more or less chronologically and with a single narrative voice. The *Nihon Shoki* was intended to establish Japan on a world, or at least regional stage, on the wings of which loomed the Chinese juggernaut. It was composed in Chinese in a more explicit attempt to imitate Chinese historiography, including the tendency we noted earlier in Sima Qian to include multiple versions of the same event, introduced by phrases such as 'another work says' or 'in another place it says'. Its authors clearly used Chinese histories such as the *Hanshu* and *Hou Hanshu* as both models and sources: the work borrows sections from Chinese works and converts them into speeches by Japanese rulers. Finally, whereas the *Kojiki* provides minimal dating, the *Nihon Shoki* is almost relentlessly chronological down to the specific day (see Extract 8).

By 901 the *Nihon Shoki* had been augmented by the five other Chinese-language works, again modelled on *guoshi* and *zhengshi*, that with it form the Six National Histories or *Rikkokushi* (see Box 8). As with their progenitor, the later five histories are annalistic in organization (though unlike *Nihon Shoki* they do not omit any year); they focus principally on the court, the emperors and the nobility; and they display a geographical bias towards the central part of Japan. They exclude the *Nihon Shoki*'s account of mythical antiquity but include verbatim reportage of government decrees and appointments, sometimes ignoring matters elsewhere in the country that might, to us, seem more important.

8: History in Early Japan: *Nihon Shoki* on the Emperor Temmu

28th day. The Emperor went to Wasami. He returned after having inspected the military arrangements.

29th day. The Emperor went to Wasami and issued his commands to the troops through the Imperial Prince Takechi. The Emperor then went back again to Nogami, and abode there.

On this day Wofukehi, Ohotomo no Muraji, had secret conference with Kumage, Sakano-he no Atahe, the officer in charge [of the palace during the emperor's] absence. Addressing himself to one or two of the Aya no Atahe, he said: – 'I shall pretend that I am the Imperial Prince Takechi, and at the head of some tens of cavalry soldiers, will issue forth and approach the camp from the road north of the Temple of Asukadera. So do you co-operate with me secretly.' Having done so, he marshalled his troops at the house of Kudara and issued forth from the South Gate. In the first place he caused Kuma, Hada no Miyakko, in his waist-cloth, to mount a horse and gallop into the camp west of the Temple and say to them: – 'The Imperial Prince Takechi has arrived from Fuha, followed by a numerous armed force.' Hereupon Prince Takazaka, who had charge of the Palace in (the Emperor's) absence, Momotari, Hodzumi no Omi, who had been sent as a messenger to levy troops, and oth-ers repaired to the tsuki tree west of the Temple of Asukadera and encamped there. But Momotari remained at the arsenal of Woharida, where he transported arms to Afumi ...

Selected from *Nihongi* XXVIII.12, in *Nihongi: Chronicles of Japan from the Earliest Times to A.D. 697*, trans. W. G. Aston, 2 vols. in 1 (Rutland, VT and Tokyo: Charles E. Tuttle Co., 1972), vol. II, 310; par-enthetical insertion is the translator's, bracketed insertion is mine, drawn from the translator's notes which have been otherwise omitted. The selection recounts events in AD 672, early in the reign of Temmu.

In 713 the government also ordered the compilation of local histories (*fudoki*) of various provinces of which one, the *Izumo Fudoki* (comp. 733), has survived intact and fragments or sections of others remain. Some other works fell outside the Confucian mainstream, such as Imibe Hironari's *Kogoshūi* ('Gleanings from Ancient Japanese Stories', comp. 807), and the *Shinsen Shōji Roku* ('New Selec-tion and Record of Inherited Titles and Family Names'), a genealogical work of the early ninth century. Imibe's work, through which ran a resentment of Chinese influences on Japanese culture, is interesting for its passage reconstructing Japan's earliest history and its relation to oral tradition:

... I have heard that in ancient times, when Japan had no written script, everyone, noble and base, old and young, performed every duty by word of mouth, forgetting nothing. Since the introduction of writing to Japan, people have not been fond of talking about the ancient past. Thus, people studied the sterile learning of China and mocked their own

Box 8   *Rikkokushi* ('Six National Histories')

The Six National Histories are, in chronological order of completion: *Shoku Nihongi* ('Chronicles of Japan Continued', comp. 797) a Nara period continuation of *Nihon Shoki*, covering the years 697–791; *Nihon Kōki* ('Later Chronicles of Japan', comp. 840 and covering 792–832); *Shoku Nihon Kōki* ('Later Chronicles of Japan Continued', comp. 869 and covering 832–50); *Nihon Montoku Tennō Jitsuroku* ('Veritable Records of Emperor Montoku of Japan', comp. 879 and covering 850–8); and the *Nihon Sandai Jitsuroku* ('Veritable Records of Three Reigns of Japan', comp. 901 and covering 858–87). They are collectively some-times known, confusingly, as the Five National Histories (i.e. the six, minus *Nihon Shoki*). Each of these was directed by a Chief Compiler, invariably a member of the dominant Heian family of Fujiwara (regents for the emperor beginning in 858), who presided over an authorial team. One is reminded that the history of collec-tive scholarship has not always been a smooth one. Fujiwara Tokihira (871–909), Chief Compiler of the last of the national histories, was forced to take on a co-Chief: but he soon contrived to have his rival exiled!

ancient traditions. They altered the old way of doing things, neglecting various aspects of the past. When people inquire into the customs of the past, they cannot find the truth concerning them.[20]

This suspicion of writing and its corrosive effect on memory and tradition (pre-viously articulated in Plato's dialogue, *Phaedrus*), and the further association of writing with cultural imperialism, is a theme we will run into again, during the period of European expansion in the early modern era.

We saw in ancient Europe that prose historiography emerged in places from poetic and epic foundations, and that its early functions of entertainment and commemoration only gradually took on a more serious moral and didactic pur-pose. In Japan, the trend was virtually the reverse. Japanese historiography com-mitted early to the notion of deriving lessons, both moral and practical, from the past, while only at a later stage during the Heian and Kamakura periods did a more entertaining and poetic use of history develop (see Chapter 3 below). This difference perhaps derives from history's much earlier tie to imperial power and to the influence of Chinese models. The early Japanese historians lay praise on good emperors and blame on the bad ones, such as Buretsu (r. 498–506), of whom *Nihon*

Shoki records that 'he worked much evil, and accomplished no good thing'. Like Tacitus' emperor Domitian, Buretsu 'never omitted to witness in person cruel punishments of all kinds, and the people of the whole land were all in terror of him'.[21] The metaphor of the 'mirror' occurs once again, for instance, in the dedication to the emperor by the author of *Shoku Nihon Kōki*, one of the national histories:

I hope that beautiful things will be widely known and wise actions will be taught so that both may be lessons for succeeding generations. Using great and good men creates a mirror for succeeding generations by commending good and rejecting evil.[22]

In the next chapter we will find that the image of the mirror is a recurrent one across much of Eurasia. Far from viewing the 'real' past as indistinguishable from fiction, and their hands untied from any obligation to canons of truth, most medieval historians, a modern scholar suggests, saw their history as a kind of looking-glass through which the past could be relayed to the reader, unadorned and un-edited, in all its untidy wealth.[23] This point brings us back to Latin Europe.

Historiography in the Latin West during the Ninth and Tenth Centuries

The settling of kingdoms in western Europe during the eighth and ninth centuries more or less brought an end to the period of migrations, some semblance of territorial if not yet fixed or national boundaries, and the establishment of aristocratic and royal houses. By the year 1000 it is possible to speak of countries called 'England', 'Scotland' and 'France', all of whom had kings, even if hereditary succession had not quite eradicated the older Germanic practices of elective monarchy. Other geographic regions would remain divided for many centuries to come. The heirs to the Frankish empire of Charlemagne fought among themselves, like the Diadochi of old. By the early tenth century, what passed for imperial power in Latin Europe rested with the Ottonians, a German Saxon line, while the French, as the northwestern Franks were now called, were ruled by the Capetians. An England unified by the kings of Wessex would spend two centuries defending itself against incursions from the Norsemen and Danes. The Iberian Peninsula, previously united under the Visigothic monarchy of Toledo, had meanwhile disintegrated into several competing kingdoms which now included a powerful Muslim presence in Andalusia.

The ancient heritage, refracted through patristic and early medieval scholarship and a good deal of its textual wealth scattered or lost, was reinvigorated during the Carolingian Renaissance of the ninth century, as was an interest in classical rhetoric. Monastic historiography would benefit directly from this revival. At the same time, knowledge of the classical past remained a bit like an out-of-focus photograph: the general shape was apparent but the outlines and details were blurred. With no obvious external evidence that the world was socially and otherwise a very different place than it had been in antiquity, great historical figures such as Julius Caesar or Alexander were readily imported into literary genres such as the *romans d'antiquité*. There they became medieval chivalric heroes, hardly distinguishable from a Christian figure such as Charlemagne or, two centuries later, the Spaniard El Cid. Both of those characters in turn became chivalric icons in military-oriented epic literature such as the French *chansons de geste* (eleventh to twelfth centuries) and the Castilian *El Cantar del Mio Cid*, works which recount the earliest episodes in the long and difficult relations between Christianity and Islam.

Historiographically, it becomes possible at this point to highlight some major developments. The first and most important is a pluralisation of genres, beyond the older distinctions between universal history and ecclesiastical history, but without anything like the classical Greek or Chinese strict attention to form. A spinoff of sacred history was the saint's life (usually known as 'hagiography', a term that does not really do it justice), which commemorated the piety and deeds, including miracles, of Christian martyrs, monks and hermits, and soon spread to cover scholars and secular clergy such as bishops. Bede, who included such lives in his *Ecclesiastical History*, also wrote a separate example in his *Life of St Cuthbert*; Alcuin wrote a life of Willibrord; and the eleventh-century saint and philosopher St Anselm would be captured in a life by Eadmer. These works may have depicted saints, but they were much more than hagiography, since they celebrated the literary and often the political achievements of their subjects, some of whom had been powerful churchmen. The success of monarchs such as Charlemagne and England's Alfred the Great produced a number of individual royal biographies, such as Einhard's and Notker Balbulus' of the Frankish emperor (the latter of which liberally embellished the facts and thereby inaugurated Charlemagne's transformation from historical figure to chivalric folk hero), and two lives of his successor Louis the Pious. Lesser mortals also had their lives commemorated, as Wipo of Burgundy (*fl.* early eleventh century) did for the Emperor Conrad II. The relation between these lives and the more common form of annals is complex and variable. Einhard (c. 770–840) seems deliberately to have avoided an annalistic approach to his life of Charlemagne, and chose to imitate Suetonian biography; his own English reader Asser (d. 908/9), three generations later, would include in his *Life of Alfred* extensive passages and frequent *anno domini* dates drawn from a work known to us as the *Anglo-Saxon Chronicle*.

The *Anglo-Saxon Chronicle* exemplifies a further development in both halves of Christendom, Latin and Greek, namely the first appearance of historiography written in vernacular languages. Some of these were newly composed works while

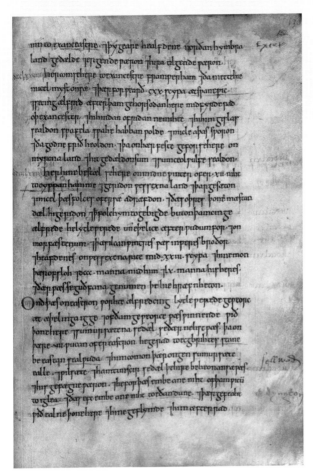

Figure 11 | Excerpt from the text of the *Anglo-Saxon Chronicle*. This manuscript was probably copied at Abingdon Abbey *c.* 1046; the last paragraph describes King Alfred the Great's defeat of the Danes at Edington in AD 878.

others were translations of Latin and Greek texts. A number of eastern European regions, including the future Bohemia, Bulgaria and eventually Russia would produce historical or pseudo-historical/semi-legendary works (such as the Legends of Sts Cyril and Methodius) in a language known as Old Church Slavonic, ancestor of several of the modern Slavic tongues. But on the whole, vernacular works would remain very rare for quite some time: the *Anglo-Saxon Chronicle* (Fig. 11) is the name given to a series of manuscripts that began towards the end of Alfred the Great's rule and which was continued until the mid-twelfth century by successive anonymous annalists. It is virtually unique in the West at this juncture as an ongoing national history composed in a vernacular language. Latin remained the language of learned discourse, and the literary order, the clergy, continued to use that language for their histories, reflecting the larger Latin Christendom that was both the context for their activity and the extended audience for their works. But the Latin and Germanic tongues had also produced vigorous new languages such as Old English, Old French, Spanish and Italian, which in time would find their way into histories and eventually be seen as the principal bearers of their people's ethnicity.

No period in the history of historical writing has been so ill-judged as the Middle Ages, even by those who acknowledge the brilliance of the exceptional figure like Bede. In part it is because we have been conditioned for nearly five centuries – apart from the romantic flirtation with the medieval in the nineteenth century – to regard the Middle Ages on almost every front as a colourfully peculiar digression from the main course of European history, a popular impression that has been enormously tough to dispel. And it is scarcely a popular view only: so far as historiography is concerned, modernity has tended to swallow wholesale the disparaging comments of Renaissance humanist historians who had a vested interest in repudiating their medieval precursors at the same time that they were labouring to imitate the rediscovered ancients. This contempt for medieval history-writing was pervasive if not universal in Europe from the fifteenth to the late eighteenth century, with monastic chronicles (superstitious monks!), urban annals (trivial details!) and national histories (invented heroes!) forming an unholy trinity of historiographical offenders.

This smugness would itself be risible did it not betray a serious and profoundly misleading tendency to judge all historical writing by modern standards. Yet one cannot dismiss such sentiments altogether, even while rejecting their value-laden conclusions. Though one can find it fascinating, medieval historiography nonetheless looks odd. In a group of European historians that includes Thucydides or Tacitus at one end and Leopold von Ranke or Karl Marx at the other, virtually any historian writing between the fifth and the fifteenth centuries will seem very different. This is in part because medieval historiography has nearly always been considered in a comparison group that includes only the Western tradition, but though a cross-cultural juxtaposition with Chinese or Islamic histories may ameliorate this impression, it does not remove it. Various explanations have been adduced for the oddities of medieval histories, including William F. Brandt's suggestion that the texts simply reflect their authors' radically different (from our own) mode of perceiving the world and how it works, causally and ethically. Nancy F. Partner, building on a line of argument originating with the great literary critic Erich Auerbach, has stressed the differences in literary construction, rather than the content:

... [I]t is always the paratactic arrangement of medieval historical narrative that is at the heart of everything we find most difficult about it and which ultimately defies understanding. Compared with the narratives of antiquity which served as models, medieval narrative seems terribly slack and fallen-off from any aesthetic or intellectual standard.[24]

One of the most salutary developments of the past generation in many areas of historiography, and in particular the study of medieval historiography, has been the shift away from the older fixation of their great nineteenth-century editors on appraising the accuracy of past historians (a branch of *Quellenkritik*) and the reliability of their information, or tracking down their sources (*Quellenforschung*), and a much greater concern with the shape, argumentative structure and style of individual historical texts, and careful attention to the announced intentions of their authors. This approach has in turn made medieval historians' complex relations to their own ancient precursors rather more clear. The Middle Ages had available, especially in Latin Europe, a partial and disrupted classical heritage. On the one hand, they knew of and practised the teaching of classical rhetoric via authors such as Quintilian and were aware of distinctions in genre, as noted in Isidore earlier. A later historian, the Anglo-Norman Orderic Vitalis, would protest that his history was neither fictitious tragedy nor 'wordy comedy' but simply a record of different sorts of events for attentive readers.[25] On the other hand, such awareness seems rarely to have been translated into historiographic practice. The very word *historia* now applied indiscriminately to secular history, religious history and to the historical books in the Bible. The term would soon include romance and other fictional works, and it is far from clear that medieval audiences made a distinction between the two or that they were bothered by the overlap.

The further from antiquity they found themselves, the greater the difficulty writers of history had with fitting accounts of newly emerged monarchies into the box of classical models. One trouble lay in the modest supply of such models. It is certainly not true that medieval historians were ignorant of ancient historiography, its practices and values, or that classical works were uniformly 'lost' till the Renaissance. To the contrary, there is a visible line – albeit sometimes a dotted and jagged one – from the ancients to the humanists, via the 'classicizing' late antique historians, down through most of the Middle Ages, including twelfth-century *romans d'antiquité* and thirteenth-century adaptations or translations of Lucan, Sallust, Suetonius and Caesar. Classical rhetoric and its devices, including the time-honoured device of the invented speech, were routinely pressed into service, and most chroniclers probably believed that their work had moral or didactic value, and gave thought to their audience. The early ninth-century court historian Nithard (d. 844) wrote an account of events during the final years of the Carolingian state, in which he had been personally involved. This is patterned after ancient histories – he had read Sallust in particular – and, like many of those, aims to preserve these recent events for the benefit of both contemporary readers whom he wished to persuade and posterity. Richer (*fl.* late tenth century), a monk of Saint-Remigius who constructed his national history of tenth-century France from a mix of oral information and research into earlier works, saw himself as operating within a tradition of Roman writers that included Julius Caesar, Cicero and Sallust as well as late antique historians such as Orosius.

Yet these classical tools rarely formed a complete kit. Few ancient historians apart from Sallust were known in whole, and the fragments and paraphrases contained in early medieval successors such as Bede or Gregory of Tours, or quoted by Byzantine scholars, were informative on a factual level but not much of a help to writing. Aristotle's distinction between history and tragedy was known, but not its source nor its full text containing Aristotle's doubts about history's practical utility. If antiquity itself remained, as suggested above, like a blurry photograph, the connection between medieval writers and their surviving classical sources can similarly be likened to another feature of modernity, the broken telephone: our chroniclers were on the listening end of a conversation with antiquity in which the line went repeatedly dead in the middle of sentences, or introduced intermediary and intrusive voices from points along the way.

The easiest solution to this problematic relation with a fragmentary ancient heritage was to avoid the question of genre altogether and divide their subjects in different ways, sometimes reflecting the medium in which it was preserved. Some grouped materials broadly chronologically into books (*libri*) subdivided into briefer headings (*capituli*, whence derives our word 'chapters') as did, for instance, Eusebius, Bede and Otto of Freising. Or, increasingly, authors could fall back on that tried and true unit of historical organization, the annal. As has been pointed out already, this was not the invention of unimaginative monks incapable of writing a continuous history in the classical style, and from whom history had to be rescued with the rediscovery of classical Latin models in the Renaissance. Rather, as we have seen, annals were *themselves* an ancient form: we have noted them in Han China where they had primacy of place over other categories of history. More directly relevant, since the medieval European annalists had at this point no knowledge of Chinese historiography, were the Roman civic annals, their late antique successors, and especially the Easter Tables mentioned earlier in connection with Bede. Annals and their expanded form, chronicles, solved all manner of problems at once. Chronology was straightforward, major dates and calendrical issues having been established by the string of chronographers from Eusebius to Bede. All that needed to be done, whether the annalist was recording contemporary events or arranging earlier sources into a chronicle of the past, was to create a list of years and then add events that transpired in those years where they belonged. In such a manner did one of Richer's sources, Flodoard (894–966), the archivist of Rheims Abbey, patiently record occurrences annually from 919 to 966.

The use of annals freed the writer from having to do a number of things that we might see as important for a historian: to discriminate between the important and the ephemeral; and to tell the story of an event or a chain of events that lasted, as most do, beyond the bounds of a single year. We have seen and will see again the various ways in which the Chinese solved this problem. Medieval European authors by and large did not even recognize that a problem existed, and it has been plausibly suggested that there was good reason for this: that medieval annalists believed that the 'real' event to be the year itself, as the numerical sign of the unfolding of God's will in chronological order, and not the disparate, mundane occurrences that transpired within that year.[26]

Annals tended to have similar contents, ranging from reportage of omens and comets or severe storms, to the travels and wars of individual kings (and details on where they spent particular parts of the year such as Christmas); other matters, including comments on the lessons to be drawn from a particular event, or comparisons across time, were very much dependent on the skill and creativity of the historian and his ability to think outside of this almost literal 'box'. The *Annales regni Francorum* ('Royal Frankish Annals') of the Carolingian court was one of several sets of annals to appear in the ninth and tenth centuries. Covering the period from the 790s to 829, they may or may not have been 'official' history insofar as Charlemagne and his court were known to be interested in history, and insofar as their author or authors may have had privileged access to information on military campaigns. Consider this annal for the year 803, which is rather typical, down to its almost sing-song use of Christmas as a transition point between years:

803
    In this winter there was an earthquake around the palace and in neighboring areas and a large death toll was the result.

    Winigis was released from captivity by Grimoald, and the emperor's emissaries returned from Constantinople. Along with them came envoys of [Byzantine] Emperor Nicephorus, who ruled the commonwealth at that time, for they had deposed [the Empress] Irene after the arrival of the Frankish embassy. The names of the envoys were Bishop Michael, Abbot Peter, and the candidate Calistus. They met the emperor at Salz on the River Saale and received a written proposal for peace. They were dismissed with a letter from the emperor and returned by way of Rome to Constantinople.

    But the emperor [Charlemagne] marched into Bavaria and, after settling the affairs of Pannonia, returned to Aachen in the month of December and celebrated Christmas there. And the date changed to
804[27]

This kind of flexibility was hard to resist, and while other forms of historical writing, including biography, continued, annals soon became the favoured mode of recording current events and of organizing past ones.

CONCLUSION

By the end of the tenth century, annals – either in the form of the most rudimentary list of years with annual officials, or in more expansive chronicles – had become *the* dominant form of European historiography in any language. The next few hundred years would see that situation continue, but they would also witness the significant expansion of historical writing beyond clerical hands, and a growing enthusiasm for history on the part of the military aristocracy and, eventually, an emerging urban mercantile elite. At the same time, as the volume of record-keeping increased with the advent of more formal institutional apparatus (courts of law, royal exchequers and an odd new educational facility, the university), the balance between oral and written sources, also observable in Islam and in East Asia, would begin to shift in the direction of the written record, though a repudiation of the authority of the oral still lay many centuries ahead.

The rising interest in the past both as tool and as entertainment was also occurring in other parts of the world during a half millennium of persistent and usually violent conflict within and, increasingly, between different civilizations.

Notes

1 Example taken from Warren Treadgold, *The Early Byzantine Historians* (Basingstoke, 2007), 28.

2 Jill Harries, 'Sozomen and Eusebius: The Lawyer as Church Historian in the Fifth Century', in Christopher Holdsworth and T. P. Wiseman (eds.), *The Inheritance of Historiography 350–900* (Exeter, 1986), 46–52, at 46.

3 Anthony Grafton, *Forgers and Critics: Creativity and Duplicity in Western Scholarship* (London, 1990), 23.

4 Bede, *The Reckoning of Time*, trans. Faith Wallis (Liverpool, 1998), Book V, ch. 66, 157–237.

5 Chase F. Robinson, *Islamic Historiography* (Cambridge, 2003), 188.

6 Ibid., 39.

7 Bernard Lewis, *From Babel to Dragomans: Interpreting the Middle East* (Oxford, 2004), 412.

8 Tarif Khalidi, *Arab Historical Thought in the Classical Period* (Cambridge, 1994), 133.

9 Robinson, *Islamic Historiography*, xxiv, 24, 139.

10 Often meaning specifically religious knowledge; the derivative 'ulema' (alt. 'ulama') denotes the learned religious elite, i.e. those Muslims who have acquired religious knowledge.

11 Khalidi, *Arab Historical Thought*, 84.

12 Quoted ibid., 167–8.

13 Quoted in translation by Khalidi, *Arab Historical Thought*, 74.

14 Quoted by Denis Crispin Twitchett, *The Writing of Official History under the T'ang* (Cambridge, 1993), 14–15 (transliterated Chinese omitted here).

15 Quoted in David McMullen, *State and Scholars in T'ang China* (Cambridge, 1988), 178.

16 Liu Zhiji [Liu Chih-chi], 'Understanding History: The Narration of Events', trans. Stuart H. Sargent, in *Renditions* 15 (1981): 27–35, quotation at 30–1. I owe this reference to Dr Zeb Raft.

17 Peter Nosco, *Remembering Paradise: Nativism and Nostalgia in Eighteenth-Century Japan* (Cambridge, MA, 1990), 174–5; see also John Harrison (ed. and trans.), *New Lights on Early Medieval Japanese Historiography: Two Translations and an Introduction* (Gainesville, FL, 1959), 7 n. 2.

18 Not to be confused with the *Kujiki* composed a few hundred years later.

19 Both are available in English translations. *Kojiki*, trans. Donald L. Philippi (Tokyo, 1968) and *Nihongi: Chronicles of Japan from the Earliest Times to A.D. 697*, trans. W. G. Aston (Rutland, VT and Tokyo, 1972).

20 Translated in John R. Bentley, *Historiographical Trends in Early Japan* (Lewiston, NY, 2002), 67. See alternative translation in *The Kogoshui or Gleanings from Ancient Stories*, trans. and ed. Genchi Kato and Hikoshiro Hoshino (Sanseido, 1924), 15–16.

21 Quoted by John S. Brownlee (ed.), *History in the Service of the Japanese Nation* (Toronto, 1983), 44–5.

22 Quoted by Kawasaki Yasuyuki, 'The Records and Mirrors', in Harrison (ed. and trans.), *New Lights on Early Medieval Japanese Historiography*, 13–18, at 14.

23 Gabrielle Spiegel, *The Past as Text: The Theory and Practice of Medieval Historiography* (Baltimore, 1997), 101.

24 William J. Brandt, *The Shape of Medieval History: Studies in Modes of Perception* (New Haven, CT, 1966); and Nancy F. Partner, 'The New Cornificius: Medieval History and the Artifice of Words', in Ernst Breisach (ed.), *Classical Rhetoric and Medieval Historiography* (Kalamazoo, MI, 1985), 16–17.

25 Partner, 'The New Cornificius', 15.

26 Hayden White, *The Content of the Form: Narrative Discourse and Historical Representation* (Baltimore, 1987), 14–15.

27 *Royal Frankish Annals and Nithard's Histories*, trans. B. W. Scholz with B. Rogers (Ann Arbor, MI, 1970), 83.

c. 940–1030	Ibn Miskawayh's *Tajārib al-Umam* ('Experiences of the Nations and Succession of Endeavours')
c. 1000	Murasaki Shikibu's *Genji Monogatari* ('Tale of Genji')
1060	*Xin Tangshu* ('New History of the Tang')
c. 1084	Completion of Sima Guang's *Zizhi Tongjian* ('Comprehensive Mirror in Aid of Government')
c. 1120 to c. 1143	William of Malmesbury's *Gesta regum anglorum* ('Deeds of the English Kings'), *Gesta pontificum anglorum* ('Deeds of the English Bishops') and *Historia novella* ('New History')
c. 1148–9	Kalhaṇa's *Rājataraṅgiṇī* ('River of Kings')
c. 1136	Geoffrey of Monmouth's *Historia regum Britanniae* ('History of the Kings of Britain')
c. 1220	Jien's *Gukanshō* ('Jottings of a Fool')
c. 1281	Ilyŏn's *Samguk Yusa* ('Memorials and Legends of Three Kingdoms')
1274–1461	*Grandes Chroniques de France* ('Great Chronicles of France')
c. 1300	Rashīd al-dīn's *Jāmi 'al-tawārīkh* ('Compendium of Chronicles')
c. 1305 to c. 1309	Joinville's *Chronicle of the Crusade of St Louis*
1307	Ma Duanlin's *Wenxian tongkao* ('Comprehensive Investigation of Literary Traditions')
c. 1369–c. 1400	Froissart's *Chronicles of France, England and Nearby Countries* is compiled in stages
1339	Kitabatake Chikafusa's *Jinnō Shōtōki* ('Record of the Legitimate Succession of Divine Sovereigns')
1375–8	Ibn Khaldūn's *Muqaddimah* ('Introduction to History')
1498	Philippe de Commynes completes his *Memoirs*

3 | An Age of Global Violence, c. 1000 to c. 1450

Introduction

In our last chapter we traced the development of three distinctive historical cultures, the early medieval Christian European (in its Latin and Greek divisions), early Islamic and contemporary East Asian. We also highlighted certain themes in historical thought and writing, among them the quest to establish what may be called a 'usable past', something that did not feature very prominently in Western antiquity, occasional figures like Polybius excepted. This chapter carries that theme further but opens up another one, that of gradually increasing intercultural contact. The emphasis of this chapter's title should thus fall on the word 'global' rather than 'violence'. A violent period the first half of the second millennium AD surely was: its list of confrontations includes the Crusades and a number of anti-heretical campaigns, further nomadic conquests in the East by the Mongols, the advance of the Ottomans at the expense of the Byzantine Empire and the final end of that polity in 1453. Internally, nearly every region or nation faced both wars of territorial aggrandizement or dynastic succession, such as the English 'Wars of the Roses'. China and Japan endured similar turmoil in the Far East: the former witnessed further dynastic change and the imposition of Mongol rule for a century, and the latter a period of mounting tension between the old nobility and emperor on the one hand and the rising samurai class on the other. Islam for its part had to contend with aggressive Christian counter-offensives in Spain and the Holy Land, with defeat by the Mongols in the East, and with the dissolution of Muslim unity in the aftermath of the Abbasid caliphate.

With all of this it is true that the period was probably no more or less bloody than the previous six centuries, and the loss of life through war assuredly pales against the carnage of the twentieth century – or even against the devastating population reduction wrought by the bubonic plague (or 'Black Death') in the mid-fourteenth century. What *is* different is that there was a good deal more intercourse between different parts of the world than there had been previously, not only within Europe, where classical civilization and 'barbarian' tribes had long had contact, but now also between Europe and the rest of the world, including, at the very end of the period, two entirely new continents in the Americas. Conflict with Islam, under way intermittently since the seventh century, achieved new levels of intensity with the Crusades, and the quest for oriental wealth exposed Europeans to the civilizations of China, Persia and India. Islam itself spread into India and further into Africa. The process of religious conversion played a small but significant role in the exchange of cultures, sometimes with an effect on historical outlooks. Thus a twelfth-century Jewish convert to Islam, Samaw'al al-Magrhibī, pursued the writing of history as a means to critique his former co-religionists; he thereby also abandoned the predominant attitude of rabbinic Judaism towards history, expressed by his contemporary Moses Maimonides, who had pronounced 'books found among the Arabs describing historical events ... a waste of time'.[1]

Notwithstanding such examples, the impact of these contacts on the writing of history was for now rather limited: Italian merchants did not bring back with them Chinese practices of history-writing; the Chinese Muslim Ma Huan (d. c. 1451), venturing to Southeast Asia, India and the Persian Gulf during the early fifteenth century, did not take home the historical writings and tales that existed there; and though Islamic historiography was known to the Christian world, for instance in the chronicles of Moorish Granada, it was not adopted by Europeans. But the almost constant state of warfare that existed in one part of the world or another during these four and a half centuries in itself occasioned a great deal of historical writing, including another wave of 'proto-national' accounts of the past in parts of Europe and Asia that had not produced them previously. If the nineteenth century was Europe's great age of historiographic nationalism and of the romantic celebration of the medieval, then it owed much to the Middle Ages and to the incipient or even unintended patriotism of now-obscure tomes like the *Kronika Dalimilova* (comp. 1308–14), the first historical work to be written in Czech. The rediscovery, editing and publication of European chronicles in Latin and vernacular languages, undertaken by nineteenth-century scholars such as Germany's Georg Heinrich Pertz and England's William Stubbs, was the work of modern scholars for whom the medieval inheritance formed the bedrock under their own sense of national identity. Finally, a further development was the appearance, for now sporadic, of historians writing histories of other cultures and peoples not their own, most notably in the Muslim scholars' attention to Indian and Mongol pasts. 'Universal history' was not yet multicultural, but it was getting more difficult to tell one people's story without reference to that of its neighbours.

Classical Islamic Historiography to the Fifteenth Century

By the ninth century, though Islamic history was still written principally in Arabic, the religion's learned language, Islam had long ceased to be predominantly a religion of the Arabs alone, and within 300 years after that Persian would rival Arabic as a literary (though not theological or scientific) language in central Eurasia. The 'classical' period of Islamic historiography would produce a great deal of writing by Persians, particularly under the Ghaznavid dynasty of the eleventh and twelfth centuries. This succeeded a pre-Islamic Persian tradition of epic that culminated in the post-conquest *Shahnama* ('Book of Kings') by Firdawsi, which was completed in AD 1010. An enormously popular work tracing Zoroastrian Iran from its beginnings to the Arab conquest, Firdawsi's poem is built on a pre-existing genre of prose Shahnamas and it would influence not only later histories but the development of the Persian language itself. Persian Muslim historiography would also continue the departure from strict attention to *ḥadīth* and the adoption by many historians of a rather more secular intellectual outlook characterized by *adab*; it tended to undervalue biography compared with its Arabic counterpart. The Persian approach to history as a branch of the tree of scholarship, rather than as handmaiden to theology, is embodied by the prolific scientist, geographer and polymath Abū'l Rayḥān Muḥammad ibn Aḥmad al-Bīrūnī (973–1048), much of whose life was spent in India. Al-Bīrūnī, who wrote in both Arabic and Persian, employed his mathematical and philological knowledge to the resolution of calendrical and chronological conflicts between the world's nations; he also exemplifies a sceptical turn of mind with respect to remote and legendary history, and in particular to mendacious genealogies of the sort that arise in times of social ferment, when familial and dynastic shifts require the construction or invention of a noble past. His derisive comments on those who 'invent laudatory stories and ... forge genealogies which go back to glorious ancestors' both echoes Hecataeus of Miletus and presages European critics of such creativity from the twelfth to the nineteenth centuries.[2]

Firdawsi had captured the cyclical course of political history in his account of successive Persian regimes or *dawla*s, a word that literally means 'revolution' or 'alteration' but in an extended sense means 'dynasty' or 'state'. A cyclical view of history had not heretofore been characteristic of Islam, but the religious sense of a finite world unfolding in a linear story was now running up against the observable fact of political ebbs and flows as once-strong states succumbed to civil strife and loss of authority. Persian historians wrote in a world in which the influence of the Abbasid caliphate had dissipated and real power was wielded by a number of local or regional dynasties, while common Islamic identity was maintained through other means, for instance through the madrasas, Muslim seminaries that first appeared in the tenth century. Beginning at virtually the same time, the Samanid dynasty (819–999) both promoted Islam in Persia and encouraged a literary revival parallel to that in the ninth-century Carolingian Empire. This Renaissance continued under the Ghaznavids, a Turkish dynasty, with some shifts in focus away from the Iranian heritage, and a notable if temporary decline in the literary dominance of Firdawsi. One of the by-products of a multiplicity of ruling powers in Islam was a secularization, of sorts, in historical writing – a turn away from a religiously based account of the past, written by clerics and jurists, to one written from within chanceries and organized by dynasties, with a preponderance of work appearing as dynasties weakened, as would be the case under both the Ghaznavids and their Saljuq successors.

Ethnic interests cut across the grain of religious affiliations, as historians such as 'Abd al-Ḥay Gardīzī (fl. early eleventh century) wrote about the Persian rather than a broader Islamic past. The political interests of most of these historians, and their almost Polybian emphasis on a 'pragmatic' history, are illustrated by the prolific early eleventh-century historian Ibn Miskawayh (d. 1030), another former official, who departed from the mainstream by placing God outside the course of human events. His Tajārib al-Umam ('Experiences of the Nations and Succession of Endeavours') is a universal history of Muslim regimes which stresses the utility of history in words we have seen before. 'Having examined the histories of nations and lives of kings … I found them to contain useful experiences in events which still recur and may be expected to recur in similar ways such as the origins of states and kingdoms, the later incipience of disorder, the measures taken to redress matters … or the neglect … leading to weakness and destruction.'[3] Others such as Abu'l Fazl Bayhaqī (995–1077), a chancery official and admirer of Miskawayh, retired from public life to write history. As part of a much longer work that does not survive in full, Bayhaqī wrote a history of the reign of the Ghaznavid shah Mas'ūd I (r. 1031–41); his work contains elaborate descriptions of administrative practice in the chancery that slow the narrative (one thinks of perennial reader complaints about descriptions of whaling life that interrupt the plot of Herman Melville's Moby Dick). He was capable, however, of sharp judgments on writing about the past, and on its possible sources. There is something almost Thucydidean in Bayhaqī's crisp declaration that 'The history of the past is of two sorts, without a third: one must either hear it from someone or read it in a book.'[4]

The differences between dynastic and religious or ḥadīth-based historiography were not formalized and should not be over-stated: even a court historian-cum-propagandist such as Abū al-Ḥusayn 'Utbi (961–1036 or 1040), whose primary focus was to legitimize his Ghaznavid masters and their succession, reaffirmed an older dictum that 'religion and kingship are twin brothers'.[5] Nor did the dynastic type of historiography continue indefinitely among the Persians. It waned under

Box 9   Mongol Chronicles

A nomadic people, the Mongols developed their own historical writing, early specimens including the thirteenth-century *Mongyol-un niyuca tobčiyan*, a text usually known in English as 'The Secret History of the Mongols'. This begins with a supposititious genealogy of the warrior Temüjin, the future Genghis Khan. There is little sign of further historical writing in this vein among the China-based Mongols during the late thirteenth and early fourteenth centuries, the period of their Great Khans' rule as the Yuan dynasty. However, the late sixteenth and early seventeenth centuries witnessed a revival and produced several specimens of chronicles similar to the *Secret History*. These included the *Altan Tobči* ('Golden Summary', 1655), which begins with a section on events leading up to the death of Genghis Khan and continues through the Yuan period and the decline of Mongol power, ending in the early seventeenth century; and the collection of chronicles known as *Erdeni-yin Tobči* ('Precious Summary'), written about 1662, a work drawing on Mongol, Chinese and Tibetan sources.

the less literarily inclined Saljuqs, during whose rule administrators wrote history principally for other administrators rather than for the rulers themselves, producing specimens of a genre known in Europe as the 'mirror for princes', usually a collection of anecdotes and examples digested for easy learning. But the general point is this: history in the larger Islamic world was no longer exclusively about Islam only, nor was its gaze always fixed on the Prophetic period. Stimulated both by internal dissension and by the conflict with Christianity, historians lost that indifference to contemporary events which had characterized the earliest Muslim historical writing.

As it happens, the defining conflict for late medieval Islam was not that with Christian Europe, but rather with the Mongols to the east. One branch of this nomadic people, the Golden Horde, had already conquered much of Russia in the 1240s. Another sacked Baghdad in 1258 and executed the last Abbasid ruler and his family, killing with them the ideal of a universal Muslim caliphate. A warlike non-Muslim people who came into contact with Persia to the west and China to the east in the course of the thirteenth century, the Mongols had their own sense of universalism; a divine entitlement to world rule given to Genghis (or Chinggis) Khan and his successors provided the theme of much of their early historical writing (see Box 9 and Extract 9).

extract

9: Mongol Historical Writing: *Altan Tobči*

These were celebrated as the Five Cakravarti Kings. The son of Perfect Splendid King was Deliverer King. His son was Delivering Conserving King. His son was King Seküni. His son was King Küsi. His son was King Great Küsi. His son was King Good-at-Seeing. These are the family of kings who descended from the golden line of King Maha Samadi. His son was King Well Born. The last of the Kings who descended in the line one by one from this king was King Lion Jaw. His sons were Pure Food King, White Food King, Agreeable Food King, and Rasâyana Food King ....

It is said that, because Rahuli became a priest, the line of Pure Food King was extinguished, but in many chronicles it is taught that it was not extinguished. More than one thousand years after Buddha had passed into Nirvana, those who flourished on the snowy eastern slopes from the golden line of King Maha Samadi were as follows. There were five sons of the king called Sarba, son of King Kusala of Magada in India. The youngest son, at birth, had turquoise blue hair; his hands and feet were flat; his eyes closed from below upwards. They said to each other: 'He is not like (one who has had) a previous incarnation.' Putting him into a copper box, they threw him into the River Ganges. Between Nepal and Tibet an old man of Tibet picked up the box from the bank of the river and opened it ....

Selection from *The Mongol Chronicle Altan Tobči*, ed. and trans. C. R. Bawden (Wiesbaden: Otto Harrassowitz, 1955), 111–12. Editorial notes omitted. The selection is taken from the beginning of the chronicle, which commences with an account of the ancient kings of India from whom the Khans traced their descent.

Aside from the dominant Yuan branch that ruled China, the Mongol expansion had established a number of subordinate Khanates in Persia and Central Asia under the sons of Ghenghis, regimes which swung towards the Islamic rather than Chinese style of historiography. The Ilkhans who ruled much of Iran in the thirteenth and early fourteenth centuries produced a strong tradition of narrative historiography in Persian. The Timurid dynasty, which sprang from the late fourteenth-century Chaghatāyid warlord Tīmūr Bārlās or Tamerlane (d. 1405), ruled much of the region during the fifteenth century and had an especially strong interest in history. The illiterate Tīmūr, we are told (by a hostile Arabic biographer), 'was assiduous in listening to the reading of chronicles, the stories of prophets ..., the deeds of kings, and the accounts of men of the past'.[6] He was constantly accompanied on his travels by secretaries assigned to record his sayings and utterances, which were read back to him for verification before being converted into histories written in Turkish or Persian, few of which, regrettably, have survived. Tīmūr had a number of historians at his disposal and multiple versions of his career were composed. Among others, he commanded the captive historian Niẓām al-Dīn ʿAlī Shāmī (d. before 1409) to write a history of his rise to power. This work, the *Ẓafar-nāme*, was based on both literary and oral sources, and, as continued by later writers, formed the core of the biographical tradition about the conqueror which provided the focus for Timurid historians through several generations, during which time their works would become progressively more islamicized.

Islamic influence continued to spread throughout the Middle Ages into other regions, including its western European beachhead in Spain, as well as Egypt, parts of sub-Saharan Africa and India. Muslim-authored histories of those regions and of particular localities (for instance, Aleppo and Damascus in Syria) appeared throughout the later Middle Ages, and as in Persia administrators and officials were the likeliest to have the inclination and the access to information to become historians. Baibars al-Manṣūrī (d. 1324 or 1325) was a former soldier and administrator in the Mamluk sultanate, where history was written in Arabic.[7] Political life in the Muslim world could be as unpredictable as in Christendom, and the old Thucydidean pattern of the fallen magnate or minister turning to history as a form of self-exoneration repeated itself with him. Manṣūrī had a tumultuous career that saw him gain, lose and regain influence several times as sultans changed. In his case, both the active participation in governance and military campaigns, and the forced periods of retirement, were productive; he left a general history of Islam to 1323 (the *Zubdat al-fikra fi taʾrīkh al-hijra*) and a series of extracts from that work arranged into a history of the Bahri dynasty, the first of the Mamluk regimes. A century and a half later, Abū l-Maḥāsin ibn Taġhrī Birdī (d. 1469–70) continued this trend by turning his family's connections into something like an official position of court historian.

As a record of what actually happened in the past, Muslim historical writing of these centuries compares very favourably with the best chroniclers of Christendom and exceeds it in attentiveness to detail and accuracy, for instance the 'Obituaries of Eminent Men', a great biographical dictionary by the Kurdish-born Ibn Khallikān (1211–82), and the travel writings (themselves a major source for Muslim social history) of the peripatetic Ibn Baṭṭūṭa (1304–68/69 or 1377), an Arabic-writing Berber from what is now Morocco, whose *Rihla* ('Travels') remains a foundational text for modern world history.[8] Like the European invaders, Arabs such as the Damascene mayor Ibn al-Qalānisī (*c.* 1073–1160) (Extract 10) and Saladin's minister ʿImad al-Din (1125–1201) wrote about the Crusades, though they did not regard those wars as anything other than the latest in a series of struggles against the infidel. Ibn al-Athīr (1160–1233), another chronicler of the Crusades, was a religious scholar and author of a biographical dictionary on the companions of the

10: The Crusades from a Muslim Perspective: the Chronicle of Ibn al-Qalānisī

AH 501

(22nd August, 1107, to l0th August, 1108)

In this year Baldwin, king of the Franks, collected his broken faction and God-forsaken army and marched on the port of Tyre. He encamped in face of the town and began the construction of a castle in its outskirts on Tell al-Ma 'shūqa. He remained for a month, after which the governor of the town purchased his withdrawal for seven thousand dinars, and he took them and withdrew.

In this year also the Sultan Ghiyāth al-Dunyā wal-Dīn Muhammad, having [defeated and slain Sadaqa b. Mazyad, and] settled the affairs of al-Hillah, set out to return to Isfahān at the beginning of the month of [Shawwāl]. Before setting out he laid it as a duty upon the amīr Mawdūd and the 'askar to march on Mosul, reduce it by siege, and take possession of it. Mawdūd and the army therefore proceeded on their way and encamped before Mosul. Now Jāwalī, lord of the city, had driven out most of the people, and his troops had behaved themselves ill in it and committed every kind of excess. So he betook himself to al-Rahba and deputed one of his officers in whom he had confidence to remain in Mosul and defend it. The 'askar of the sultan had remained before it for some time, when seven of the townsmen resolved upon conniving at its capture, and opening one of the city gates delivered over the town to Mawdūd. Upon entering he made a great slaughter of the troops of Jāwalī, but gave quarter to the garrison in the citadel, and dispatched them and all that was with them to the Sultan.

Selection from *The Damascus Chronicle of the Crusades Extracted and Translated from the Chronicle of Ibn al-Qalānisī*, extracted and translated by H. A. R. Gibb (London: Luzon, 1932), 82–3. Gibb's notes have been omitted.

Prophet as well as a monograph on the Zangids, a sub-Saljuq dynasty; his most ambitious work was a universal history covering the Islamic world from Creation through Persian and Roman empires up to the Prophet, and continuing annalistically up to 1233. Its later sections reflect an Islam already struggling in the wake of the Mongol invasions of the Muslim world during the early 1220s. Over the next century, a number of Muslim historians would chronicle the Mongol ascent from within. The Persian 'Ala-ad-Din 'Ata-Malik Juvaini (1226–83) served in the capital of the Great Khan before returning to Baghdad as governor and composing an incomplete *Ta' rīkh-i jahān-gushā* ('History of the World Conqueror') about Genghis Khan.[9] Rashīd al-dīn (1247–1318), a Persian converted from Judaism to Islam, also served Persia's Mongol rulers until political intrigues occasioned his execution;

Figure 12 | At the Court of the Khan. Double-page miniature (left half). Illuminated manuscript page from Rashīd al-dīn's *Jāmi 'al-tawārīkh* ('Compendium of Chronicles'), a universal history. Manuscript dates *c.* 1330 AD.

his *Jāmi 'al-tawārīkh* ('Compendium of Chronicles') is a vast universal history (Figs. 12 and 13) especially full of details on the Mongol regime, and exemplifying a high degree of awareness of the world's multiple cultures.

The Mongol warlord Tīmūr found himself on one occasion being interviewed by a Tunisian Muslim whose name is among the most famous in the history of historical thought. Ibn Khaldūn (1332–1406) is deservedly praised, though he was less unique a figure than admiring Westerners, unfamiliar with Islamic historiography of the previous seven centuries, attest. He is more correctly seen as a culmination of the philosophical tendencies previously observed in al-Masūdī, and indeed the more practical, methodological aspects of writing a history, not emphasized by Ibn Khaldūn, were being addressed more directly, and at almost the same time, by a Persian contemporary named Shams al-Ijī (*fl.* 1380s). Ibn Khaldūn was not unacquainted with methodological questions as the author of a long history, the geographic reach of which extended as far as northern Europe. His fame has traditionally rested not on the history itself

Figure 13 | Genghis Khan dividing his empire among his sons. From a Mughal-age manuscript of Rashīd al-dīn's *Jāmi 'al-tawārīkh* ('Compendium of Chronicles), c. 1596.

but rather on its prolegomenon or *Muqaddimah* ('Introduction to History'),[10] an ambitious attempt to work out the many factors underlying historical change including customs, manners, climate and economics. 'It should be known that history, in matter of fact, is information about human social organization, which itself is identical with world civilization', writes Ibn Khaldūn at the beginning of the *Muqaddimah*. 'It deals with such conditions affecting the nature of civilization as, for instance, savagery and sociability, group feelings, and the different ways by which one group of human beings achieves superiority over another.'[11]

Ibn Khaldūn's idea that individuals and groups that come to power are animated by a group spirit or *'asabiyya* (which in itself often works against the maintenance of that power and must be suppressed) has counterparts in much later European writers such as Herder, while his belief that regimes once consolidated will almost inevitably become divided or corrupted and fall echoes the cyclical politics of the Greek Polybius. Much of the *Muqaddimah* is taken up with a survey and analysis of different types of government and social arrangements, including the various ranks and offices of caliphal administration, and with the articulation of certain types of 'laws', or at least generalizations on which one can make reasonable prognostications since it is human nature to want to know the outcomes of things that concern us. This is 'especially great with regard to events of general importance, and one wants to know, for instance, how long the world or certain dynasties are going to last'. Unfortunately, many of the means used to predict such matters are unreliable or have been proved wrong, such as the traditionists' belief that the world would last only five centuries after the coming of Islam. Generalizations based on observation of human behaviour are a safer bet, and the study of cases illustrates certain rules of power, such as that dynasties have a natural life-span, like individuals; that once in power, a dynasty may be able to dispense with 'group feeling'; that 'the first (perceptible)' consequence of a dynasty's senility is that it splits; and that the rise of a new dynasty usually follows through perseverance during the decline of its predecessor, rather than sudden action.[12]

Ibn Khaldūn's overall approach to history, which has sometimes been termed sociological, puts him in fine company with Europeans of a much later date such as Vico and Montesquieu (see Chapter 6 below). His analysis of power also anticipates a historical generalist of the sixteenth century, Florence's Niccolò Machiavelli. But the *Muqaddimah* is not only about the macro-questions of historical processes and influences. Since the ninth and tenth centuries, when theologians had challenged both the utility and reliability of history, its practitioners had fought back, typically articulating in their prefaces the basis of their methods and assumptions. Ibn Khaldūn, though his remarks are much more extensive, fits into a pre-existing tradition of thinking about what history as a branch of study should involve, and where its weaknesses lie. At the very opening of his book, Ibn Khaldūn ponders the limits of historical truth – or rather, of untruth. Historical knowledge is afflicted by several kinds of falsehood, of which the first is 'prejudice and partisanship', by which he really meant unthinking allegiance to a particular sect or opinion within Islam. Further kinds of falsehood are occasioned by a range of human weaknesses – reliance upon transmitters of testimony without proper examination of the transmitters themselves, ignorance of the purpose of an event, baseless reliance on the truth of an event, the inclination of historians to embellish accounts in order to flatter the powerful and, above all, 'ignorance of the various conditions arising in civilization'.[13] All of these are themes that would be explored at a theoretical and philosophical level by later Europeans, but not for the most part in the medieval chroniclers that preceded them.

Europe from the Crusades to the Early Renaissance

At the distance of a millennium, the most important cultural change to occur during Europe's 'high' Middle Ages between the tenth and the thirteenth centuries lay in communications, specifically a transition away from the predominantly oral culture of earlier centuries towards one in which written texts and documents carried considerably more weight, and in which their preservation, transmission or even, when necessary, fabrication became necessary. This shift had profound implications for historiography. Most obviously, literacy gradually expanded beyond the upper clergy and monasteries. Systematic record-keeping increased, as the quantity of surviving documents demonstrates: commitments and promises once made by ritual or personal contact were now also preserved on paper or parchment.[14] This has produced a wealth of material for the historians of later centuries, though it should not be regarded as complete in any sense: just as archivists today have to be selective in what they retain, their early second millennium forebears often jettisoned materials that no longer seemed relevant, thereby eradicating their memory permanently. Furthermore, oral means of communication remained in vigorous use in the transmission of historical narratives, especially in song and poetry, and for the next several centuries history would float between oral/aural modes of transmission and cognition on the one hand and written/visual ones on the other, with traffic between them in both directions as written history fed into oral tradition and thence back into writing. A simple manifestation of Europeans' vestigially oral mindset is the tendency of many historians to think of the words that they wrote as matter to be listened to, not seen. 'I am going to tell you a great tale,' begins one fourteenth-century chronicle of lost Frankish glory, 'and if you will listen to me, I hope that it will please you.'[15] Tensions between the oral and the written would eventually figure in European encounters with New World pasts (see Chapter 5 below).

A further consequence of this complex communicative situation, and of the relative increase in writing's status, was a broadening of the older search for a usable past. Certain groups increasingly felt pressed to preserve, find or even produce from scratch historical documents in support of particular claims or assertions they wished to make about their present status and its roots in a remote or even immemorial antiquity – some documents were indeed taken not as foundational in their own right but rather as later codifications of traditional or customary rights and privileges granted at some unspecified earlier time. This documentary turn had benefits, of course, in the generation of new kinds of historical writing, but it also had pernicious side-effects, since it generated a scholarly cottage industry of textual forgery, a practice that began its life in antiquity, but now flourished seemingly unchecked. If a supporting document was now useful, if not quite *de rigueur*, in this newly textual culture, then one often needed to be produced for inspection. Where it could not be found, or had never existed at all but 'ought to have', and even where its meaning was simply not clear enough, there were talented calligraphers and scholars willing to generate such a document *ex nihilo*, or creatively emend it, whether a cartulary containing records of monastic land transactions, the genealogy of an aristocratic family (a practice that would endure well past the Middle Ages) or, in the most famous case of all, the Donation of Constantine.

A celebrated document widely cited to bolster the papacy's secular power at a time of chronic conflict between temporal and spiritual authorities in Latin Christendom, the Donation was probably composed in the late eighth or early ninth century, and presented itself as a genuine fourth-century gift of authority over Latin Europe from the Emperor Constantine to Pope Sylvester I. The demolition of its veracity proved a lengthy process during the early Renaissance, but for now the key points the reader should bear in mind are twofold: first, that most forgeries, the Donation among them, were probably not created maliciously or with intent to deceive but with a desire to provide documentation in support of claims fervently held to be true; and second, that for the medieval European, there was no easy test by which falsity and truth could be assessed, whether it came from a written text, a picture or the word of witnesses. A by-product of this situation is that those who told histories, and those who listened to or heard them, while often concerned with the veracity of what was said, kept their concerns at the level of particularity. They evaluated the truth of this or that account of an event, including miraculous occurrences, and the reliability, principally judged by moral reputation and social standing, of the individual rendering the account to the historian where he had not observed it at first hand. Rarely did historians or their readers pause to consider the accuracy or veracity of a whole genre of writing, and much less still did they explore the epistemological issues, such as the very possibility of accurate knowledge of the past, that would emerge in later centuries.

This in part helps to explain the almost total absence of what we would now call historical theory, or philosophy of history, and even of a systematic elucidation of historical genres, in medieval Europe. Occasional comments on the utility of history there were: the twelfth-century historian and political philosopher John of Salisbury (c. 1120–80) produces historical examples throughout his *Policraticus*, and extols the commemorative value of written records and inscriptions, without which the past would be lost;[16] various chroniclers solemnly testify to the value of their exercise. But late medieval Christendom produced no single historical thinker of profound originality, nor any extended reflection on history. With a couple of notable exceptions, such as the prophetic mystic Joachim of Fiore (c. 1135–1202)

Box 10   Historical Speculation in the Medieval West

While a truly original and wide-ranging philosophy of history was largely missing from medieval Europe, there are two notable exceptions to this rule. Joachim of Fiore (c. 1135–1202), a Calabrian monk, developed a millenarian theory of three successive ages of history based on the three persons of the Trinity: an age of the Father (from Creation to Christ), an age of the Son (which he prophesied would end in 1260) and an age of the Holy Spirit. Hugh of St Victor (1096–1141), a scholastic synthesizer, wrote a world history which he arranged – quite unusually – topically rather than chronologically, the *Liber de tribus maximinis circumstantiis gestorum, id est personis, locis, temporibus* ('Book of the Three Main Circumstances of History, Namely Persons, Places, Times'). But Hugh is best known for postulating in his other works a three-stage scheme for human history, within which humans actually develop both mentally and in their relation to God.

and the scholastic Hugh of St Victor (d. 1141) (see Box 10), it is also striking that Europe produced very little 'historical thought' in the sense of wide-ranging philosophizing about or reflection upon the cumulative meaning of the past, as opposed to the proper method of its narration. There is no Latin counterpart to Ibn Khaldūn.

Notwithstanding this theoretical paucity, medieval men, and the occasional woman, generated a ponderous quantity of history. By the thirteenth century, when the Dominican friar Vincent of Beauvais (c. 1190–1264) attempted an encyclopedic survey of knowledge, one of his series of *specula* (mirrors) was entitled *Speculum historiale*, itself another world history cast as a mirror. Vincent's *specula* were collectively intended to perform something of the same role that Isidore of Seville's *Etymologies* had 600 years earlier. But Vincent and Isidore lived in very different worlds. By 1000, the high tide of barbarian migration was long over, with the notable exception of the Scandinavian assaults in the north of France and throughout England; by Vincent's day, two centuries later, the Vikings and Normans too had vanished from the stage, assimilated into the countries they had settled in, despite a flurry of *gesta* and other histories intended to commemorate their great deeds. Between 1095 and 1291 the epicentre of military activity, and consequently of historical writing, would shift eastward, its dominant engine being a new round of engagements with the Muslim world.

Islam had made contact with Christian Europe early, its forces at one point advancing well into France. While this unquestionably produced useful cultural cross-fertilization in both directions, it also generated conflict between two expansionist religions, though a good deal of the warfare involved less spiritual motivations than territorial ambitions and aristocratic martial impulses thinly garbed in the cloak of holiness. The flashpoints were particular hotspots such as the Iberian peninsula, into which North African Muslims or 'Moors' had expanded by the early eighth century, and the borders of the Byzantine Empire, which would finally fall in 1453 to the dominant Islamic power of the fifteenth through nineteenth centuries, the Ottoman Turks. But nowhere was such conflict more productive of historical writing than in that recurrent battleground, the Holy Land, during the period of the 'Crusades' from the late eleventh to the late thirteenth centuries.

To modern eyes a rather unpleasant early chapter in the history of relations between Christianity and Islam (and one that irreparably damaged relations between Greek east and Latin west), the Crusades were nonetheless productive of an enormous wealth of historical writing on both sides of the conflict. The obscure Robert the Monk's history of the First Crusade, complete with a supposedly verbatim recitation of Pope Urban II's call to arms at the Council of Clermont, set the tone, but another early writer deserves our attention. William of Tyre (c. 1130–90) set the bar high for subsequent Crusade chroniclers. William was a native of Jerusalem, an archbishop and a seasoned author who had previously written several historical works, mostly now lost. It is on his *Historia rerum in partibus transmarinis gestarum* ('History of Deeds Done Beyond the Sea') that his reputation rests. Composed at the request of Amaury I, king of Jerusalem (r. 1163–74), it covered nine decades of events from the preaching of the First Crusade in 1094 up to 1184. William's intent was both to praise the champions of the first two Crusades and to encourage readers in his present to renewed commitment to the cause. This was a long book, filled with vivid geographical descriptions and frequent allusions to and quotations from classical and Christian authors. These references were largely decorative – as William admitted, he was in uncharted territory, with 'no written source, either in Greek or Arabic' and thus had to depend for his information 'upon tradition alone'.[17] The work would influence many later accounts of the Crusades, which incorporated his account of the First Crusade into their own. A taste of the historian's frank evaluation of evildoers, and of his considerable dislike of the Byzantine forces, Greeks and their emperor, can be seen in his comments on Taticius, a Saracen-born member of the Byzantine imperial household, under the title 'One Taticius, a servant of the emperor, a very crafty man of notorious wickedness, becomes associate with our leaders.'

Throughout the later Middle Ages, wars, both international and domestic, provided the single most potent stimulus for the writing of history, especially aristocratic chronicles ('aristocratic' implies audience and subject rather than author), increasingly presented in vernacular tongues. The northern English knight Sir Thomas Gray (d. 1369?), for instance, captured by the Scots in 1355, would pass his period of captivity in Edinburgh, where a good library allowed him to write his *Scalacronica* ('Ladder of Histories'). Written in Anglo-Norman French, *Scalacronica* traces British history from its beginning to Gray's own time, for which he was able to supplement his literary sources with personal recollections and information given to him by his own father. Gray, discussing himself in the third person, tells us of his historical awakening amidst books and boredom:

He perused books of chronicles, in verse and prose, in Latin, French and English, concerning the deeds of our ancestors, at which he was astonished. And it weighed heavily upon him that he had not previously known more about the sequence of the centuries. So, as he had hardly anything to do with his time, he became curious and contemplated how he might deal with and convert into more succinct form the chronicles of Great Britain and the deeds of the English.[18]

Others, less interested in the past as such, focused specifically on their immediate military experiences: the Catalan Ramón Muntaner (c. 1270–1336) wrote a detailed account of his life as a soldier. The Castilian nobleman Pedro or Pedro López de Ayala (1332–1407), who like Gray had an early career marked by lengthy imprisonment (in this case by the Portuguese), returned home to the position of chancellor; he turned in retirement to history, producing a translation of parts of Livy, a family genealogy and the collection of chronicles known as the *History of the Kings of Castile*. Much further down the social ladder, the Picard knight Robert de Clari authored a history of the Fourth Crusade, ending at a new low point in relations between the Crusaders and their sometime Byzantine allies, the sack of Constantinople (1204).[19] Clari's work is part contemporary account, part history, based on his own participation in the Crusade but also on tales he had heard in his travels. But he understood that he was acting as a historian, that is, as the narrator of a *histoire* which was, to the best of his knowledge, truthful.

The two most famous lay-authored histories to emerge from the Crusades were both by men of higher birth than Clari. The first of these was Geoffroy de Villehardouin (c. 1150 to c. 1213), who dictated in 1207 his own eyewitness account of the seizure of Constantinople three years earlier. It is one of the oldest extant texts in Old French, its style originating as much in the *chansons de geste* of an earlier age as in the chronicle. Over half a century later the second of these men, Jean de Joinville (1224–1317), wrote an admiring if critical account of King Louis IX (r. 1226–70), whose close companion he had been during the Seventh Crusade; Louis had unwisely ignored his friend's advice on more than one occasion, proceeding on a further Crusade in 1270 during which the king perished.

History composed in this key appealed to both rulers and their fighting nobility, alike members of a single social 'order' or 'estate'; it celebrated wealth, plunder and bloodshed, commented matter-of-factly about military victories without much sensitivity to the human cost or to the morality of conqueror or victim. But at the same time, it perceived a wider significance to human actions. Louis IX is an example of heroism and martial valour, but he and others like him are also personifications of the larger struggle between Christianity and Islam, and physical embodiments of that even larger, heavenly struggle between light and dark. Joinville's account begins with Louis' virtues and his piety, with examples of his devotion rather than of his courage. While this is to some degree formulaic, it suggests that he had envisaged Louis as more than a powerful king and warrior. Rather, he saw the king as a soldier in the manner of Christ himself, pious and holy as well as brave:

In the name of God Almighty, I, John, Lord of Joinville, seneschal of Champagne, dictate the life of our holy King Lewis; that which I saw and heard by the space of six years that I was in his company on pilgrimage oversea [sic], and that which I saw and heard after we returned. And before I tell you of his great deeds, and of his prowess, I will tell you what I saw and heard of his good teachings and of his holy words, so that these may be found here set in order for the edifying of those who will hear thereof.

This holy man loved God with all his heart, and followed Him in His acts; and this appeared in that, as God died for the love He bore His people, so did the king put his body in peril, and several times, for the love he bore to his people; and such peril he might well have avoided, as you shall be told hereafter.[20]

Whether it concerned Crusades or warfare among Christians, the aristocratic account of history's battles bespeaks a very different mindset from the Latin clerical chronicles. Perhaps the most widely read aristocratic works both at that time and since have been the narrative by Jean Froissart (1337? to after 1405) of the first phases of the Anglo-French Hundred Years' War (1337–1453) and the various vernacular Scots' accounts, in verse and prose, of the Scottish wars of independence against the English. Froissart's *Chronicles of France, England and Nearby Countries* is a classic of European historiography, extraordinarily readable and entertaining. Froissart himself was a priest who had spent a good deal of his life in royal and noble households, and had absorbed the values of their inhabitants. It is not surprising that his *Chronicles* are much closer in both subject and language to Villehardouin and the thirteenth-century romances than to the Latin clerical chronicle.

Yet while Froissart wrote in the vernacular and shared with the Crusade-era writers a common martial and honorific ethos, there are some significant differences between his work and that of a Joinville, differences which suggest changes in how the past was perceived, and which reflect a shift in the scope of historical writing during the late Middle Ages. With respect to the former, it has been suggested that late medieval historians, both clerical and lay, had abandoned a metaphorical view of the human past in which events on earth connect 'vertically' to the 'eternal history' above, and in which layers of allegorical and symbolic meaning could be adduced like a series of musical chords. Miracles and portents had provided specific points of contact between the two – as John of Salisbury had put it in his *Historia pontificalis* ('History of the Popes'), 'the invisible things of God may be clearly seen by the things that are done'. In its place, a 'horizontal' conception of history as a highly visual sequence of images placed back to back has taken its place, with an emphasis on vivid description and reportage rather than on searching inside events for some wider significance.[21] Another way of putting it might be that the early 'realism' of the post-Augustinian tradition, with its close relation between City of God and City of Man, has been displaced by an Ockhamist nominalism in which there are only individuals and history is a sea of discrete occurrences without any particular pattern. Nancy Partner's verdict is that at some point in the twelfth century, it simply became harder to write 'Christian' history in the sense that Eusebius and the Church Fathers had conceived of it.[22]

These broad distinctions can be over-stated. What is not in doubt, however, is the lowering of historians' sight lines. At the end of the Crusades, and with them their historians' almost instinctual perception of warfare as a localized version of sacred conflict, the focus of much historical writing becomes decisively narrower. 'Christendom' is replaced by individual kingdoms or principalities, and a chivalric hero such as St Louis or even Charlemagne becomes less a soldier of the Church than a leader of his people. If there were no 'nations' in the modern, post-nineteenth-century sense of the word, there were at least national or patriotic sentiments. There is an observable trend, beginning no later than the mid-twelfth century, towards the redeployment of historical talents on to specific kingdoms' pasts and to intra-Christian conflicts. Universal history, having peaked in the twelfth century, by no means disappeared. It was read at late medieval courts, and provided an obvious channel through which clerical authors could offer secular princes advice; new examples appear right through the period. But even its authors narrowed their focus down to imperial or national history as they approached their own times: their universality tended to be temporal and theological rather than spatial. Conversely, chroniclers of the twelfth to fourteenth centuries, such as the secular cleric Saxo Grammaticus, not all of whom were comforted by the growth of hereditary monarchical authority (which occurred just as often at the expense of the Church as of feudal magnates), continued to situate nationally based accounts within a Eusebian framework of *historia mundi*.

There are similarly great examples of ecclesiastical history, such as the enormous *Historia ecclesiastica* by the Anglo-Norman Benedictine monk Orderic Vitalis (1075–1142), which range widely, continuing to use the Church as the common link between multiple political realms, and envisioning mundane events as signposts along an eschatological highway, but universal history in the Eusebian mould was in decline. By the mid-fourteenth century, the English monk Ranulf Higden (c. 1280–1364), in writing his *Policronicon* (the closest thing to a late medieval historical 'bestseller') was providing a summation of world history rather than a new contribution to it. The huge subsequent popularity of that work, soon translated into English, suggests a ready market for a 'quick summary' of the universal story rather than the continued vitality of the genre. The expansion of readership into the laity was beginning to feed back into the writing of history, and readers' interests were beginning to influence authors' choice of subject, a trend that would be significantly enhanced by the arrival of printing.

The varieties of historical literature were beginning to proliferate. Even those of clerical authorship were putting some water between themselves and the home port of the Eusebian world history. Among the regional variants that do not have obvious counterparts elsewhere, the twenty-three Norse (Norwegian and Icelandic) sagas of the twelfth to fourteenth centuries (initially an oral record but committed to writing after about 1150) present an especially interesting departure from the prose chronicle and form a link between the world of the annalist and that of the heroic poet; they are the major source for modern Norway's medieval past, though allowances have to be made for the propagandistic role they were designed to serve. Culminating in Snorri Sturluson's (1179–1241) compendious *Heimskringla* ('History of the kings of Norway') (Extract 11), itself a reference point for Norwegian national consciousness in much later centuries, the sagas existed alongside Latin prose works such as Saxo Grammaticus' (c. 1150 to after 1216) *Gesta Danorum* ('Deeds of the Danes', a work which drew on old Danish poems engraved on rocks), vernacular chronicles such as Aelnoth's *Krönike* (c. 1120) and Sweden's series of rhymed royal chronicles. Ultimately, however, prose annals and chronicles, and the occasional verse chronicle, would prove the most common form of historical writing through much of the Middle Ages, with the constraints that year-by-year accounts (without the Chinese convention of accompanying biographies) impose on representing the past as a series of continuous events.

Outside of Crusader literature, the preponderance of histories written during the twelfth, thirteenth and early fourteenth centuries almost invariably concern a particular nationality/ethnicity or region, whether arranged as *gesta* (a story focused on exemplary lives and especially deeds), annals or non-annalistic history. The historians of England may serve as an example. William of Malmesbury (c. 1095 to c. 1143), widely regarded as one of the more perceptive and critical of medieval

11: Norse Historical Writing: Snorri Sturluson's *Heimskringla*

In this book I have had old stories written down, as I have heard them told by intelligent people, concerning chiefs who have held dominion in the northern countries, and who spoke the Danish tongue; and also concerning some of their family branches, according to what has been told me. Some of this is found in ancient family registers, in which the pedigrees of kings and other personages of high birth are reckoned up, and part is written down after old songs and ballads which our forefathers had for their amusement. Now, although we cannot just say what truth there may be in these, yet we have the certainty that old and wise men held them to be true .... [A description of some of these earlier sources follows.]

Iceland was settled in the time that Harald Fairhair was the King of Norway. There were scalds in Harald's court whose poems the people know by heart even at the present day, together with all the songs about the kings who have ruled in Norway since his time; and we rest the foundations of our story principally upon the songs which were sung in the presence of the chiefs themselves or of their sons, and take all to be true that is found in such poems about their feats and battles: for although it be the fashion with scalds to praise most those in whose presence they are standing, yet no one would dare to relate to a chief what he, and all those who heard it, knew to be a false and imaginary, not a true account of his deeds; because that would be mockery, not praise.

The priest Are hinn Frode (the Wise [1067–1148]), a son of Thorgils the son of Gellir, was the first man in this country [i.e. Iceland] who wrote down in the Norrön [i.e. Norse] language narratives of events both old and new. In the beginning of his book he wrote principally about the first settlements in Iceland, the laws and government, and next of the lagmen [law-speakers, the highest civic officials, who recited one-third of the laws in each year of a three-year term], and how long each had administered the law; and he reckoned the years at first, until the time when Christianity was introduced into Iceland, and afterwards reckoned from that to his own times. To this he added many other subjects, such as the lives and times of kings of Norway and Denmark, and also of England; besides accounts of great events which have taken place in this country itself. His narratives are considered by many men of knowledge to be the most remarkable of all; because he was a man of good understanding, and so old that his birth was as far back as the year after Harald Sigurdson's fall [in 1066]. He wrote, as he himself says, the lives and times of the kings of Norway from the report of Odd Kolsson, a grandson of Hall of Sida. Odd again took his information from Thorgeir Afradskoll, who was an intelligent man, and so old that when Earl Hakon the Great was killed (995) he was dwelling at Nidaros – the same place at which King Olaf Trygvesson afterwards laid the foundation of the merchant town of Drontheim which is now there.

The priest Are came, when seven years old, to Haukadal to Hall Thorarinson, and was there fourteen years. Hall was a man of great knowledge and of excellent memory; and he could even remember being baptised, when he was three years old, by the priest

Thangbrand, the year before Christianity was established by law in Iceland. Are was twelve years of age when Bishop Isleiv died [in 1080], and at his death eighty years had elapsed since the fall of Olaf Trygvesson. Hall died nine years later than Bishop Isleiv, and had attained nearly the age of ninety-four years. Hall had traded between the two countries, and had been in partnership in trading concerns with King Olaf the Saint, by which his circumstances had been greatly improved, and he had become well acquainted with the kingdom of Norway. He had fixed his residence in Haukadal when he was thirty years of age, and he had dwelt there nearly sixty-four years, as Are tells us. Teit, a son of Bishop Isleiv, was fostered in the house of Hall of Haukadal, and afterwards dwelt there himself. He taught Are the priest, and gave him information about many circumstances which Are afterwards wrote down. Are also got many a piece of information from Thurid, a daughter of the gode Snorri. Thurid was wise and intelligent, and remembered her father Snorri, who was nearly thirty-five years of age when Christianity was introduced into Iceland, and died a year after King Olaf the Saint's fall [i.e. 1030]. So it is not wonderful that Are the priest had good information about ancient events both here in Iceland, and abroad, being a man anxious for information, intelligent, and of excellent memory, and having besides learned much from old intelligent persons.

Selected from author's preface to Snorri Sturluson, *Heimskringla: Sagas of the Norse Kings*, trans. S. Laing, revised by P. Foote. (London: J. M. Dent, 1961), 3–6. Bracketed interpolations are mine, drawn from Foote's notes, which are otherwise omitted.

monastic chroniclers, wrote a number of historical works over a career mainly spent as a librarian. These included a life of St Dunstan and two major works, the *Gesta regum anglorum* ('Deeds of the English Kings') and *Gesta pontificum anglorum* ('Deeds of the English Bishops'). Later in life William added his *Historia novella* ('New History') concerning the years 1125–42. All of these works are devoted to the history of England, the past of which is taken as naturally involving both ecclesiastical and secular matters. The same applied to Henry of Huntingdon (c. 1080 to c. 1155) in the mid-twelfth century and to the long sequence of monks at St Alban's Abbey from Roger of Wendover (d. 1236) and Matthew Paris (c. 1200–59) in the thirteenth century down to Thomas Walsingham (d. c. 1422) in the early fifteenth century: all were relentlessly Anglocentric, however variable the quality of their judgment and use of sources or originality of their writing.

Where national pride and royal ambition went, historians were likely to follow, and many historical works had the direct support or at least tacit encouragement of the monarch. While later English and French rulers are known to have taken an interest in history, very few Europeans, outside Byzantium, can compare with the hands-on historiographic activity of a number of Spanish kings virtually from

Visigothic times up to the arrival of the Habsburgs in the sixteenth century. When Fernando III of Castile (r. 1217–52) wanted to read a history of Spain he turned to a leading prelate, Rodrigo Ximénez de Rada, archbishop of Toledo who, with some subordinates' help, produced the *De rebus Hispanie*. Throughout the later Middle Ages, the various Spanish monarchies (Castile-Léon, Aragon and Catalonia, and Navarre) would generate an enormous quantity of writing, some of it by the kings themselves, more sponsored by the crown, and still other independent texts which might nonetheless draw on official works. Among the most celebrated are those compiled under the direction of Alfonso X 'The Learned' of Castile and Léon (r. 1252–84), including a vast six-book universal history called *General Estoria* and the *Estoria de España*. Alfonso's 'history workshop' – the arena of several competitive and argumentative minds rather than a table for simple 'scissors-and-paste' assemblage – generated a number of other works over the ensuing decades, all of which constitute what is known as the Alphonsine Chronicles. The kings of Aragon and Catalonia were just as active. Pedro IV 'the Ceremonious' of Aragon (= Pere III of Catalonia; r. 1336–87) was, for his time, a history 'buff' who read incessantly and confessed that history was 'the main interest of his life'. Apart from the autobiography of his ancestor Jaime I (r. 1213–76), Pedro read carefully a set of chronicles of the kings of France. His wider reading included Orosius, Isidore of Seville and the histories of even northern countries, though he appears to have had little interest in the authors of classical antiquity. But Pedro was not content simply to read, and he is known to have had compiled (and perhaps even himself wrote parts of) two works, a chronicle of the kings of Aragon and one of his own reign. The latter, now regarded as a classic of Catalan literature, was the product of an ongoing and close collaboration between the king and an official, one Bernat Descoll (d. 1391).

In France, the roughly counterpart chronicle series to St Alban's or to the various Spanish royal histories was a very different product engineered at the abbey of Saint-Denis. Where the St Alban's chroniclers had been long disconnected from the English court, those of Saint-Denis were encouraged by the French monarchy to write a carefully designed history, going back to the Trojans, and celebrating the emergence of the centralized French kingdom. The abbey was a perfect incubator for such a project. Close to Paris, and a long-standing favourite of successive royal houses since the Merovingians, it already had a distinguished historiographic record and an inclination to royalism. Saint-Denis's early twelfth-century abbot, Suger (c. 1081–1151), was himself a remarkable historian, intimate advisor of the forceful king Louis VI ('the Fat', r. 1081–1137), and biographer of that king and his son. During his abbacy (1122–51) the monks compiled from earlier sources a complete history of France, the *Gesta gentis Francorum*. Later in the twelfth century another monk pulled together a set of historical notes or *cahiers*

Figure 14 | Various episodes from French history in a fourteenth-century manuscript of the *Chroniques de Saint-Denis/Grandes Chroniques de France*. Scenes include the coronation of Pharamond, the Battle of the Franks vs the Romans and the baptism of Clovis.

and outlined a plan for a new history; this seems to have been realized in a series of subsequent works like the *Nova gesta Francorum*. A practically uninterrupted tradition devoted to the Capetian kings unfolded from this time, eventually mutating into an 'official history', something that had hitherto been a rarity in Europe, certain Spanish exceptions aside. The Latin originals produced at Saint-Denis were rearranged and translated in the late thirteenth century by a monk known only as Primat into a lavishly illuminated vernacular series called the *Grandes Chroniques de France* ('Great Chronicles of France'), with additional materials added from other vernacular histories (Figs. 14 and 15).

In both the *Grandes Chroniques* and their Latin originals we have something not dissimilar to Chinese *Zhengshi* ('Standard Histories') or the early Japanese *Rikkokushi* ('Six National Histories'): a carefully woven, internally coherent national view of the past framed as an uninterrupted sequence of rulers since the election

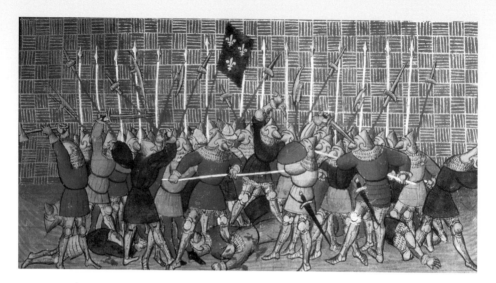

Figure 15 | Battle of Courtrai, Flanders, 1302, from a late fourteenth-century manuscript of the *Chroniques de Saint-Denis*.

of the mythical king Pharamond, a line presiding over a nobility and a larger realm whose boundaries, ethnicity and language had been largely unchanged since the first Trojan descendants had arrived. The *Grandes Chroniques* appeared in instalments beginning in 1274 and ending in 1461. Its dissemination was restricted by the monarchy, the translation being for the benefit of courtiers untrained in Latin, not a wider readership, and the printing of the *Grandes Chroniques* for the first time at Paris in 1477 brought the tradition to an end at a time when the newer humanist form of historical writing was beginning to make its presence known in France.

A consequence, and perhaps also a cause, of this historiographic nationalism, is the resurgence of semi-fictional histories in Latin providing elaborate accounts of the foundation of kingdoms and even some early theories of racial descent. The most notorious work of this sort, arising from the growing rivalry between England and France, was the *Historia regum Britanniae* ('History of the Kings of Britain'). This was composed about 1136 by Geoffrey of Monmouth (c. 1100–54), and is a pond from which many historical and literary streams flow, including virtually the whole late medieval Arthurian legend and a line of fictitious British monarchs which it would take centuries of scepticism and scholarship to depose from their imagined thrones. Picking up from Gildas and his successor, an obscure ninth-century Welshman known to us as Nennius, Geoffrey took the old stories of the origins of Britain, sidelined Nennius' biblical apparatus in favour of Trojan ancestors and then 'improved' upon his sources. Citing as his main authority a 'certain very ancient book written in the British language [i.e. Welsh]', of which there has been no trace since, Geoffrey filled in most of the chronological span in between, providing very few actual dates but, perhaps following Bede, inserting into his narrative synchronisms between events in Britain and those elsewhere, all of which made the scholarship look rather impressive. Thus a description of the reign of Ebraucus 'who was very tall and a man of remarkable strength' and to whom the foundation of the city of York would be ascribed, is followed by the information that 'At that time King David was reigning in Judea and Silvius Latinus was King in Italy. In Israel, Gad, Nathan and Asaph were the prophets.'[23] Geoffrey added a good deal more detail and colour to the information he had inherited, and took some old stories in new directions, more or less completing the reshaping of Arthur the obscure Dark Age warrior of Gildas' account into the knightly hero familiar to modernity from late medieval romancers like Chrétien de Troyes and Sir Thomas Malory.

Geoffrey's book was neither *sui generis* nor, despite its massive popularity, was it accepted whole cloth by contemporaries. He was attacked for fabrication before the twelfth century was out by a younger contemporary, William of Newburgh (1136 to c. 1201), who made the discrediting of Geoffrey's history – in large measure because it departed from the revered account in Bede – the subject of a prologue to his *Historia rerum Anglicarum*, as well as by the topographer Gerald of Wales (c. 1146 to c. 1223), who nonetheless mined Geoffrey as a historical source when it suited. Geoffrey's work came in the middle of a long-standing tradition of history-writing, the main object of which was to provide a glorious past for a particular kingdom or people. His Latin prose history quickly acquired a French-language verse counterpart in one Wace, a Norman poet whose *Roman de Brut* ('Romance of the Brute') built on Geoffrey's account to celebrate King Henry II of England's (r. 1154–89) ancestry; and a priest named Layamon would retranslate the French into Middle English. The various versions of Geoffrey's tales would spawn a whole series of 'Brut' poems and manuscripts over the next three centuries. That doubts were raised about his reliability, and that Geoffrey himself felt obliged to tie his statements to a notional ancient book, is a proof, were such needed, that the medieval mind was quite capable of discerning *fabula* from *historia*; the protestations of vernacular chroniclers in the next century that their works were to be believed because, unlike poets, their prose did not repeat lies, is another.

The key word here, however, is 'belief'. The readers of chronicles and hearers of *chansons* alike may have been able to recognize the differing 'textures' of historical writing, wherein the same work could contain matters of literal truth, those invented and those somewhere in between. In any event, they certainly did not make hard and fast distinctions between fiction and 'fact', a word that would not acquire its modern sense of a 'true thing' in any case for several more centuries. History was less a literally truthful account of genuine events thought to have occurred in a real past than 'what was willingly believed'.[24] Isidore of Seville's old notion of a kind of middle ground between truth and myth, the *argumentum* – things that *might* have happened even if they literally hadn't – is put into practice in works such as these. It allows for a zone of both credence and incredulity, of suspension of disbelief, which is wider than modernity has been able to accept.

Both patriotic sentiments and a willingness to fish in the murkiest and most unfathomable depths of history's ocean for evidence to support them can be found much further afield throughout the later Middle Ages and well into the Renaissance. Many examples come from central and eastern Europe, areas that had shown scant historiographic activity independent of Rome or Constantinople during the first millennium. The Bohemian priest Cosmas of Prague (1056–1125) laid the grounds for later generations of Czech nationalism by summarizing several centuries of legends and saints' stories in the *Chronica Bohemorum*, tracing his people's origins back to one 'Bohemus'. A variety of Polish works in both Latin and Polish, such as the twelfth-century *Kronika Anonima zwanego Gallem* ('The Chronicle of the Anonymous called Gallus', comp. 1113–17), a *gesta*-style work founded on a combination of oral tradition and earlier writings, would appear from the twelfth to the fifteenth centuries; they culminated in Jan Długosz's (1415–80) *Annales seu Cronicae incliti Regni Poloniae* ('Chronicles of the Glorious History of Poland'), a ten-volume work (1455) covering all of Polish history from legendary times to the year of its author's death. In Arpád-dynasty Hungary, the court cleric Simon of Kéza compiled in the 1280s a *Gesta Hungarorum* ('Deeds of the Hungarians') for his master, King Ladislas IV 'the Cuman' (r. 1272–90). His work finds the remote origins of the Hungarians not in the Trojans but rather in the 'Huns dwelling in Scythia'. Like Geoffrey of Monmouth, Simon was willing to interpolate created dates and episodes in order to avoid unseemly gaps or provide linkages where the evidence did not run; he even ingeniously turns Attila, who had been traditionally integrated into Christian history as an Assyrian-like 'scourge of God', into an unlikely ally of the papacy.

To the southeast, the impressive line of early Byzantine political historians and chroniclers had dried up temporarily in the seventh century. It remained that way through the eastern empire's most expansive period from the ninth to the eleventh centuries, when the initial advances of Islam had been arrested and before the Ottoman onslaught of the fourteenth and fifteenth centuries, a period that also saw extensive civil war within the empire. Rather like the pattern already noted in the Persian dynasties of the age, a significant revival in historical writing occurred just as Constantinople's political and military fortunes were beginning their long downward slide in the eleventh century. The memoirs of court life by the court official-turned-monk Michael Constantine Psellus (1018 to c. 1078) inaugurated this new phase of Byzantine historical writing which would peak in the next quarter-millennium under the Comnenian and Palaiologan dynasties. In contrast to the historians of the age of Procopius, a disproportionate number of the newer writers were persons of very high or even royal status.

The Emperor John VI Cantacuzenus (r. 1347–54) was so far as we know the only Byzantine emperor to write his own long life, but neither the first nor the most illustrious member of an imperial family to turn to history. Among these, the princess Anna Comnena (1083–1153) merits particular attention as one of the very few women in Europe to write, openly over her own name, a history of substantial length before the eighteenth century. The empire – Anna still refers to it as 'Rome' – had entered a newly expansive and resurgent phase under her father Alexius I Comnenus (r. 1081–1118), the very same ruler so detested by the Crusade chronicler William of Tyre. There is no doubt that his daughter's book is an admiring homage to Alexius' deeds, nor that she just as strongly disliked his successor, her brother John II Comnenus. Anna admits herself in introducing her book, which she entitled the *Alexiad* in conscious imitation of Homer, that her intent was to ensure that these achievements would not be lost to oblivion. Among its other features, her work shows a striking attentiveness not only to the details of military campaigns, but to the technology of war.

The influence of the Byzantine Empire and the Orthodox Church extended beyond its Mediterranean and Balkan boundaries into more northerly parts of Europe, among them Russia, where historical writing proved to be relatively rare before the thirteenth century. By the early fifteenth century, when Muscovy was beginning to consolidate, a more robust tradition emerged, though comprehensive chronicles covering all of Russia come to an end in the 1480s. Prior to this, various localities produced annals, as did the assorted minor principalities that had sprouted off from Kiev, of which the most notable is the series of chronicles composed in the Novgorod Republic to the north of Rus' (Extract 12).[25] The most important of all medieval Russian histories, once ascribed to a monk named Nestor but now believed to have been the work of several authors, is called the *Russian Primary Chronicle* (also known from its opening sentence as 'a Tale of Bygone Years'). Compiled in the early twelfth century in Kiev, and surviving in two much later redactions from the fourteenth and fifteenth centuries respectively, the *Primary Chronicle* exerted an influence over subsequent Russian historiography that few western European chronicles could claim in their own realms, simply because of its prominence in a narrow field. It became almost standard practice in subsequent centuries to include a copy of the *Primary Chronicle* as the first part of any new historical work.[26]

This was also a period, beginning with Villehardouin and continuing with Froissart, during which western European vernacular historical writings began to appear with much greater frequency than in the previous six centuries. We

12: History in Medieval Russia: the Chronicle of Novgorod

AD 1355. AM 6883. The Metropolitan Alexi arrived in Russia, having been appointed in Tsargrad.

AD 1356. AM 6864. A stone church to the Annunciation of the Holy Mother of God was erected in Ilya Street.

AD 1355. AM 6863. *Vladyka* [= Archbishop] Moisei erected a stone church to St Mikhail in the Skovorodka [a district of Novgorod].

AD 1356. AM 6864. They erected a stone church to St Georgi in the Lubyanitsa [Street] where formerly a wooden church had stood. The same year they erected a church to the Forty Saints, of stone; the previous one had also been of stone, but had collapsed from old age and from the great conflagrations. ...

AD 1376. AM 6884. For the second time in three years the Volkhov flowed backwards, seven days. The same spring the Metropolitan Mark from the Holy Mother of God, from Mount Sinai, arrived in Novgorod, seeking charity. ...

AD 1379. AM 6887. Eight streets were burnt down in Novgorod, the fire breaking out in Lukin Street, and twelve churches, the fire extending to Chudinets Street.

The same year the Tartars came into the Russian Land, against the *Veliki Knyaz* [= Prince] Dmitri. And the *Knyaz* went out against them, and it was on the Ovozha river, and there both forces met and God aided the *Veliki Knyaz*, and the Tartars turned shoulder and fled.

The same year they founded two stone churches: one to the Holy Mother of God in the Mikhalitsa [Street] and the other to the Holy Frola and Lavra in Lyudogoshca Street.

Selected from *The Chronicle of Novgorod 1016–1471*, trans. R. Michell and N. Forbes, Camden Society third series 25 (London: Camden Society, 1914), 156–8. Bracketed interpolations of the word 'Street' are translators'; others are mine, drawn from editorial notes which have otherwise been omitted. This extract, with dates given both *anno domini* and *anno mundi*, illustrates a number of features commonly associated with medieval historical writing. Note the brevity of several of the annals; the keen interest in church construction (this was the work of clerics); and above all the 'paratactic' structure wherein one event is grafted on to the previous one without necessary connection or any apparent sense of priority or scale of significance. The Tartar invasion of 1379 is thus sandwiched between two local events, a fire and the foundation of two new churches. Note also that the text backtracks at one juncture from 1356, back to 1355, and then back to 1356.

noted in the previous chapter that historical writing in non-classical tongues was quite rare across first-millennium Europe. By the fifteenth century, a much larger corpus of non-Latin European historical writings existed: the Scandinavian sagas (Figs. 16 and 17); Old Church Slavonic chronicles in the Grand Duchy of Lithuania (a large late medieval principality including parts of modern Lithuania, Belorus, Ukraine, Poland and Russia) and other parts of central and eastern Europe; the

Figure 16 | Sigurd kills Regin, detail from the Saga of Sigurd Favnesbane, twelfth century. Wood carving from the Hylestad stave church, Setesdal, Norway.

Old French *chansons de geste* and verse histories; aristocratic prose chronicles in the thirteenth century (such as the *Chroniques des rois de France* and *Histoire des ducs de Normandie et des rois d'Angleterre* and their successors); the militaristic histories of the fourteenth and fifteenth centuries; and the urban chronicles of the newly emergent towns and cities of northern Italy, the German lands and England. Latin remained the preferred language of clerically authored historiography, but even among the clergy the vernacular was sometimes used, as for instance in a number of Anglo-Norman and Middle English chronicles of the late thirteenth and fourteenth centuries. Indeed in some corners – notably Iberia – Latin no longer even commanded pride of place as the 'learned' tongue, many clergy being unable to read it. Nor was an 'international' readership of individual chronicles dependent upon Latin, a good example being the so-called *Chronicle of Morea*, a fourteenth-century work concerning Frankish achievements in the Greek principality of Achaea, which exists in separate Greek, Aragonese, Italian and French versions. The days of Latin's historiographic near-monopoly were drawing to a close in western Europe, though it remained the language of international scholarship for several more centuries.

Figure 17 | Illustration from the collection of Icelandic sagas, the *Flateyjarbók*, from the Saga of Olaf Tryggvason, here depicted killing a wild boar and a sea-ogress. Late fourteenth-century manuscript. Stofhun Arna Magnussonar a Islandi, Reykjavik, Iceland.

The readership and authorship of historical literature were both expanding modestly throughout Europe, and this, too, drove an increase in vernacular-language writing. Urban readers were acquiring an interest in their communities' pasts, and what often began as records of civic officials evolved in the fourteenth and fifteenth centuries into urban chronicles, most of which were written in tongues other than Latin (see Box 11). Another sector of the laity, the aristocratic houses of the great feudal kingdoms, continued to develop an interest in both history and – especially as new families rose in rank and prosperity – genealogy that would be

Box 11   Urban Chronicles

Emerging from a context largely unconnected with either clerical or aristocratic historical writing was the urban or town chronicle, so-called for its authors who lived in and wrote about the world of commerce and civic politics. The urban chronicle first sprouted in Italy in the eleventh and twelfth centuries, flourished in the thirteenth and fourteenth centuries and fully blossomed elsewhere in Europe during the fifteenth and early sixteenth centuries. Often developing from lists of civic officials or simple annals, and mainly written by laymen, these chronicles recorded local events in varying degrees of detail and were an important counterpart, for the emerging middling sort of merchants and townsmen, to the more learned chronicles of the monastic and secular clergy, or to aristocratic works. Of particular note was the Florentine merchant and sometime soldier Giovanni Villani (c. 1275–1348) who set out to write a chronicle that, unlike previous Florentine chronicles, had an overarching theme, which was the greatness of Florence and its place as rightful successor to the greatness of a now-decaying Rome. With its identification of causes in human actions and motives rather than only providence, and its ruminations on the significance of fortune in the rise and fall of men and states, Villani's *Istoria* edges us closer to humanist historiography. Nowhere did the urban chronicle proliferate more than in German-speaking territories, and the volume produced was of such a scale that the mid-nineteenth-century project to publish them has not yet completed its work. A great many of the authors were not native to the places about which they wrote and they were also occupationally diverse. Many towns even had an official chronicle, kept up over multiple generations: the successive fifteenth-century authors of the Council Chronicle (*Ratschronik*) of Lübeck, all of them clergy, built on a pre-existing work by a local Franciscan. The fifteenth-century urban chronicles, in contrast to earlier examples, were mainly a category of works written or printed *in* a town, rather than a type of history *about* a particular town. The cartographer Hartmann Schedel's *Nuremberg Chronicle* (1493) is so-called not because it was about Nuremberg (it was actually a universal history, written in Latin) but because it was published there. The urban chronicles often tell us less about the towns themselves than they do about the awakening public interest in history, which was now spreading unmistakably beyond its traditional audience of royal and aristocratic courts and monastic scriptoria.

Figure 18 | Genealogical table of the Saxon kings and emperors (top row: Dukes Brun, Ludolf and Otto of Saxony), from Ekkehard von Aura, *Chronicon Universale*. Miniature on parchment, c. 1100–50, Corvey, Germany.

sustained for two or three centuries (Figs. 18 and 19). The same level of creativity that had spun tales of Brutus and Francion and chronicles of the Crusades would be deployed to provide noble families with genealogical rolls and sometimes full-scale histories reaching back to Noah or Adam, or to Brutus and thence the Trojans. In the emerging 'national monarchies' of western Europe patriotic histories such as the *Brut* multiplied in the fourteenth and fifteenth centuries. Robert Mannyng of Brunne, an Englishman who completed a *Chronicle of England* in 1338, traced England's origins back to Brutus in his genealogical narrative. Aristocratic libraries collected copies of chronicles, and some appear to have been genuinely interested in their contents. The dukes of Burgundy, the spectacularly wealthy rulers of much of northern France and the Low Countries, developed a remarkable collection of historical materials, with the history of France given pride of place. Duke Philip the Good's (r. 1419–67) court in particular regularly hosted historians

Figure 19 | Family tree of the royal Nemanjic dynasty, Serbia. Byzantine fresco, 1346–50. Decani Monastery, Decani, Kosovo.

seeking to present their work to him, and the duke sponsored a host of chroniclers. The pay for their labours was often not especially good: Enguerrand de Monstrelet (c. 1400–53) received only a modest sum for his lengthy continuation of Froissart.

The sort of martial chronicle that had been perfected by Froissart in the fourteenth century had imitators in the fifteenth such as Monstrelet and Georges de Chastellain (1405?–75). A client of Philip the Good, Chastellain was among those late medieval historians actually granted 'official historian' status by his patron – official in the limited sense that he was actually appointed to the position, for which he received remuneration, by the duke himself. The retention of official historians by princes or by independent city states was a relatively new trend that would enjoy considerable favour at the courts of the Italian Renaissance (see Chapter 4 below). The role of court chroniclers was multiple: to commemorate past heroic events; to chronicle the life and grandeur of the court of their own day; and to use history as a *miroir*

Figure 20 | Caesar landing in Britain, from an illuminated Flemish manuscript of Jean Mansel, *La fleur des histoires*, c. 1454–60.

in which their aristocratic readers could see themselves reflected, and on whose contents they could fashion their own pursuit of future immortality. These works were intended both for private reading and for public recitation, with considerable attention to language and rhetorical display. Historians like Chastellain and Olivier de la Marche (1425–1502), Paul Archambault has aptly remarked, were able to maintain their dukes in a state of 'hypnotic narcissism' while at the same time reminding them that they were competing for fame with Old Testament monarchs, Roman emperors since Caesar (Fig. 20) and all the past rulers of France from Clovis and Charlemagne to their own Burgundian predecessors.[27]

But courtly historical writing was not all about flattery and display. By the mid-fifteenth century, in the context of the struggles of the French crown with English power and with Burgundian independence, one begins to discern a sharper political analysis in certain historians such as Thomas Basin (1412–91) and Philippe de Commynes

(1447–1511), who anticipate in many ways the flavour of Renaissance humanist historiography. Basin, a priest and eventually bishop who had studied at the University of Paris, spent time at Rome where he met the humanists in the circle of Florentine chancellor Poggio Bracciolini. This turned him away from the vernacular writing that had featured so prominently at aristocratic courts, but he was not content to revert to the older traditions of Latin annals. The *History of Charles VII and Louis XI* that Basin eventually wrote in Latin took as its models not the chroniclers of past centuries but more remote classical authors such as Livy and Sallust. In it the historian quotes frequently from Seneca and Cicero, drawing comparisons between recent and ancient events and deriving political and military lessons therefrom. Far from flattering authority, it conveyed sharp criticism of the formidable Louis XI (r. 1461–83), perhaps not surprising given that Basin had fallen afoul of the 'spider king', and spent the last third of his life either out of favour or in exile. Notable features of this kind of 'politique' analysis include: a much closer attention to the precise causes of events, both on the battlefield and in the diplomatic intrigues of court; a more ruthless selection among them; the avoidance of extended passages describing scenes of display; the reappearance of 'fortune' as a significant agent of random change; and the beginnings of a psychological analysis of major figures, especially rulers.

Commynes provides perhaps the best illustration of the same features, and a return to the larger international canvas of previous centuries. Like the most accomplished Italian historian of the next half-century, Francesco Guicciardini, and hearkening back to Polybian *symploke*, Commynes saw the interplay of individual nations as part of a larger whole, namely Europe, though he did so from the vantage point of a firm adherent to Louis XI and his successor Charles VIII (r. 1483–98). Writing some time after Louis' death, and frequently intruding his own persona into the narrative, Commynes was relatively free to portray his former master 'warts and all'. He warns the work's patron Angelo Cato, archbishop of Vienne that he is likely to find episodes 'not at all to Louis' credit'.[28] His portrait is a balance of virtues and flaws, and Louis comes off looking shrewd and politic rather than merely crafty and deceitful. In comparing this with the rather negative evaluation of duplicity one finds in chroniclers only a couple of centuries or so previously (one recalls William of Tyre) it is clear that we are no longer in the world of devout piety and chivalry. We have arrived in the world of Machiavelli.

Chinese Historiography from Song to Yuan

As the end of the Han dynasty had produced a period of disunion, so too was the close of the Tang in 907 followed by a shorter time of instability (the 'Five Dynasties and Ten Kingdoms'), during which historiographical activity continued with rather more inconsistent official sponsorship: it would take until 945 for an early version of the Tang Standard History to be completed. Stability returned with the ascension in 960 of the Song, who would preside over an enormous population expansion along with great scientific and technological achievements, all conducted in the face of barbarian threats from the north.

If the Tang had created a state apparatus for the production of history, the historiographic contribution of the Song was in some ways even more formidable. Song historians have been praised for their work on the tools of 'modern' historical thinking. While we do not wish to fall into the trap of judging past histories by the metrics of nineteenth-century Germany, there is no doubt that considerable reflection on concepts such as anachronism and the use of evidence, all dear to modern historians' hearts, occurred during these centuries. Song historians compiled the mandatory Veritable Records of each emperor, and they further developed the writing of gazetteers or *fangzhi* for individual administrative regions, including bibliographical, geographical, genealogical, biographical, historical and social information. They also produced no less than six comprehensive *guoshi* ('national' histories in the limited sense that they comprised both ruling regimes and their territories), complete with annals, monographs and biographies. *Nianpu*, free-standing or collective annalistic biographies, first appear under the Song, while the older Buddhist tradition of biographies continued, including collections such as the 'Biographies of Eminent Monks' assembled by Zan Ning (c. 919 to after 988) in 988 at the request of the emperor. Buddhism, a South Asian import, had on the whole been compatible with Chinese religions (especially Daoism) and with Confucian society; Buddhist historiography proved similarly adaptable and did not differ remarkably from the mainstream of Chinese historical writing, tending to borrow both its methods and sources. It is also at this time that history-painting, sporadically practised under the Han and Tang (and rare in Europe before the Renaissance) experienced a revival.[29]

While much of what the Song historians did was to continue along the path laid out by their predecessors, intellectuals such as Ouyang Xiu (1007–72) developed a distinctive school of 'Song Learning', which paid closer attention to literary style and problems of composition. Ouyang, a member of the History Bureau and thereby a participant in the compilation of the *Xin Tangshu* ('New History of the Tang') – a significant improvement in both quality and source-base from an earlier *Jiu Tangshu* ('Old History of the Tang') – also wrote works independently, such as his sole-authored *Wudai shiji* ('Historical Records of the Five Dynasties' or sometimes 'New History of the Five Dynasties'), first published posthumously in 1077. Moreover, Ouyang assisted in the creation of an annotated catalogue for the imperial library, and his work continued the long-standing tradition, going back to Confucius, of bestowing praise or blame on figures from the past. He urged his students to discard traditions and sections of texts that could not be fully authenticated, thereby preceding by four centuries the kind of philological scholarship whose invention is usually ascribed to the Italian Renaissance. Finally, Ouyang introduced the use of inscriptions and archaeological evidence as a check on the veracity of textual histories some four centuries before this occurred in Europe.

Ouyang's equal as an innovator and thinker, and his superior as a stylist and writer, was perhaps the greatest historian since Sima Qian, another member of the Sima family, Sima Guang (1019–86). A politician and official of high standing until rivals drove him into retirement, Sima was also a formidable lexicographer. As a historian, he produced works on a variety of subjects, but his major legacy was the vast text, nearly two decades in the making, that goes by the name of *Zizhi Tongjian*.[30] This title was given to the work by Sima's own admiring and financially supportive emperor after the historian had recited some early sections of it at court. The title is usually translated as 'Comprehensive Mirror in Aid of Government', and the emperor himself gave voice to a very old Confucian notion of the past as mirror on the present in introducing Sima Guang's history with the remark 'The Mirror of Yin is not far off. It lies in the age of Hsia [Xia].'[31]

Sima Guang had inherited some of Liu Zhiji's Tang-era dissatisfaction with the limits and quality of the Standard Histories, among which was surely their inability to capture a wider span of history than a single dynasty (a problem that would continue to trouble nineteenth-century Chinese scholars who would, however, seek solutions from entirely outside their country). He aspired to write a comprehensive (*tong*) general history of China back to the Warring States era; when finished, it covered the years 403 BC to AD 959. Where Sima Qian had solved the problem of organization by cutting his material multiple ways into annals, chronologies, biographies and so on, Sima Guang chose a simpler route which eliminated redundancy of coverage in order to bring into prominence the lessons of the past, that of a straightforward chronological account along the model of the Zuo Commentary. He pressed the need to examine original evidence where possible rather than later works – an early articulation of the distinction between primary and secondary sources – and he shared Ouyang's severe scepticism towards the invocation of the supernatural as a causal agent.

The success of the *Zizhi Tongjian* was such that it inspired imitators and successors, such as Zhu Xi (1130–1200), author of a more explicitly didactic version of Sima Guang's *Comprehensive Mirror*, and Yuan Shu (1131–1205). Zhu Xi, an unorthodox, iconoclastic and highly philosophical writer (and a founder of what is known as neo-Confucianism which would exercise a rather restrictive influence in coming centuries), reflected on the relation between the classics and history, coming down decisively on the priority of the former. The classics and the lessons they taught had to be mastered before one turned to post-Confucian history, which was less a separate field than the practical arena in which to play out moral principles gleaned elsewhere. Critical of historians ancient and modern, including even Sima Qian, Zhu felt a nostalgia for the distant past and an empathy for its inhabitants which sounds remarkably like Italian humanists' longing for antiquity two centuries further on:

I was born a thousand years too late!
My best friends lived a thousand years ago.[32]

Yuan Shu, Zhu's junior by a year, had perhaps a more ordinary mind, but he contributed a significant innovation in the organization of historical knowledge. Yuan, a historian of the Southern Song period, sought to improve on the rather relentless chronology of Sima Guang, from which it was often difficult to isolate the story of a particular event across annals. Yuan's *Tongjian jishi benmo* reorganized some of Sima Guang's most significant events or episodes (rebellions, dynastic changes and so on) into discrete and self-contained accounts. This inaugurated yet another new historical genre, the *jishi benmo* (narratives of the beginnings and ends of events). Meanwhile, the break with dynastic history in the direction of Sima Guang-style general history continued with Zheng Qiao's (1104–62) *Tongzhi* ('Comprehensive Treatises'), a comprehensive history of China from antiquity to the Tang, written in the annals–biography format, but with summaries replacing Sima Qian's monographs; its preface also contains the first extended theorizing about historical writing since the time of the *Shitong*. While the same moral economy of praise and blame that had been a core characteristic of Confucian historiography since the *Chunqiu* remains evident, there has been movement away from an overwhelming emphasis on the ethical conduct of individuals to the role of institutions and political arrangements in determining the course of History; and attention to great past failures in governance, at one time deemed unworthy of commemoration, now became a legitimate subject for the historian.

The rearrangement of history into different formats, including topics, furthered the trend towards making it a tool of social and economic policy and not merely personal wisdom: this was the high watermark in China of what has been called 'historical analogism', during which over a millennium of experience was available to statesmen and imperial servants seeking the solution to present problems in the past. The literary legacy of this Song focus on the practical lessons of history and on the distillation of erudition into a usable past was an efflorescence of topically arranged books such as encyclopedias, and innovative genres such as the 'imperial policy chronicle' (a sort of cross between Sima Guang's *Comprehensive Mirror* and Du You's late eighth-century *Comprehensive Institutions*). Knowledge of history became a critical part of the Chinese educational system all the way up to the imperial court. When we come in a later chapter to the genteel Victorian English undergraduate historical education of future politicians and members of

Figure 21 | Civil service examinations under the Song dynasty. Manuscript page from a seventeenth-century history of the lives of Chinese emperors.

the colonial office, and to the German bestowal of civil service ranks on its professional historians, it will be worth remembering that the Chinese had got to this point nearly a millennium earlier (Fig. 21). Students in the prefectural school system during the 1080s would be asked examination questions involving the discussion of the *Chunqiu*, *Shiji*, both Han histories and several subsequent works of history and historical criticism. This, as one scholar has noted, is 'roughly comparable to asking for an evaluation of Herodotus, Thucydides, Livy, Tacitus, Gibbon, Bede, Bury, Croce, and Hegel'.[33] A system of imperial lectures or seminars on the lessons of history, and regular recitations of Sima Guang's and other works, would endure till the empire's end in 1911. At the same time, history became even more thoroughly embedded in the preparation of candidates for civil service examinations.

A movement in the early twelfth century to refocus pedagogy at all levels on the classics at the expense of history (the position later adopted by Zhu Xi) led to the works of Sima Guang and other historians being publicly proscribed in 1105, but an unfavourable turn of events would eventually reverse this. Much of the northern half of the empire was lost in the twelfth century to the Jurchens, who established the Jin dynasty; they in turn were supplanted in the early thirteenth century by the Mongols, a nomadic people who over the next few decades also conquered the south of China, and established the Yuan dynasty (1260–1368). The Southern Song endured until 1279, and its new emperor almost immediately restored the old history curriculum, the imperial seminar and public readings of Sima Guang – the recent Chinese defeats having been laid squarely at the door of the classicizing reformers who had tried to eliminate history from education.

With the arrival of the Jin and the Yuan, two successive dynasties would be composed of ethnic foreigners. These dynasties faced the usual problems of legitimation that had attended every such change, now complicated by their linguistic and cultural foreignness. How to establish a usable and supportive past? The answer by and large was to embrace wholesale the language and historiographical apparatus of the conquered and put it to work – in a sense, to appropriate the practices of the Chinese without losing their own identity in the process. Thus the Jin emperor Shizong (r. 1161–89), who was especially fond of Sima Guang's work, decided that history offered a much clearer form of education than the Confucian classics. The Jin regime had in 1128 mandated the writing of a history of its people, and imitated their southern neighbours in the establishment of an Office of Records and a Bureau of Compilation – once again splitting off the recording from the writing of history. Like any new dynasty, they sponsored the composition of the Standard History of their predecessors, a minor northern dynasty called the Liao. The Yuan, who unlike the Jin had complete control over all China after 1279, similarly embraced the historiographical traditions they found, rather than continue their own chronicling traditions (see above and Box 9). To this end, they pressed many of the former Jin and Song literati into service. The first Yuan emperor, Khubilai Khan (r. 1260–94), ordered the merging of all the local gazetteers into a single common national administrative compendium, and he accepted the obligation to produce Standard Histories of the preceding Jin, Liao and Southern Song. Owing to disputes about the legitimacy of these various dynasties, their histories would not be completed until the mid-fourteenth century, by which time the Yuan themselves were on the brink of extirpation.

Forms of history outside the structures of government flourished under the Yuan, including some of the great romances or historical novels, intended to retell the events of official history in a more entertaining way. Luo Guanzhong's novel *Sanguo Yanyi* (a title usually rendered in English as *The Romance of the Three*

Kingdoms) was written towards the end of the Yuan and start of the Ming. One of the four great classic Chinese novels, it would eventually be a favourite of Nurgaci, founder of the Qing dynasty in the early seventeenth century. Luo's fiction looked backwards to an earlier period of uncertainty, the waning of the Han dynasty in the early third century. Oral tales survived from that epoch but its author appears also to have consulted historical works such as Chen Shou's third-century *Records of the Three Kingdoms*, which had featured especially vivid physical descriptions of its figures. Genealogies easily trip from characters' tongues, and battles are narrated in realistic detail.

Private history-writing, well established under the Song, also continued since not all of the servants of the former regimes were willing to be co-opted, and the new rulers were remarkably tolerant of works nostalgic for the Song. The Jin loyalist Yuan Haowen, for instance, retired from public life and devoted the rest of his days to poetry and to the collection of oral evidence concerning the Jin heritage, captured in his *Guiqian zhi* ('Retirement Memoirs'). Another, Ma Duanlin (1254–1324 or 1325) similarly refused to serve the Yuan and instead focused on writing a comprehensive cultural history of China, stressing the continuity to be found in native institutions which could endure the vicissitudes of dynastic rise and fall, but which revealed little by way of a meaningful pattern. Ma's *Wenxian tongkao* ('Comprehensive Investigation of Literary Traditions') is notable for its attention to economic and social change and its sensitivity to long-term development and major ruptures in continuity such as the Qin ascension. Like Ibn Khaldūn, Ma merits comparison with much later historical thinkers such as the 'stadial' historians of the eighteenth-century Scottish Enlightenment.

Japan and Korea from the Tenth to the Fifteenth Centuries

By the late tenth century, the rather mechanical replication of Chinese dynastic histories in Japan was beginning to wear thin. The office in charge of producing a planned continuation of the *Rikkokushi* was abolished in 969. There are several reasons for this, but the most important is that in fundamental ways the Chinese system of historical writing, and in particular the use of the dynasty as the basic unit of the Standard History, was ill-suited to Japan. From the Japanese point of view, all emperors belonged to the same dynasty, being directly descended from Jinmu: both the *Kojiki*'s collected tales and the more chronologically organized *Nihon Shoki* presume the continuity of the imperial line rather than the cycle of dynastic rise and decay that characterizes the Chinese Standard Histories. Notwithstanding a number of minor rebellions, there was relatively little instability before the twelfth century. Changes in lineage within the dynasty were duly noted, and even the cycle of 'good first emperor/bad last emperor' was transplanted from China to Japan; but these changes did not constitute for the writers a major shift in the 'Mandate of Heaven'. This linealism, and a degree of resistance to Chinese cultural dominance in spite of the influence of Confucianism, ensured that while its language was initially borrowed, the edifice of Chinese historical writing was not reconstructed wholesale in Japan. This proved useful when the illusion of imperial divinity was seriously challenged in the twelfth century by the pronounced shift of power to the feudal warrior or samurai class, who found that they too could press history into service on their side. The *Azuma kagami* ('Mirror of the East') may serve as an example. A rather minimalist chronicle of the events it describes, written from the point of view of the shogunate rather than the emperor, *Azuma kagami* was a late thirteenth-century product of the Kamakura bakufu, which produced a number of works justifying its rule, in a sense taking over the 'official' history once owned by the imperial court.

But this sort of governmentally inspired work no longer existed alone. Beginning in the eleventh century, about midway through the Heian period (794–1185), a different type of history, written in Japanese, began to appear in the form of *monogatari* stories in prose or verse. Some of these are closer to fiction than to history, providing another instance of the resistance of many earlier historical cultures to the imposition of rigid boundaries between the two. When Murasaki Shikibu (c. 973 to c. 1014 or 1025) penned the most famous of these, *Genji Monogatari* ('Tale of Genji'), which concerns a fictitious prince, she had one of her characters justify the work's explicit departure from the national histories (and the perceived aridity of their Chinese models) by noting that whereas the tales recounted all that had happened since the age of the gods, the National Histories covered 'only one aspect of events'. Her writings earned her the honorific title Nihongi no Mitsubone, 'Lady Chronicle of Japan', supposedly because her fiction appeared accurately to describe life in court circles.[34] Other *monogatari* come closer to history in the sense that they at least portray real events, albeit fictitiously reconstructed as in a historical novel: *Heike Monogatari*, for instance, is set during the civil wars between rival clans in the late twelfth century. The *Rekishi Monogatari* or historical tales is a specific group of six works written by independent scholars and courtiers, often Buddhist-influenced, sometimes following the chronicle form but departing considerably from the National Histories in scope and tone, and sometimes featuring a first-person narrator. The first work in the *Rekishi* sub-genre, the *Eiga Monogatari* ('Tale of Flowering Fortunes'), which dealt chronologically with events in the life of a leading nobleman, Fujiwara Michinaga, was composed, like the *Tale of Genji*, by a woman or several successive women over a period of roughly a century beginning about 1028. Many other types of *monogatari* were biographically or thematically organized. A number, such as the group known as *Gunki monogatari*

('War Tales') dealt with violent conflicts, and were often recited orally (not unlike the Homeric epics or the *chansons de geste*, which they resemble for their heroic values) before being committed to writing in prose form and often also painted. There are five of these works extant, mainly dating from the twelfth century. The last in the series, and the longest, was *Taiheiki* ('Chronicle of Great Peace'), written somewhat later, in the mid-fourteenth century. All were the work of unknown or multiple authors, principally monks; again like the Homeric epics, they were handed down orally and then revised or complemented many times before they reached their final forms. Their authors show a familiarity with Chinese histories and episodes therein, which are dropped into the narrative to provide comparisons with Japanese occurrences and personalities. As with the Six National Histories earlier, the tendency of Japanese readers before the nineteenth century was to read the *Gunki Monogatari* and *Rekishi Monogatari* as literal, chronological history. The highly positivist scholarship of the late nineteenth century, which produced numerous debunkers and revisionists across the globe, was less kind: the iconoclastic historian Kume Kunitake, whose misadventures with imperial censorship will concern us much further on in this book, regarded the *Taiheiki* as utterly worthless in historical terms though more recent scholarship has been more forgiving. We can appreciate it, however, as a window into the Japanese historical mind a little over a century before it first came into sustained contact with the West (Extract 13).

Apart from the *Eiga Monogatari*, the most widely read among medieval Japanese historical writings were the *Gukanshō* ('Jottings of a Fool', c. 1220) by the Buddhist monk Jien, and another work in the *Rekishi Monogatari* genre, the twelfth-century *Ōkagami* ('Great Mirror'), whose author was influenced by the *Eiga Monogatari*. Jien (1155–1225), a leader of the Tendai Buddhist sect, wrote in a time of great turmoil, which drove him to search the past for underlying patterns. Apparent public indifference to the causes and consequences of a particular conflict, the Hogen rebellion of 1156, inspired Jien to look, on the eve of another such storm, the Shōkyū war (1219–22), for some sort of predictability in history, or at least a lesson that those contemplating war could heed. Jien's scope was wide, proceeding from Jinmu down to 1219, but it is his reflections on 'reason' as an underlying cause of events in the Japanese past that are of greatest interest. He wrote in Japanese, not Chinese, he admitted, 'to make it possible for the reader to comprehend the changing conditions of the world' at a time when he saw little understanding or true scholarship, and envisaged an immediate future that was 'inexpressibly dangerous'. Jien, who had observed the gradual emergence to power of the warrior class, had the Buddhist's Brahmin-derived overarching sense of long-term cosmic decline, paralleled by a deterioration in human matters since a 'legitimate age' in the tenth century 'when all was fortunate', though he also acknowledged

13: Fourteenth-Century Japanese Historical Epic: *Taiheiki*

It is the way of the morning sun that without evil intent it robs the lingering stars of their radiance. Even so was it in the estates of the land, where stewards grew strong and land-holders grew weak, although the military in no wise sought to dishonor the court. Likewise in the provinces the protectors were respected, but the governors were held lightly. Year by year the court declined; day by day the military flourished.

The generations of emperors thought always, 'Would that the eastern barbarians might be struck down!' For it was in their hearts to comfort the spirit of the imperial exile of Shōkyū; likewise, they sorrowed to think upon the court's power, how it wasted and became as nothing. Yet they abode in silence, troubled that the design was beyond their compass or the time was not fitting. But then came the day of the lay monk Taira no Takatoki Sōkan, the former governor of Sagami, a descendant of Tokimasa in the ninth generation. Then indeed was change close at hand in the mandate of heaven and earth! The deeds that Takatoki did were exceedingly base, and he was unashamed before the scorn of others. Without righteousness did he govern, not heeding the people's despair. By day and by night, with wanton acts he dishonored his glorious ancestors under the ground; in the morning and in the evening, with vain merriment he invited ruin in his lifetime. Fleeting indeed was his pleasure, even as the pleasure of Duke I of Wei who carried cranes; near at hand was his regret, even as the regret of dog-leading Li Ssu of Ch'in! Those who saw knit their eyebrows, and those who heard uttered condemnations.

The emperor of that time, who came forth from the womb of Dattemmon'in, was Go-Daigo, the second princely son of Go-Uda-in, set upon the throne in his thirty-first year by design of the governor of Sagami. In his reign this emperor obeyed the way of the Duke of Chou and of Confucius, properly observing the three relationships and five virtues; nor was he neglectful of the myriad affairs and hundred offices of his government, but followed the uses of Engi and Tenryaku. Hopefully the four seas gazed upon his aspect; with joyful hearts the myriad folk bowed before his virtue. In truth he revived forgotten things and rewarded all that was good, so that shrines and temples flourished, and [the Buddhist sects of] Zen and Ritsu, and fulfillment blessed the great teachers of the revealed and secret ways of Buddhism and the truths of Confucius. There was no man but praised his virtue and exulted in his goodness, saying, 'Surely this is a heaven-endowed emperor, an earth-ruling sovereign.'

Selected from *The Taiheiki: A Chronicle of Medieval Japan*, trans. and ed. Helen Craig McCullough (1959; Rutland, VT and Tokyo: Charles E. Tuttle Co., 1981), 5–6, reprinted with permission from Columbia University Press; bracketed insertion drawn from editorial notes which are otherwise omitted. The selection comes from near the beginning of the work. Note the authors' familiarity with Chinese

history, which is specifically adduced as an analogy; note also the sharply contrasting moral judgments concerning the evil former governor Takatoki, head of the Hōjō clan in Kamakura, and the duti-
ful emperor, a pious Buddhist and faithful Confucian. The emperor, deposed in 1331, would recover
and in 1333 briefly seize authority back from the Kamakura shogunate till 1336; he died in 1339.
Compare this account with that at the end of *Masukagami*, a more subdued version of the end of the
Kamakura shogunate: *The Clear Mirror: A Chronicle of the Japanese Court during the Kamakura Period*
(1185–1333), trans. and ed. George W. Perkins (Stanford University Press, CA, 1998), 183–220.

extract

occasional periods of improvement. Just as Buddhist Law had entered its third and
final stage, so had Japan progressed through an ancient and middle age to a 'Final
Age'.[35] Great disorders in the remote past, such as a series of imperial assassina-
tions, were signs of the coming end in Jien's own future.

The Hogen Rebellion, thought Jien, had ushered into existence an age of warriors whose values and ambitions were at odds with the rule of benevolent emperors and their regents, properly advised according to Buddhist principles. The way
forward in Jien's time lay in some kind of modus vivendi between the warriors
and the emperor governing through the nobility – his occasion for writing was to
advance the argument that the divine will had predestined a child of his own clan
named Kujō Yoritsune to rule on behalf of the emperor as both regent and shogun,
balancing the interests of both. It is difficult not to see some of the same concerns
that arose in late Roman historiography and which would recur in subsequent
times – how to reconcile a theoretically divine imperial power with the reality of
a military determined to have direct influence on governance. The past itself was
an ongoing process not of accidents and contingencies, but of the working out
of something like 'Reason'. This was not, it should be stressed, the same sort of
'Reason' that Enlightenment *philosophes* of the eighteenth century or Hegel in the
early nineteenth century had in mind but rather a law of the cyclical rise and fall
of things (including states) within a longer phase of decline. 'Reason' consists of
both divine and human elements, and the human inability to comprehend divine
Reason – the working out of events – is in itself an explanation for the degeneration of things on the mundane plane.

The *Ōkagami*, which is framed as a conversation between two very old men,
is another Buddhist-infused history; it shared Jien's notion of decline, and the
conviction that the world was well along in *mappō*, the last of the Buddhist Three
Ages, a 10,000-year era of decay.[36] Although it is the first Japanese-language historical work to imitate the annals–biography form of Chinese Standard Histories
(without Sima Qian's full apparatus of chronological tables, hereditary houses and
treatises), the *Ōkagami* was a privately written work, not an official history like

the *Rikkokushi*. Also unlike the National Histories (and like Jien's *Gukanshō*), the *Ōkagami* and its successor works were written in Japanese, and by individuals rather than committees. Composed by an unknown eleventh-century author, the *Ōkagami* was yet another work specifically to appropriate the idea of the reflective value of history. The image of the mirror, inherited directly from Chinese Confucian historiography, is repeated in three of the later *Rekishi* or *kagami-mono* ('mirror pieces'), *Imakagami* ('Mirror of the Present Age', c. 1170), *Mizukagami* ('Water Mirror', comp. c. 1185–98) and the anonymous fourteenth-century *Masukagami* ('Clear Mirror'). While there is an entertaining aspect to some of this literature, there is no mistaking the overtly political and often propagandistic tone in much of it.

In the *Jinnō Shōtōki* ('Record of the Legitimate Succession of Divine Sovereigns', comp. 1339), however, we have almost come full circle back to the original Japanese use of history in the eighth century to legitimize the imperial regime, and the work was much cited over the next several centuries as a call for loyalty to the emperor. One difference is that the author of this work, Kitabatake Chikafusa (1293–1354), is one of the few medieval Japanese historians, apart from Jien, about whom we know more than his name. Another is the much sharper polemical edge. Chikafusa was a former imperial advisor, warrior and nobleman who seems to have undertaken the task of writing his work while under siege in his home province and with access to only one work, 'an abridged imperial genealogy', though he was able to revise it a few years later. The *Jinnō Shōtōki* is a review of the entire history of the imperial line, emperor by emperor, ending with the death of Emperor Go-Daigo (r. 1318–39) in the year the work was composed. Chikafusa's history was an unashamedly partisan attempt to promote support for the emperor, as a schism of imperial courts followed the failure of the Kemmu Restoration. Chikafusa was an implacable foe of the Northern Court shogun Ashikaga Takauji ('a thief without merit or virtue') and of the warrior class generally,[37] but he was nonetheless able to accept the reality that there had indeed been bad or weak emperors. Written during a period of resurgent Shintoism, which defined Japan as *Shinkoku* ('Land of the Gods'), its author was familiar with but rejected the Buddhist ideas of change to be found in a work such as *Gukanshō*, and he eschewed Jien's notion that Japan had a temporally limited future. He turned to remote antiquity less for auguries of that future than for guidance in the present.

Jinnō Shōtōki begins with its author's confident declaration that 'Great Japan is the Divine Land. The heavenly progenitor founded it, and the sun goddess bequeathed it to her descendants to rule eternally. Only in our country is this true; there are no similar examples in other countries. This is why our country is called the Divine Land.' This status as a favoured people was inseparable for Chikafusa from the principle of imperial rule, which was under divine protection. Chikafusa knew his Chinese history from works such as the *Shiji* and *Hanshu*, and he contrasted the kind of dynastic change that China had experienced and the resulting 'unspeakable' disorder with the stability of Japan's imperial line. Japan would always return to the same ruling house – even diversions into separate lineages were merely tributary streams which would eventually return to the main river. 'In our country alone has the imperial succession followed in an unbroken line from the time when heaven and earth were divided until the present age. Although, as is inevitable within a single family, the succession has at times been transmitted collaterally, the principle has prevailed that it will invariably return to the direct line.'[38] This notion of Japan's special status is worth highlighting here for two reasons: first, because we will see the theme recur in later Japanese historical thought; and second, because it resembles 'exceptionalist' arguments made in other parts of the world at different times, from the Israelite notion of a covenanted or 'elect' Chosen People through Frankish monarchs' perceptions of themselves as latter-day Old Testament monarchs and Bede's view of the Anglo-Saxons as an elect people, down through early modern Protestant providentialism, to modern German nationalism with its notion of a *Sonderweg* ('separate path') and American convictions of Manifest Destiny.

Sandwiched on a peninsula between the Chinese mainland and the Japanese archipelago lies Korea, for the past six decades divided into North and South. Its modern division is not unprecedented. Although the founding of the first Korean kingdom of Kojosŏn, according to legend, can be traced back to one Tan'gun Wanggŏm (Dangun Wanggeom) in 2333 BC, historical Korea, like Japan, was a more recent creation. The Korean people, much like the pre- and post-Han Chinese, had a divided country before the Silla kingdom, a Tang client state, overcame its rivals in the mid-seventh century to take control of most of the country. Its successor, the Koryŏ (Goryeo) kingdom (935–1392), whose fourth ruler was the first to style himself 'emperor', was roughly coterminous with the Song and Yuan in China. The Koryŏ expanded their control to the northern part of Korea before they in turn were supplanted by the Chosŏn (Joseon) kingdom and its Yi dynasty (1392–1910).

The third East Asian country to develop historical writing, Korea has historically been vulnerable to intermittent exogenous influences from China, Japan and eventually the West; both Korean antiquity and its past independence remain even today prickly issues for historians, archaeologists and politicians. Like Japan, Korea was strongly affected by Chinese historiography through much of the premodern period and adopted many of its practices, including the institution of court diarists who, armed with brush and bronze tablet, followed their monarch around and faithfully recorded his words and actions: the dogged determination of the historians to attend the king at every turn was frequently resisted by monarchs such as T'aejong (r. 1400–18), the third Yi ruler, who tried unsuccessfully to ban them from the court. A temporary 'History Purge' occurred in 1498 under the rule of Yŏnsan-gun (r. 1494–1505), but the historians had the last laugh when the king was deposed in 1505.

Like China and unlike Japan, Korea recognized distinct dynasties, and the annals of each reign (*sillok*) are the counterpart to Chinese Veritable Records (*shilu*). The *chongsa* or dynastic histories of early Korea are similarly comparable to the Chinese *Zhengshi* which actually provided the earliest source material for Korean history. Historical records were maintained from the fourth century AD: the Silla kingdom, for instance, kept records known as the *Silla Kogi* and a history is known to have been compiled in 600 by Yi Mun-jin of the Koguryŏ kingdom; and Korean writings may even have influenced the Japanese *Nihon Shoki* in the eighth century. Virtually none of this first-millennium material has survived. The earliest example still extant of Korean history-writing, compiled in the Koryŏ period (935–1392), is Kim Pu-sik's *Samguk Sagi* ('History of Three Kingdoms', 1145); this used both now-lost Korean sources and Chinese writings (including the *Hou Hanshu*) and is clearly modelled on Chinese Standard Histories. The Koryŏ dynasty, following earlier Tang Chinese practice, established a History Office in the tenth century; this bureaucracy was considerably expanded during the ensuing Chosŏn kingdom, and in the fifteenth century a group of scholars led by Chong In-ji (1418–50) completed the *Koryŏsa*, a dynastic history of the Koryŏ.

Chosŏn historians would eventually produce a whole series of *sillok* for each reign covering nearly five centuries up to 1863. As with the Chinese Veritable Records, *sillok* were carefully guarded so that even the reigning monarch was denied access to them in order to protect against interference; and the diaries on which they were based were also kept out of sight, stored in the private dwelling of the historian, a practice which continued into the early Chosŏn period. When the pious Confucian King Sejong (r. 1419–50), a supporter of the historians, asked to see in advance the *sillok* being compiled of his predecessor, T'aejong, he was warned against this by his ministers, since such an act would encourage future monarchs to revise their historians' work and the historians themselves to refrain from writing the complete truth. The Korean king also formally lacked the Chinese emperor's power of appointment and was obliged to accept the nomination of the outgoing historian. Historians were selected from the *yangban*, a hereditary caste of Confucian intellectuals that would administer Korea up to the twentieth century, and whose interests often diverged from those of the emperor.

Again as with China, however, the presence of an official bureaucracy, and the intentional destruction of preliminary materials once a history had been completed, could not prevent alternative or private interpretations of the past from being written. A more Korean-focused tradition of historical writing emerged in the

14: Historical Writing in Thirteenth-Century Korea: Ilyŏn's *Samguk Yusa*

During the reign of Pŏpmin (King Munmu, thirtieth Silla sovereign, 661–681), the King issued a decree: 'When King Kuhyŏng, in the ninth generation of descent from the founder of Karak-kuk, surrendered to Silla, he brought with him to Kerim (Kyŏngju) his crown prince, Sejong. Sejong begat Solukong, Solukong begat Sŏun-Chapkan, Sŏun-Chapkan begat Queen Munmyŏng, and Queen Munmyŏng gave birth to me.[39] The founder of Karak-kuk is therefore my ancestor of fifteen generations ago. Though Karak was destroyed long ago, his shrine still exists today. Ye, my local subjects, must enshrine his tablet in the national sanctuary with those of my royal predecessors and offer annual sacrifice to his noble spirit at his shrine.'

The King dispatched a messenger to the ruins of Karak-kuk to set apart thirty 'kyŏng' (furrows?) of fertile rice land to support the caretaker of the tomb and pay for the ceremonies. Kaeng-se Kŭpkan, in the seventeenth generation of descent from King Suro, was appointed caretaker, to offer wine, rice cakes, tea and sweets to the royal spirits on the five annual memorial days fixed by King Kŏdŭng.

From the time King Kŏdŭng first established the royal resting-place at his palace until the reign of King Kuhyŏng the sacrificial offerings at King Suro's tomb continued for 330 years, after which they were suspended from time to time until King Munmu of Silla decreed their resumption.

In the closing days of Silla a local official called Ch'ungji-Chapkan took control of Kŭmgwan fortress and styled himself General-Magistrate of the city. One of his subordinates, Yŏngkyu-Agan, was in the habit of offering sacrifices to obscene idols at the shrine of King Suro. While he was engaged in invoking these gods' blessings on his family one day, a heavy beam fell from the ceiling and crushed him to death.

The General-Magistrate was frightened almost to death. He had a portrait of King Suro painted on a three-foot length of silk embroidered with a twisting dragon, hung it on the wall with an oil lamp burning before it and worshipped it daily, morning and evening. After three days tears of blood fell like rain from both eyes of the portrait and made a deep pool on the ground. He then took the portrait to King Suro's shrine and burned it there. Summoning a descendant of Suro named Kyurim, He said, 'One misfortune rides on the neck of another in my family. The King's spirit is angry at me because of my disrespectful worship of his portrait. I feared to look at it and burned it, and now perhaps his ghost will strike me dead. I wish you to resume the sacrificial ceremonies as before.'

Kyurim consented, and conducted the rites regularly thereafter until his death after a long life of eighty-eight years. But while his son Kanwon-kyŏng was worshipping at the shrine on a May Day, Yŏngkyu's son Chunp'il went mad. He jumped into the shrine, kicked away the sacrificial food and spread another table with his own offerings. – Before he had offered the third cup of wine to his obscene idols he was taken ill, and died of insanity on the way home.

There is an old saying, 'Obscene idols send down calamities instead of blessings on the offerer of sacrifice.' This refers to Yŏngkyu and Chunp'il, the disrespectful father and son.

Selected from Ilyŏn (Iryŏn), *Samguk Yusa: Legends and History of the Three Kingdoms of Ancient Korea*, trans. Ha Tae-Hung and Grafton K. Mintz (Seoul: Yonsei University Press, 1972), section 58, 164–5. Note the same theme of 'bad ends awaiting those who blaspheme or do evil' which occurs in the Christian tradition.

thirteenth-century Buddhist monk Ilyŏn's (1206–89; alternative transliteration, Iryŏn or Ilyeon) *Samguk Yusa* ('Memorials and Legends of Three Kingdoms'). Composed in Chinese at a time when Korea was under Yuan rule, it was nevertheless a celebration of Korean nationality. A Korean counterpart of Japan's Jien, Ilyŏn subscribed to the dominant Confucianism endemic in nearly all Chinese-influenced historiography; but since he was no official and wrote his work privately and mainly for recreation, he was freed of the obligation to follow the models of Chinese historiography. Ilyŏn was fascinated by the early history of Korea, in particular the three early kingdoms of Silla, Koguryŏ and Paekje, the establishment of which he pushed back to the time of China's Han, which all three survived by several centuries.[40] He records the legend of Tangun, born of a bear-turned-woman, and the supposed ancestor of all Koreans. With its mixture of history, folklore, custom, anecdotes and foundation legends, often drawn from unnamed 'old books' and now untraceable, it is not unlike Geoffrey of Monmouth's *Historia regum Britanniae*. And throughout the world, the next two centuries would challenge the veracity of such beliefs while working towards a more rigorous distinction between fact and fiction (Extract 14).

India and Tibet

While imported Buddhism successfully coexisted with Confucianism in China and both Confucianism and Shinto in Japan, it was in decline in its South Asian home, where both it and other indigenous faiths were confronted by an alien religion, Islam, at the outset of India's 'early medieval' period (eighth to thirteenth centuries). There had been a marginal Muslim presence in India virtually since the time of Muhammad, including visitors such as al-Bīrūnī, and various incursions by Turks and Arabs in the tenth through twelfth centuries, but Islamic India really dates from the establishment of a number of Muslim regimes, beginning with the Delhi Sultanate (1206–1526). A series of dynasties that ruled northern India from Delhi for three centuries, the Delhi Sultanate was only one among a number of regional Muslim states which arose in India during the thirteenth to fifteenth centuries, the next most significant being the Deccan sultanates (1490–1596), of South-central India. The Muslim chroniclers attached to these courts introduced a very different historical thought, and a tradition of Islamic history-writing already several hundred years old. Several historians would write about India in the next two centuries, including the prolific Amīr Khusrau Dihlawī (1253–1325) and Isami, an aristocratic court historian of the early fourteenth century who used his reign-by-reign celebration of earlier sultans to comment on the depravity of Muhammad Tughlaq (r. 1325–51) and promote the interests of the nobility.

Among these Indo-Muslims no historian has enjoyed as high a reputation as Żiyā al-Dīn Baranī (fl. 1284 to after 1357), both for the thoroughness in recording contemporary information which makes him a useful source, and also for his philosophic outlook, which one modern scholar has remarked lifts him 'right out of the ranks of mere compilers of chronicles'.[41] A member of the Delhi ruling elite, he completed his Ta'rīkh-i Fīrūz Shāhī ('History of Shah Firuz') in 1357, when he was in his seventies, amid a forced retirement, a circumstance reflected in the bitterness colouring his writing. But Baranī had reflected seriously on the purposes of history, the 'queen of the sciences' and highest form of learning other than those dealing with the Qur'an or the laws. He outlines seven different reasons for studying history: it bestows familiarity with sacred texts and with a stock of examples; it is the twin brother of ḥadīth and helps confirm its testimony; it strengthens reason and judgment by forcing us to confront the experience of others; it comforts the powerful in times of stress because it shows that there are tried solutions to most problems; knowledge of it will induce patience and resignation in good Muslims; it clearly delineates the contrasting characters of the virtuous and pious and the evil, displaying the consequences of good and bad behaviour and thereby induces rulers to behave themselves; and finally, as a foundation of truth, it will present ordinary readers with valuable examples and encourage them to take a righteous path. The duty of the historian is itself a moral one, to inculcate history's lessons. His own work, Baranī promises, serves a variety of purposes, providing an account of kings, a law book, a source of precepts and advice for rulers, and an accurate version of the past. In his corollary statement that 'history is a science that requires no proofs so long as the historian is a trustworthy person', trustworthy really means 'of respectable birth': Baranī anticipated much later European attitudes to scientific and historical truth which located epistemological authority in the social standing of its speakers.[42]

Outside the Sultanates, Hindu and Buddhist modes of historicity remained dominant. We saw in Chapter 1 that the historical thought of ancient India, contrary to popular belief and the propaganda of outsiders from al-Bīrūnī to James Mill, did in fact produce historical literature, though of a very unfamiliar kind. The most frequently cited exception to this pattern is a twelfth-century text that actually resembles a chronological 'history', the Sanskrit-language *Rājataraṅgiṇī* ('River of Kings', comp. c. 1148–9) by Kalhaṇa (*fl.* mid-twelfth century).[43] This verse composition, an example of the broader genre of *vaṃśāvalis*, covered the history of Kashmir from remote antiquity to the author's own time and was derived from legends, oral traditions, written records and inscriptions; it refers to other histories from which its author drew, suggesting that it was not, in its time, *sui generis*. Kalhaṇa pays tribute to the role of the poet, who alone is 'capable of making vivid before one's eyes pictures of a bygone age' but he also describes his methods and views on history at the outset:

Although owing to the exigency of the length of the narrative a variety of events have not been set down in detail, there should still be in this poem enough material for the delectation of the right-minded.

That man of merit alone deserves praise whose language, like that of a judge, in recounting the events of the past has discarded bias as well as prejudice ....

When they [i.e. his predecessors in recounting this history], who had pieced together the history of the kings, each one as he saw it, had gone to their rest, what kind of skill is it on the part of those born in later times that they should add to the narrative? Hence my endeavour will be in this narrative of past events to repair by all manner of means where there is error.

The voluminous works in fragments containing the early history of the kings were epitomized in Suvrata's composition so that they may be remembered.

The style of Suvrata being irksome, owing to the fault of pedantry, his composition, though it has acquired celebrity, is lacking in the art of the exposition of the theme.

While owing to an incomprehensible lack of care in the work of Kṣemendra [an eleventh-century author], known as the List of Kings, even a portion is not free from error, although it is the composition of a poet.

Moreover, eleven works of former savants containing the annals of royalty have been scrutinized by me as well as the views of the Sage Nīla.

By the inspection of ordinances of former kings relating to religious foundations and grants, laudatory inscriptions as well as written records, all wearisome error has been set at rest.[44]

This passage hits on a number of areas familiar to us already: the errors of illustrious predecessors; the need to consult various sources; the importance of style; and the educative function of the historian. The more acute sense of time that one finds in the body of a work like Kalhaṇa's may be attributable to Buddhist influences, though a Buddhist 'era' analogous to that in the Christian or Muslim calendars never achieved common historiographical usage in either South or East Asia. We should be cautious, however, about assuming that this chronicity must have had non-Hindu influences, and in awarding Kalhaṇa, who certainly saw himself as a poet, the title of 'true' historian within a historiographical framework that sets history in one corner and myth or poetry in the opposite. The polarity is itself one of Western creation which does not fit well with the South Asian capacity, already demonstrated in the Vedic tradition, to mix truth and myth liberally.

To India's north, the mountainous Central Asian kingdom of Tibet which lies between India, Nepal and China, emerged as a regional power from the seventh century, during which time Buddhism established itself more firmly than in any other region. Buddhist scholarship produced (in both Tibetan and Sanskrit) a number of histories, and it has been observed that in many of them, the indigenous Tibetan national story has been overwritten by religious history, rather in the way that the Maurya King Asóka was turned into a Buddhist hero in the second-century *Legend* – or, to draw a comparison from much further afield, the way in which the Emperor Constantine's Christian connections eventually outshone in medieval European histories his secular achievements. Thus some kings who had little affiliation with Buddhism are elevated in the fourteenth-century *Gyalrab Salwa'I Melong* ('Clear Mirror on the History of the Dharma') by Sakyapa Sonam Gyaltsen (1312–75) into major religious figures. The very long history known as the *Deb-ther sñon-po* ('Blue Annals') was the work of an aged translator and compiler 'Gos lo-tsa-ba gzhon-nu-dpal (1392–1481) who used and frequently simply copied earlier sources such as *rnam-thar* (lives) by religious teachers, not all of which are still extant. The author did, however, pay close attention to the lineages of the early Buddhist teachers and to chronology, calculating dates backward and forward from the named year (corresponding with AD 1476), when he was writing. He provided life-spans of the individuals whom he named including birth and death years.

The three sons of dPyan-sna dPal-chen: the first (was) sPyan-sna Kun-rgyal (who lived for) 35 years, between the year Earth-Serpent [1269 CE] and the year Water-Hare [1303]. The second (son) Yontan rgyal-mtshan (lived for) 54 years, between the Iron-Horse [1270] and the year Water-Hog [1323]. The youngest son Drin-can-pa (lived for) 63 years, between the year Water-Bird [1273] and the year Wood-Hog [1335].[45]

The literary effect of hundreds of passages, dense with information such as this and with commentaries on the deeds and teachings of particular notables, is to make the work very heavy-going, but the author had preservation of information rather than entertainment in mind. It is nonetheless true that the dates in the *Blue Annals* and the names of Tibetan rulers can be verified in other Tibetan chronicles and by comparison with events described in Chinese histories dealing with Tibet. Together with an earlier *History of Buddhism* by Bu-Ston (comp. c. 1322) the *Blue Annals* has become the principal source of information for later histories of Tibet.

CONCLUSION

This and the preceding chapter have covered well over a millennium of historical writing and ranged around Eurasia and northern Africa. Some key themes are worth highlighting here before we move on to the early modern era and a significant expansion of our geographic scope. The first point is that historical writing from late antiquity to the mid-second millennium AD flourished alike in circumstances of political and social instability, or in times of good order. The second is that religion and secular interests cut across each other rather than dwelling in entirely separate spheres, an interplay manifest in historiography from most of the regions examined. The third is that the cumulative achievements of Western historical writing to this point, when set against those of China and Islam, suddenly seem much less impressive than they appear when examined on their own. While there were capable chroniclers, lay and clerical, in significant numbers, historiography remained confined to a relatively limited number of forms. In contrast, the variety of different genres developed by the Chinese in particular – including encyclopedias, biographies and historical novels – and the Song historians' sophisticated linking of history and philosophy commands our respect. And there is similarly little in Christian Europe to compare with the intellectual range, perceptive observations and capacity to generalize that Islam produced in Ibn Khaldūn.

Mention of such comparison brings us to the fourth, and most important point: that many historians were already aware of, and a few were substantially influenced by, other cultures, whether one thinks of Christian–Muslim contacts, Muslim–Mongol, Sino–Mongol or Indo–Muslim. The extent of this contact would increase considerably in the next three centuries. During this next period, the reality of two large unexplored continents in the Americas, combined with more sustained ventures to the Far East, forced Europeans to rethink their picture of the world's history. It also made them realize that their own modes of historicity, themselves experiencing a protracted period of rapid change and unprecedented expansion, were neither entirely unique nor universally shared.

Notes

1 Adnan Husain, 'Conversion to History: Negating Exile and Messianism in al-Samaw'al al-Maghribī's Polemic against Judaism', *Medieval Encounters* 8:1 (2002): 3–34, at 3–4.

2 Julie Scott Meisami, *Persian Historiography to the End of the Twelfth Century* (Edinburgh, 1999), 21.

3 Quoted by Tarif Khalidi, *Arab Historical Thought in the Classical Period* (Cambridge, 1994), 173.

4 Meisami, *Persian Historiography*, 80.

5 Ibid., 55.

6 John E. Woods, 'The Rise of Tīmūrid Historiography', *Journal of Near Eastern Studies* 46:2 (1987): 81–108, at 82; E. A. Polyakova, 'Timur as Described by the 15th Century Court Historiographers', *Iranian Studies* 21 (1988): 31–44.

7 The Mamluks (a term that refers to a warrior class of former slaves) were the last vestige of the Abbasid line; a series of Mamluk dynasties ruled Egypt from the mid-thirteenth to the early sixteenth century.

8 Pamela Kyle Crossley, *What is Global History?* (Cambridge, 2008), 23–4.

9 'Ata-Malik Juvaini, *The History of the World-Conqueror*, trans. J. A. Boyle, rev. edn (1958; Manchester, 1997).

10 Khalidi, *Arabic Historical Thought*, 222–3 argues, contrary to convention, that the history, typically regarded as a lesser work than its prolegomenon, is in fact a well-structured working out of ideas outlined in the *Muqaddimah*.

11 Ibn Khaldūn, *The Muqaddimah: An Introduction to History*, trans. F. Rosenthal and abridged N. J. Dawood (Princeton, NJ, 1967), 35.

12 Ibid., 98–9, 259–61, 244, 252–3.

13 Ibid., 36–7, 98–9.

14 See variously P. J. Geary, *Phantoms of Remembrance: Memory and Oblivion at the End of the First Millennium* (Princeton, NJ, 1994); M. T. Clanchy, *From Memory to Written Record: England 1066–1307*, 2nd edn (Cambridge, MA, 1993); and B. Stock, *The Implications of Literacy* (Princeton, NJ, 1983).

15 *Crusaders as Conquerors: The Chronicle of Morea*, trans. Harold E. Lurier (New York, 1964), 67.

16 John of Salisbury, *Policraticus*, ed. and trans. Cary J. Nederman (Cambridge, 1990), prologue, 3.

17 William of Tyre, *A History of Deeds Done Beyond the Sea*, ed. and trans. Emily A. Babcock and A. C. Krey, 2 vols. (New York, 1943), 56.

18 Quoted in Antonia Gransden, *Historical Writing in England*, 2 vols. (Ithaca, NY, 1974–82), vol. II, 93; *Sir Thomas Gray: Scalacronica*, trans. and ed. A. King (London, 2007), 2.

19 Robert of Clari, *The Conquest of Constantinople*, trans. E. H. McNeal (1936; New York, 2005).

20 *Joinville's Chronicle of the Crusade of St. Lewis*, Book I, in Villehardouin and Joinville, *Memoirs of the Crusades*, trans. F. Marzials (London, 1908), 139.

21 Paul Archambault, *Seven French Chroniclers: Witnesses to History* (Syracuse, NY, 1974), 78–9.

22 Nancy Partner, *Serious Entertainments: The Writing of History in Twelfth-Century England* (Chicago, 1977), 229; Salisbury quote on 212.

23 *The History of the Kings of Great Britain*, trans. L. Thorpe (Harmondsworth, 1966), 79.

24 Suzanne Fleischman, 'On the Representation of History and Fiction in the Middle Ages', *History and Theory* 22 (1983): 278–310, at 305; and Maurice Keen, 'Chivalry, Heralds, and History', in R. H. C. Davis and J. H. M. Wallace-Hadrill (eds.), *The Writing of History in the Middle Ages* (Oxford, 1981), 394–5.

25 *The Chronicle of Novgorod 1016–1471*, trans. R. Michell and N. Forbes (London, 1914).

26 *The Russian Primary Chronicle: Laurentian Text*, trans. S. H. Cross and O. P. Sherbowitz-Wetzor (Cambridge, MA, [1953]).

27 Archambault, *Seven French Chroniclers*, 78–9.

28 Philippe de Commynes, *Memoirs: The Reign of Louis XI 1461–83*, trans. Michael Jones (Harmondsworth, 1972), 57–8.

29 I owe this information to my former colleague Professor Walter Davies of the University of Alberta.

30 Chapters 69–78 of the *Zizhi Tongjian* have been translated into English as *The Chronicle of Three Kingdoms (220–265)*, trans. Achilles Fang and ed. Glen W. Baxter, 2 vols. (Cambridge, MA, 1952).

31 Quoted in Conrad Schirokauer, 'Chu Hsi's Sense of History', in Robert P. Hymes and Conrad Schirokauer (eds.), *Ordering the World: Approaches to State and Society in Sung Dynasty China* (Berkeley, CA, 1993), 205.

32 Quoted ibid., 202.

33 Robert M. Hartwell, 'Historical Analogism, Public Policy and Social Science in Eleventh and Twelfth Century China', *American Historical Review* 76 (1971): 696–7, 701, 710.

34 Quoted in the translators' introduction to *A Tale of Flowering Fortunes: Annals of Japanese Aristocratic Life in the Heian Period*, trans. W. H. and H. C. McCullough (Stanford, 1980), 7.

35 Delmer M. Brown and Ichirō Ishida (trans. and eds.), *The Future and the Past: A Translation and Study of the Gukanshō, an Interpretative History of Japan written in 1219* (Berkeley, CA and Los Angeles, 1979), 23, 198–9.

36 Following the first two ages, each a millennium, of the 'former' and 'middle' times of the Law.

37 *A Chronicle of Gods and Sovereigns*, trans. H. Paul Varley (New York, 1980), 269.

38 Ibid., 16, 49, 60.

39 The *Samguk Sagi* says that Kim Yu-sin's sister Munhŭi was the consort of King Muryŏl and the mother of King Munmu. It also states, however, that Kim Yu-sin's father was Sŏyŏn, also called Sŏun. The 'Sŏun' in the genealogy given here is possibly a corruption of Sŏhyŏn.

40 Several centuries earlier than modern Korean historians believed these kingdoms developed.

41 Peter Hardy, *Historians of Medieval India: Studies in Indo-Muslim Historical Writing*, 2nd edn (New Delhi, 1997), 20.

42 Quoted in Harbans Mukhia, *Historians and Historiography during the Reign of Akbar* (New Delhi, 1976), 16.

43 The work was continued right up until the early seventeenth century by four other
   Sanskrit-language historians who followed Kalhaṇa: Jonaraja (early fifteenth century),
   Srivara (later fifteenth century), Prajyabhatta (early sixteenth century) and Suka (early
   seventeenth century).
44 From Kalhaṇa, *Rājataraṅgiṇī: The Saga of the Kings of Kasmīr*, trans. R. S. Pandit (1935;
   New Delhi, 1968), 4–5 (first Taranga or section, verses 3–15).
45 *The Blue Annals*, ed. G. Roerich (Calcutta, 1964–5).

4

History in the Early Modern Empires

Europe, China, Islam

Introduction

It is a theme of this book that 'history' can occur in a variety of shapes, forms, languages and modes of communication. Virtually all of the historical cultures observed up to this point postulated a close connection between writing and the representation of the past, though we have also seen that a good deal of history was recounted orally, from the Greeks through the Norse sagas. Western histories of historiography have adopted, virtually without question, the assumption that writing is a precondition for history – *pas d'écrire, rien d'histoire* – and the derivative conclusions that, therefore, any people without a writing system cannot have 'real history'. After two generations of work by Africanists on oral tradition and by Latin Americanists on indigenous forms of historical representation, that position is surely no longer sustainable. Granted, a history remembered or a history conveyed principally through picture or symbol is not the *same* as a history contained in an alphabetic text, and is subject to different sorts of limitations and possibilities. But it can no longer be seriously put that the pre-modern world beyond Eurasia consisted of 'peoples without history', any more than it can be claimed that books and paper (as opposed to stone, wood, parchment – or, for that matter, floppy disks) are indispensable as vessels for the containment of compositions about the past. In short, as one recent commentator has asserted, it is 'deeply simplistic and ultimately false to divide societies (or cultures) into those that are historical and those that are not'.[1]

It is necessary to be explicit about this point as we leave the Middle Ages behind and encounter the profound tremors that began with the Renaissance, continued with the Reformation and ended in the intellectual ferment of the seventeenth century. In the history of historiography, the achievements of the Renaissance humanists and their heirs have been honoured with a special place, second only perhaps to the great discipline-founders of history's 'golden age', the nineteenth century. Given this, it becomes especially hard to resist seeing the early modern era, from about 1450 to 1700, as defined by anything other than the triumph of humanism, philology, a sense of distance from the past and a partial return to classical narrative models. These developments were momentous, and have been justly celebrated, but if we widen the lens to include equally sophisticated historical cultures to the east, they lose some of their presumed uniqueness.

A second theme of the book is the process whereby disparate and disconnected historical cultures gradually became aware of and intermittently interacted with one another. Trans-regional economic and cultural cross-fertilization had been at work for several millennia by the sixteenth century on all the world's inhabited continents. Religious conversion (voluntary or involuntary) and trade, along older pathways such as the Silk Roads and through cities and ports, had ensured that echoes of one civilization could be found far from its homeland, the spread of Buddhism, Christianity and Islam providing major examples. So did warfare, and in nearly every case of conquest there were also instances of resistance or mere outward conformity to alien values. The empires of middle and late antiquity, Persia, Rome, Han China, Maurya India, had been multiethnic and complex, as were their Byzantine, Mongol and Arabic successors. By the end of the sixteenth century the known globe would be much larger, but it would still be dominated by transnational states, both literal empires (in the formal sense of 'being ruled by an emperor') and republican or monarchical regimes with 'imperial' ambitions. Some of the empires, such as those of the Mughals, Ottomans and Spanish Habsburgs, were new; others, like the German-dominated Holy Roman Empire, were old. A few (Spain, Portugal, France) complemented European conquests with overseas expansion while others (England, the Dutch Republic) gradually turned their back on the continent and focused on the Americas or Asia. Most of these states remained multilingual, religiously diverse and ethnically mixed. Contact and exchange thus occurred within the boundaries of these empires, between them, and outside them with countries beyond their orbits, not least of all in the continents that lay between the Atlantic and Pacific, blocking the Europeans' dream of a western oceanic route to the Orient.

The early modern period would see considerably greater exposure than the late medieval of one civilization to another's pasts and its methods of preserving them. The consequences of this were uneven. European historians, like European missionaries (not infrequently the same people), continued, for the time being, to have at best a marginal impact on their Asian counterparts. Out in the Atlantic, in the Americas and in sub-Saharan Africa, it was a different story. There, the process of contact, linked not merely to commerce but to conquest and religious conversion, proved much more potent – at times aggressively destructive but also creative. Similarly, the greater Islamicization of India achieved by the Mughals, though not nearly as thorough as the Christianization of American conquests, did have lasting effects on the historical writing of South Asia. In our next chapter, we will visit the areas into which Europe expanded between the fifteenth and seventeenth centuries, in particular the Americas, where Europeans would find very different forms of historical memory and historical representation. The present chapter is concerned with what the Europeans themselves, and the great empires of the Islamic and Asian worlds, had developed.

Renaissance and Seventeenth-Century Europe

In 1487, five years before his own death (and the more memorable occurrences of Columbus' first voyage and the driving of the Moors from their last stronghold in Granada), a Castilian named Diego Rodríguez de Almela (1426–92) had printed, in his home town of Murcia, a little book he had written called *Valerio de las estorias escolásticas e de España* ('A Valerian Compilation from Sacred Histories and Histories of Spain'). This renders the famous deeds of Spain's historical personages through the ages, accompanied by a supporting cast of biblical figures, as examples to illustrate moral points in the manner of the first-century AD Roman moralist and rhetorician Valerius Maximus. Almela himself is a minor footnote in the history of history. A mid-ranking priest who was in the patronage of a powerful bishop, he for a time served as chaplain to Isabella of Castile, and as a propagandist to the queen and her husband Ferdinand of Aragon, both of whom had more notable writers in their talent pool.[2] Among his other pastimes, Almela collected and abridged histories, generally showing a blithe disregard for chronology; his *Compendio historial*, drawn from early royal chronicles, was justifiably ignored. But with the *Valerio*, written many years earlier, he hit on a modest bestseller, by late fifteenth-century terms. Reprinted sixteen times before 1600 (after which its popularity waned), Almela's book would be widely read both in Spain and in the New World. It would be only one of a number of Renaissance texts to find in the past, and in the lives of worthies recent or remote, illustrations of moral principles; Niccolò Machiavelli's *The Prince*, written some three decades later, though focused on political reality rather than abstract morality, is not remarkably different in its approach, which begins from precept and then finds its practical exemplification in episodes from the past.

Almela, though very far from being among the best historians of the era, thus exemplifies the Renaissance outlook on history as a pool of examples. Historians from the fifteenth to the seventeenth century believed overwhelmingly that the primary purpose of history was didactic. While medieval writers considered history to have an educative function, its place in their hierarchy of learned culture was middling at best. The Renaissance promoted history several rungs up the intellectual ladder and made it in equal parts a stern enforcer of the status quo and a powerful weapon to brandish in pursuit of radical and often violent change. As one scholar has written, 'history put human beings in charge of their own affairs and gave them the liberty to differ ... In those days, history was the stuff of revolution.'[3] Knowledge of the past itself promoted change. However, it was just as much the stuff of kings and their ministers, and across Europe, the old medieval 'mirror of princes' literature got a second wind. Europe was not unique in this respect: the three great Islamic empires to the east (see below), the Ottomans, Safavids and Mughals, each had their equivalents of historically informed 'advice literature'.[4]

Renaissance humanists enthusiastically appropriated Greek and especially Roman authors as their models of style, genre and suitable content. This was true across many areas of intellectual activity from the mid-fourteenth century on, but the rediscovery of classical texts and categories would have wide-ranging effects on historical thought and writing, not least because from the mid-fifteenth century, the advent of printing permitted the easier replication of texts in larger numbers. Over the course of two centuries this would also create something new: a public appetite for history well beyond the princely courts and noble households. Yet history still remained overwhelmingly the property of only one sex, a historic imbalance now deepened by emerging notions of gender and reinforced by humanist works which parroted the ancient notion that the historian must be a *man* of affairs living in the public arenas of politics, battlefields and commerce, not the private spheres of children, religious devotion and domesticity (see Box 12).

Intellectual and cultural historians have long suggested that the Renaissance signalled a shift in thinking about the past in relation to the present. What were the hallmarks of this? First, a mounting sense of remoteness from classical times and an accompanying urge to reconnect with them bestowed a temporal perspective absent in much medieval writing. This took longer to mature than is usually acknowledged, but by the early seventeenth century a 'sense of anachronism' is routinely if inconsistently discernible in various media, for instance in art and in drama: it was increasingly difficult to portray Julius Caesar or Alexander the Great as medieval Crusaders or Renaissance *condottieri* without at least being aware that this was an artifice. This new sensitivity did not occur equally fast across all Europe: the acute awareness of change, of ruptures between past and present, that one finds in Florentine historians of the sixteenth century is rather less obvious in their Venetian counterparts, fixed on the imagined stability of their aristocratic republic; it is nearly absent in contemporaneous Spain, where one historian, Pedro Mexía, could publish a bestselling account of the Roman emperors from Augustus

Box 12   Women and History in Renaissance Europe

There are signs of a female interest in the past, beginning with the early fifteenth-century scholar Christine de Pizan and continuing through the seventeenth century. Women were highly active as readers of history during this time. Humanist writers on education such as Leonardo Bruni would recommend history, somewhat selectively, as a suitable topic for female edification. Women also began, more slowly, to write about the past themselves. Much of this writing occurred within older forms, such as the chronicle, or in philological and antiquarian research into the past, and it often eschewed the political and military concerns of male historians. The late medieval and Reformation periods, for instance, saw northern European women active as chroniclers and memorialists, especially nuns in a number of Catholic religious orders, who wrote for a combination of hagiographic, familial, commemorative and institutional motives. By the later seventeenth century, women were beginning even to venture cautiously into the writing of full-blown narrative histories, though generally cloaked under some other name such as 'Lives'. The English Puritan Lucy Hutchinson wrote such a work around the life of her husband, an officer in the English Civil War. Women were also frequently the sources of oral information used by male authors: the mestizo historian Garcilaso de la Vega, El Inca (see Chapter 5 below), refers specifically to having taken his information about the early Incas from his own mother and those of his friends, and seventeenth- and early eighteenth-century English local historians did likewise. This early inclination of women to involve themselves in family history, and their increasing comfort working in an archival setting, would quietly blossom by the eighteenth century into a much broader interest in the past.

to Charles V as if these were all members of the same line, a Japanese-style single dynasty without even the minor gear-shifting of the *translatio imperii*.

A more period-specific visual sense of the past was slower to develop, though archaeological discoveries, especially the ruins of Rome and of former Roman encampments across Europe, soon stimulated this too. The art of the time displays an ambivalence to this new perspective with respect to antiquity, often simultaneously recognizing the distance and eliding it, as in the *Alexanderschlacht*, a painting Duke William IV of Bavaria commissioned in 1528 (Fig. 22). In it the artist Albrecht Altdorfer (who had consulted the court historiographer, who in turn

Figure 22 | *Die Alexanderschlacht*, or 'The Battle of Alexander at Issus', 333 BC. Painted by Albrecht Altdorfer, 1529.

had looked in the first-century AD biographer Quintus Curtius Rufus) painted an ancient battle in a temporally neutral and dateless *Historie* which to the viewer invokes more recent episodes such as the 1525 Battle of Pavia. The routine placing of patrons' likenesses in secular and biblically themed painting, sometimes with period-appropriate dress, sometimes not, is another example. It is as if, having un-covered a vast distance, artists were searching for the visual equivalent of a worm-hole through which different temporal planes could be viewed simultaneously.

Much more quickly, however, there developed a sense of *linguistic* change. The humanists of the fifteenth century followed the fourteenth-century poet Petrarch

Box 13   **The Donation of Constantine**

No fakery crashed to earth more loudly than the notorious Donation of Constantine. It was not news that this was a work of doubtful provenance – it had been a suspicious annoyance throughout the late Middle Ages. But philology gave to its adversaries, previously armed only with logical clubs, a sharp new rapier, wielded most deftly by Lorenzo Valla. One of the great textual scholars of his or any age, Valla's philological achievements ran far beyond his demolition of the Donation and one or two other *faux*-antique texts. In the 1430s and 1440s, while in the employ of Alfonso 'the Magnanimous', king of Naples, Valla both started a narrative history of the Aragonese conquest of Naples and used his philological skills to demonstrate precisely and definitively that the Donation included language completely inconsistent with its supposed age of composition. Valla's demolition job proved definitive, and over the next three centuries there would be many more philological explorations of the legitimacy of an inherited ancient or medieval text, or clarifications of its true period of origins.

in acknowledging the desert of a *medium aevum* standing between them and the vanishing point of antiquity back towards which they stared (it is from this recognition that the modern Western tripartite division of time into antiquity, the 'Middle' Ages and modernity was born). Above all, they were devoted in the first instance to the restoration of Latin to its classical purity, though the notion that a language could be transplanted in an archaic and frozen form on to a different era actually negated 1,500 years of gradual change and introduced a different sort of anachronism. One of the early consequences of this new study of language was the realization that all was not well with the textual and documentary heritage of the previous twelve or so centuries. Perhaps the most notorious of these was the Donation of Constantine, discredited by the greatest philologist of the mid-fifteenth century, Lorenzo Valla (c. 1407–57) (see Box 13). Other forgeries created in the Middle Ages soon began to fall by the wayside, including the histories of an infamous textual mischief-maker named Giovanni Nanni (c. 1432–1502), better known as 'Annius of Viterbo'. Annius became an object of contempt to several philologers who methodically tried to discredit his *Antiquities*, a work which claimed to include, among others, the lost texts of Manetho and Berossus (see Chapter 1 above). The textual editor Isaac Casaubon (1559–1614), a French Protestant exiled in England, performed a Valla-like analysis of yet another fraud, the *Corpus*

Hermeticum, a recently rediscovered set of works ascribed to a fictitious Egyptian contemporary of Moses, redating them to late antiquity. In this attack on fakery, the cure was not always better than the disease, and there was madness in a good deal of this 'method': Johannes Goropius Becanus (1519–72) wanted to demolish Annius simply to clear the way for his own pet theory that the Dutch had once inhabited the Garden of Eden. For many spurious or misdated texts, the process of exiting the stage of true history was a long one, not least because the forgers themselves were often men of talent and knowledge. And there was a further problem: if a source was thoroughly discredited, what was to be put in its place? The early modern mind, even more than the medieval one, was uncomfortable leaving gaps in the record.

The rediscovery of particular ancient historians, and ebbs and flows in popularity among them, restored the writing of biography and history as continuous narrative, in neoclassical Latin and vernacular languages, in place of the chronicles that had dominated for the past several centuries. The humanists, who had an interest in promoting the superiority of their manner of writing history (often with a whiff of social snobbery towards their less learned chronicling brethren), did a superb hatchet job on their immediate predecessors, one which modernity has had a tough time seeing past. 'Stupid, inexperienced, foolish scribblers', the German humanist Johannes Aventinus (1477–1534) called the chroniclers,[5] while a few decades later an Englishman would annotate his copy of Livy with criticism of the 'many asses who dare to compile histories, chronicles, annals, commentaries.'[6] Chronicles by no means disappeared, and their loss of popularity occurred at widely varying paces from one end of Europe to another – Spain's humanists, though outwardly adopting classical models, were initially more influenced by the northern Renaissance occurring in other parts of the Holy Roman Empire than by Italy, and there was thus rather less repudiation there of the chronicling heritage. In England, early experiments in Italianate historiography failed to catch on, and it would not be till very near the end of the sixteenth century that classically modelled historical writing became firmly established.

This was not just the slower arrival of new fashion in the more remote corners and backwaters of Europe: there were legitimate reasons for keeping the old-style chronicler in business, especially as humanist historical writing became increasingly selective and elitist in its focus and, in some realms, tied itself to the coattails of ruling princes or ambitious patricians. The chronicle's inclusiveness and freedom from the reintroduced tyranny of classical poetics made it the genre of choice for those, such as the collaborators in that cornucopia of British history known as Raphael Holinshed's *Chronicles* (1577 and 1587), who wished to include a wide variety of materials, especially stories about the middling sorts of folks who fell below the radar of humanist historical narrative. As they had been doing for two centuries or so in Italy and Germany, chronicles also offered an excellent outlet for the civic consciousness of growing northern European cities, and in the more remote parts of the continent retained their dominant position rather longer. Russia, for instance, largely missed both the Renaissance and the accompanying printing revolution, though classical and western European historians were certainly read in Muscovy – the Jesuit-educated Croatian scholar and pan-slavist, Juraj Križanić (Yuriy Krizhanich, c. 1618–83) took Livy, Plutarch and Polybius with him into Siberian exile in the 1660s. For the most part, however, the historiographic tradition that began with the *Primary Chronicle* only ended with the mammoth *Nikonian Chronicle* completed at the court of Ivan IV, the Terrible (r. 1547–84).[7] Urban chronicles endured in many cities, Frankfurt am Main for instance, right through the eighteenth century. But these survivals should not obscure the crucial point: throughout much of Europe, the chronicle first lost the privileged position it had enjoyed for several centuries, and soon became the backward, lumbering poor cousin of a slicker, more literary form of historical narrative favoured by the educational elites and their most powerful readers.

The models for this new history were to be found in antiquity. Recovering the classical heritage essentially meant finding and then emending old texts into modern manuscripts that gave the most accurate reading of the author possible. This salvage effort rarely meant finding a completely unknown ancient author, but it frequently involved finding, buried in a manuscript long preserved in a monastic house, new works, additional sections of known works and older versions of texts by authors such as Livy. One by one, reformed Latin editions of Roman historians appeared. The Greeks were not far behind as émigré Byzantine scholars trained attentive Italian pupils; thus Poggio Bracciolini would translate Xenophon and parts of the *Historical Library* of Diodorus Siculus, in addition to composing his own Latin history of Florence. By 1700, some 2,355 editions of twenty Greek and Roman historians were in print,[8] the latter being by a wide margin more frequently published than the former. Although as early as 1500 some humanists were grumpily warning against becoming slaves to Cicero, the spectres of the ancients lurked at the shoulder of their early modern successors, as if ready to chide them in their efforts. Both the quantity of classical work and its quality made Renaissance writers reluctant to reinvent the ancient wheel of historiography – what vain fool thought he could improve, at some centuries' distance, on Tacitus and Livy? So instead, they turned to narrating the post-classical past, and to non-narrative, 'antiquarian' types of scholarship that we will take up shortly.

The beginnings of humanist historical narrative, in Latin, and modelled on the ancients, are by consensus located in the early fifteenth century. Leonardo Bruni of Arezzo (c. 1369–1444) is justly singled out both for the quality of his historical writing and the originality of its form. Chancellor of the Florentine Republic from

Figure 23 | Sallust, depicted in fresco, c. 1500–3 by Luca Signorelli (1441–1523). Duomo, Orvieto, Italy.

1427 till his death, Bruni had begun his history nearly twenty years before, supposedly inspired to write it by the momentous occasion, in the years around 1400, of Florence's underdog victory over neighbouring Milan. The *Historiae Florentini populi libri xii* ('Twelve Books on the History of the Florentine People') was presented to Florence's ruling council in 1439; its author's self-conscious realization that he was doing something fundamentally different from the chroniclers of a previous age, and his rhetorical demotion of earlier works to the status of mere compilations which his shaping pen would turn into true history, signalled a conscious and intentional break with the medieval chronicle. 'History', Bruni notes in his preface, 'requires at once a long and connected narrative, causal explanation of each particular event, and the public expression of one's judgment about every issue.'[9]

Bruni had already translated a few of the Greek historians into Latin, including Polybius, Thucydides and Sallust (Fig. 23), all of whom made a strong impression on him. His own *History* was known both for its confident Latin style and its apparent scrupulous accuracy. While it was based on earlier chronicles, it may have been supplemented with direct research in the archives. Critical of his sources, he was well aware of their discrepancies and conflicting stories. The organization of the *History* is also innovative. Though Bruni follows a year-by-year chronological order, it is a modification of the annalistic form of the ancient Romans, Livy among them, not a continuation of late-medieval Florentine chroniclers such as Giovanni Villani. He also brought back to prominence that characteristic feature of classical historians, the invented oration, which another humanist, Giovanni Pontano, would eventually call the soul of history. The *History* was recognized as brilliant at the time, and its admirers in other cities optimistically proclaimed that it heralded the arrival of a new age of Livy. Locally, the reception of his history was so positive that Bruni is perhaps the first figure since antiquity to have been commemorated publicly for his historiographic achievement: the citizens of Florence erected a marble monument in the church of Santa Croce in which the great humanist is captured recumbent, holding his history to his chest.

Bruni did not simply mimic classical historiography; he lived at a different time, and came to his historical outlook not only through what he read but through his personal experiences. Conversely, while it is tempting to regard Bruni methodologically as a proto-modern, a member of a chain of greats stretching from Thucydides to the critical scholars of the nineteenth century, this is to go too far in the other direction. For all his interest in the past and his willingness to demolish legend, the Florentine chancellor was no dispassionate practitioner of history for history's sake: both in the history and elsewhere he asserts that it is the first duty of the historian to provide guidance for modern problems. The 'usable past' of the Middle Ages was still very much in play, now in the context of public service.

The story was the same in Venice, Milan, Ferrara, Mantua, Rome and other cities from the mid-fifteenth to late sixteenth centuries. Most of the historians of this day are now largely forgotten, but several were outstanding and wide-ranging scholars like the great textual editor (and another Florentine chancellor) Poggio Bracciolini (1380–1459) and, a century later, Paolo Giovio (1483–1552), who is notable among other things for establishing a classically modelled sub-genre of 'histories of one's own time'. By the end of the fifteenth century, a number of humanists had also written letters or prefaces to longer works, outlining the value of history, and the new scholarship had even produced its first theoretical forays into the proper style and content of history, and on the nature of historical truth, contained in the Neapolitan Giovanni Pontano's (1426–1503) dialogue *Actius* (1499) and in the brief *Praelectiones de historia* (1471) by Pomponio Leto (1425–98), an eccentric former pupil of Valla who carried his love of antiquity so far as to establish his own academy, the members of which met in Leto's Roman house and addressed each other by classical names.

The political crises and religious wars that afflicted Europe for nearly three centuries provided a profound stimulus to historical writing in general and to thinking about the etiological or *linear* relationship between past and present – the road that brings us from then to now – in particular. To use our earlier metaphor, it helped transform the past from a lake into a river, a revisioning that the eighteenth century would solidify. Time and again in early modern Europe the conventional, exemplary use of the past gave way, in the face of violent political or social change, to explanation of the origins of the world in which contemporaries lived. In early sixteenth-century Italy, several decades' worth of grand humanist narratives *après* Livy had already been produced; historians had almost run out of things to write about when the French and Spanish invasions forced a refocusing of their attention on recent events. Another Italian, Enrico Caterino Davila (1576–1631), provided a similar account of the French religious wars of the late sixteenth century in which he had participated, while the moderate politician Jacques-Auguste de Thou (1553–1617) recounted recent French history using Paolo Giovio's genre of a *History of his Own Time*. Mid-seventeenth-century English historians abandoned the Elizabethan and Jacobean practice of writing 'Lives and Reigns' of medieval kings and produced a rash of histories about the early Stuarts themselves and the civil wars that now beset them. When Edward Hyde, Earl of Clarendon (1609–74), advisor to the executed King Charles I (r. 1625–49) and later Lord Chancellor to his son, set about writing an account of those wars during two separate periods of exile, he renounced looking any further back for causes than the start of his martyred royal master's reign. Clarendon's *History of the Civil Wars and Rebellion*, unpublished until the early eighteenth century, would come to be regarded by many readers as the English-speaking world's closest replication of a Thucydidean narrative.

The contrast between these two ways of looking at the past is nowhere better illustrated than by comparing two near-contemporary Florentine historians caught in the transition from republic to monarchy and the disorders of war and invasion, Francesco Guicciardini (1483–1540) and the more notorious Niccolò Machiavelli (1469–1527), each of whom wrote histories of Florence and, in Guicciardini's case, a lengthier history of Italy. Both men authored works of political wisdom, Machiavelli memorably yoking together examples from the recent and remote past in *The Prince* and *Discourses*. Few passages illustrate the Renaissance's intense love affair with antiquity, and its sense that it was conducting a dialogue with the great authors of the past, so much as Machiavelli's description, written during his political eclipse, of his evenings of repose:

When evening comes, I return home and enter my study, on the threshold I take off my workday clothes, covered with mud and dirt, and put on the garments of court and palace. Fitted out appropriately, I step inside the venerable courts of the ancients, where, solicitously received by them, I nourish myself on that food that *alone* is mine and for which I was born; where I am unashamed to converse with them and to question them about the motives for their actions, and they, out of their human kindness, answer me.[10]

Figure 24 | Francesco Guicciardini. Nineteenth-century statue of the Florentine historian sculpted by Luigi Cartei. Uffizi, Florence.

Guicciardini (Fig. 24 and Extract 15), Machiavelli's more pessimistic junior, had as a young man written a history of Florence; but he grew less interested than Machiavelli in pursuing the history of his city back to barbarian times than in narrating the unfolding of its and all Italy's current troubles (the invasions by French and Spanish armies and the erosion and collapse of republican independence). Perhaps as a consequence of this Thucydidean focus on the very recent past, he was more attentive to detail and, unusually for his day, more sceptical about the capacity of past examples to serve the present, owing to variations of circumstance between superficially similar historical situations. 'How wrong it is to cite the Romans at every turn', he commented in his *Ricordi*, a set of maxims and thoughts. 'For any comparison to be valid, it would be necessary to have a city with conditions like theirs, and then to govern it according to their example. In the case of a city with different qualities, the comparison is as much out of order as it would be to expect a jackass to race like a horse.' This is an important insight that anticipates much later 'historicist' thinking on the uniqueness of discrete historical events and

15: The Spread of Humanist History in Northern Europe: Fenton's Translation of Guicciardini

extract

Having in hand to write the affairs and fortunes of Italy, I judged it convenient to draw into discourse those particularities that most nearest resemble our time and memory, yea even since the self princes of that country calling in the armies of France, gave the first beginning to so great innovations. A matter, for the variety, greatness, and nature of such things, very notable, and well worthy of memory: and for the heavy accidents, hateful, bloody and horrible; for that Italy for many years was travailed with all those sorts of calamities with the which principalities, countries, and mortal men, are wont to be afflicted as well by the just wroth and hand of God, as through the impiety and wickedness of other nations. The knowledge of these things so great and diverse, may minister many wholesome instructions as well to all men generally, as to every one in particular, considering that, by the trial, consent and demonstration of so many examples, all princes, people, and patrimonies may see (as a sea driven with diverse winds) to what inconstancy human things are ordained, and how harmful are the ill measured counsels of princes, many times prejudicial to themselves, but always hurtful to their people and subjects, especially when they are vainly carried away either with their singular errors, or private covetousness, without having any impression or remembrance of the ordinary changes of fortune, whereby turning to the domage and displeasure of others, the power which is given them for the safety, protection, and policy of the whole, they make themselves, either by want of discretion, or too much ambition, authors of innovations and new troubles.

Selection from the opening page of Geoffrey Fenton's 1579 English translation of Francesco Guicciardini's *Historia d'Italia*, as *The historie of Guicciardin: conteining the warres of italie and other partes* (London: T. Vautroullier, 1579), 1. Spelling has been modernized from Fenton's Elizabethan English. Print ensured that histories had a much wider availability than during the Middle Ages, a typical edition by 1600 being 1,000 to 1,200 copies. Translations such as this ensured that readers without reading ability in a historian's language could still read a number of histories from other countries, especially France or in this case Italy.

---

the incommensurability of different historical epochs.[11] It is no coincidence that Guicciardini, who also rejected his predecessors' reliance on earlier chronicles in favour of source materials from the Florentine archives, eventually found a modern disciple of sorts (albeit a critical one) in the great nineteenth-century German historian Leopold von Ranke.

The discovery of non-archival – but no less 'historical' – sources including physical ruins, statuary, coins and buildings in Italy and elsewhere nurtured an ancillary branch of historical study often referred to by the generic title 'antiquarianism'. Its origins lay in philology, but also in sensory perception of the remnants of lost times, both linguistic and tangible, and the rupture with the past, especially (at first) the classical past that they signified. Antiquarianism took various forms in different countries, but beginning with Biondo Flavio's (1392–1463) mapping of the topography and antiquities of Roman-era Italy, the results of which he called *Italia illustrata*,[12] its practitioners engaged principally in inquiries into what might be called the non-narrative past. Characteristically, they exploited non-traditional types of evidence such as coins rather than earlier chronicles or even documents. The Frenchman Guillaume Budé (1467–1540) had already explored ancient coins and units of measure in his *De asse et partibus eius* (1514). Others such as the Vatican-based Augustinian scholar Onofrio Panvinio (1530–68) and the Castilian crown historian Ambrosio de Morales (1513–91) followed, gleaning inscriptions from coins, tombs, sherds and steles, and cataloguing the Roman antiquities in their region or country. Major discoveries such as that of the Roman *Fasti* (lists of magistrates and winners of triumphs, excavated in the 1540s) seemed to open up an alternative and more direct passage to the remote past, one less dependent on the historians of antiquity.

By the end of the seventeenth century, antiquarianism had, rather like its more prosperous sister, history, become an umbrella concept for a variety of different activities, from the archaeological study of ancient monuments and prehistoric monoliths, to the deciphering of tombstones, coins and medals, to the cataloguing of natural rarities, including fossils. Local historians in England and elsewhere contributed studies of individual towns or regions and their antiquities, a genre usually known as 'chorography'. The packrat tendencies of late Renaissance 'virtuoso' collectors like France's Nicolas Fabri de Peiresc (1580–1637) or Turin's Cassiano dal Pozzo (1588–1657), though they began as 'curious' collections of things both rare and ancient, man-made and natural, began to merge with the kinds of scientific inquiries practised by the European academicians of the later seventeenth century. By the end of the century, numismatists such as Ezechiel Spanheim (1629–1710) had turned coins and medals from mere decorative illustrations in narrative histories into actual sources of data. Similarly, the early fixation of many antiquaries on heraldry and genealogy had turned by 1700 into an activity that looks a little more like modern archaeology. A good example of the systematic approach applied to man-made objects (in this case to ancient culture as revealed by its artefacts) was Bernard de Montfaucon's (1655–1741) *L'Antiquité expliquée et représentée en figures*, published between 1719 and 1724. Antiquarianism had also evolved on another front so that it pressed up against and often overlapped with another new discourse, 'natural history', and by the early eighteenth century it had acquired the classificatory and empirical inclinations we associate with contemporary scientists such as Linnaeus.

Not all of this erudite scholarship was peripatetic, or even concerned with physical artefacts beyond book or manuscript. A good deal of it was focused, in the manner of Valla or Casaubon, simply on sorting out truth from fiction. In some

cases, sheer common sense incited disbelief. Even a pillager of Livian periods like
Venice's Marco Antonio Sabellico (1436–1506) found it tough to swallow wholesale the story of Romulus' and Remus' infantile adventures among wolves and
shepherds; a century later the much-travelled German geographer Philip Cluverius
(1580–1622) was even more sceptical of the entire Roman monarchical period
on the grounds that the sources for these could not possibly have survived the
city's sacking by the Gauls in 390 BC to have been used by Livy and his predecessors.[13] In other instances more elaborate philological weaponry was deployed, and
among the victims of this purgative campaign, a notable casualty was the good
ship Troy, which having come unscathed through the Middle Ages sailed happily
on till at least the mid-sixteenth century, carrying its multinational crew of Francion, Brutus and friends. At that point, it attracted an international wolf-pack of
humanist sceptics including the German Beatus Rhenanaus (1485–1547), the Italian Polydore Vergil (c. 1470–1555) and a series of French *érudits*. But the Trojans
had their defenders, even now, for humanist opinion was far from unified on this
point, and not always accurate in offering alternatives. The mid-fifteenth-century
historian Enea Silvio Piccolomini (1405–64; from 1458 Pope Pius II), among others, rejected the lingering medieval notion that the Trojans were the ancestors of
the Ottoman Turks (now seeking vengeance on the Byzantine descendants of their
ancient Greek foes) merely to substitute a more suitably barbarous Scythian parentage.[14] Robert Gaguin (1433–1501), an early French humanist historian, doubted
the Trojan origin of the Franks but not the idea of a foundational king Francion
or Francus. Polydore Vergil had argued against the Trojans merely on the basis
of silence in the classical sources; he was pilloried by nationalistic English and
Welsh critics (many of them competent philologists in their own right) reluctant to
part with either Brutus or the somewhat more defensible later hero, King Arthur,
and ironically capable of using good, if wrong, philological arguments in favour
of such a genealogy. So the Trojan hulk still took some time to sink, and it even
threatened to right itself during the seventeenth century when nationalist sentiments required its support, most notably in France. But the trend was clear, and
by 1700 the grip of inherited beliefs in founding kings, postdiluvian giants and
migratory ancient princes had been loosened among the scholarly elite.

Popular culture remained a different matter, and the various chapbooks, ballads
and broadsheets that circulated through Europe well into the eighteenth century,
including the French *bibliothèque bleue* of cheap print, peddled a mixture of romance, legend and history that fed into and sprang back out of oral culture. It is
not that contemporary Europeans did not realize the difference. To the contrary,
the successors to Valla and Bruni were as adamant as any late nineteenth-century
Rankean that fiction was one thing and historical truth another. The problem was
that the authors of fictions tended to portray themselves as real historians, an

effective gambit in a period of low literacy and very limited historical education. The Renaissance retellers of tales such as *Amadis of Gaul* and *Guy of Warwick*, and the French romancers who followed in the late seventeenth century (and English novelists of the eighteenth), would formalize this ironic posture by entitling their own works 'histories'.

Another problem lay in the establishment of precise timelines for the events of history, especially ancient history, and the reconciliation or 'synchronism' of events in different parts of the world and their calendars. If philology was a difficult but respected form of knowledge, the physics of the age, historical chronology was its string theory, briefly at the cutting edge of scholarship. The vast early modern treatises on the dates of Assyrian monarchs and the years of Roman consuls and Greek archons now seem both inaccessible and recondite, and the chronologers included millenarians among their number, some with bizarre and unsupportable theories to explain away problems in the calendar. Others made quirky attempts to fix with certitude dates such as the first day of Creation – perhaps most famously assigned by the Irish archbishop James Ussher (1581–1656) to twilight on 23 October 4004 BC. But chronology also attracted minds of genuine brilliance, with superior learning in languages, history and even astronomy, from Joseph Justus Scaliger (1540–1609), the greatest philologist of his day, and John Napier (1550–1617), a Scottish millenarian who incidentally invented logarithms to assist in his chronological calculations, all the way down to Sir Isaac Newton (1643–1727).[15]

Little of the most sophisticated chronological work, however, found its way into most universal histories, and some, like Johann Sleidan's (1506–56) *De quatuor summis imperiis* ('Concerning the Four Great Empires') or Sir Walter Ralegh's (1552–1618) *History of the World* clung firmly to the simpler periodization provided by the Four World Empires. Universal history in this older form – though not all efforts at global history – would experience its final bloom in a strange, transitional work of the late seventeenth century, Jacques-Bénigne Bossuet's (1627–1704) *Discourse on Universal History*. The book was nominally written for the French dauphin, whose tutor Bossuet had been for several years. Appointed a bishop in 1681, Bossuet was a perennial controversialist whose *Histoire des variations* (1688) was a significant entry in the heated disputes between Catholic and Protestant historians in late seventeenth-century France. He used the opportunity of the *Discourse* to reassert the reliability of the biblical account of history in the face of late seventeenth-century critical scholarship and the early manifestations of deism, while taking shots at more traditional foes such as Jews, late antique heretics and (more subtly) Protestants. Bossuet combined chronology, sacred history and the secular political history of the world all within the covers of one accessible volume, its tone dogmatic but reassuring, giving the reader just enough

16: Bossuet on the Uses of Universal History

Even if history were useless to other men, princes should be made to read it. For there is no better way to show them what is wrought by passion and interest, time and circumstance, good and bad advice. Histories deal only with the deeds that concern princes, and everything in them seems to be made for their use. If they need experience to acquire the prudence of a good ruler, nothing is more useful for their instruction than to add the examples of past centuries to the experiences they have every day. While ordinarily they learn to evaluate the dangers they encounter only at the expense of their subjects and their own glory, history will help them form their judgment on the events of the past without any risk ....

He who has not learned from history to distinguish different ages will represent men under the law of Nature or under written law as they are under the law of the Gospel; he will speak of the vanquished Persians under Alexander as he speaks of the victorious Persians under Cyrus; he will make the Greeks as free at the time of Philip as at the time of Themistocles or Miltiades, the Roman people as proud under Diocletian as under Constantine, and France during the upheavals of the civil wars under Charles IX and Henry III as powerful as at the time of Louis XIV, when, united under that great king, France alone triumphs over all of Europe ....

This kind of universal history is to the history of every country and of every people what a world map is to particular maps. In a particular map you see all the details of a kingdom or a province as such. But a general map teaches you to place these parts of the world in their context; you see what Paris or the Ile-de-France is in the kingdom, what the kingdom is in Europe, and what Europe is in the world.

In the same manner, particular histories show the sequence of events that have occurred in a nation in all their detail. But in order to understand everything, we must know what connection that history might have with others; and that can be done by condensation in which we can perceive, as in one glance, the entire sequence of time.

Selection from 'The General Plan of this Work', in Jacques-Bénigne Bossuet, *Discourse on Universal History* [1681], trans. E. Forster, ed. O. Ranum (Chicago and London: University of Chicago Press, 1976), 2–4.

knowledge to understand the workings of providence in history. Bossuet certainly knew the major works of seventeenth-century chronologers; he endeavoured to present events in a single common timescale, with dates provided parenthetically both BC and *anno mundi* till the birth of Christ, and thenceforth *anno domini* (Extract 16). Underpinning the whole is a global, though Gallocentric, view of history that would provide a point of departure for the very different universal history of the Enlightenment.

The oddities of Bossuet's *Discourse* are even starker when seen in the context of two centuries of French critical scholarship. Philologists and antiquaries from Budé in the early sixteenth century to Jacques Cujas (1522–90) and François Hotman (1524–90) half a century later had studied both language and law (in particular Roman law). Many of them practised the humanist method of legal philology known as the *mos gallicus* (or 'French method' of scholarship), as opposed to the older, late medieval *mos italicus* which had provided commentaries or 'glosses' on Roman legal writings, the contents of which were taken as abstract and timeless principles. Collectively, Cujas, Hotman, François le Douaren (1509–59) and several others formed what amounted to a 'French school of historical study'. This was not a literal 'school' (though many of its adherents were based at the University of Bourges) but rather a distinctive approach to sources that initially stressed textual editing, fixing the historical meaning of words and documents, and understanding laws as time-bound creations of a specific period. It eventually broadened its scope to include the comparison of different legal systems, for instance Roman civil law and local customary law. By the late sixteenth century, a relatively detached study of esoteric points of Roman law had become more urgent in the 'real world', as France ripped itself apart in religious wars. Both there and elsewhere philology was pressed into service to identify the historical basis for certain legal claims, and even to construct cases for the overthrow of tyrannical or (from the Catholic perspective) heretical princes. Hotman did this for the Huguenots in his *Francogallia*, and George Buchanan, the leading Scottish philologer and poet of his generation (1506–82), did so in his great history of Scotland as well as a tract *De iure regni apud Scotos* ('On the Law of Kingship among the Scots'). A succession of seventeenth-century English jurists and pamphleteers argued the issues of whether the Norman Conquest of 1066 had been a 'real' conquest, whether institutions such as parliament preceded it and whether the common law of the land dated from time immemorial, all of which had real implications for contemporary political debates. Even that new upstart, the Dutch republic, built its own 'Batavian myth', a set of laws and freedoms violated by Spain's Philip II, against whom they had justly revolted, or so said the authority on international law and sometime historian Hugo Grotius (1583–1645) in his *De antiquitate reipublicae Batavicae* (1610). During Europe's Enlightenment, no discipline would prove more relevant to historical thinking than law, as one jurist after another turned comparative knowledge of legal systems into broader generalizations about the ascent of man. Seventeenth-century writers on law such as Grotius, John Selden, or the Saxon scholar Samuel Pufendorf (1632–94, briefly Historiographer Royal at the Swedish Court) provide a crucial link between Renaissance legal humanism and the speculative achievements of Scottish, French and German philosophers of history in the eighteenth century. Pufendorf, a narrative historian as well as a legal theorist, issued perhaps the most resounding rejection of the *translatio imperii* in his pseudonymously published work *The Present State of Germany* (1677):

By all that has been said, it will appear how [childishly] they are mistaken, who think the Kingdom of Germany has succeeded in the Place of the old Roman Empire, and that it is continued in this Kingdom; when in truth, that Empire which was seated at Rome, was destroyed many ages before Germany became one Kingdom .... But the different Coronations [and inaugurations] which belong to them do not obscurely shew, that there is a real difference to be made between the Roman Empire and the Kingdom of Germany.[16]

There was a further dimension to all of this, an epistemological one, in the buoyant optimism of some historians that the past could indeed be recovered and represented accurately. One of these, Henri de la Popelinière (1541–1608), even wrote a complete 'History of histories, with the idea of perfect history', sometimes credited (wrongly) as the first tract about the history of historical writing. Another, Jean Bodin (1530–1596), wrote a widely read *Methodus* ('Method') for the reading and understanding of history. This was intended to guide the reader through the thorny thickets of past historians, even providing a chronological bibliography of histories, but the *Methodus* went well beyond this. Bodin was concerned to identify rules for the 'correct evaluation' of histories and (like Polybius) the types of government, 'since history for the most part deals with the state and with the changes taking place within it'.[17] He also wished to dispel certain timeworn schemes such as the 'Four Monarchies', inherited from the Middle Ages and now reappropriated by writers of apocalyptic literature and Protestant propagandists. This was fatally flawed in Bodin's opinion by its conflating of some empires and the ignoring of several others; it had no room, for instance, for 'the monarchy of the Arabs, who forced almost the whole of Africa and a great part of Asia' to adopt their language and religion, or for the Tartars (that is, the Mongols). A European had thus recognized the inherent Eurocentrism of history as practised up to his own time (see Box 14).

The relationship between historians and authority began to change in the early sixteenth century as monarchies consolidated their authority, and big states gobbled up smaller ones. With the notable exception of Venice, much of Italy, the home of humanist historiography, had by 1520 fallen into the Habsburg orbit, and the former republics became subjects of 'princes', the various dukes, grand dukes and other magnates who imposed hereditary rule on previously independent city states; southern Italy, principally the 'kingdom of Naples', had been part of the Spanish Empire for an even longer period. Despite the fact that these 'despots'

Box 14   The *ars historica*

As a manual on reading history, Jean Bodin's *Methodus* soon had plenty of company. He was simply the most politically astute and philosophical among a number of writers determined to impose order on the proliferating species of writing about the past, now threatening to bolt from their classical cages, and to offer guidance to bewildered readers. Describing the genres and forms of history according to well-defined categories, these late sixteenth-century authors of *artes historicae* (arts of history) hearken back, via *quattrocento* musings like Pontano's *Actius*, to Lucian's *How to Write History* in the second century. The Europeans thus largely overcame, in the sixteenth century, their earlier reluctance to theorize about the writing of history. Worshipping at the altar of the ancients impelled them to pay attention to both style and genre, an inclination that turned into a necessity by the century's mid-point when the printing press had multiplied enormously the availability of historical texts. The durability of frauds and pseudo-texts, such as those of Annius of Viterbo, made this a treacherous forest and a host of little books appeared from historically minded *trattatisti* claiming to provide guidance through the woods. The Dutch Protestant Gerhard Vossius (1577–1649) turned the genre in a bio-bibliographical direction in the 1650s with his twin volumes, *De historicis graecis* and *De historicis Latinis* (1651), and subsequent authors began to write manuals devoted more especially to the emerging 'ancillary' disciplines such as numismatics and palaeography, leaving behind the more philosophical reflection practised by Bodin and some of his contemporaries.

were also keen supporters of history (Fig. 25), it has sometimes been suggested that Renaissance historiography lost some of its civic energy in the era of increasingly absolutist monarchs. Certainly historians all across Europe were sensitive to lines they could or should not cross, but this was scarcely new: Bruni had prudently eliminated from parts of his *History* some incidents potentially embarrassing to the powerful Medici. The oft-retold story of the historian Cremutius Cordus, put to death under the Emperor Tiberius (r. 14–37) for praising Julius Caesar's assassins, may have made many a quill quiver in its holder's hand. Jean Racine (1639–99), the great French poet appointed historiographer royal in 1677, would gloss his notes on that Tacitean episode with the comment 'Fear and hatred are the plagues of history.'[18]

Figure 25 | The humanist Antoine Macault reads from his translation of Diodorus Siculus in the presence of Francis I, king of France. From *Les trois premiers livres de Diodore de Sicile*, trans. A. Macault, 1534, parchment.

Following Caesar, or even Commynes, publishing memoirs or commentaries was especially risky, and writers of contemporary or recent history in all parts of Europe had to tread carefully unless, like the Czech historian William Count Slavata (1572–1652), they enjoyed privileged royal sponsorship. Even with such protection, caution was essential. The mild-mannered English schoolmaster-turned-herald William Camden (1551–1623), hired by King James I's government to write a semi-official Latin life of James's predecessor, Queen Elizabeth, had to dance delicately around certain issues such as the execution of the new king's mother, Mary Queen of Scots. Camden's French counterpart and correspondent, Jacques-Auguste de Thou, had to withstand not only recriminations from the crown but from the living survivors of persons named in his text. But the degree of censorship and fear should not be overstated and there are counter-examples of historians, freed from monarchical oversight, speaking their minds and even going to the opposite extreme in order to vilify a ruler. The exiled former friend and advisor of Ivan the Terrible, Prince Andreii Mikhailovich Kurbskii (1528–83), wrote a historical attack on the tsar worthy of Procopius,[19] just as a disgraced English courtier named Anthony Weldon ridiculed James I in a Suetonian portrait conveniently published just after the regicide of that king's successor, Charles I.[20]

There was not yet, of course, anything like total freedom of historical opinion, or even the idea that historians ought always to have such liberty. The Modena-born expert on Roman antiquities Carlo Sigonio (1524–84) found his editions of Livy and the Roman *Fasti Consulares* to be harmless, but he ran afoul of the Catholic church when he moved on to late antique and medieval Italian and ecclesiastical history with his 1571 *Historiae Bononiensis libri VI* ('Six Books on the History of Bologna'), eventually banned from publication by Pope Pius V. The English lawyer and antiquary John Selden's (1584–1654) remarkable synthesis of antiquarian erudition and narrative, *The Historie of Tithes* (1618), was attacked for its perceived hostility to clerical property. The Venetian priest Paolo Sarpi (1552–1623) fell afoul of Rome for his critical *History of the Council of Trent*; translated into English and pseudonymously published, it would become one of the most admired histories of the seventeenth century and the exemplar of a detached, 'impartial' narrative. The *frondeur*-turned-*historiographe* François Eudes de Mézerai (1610–83) was already a frequent target of criticism from the vigilant eyes that policed proper French style and found his prose unworthy of the French Academy; he also fell afoul of Louis XIV's minister Colbert when he published the third volume of his *L'Abrégé chronologique, ou extrait de l'histoire de France* ('A Chronological Summary or Extract from the History of France', 1667–68) and included an account of the origins of certain taxes that did not accord with royal policy. Choosing the wrong side in debates about the origins of a people or its modern heirs could have as serious consequences as the libelling of a living monarch. In Sweden, newly independent of Denmark, King Gustav I Vasa condemned the Lutheran priest and historian Olaus Petrei (Olof Petersson, 1493–1552) for apparent criticism in the latter's *En Svensk Crönika* ('Swedish Chronicle'). Asserting that the Franks were originally Germans and not Trojans earned Nicolas Fréret (1688–1749) a few months in prison as late as 1714, even though learned culture had dispensed with Troy, Francion, Brutus and their friends for over a century.

The converse of censorship in history was history explicitly written as panegyric or propaganda, a practice that the Renaissance took up from previous times and expanded considerably, aided by the printing press. Much medieval historical writing had been undertaken as propaganda for one side or the other in disputes such as the long-running papal–imperial or Anglo–French rivalries. Various Renaissance and seventeenth-century Italian courts had employed humanists to write elegant Latin histories explicitly favourable to their regimes and intended to ensure that a positive image of their achievements would be passed down as fame to posterity. History was the favoured vehicle of Fame, whether good or ill, and nowhere more so than in seventeenth-century France. In continuing the late medieval *Grandes Chroniques* tradition, the French produced all on their own an enormous number of such works, either by 'historiographers royal' or by those aspiring to such appointments; a stream of official or semi-official writers stretches from Robert Gaguin and Paulo Emili at the end of the fifteenth century, to Mézerai and Paul Pellison-Fontanier. Throughout the seventeenth century, history plays, poems, spectacle and the prose narratives of the historiographers royal provided much of the lustre surrounding the Bourbon monarchs of France, culminating in *le roi soleil*, Louis XIV (r. 1643–1715).

The propaganda potential of works in both Latin and vernacular languages, even in an era of limited literacy, was enormous, and it was deployed for a wide range of purposes from territorial aggrandizement to the legitimizing of shaky authority. England's Henry VII (r. 1485–1509) used history effectively to blacken the memory of Richard III, the Yorkist king he had displaced. In the emerging Russian state of the sixteenth century, chroniclers followed some of their medieval predecessors in casting Moscow as a New Israel and (rather later, and to a lesser extent than once supposed) even a Third Rome; absorption of Ukraine in the seventeenth century generated Innokentii Gizel's (d. 1683) *Synopsis*, stressing the historical solidarity between the two countries. By the middle of the seventeenth century, this history-for-hire business had gone 'out of court'. Hack writers and mercenary polemicists were in great demand from kings, cities, ministers and institutions, their services available to the highest bidder; conversely, their enmity was to be avoided at the risk of a published history, unfavourably told, with the dirt flung far and wide in print. The prolific Milanese Gregorio Leti (1630–1701), many of whose works wound up on Rome's Index of Prohibited Books, scared some potential subjects so badly that he was paid off in order *not* to write their histories. The Peruvian-born Luca Assarino (1602–72), official historian to the Bavarian Palatinate, used his position of strength to send his work out to authorities in Genoa and Venice, promising favourable coverage for a price, and hinting at the opposite if appropriate rewards were not forthcoming – the Venetians were given the warning of an unpublished draft especially critical of their conduct in a recent war.

With the Protestant Reformation in Europe, and a century of religious warfare erupting soon after, the inherently polemical capacity of historical writing reached new levels. It was no longer used to promote mere conflicting perspectives or scholarly differences, however vicious, over particular points of fact, but something qualitatively different. The public display of opposed interpretations – what we would now call 'ideology' – began for the first time to splinter historical writing into recognizably conflicting camps, now able to conduct their campaigns in print, the powerful new Weapon of Mass Instruction. Early Protestant reformers, needing to discredit the papacy and the medieval church generally as one long decline from apostolic purity, provided histories such as the multivolume *Ecclesiastica historia*, familiarly known as the *Magdeburg Centuries* (1559–74), so-called after the city in which it was printed and its organization into hundred-year periods. A collaborative venture directed by the Croat reformer Matija Vlačic (Matthias Flacius Illyricus, 1520–75), the *Centuries* recounted the survival of the true church across centuries of papal tyranny. It rapidly found imitators such as the English Protestant John Foxe, whose *Acts and Monuments* (1563), a combination of ecclesiastical history with latter-day martyrology, became a frequently reissued indictment of Catholic persecution and papal tyranny; its influence on anti-Catholic feeling would endure for generations.

Catholic Europe responded in kind, for instance in the *Annales Ecclesiastici* ('Ecclesiastical Annals', 1588–1607) by Cardinal Cesare Baronio. Intended as both a latter-day Eusebius (whose chronology and text both feature prominently in the *Annales*) and as an antidote to the Protestant version of the past contained in the *Magdeburg Centuries*, the Catholic cure outperformed the Protestant disease by a wide margin. Where the *Centuries* was reissued only a couple of times, Baronio's riposte proved a bestseller, reprinted, abridged and continued in dozens of editions up to the nineteenth century. Partisanship would become virtually routine in historical writing during the religious wars across Europe and Britain during the late sixteenth and seventeenth centuries, although, paradoxically, individual authors continued to stress their own impartiality and the bias or falsity of their opponents: from the fifteenth to the eighteenth centuries historians routinely declaimed on the need for a historian to be above 'party', to write *sine ira et studio*, at the very time that conflict among historians was both becoming institutionalized and being played out in the public sphere of print. The other significant feature of church histories, and of historical polemic that drew upon them, is that, like the ecclesiastical histories of late antiquity, they largely ignored the canons of narrative and style so thoroughly worked out by the humanists for the presentation of evidence. Thus the vast trove of histories with a religious focus is loaded with extended quotations, letters, documents and tracts reproduced verbatim. Their authors wanted to win their cases, and the best way to do that remained to drown one's opponent in the evidence of the past.

It is easy to look back at much of this material and recognize its obvious slant, yet it would be a gross error to ignore it, given what it tells us about contemporary uses of the past. Although openly hostile to alternative views, and often naively supposing that a correct or 'perfect' version of the past was achievable, the strength of their convictions led many of these authors to undertake careful research in order to buttress their cases. Indeed, ecclesiastical erudition deployed in the service of faith continued to drive some of the best scholarship of the late sixteenth and seventeenth centuries, as a defence not just against alternative religious beliefs but against the potentially more serious threat posed by a growing subversive tendency called 'pyrrhonism' – essentially a deeply sceptical attitude towards the possibility of recovering the past. Derived ultimately from the ancient writer Sextus Empiricus (*fl.* late second/early third century AD), this was first articulated in passing by the German humanist Henry Cornelius Agrippa (1486–1535), who rather breezily asserted that 'Historiographers do so much disagree among themselves, and do write so variable and diverse things of one matter, that it is impossible, but that a number of them should be very liars.'[21] This was not quite a rejection of history – note that Agrippa only suggests that *some* historians must be liars – and for a time there was little take-up of such ideas. A more profound pyrrhonism began to arouse heightened concern following the publication in 1560 of Francesco Patrizzi's (1529–97) *Della historia diece dialoghi* ('Ten Dialogues on History'), a work which seemed to conclude that history was on the whole a safe bet but pointed to all manner of pitfalls from unreliable sources to deliberate manipulation, and especially François de la Mothe le Vayer's (1588–1672) essay *Du peu de certitude qu'il y a dans l'histoire* ('Of the Uncertainty of History'), which mused on how a classic episode, for instance Caesar's account of the Gallic Wars, would have looked if told by the Gauls. The Elizabethan courtier Sir Philip Sidney, building on Aristotle's ancient preference for poetry over history, asserted the superiority of the poet's world of 'what might be' over the historian's limited and ultimately untrustworthy vision of what was – or actually may only have been.

Building on the chronological works described above and on two centuries of philological technique, the Maurists, French Benedictines at Saint-Germain-des-Prés and other houses, set out to defend the reliability of history, especially church history, through exhaustively rigorous scholarship. They produced editions of the Church Fathers, based on original sources, but their principal contribution was in the formalization of practices connected with the emerging 'ancillary disciplines'. These were the technical skills needed for dealing with late antique and medieval documents, in particular systematic palaeography (interpretation of historical scripts and hands) and diplomatic (knowledge of the structure, layout and conventional formulae of documents). The Bollandists – Belgian Jesuits – commenced the *Acta Sanctorum* ('Acts of the saints'), organized as a month-by-month calendar of feast days, in order to set the lives and deeds of the historical saints on a sounder scholarly footing. Their project continues today and significantly improved the level of source editing then practised.

The most famous among these late seventeenth-century *érudits* is the Benedictine Jean Mabillon (1632–1707), whose major methodological text was intended to defend particular documents whose authenticity had been challenged by another savant, the Bollandist Daniel von Papenbroek (or Papebroch, 1628–1714). Only accidentally did this turn into a wholesale defence of the possibility of accurate history. Mabillon's *De re diplomatica libri VI* ('Six Books on Diplomatic'), which focused on the authenticity of medieval charters, illustrates the shift in focus within the *ars historica* (see above, Box 14) from ruminations about history or its literary merits towards nuts-and-bolts, 'coal-face' work on its sources, though for now mainstream historical narrative remained largely impervious to these developments.

Despite the uncharitable comments of historians of the seventeenth and early eighteenth centuries against document-mongering antiquaries, there was philosophy behind all this erudition, as there had been in the time of Bodin. Mabillon, for one, echoed the older *trattatisti* (a term sometimes applied to the authors of the *ars historica*) in a chapter entitled 'On studying sacred and profane history' in his *Treatise on Monastic Studies* (1691), which defends the utility of historical studies for the religious and outlines the most useful histories for a monk with limited time, along with warnings of traps laid by false histories 'such as the histories of Manethon [*sic*], of Berosus, and others fabricated by Annius of Viterbo and similar impostors'.[22] Such tendencies in evidentiary criticism could, however, have unintended consequences in nurturing unbelief. Both scepticism towards history and the various attempts to limit or contain it coexisted in a complicated debate in which there could be no winner, merely continuing point and counterpoint. The flood of knowledge intended to cleanse the Augean stables of error simply promoted further doubt: the Jesuit numismatist Jean Hardouin (1646–1729) concluded from his study of classical texts and ancient coinage that most of the ancient heritage of arts and letters, even some ecclesiastical texts, were fictions created by medieval monks. The same scepticism that appears in earlier antiquaries' worries about the Trojan legend, in Bodin's dismissal of the old 'Four Monarchies' periodization and in the loosening grip of interpretative frameworks like the *translatio imperii* eventually produced doubts about things previously unassailable. In particular, the literal truth of the Old Testament as a historical source came into question, accompanied by attacks on dogma, such as that mounted by the German pietiest and mystic Gottfried Arnold (1666–1714) in his *Unparteyische Kirchen- und Ketzer-Historie* ('An Impartial History of the Church and Heresies', 1699–1700) and by Deism which was ultimately willing to treat the Old Testament as simply another vessel of the world's myths.

The pyrrhonist tendencies of the later sixteenth century produced in the seventeenth century both reactive affirmations of received traditions (such as Bossuet's) and more thoughtful attempts to address what was now an urgent problem, the very reliability of not just specific traditions, but of *any* historical knowledge.

Some of these efforts had a more secular focus. Francis Bacon's (1561–1626) empirical attempt to build truths from individually verified 'facts' applied, in his judgment, both to the realm of the past and the realm of nature, both of which were best represented by 'histories' – echoes of the old Herodotean notion of a discovery or inventory can here be heard. The Italian philosopher Tommaso Campanella (1568–1639) saw history as the map of experience, both natural and man-made, and even gave it priority over logic and grammar. The French philosopher René Descartes (1596–1650) came at the issue from precisely the opposite perspective. He addressed the problem of moving firm knowledge from the human mind to the exterior world through a process of deduction, but his solution to pyrrhonism in areas like mathematics and religion did little to buttress confidence that knowledge of the past could be similarly verified. Descartes himself vigorously challenged the certainty of any statement not rendered by formal means, which threatened to knock history off the ladder of learned arts that it had only recently scaled.

A recurring controversy in these centuries was the so-called *querelle* (quarrel) between the 'ancients' and the 'moderns'. This began in the sixteenth century with a revolt against the early humanists' rather slavish devotion to imitation of the classics, and continued to develop against a backdrop of significant social and economic change, which some writers refused to accept as inexorably negative. At its core an ongoing argument about the relative merits of modern writers compared with their ancient predecessors, the *querelle* had expanded by the end of the seventeenth century into a wider debate about 'progress' in human learning. It soon took account of the emerging natural sciences, where technology had clearly invented tools (the compass, gunpowder and printing were the examples most often cited) that antiquity had lacked. The growth of scepticism towards received knowledge, and the belief that reason and experience must take precedence over, or at least be adduced to clarify, the revealed truth in scripture, was related to the *querelle*, even if it did not necessarily choose sides. As applied to history, the sceptical tone of the late seventeenth century is perhaps most famously represented in Pierre Bayle's *Dictionnaire historique et critique* ('Historical and Critical Dictionary'), a celebrated book that appeared in the middle of an especially intense period of intellectual speculation and rampant doubt. Bayle (1647–1706) was among the many French controversialist-historians driven abroad for reasons of religion. His *Dictionnaire* appeared in several editions beginning in 1697, and was enormously influential in subsequent decades, though its approach to historical truth – a relentless series of demolition exercises and controversial statements about a wide variety of topics and persons – would ultimately be rejected, since it seemed powerless to erect anything in place of the truths that it challenged. Bayle was scarcely alone in his doubts, however, especially with respect to the status of scripture as a historical source. Another Frenchman, Isaac de la Peyrère (1596–1676), had anticipated this position in 1655; he concluded that the Old Testament chronologies were irreconcilable with the existence of non-biblical peoples and even postulated the existence of a pre-Adamite race. The Jewish-born Dutch philosopher Baruch or Benedict Spinoza (1632–77) antagonized his parents' religion by proposing that the Pentateuch was the work not of Moses but of a much later, post-Exilic author. Churchmen were especially active participants on both sides of these discussions. The French priest Richard Simon (1638–1712) advanced Spinozan doubts as to Mosaic authorship in his *Histoire critique du Vieux Testament* ('Critical History of the Old Testament', 1678). The Swiss-born preacher and professor of ecclesiastical history, Jean Le Clerc (1657–1736), a prolific writer based in Amsterdam, questioned the notion that the scriptures had been directly inspired by God. The son-in-law of the hack-historian Gregorio Leti, Le Clerc took the correction of historical error as a watching brief. The English cleric Thomas Burnet (c. 1635–1715) tried to merge contemporary geology with theology in treating Noah's flood as a historical event, two centuries of philological refinement having now been reinforced by the physical evidence of fossils, bones and other artefacts.

The atmospheric pressure and velocity of erudite knowledge is well captured in the letters between scholars, in the interconnected activities of the many European academies and societies that were founded at this time, and in the earliest journals that circulated learned work in print. There was also intense activity in the area of source publication and criticism. This included both ancient materials and (with an interest not shown previously) those from the Middle Ages, such as the sources of French history edited by the Maurists, or the scholarship in hagiography and imperial Roman history by the Jansenist scholar Louis-Sébastien Le Nain de Tillemont (1637–98), whose writings would prove indispensable to Edward Gibbon in the next century. And a foretaste of the nineteenth century's publication of medieval sources was provided by the works of a prolific Italian priest, the archivist and librarian Lodovico Antonio Muratori (1672–1750).

As the eighteenth century opened, the European historiographical map had been utterly transformed from its appearance less than 300 years before. We can summarize the reasons for and evidence of the change: generation after generation of philologists, the emergence of antiquarian 'erudition', a keener sense of the differences between epochs, the alternately stimulating and limiting influences of ideology and religion, and the willingness to look seriously at the foundations of historical knowledge – all of this magnified through the mechanical marvel of print, the arrival of history as a vendible commercial genre, the virtual extinction of the chronicle as a viable literary form and a considerably higher literacy rate in many parts of the continent. But the map of the world had also been redrawn, and Europe's expansion both eastward and westward would have a further potent impact on historical thought and writing.

Chinese Historical Writing under the Ming

In 1580, an Augustinian priest arrived in Ming China on a mission from Philip II of Spain. Juan González de Mendoza (1545–1618) would spend three years in China before moving on to Mexico and finally back to Spain. Mendoza, a former soldier, was one of many Catholic missionaries to sojourn in China, and in 1586 he became the first European to publish in print a history of the land known to the West for centuries as Cathay. Translated the same year into Italian and soon after into English, the *History of the Great and Mighty Kingdom of China* would become the principal introduction for many readers to the history of the giant in the Far East.[23] By the time Mendoza arrived, the Ming dynasty was already over two centuries old and in rapid decline, the last stages of which would be vividly chronicled for European audiences by a later missionary, the Jesuit Bernard de Palafox y Mendoza (1600–59). The Ming collapse in 1644 brought to a close the final dynasty of Han ethnicity and ushered in the last of all Chinese imperial regimes, the Jurchen (or Manchu as they became after 1636) Qing dynasty. The Ming had themselves recovered China from foreign hands in 1368 when the Mongol Yuan had abandoned China. This restoration of indigenous rule, despite a massive military and naval expansion, proved shaky, and for much of its slightly less than three centuries in power the dynasty was beset both by internecine, factional struggle and by continued pressure from 'barbarians', including the heirs to the ousted Mongols, and neighbouring Southeast Asian countries such as Thailand and Vietnam.

This is also the period during which the Chinese, who already had a sporadic history of encounters with Europe, now came into more intense contact with its culture, especially through missionaries such as Mendoza and the shrewd Jesuits Matteo Ricci and Giulio Aleni. Ricci (1552–1610), whose long sojourn in China under the name Li Madou would eventually earn him an entry in the Ming Standard History, is remembered for his efforts to bridge the gap between Chinese and European cultures and his posthumously published history of the Jesuit mission. He interpreted traditional Confucianism – which he was instrumental in introducing to the West – as an essentially monotheistic ethical system into which he simply had the task of injecting the concept of Christ the Son, while ignoring apparently countervailing currents such as Buddhism and neo-Confucianism. This adaptation applied to history as well, where there was a double bind: reconciling Chinese records not only with the Bible, but also with the new chronology of ancient kingdoms developed by philologists such as Scaliger (see above). Another Jesuit missionary, the cartographer Martino Martini (1614–61), in a 1658 history of ancient China, placed the ancient emperor Fuxi in European chronology, at the early third millennium BC; others identified the emperor with Adam, or Noah, or other prediluvian figures, and the twenty-fourth-century BC flood under the Emperor Yao as identical with the Noachic Deluge. By the end of the seventeenth century, Western knowledge of China had considerably increased, extending to some familiarity with its historical writing. Gottfried Wilhelm Leibniz (1646–1716), one of Europe's most distinguished polymaths, fashioned two centuries of information about China into a full-blown Sinophilic philosophy. He developed an astonishingly accurate – given that he read no Chinese – and sympathetic understanding of Chinese thought, and called for greater exchanges of knowledge between China and Europe, a 'commerce of light'.

The Ming had come and gone by Leibniz's day, their lovely porcelain both an iconic survivor of the dynasty and a metaphor for its fragility. Philosophy had flourished, with a multitude of different schools developing, described early in the succeeding Qing dynasty by the aging former Ming loyalist, Huang Zongxi, in his comprehensive intellectual history of the age, completed in the 1670s, *Mingru xuean* ('Records of Ming Scholars'). Although Huang disparaged other branches of Ming learning,[24] literacy had increased dramatically under the dynasty, as it was doing in early modern Europe. Books were much more widely available, leading to a growth in personal libraries and the circulation of historical works, including some of the Standard Histories, outside the courtly circle of literati to which they had been previously confined. Whereas historical study in previous eras focused largely on past dynasties, Ming historians took a considerably greater interest in the recent past. As in Europe, genres continued to proliferate, and when the Standard History of the dynasty was eventually written, a bibliography of Ming works named ten varieties of historical writings, organized around 1,378 categories, and amounting to nearly 28,000 fascicles. Students in sixteenth-century civil service examinations were asked to reflect on the relative merits of chronologically organized histories as compared with more topically arranged works such as Sima Guang's *Comprehensive Mirror*, recalling the tensions between erudite research and narrative in the West at about the same time.

Despite its prodigious quantity, Ming historiography was a mixed bag when compared with the achievements of the Tang and the Song. On the one hand, more contemporary and near contemporary critiques of official history-writing have survived than in former periods, as have more of what we would deem 'primary sources', in particular the Veritable Records of individual reigns. Moreover, by the sixteenth century, a critical attitude to documents was beginning to appear in the work of less tradition-minded scholars like Wang Shizhen (1526–90; see further below). On the other, there was little sign of further innovation in official historiography, especially in the first century or so of the dynasty when the strict traditionalism of Zhu Xi's twelfth-century neo-Confucianism again dominated intellectual life. Even within the parameters laid down by the earlier dynasties, the practice of official history-writing is generally held to have been inferior; the Ming scholars' Standard History of the Yuan is an especially weak effort. This may have been because of the alien nature of the Yuan dynasty (and residual contempt for it), and a lack of understanding of the Mongol sources, but it is just as likely because of the inordinate haste with which its 212 books were composed in barely a year (1369–70), owing to the compilers' fear of Taizu (the Hongwu Emperor, r. 1368–98), a severe and cruel figure known for punishing officials who had disappointed him. Widely regarded as one of the poorest of the Standard Histories, the deficiencies of the *Yuanshi* were so glaring that it was eventually rewritten in the twentieth century.

There were also changes in the organization of scholarship. The previously independent History Bureau was attached to the Hanlin Academy, a Tang-founded institution with a mandate much wider than historical writing. The Ming ensured the survival of the Veritable Records of individual reigns through an orchestrated process of copying, ceremonial presentation of the master copy to the emperor according to rules laid down in 1403, and taking greater care in their storage. While the construction of daily records or *rili* was initially mandated, the Ming abandoned the long-standing practice, dating back to the Zhou, of recording the daily affairs of court in the 'Diaries of Activity and Repose'. When these disappeared in the 1390s (to be partially restored in the 1590s, late in the dynasty), they took the *rili* with them and thus the basic source from which future historians could write an accurate history of the Ming. This forced the authors of Veritable Records to rely on other types of document such as edicts and memorials for all but about a hundred years of the regime. The weakening of official history was not lost on contemporary scholars such as Wang Shizhen, who observed that 'the national historiography never failed in its task to such an extreme degree as under our dynasty'. Against all this must be weighed both the spreading of historical interests more widely and the encouragement of a number of large encyclopedic works such as the 12,000-volume *Yongle Encyclopedia*.

The most serious criticism of Ming official history was that it was prone to the spectre of political interference to an extent that had not (or so it was supposed) been true under previous dynasties. Cases occurred of previously sealed records being opened and rewritten, for example the Veritable Records of the dynasty's founding Hongwu Emperor. When the latter's successor Jianwen was deposed only four years later by his uncle the Yongle Emperor (r. 1402–24) and then mysteriously disappeared, Yongle decided to rewrite history, burning the records that attested to the legitimacy of his ousted predecessor, having new ones written and then, worried that the new records were themselves inadequate, having them in turn revised. The deliberate revision of events by a single emperor was, however, not the only flaw. The old tendency to glorify the achievements of successful emperors, especially the founders of new dynasties, and vilify the morally deficient, the usurper and the tyrant, came to the fore; Taizu himself became the subject of hagiography, a superhuman, semi-divine figure who rose from humble monk to return China to native rule, complete with visions and direct revelation to him of the Mandate of Heaven.

Paradoxically, the very weaknesses of Ming official historiography promoted creativity in other scholarly spheres. Most notably, private historiography, hitherto a relatively minor proportion of the Chinese historical output, increased substantially under the Ming, sometimes authored by the very same individuals who also contributed to official writings. Song Lian (1310–81), a compiler of the much-maligned *Yuanshi*, was an erudite scholar who, when operating beyond the imperial gaze, was capable of writing good history with criticism only shallowly cloaked by flattery. His *Records of the Sagely Rule of Hongwu* compared the reign of Taizu to that of the revered first Han emperor, but criticized the emperor's severity. Another functionary, Qiu Jun (1421–95), contributed to several officially sponsored works including Veritable Records of two reigns, but he was able independently to write a much more original and insightful work, the *Shishi zhenggang* ('The Correct Bonds in Universal History'), offering philosophical reflections on the course of Chinese events since the Qin.

The volume of privately authored history grew dramatically in the latter half of the dynasty; there were so many unauthorized histories and family chronicles, one commentator observed, that the oxen bearing them perspired and they filled a storage house to the rafters. The boundary between the private and the official is not precise, since authors like Song Lian who contributed to the project of official history also wrote works on their own. Moreover, the extensive copying of the Veritable Records and the relaxation of secrecy concerning them meant that private historians now had access to this most official of regnal histories. But despite the availability of previously restricted sources, many private historians had at best a single vantage point on the past, incomplete information and the freedom to operate without the correction of scholarly peers: in our terms, private historiography was rather like an unrefereed publication, and inspired less confidence. Wang Shizhen, a critic of official history in the sixteenth century, saw both strengths and weaknesses in its private counterparts. He aptly commented that

Official historians are unrestrained and are skilful at concealing the truth; but the memorials and laws they record and the documents they copy cannot be discarded. The unofficial historians express their opinions and are skilful at missing the truth; but their verification of right and wrong and their abolition of taboo of names and things cannot be discarded. The family historians flatter and are skilful in exceeding the truth; but their praise of the merits of [the] ancestors and their manifestations of their achievements as officials cannot be discarded.[25]

More important than the proliferation of private historical writing in itself was the spread of a much more critical attitude to historical writing in general, whether it issued from the Hanlin Academy or from independent authors writing for a popular audience. This was not without precedent. Liu Zhiji's withering criticism of the Tang History Bureau nearly a millennium earlier was echoed in the late Ming historian Tan Qian's (1594–1658) denunciation of the works previously written on the Ming, and in his widespread travels across China in search of reliable sources for what became his own massive history of the dynasty, which Tan completed under the Qing. The difference between criticism during the Tang and that under the Ming is one of scale. Liu had focused on the weaknesses of the History Bureau in particular; Ming critics attacked the entire collaborative history enterprise, along with much else, in works like Wang Shizhen's *Shisheng kaowu* ('A Critical Treatise on the Errors in Historical Works'). The period also witnessed, in tandem with the spread of historical readership and increase in the availability of texts, a proliferation of public debate about the past that resembles the pattern we have seen in contemporary Europe.

Something like French historical scepticism and relativism also emerged in China at this time, the pyrrhonism of late sixteenth-century European sceptics being mirrored in the plaintive cry of Zhang Xuan (*fl.* 1582) that 'Writing a truthful history is difficult!'[26] La Popelinière, Bodin and Bayle each have counterparts of sorts during the Ming, though it is rather unlikely that the Chinese authors, despite Western contact, knew of their French opposite numbers or vice versa. La Popelinière's *L'histoire des histoires* was answered by his older contemporary Bu Dayou's (1512 to c. 1602) *Shixue yaoyi* ('Essential Meanings of Historical Learning'), which described the institutions for official history-writing and its rules, and then proffered critiques of the great historians from Sima Qian through Sima Guang. If Bu was China's La Popelinière, then Qu Jingchun (1507–69) was its Bodin, offering in his *On the Merits and Deficiencies of Historical Learning from Past to Present* a systematic and at times harsh criticism of both the Standard Histories and exegetical works such as Zhu Xi's twelfth-century commentary on Sima Guang. Qu outlined 'four responsibilities' of a historian that read like the mantra of the modern professional association: focusing on the task at hand against other distractions; being patient and deliberate rather than hasty; having a sense of professional devotion to his craft; and collecting sources assiduously such that all publicly available ones are consulted.

Even Pierre Bayle, that pugnacious pre-Enlightenment puncturer of historical myths, finds his match in two Ming authors, both active nearly two centuries before his own time. Zhu Yunming's (1461–1527) *Records of Wrongful Knowledge*, completed in 1522, is a bold attack on historiographic orthodoxy and deflater of great names, for instance showing the founders of the Shang and Zhou dynasties to have been less the selfless destroyers of tyranny and agents of the Mandate of Heaven of popular tradition and more like brutal opportunists and thugs. One of Zhu's successors, Li Zhi (1527–1602), went even further down this sceptical path, so much so that he was thrown into prison, where he committed suicide, for 'daring to propagate a disorderly way, deceiving the world and defrauding the masses'. His openly provocative and aptly named *Cangshu* ('A Book to be Concealed'),[27] organized something like a Standard History, included both annals and 800 biographical sketches. Apart from his judgments on individuals and their motives, which often run diametrically against received opinion, Li promoted something like the 'relativism' that has been noted in Renaissance France, an impatience with universals and what we would now call 'essentialism', noting that what is meritorious to one age may not be to the next, and repudiating the attribution of virtue to past figures on the basis of timeless values. His ability to think beyond the individual indeed makes him the superior of the contrarian Bayle and puts him in the ranks of those, like Bodin and Ibn Khaldūn, who have thought more widely and systematically about the past and how we in subsequent ages see it.

Heirs of Tīmūr: Islamic Historiography among the Safavids, Mughals and Ottomans

The rollercoaster of Mongol triumph and collapse, apart from its impact in China, had left Islam politically divided under a number of successor states to the old Abbasid caliphate. In 1501, what is now Iran came under the rule of one Ismaʻil, who crowned himself Shah, inaugurating the Safavid dynasty (1501–1736). This was the first native dynasty (though it had spent recent centuries in Kurdistan and Azerbaijan) to rule Persia since the seventh century. Among other things, the Safavids, whose origins lay in Islamic Sufism, turned a previously Sunni Muslim population towards the Shiʻism that characterizes modern Iran, and they kept Persia outside the gravitational pull of the Ottoman Empire. Like other new dynasties, the Shahs had an interest in promoting favourable accounts of their origins, and they had inherited a long-standing Islamic practice of using genealogy as a legitimizing authority, a habit shared with European noble and royal houses.

Although they are not remembered as great supporters of Persian literature more generally, historical writing prospered under the Safavids. Ismaʻil (r. 1501–24) himself commissioned separate histories from two 'men of the pen', Sadr al-Din Sultan Ibrahim Amini Haravi and Ghiyas al-Din Khvāndamīr. The commissioning of histories continued under Ismaʻil's successor Tahmāhsb (Fig. 26), peaking under the reign of Shah ʻAbbās I (1588–1629). Long dismissed by orientalists such as the influential Briton E. G. Browne (1862–1926) as 'dull and arduous reading' because

Figure 26 | The Persian Shah Tahmāhsb receives the Mughal Emperor Humayyun. Safavid mural, mid-seventeenth century. Chihil Sutun (Pavilion of Forty Columns), Isfahan, Iran.

of their prolix style and obsession with military matters, the Safavid historians have been rehabilitated by more recent scholarship. The best known example, *Tā'rīkh-I 'Ālam-ārā-yi 'Abbāsī* ('The World-Adorning History of 'Abbās'), was the work of a 'Munshī' or chancery scribe called Iskandar Beg (c. 1560–1632). Like Leonardo Bruni and so many other Renaissance Italian officials-turned-historians, Iskandar Beg put his public experience and his privileged access to official records to good use. Completed in 1629, his *Tā'rīkh* is perhaps the most important source for Safavid history, its introduction reaching back beyond the reign of 'Abbās, the fifth Safavid Shah, to the dynasty's origin. Most of the work focuses on the Shah himself, its subjects ranging from battles, rebellions and court politics to the inclusion of short biographies. Iskandar Beg's work is regarded as one of the finest examples of Persian historiography, notable for both its literary quality and its author's Thucydidean claim to rely only on his own knowledge or that of direct participants in events (Extract 17).

17: Persian Historical Writing under the Safavids: Iskandar Beg Munshī

Events of the Year of the Fowl, corresponding to the Muslim Year 1006/1597–98, the Eleventh Year of the Reign of Shah 'Abbas.

New Year's Day occurred this year on Friday, 2 Sa'bān 1005/21 March 1597. The Shah was at Qazvin, and the weather, for once, was unseasonable, with an overcast sky and steady rain. Winter had not relaxed its grip, and the New Year's festivities had to be postponed for several days because of persistent snow and rain. When the weather at last improved, the Shah held his customary New Year's audience in the Čehel Sotūn hall of the royal palace. Monarchs and princes from many parts and foreign ambassadors were received by the Shah, and offered their felicitations on the occasion of the New Year.

An auspicious event which occurred this year was the birth of the Shah's son, Sultan Moḥammad Mīrzā. Messengers were sent to all parts of the empire to announce the glad news; kettledrums were beaten for several days, and high and low, young and old made the prince's birth an occasion for futher merry-making. Every day the Shah played polo in the Meydān-e Sa'ādatābād, and took part in archery contests. Then, his holidays over, he turned his attention once more to affairs of state ....

[Further on Iskandar Beg relates the Shah's campaign against the rebellious governor of Lorestān later that year, taking up a plot thread begun earlier.]

Shāhverdī Khan, conscious of his past misdeeds and afraid the Shah would march against him, avoided going to Korramābād because it was too close to Borūjerd and Sīlākor. This year, however, because of the excessive heat, and on the advice of his senior chiefs, he had come to Korramābād ....

Shāhverdī Khan never slept peacefully at night, because he knew it was only a matter of time before the Shah moved against him. He had stationed spies to send him word the moment the Shah left Qazvin. In order to put him off guard, the Shah informed only his personal retainers and *moqarrabs* of his real intention, and pretended to the rest of his troops that his destination was Isfahan.

Selection from Eskandar [Iskandar] Beg Munshī, *History of Shah 'Abbas the Great*, trans. Roger M. Savory, 2 vols. (Boulder, CO: Westview Press, 1978), vol. II, 711, 717–18, diacriticals simplified and Savory's notes omitted.

As in Han China centuries earlier, court astrologers played a significant role in Safavid historiography, their functions including both the prediction of auspicious days and the recording of events. The historians themselves, whose works have titles like *The Gist of Histories*, *The Most Beautiful of Histories* and *The Quintessence of Histories*, formed dynasties of their own: both the son and great-grandson of Khvāndamīr would write their own works, as did the son and grandson of the court astrologer and historian Jalal al-Din Munajjim Yazdi, who had authored a history of Shah 'Abbās. The majority of histories written prior to 'Abbās' reign were general works with an ambitious scope equivalent to the Western 'universal history' – an especially prominent genre in early modern Persia. The long familiarity of Muslims with Judeo-Christian culture ensured that their vision of history prior to Muhammad (which features the Fall, Noah and the Flood and other Old Testament episodes) and that of European chroniclers were not remarkably different. There was considerable overlap between Christians and Muslims in the writing of universal or world history, marked by the sharing of certain chivalric heroes, especially Alexander the Great (in Arabic, Iskandar). Later in the dynasty there also appeared historical fiction and drama, both features of contemporaneous European and Ming historical culture.

Safavid-era authors, like their early Islamic predecessors, paid a great deal of attention to genre. Although there is nothing quite comparable in contemporary Islam to Europe's *ars historica*, historians routinely used extended prefaces to explain their intent in writing their work. At roughly the same period that the Neapolitan Giovanni Pontano was penning his *Actius*, the historian Fadl Allah ibn Ruzbihan Khunji (1456–1521), a Sunni opponent of the Safavids who had fled Persia for Uzbekistan, outlined no less than eight types of historian: historians writing histories commencing with Adam; writers of lives of the prophets; collectors of reports on the prophet; authors of lives of the prophet's followers; annalists recounting events year by year from the Hijra to their own day; compilers of alphabetic dictionaries; historians of classes of doctors of law; and authors of dynastic histories. With 'Abbas, a new vogue for dynastic history set in, and only one of the seven major narratives written during the reign was a general or universal history. There also continued, from its thirteenth-century origins, a Persian version of local history, devoted to towns or provinces and the customs of particular ethnic groups such as the Kurds. The chorographies of early seventeenth-century England (and, despite their explicitly political purpose, the proliferating Ming *fangzhi*) have rough counterparts in books such as Ja'far bin Muḥammad bin Ḥsan Ja'farī's *History of Yazd* (early fifteenth century) and the *Compendium of Mufīd* by Muḥammad Mufīd Mustaufī Bāfqī Yazdī, a history of the same city from Alexander the Great to Shah Suleyman I (r. 1666–94), complete with topographical notes and biographical remarks.

By the late fifteenth century, the Muslim presence in India was well established, and Islamic historiography had begun to proliferate in the subcontinent. Early in the sixteenth century, a Timurid leader named Zāhir ud-Dīn Mohammad, better known as Babur, invaded and conquered much of India, absorbing (1526) the remnants of the Delhi Sultanate. Babur, who claimed descent both from Tīmūr and Genghis Khan, thereby founded the Mughal (a Persian word derived from 'Mongol') dynasty which would rule much of northern and central India until the advent of British colonial rule in the late eighteenth century. With them the Mughals brought both the ancestral veneration of Tīmūr himself, whose exploits provided a mirror for several generations of Central and South Asian potentates, and the past century's heritage of historical writing. It is no accident that several of the conventions of Safavid writing, including formulaic prefaces and declarations by the historian of the 'inspiration' that led him to write, are repeated by the Mughal historians, since Persian was their preferred tongue for both literature and administration. Both Safavid and Mughal historians turned with regularity to the same models, notably an early fifteenth-century history by Niẓām al-Dīn 'Ali Shāmi, the *Ẓafar-name*. At virtually the same time that their Christian counterparts elsewhere in India were wrestling with indigenous South Asian sources and finding them wanting, so too were Muslims like the Persian Ferishta (born Muhammad Qasim Hindu Shah, c. 1579 to after 1623). Ferishta, who lived in Bijapur till 1623, was assisted by its history-loving Muslim ruler with the assembly of materials, and used Hindu sources such as the *Mahābhārata* (in Persian translation) to write accounts of India before and since the advent of Islam, but expressed irritation at that ancient epic's thirteen different accounts of the creation of the world, 'not one of which is sufficiently satisfactory to induce us to adopt it in preference to another'.[28] Historians such as Ferishta were for the most part unable to escape casting these within traditional Islamic historiographical genres, specifically the history of holy war against an idolatrous and simple Hindu population. As one author has commented recently, if we are looking for the early modern version of Orientalism, the creation and diminution of a foreign 'other' in India, then the first place to look is not to Europeans but the Muslim historians of India.[29]

In fact, history was already well established in the South Asian 'ecology of genres', and historical awareness on the periphery of the Mughal domains continued to grow through the sixteenth, seventeenth and eighteenth centuries, with an apparent increase in the features that writing can enable, such as factuality, precise names and an attention to the connectedness of events. These genres were sufficiently fluid and open-ended that they could permit the trading and sharing of particular stories: just as in Europe the same tale could feature in local oral tradition, vernacular urban chronicle and Latin humanist history, so episodes and figures from one region or language group were portable and could surface elsewhere, in other tongues and entirely different formats. The polyglot village literati or *karaṇams* of southern India, taking advantage of increasing literacy and the transition of information from inscriptions to paper, palm leaves and other portable media, composed a distinctive prose historiography in vernacular languages like Marathi, Telugu and Rajasthani, as well as 'official' tongues such as Persian. In states such as Mārvāra (in what is now part of Rājasthān, northwestern India) dominated by the *Rajput* warrior caste but subject to the Mughals from the mid-sixteenth century, several different types of prose history developed out of the oral *bātām* or 'tales' about particular conflicts, or episodes from the lives of local heroes; these were recited by semi-professional bards or *Cāraṇas* ('one who transmits fame and renown'). These include two written types of genealogical history, *vaṃśāvali*s ('line of descendants') and the *pīḍhiāvalī* ('series of generations'). The chronicles known as *khyāta* first appeared in the late sixteenth century. Rooted in the oral genealogies kept by royal courts since earliest times, and showing some influences from Mughal historiography, they can be placed in a continuous tradition along with the *purāṇa*s and epics; they may have been intended to promote local elites in the eyes of the Mughal emperors. The earliest extant *khyāta* is a collection of tales and genealogies associated with an administrator known as Mumhata Naiṇsī Jaimaloṭ Naiṇsī (1611–70), scion of a family of professional administrators, who governed in Jodhpur during the 1650s and 1660s before he fell from favour and committed suicide. His major historiographical legacy, the *Naiṇsī rī Khyāta* ('The Chronicle of Naiṇsī'), probably initiated in 1648, is a history of all the major clans and their descent lines from their founding to the mid-seventeenth century, when they were first written down. A related genre is the *vigata* ('gone away' or 'deceased'), sometimes simply a list of names but in other instances a more literary history of a single clan. As with many of the other historical writings we have seen on the cusp between orality and literacy, none of these should be treated as a defective form of 'objective history', since they involve a phenomenon that modern students of oral tradition call 'telescoping', the creative extension or truncation of lines to bring them into conformity with present circumstances. Those who wrote them and recited them saw themselves as preservers of a living tradition, not 'historians' in our sense.

There also exists a distinct variety of historical writing among the Maratha people of western India, who established an empire of their own in the late seventeenth century with the coronation of their ruler Shivaji (d. 1680). Marathi literati and prominent families kept chronicles to assert their property claims in which are included dates and notes of important events; in one case, the information was then used to write a *karina* or history of the family's land acquisitions – a process not unlike that followed by the Italian worthies who kept household *ricordanze*, or the family chroniclers of early modern Germany. Another Marathi genre, the *bakhar*s (chronicles and biographies), examples of which first appeared in the sixteenth century, became more common near the end of the seventeenth century and continued to be written well into the period of British imperial governance; up to 200 *bakhar*s have been thought to survive among which about 70 have been published. Originating in the narratives constructed by plaintiffs or defendants in judicial disputes, the *bakhar*s emerged as literary accounts at a time when Marathi-speaking locals felt compelled to develop 'coherent narratives of local pasts' in the face of mounting royal influence. A famous *bakhar* concerning Shivaji, for instance, was written in 1694 at a time of renewed danger from the expansionist Mughal Emperor Aurangzeb. Over the course of the next century, as Maratha influence in the subcontinent increased, *bakhar* authors expanded their regional focus, with some of their works virtually constituting national Maratha histories. While the reliability of some of these works as chronological sources for the periods they depict is questioned by modern scholars, they are indisputably intentional attempts to capture and narrate events from the past.

By the later sixteenth century, Perso-Islamic cultural influences on historiography had spread with the Mughal domain. The Sanskrit-language Kashmir chronicles that had followed Kalhaṇa in the thirteenth century were rendered into Persian during the sixteenth, and augmented by new works in Persian such as the anonymous *Bahāristān-i-Shāhī* (completed 1614), and the sixteenth-century autobiographical history of the Central Asian Mughals, *Tā'rīkh-i-Rashīdī* ('History of Rashīd'; comp. *c.* 1541–44) by the warrior Mīrzā Muhammad Haidar (1499 or 1500–51).[30] Haidar's kinsman, the Emperor Babur himself composed or dictated a detailed autobiographical history of his times, the *Baburnama*, a practice which his great-grandson, the fourth Mughal Jahangir (r. 1605–27), would eventually emulate. Babur inaugurated a string of 'namas' (a nama being literally a 'book', though the word can be understood as 'history' or 'chronicle'). The first of these was the *Humāyūn-Nāma* (Extract 18), an account by Babur's daughter, Gul-Badan, of parts of her father's reign and that of her brother, the second Mughal emperor, Humāyūn. This in due course was followed by the *Akbarnama* ('Book of Akbar') (Fig. 27), the work of Abu'l Fazl 'Allami (1551–1602), a colourful figure known for his learning, his self-confessed arrogance and a prodigious appetite for food. Abu'l Fazl was minister to Babur's grandson Akbar (contemporary with Persia's Shah 'Abbās) and served as that emperor's trusted advisor for many years, interrupted by a brief period of disfavour, before finally being assassinated at the behest of the crown prince, the future emperor Jahangir. Abu'l Fazl brought together a variety of sources in the *Akbarnama*, a work also notable for its many interesting reflections on the nature of history, which he conceived of as both a philosophical, rational genre and as a source of solace for grief in the present. He also joins the list of those historians, from Thucydides to T. B. Macaulay, who have had a sufficiently high degree of confidence in their own abilities to declare that they were writing at least in part to 'leave future generations a noble legacy.'[31]

18: A Mughal Princess Writes History: Gul-Badan Begam's *The History of Humāyūn*

Mīrzā Kāmrān had gone as far as Bhīra and Khūsh-āb when Adam Ghakkar, by plot and stratagems, captured him and brought him to the Emperor.

To be brief, all the assembled khans and sultans, and high and low, and plebeian and noble, and soldiers and the rest who all bore the mark of Mīrzā Kāmrān's hand, with one voice represented to his Majesty: 'Brotherly custom has nothing to do with ruling and reigning. If you wish to act as a brother, abandon the throne. If you wish to be king, put aside brotherly sentiment. What kind of wound was it that befell your blessed head in the Qibchāq defile through this same Mīrzā Kāmrān? He it was whose traitorous and crafty conspiracy with the Afghans killed Mīrzā Hindāl. Many a Chaghatai has perished through him; women and children have been made captive and lost honour. It is impossible that our wives and children should suffer in the future the thrall and tortures of captivity. With the fear of hell before our eyes (we say that) our lives, our goods, our wives, our children are all a sacrifice for a single hair of your Majesty's head. This is no brother! This is your Majesty's foe!

To make an end of words, one and all urgently set forth: 'It is well to lower the head of the breacher of the kingdom.'

His Majesty answered: 'Though my head inclines to your words, my heart does not.' All cried out: 'What has been set before your Majesty is the really advisable course.' At last the Emperor said: 'If you all counsel this and agree to it, gather together and attest it in writing.' All the āmirs both of the right and left assembled. They wrote down and gave in that same line ...: 'It is well to lower the head of the breacher of the kingdom.' Even his Majesty was compelled to agree.

When he drew near to Rohtās, the Emperor gave an order to Sayyid Muhammad: 'Blind Mīrzā Kāmrān in both eyes.' The sayyid went at once and did so.

Selection from Gul-Badan Begam, *The History of Humāyūn* [*Humāyūn-Nāma*], trans. Annette S. Beveridge (1902; Delhi: Low Price Publications, 1996), 200–1. This selection, which omits Beveridge's notes, comes from the very last portion of Gul-Badan's manuscript, which ends abruptly in mid-sentence. Diacriticals have been simplified.

At precisely the same period that court-sponsored histories were in vogue in Renaissance Europe, the same feature can be observed in Mughal India, and the appointment of Abu'l Fazl by Akbar inaugurated the policy of having an official historiographer write the history of the empire; the practice would be maintained until the last great Mughal emperor, Aurangzeb 'Alamgir (r. 1658–1707). So, too, were the genealogical interests of the Safavids emulated by their Mughal cousins.

Figure 27 | Babur leaving Kabul to attack Kandahar. Miniature from an early seventeenth-century manuscript of the *Akbarnama*.

At the very same time that such genealogical fancies were reaching an absurd-ist level, a world away, in India's future colonizer England, Abu'l Fazl was busy tracing Akbar's pedigree back via Tīmūr all the way to Adam: chapters 14, 15 and 16 of the *Akbarnama* consist of an elaborate series of fifty-two biographies begin-ning with the first man and ending with the forty-sixth year of Akbar's own reign, for Abu'l Fazl the apogee of civilization. The mild note of scepticism towards the full story of Adam as 'hero' echoes the growing global tension between sacred his-tory and observed nature.

It is well known that [Adam] came into existence about 7000 years ago through the perfect power of God, without the intervention of a father's loins or a mother's womb and that he was equably compounded of the four elements .... Adam was of lofty stature, of a wheaten colour, had curling hair and a handsome countenance. There are different accounts of the stature of this patriarch, but most agree that he was sixty cubits high .... Historians have told many strange and wondrous things about this hero and though there be no difficulty about the extent of God's power, yet experienced and practical men of the world, on looking to the course of nature, rather hesitate about accepting them.[32]

Abu'l Fazl's writing is overwhelmingly panegyrical of Akbar, whose patronage of historians was equal to that of any contemporary Italian despot. Akbar cleverly employed a number of historians to extol the virtues of a strong monarchy amid struggles with both nobility and theologians, and to glorify his personal achievements.

Akbar's personal interest in history pales, however, besides that of his favourite grandson, the fifth Mughal emperor, Shah Jahan (r. 1628–58; d. 1666). Best known as the builder of spectacular but ruinously expensive buildings such as the Taj Mahal, Shah Jahan was ultimately deposed and imprisoned by his own son Aurangzeb. Notwithstanding his humiliating end, Shah Jahan held a very grand sense of his own place in History, not unlike a younger contemporary who was just beginning his long reign several thousand miles away, France's Louis XIV. Determined to leave monuments to his successes in manuscript as well as marble, he commissioned a number of court chronicles. This was no arms-length commission. In an age of court-sponsored histories and intellectually engaged princes throughout the world, the emperor was the outstanding micromanager, unable to stay out of the way. He appointed and then dismissed one chronicler after another from the literary elite at his court, before settling on Mirza Amina Qazwini, who, appointed court historian in 1636, outlasted his predecessors and succeeded in writing the first 'decade' of the reign. Shah Jahan had very precise ideas about the shape of his history: it was to be divided into volumes, each containing a decade, since he thought the number ten especially auspicious – he was the tenth ruler in direct succession to Tīmūr.

Working for the emperor was akin to hitting a moving target. Before Qazwini had finished his decade, Shah Jahan had changed his mind about the organization of the history: beginning with the eleventh year, regnal years were to be calculated on a lunar cycle instead of the previous solar calendar. This was probably motivated by the emperor's sudden burst of Muslim piety, and it soon led to unhappiness with the way in which Qazwini had narrated the early part of the reign. The unfortunate man was dismissed about 1638 and replaced by an older literary master, Shaikh 'Abd al-Hamid Lahori, whose prose style resembled that of the great Abu'l Fazl. Lahori was fetched back from a provincial retirement to assume the position of court historian. He stayed in his post till old age forced him to stop writing and give way to his own pupil, Muhammad Waris, who completed the task, depositing the third and final volume in the Royal Library in March 1657. In contrast to the luckless Qazwini, Lahori's rewards were substantial – 4,000 rupees in 1647 and the bonus gift of an elephant a year before that. The end product, entitled *Padshah Nama* ('Chronicle of the King of the World'), runs to nearly 3,000 pages, arranged chronologically, but with accounts of every public activity of the emperor and of battles, lists of the nobility, verbatim transcripts of documents and letters, and biographies of notable figures. Not surprisingly given Shah Jahan's ego, the authors suppressed all evidence of defeats and setbacks and extolled the emperor to the point of apotheosis. *Padshah Nama* was flattering and hyperbolic even by the standards of the most sycophantic of French *historiographes du roi*. It was also far too large to be useful, and in 1657 a nobleman named 'Inayat Khan, Superintendent of the Royal Library, summarized it, in a style closer to that of Qazwini's original text, so that the ordinary literate person could read it. The *Mulakhkhas* (which means 'abridgement') proved far superior to its parent, and has become known as the *Shah Jahan Nama*, a name it shares with several other histories of this Mughal's reign. Ironically, this textual testament to Shah Jahan's greatness would be completed at the very moment that the emperor was being elbowed aside by his ambitious son.[33]

By the time of the Mughal entry into India, Islam already had a new Western standard bearer in the Ottoman Turks. The rise of the Ottomans, former Mongol vassals, began in early fourteenth-century Anatolia, and they expanded their dominion in southern Europe over the following century, culminating in their defeat of the beleaguered Byzantine Empire and capture of Constantinople in 1453. Despite frequent periods of weakness they became the favoured eastern bogeyman for Europeans through the late seventeenth century, filling the role that the Mongols had played for central Eurasia in an earlier age. Consequently virtually no other oriental power received as much attention from European writers. A whole sub-genre of 'Histories of the Turks' and speculations *de origine Turcorum*, beginning in the fifteenth century and continuing with Paolo Giovio's widely translated *Comentario de le cose de' Turchii* ('Commentary on Turkish Matters', 1532), spread through the filter of Italian writers to the rest of Europe, to be picked up in later times by the English schoolmaster Richard Knolles (d. 1610), the seventeenth-century diplomat and traveller Paul Rycaut (1629–1700) and the Moldavian prince Dimitrie Cantemir (1673–1723).[34] So significant a threat did the Turks seem to Renaissance Europeans that some humanists and propagandists even rewrote the history of past medieval Islamo-Christian conflicts to render medieval Arabs or 'Saracens' more benign.[35] On the principle of 'my enemy's enemy is my friend' they revised history to turn other Muslim peoples, in particular the Persians, into civilized potential allies against a common Ottoman foe; a few even romanticized recent

Asiatic conquerors such as Tīmūr and, later, the Safavid founder Shah Ismaʻil into Alexander-like heroes.[36]

Although, unlike the Mughals, the Ottomans were not literal descendants of Tīmūr, the warlord's inspiration also hovered over their culture: it has even been suggested that the shock of Sultan Bayezid I's defeat at Tīmūr's hands (1402) and subsequent strife among the sultan's sons drove Ottoman historical consciousness, previously exemplified by scattered poems and tales, mainly conveyed in oral tradition, to find a new form in writing. Almost from the moment of the Ottoman recovery from this crisis, significant historical works appeared in Anatolia, principally focused on the successes of the Ottomans themselves. The efforts of the early fifteenth-century sultans retroactively to justify their elimination of rivals, exemplified by ʼAbduʼl-vasi Çelebi's (*fl.* 1414) account of the accession of Mehmed I, bear comparison with the slightly later histories written in Sforza Milan and Yorkist and Tudor England. This chronicle tradition continued with works by Âşikpaşazade or Aşiki (1400 to after 1484) and the obscure Mevlana Neşri (d. *c.* 1520), who synthesized many of the sources up to his own time. These 'Chronicles of the House of Osman', the authors of many of which remain unknown, typically added annals of contemporary events to earlier history derived from other sources. The chronicles (*tarih*; plural *tevârîh*) were supplemented and in some cases overlaid by other sources. These include royal calendars (the oldest extant examples of which date from the early fifteenth century) containing historical lists, and poems and oral traditional accounts reaching back to a heroic age of Muslim warriors, which provide a backdrop of legend, folklore and pseudohistory. Few of these at this point exhibit a narrowly 'court' perspective; even Âşikpaşazade, who was encouraged by Bayezid II's (r. 1481–1512) wish to have his ancestors' achievements recounted, held no official position. The tensions between the Ottoman house and the Turkish warrior class can be gleaned from the divergent accounts in the chronicles. In a striking metaphor, Cemal Kafadar has suggested that looking to such works as an incremental tradition of embellished fact, with earlier accounts presumed to be more reliable versions of later ones, is rather like seeing historiography as the progressive layers of an onion, radiating out from a true historical core.[37] This can be misleading, since successive chronicles, even if borrowing from earlier ones, often represent different points of view. They are thus closer to garlic, a series of connected but separate cloves, than they are to onion. Given what we know about the equally variable agendas and perspectives of contemporary historians in western Europe, this seems a persuasive caution.

Sixteenth-century Turkish literati, not unlike their humanist counterparts to the west, objected to both the language and the content of the chronicles and to their simple style, suffused with nostalgia for an earlier era of free-ranging warfare, as incompatible with a centralized bureaucratic regime. Sultan Bayezid II initiated a change in historical styles when he commissioned the first two histories devoted specifically to the Ottomans. Idrîs-I Bidlîsî (d. 1520), a Kurdish chancery official who had fled Safavid Persia, wrote the first of these, *Hasht Bihisht* ('Eight Paradises'), in literary Persian; this led to the sultan's commissioning of a second history by the scholar Kamalpaşazade (d. 1534), in Turkish prose. After a dry spell for several decades, further commissions followed with Suleyman the Magnificent's (r. 1520–66) creation in the 1550s of the position of *şehnāmeci* or court-writer – the name derives from Firdawsi's *Shahnama* – to write a new dynastic history in Persian. This early venture into official history was not terribly successful: the fifteen works produced were mainly poorly written propaganda pieces in verse, though presented in beautifully illustrated manuscripts. Five men held the post of *şehnāmeci* in succession, the first two being poets who aspired to Firdawsi's epic style; the language of composition had changed to Turkish by the end of the sixteenth century, and later *şehnāmeci* (or *sehnameji*) were drawn from other professions, especially the *kātibs* or bureaucrats. The *şehnāmecilik* (the office itself) ceased to function early in the reign of Sultan Ahmed I (r. 1603–17), though a few subsequent works in the genre were produced through the first half of the century. One or two *şehnāmeci*, such as Seyyid Loḳmān, were quite prolific and enjoyed a close connection with their sultans (in Loḳmān's case, Murad III). But the works were ill-received by other historians and often available only in inaccessible formats; beautifully illustrated copies of Loḳmān's *Quintessence of Histories* (Fig. 28), for instance, were given by Murad to visiting dignitaries but otherwise not widely circulated. Ultimately the *şehnāmeci* were unsuccessful in establishing an imperially sanctioned 'hegemonic voice' in historiography.[38]

The Ottomans finally established 'official' history in the stricter sense of an office of state historiographer (*vak'a-nüvis*) only in the late seventeenth century; they were more successful in the eighteenth century at controlling perceptions of the past, not least because of the easing of previously tight restrictions on printing, and the publication of many official chronicles by the Imperial Press. By this time, they had become vehicles for the promotion of a now-solidified Ottoman state, rather than courtly writings tied to the sultans, who had by this time lost a good deal of their personal power. There was also a movement during the seventeenth century away from explorations of the origins of dynasties and towards the coverage of more recent history. At the same time, the older judicial elite whose names had dominated biographical dictionaries began to lose place in those works to viziers, ministers and secretaries. Thus, argues Baki Tezcan, the 'new' Ottoman official histories of the eighteenth century emerged hand in hand with a state very different from the sixteenth-century monarchy.[39]

Figure 28 | Surrender of Belgrade, 1521. From Loḳmān, *Hunername*, on the military campaigns of Suleyman the Magnificent. Ottoman, 1588.

Unofficial histories in verse and prose appeared throughout the period, with the reigns of Selim II (r. 1566–74) and Murad III (r. 1574–95) being especially fertile. These works included Turkish-language continuations of the old 'Chronicles of Osman' (such as that by Grand Vizier Lutfı Paşa) and accounts of single events or of a particular sultan's reign. Increasingly self-aware of their great power status, which they likened to both Rome and China, the Turks also came, somewhat late, to an interest in 'universal history', borrowing the model from late medieval historians such as Ibn al-Athīr, Juvaini and Rashīd al-dīn. These general histories (mainly composed in Persian or Arabic) ranged in size from the grand example of the Anatolian teacher Şukrullah's *Bahjat al-tavârîkh* ('Splendour of Histories') to a brief Turkish-language epitome of world history by Suleyman's chancellor, Ramazanzade Mehmet Paşa, which appeared in the 1560s.

There are obvious parallels to be drawn both with China's mandarin-dominated historical writing (and its evolution under the Tang from informal sponsorship to explicit arm of government) and, more remotely, with the less bureaucratically organized civic and princely historiography of many European states. The Chinese practice of maintaining court diaries as the source for imperial Veritable Records has a counterpart in the day-books of court activity or registers that would subsequently be transformed into histories. The major Turkish histories of the late fifteenth, sixteenth and seventeenth centuries, even when written unofficially, were often the labour of ministers or bureaucrats. These included the chancellor Mustafa Çelebi Celâlzade (*c.* 1490–1567), the bibliographer and geographer Kâtip Çelebi (1609–57) and the Hungarian-born Ibrahim Peçevi (1574–1650). Peçevi, a provincial functionary, was among the earliest Ottoman historians to use European sources. He shared with Kâtip Çelebi a cosmopolitan outlook, the latter having collaborated with a former Christian priest to gain information on Europe for his works. Kâtip Çelebi is of interest for his praise of brevity and completeness of information over literary style.[40] Insofar as the Turks experienced a counterpart of Europe's quarrel between rhetoric and erudition, his *Fezleke* (the Turkish translation and expansion of a history he first wrote in Arabic) places him on the side of the scholars rather than the narrators. Istanbul bureaucrat Mustafa Na'îmâ (1655–1716) wrote an important history of the empire in the first half of the seventeenth century, the *Tarih-i Na'îmâ* ('The History by Na'îmâ'). Generally regarded as the first of the new official chronicles, it remains one of the most cited sources for that period; its author's views on the reasons for writing history and the ways in which it should be done look remarkably similar to any European *ars historica* of the day (Extract 19).

Like its Mughal and Safavid contemporaries, the Ottoman Empire was a multilingual and multiethnic state. Accordingly, Ottoman historiography embraced writings in languages other than Turkish by ethnic minorities including Kurds (such as Idrîs-I Bidlîsî, mentioned above), Armenians and Arabs, as well as Greeks in the conquered Byzantine territories. It is worth noting, too, that the interest of western European historians in Turkish matters was reciprocated by their Ottoman counterparts, who sometimes wrote about the non-Ottoman world. Kâtip Çelebi was a frequent observer of and commentator on continental affairs, while one İbrahim Mülhemi devoted a chapter to French history in his, *Murâd-nâme* ('The Book of Murad [IV]'), which despite its title was designed as a universal history. In 1572 two chancery officials had compiled *Tevârîh-i Pâdishâhân-i Frânçe* ('Chronicles of the Kings of France') from several French sources, covering the period from the legendary Frankish king Pharamond to their own day.[41]

19: Mustafa Na'îmâ on How and Why to Write History

In the mirror of the innermost hearts of men of keen intellect, it is clear and plain and manifest and evident that the science of history and the science of biography are the quintessence of instruction and information and the elixir of excellent qualities and intellects, an august and great study whose subject is of universal utility, for it teaches those happenings and lessons which have been manifested in the world, from the earliest periods up to this very moment, and it expounds those occurrences, good and bad, which have transpired in creation from the covenant of Adam to this time. History has ever been common fare among the peoples and nations, a subject esteemed and of currency within the various estates and *millets* of mankind, approved and sought after by great sultans and noble rulers, the solicitude and desire of outstanding men of fame and renowned men of wisdom.

It is a science of much usefulness, appertaining to the common good. It increases the livelihood and the keenness of scholars' intellects, makes the attentiveness and penetration of wise men broader, puts the commonality into possession of the story of what has happened aforetime, and gives the elite knowledge of secrets which would otherwise be concealed ....

Certainly a man who will not be content with primitive traditions about what happened in history is not a man to be duped by sophistries and silly stories and tales of every sort. Instead, he will infer what is missing on the basis of the data which he has, and will derive the lacking circumstances from those with which he is acquainted. Through much experience and much application he reaches a point at which he can foresee what will be the results of actions, provided he understands the men who do those actions, and can comprehend the affairs of great men, provided he knows what the causes prior to those affairs were. In his mind's mirror, the consequences of circumstances become clear, and the forms of good and evil distinct, as if by intuition ....

There are certain vital conditions and important rules for those who record events and for those scholars who write history:

First: They must be reliable in what they say, and must not make foolish statements or write spurious tales. If they do not know the truth about any particular question, they should address themselves to those who have fathomed, it, and only then put down whatever they have ascertained to be the fact.

Second: They should disregard the disquieting rumors which are gossiped about among the common people. Instead they must prefer the reliable, documented statements of men who knew how to record what actually did happen .... How often do men of feeble intellect base their conclusions upon their own fallible imaginings! ...

Third: Whatever the sphere of human life to which the question of which an historian is treating belongs, he should not be content simply to tell the story but should also incorporate useful information directly into his narrative. It is of no great consequence merely to recount campaigns and seasons of repose from campaigning, arrivals and departures, appointments to office and removals from office, and peace and war. Rather, historians ought first to inform themselves, from those who have proper information concerning the question in hand, of what was the divinely ordained condition of any age in history; of how, in a given century, the affairs of men were going forward, and in what direction, of what ideas and counsels were predominating in problems of administration and finance – in short, the historian must first ascertain what it was they believed to be the best course in the conduct of the war and in making terms with the foe, what were the causes and the weaknesses which were then bringing triumph or entailing destruction. Then, after an historian has ascertained all these things, he should present his findings on the basis of their reliability. When this has been accomplished, later readers will be able to avail themselves of the different benefits of experience's teachings ....

Selections from Lewis V. Thomas, *A Study of Naima*, ed. N. Itzkowitz (New York University Press, 1972), 110–13.

CONCLUSION

The period from the mid-fifteenth to the late seventeenth century had seen among other things a voluminous increase in the number of historical works written, a multiplication of genres and sub-genres (and considerable effort expended on sorting them out in both Europe and Asia), a significant growth in historical readership in most parts of the world and the accompanying capacity, especially in the West, to replicate texts through the printing press. The use of history as an explicit tool for the establishment of new regimes and as an underpinning for monarchical and religious authority had also increased dramatically from earlier centuries. In Europe, history had made the transition from a secondary branch of knowledge to a literary form of steadily increasing stature; in China, where it had enjoyed a high status for much longer, private historical writing had increased. In the Muslim world, the ruling houses of India, Persia and the Ottoman Empire had abandoned the religious focus of much early Islamic historical writing and redeployed history, much like contemporary European princes, as an instrument of monarchical authority and centralized state-building.

A fitting place to close this chapter is with a further Turkish functionary-turned-historian. Mustafa Âli's (1541–1600) *Essence of History* (see Box 15), one of several histories by this author, was intended as a continuation of works by his former mentor, Celâlzade, and a contribution to the older, distinguished tradition of Islamic world history that included the likes of Rashīd al-dīn, and to which the Ottomans were relative newcomers. Âli had a tempestuous career marked by recurrent

Box 15   Mustafa Âli's *Essence of History*

Âli conceived of the *Essence* as a building resting on four 'pillars', or volumes, dealing successively with cosmography and the creation of man, Islamic history from
before the Prophet to the Mongol invasions, the Mongol and Turkic dynasties and,
finally, the Ottoman dynasty. His lengthy introduction to the work, explaining his
purpose in writing it, also listed his sources and his ideas on history. On the whole
generous to his immediate predecessors, he was contemptuous of earlier chroniclers
and especially the contemporary *şehnāmecis* whom he dismissed as clumsy scribes
and authors of fiction. Âli wrote his general history without official sponsorship in
the 1590s, motivated by a combination of career failures and dissatisfaction with
the state of the empire under Suleyman's successors. This was a period of moderate
decline for the Ottomans, and it coincided with the more widespread millenarian
feelings that attended the years around the thousandth anniversary of Islam, which
on the Muslim calendar fell in 1591–2. Âli organized his book unusually, with a
mixture of chronological and topical sections, and it included biographies within
the overall structure, as well as events which were numbered rather than arranged
annalistically.

losses of office which inevitably remind us of some of his European counterparts
of this period, officials or ministers who turned to history such as England's Francis
Bacon, or Florence's Machiavelli; his case also reminds us of an earlier disappointed Muslim, Delhi's Baranī (see Chapter 3 above). Like many of his medieval
Muslim precursors, Mustafa Âli had to wrestle with the tension between Islamic
universalism and regional or dynastic particularism: the Ottomans, like medieval
Roman emperors both west and east, and their own Mongol forebears, subscribed
to a view of world monarchy that privileged one branch of their religion, but
refused to subordinate itself to theological interests. The early modern era had
seen theological fragmentation across various parts of the world, and the capacity of historians to take a 'universal' approach to the past was increasingly being
strained. Yet as the seventeenth century wound down, however, what we might
call 'universalism' was about to return as both a political problem and as a view
of history. To understand fully the origins of this, and of the comparative, generalist, sociological and cultural history that we associate with the Enlightenment,

we must look to parts of the globe we have yet to visit, and to the rethinking of history that encounters with them provoked.

Notes

1 Sanjay Subrahmanyam, 'On World Historians in the Sixteenth Century', *Representations* 91 (2005): 26–57, at 27.

2 Brian Tate, 'The Rewriting of the Historical Past: Hispania et Europa', in Alan Deyermond (ed.), *Historical Literature in Medieval Iberia* (London, 1996), 85–103.

3 Constantin Fasolt, *The Limits of History* (Chicago, 2004), xiv.

4 Douglas A. Howard, 'Genre and Myth in the Ottoman Advice for Kings Literature', in V. H. Aksan and D. Goffman (eds.), *The Early Modern Ottomans: Remapping the Empire* (Cambridge, 2007), 137–66.

5 Gerald Strauss, *Historian in an Age of Crisis: The Life and Work of Johannes Aventinus 1477–1534* (Cambridge, 1963), 80.

6 Virginia F. Stern, *Gabriel Harvey: His Life, Marginalia and Library* (Oxford, 1979), 152.

7 *The Nikonian Chronicle*, ed. Serge A. Zenkovsky, trans. S. A. and B. J. Zenkovsky, 5 vols. (Princeton, NJ, 1984–9).

8 P. Burke, 'A Survey of the Popularity of Ancient Historians, 1450–1700', *History and Theory* 4 (1966): 135–52, at 136.

9 Leonardo Bruni, *History of the Florentine People*, vol. I, Books I–IV, ed. and trans. J. Hankins (Cambridge, MA, 2001), 5.

10 Machiavelli to Francesco Vettori 10 December 1513, in *Machiavelli and his Friends: Their Personal Correspondence*, ed. and trans. James B. Atkinson and David Sices (De Kalb, IL, 1996), 264.

11 F. Guicciardini, *Maxims and Reflections of a Renaissance Statesman (Ricordi)*, trans. M. Domandi (Gloucester, MA, 1970), 69.

12 *Biondo Flavio's Italia Illustrata*, ed. and trans. Catherine J. Castner, vol. I: *Northern Italy* (Binghamton, NY, 2005); Nicoletta Pellegrino, 'From the Roman Empire to Christian Imperialism: The Work of Flavio Biondo', in S. Dale, A. W. Lewin and D. J. Osheim (eds.), *Chronicling History: Chroniclers and Historians in Medieval and Renaissance Italy* (University Park, PA, 2007), 273–98.

13 H. J. Erasmus, *The Origins of Rome in Historiography from Petrarch to Perizonius* (Assen, 1962).

14 Margaret Meserve, *Empires of Islam in Renaissance Historical Thought* (Cambridge, MA, 2008), 22ff., who points out that this idea was less prominent among humanist historians as an explanation for the Turks than has generally been believed.

15 Frank E. Manuel, *Isaac Newton, Historian* (Cambridge, MA, 1963).

16 Samuel Pufendorf, *The Present State of Germany*, trans. Edmund Bohun (1696), ed. M. J. Seidler (Indianapolis, 2007), 46. I have romanized italics in the extract.

17 Jean Bodin, *Method for the Easy Comprehension of History*, trans. B. Reynolds (New York, 1945), 153.

18 Orest Ranum, *Artisans of Glory: Writers and Historical Thought in Seventeenth-Century France* (Chapel Hill, NC, 1980), 286.

19 *Prince A. M. Kurbsky's History of Ivan IV*, ed. and trans. J. L. I. Fennell (Cambridge, 1965).

20 Anthony Weldon, *The Court and Character of King James* (London, 1650).

21 Henry Cornelius Agrippa, *Of the Vanitie and Uncertaintie of Artes and Sciences*, trans. C. Dunn (Northridge, CA, 1974), 35 (spelling modernized by present author).

22 Jean Mabillon, *Treatise on Monastic Studies*, trans. J. P. McDonald (Lanham, MD, 2004), 153.

23 Juan González de Mendoza, *The History of the Great and Mighty Kingdom of China and the Situation Thereof*, trans. Robert Parke (1588; London, 1853).

24 Huang Zongxi (Tsung-hsi), *The Records of Ming Scholars*, trans. Julia Ching with Chaoying Fang (Honolulu, 1987), 45–6.

25 On-cho Ng and Q. Edward Wang, *Mirroring the Past: The Writing and Use of History in Imperial China* (Honolulu, 2005), 214.

26 Ibid., 217.

27 Ibid., 219.

28 Muhammad Qasim Ferishta, *History of the Rise of the Mahomedan Power in India till the Year A.D. 1612*, trans. John Briggs, 4 vols. (London, 1829), vol. I, xlv (author's introduction).

29 Joan-Pau Rubiés, *Travel and Ethnology in the Renaissance: South India through European Eyes, 1250–1625* (Cambridge, 2000), 286.

30 *Bahāristān-i-Shāhī: A Chronicle of Mediaeval Kashmir*, trans. K. N. Pandit (Calcutta, 1991); Mīrzā Muhammad Haidar, *A History of the Moghuls of Central Asia*, trans. E. D Ross and ed. N. Elias, 2 vols. (New Delhi, 1998).

31 Sudipta Sen, 'Imperial Orders of the Past: The Semantics of History and Time in the Medieval Indo-Persianate Culture of North India', in Daud Ali (ed.), *Invoking the Past: The Uses of History in South Asia* (New Delhi, 1999), 239.

32 *The Akbarnama of Abu'l Fazl*, trans. H. Beveridge, 3 vols. (1907; Calcutta, 2000), vol. I, 155–6.

33 *The Shah Jahan Nama of 'Inayat Khan: An Abridged History of the Mughal Emperor Shah Jahan, compiled by his Royal Librarian*, trans. A. R. Fuller, ed. W. E. Begley and Z. A. Desai (Delhi and Oxford, 1990).

34 *Dimitrie Cantemir: Historian of South East European and Oriental Civilizations*, ed. A. Duțu and P. Cernovodeanu (Bucharest, 1973), an abridgement of Cantemir's *History of the Ottoman Empire*.

35 A practice begun as early as the Crusade historian William of Tyre, who differentiated among less and more threatening Muslim peoples: Meserve, *Empires of Islam*, 161.

36 Ibid., 203–37.

37 Cemal Kafadar, *Between Two Worlds: The Construction of the Ottoman State* (Berkeley, CA, 1995), 99–101.

38 I am grateful to Professor Baki Tezcan for this point.

39 Baki Tezcan, 'The Politics of Early Modern Ottoman Historiography', in Aksan and Goffman (eds.), *The Early Modern Ottomans*, 180–4, 196–7.

40 Born Mustafa bin Abdullah; Kâtip Çelebi is an honorific in which Kâtip is a title or epithet meaning 'secretary' while Çelebi denotes a man of learning.

41 *La première histoire de France en turc ottoman: Chronique des padichahs de France, 1572*, ed. and trans. Jean-Louis Bacqué-Grammont (Paris, 1997). I owe references in this paragraph to Baki Tezcan.

Transatlantic Histories
Contact, conquest and cultural exchange
1450–1800

Introduction

Somewhere in the Ottoman Empire about the year 1580, one of Mustafa Âli's contemporaries was struck by the evidence of 'novelty' in his own time, exemplified by
the printing press. He decided to write a history of an even bigger novelty, the New
World that had opened up across the Atlantic. We don't know the identity of this
perceptive author, but he had recognized the significance of the sixteenth-century
'discoveries', and there is evidence that he collaborated with an Italian-speaking
Spaniard in writing his book. The *Tarih-i Hind-i Garbi* ('History of the West Indies')
was intended for a royal audience, and the beautifully illustrated presentation copy
prepared for the relentlessly womanizing but endearingly bibliophilic Sultan Murad
III (r. 1574–95) may have been polished up by the poet Emîr Mehmet es-Suudî,
whose name appears on the manuscript though he was almost certainly not its
author.[1] As a specimen of the historian's craft, *Tarih-i Hind-i Garbi* is not very
remarkable. Yet it illustrates both that the impact of the European oceanic explorations was being felt outside Europe, in a land that itself had no transatlantic engagements, and that histories from one culture could be adapted into the language
and the generic forms of another. The interest of our anonymous Ottoman historian
in the wider world is not surprising in itself. Muslim authors often provided, as they
had throughout the Middle Ages, the most frequent point of contact between East
and West. Many continued to travel extensively, in the tradition of al-Bīrūnī and
Ibn Baṭṭūṭa; perhaps the most popular text about Africa to be read by sixteenth-
century Europeans was the creation of al-Hasan al-Wazzan (better known as Leo
Africanus, *c.* 1494 to *c.* 1554), a Spanish-born Muslim who converted to Christianity and then back to Islam, and who would spend time in both Catholic Rome and
Muslim North Africa.

Geography, the study of place and space, has nearly always been related to history, the study of past times. That connection has never been more influential than between about 1450 and 1700. Ultimately, the uncertainties affecting European thinking about the past in general, about chronology, and about the proper forms in which history should be cast, would be magnified by two centuries of overseas exploration. In the early decades, however, the contacts had nearly the opposite effect: they offered evidence in support of long-held beliefs. The discovery of other peoples, especially primitive indigenous cultures – both completely 'savage' tribes such as the Brazilian Tupinamba (whom the Calvinist explorer Jean de Léry thought the descendants of Ham), and more advanced 'barbarian' societies such as the Incas and Aztecs – would complicate inherited schemes for the periodization of history and the Creation story, as La Peyrère would later demonstrate, not least because most of those who initially wrote about this 'new' world were quite convinced that it actually wasn't. Columbus went to his grave convinced that he had found part of Asia. A Portuguese explorer who arrived in Ethiopia in 1490 brought with him a letter from his monarch addressed to 'Prester John', the shadowy Christian king that medieval legend supposed to rule in Africa. A century later the Portuguese Jesuit Manuel de Almeida (1580–1646) began his history of Ethiopia with a discussion of Prester John's name.[2] One of the first chroniclers of the New World, Gonzalo Fernández de Oviedo y Valdés (1478–1557, usually referred to as Oviedo), who had a dim view of the natives he encountered in the Antilles, applied both late antique history and Aristotelian syllogism to his depiction of the Taino, their indigenous inhabitants, whom Columbus had reported to be cannibals. Because both the Taino and the ancient Thracians practised polygyny, and because Eusebius had said that the Thracians also sacrificed foreigners, Oviedo concluded that logically, the Taino must also routinely kill their visitors.

What was outwardly new was thus slotted into categories quite old, and contextualized within the boundaries of learned and popular tradition. Legendary figures, monsters, the Garden of Eden, fountains of youth, King Solomon's mines, cannibals and Amazon women all seemed to be borne out by discoveries in the Americas, Africa and the East Indies, and some truly wild speculations, stimulated by late medieval frauds like Annius of Viterbo's pseudo-Berossus, would eventually explain the native inhabitants as lost citizens of Atlantis, or exiled Israelites, or some subsidiary branch of the sons of Noah. It was, David Brading writes, 'as if the classics had come to life, with the accounts of modern travellers confirming the picture of the first men already drawn by ancient poets and satirists'.[3] The theoretical justification of imperial and ecclesiastical power overseas rested on the assumption that the Americas and other hitherto unknown terrains were in fact part of the Old World, had been alluded to in ancient legends and romances (as well as in scripture and in classical geography), were subject to the same authority as European lands and were occupied by popula-tions sharing universal human values, though much more primitive in behaviour.

This chapter explores the historiographic consequences of two centuries of dis-covery, including the development of new genres capable of capturing a world that did not, in the end, easily fit into conventional European categories, and the impact on Europeans and native populations alike of the confrontation between radically different modes of representing the past. It focuses on three different transatlantic experiences: first, European (and especially Spanish) writings about the Americas; second, indigenous and mestizo versions of the past; and finally, the beginnings of North American historical writing up to the American Revolution. This sets the stage for the eighteenth-century distancing of Europe, and its own historical sensibility, from that of 'barbarians' and 'savages', during an age much given to histories of social development. And it provides a prologue to our discussion in Chapter 8 below, of the much more comprehensive spread of European historiography, converted during the nineteenth century into a professional discipline, across the planet.

European Historical Writing about the Indies and Americas

Apart from earlier Viking ventures depicted in medieval sagas, the first systematic explorers of the Atlantic world were the Portuguese, whose ventures were bent more towards commerce than conquest. Preceding both their Spanish neighbours and hired Italian mariners such as Columbus into serious maritime exploration by half a century, Portuguese ships sailed down to the Guinea coast during the later fifteenth century and then, by 1498, as far as India. While the Treaty of Tordesil-las (1494) left Brazil on their side of a papally arbitrated line of demarcation, the geographical orientation of the Portuguese remained predominantly eastward, in Africa, India and China, where they established an enclave at Macao.

Unlike the Castilians, Aragonese and Catalans, the Portuguese had produced relatively little historical writing prior to the early fifteenth century, when King Duarte (r. 1433–38) commissioned one Fernão Lopes (c. 1380 to c. 1459), for-merly the secretary and archivist to his father King João I, as principal chroni-cler of the realm, charging him to 'put into chronicles the stories of the kings of old time'.[4] Lopes' notarial training gave his work a documentary foundation that distinguishes it from contemporaneous court historiography in many other jurisdictions. The earliest Iberian account of Portuguese expansion came from Lopes' immediate successor, Gomes Eanes de Zurara (c. 1410–74), who in 1448 authored a chronicle of the conquest of Guinea in West Africa. Though this did not maintain Lopes' documentary enthusiasm (Zurara praised Lopes in one breath while repudiating with the next his predecessor's stylistic offence of extensive transcription), it remains a rare and useful source for the exploratory initiatives supported by Duarte's younger brother, Prince Henry 'the Navigator' (1394–1460).

The Portuguese had more interest in India, Southeast Asia and Africa than did the Spanish and were the dominant European power in those regions until absorbed temporarily by Spain (1580–1640) and subsequently pushed out by the Dutch and English. Fernão Lopes de Castanheda (d. 1559, not to be confused with his similar-named fifteenth-century predecessor) had actually visited India as a young man, and having spent 'all my youth in learning, and gave myself greatly in reading of ancient histories', was inspired to write the history of the Indian discoveries.[5] Castanheda's rival, Gaspar Corrêa (c. 1495 to c. 1563), a former sailor-turned-secretary, also went to India in his youth and, all told, would spend over fifty years there. He wrote an unfinished history, the *Lendas da India*,[6] which deplored the government of Portuguese India, overrun by 'murderers who go home without any fear of being punished'.[7]

As the Spanish would later do in New Spain and Peru, so the Portuguese encountered indigenous knowledge of the past in Africa and the Indies that was difficult to reconcile with either their Christian notions of world history or their hardening sense of the boundary between myth and 'fact', but which they were often obliged to use in the absence of alternative sources. A Portuguese chronicler who visited the Moluccas (now the Maluku islands) in the Malay archipelago, recorded its inhabitants' belief that their founding rulers had been hatched from four serpents' eggs. 'This is said to be the origin of all the kings of these islands ... One may believe it if he wants to, as also that story of the serpent; they insist that it is true, as they do with all their poetic fables, which are very much in vogue with them.'[8] João de Barros, known as the 'Portuguese Livy' (c. 1498–1570), ventured to both East Africa and southern India during his career, sometimes using indigenous histories. Barros was simultaneously the author of both romance and history, and well aware of the difference between the two. He raised the classic distinction between *verum* and *fabula* in order to dismiss the historical writings that he encountered in Malabar as 'fables like those of the Greeks and the Latins'.[9] Another historian, a horse-trader named Fernão Nunes, was so struck by the South Indian Vijayanagara (or Bisnaga) Empire that he undertook to write its history. Since he read neither Sanskrit nor Dravidian, he was dependent on native readers and interpreters for information from local chronicles.[10] Diogo do Couto (1542–1616), the more humanistically trained historian who followed Nunes, similarly used indigenous chronicles both in India and Sri Lanka, but unlike Nunes, he felt compelled to reconcile the Vijayanagaran accounts with European ones, thereby muddling the chronologies of both.

In the course of the sixteenth and seventeenth centuries the other European powers, France, England and the Dutch Republic, produced exploration histories of their own, such as Johannes de Laet's (1593–1649) history of the Dutch West India Company (1644). The Frenchman Charles Rochefort (c. 1605–90), for instance, authored a *Histoire naturelle et morale des Iles Antilles de l'Amerique* ('Natural and Moral History of the Antilles Isles in America', 1658), and the German Gaspar Ens (*fl.* 1570–1612) an *Indiae occidentalis historia* ('History of the West Indies', 1612). Perhaps the most famous account of the Tupi of Brazil is that by another German, Hans Staden (c. 1525 to c. 1576). Staden, a soldier in Portuguese employ, spent several months in Tupi captivity; his 1557 'true history' or travel memoir, illustrated by woodcuts, became something of a bestseller for its sensational accounts of cannibalism.[11]

The historical literature on the Americas was the work not only of the clergy, who still dominated historical writing in sixteenth-century Europe, but also of a number of laymen, especially the many Spanish administrators and jurists who wrote briefs and reports (*relaciones*) which included a good deal of historical information about their territories and indigenous inhabitants. Some came from a humble background, among them a number of *soldados cronistas* who would, at home, have been unlikely to engage in a humanist historiography increasingly the preserve of the middling and upper classes. This group, principally former officers, included the anonymous author of a report of Francisco Pizarro's exploits in Peru published in 1534, and the better known Pedro Cieza de Léon (1518 to c. 1554 or 1560), a soldier who travelled extensively through Peru. Cieza de Léon's *Parte primera de la chronica del Peru* ('The First Part of the Chronicle of Peru') ranges more widely than its title indicates, and is full of oral information from Andean informants about their own culture and history. It was widely published in several languages and more than any other book cultivated the idea of the Incas as sophisticated rulers who had imposed a level of civility on the much more primitive peoples whom they had subjugated a century earlier. A counterpart in Mexico to Cieza de Léon was Bernal Díaz del Castillo (1496–1584), an unsuccessful conquistador famous less for his exploits under Cortés than for the *Historia verdadera de la Conquista de la Nueva España* ('True History of the Conquest of New Spain', 1632), which he set down largely from memory. An old man of eighty-four, without sight or hearing, by the time he wrote his brief preface, Díaz declined to provide a 'lofty' prologue in humanist fashion, promising simple eyewitness description and bequeathing the story to his children, having 'gained nothing of value' in his life.[12]

As expeditions multiplied, they almost inevitably generated their own historians. Prominent examples include Alvar Núñez Cabeza de Vaca's 1542 *Relación* of his near-disastrous expedition to Florida and Xenophon-like march through the southwest to the Pacific coast, and Antonio de Morga's (1559–1636) *Historia* of the Philippine islands (1609). The Franciscan missionary Diego López de Cogolludo's (c. 1612–65) *Historia de Yucathan* was a combination of political history, a narrative of Franciscan conversion efforts and, most interestingly, observations on the civilization and customs of the Maya, whom Cogolludo – who had taken the trouble to learn Mayan – thought must be descended from the ancient Carthaginians.

Enrique Florescano has suggested that the vigour, flexibility and sincerity of the first generation of writers about the New World was soon displaced by the artificiality of subsequent generations of official historians, classically trained, who turned the remembrance of the past into a 'bookish experience' containable within an established but narrow Renaissance genre.[13] There is some truth to this, looking at the social and educational background of later writers, but the chronology behind this assertion does not entirely support it. Scholarly writing about the New World began very early, overlapping with the experiential narratives, with a man who never saw the Americas in person, Pedro Mártir de Anglería or Peter Martyr d'Anghiera (1457–1526), a Lombard who spent most of his adult life in Spain. Like so many Italian humanists of the previous century, Martyr, a one-time soldier-turned-priest, found himself in a secretarial position (in this case to the Council of the Indies from 1520). This led to a commission from King Carlos I (from 1519 the Holy Roman Emperor Charles V) to write a history of the discoveries. Although it covered other matters such as geography and the natural features of the Americas (thereby blurring the boundaries between Plinian natural history and historical narrative), his work was in most respects textbook Renaissance historiography, its Livian inspiration indicated by its organization into decades.

The first books of Martyr's *De orbe novo* ('Decades on the New World') were published in Latin in 1516, and expanded in subsequent editions. It was probably the earliest attempt to domesticate the 'wild' past of the new territories by integrating it into European history. The natives could not, in a biblical interpretation of world history, be seen as utterly alien; it was easier to turn their culture into the remnants of a lost 'golden age'. Peter Martyr proved only the first of several historians willing to write about the discoveries without ever venturing in person to the New World. Others include Antonio de Herrera y Tordesillas (c. 1549–1625), a lifelong Habsburg functionary and prolific author of histories of France, England and Scotland. Herrera was appointed Cronista Mayor de Indias by Philip II in 1586, one of a long line of such official historians stretching into the eighteenth century. He was charged with defending Spain against increasingly sharp foreign critiques of its conduct in the Americas. As Cronista, Herrera enjoyed privileged access to state documents, which he exploited in his encyclopedic *Historia general de los hechos de los Castellanos en las islas y tierra firme del Mar Oceano* (1601–15). Better known by its English title, *The General History of the Vast Continent and*

Islands of America, it contained a chronological narrative, again organized by decades, of the period from Columbus to the mid-1550s, mixing documentary research on the one hand with heavy borrowing, to the point of near plagiarism, from Cieza de Léon and others.

Herrera's relentless devotion to telling his story in strict chronological order brought out a tension created when a set of genres in the process of being fine-tuned to contain European experiences had to be pressed into service to represent completely foreign terrain, and where practical information rather than the provision of heroic or moral models was often the principal goal. Much of the Conquest historiography was read by its target audience – kings, ministers, senior clergy – neither for entertainment nor exemplarity, but for more practical, informational purposes. When Francis Walsingham, Elizabeth I's secretary of state and a rabid opponent of Spain, read Thomas Nicholls' *The Conquest of the Weast* [*sic*] *India* (1578), a translation of López de Gómara, it is unlikely that he did so merely to while away the hours. The humanist-trained among the early historians were aware of the conflict between providing a comprehensive and informative treatise on the New World and meeting the requirements of classical genres. In particular, the question of how much geographical description should intrude on a chronological narrative had to be confronted. For Pedro Sarmiento de Gamboa (1532? to 1608?), a late sixteenth-century cosmographer commanded by the Viceroy of Peru to write a general history of the province (with special emphasis on the viciousness of the Inca royal line), the solution was the old classical and medieval one of simply providing an introductory section on the land and people before launching into a narrative:

When historians wish to write, in an orderly way, of the world or some part of it, they generally first describe the situation containing it, which is the land, before they deal with what it contains, which is the population, to avoid the former in the historical part. If this is so in ancient and well known works, it is still more desirable that in treating of new and strange lands, like these, ... the same order should be preserved.[14]

For many others, however, a prefatory treatment was insufficient, and their histories integrated sections on customs, geography, beliefs and commerce into the divisions of the book as a whole. The inclusion of geography and history together in ways rather different than conventional humanist narratives proved trend-setting, and many of the most important histories of the New World are much more than chronological accounts. The discoveries, quite apart from their impact on the understanding of human history, thereby mitigated some of the rigidity in the genre boundaries of this classicizing age. One of the most widely translated of all sixteenth-century works in any genre, Nicolás Monardes' (c. 1512–88) *Historia Medicinal* took this 'natural history' stream in one direction, towards the study of medicine, its author, a well-known Seville physician, having spent time in the Americas collecting and studying specimens of plants and animals. The inclusion of physical features, plants, animals and eventually local human customs encouraged from the beginning a more open-ended historical writing with room for the non-political and un-narratable. In a way, it constituted an efflorescence of Herodotean-style history at a time which principally valued the straightforward, tightly constructed narrative inherited from Thucydides.

Oviedo, the first historian who actually spent time in the Indies (as the Americas were to be called by Europeans for some time), was also the earliest to write about it in Spanish, and he, too, decided to include chronological history under the umbrella of natural history. Oviedo went to the New World in 1512 and apart from visits back to Spain, remained there as a crown representative. The brief *Sumario* that he wrote on one of his visits was expanded into his *De la natural hystoria de las Indias* ('On the Natural History of the Indies') and was intended initially as a corrective to Martyr's account. This work led to Oviedo's appointment in 1532 as 'chief chronicler' of the Indies, which gave him access to information beyond his own extensive experience. The results of this were set out in his magnum opus, the *Historia general de las Indias* ('General History of the Indies'), the first fifteen books of which were published at Seville in 1535 and eventually further expanded to a total of fifty books. While his geographic breadth was wide, Oviedo's historical narrative, like Martyr's, emphasized events only since the discovery; substantial inquiry into the past before contact awaited the attention of the next generation of writers. His work also illustrates the half-classical, half-medieval roots underlying historical accounts of the discoveries, even when they were trumpeted as an achievement that had outdone the ancients: Oviedo, a former writer of romance, saw Cortés as a latter-day Julius Caesar (in his medieval, knightly incarnation), and sought evidence for an earlier, pre-Columbian Spanish conquest in so dubious a place as the pseudo-Berossus. As Anthony Pagden notes,[15] Oviedo's double identity as a fiction writer was a potential problem for both him and other narrators of the fantastic world overseas. How could one reassure the literate public – in this time of uncertain frontiers between history and romance, when the authors of that popular Spanish fiction *Amadis de Gaula* routinely compared themselves to Livy – that what they were reading was the genuine article, *historia verdadera*, and not a newer version of that celebrated medieval potpourri of the incredible, Sir John Mandeville's *Travels*?

The writing of chronological histories that concentrated on events required a narrowing of focus and a familiar peg on which to hang the narrative, that peg being provided by the Conquests, commencing with Cortés' triumphs in Mexico between 1519 and 1521 (Fig. 29). Peering back before the Spanish arrival was harder, and required some understanding of native tongues, in particular Nahuatl, the dominant language family in Mesoamerica. Although the humanist Francisco

Figure 29 | The arrival of Cortés in Mexico, depicted in Codex Azcatitlan. Manuscript Mexicains n 59–64.

López de Gómara (1511–64) never set foot in Mexico, he later served as Cortés' chaplain and used his employer's information as the major source for his account of the Conquest, the *Historia de la Conquista de México* (1552). This work was almost immediately joined to another he published in the same year, *Historia general de las Indias*, which now included Peru, concerning which he had considerably less reliable information. Like the histories by Oviedo and Martyr, this was organized spatially and included information on the natural features, native language and customs, book-ended between opening and closing chapters on the birth and death of Cortés himself. Not surprisingly, this is complimentary to Cortés who is presented as a great figure of History along the lines of Alexander the Great and Julius Caesar; the Conquest itself figured in the histories of both Spain and of the Church, since it had advanced Christianity, much as the religion had been disseminated over a millennium previously in barbarian Europe. The lavish praise of his master proved politically incorrect, since the Cortés family was by now out of favour, and orders were issued to withdraw Gómara's history, though not before it exerted a significant impact on its readers.

Francisco Cervantes de Salazar (c. 1514–75) was a historian of much the same species as Gomára, but he holds the distinction of being the first to write a narrative history of New Spain while actually residing there. Initially commissioned by the crown to write a chronicle, he succeeded only in producing six books which remained unpublished until the twentieth century, though his 1560-published *Dialogues* also presented information on the Mexican peoples. The stream of works concentrating more narrowly on the Conquests would continue right through the sixteenth and seventeenth centuries, generating titles such as Antonio de Solís y Ribadaneyra's (1610–86) *Historia de la Conquista de México* (1684), another publication by an 'official' historian, and perhaps the single most widely read account of the Conquest, not least because of its author's flare for the dramatic – he had been a playwright earlier in life.

Peru was colonized slightly later and in a much less orderly fashion, its government never quite achieving the stability of New Spain. Conquest there quickly turned into civil war between rival groups of conquistadores. Their initial leader, Francisco Pizarro, who was assassinated amid these struggles in 1541, was himself illiterate and left no personal account of events, but there were plenty to fill this breach, including his successive secretaries Francisco de Xerez and Pedro Sancho, both of whom wrote early reports on the campaign against the Incas. Official or semi-official histories began to appear from mid-century, starting with Agustín de Zárate's (c. 1492 to c. 1560) *Historia del Descubrimiento y Conquista del Perú* ('History of the Discovery and Conquest of Peru'). A cautious account of the civil war, by a royal minister who had spent two years in Peru trying to avoid taking sides, it was 'official' only in the sense that its publication was commanded by the future King Philip II (r. 1556–98) in 1555, who had read it in manuscript. A soldier during the civil war, Diego Fernandez (c.1520 to c. 1581) was commissioned by the Council of the Indies while still in Peru to narrate those events; he completed the *Historia del Perú* in Spain only to have it banned through legal action by the Pizarro faction.

From the beginning, would-be historians in South America were heavily dependent on native informants for pre-contact history. This put them in an awkward position. On the one hand, they needed to dismiss the religious and ritualistic aspects of Andean history as both false and morally repugnant. On the other, they could not throw out all native information since it was virtually their sole source. The quandary is illustrated by Pedro Sarmiento de Gamboa:

As these barbarous nations of Indians were always without letters, they had not means of preserving the monuments and memorials of their times, and those of their predecessors with accuracy and method. As the devil, who is always striving to injure the human race, found these unfortunates to be easy of belief and timid in obedience, he introduced many illusions, lies and frauds .... By chance they formerly had some notice, passed down to them from mouth to mouth, which had reached them from their ancestors, respecting the truth of what happened in former times.

To Sarmiento's credit, he decided that although many of the stories he heard were fables, because they were believed by the natives, it was essential to 'write down what they say and not what we think about it'. Consequently, despite his misgivings, his history, which remained unpublished till the early twentieth century, can now be taken as a reasonably accurate record of Andean attitudes to the past in the mid-sixteenth century.[16]

The seventeenth century would produce further histories of the Incas, their downfall and the early rule of the Spanish. As in New Spain and Europe, historians were growing more reluctant to trust oral sources. Bernabé Cobo (1582–1657), a Jesuit who spent most of his life in Spanish America, was deeply sceptical of information from natives and chose, despite his long residency in the New World, to base his *Historia del Nuevo Mundo* ('History of the New World') principally on earlier written sources and other recent histories. He warned against reliance on uninformed 'country people' who should not be expected to have accurate information about the Inca government, and suggested that only those who actually lived in Cuzco, the Inca capital, could be trusted. On the other hand, he was much more enthusiastic about visual evidence, such as 'the painting that they had in a temple of the sun, next to the city of Cuzco, where portraits were painted showing the lives of each one of their kings with the lands that he conquered', which probably derived from an earlier 'history' on a tapestry that he had seen.[17]

The richness of this New World historiography provided another episode in that ancient, recurring struggle between the impulse to write particular histories of anything or any place, and the need to generalize effectively and construct a comprehensive universal history embracing all regions. The same problem that classical European and early Chinese imperial historians had faced in integrating barbarian peoples into their own past (taken as providing the core of a universal history) now repeated itself but on a vaster, transoceanic scale. Both a push and a pull drove a few authors to try to synthesize the disparate histories of the Indies, East and West, into a general history, one that in turn could be plugged easily into the even larger inherited master-narrative. They did not, one recent writer has commented, so much wish to erase the indigenous memory of the past as to translate it into a European frame and thereby 'drag' it into Christian history.[18]

The pull in this drag was largely careerist and commercial: there was a market for summary, synthetic works as much as for the accounts of particular events or regions, fuelled by print and by a growing literate public thirsting for easily accessible information and newly interested in histories of varying sorts, as we saw in the previous chapter. The push was even more powerful and came principally from the Church, which was as anxious to situate heathen natives within a biblical account of the world as it was to bring them to Christian faith; as Gómara would state in the foreword to his *Historia general de las Indias* in 1552, the discovery of the New World was the most important event since the birth of Christ. The earliest missionary-historians, Andrés de Olmos (c. 1480–1570) and Toribio de Benevente (c. 1500–69, called 'Motolinía', a name meaning 'poor one' in Nahuatl, which he adopted with pride from the natives he encountered), envisaged the discoveries as falling into a broader Franciscan apocalyptic narrative; according to this, the conversion of the Indians would provide the prelude to a more general reform and the achievement of a Christian utopia on both sides of the Atlantic.

The ecclesiastical 'push' quickly came to 'shove' with the advent of the Counter-Reformation, since it now became essential to ensure that it was the right kind of Christianity, and the Roman Catholic rather than Protestant version of the past, that would be planted across the seas. One approach, arising in part from competition among the various religious orders, was to write histories of the furtherance of Catholicism in different provinces of the New World, often from the point of view of a particular order. The Lima-based Dominican Juan Meléndez (*fl.* 1680s) did this in a three-volume history of religion in Peru which gives pride of place to the Dominicans, while the Jesuit Francisco Jarque provided a comparable account of the Society of Jesus' promotion of Christianity in the province of Paraguay, including observations of native religious practice. These ostensibly church histories were conceived as segments of universal history, as much as ecclesiastical history of the previous twelve centuries had been. Thus the Franciscan Juan de Torquemada's (d. 1664) *Monarquía indiana* ('The Indian Monarchy', 1615) covered both religious and secular history, turning the story of the pre-Conquest natives into the equivalent of the Israelite captivity in Egypt, with Cortés as the deliverer ordained by God to destroy the Aztec Empire because of its idolatry, and the Franciscans as creators of a new Eden – now sadly turned, through the colonists' abuse and decadence, into a new Babylon.

Among the clerical authors of general histories, three merit special mention: Bartolomé de Las Casas (1474–1566), José de Acosta (1540–1600) and Bernardino de Sahagún (1499?–1590), respectively a Dominican, a Jesuit and a Franciscan. Las Casas has had enormous appeal to later generations because of his early criticism of Spanish mistreatment of the natives (including forced conversion to Christianity), which led this erstwhile adventurer to become a friar and commit his life to their protection. His works aroused antagonism at the time, running counter to the anti-Indian sentiments of lay historians such as Gómara and to the efforts of fellow clergy engaged in the business of conversion. Modernity has learned to take his statements with a large grain of salt, even when sympathizing with the motives behind them.

Box 16   Las Casas' *History of the Indies*

Las Casas commanded that his unfinished *History of the Indies* not be published until at least forty years after his death and it would not appear in print until 1875. It contains many of the same ideas found in his *Brief Relation of the Destruction of the Indies* and it was chanted in the same angry voice; he intended by it to arouse support for the welfare of the natives. Organized into decades, commencing with Columbus, the text of the *History* begins with a prologue (written in 1552) that has all the features of humanist historiographical discourse: a statement about the uses of history; reference back to the great historians of classical antiquity; and a discussion of his own motivation in writing. Las Casas was driven to write the history by his negative reaction to Oviedo's *Natural History of the Indies*, published in 1526, and the two men would become fierce opponents with Oviedo arguing for a very negative view of that native intelligence which Las Casas now defended. Las Casas' own tactics in debate reveal both the strengths and weaknesses of ethnography within a Renaissance context. While Las Casas enthusiastically praised the Aztecs as a superior, if still barbaric, civilization, he did so entirely within a categorical universe defined by classical culture, invariably evaluating them by comparison with Greece and Rome.

Las Casas wrote a number of works, including an unfinished *Historia general de las Indias* ('General History of the Indies') (see Box 16). Much of his fame, however, rests on his *Brevísima relación de la destrucción de las Indias* ('A Brief Relation of the Destruction of the Indies', 1552). The *Brief Relation* was a passionate defence of native rights which had the unintended consequence of reinforcing Protestant countries' anti-Catholic propaganda. This in turn fed the wider 'Black Legend' of Spanish atrocities in Europe and the Americas. So vituperative was its tone, and so strong its doubt of the merits of forcibly converting the natives, that it was attacked as untruthful and anti-Spanish by other missionary-historians, most notably Motolinía, a bitter foe who at one point denounced Las Casas to Charles V.

José de Acosta was of a later generation, and a member of the Jesuits, the new religious order associated closely with the Counter-Reformation (and which would produce his younger Italian contemporary, the missionary to China, Matteo Ricci). Acosta's much-translated *Historia natural y moral de las Indias* ('Natural and Moral History of the Indies', as it has become known in English)[19] appeared in Spanish in 1590 and was the result of both his philosophical training and time spent in both Peru and Mexico. As the title suggests, it continued in the tradition of combining natural history with narrative, and it did this so well that it was praised over two centuries later by the great German naturalist Alexander von Humboldt. Acosta is credited, among other things, with articulating the notion of a land bridge between Asia and America whence came natives who had deteriorated into degrees of primitivism, thus bringing him into accord with the generally accepted modern notion of transcontinental migration (even though Acosta reached this conclusion from entirely fallacious assumptions built on biblical and Noachic theories of descent). From our point of view, the most interesting features of his book are its moderately adulatory history of pre-contact native cultures, especially Aztec and Inca, and Acosta's reminder to his readers that the kind of bloodthirsty barbarity that these appeared to exhibit, including human sacrifice, had also featured in the European past (a point which Las Casas too had made). 'Any history, if it is a true one and well written, brings no little profit to the reader', Acosta wrote, stressing the importance of understanding the native past as a precondition for effective evangelizing. 'There are no peoples so barbaric that they do not have something worthy of praise, nor are there any people so civilized and humane that they stand in no need of correction.'[20]

Acosta divided 'barbarians' – that is, non-Christians – into three distinct groups: the civilized (including Chinese, Japanese and certain peoples of India) who had laws, government, writing and records of the past; the semi-civilized (including Aztecs and Incas) who had government, religion and some recollection of the past but neither books nor script; and finally, the completely savage, devoid of government, religion, law and writing. While these sorts of divisions and even a notion of progress from one stage to the next were not entirely new, the wide purview of Acosta's comparison, which includes Asian peoples, is of interest – a product of his order's global evangelizing ambitions. It is also notable for its insistence on the supremacy of observed experience over tradition in explaining or describing the new territories, their peoples and their natural history. Despite his ruthlessly strict adherence to the necessity of the Church to human salvation, Acosta points both backward to Aristotelian visions of the plenitude of nature and ahead to the comparativist eighteenth-century *histoire des moeurs*, even though this thorough-going providentialist, completely convinced of Spain's destiny to bring Christian monarchy across the seas, would have found the values of a Voltaire completely repugnant.

Among the most interesting of all of the sixteenth century's Spanish New World historians is Sahagún, a Franciscan whose surname derives from the town in which he was born in 1499 or 1500. He arrived in New Spain in 1529 and spent most of his very long life in various Mexican locations. Sahagún was among the generation of missionaries who mastered indigenous tongues and then used the Roman alphabet to represent native languages such as Nahuatl that had previously known no alphabetic equivalent. Sahagún pursued the earlier linguistic efforts of his fellow Franciscan, Motolinía, and the thrust of Franciscan education would be in Latin and Nahuatl rather than Spanish. A philologist and humanist pedagogue, his approach to native education, teaching the young so that they in turn could instruct their parents, had the beneficial side effect of producing very quickly a robust supply of intelligent boys who could read and write both Nahuatl and Latin, and who could translate Christian texts into the former.

Sahagún was no liberal sympathizer with native religions and practices: like most missionaries, he genuinely regarded them as superstitious evils that God had now sent Christianity to suppress. It must have chafed to have his manuscripts confiscated, late in life, when he ran afoul of the Inquisition's post-Tridentine measures to sequester and destroy suspicious and heterodox materials, including ethnographic treatises. Fortunately, through a series of accidents, a single copy of Sahagún's magnum opus has survived, unlike several other histories known to us by name but swept to oblivion in the last quarter of the sixteenth century. At some point, probably in the late 1530s while he taught at the new Colegio de Santa Cruz de Tlatelolco, Sahagún conceived the idea of writing a general history of New Spain. Unlike many other historians, he refused to rely strictly on his own observations and information, but took advantage of the native Nahuatl-speakers among his students, who became research assistants, even collaborators. Sahagún used extensive oral information, and his cohort of bilingual youth extended his reach considerably. The result, which he and his native assistants began to compile in Nahuatl in the 1550s and expanded into a Spanish version in the 1570s, is a vast and wide-ranging work. Conventionally referred to now as the Florentine Codex after the solitary manuscript in which it survives, Sahagún called it the *Historia general de las cosas de Nueva España* ('General History of Things in New Spain'). Its twelve books run the gamut of possible subjects – it hearkens back well past Renaissance humanism to an older medieval tradition of encyclopedic knowledge – but the focus throughout is native culture and history, not simply the Spanish experience in the area. Beginning with a book on the Aztec gods (carefully justified as knowledge necessary to the combating of such pagan beliefs), it continues with sections on rituals, beliefs about the afterlife, astrology, native 'moral philosophy', social organization, customs and flora and fauna.

The twelfth and final book, completed by 1579, is a summary history of the Conquest of Mexico which, as Sahagún says in his address to the reader, differs from the many other histories already available because 'I wanted to write about it in the Mexican language, not so much in order to extract some truths from the very Indians who took part in the conquest as in order to set down the language of the things of war and of the weapons that the natives use in it, so that from there one can take appropriate words and expressions for speaking in the Mexican language on this topic.'[21] In short, the principal goal was not historical truth in the natives' own words but a furtherance of the accurate acquisition by Europeans of the language. However, he adds, it is not an unimportant benefit that 'those who were conquered knew and gave an account of many things which transpired among them during the war of which those who conquered them were unaware', and that this was done while many of the participants, mainly 'persons of good judgment' whom he believed 'told the truth', could bear witness. Sahagún refers to himself variously as author of the work and as 'compiler' but it is clear that he did not do it alone. He assembled his manuscript by collecting, over the course of his life, statements and testimonials from natives of high rank and the old. His assistants transferred these as they were spoken into written Nahuatl, and then helped him to shape the material; the entire process took over twenty years, and another twelve before a Spanish version was complete. The recitation of history in Book Twelve is by and large written from the native perspective. In 1585 Sahagún revised his narrative of the Conquest into a new version which features more of his own views and contains a pro-imperial panegyric of Cortés; this was probably done for political reasons, in particular his wish to defend the Franciscan version of the Conquest and his order's alliance with Cortés. A collaborative project giving voice to the natives thus metamorphosed into a sanitized humanist narrative, complete with Thucydidean speeches providing the Spanish perspective. By the 1580s, with the Franciscan enterprise in jeopardy, Sahagún could no longer afford to let the indigenous past speak for itself.

Indigenous and Mestizo Histories from the Americas

Sahagún's collaborations with native interpreters remind us that there were two sides to the Conquests, and leads into the question of how the indigenous peoples saw their own past, both before and after they were introduced to gunpowder, Christianity and devastating Old World diseases. The degree to which the introduction of Western historiography eradicated or distorted native historical thinking and its representations is fiercely contested. Postcolonial scholars have criticized the attempted appropriation of indigenous writings, the imposition of Renaissance literacy and the extirpation of both oral and pictorial forms of historical representation. Thus Enrique Florescano asserts that the Mesoamerican conquests, and especially the introduction of alphabetic writing, demonstrates that 'not only is the history of the conquered written by the conqueror, but the conquered's own historical tradition is first suppressed and then expropriated by the conqueror, who

Figure 30 | Lunar goddesses, Mayan manuscript, twelfth century. From the Dresden Codex, fo. 20.

converts it into a reading that only the victor can carry out'.[22] Perhaps so, but the natives proved able to adapt their historical thinking to literacy; moreover, the histories that travelled back to Europe were far from unaffected by the 'conquered' culture. Sahagún's great project is a prominent but not solitary example.

The natives colonized by the Europeans had, contrary to the belief of many of their conquerors, a well-developed sense of their past and various means, graphic and oral, to represent it. Starting about 500 BC, the Maya, Mixtec, Zapotec, Aztec and other Mesoamerican peoples had developed non-alphabetic writing in a combination of pictographic, logographic, ideographic and phonetic elements, carved on monuments or written on various portable media – animal skins, bark and cloth (Figs. 30, 31 and 32). Archaeologists have uncovered remnants of Mesoamerican commemorative paintings and carvings from as far back as a millennium before the Conquest, some of which mark dates in the native calendar. One scholar has concluded from pictographic evidence that Mesoamericans 'clearly had a

Figure 31 | Wooden calendrical slit drum (*teponaztli*), Mixtec, Mexico. The scene depicts a battle between two cities and is carved with figures and calendrical inscriptions in the same style as used in Mixtec screenfold codices.

notational system that allowed them to record the facts of the present and the past and to look towards the future'.[23] The degree to which natives made use of this is a matter of judgment, but regardless of the intensity of interest in the past, knowledge of it was undoubtedly undercut or modified by the purging of old rituals and the renaming of towns for Christian saints, or the intermixing of native and European cultural practices. Prior to the invasions, the Mesoamericans had also developed calendrical systems to reckon the days and years. Mayan time-reckoning had included a linear calculation or 'long-count', with a firm beginning date equivalent to 3114 BC, in addition to a repeating cycle of years. This system probably goes back several millennia and came into general use during the Maya Classic period (third to eighth century AD), but it can be definitively traced from stone inscriptions of the first century BC. Mayan glyphs (a hieroglyphic writing system of about 500 signs, dating from the late Pre-Classic period, before AD 250), recount a dynastic history for the centuries from 250–900, and recorded dates can be found from early in the first century AD. Paper from bark was developed perhaps as early as the fifth century, and with it the possibility of making 'books',

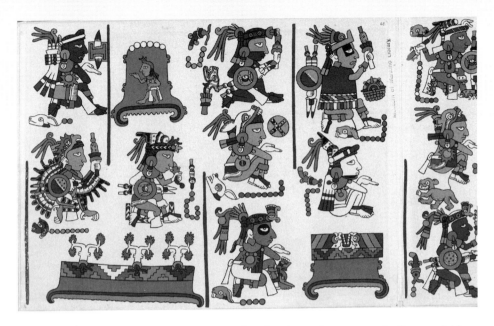

Figure 32 | Codex Zouche-Nuttall. Facsimile of codex, a forty-seven-leaf screenfold paper manuscript, painted, after 1320; Mixtec late post-classic period, c. 1200–1521. This contains two narratives: one side relates the history of important centres in the Mixtec region; the other, starting at the opposite end, records the genealogy, marriages and political and military feats of the Mixtec ruler Eight Deer Jaguar-Claw.

typically in gatefold format, such as the Dresden Codex, one of the handful of these pre-Conquest documents surviving to the present.

Acosta would later compare European, American and Asian writing systems in his *Natural and Moral History*,[24] but he waxed sceptical on the Amerindian sense of the past when sent a Mexican chronicle by Juan de Tovar in 1586–7. 'In the first place, what certainty or authority does this relation or history possess?' he asked. 'In the second place, since the Indians did not have writing, how could they preserve such a quantity and variety of matters for so long a time?' Extant central Mexican codices all apparently date from post-Hispanic times, including the Codex Mendoza, painted about twenty years after the arrival of Cortés, and intended as a record of the Aztec rulers and their conquests. They cannot be read as if they were chronological histories, since they contain myth and legend mixed in with events that may actually have occurred, but let us remember again that Europeans were themselves struggling to map the boundaries of history and fiction at this very time. The Boturini Codex, painted about the same time, tells the story of the mythical Aztec journey to the valley of Mexico. The Codex Chimalpopoca

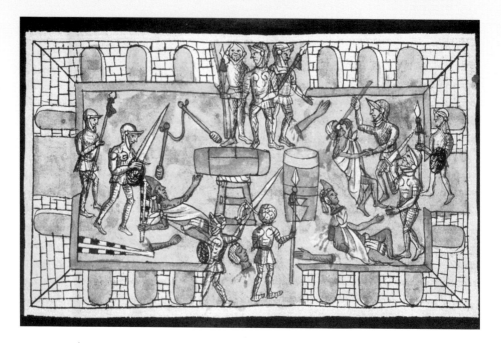

Figure 33 │ Massacre of the Aztecs. Miniature from Fray Diego Durán, *History of the Indies of New Spain*, fo. 211, 1579.

contains two anonymous works, the *Annals of Cuauhtitlan* (or Quauhtitlan, a town north of Mexico City) and the *Legends of the Sun*, both of which stretch back into remote antiquity. The author of the *Annals* had access to both now-lost pictographic sources and oral accounts. The author of the *Legends* so clearly relied on painted histories that, his modern editor observes, it seems as if he is pointing at them over the reader's shoulder as he describes them.[25] When the Spanish lawyer Alfonso de Zorita visited the Guatemalan highlands in the 1550s he was able to discover details of the natives' ancient governance 'with the aid of paintings which they had which recorded their history for more than eight hundred years back, and which were interpreted for me by very ancient Indians'. Sahagún refers to the 'old men, in whose possession were the paintings and recollections of ancient things', on whose information he rested his assertion that the Mesoamericans were not indigenous but rather earlier migrants from the north.[26] Diego Durán (c. 1537–88), the Dominican author of one of the earliest histories of the Aztecs (Fig. 33), was convinced that 'these natives are part of the ten tribes of Israel that Shalmaneser, king of the Assyrians, captured and took to Assyria in the time of Hoshea, king of Israel, and in the time of Ezekias, king of Jerusalem', an idea that has enjoyed a peculiarly long currency.

From Durán's perspective, the natives' own ideas of their origins were 'clearly fabulous' and demonstrated that they were ignorant of their beginnings. But on the other side of this determination to find a biblical origin for them lay Durán's more open-minded attitude to native accounts of recent times. He reveals a genuine determination to use both painted histories and conversation with informants, conducted in Nahuatl, to enrich his account. He went so far as to cite an indigenous *historiador real*, one Cuauhcoatl, who lived during the reign of Moctezuma II, the last Aztec monarch:

Motecuhzoma [*sic*] ... called the royal historian, an aged man called Cuauhcoatl [Eagle Serpent], and addressed him: 'O ancient father, I desire to know the true story, the knowledge that is hidden in your books about the Seven Caves where our ancestors, our fathers and grandfathers, lived, and whence they came forth. I wish to know about the place wherein dwelt our god Huitzilopochtli and out of which he led forefathers.'

'O mighty lord,' answered Cuauhcoatl, 'what I your unworthy servant, can answer you is that our forebears dwelt in that blissful, happy place called Aztlan, which means "Whiteness"....'

Cuauhcoatl continues with a story of the lives of the Aztec forebears, their travels, trials and agricultural practices: 'And this is the story told by our ancestors, it is what I have found [painted] in our ancient books.'[27]

Despite the interest of early observers, much of the pictorial heritage of the Aztecs and later the Maya met with a bad end. Although they survived longer than the ancient religious books, which were almost immediately consigned to the flames, and though new specimens were being created throughout the sixteenth century, indigenous pictorial history suffered from neglect or concerted destruction. This phenomenon was not utterly alien to the peoples affected; while the depredations of the Conquest should be neither whitewashed nor underestimated, much historiographical purging and distortion had occurred among the natives before a single Spaniard had set foot on their shores. Around 1430, for instance, the rulers of the newly hegemonic Aztec city of Tenochtitlan decided to burn old pictographic histories because they contained 'falsehoods' and did not accord with the Aztec vision of the past:

Their history was kept.
But then it was burned:
When Itzcóatl ruled in Mexico.
A decision was made.
The Mexica lords said
It is not wise for all those people
to know the paintings ....
Because a lot of lies are kept there, and in them many have been held as gods.[28]

Interference with pre-existing records was also practised, as was outright fabrication. Mixtec rulers, who organized their codices by event rather than by year, are known to have had some of these repainted in order to insert themselves retroactively into genealogies to which they did not belong. At least one Mayan leader claimed to be the son of a woman who had taken office when 800 years old. The Maya and Zapotec would deface or destroy stone monuments whose messages no longer supported current political reality. In this respect, the Mesoamerican natives were not so very different from their European counterparts of about the same period. They shared a reverence for ancestors and birth status, and many of their pictorial texts, like ancient manuscripts in the possession of great noble families of Europe, were respected precisely because they were thought to contain the words of illustrious forebears. A poem included in the *Crónica Mexicayotl* by an early seventeenth-century historian of Aztec descent, Fernando or Hernando Alvarado Tezozómoc, proclaims the faith in ancestral utterances:

Thus they have come to tell it,
thus they have come to record it in their narration,
and for us they have painted it in their codices,
the ancient men, the ancient women.
They were our grandfathers, our grandmothers,
our great-grandfathers, great-grandmothers,
our great-great-grandfathers, our ancestors ....[29]

There is a further respect in which native historians resembled medieval chroniclers, and in this instance to the discomfort of humanist-trained Europeans. Truth and falsehood were not terms that lined up neatly with 'history' on the one hand and 'myth or legend' on the other. Truth, to the Aztec mind, was what suited the speaker, whether it had occurred or not. This is not so very different from the 'truth is what is true now' attitude of many earlier European writers – recall the medieval inclination to invent documents that supported something believed to have happened – but it would be increasingly suspicious to later generations of Europeans inclined to doubt, criticism and the philological exposure of frauds.

The Spanish would step up the pace of destruction, with different motives. Nevertheless, the suppression of native historical memory was far from complete, even where pursued most vigorously. Traces of pre-Conquest and early post-Conquest historical thinking have survived into modernity, to be recovered from the distant descendants of pre-Conquest Amerindians, frequently by ethnohistorians, archaeologists, art historians and linguists rather than historians. The ethnolinguist Dennis Tedlock, translator of *Popol Vuh*, the Maya 'Book of the Dead', found his fieldwork in Guatemalan villages such as Momostenango ('Before the Building') and personal encounters with modern 'daykeepers' essential to the project of translation. Similarly, ethnohistorian Joanne Rappaport has studied memories of the indigenous past going back several centuries through engagement with modern Andean natives. Susan Niles has found traces of Inca narrative history in surviving buildings and shrines in Peru.[30]

The Conquest failed to eliminate indigenous historical memory for a number of reasons, one being the ambivalent approach of numerous missionaries, many of whom quickly realized that in order to convert the natives they needed to understand not just their language but also their sense of the past. Occasional interventions from Spain reinforced efforts to study extant codices and interview the natives, such as the 1553 decree of the Council of the Indies which authorized the questioning of 'old and experienced Indians' who should be made to produce 'any pictures or lists or any other account' of past times.[31] While a determined iconoclast like Bishop Diego de Landa (1524–79) could destroy a great deal of Mayan literature in 1562, others openly lamented their fellow clerics' purging of these texts in the name of Christianity. Through writers such as Las Casas and Sahagún, an enormous effort was put into the study of native cultures in various provinces of the New World, and the surviving product of this is a number of historical, geographical and scientific works penned in the sixteenth and seventeenth centuries by Spanish, mestizo and native authors.

The Spaniards for their part tried to make sense of the oral and written genres that they discovered among the natives by translating them into approximate European equivalents. Alonso de Molina (1514–79), author of the first Nahuatl–Spanish dictionary and an associate of Sahagún, rendered the pictographic equivalents of the Spanish *cronista* variously as *altepetlacuilo* ('community-painter'), *xiuhtlacuilo* ('year-painter') and *tenemilizicuiloani* ('life-painter', that is, biographer), while also distinguishing a further '*contador de historia*', the *tenemilizpoa*, which appears to refer to reciters of oral tradition; '*ystoriador*' (which he does not seem to have distinguished from '*cronista*') corresponded with the Nahuatl *tlatolicuiloani* or *nemiliztlatolicuiloani*. The Aztecs themselves distinguished between the speech of leaders and nobility and that used by commoners, and also between spoken words (*tlatollotl*) and written texts (*tlacuilolli*). A book was called *amatl* (after the bark-derived 'paper' they used) or *amoxtli* ('glued paper'), and the most ancient Aztec legends refer to the importance of books in their culture; their sages (*tlamatinime*) were 'owners of books'. The closest equivalent to 'history' was *nemilizamatl*, literally 'life's book'. The related phrase *Nemiliz tlatollotl* was taken by the Spanish to mean an oral chronicle or history, while *Nemiliz tlacuilolli* was rendered as a written chronicle or history. The term *huehuetlatolli*, which to the Nahuatl speakers meant 'words of the ancestors', a recitation of great deeds in the past, was inaccurately rendered by the Spanish as 'ancient histories'. A chronicle or year-by-year accounting of events, such as that found in the annals of Codex Mexicanus was, for the Aztecs, a separate type of 'year book' or *xiuhamatl* while genealogical data were contained in yet a third type of book, the *tlacamecayoamatl*.[32]

It was not only the sympathetic approach of some of the missionaries that helped to secure the indigenous heritage in the face of destruction worthy of the Qin book-burning, but native adaptability. Writing provided a medium for presenting their own history to the Europeans, and it offered the ethnic groups suppressed by the Aztecs an outlet for distinguishing themselves in Spanish eyes. It also gave indigenous writers a venue in which they could defend native practices by identifying similarities with Christianity. Just as European writers had for centuries tried to integrate myth and history through euhemerism (the explanatory reduction of pagan 'gods' into historical figures), so Mesoamerican natives practised the reverse, turning ancestors into deities, the records of this being adduced by later generations as proof of how things had been. From this it was a very short step to find linkages or equivalences between their gods and Christian saints, a process in which some of the Spanish collaborated. The above-mentioned Aztec *Annals of Cuauhtitlan* stretch back to the early seventh century AD, providing a chronology for pre-Conquest history while repudiating certain old gods as 'devils' or sorcerers. Alphabetic texts, themselves often based on now-lost indigenous books, have survived from the post-Conquest period; these were originally written down alphabetically from either a lost hieroglyphic text or an oral recitation of such a text. The Yucatec-Mayan texts known as the *Book of Chilam Balam* may have originated in the early post-Conquest period, though its earliest manuscripts date from a later time. A series of Cakchiquel authors, members of the Xahil family in what is now Guatemala, employed writing at the end of the sixteenth century to record the history of their struggles with various foreign adversaries, including their fifteenth-century rivals, the Quiché. What many of the indigenous writers who used older native sources appear to have done is to embellish their works with Christian additions (especially chronology) and Spanish words, transmitting an elastic version of the originals, most of which have been lost. Thus the *Crónica Mexicáyotl* written at the end of the sixteenth century by the Mexica historian Fernando Alvarado Tezozómoc, appears to have been a transcription of older annals.

Not only the alphabet but also the genres of European writing were appropriated by native historians, including annals. Those composed by one writer of Nahuatl, the Franciscan-educated nobleman known usually as Chimalpahín (Hispanicized as Don Domingo de San Antón Muñón Chimalpahín Quauhtlehuanitzin, 1579–1660), provide years both *anno domini* and imputed according to the *xiuhpohualli* (the pre-Conquest 'year count' or cyclical calendar): thus '9 Flint Year, 1592' is followed by '10 House Year, 1593', '11 Rabbit Year, 1594' and so on.

8 Rabbit year, 1578. In this year was when there was a procession to the [church of] the Company of Jesus, the Theatines, going to place there the relics and bones of saints which had come from Rome; the procession set out from the cathedral.

9 Reed year, 1579. In this year our precious father fray Alonso de Molina, Franciscan friar, passed away; he was our preacher. And this was when there was a sickness again (blood came from our noses). The sickness really raged; many people died. And this was also when, at Christmas, the nuns who are children of Santa Clara came to where they now are, at Petlacalco; they came from where they were first, at Trinidad; secular priests were in charge of them at first.[33]

The annals for post-Conquest times follow a pattern familiar to any reader of medieval chronicles. The rather spare entries, quoted above, for more remote years during which the adult author, a child at the time of the events recorded, was dependent on others for information, gradually broadened as he began to write annals year by year, as events occurred – or sometimes even day by day. This led generations of later readers (though not Chimalpahín himself) to consider it – somewhat misleadingly since it nowhere refers to the author's own activities – a *Diario* (diary) rather than a history. Like European annals and chronologies of the sixteenth century, and unlike both medieval illustrated chronicles and the pictorial histories of the pre- and early post-Conquest years, this work is largely devoid of images. It is also remarkable, though not unique, for its wide purview, since Chimalpahín's vision of history embraced the whole world. The events he recorded occurred in virtually every quarter of the globe, and include even a recent European tragedy, the 1610 assassination of King Henri IV of France.

By this time natives were also writing in Spanish: where Chimalpahín wrote principally in Nahuatl, occasionally deploying Spanish loan-words, his more thoroughly Hispanicized contemporary, the Texcocan mestizo, Fernando de Alva Ixtlilxóchitl (c. 1568–1648 or 1650) (Extract 20), wrote in both languages. Alva Ixtlilxóchitl had Aztec heritage but was also descended from a Texcocan prince (also named Ixtlilxóchitl) who had allied with Cortés against the Aztecs. He had a successful career in the administration of New Spain in the early seventeenth century, at one point serving as governor of Texcoco. Impressed by his knowledge of the past, the viceroy suggested that he set it down in writing. The result was a number of works ranging from a collection of songs to a history of the Chichimecas.[34] Like Chimalpahín, Alva Ixtlilxóchitl had been trained by Franciscans, reading the famous Codex Xolotl, a major source of early Mexican history, in the company of Juan de Torquemada. He typifies the ambivalence of the third or fourth generation of historians of the Americas, by which time extensive intermarriage had occurred. Alva Ixtlilxóchitl criticized the cruelties inflicted by the Spanish but at the same time extolled the Christianity that they had introduced. It is he who has given us one of the clearest statements of what his contemporaries took as the historiographical interests of the ancient Mexica:

They had writers for each genre: some who handled the Annals, putting in order the things that happened each year, by day, month and hour. Others were in charge of genealogies

20: Alva Ixtlilxóchitl's Account of the Coming of the Spanish

Some historians, especially Spaniards, write that Ixtlilxóchitl came with his army of fifty thousand men on orders of his brother, Tecocoltzin. But it was very much the reverse, according to Don Alonso Axayaca and the accounts and paintings of the natives, especially one which I have in my possession written in the Toltec language, or Mexican as it is now called, and signed by all the old chiefs of Texcoco and confirmed and certified by the other most important and old people of the city. It is these I follow in my history because they are the most truthful, and because those who wrote or painted these accounts were there personally on these occasions, and moreover some of them have told me about it orally and related the way in which it happened, people who died a few years ago and whom I reached when they were already very old. They state that Tecocoltzin already was dead on that occasion as previously stated, and that Ixtlilxóchitl was with Cortés and the others ever since they had left Texcoco.

Selection from Fernando de Alva Ixtlilxóchitl, *Ally of Cortés: Account 13. 'Of the coming of the Spaniards and the beginning of the evangelical law'*, trans. Douglass K. Ballentine (El Paso: Texas Western Press, 1969), 32–3.

and ancestors of the kings and persons of lineage .... Some of them took care of painting the limits, boundaries, and boundary lines of the cities, provinces, towns, and places, of the lots and distribution of lands ...[35]

Having collected a number of Indian codices and oral traditions from elderly informants, Alva Ixtlilxóchitl ventured in his historical writings back beyond the Conquest to ancient Mexican history, relating in turn the regime of the barbarous Olmecs (civilized by Quetzalcoatl, in this version an unnamed bearded sage sometimes identified as the Apostle Thomas), and the more civilized Toltecs, Asian émigrés and ancestors of his own Texcocan race.

To the south, in the Andes, writing was not introduced at all before 1532, and no complete narrative history of the ruling Incas predates the arrival of the Spanish, though echoes of earlier oral histories have been found in later works, and a set of paintings of Inca monarchs, commissioned by the Inca Pachacuti (r. 1438–71), awaited the Europeans. But even if they 'entirely lacked the obsessive concern with the passage of time that characterized Mesoamerica',[36] the Andeans were not a people without history. The Incas in particular had a strong interest in the past and had developed the means to preserve its memory. They had used the quipu, or coloured, knotted cords (Fig. 34), whose meaning was retained and interpreted by quipucamayocs (quipu-keepers), to record numerical data for administrative purposes, and also as cues to those charged with memorizing and performing oral

Figure 34 | Inca quipu, a series of knotted strings on a carved wooden stick. Peru or Bolivia, 1400–1532.

traditions, which were maintained through periodic performances called *cantares* (the Spanish term for their songs). Pedro Sarmiento de Gamboa, no admirer of the Inca rulers, nonetheless believed that this was a historically minded people, and that the ninth Inca, Pachacuti Inca Yupanqui, had instituted the collection of annals by sending out a summons to 'all the old historians in all the provinces he had subjugated'. In the following passage, Sarmiento outlines their methods and defends his reliance upon them:

Some may say that this history cannot be accepted as authentic being taken from the narratives of these barbarians, because, having no letters, they could not preserve such details as they give from so remote an antiquity. The answer is that, to supply the want of letters, these barbarians had a curious invention which was very good and accurate. This was that from one to the other, from fathers to sons, they handed down past events, repeating the story of them many times, just as lessons are repeated from a professor's chair, making the hearers say these historical lessons over and over again until they were fixed in the memory. Thus each one of the descendants continued to communicate the annals in the order described with a view to preserve their histories and deeds, their ancient traditions, the numbers of their tribes, towns, provinces, their days, months and years, their battles, deaths, destructions, fortresses, and 'Sinchis' [regional warlords]. Finally they recorded, and they still record, the most notable things which consist in their numbers (or statistics), on certain cords called quipu, which is the same as to say reasoner or accountant .... Besides this they had, and still have, special historians in these nations, an hereditary office descending from father to son.[37]

The mestizo historian Garcilaso de la Vega, who thought the Peruvian literary heritage equal to the Spanish, would later echo Sarmiento in asserting that the quipus had even been used to record ceremonies, rituals, laws and ordinances. Spanish officials would continue to rely on quipucamayocs and their testimony in judicial cases for several decades after the Conquest, finally rejecting them in the 1580s as they became suspicious of their accuracy and of their possible links to pre-Christian religion.

From the Spanish point of view, these forms of record-keeping were inferior to alphabetic writing, just as oral tradition was deemed less trustworthy than history, but they stopped short of dismissing them outright. In our next chapter we will see that the Enlightenment took a harder line against the possibility of deriving history from non-alphabetic sources. As in Mesoamerica, the Quechua and Aymara languages of the Andes were rendered into Latin script in the 1530s. Once again the conquered used the tools of the invaders in order both to preserve that past and to write their own versions of their colonization, despite the slowness with which they acquired oral and written Castilian. Eschewing the title of historians, they called their works *relaciónes* or *crónicas*, lower literary forms in the humanist hierarchy of genres. Among these indigenous authors was Juan de Santa Cruz Pachacuti Yamqui Salcamayhua, whose *Relación de antigüedades deste reyno del Pirú* ('On the Antiquities of the Kingdom of Peru', 1613) attempted to reconcile native historical traditions with the version of history presented in Spanish chronicles.

A few decades earlier, Titu Cusi Yupanqui (also known by the Spanish name Diego de Castro Yupangui, c. 1530–71) had also attempted to reach a modus vivendi with the Spanish missionaries while preserving Inca traditions. The heir to the Inca ruler Huayna Capac, and himself briefly head of a neo-Inca state that resisted subjugation until the 1570s, Titu Cusi was a convert to Christianity, and it is he who provided the earliest-known indigenous account of the Conquest. Titu Cusi apparently chose to have this translated into Spanish, of which he had limited knowledge, and turned into a Spanish *relación*; while this looks like a further act of submission – replacing native forms of representation with the tyranny of the European alphabet – his most recent student has argued that it was born of the delicate cultural politics of diplomacy between the Inca and the Spaniard.[38] Titu Cusi claimed that he authorized this written version because of the frailness of human memory, but since Inca mnemonic systems had previously been able to preserve the past without writing, this may rather have been a barbed comment on the Europeans' inability to preserve oral accounts with fidelity. The complexity of the process of composition aptly illustrates the 'hybrid' nature of historiography in the early post-Conquest era. Other early native accounts were similarly the result of intercultural collaboration: the history of the Conquest by Juan de Betanzos (c. 1510–76) was based in part on the oral narrative of his wife, the Inca princess Angelina Yupanqui, a sister of the Inca Atahualpa and previously the mistress of the conquistador Pizarro. Betanzos, who seems to have had little formal education, was one of the earliest Spaniards to master the Andean tongue, Quechua; he may also have derived information about particular figures from the past from a genre of oral 'life histories', a hypothesis reinforced by the similarities between his account and that of Pedro Sarmiento de Gamboa.[39]

Characteristic of these early accounts of the indigenous past are their frequent mutual contradiction and the unreliability of dates, the latter attributable in part to the cyclical vision of the past held by the pre-Columbian Andeans in common with the Mesoamerican peoples, but also to the fact that the Inca histories had operated less as records of past great events than as genealogical devices to locate a new ruler within a *panaca* (descent group) springing from the mythical Inca founder, Manco Capac. The genealogies of local peoples conquered by the Incas during their relatively brief hegemony were often appropriated into the Inca version of the past. Conversely, as in Mesoamerica, older and competing versions of history were discarded, as is a feature of oral cultures, once they no longer reflected the status quo – the victory of one descent line over another often meant not only the extermination of the losers but also the eradication of their rendition of the genealogical past.

The pluralism of native accounts and the lack of a single 'general history' was a frustration to Europeans who were growing accustomed to firm chronology and the Thucydidean goal of the single, 'correct' narrative. (One wonders what a different historical culture, that of China's Sima Qian, would have made of American indigenous accounts.) They had by the late sixteenth century marginalized their own chronicles, which had the same quality of 'polyvocality' – the representation of multiple points of view in the same text – in favour of the humanist history. Leaving these stories as conflicting voices was not, to the European mind, an attractive option, even among the earliest generations of humanists who, like François Baudouin, placed some confidence in native memory, pictography and oral tradition, or who admired, with Acosta, native calendrical skill.[40] Motolinía thought the Aztec *xiuhtonalamatl* or book of 'years and times' spoke the truth, even if it

21: A Spanish Missionary on Mesoamerican Indigenous Histories: Motolinía

There were, among these natives, as I have said, five books of figures and characters. The first tells of the years and seasons; the second, of their days and feasts during the whole year; the third, of the dreams, illusions, vanities and omens in which they believed. The fourth is the book of baptism and the names they gave the children; the fifth deals with their rites, ceremonies and omens connected with marriage. Of all these, one – the first – can be believed, because it tells the truth, for although barbarous and illiterate, these Indians were punctilious in counting the seasons, days, weeks, months, years and festivals – as will appear later. Also they depicted the deeds and histories of conquests and wars, and the succession of their great lords, the storms and noteworthy signs in the skies, and general pestilences, telling in what season and under what lord they occurred; and they list all the chief lords who ruled this New Spain until the coming of the Spaniards. All this they have in characters and figures which make it known. They call this book *The Book of the Number of the Years*, and according to what has been learned from it about the people who settled this land there were three different peoples, and even today there are some of the same names. One group they call Chichimecas, and they were the first lords of this land. The second group was the people of Colhua. The third group was the Mexicans.

About the Chichimecas we find nothing except that they have lived in this land for eight hundred years, although it is considered certain that they are much older, but that, being a barbarous race who lived like savages, they had no way of writing or representing things. The people of Colhua, we find, began to write and make records by means of their characters and figures ....

[Motolinía continues with an account of Aztec record-keeping.]

These Indians, besides recording in characters and figures the things I have mentioned, and especially the succession and lineage of the lords and of the leading families, and the noteworthy things that happened in their time, had also amongst them persons of excellent memory who remembered and could relate everything that they were asked. One of these men I met; a very clever man, I thought, and with an excellent memory, and he, briefly and without contradictions, told me about the beginnings and origin of these natives, giving me his opinion and that of the books considered amongst them as most authentic.

Selection from *Motolinía's History of the Indians of New Spain*, trans. and ed. Elizabeth A. Foster (Berkeley, CA: Cortés Society, 1950), introductory letter, 25, 29.

was 'barbarous and not written in letters', in effect conceding that the natives had achieved history without an alphabet (Extract 21).[41] Pedro Sarmiento de Gamboa, whose enthusiasm for Inca record-keeping we have already seen, was supposed to come up with a definitive version of Peruvian history for his master the Viceroy, but found, after interviewing hundreds of native informants about Inca lineages, that he was unable to establish a consensus position on many details. Pedro Cieza de León, who acknowledged that Incas (but not other Andean peoples) had a sense of the past, was nonetheless withering in his criticism. He attributed the multiplicity of accounts directly to the natives' lack of writing and reliance on memory, *cantares* and quipus; he noted that they tended to discard embarrassing failures such as the Inca Urco whose rule had lasted only a few days.

A further complication arises from the actual content of Andean perceptions of the past rather than the media of their preservation. Unlike the Europeans, they had no linear meta-story with a beginning and end but rather a lengthy imputed past consisting of cycles of different worlds, something like the vision of time we encountered in Vedic India. According to their perception of the past, 'events stand in fixed relation to each other behind and beyond the flux of experience', and are not stages along a divine road towards human salvation. But Spanish Catholics were not alone in their suspicion of native record-keeping and its authenticity. By the mid-seventeenth century, a more general hostility to non-traditional media had emerged in Europe, especially non-alphabetic writing and oral traditions arising from the 'vulgar'. Contemporaries were fully prepared to draw comparisons between exotic native barbarism and the home-grown forms that they had themselves escaped (soon to be a major theme of eighteenth-century analyses of the progress of civil society). Thus the seventeenth-century English bishop Edward Stillingfleet (1635–99), who doubted the worth of both oral tradition and non-alphabetic writing for either record-keeping or the determination of chronology, lumped native histories together with those of Eurasian heathen nations as altogether false, riddled with 'monstrous confusion [and] ambiguity'.[42]

By the seventeenth century, the events of the Spanish Conquest were rapidly falling out of living memory, displaced by more recent problems arising from governance through viceroys. At the same time the *relación*, originally the term for a legal document, had become identified with a brief historical account of past events and thus only barely distinguishable from either *historia* or *crónica*. The next generation of native historians adopted European historical genres more unambiguously to record the events of the previous hundred years. Among these, two stand out, an Andean native, Felipe Guaman Poma de Ayala (*c*. 1550 to after 1616), and Garcilaso de la Vega (1539–1616, surnamed El Inca to avoid confusion with a distant relative of the same name, a celebrated sixteenth-century poet). Both men were influenced by the worldview of Las Casas. Both were comfortable – to differing degrees – writing history in the mode of their Spanish overlords, as had their younger contemporary Alva Ixtlilxóchitl in New Spain. And both were critical of the way post-Conquest Peru had been governed. Yet their histories are very different, both from Alva Ixtlilxóchitl's and from each other's.

Perhaps no early modern historian illustrates the impact of one culture's *régime d'historicité* on another's, and the potential of the two to mix, so well as El Inca Garcilaso de la Vega. An aristocratic mestizo, Garcilaso left Peru as a young man in 1560, and spent the rest of his life in Europe. Garcilaso was thoroughly Hispanicized, and he wrote his works in polished Castilian prose. But he was also a native of Cuzco, 'formerly the Rome of that empire', and immensely proud of his Inca heritage. He could read Italian and had absorbed the historical style of the Renaissance via Guicciardini and Bodin; he repudiated the reading of romances in favour of history after studying Pedro Mexía's *History of the Caesars*. But Garcilaso was also keenly affected by the stories he had heard as a child from relatives. During visits with his mother's kin, 'the ordinary subject of conversation was always the origin of the Inca kings, their greatness, the grandeur of their empire, their deeds and conquests, their government in peace and war, and the laws they ordained so greatly to the advantage of their vassals', Garcilaso records. 'In short, there was nothing concerning the most flourishing period of their history that they did not bring up in their conversation.' During these visits, which turned inevitably to mourning the present and their 'lost empire', the young Garcilaso would listen intently to his relatives. When he was sixteen or seventeen, he issued a challenge to 'the most senior of them', his mother's uncle:

Inca, my uncle, though you have no writings to preserve the memory of past events, what information have you of the origin and beginnings of our kings? For the Spaniards and the other peoples who live on their borders have divine and human histories from which they know when their own kings and their neighbors' kings began to reign and when one empire gave way to another. They even know how many thousand years it is since God created heaven and earth. All this and much more they know through their books. But you, who have no books, what memory have you preserved of your antiquity? Who was the first of our Incas? What was he called? What was the origin of his line? How did he begin to reign? With what men and arms did he conquer this great empire? How did our heroic deeds begin?[43]

The Inca then responded with an account, which Garcilaso represents in direct quotation – though he may be writing his own version of a fictional speech – of the founding of the dynasty by Manco Capac.

Garcilaso's interests extended to the more northerly Spanish ventures in America. An early work about Hernando de Soto's failed expedition to the American southeast in the 1540s, recounted with the enthusiasm of a Xenophon, and usually referred to as *La Florida del Inca* ('The Florida of the Inca', 1605), is among the first histories of ventures into what is now Florida and the Gulf coast; its depiction of native resistance to the Spanish hearkens back to Tacitus' *Germania*. By the time he completed his most celebrated works, *Comentarios reales* ('Royal Commentaries' 1609) and its companion volume, *Historia general del Perú* (1617), Garcilaso had entirely assumed the garb of a humanist historian, enlivening his story with invented speeches, attempting to reconcile the conflicting accounts in his sources and appealing, not without some scepticism, to the authority of earlier historians such as Gómara, Zárate, Acosta and especially Cieza de León. That a mixed-blood Peruvian, living in Spain, would now rest his case not on native tradition but on the words of sixteenth-century Spaniards, taken as authoritative because of their personal experience in the lands about which they wrote, says a good deal about the nature of literary traffic by the beginning of the seventeenth century, and about the cultural hybridity of history and historians.

Garcilaso's conciliatory message, while critical of some Spanish injustices, presented his people as having much in common with the Spanish and as having voluntarily submitted to Christianity rather than being subjugated and forcibly converted. The Incas, he proposed, were not despots ruling a simple but noble population, even if some, such as Atahualpa, were demonstrably cruel: Atahualpa's atrocities, including elimination of rival family members, prompted a transoceanic comparison by Garcilaso of this form of succession with the 'evil custom of the Ottoman house'.[44] Rather, these sophisticated rulers represented a stage in the progress of the Andean peoples from savagery to government by natural law, analogous to the Roman impact on barbarian Europe. The superiority of classical heroes like Julius Caesar was attributable to the Romans' early literacy, which permitted them to disseminate stories of their deeds.

Garcilaso's keenness to promote the Andeans as a civilized people meant that his work included an enormous amount of material, oral and written, on pre-Columbian Peru. The information from his forebears crowds up against the writings of the Europeans. When deliberating on how best to recount the origin and early history of the Inca kings, 'it seemed to me that the best scheme and simplest and easiest way was to recount what I often heard as a child from the lips of my mother and her brothers and uncles and other elders about these beginnings. For everything said about them from other sources comes down to the same story as we shall relate, and it will be better to have it as told in the very words of the Incas than in those of foreign authors.' He went so far as to write to his old schoolmates for accounts of territories the Incas had conquered, which might be had from their mothers, 'for each province has its accounts and knots to record its annals and traditions, and thus preserves its own history much better than that of its neighbours'.[45] Yet despite Garcilaso's ancestry and his attentiveness to oral tradition, his work lies much closer to the European culture he had adopted than the Andean one he had abandoned: he stretched the normal genre boundaries of narrative history by venturing extensively into philology and linguistics, but in the end these are all part of the broader humanist discourse.

22: Guaman Poma de Ayala on the Origins of the Incas

The Kings of an earlier dynasty of Peru, the last of whom was called Tocay Capac Pinahua Capac, had their own coat-of-arms specially drawn to illustrate their legitimate descent from the Sun. These rulers were called *Intip churin*, which means 'children of the Sun'.

The founder of the Inca dynasty declared that his father was the Sun, his mother the Moon, and his brother the Day-Star. The idol which he worshipped was called Huanacauri. He and his family were supposed to have come from the place called Tampu Toco which means 'lodging with openings or windows'. This place was also named Pacari Tampu, indicating that it was where divine apparitions occurred. The worship of idols began in the time of the mother and wife of the founder of the dynasty, whose name was Manco Capac. Mother and son both belonged to the caste of the Serpents. This account which I have given is the true history of the origin of the Incas and all other accounts are false.

Manco Capac was not descended from the previous dynasty and had no inherited property. The name of his father was unknown. This was the reason why he called himself the son of the Sun and Moon. The truth is that his mother was Mama Huaco. This woman was a sorceress and a witch who was on close terms with demons. She was able to talk to sticks and stones, and even mountains and lakes, for they answered her in the voices of the demons. She succeeded in deluding the Indians of Cuzco and then of the whole country. Regarding her powers as miraculous, the people were content to obey and serve her. According to all accounts, she slept with the men whom she fancied, regardless of their rank.

When she discovered that she was pregnant with a son, she was advised by her demons to hide the child away and confide it to the care of a nurse called Pillco Ziza. This nurse was to take the child to one of the caves of Tampu Toco and keep it there for two years, while remaining silent about the birth. In the meantime it was to be made known that a King called Manco Capac Inca would appear and rule over the country ....

According to one legend, the Incas originally came from Tiahuanaco on the farther side of Lake Titicaca. There were four brothers, one of whom was Manco Capac, and four sisters. After reaching Pacari Tampu and in due course emerging from there again, they returned as a gesture of piety to the shrine of Huanacauri on the road from the lake. The city of Cuzco, where they settled down, was at first called Aca Mama. The later name of Cuzco means 'navel'. From the beginning, the Incas insisted on sacrifices to their own idols whose shrines were situated among the rocks, caves and mountains.

The Incas distinguished themselves by enlarging their ears, so as not to be mistaken for the common people. Only one of them, Manco Capac himself, bore the title of King.

The rulers of Collasuyu in the south followed the custom of the Incas in wearing bone earrings, head-cloths of fine wool and birds' feathers, and in piercing their flesh, but they were not considered true nobles. This was because they were lazy and failed to arrive at Tampu Toco in time for the distribution of ear ornaments which the Incas arranged in order to be able to identify their own caste. These Colla nobles were referred to as 'people with ears of white wool'.

Selection from Felipe Guaman Poma de Ayala, *Letter to a King: A Peruvian Chief's Account of Life under the Incas and under Spanish Rule*, ed. and trans. Christopher Dilke (New York: E. P. Dutton, 1978), 32–4.

As history, Garcilaso's work is not now deemed at all reliable for the facts of pre-1533 Peruvian events, but it would acquire considerable influence on South American historical consciousness in the eighteenth century. In a way, Garcilaso did for fifteenth-century Incan history what his contemporary William Shakespeare's history plays did for England during the same time: it created an enduring popular historical culture. Garcilaso fed into the *criollo* patriotism that characterizes a good deal of seventeenth- and eighteenth-century historical writing to emerge from both Peru and New Spain. Some later writers would view not merely his assertions but his politics with suspicion; as late as the 1780s he was blamed by some for having stirred up native rebellions such as that of the last Inca, Tupac Amaru, and vain attempts were made to impound all copies of the *Comentarios reales*. Yet if Garcilaso had a subversive side, it was relatively tame. Guaman Poma is a very different case. Although he too saw natives and Spanish as compatible – he wrote the Andeans into world history by repeatedly asserting that they were directly descended from Adam – there is a sharper edge to his history, so much so that he has been called the native disciple of Las Casas. Guaman Poma was of humble background, though he called himself a nobleman. Patrilineally descended from an Andean ethnic group previously subjugated by the 'usurping' Incas, he chose to stress this heritage rather than his Inca maternity. For the Europeans are not the sole villains of his piece. The Incas get as harsh a treatment as the Spanish who succeeded them (Extract 22) – it was the Incas, subjugators of neighbouring populations, who had displaced a proto-Christian monotheism in the region with paganism.

Guaman Poma wrote his *El primer nueva corónica y buen gobierno* ('The First New Chronicle and Good Government') (see Box 17) in both Quechua and Castilian, and he included numerous pen and ink drawings (Fig. 35), even a depiction of his imagined presentation of his work to King Philip III. Guaman Poma was well versed in the works of earlier Spanish historians including Las Casas and Acosta, and he freely exploited and paraphrased other histories, even those of which he was critical such as Agustín de Zárate's *Historia del descubrimiento y conquista del Perú* (1555), the source for much of his account of the Conquest. He called his own text a chronicle, and declared its utility as a source of moral examples. Yet his

Box 17   *Guaman Poma's El primer nueva corónica y buen gobierno*

Guaman Poma organized the history so that it began with an account of Peru from biblical antiquity to the Incas, followed by a second part on the Conquest; the third part, on good government, which makes up over half the book, consists of a series of observations of and comments on daily life under Spanish rule. Through-out, Guaman Poma blends biography and history in a way that does not fit the late sixteenth-century notions of genre boundaries as contained in the *artes historicae*. The book provided an outlet for his severe commentary on the injustices of Spanish rule, perhaps the example *par excellence* of a European genre being appropriated without deference to its rhetorical rules and practices, and used as the Trojan horse to deliver a subversive political message. The preservation of this history is itself the stuff of legend. Guaman Poma spent nearly three decades assembling the work, which he apparently intended to have published (he uses European typesetting conventions). Then, at the age of nearly eighty and very close to the end of his life, he trekked overland with the manuscript from his Andean home to the vice-regal capital in Lima. There he intended to present it, at least by proxy, to Philip III, who in the end probably never read it. Soon after the manuscript arrived in Spain, it was acquired by the Danish ambassador and taken to Copenhagen, where it lay buried in the Royal Library till its discovery at the end of the nineteenth century.

work, while wearing the cloak of Western historiography, and outwardly adopting its forms, is unlike any humanist history of the day. Not written sequentially, its chapters mix diachronic and synchronic treatments, and show throughout traces of its author's indigenous culture: its table of contents is divided according to the Andean decimal system, and the book employs narrative to explain the pictures rather than using the pictures to illustrate the narrative, thereby undercutting the primacy of alphabetic literacy. Though it seems as if Guaman Poma did not fully understand the conventions of European historiography, it can be argued instead that he simply adapted them to his own ends. Guaman Poma wrote, he said, both to set the record straight on the story of the Spanish Conquest and to preserve rap-idly disappearing oral narratives by translating them into written form. However, his work is just as much a polemic on a number of issues that enraged him, from flaws in the governance of the kingdom of Peru, to the evils of the clergy, the sins

Figure 35 | The *Quipucamayoc* ('Keeper of the Quipu'), from Felipe Guaman Poma de Ayala, *El primer nueva corónica y buen gobierno*, c. 1600–15.

of both Europeans and miscegenated natives, and the need for a Christian ruler to preside over the whole region under the Spanish king's authority – a post to which Guaman Poma nominated his own son. His is an early instance of a phenomenon that would occur more extensively in the twentieth century, the adoption by the colonized of Western historicity and European historical methods as tools of resistance against the colonizing powers.

Historiographically, the New World had offered historians and geographers the equivalent of particle physics' 'exotic matter': after initially failing in their valiant efforts to accommodate it within the rules of the classical–scriptural universe, they were ultimately forced to revise their theories. This would take a long time, and several intellectual routes, not all of them entirely wrong. José de Acosta's view that the natives of the Americas were not indigenous but Asiatic looks like our modern understanding of prehistoric migration, even if he constructed this theory not on solid anthropological evidence but to accommodate the natives to the theory of descent from Noah, and had to explain their lapse into savagery or barbarism as the work of Satan. The idea of the simultaneous creation of all species at a single point in time a few thousand years earlier would not be thoroughly displaced before the nineteenth century. But, as noted in our previous chapter, it was becoming clear to some that there were fundamental problems with the inherited picture of chronology. Without highly elaborate mental gymnastics, it could not explain archaeological, fossil and botanical discoveries, nor account very convincingly for the existence of previously undetected peoples. The scriptural foundation for the history of the world began to experience serious subsidence, cracking under the weight of experience. The next century and a half would witness what the late historian of science Thomas Kuhn might have called a 'paradigm shift', a period of speculation and searching to find a new master theory for the History of Man.

History in Colonial North America

A convenient passage from the Renaissance to the Enlightenment, albeit one that takes us somewhat beyond the chronological boundaries of the rest of this chapter, is provided by the historical thought and writing of British and French colonial writers in North America, where, too, Europeans discovered indigenous residents. Here, the writings of the Spaniards, especially Acosta, were influential in the formulation of North American colonial ideas about the natives they encountered. They promoted the belief that despite their record-keeping capacity, savages can have no 'civil history' in the form of a narrative of events, and must therefore be studied as a branch of natural history or, as 'philosophic' or 'conjectural' history, as the Scot William Robertson (see Chapter 6 below) would do in his *History of America*. To the examples provided by sixteenth-century Spaniards there could be added the observations of more recent travellers such as the French Jesuit Jean-François Lafitau (1681–1746), whose 1724 opus *Moeurs des Sauvages Amériquains, comparés aux moeurs de premiers temps* provided an explicit comparison between the North American natives and the tribal societies documented by Caesar, Tacitus and other classical historians. The direct linkage between the barbarians of antiquity and modern savages, summarized in the oft-quoted hypothesis that 'In the beginning all the world was America', is illustrated in Lafitau's declaration that he found text and observation mutually reinforcing. 'I have not limited myself to learning the characteristics of the Indian and informing myself about their customs and practices, I have sought in these practices and customs, vestiges of the most remote antiquity ...', he suggested. 'I confess that, if the ancient authors have given me information on which to base happy conjectures about the Indians, the customs of the Indians have given me information on the basis of which I can understand more easily and explain more readily many things in the ancient authors.'[46] As with the study of antiquities, classical authority was tough to shake off, its fit as an interpretative guide too comfortable to be easily discarded.

Lafitau, like Acosta, was a Jesuit missionary, and he too saw the natural and historical worlds through clerical spectacles. (It was a gaze certainly more sympathetic than that of a slightly later 'authority' on the Americas who never set foot in the New World, Cornelius de Pauw, in whose *Recherches philosophiques* the American natives provided living proof of the natural decline of mankind since antiquity.) Stationed in New France where he spent several years among the Iroquois, Lafitau provided a lengthy account of Indian customs – both North and South American – which specifically compared these with those of 'primitive times'. He was mainly concerned to fight atheism by showing that even the most primitive of peoples had both a concept of the divine and religious practices, but his range was considerably broader. Covering the gamut of subjects from warfare to musical instruments to funeral practices to language, Lafitau's *Moeurs des Sauvages Amériquains* had one foot in the medieval and Renaissance tradition of speculations on *origo gentis* (largely dealt with in his first chapter and then set aside) and the world of sixteenth-century travel literature, and another in the age of Enlightenment comparativism, complete with a universalist agenda in which the origins and development of monotheism loomed urgently. He has been variously praised as a founder of anthropology or criticized for stuffing indigenous and European civilization into a single framework. He used classical authors such as Pliny, Herodotus and Caesar to demonstrate the general characteristics of primitivism and to provide further proof of the Asiatic origins of the Indians. 'As it was the custom among the ancients to eat lying on couches, so it is still the custom among the South American Indians who, although they have little seats with three feet like shoemakers' stools on which they eat ordinarily, also quite often take their repasts lying in hammocks as do the North American Indians who eat seated on the same mats on which they sleep.' Snowshoes, described by Lafitau from direct observation, were to him 'another custom of the first times which came from Asia into America with the nations which transplanted themselves there', citing Strabo and Suidas for ancient examples.[47]

Seventeenth-century English colonists were aware that they shared the continent not only with the French to the north and the Spanish to the south, but also with a native population. Their coexistence was uneasy from the beginning. An important difference with the Spanish American experience, however, affected the shape of writing about colonial-native history. In North America, unlike Peru or Mexico, there was no 'Conquest' to relate – though there were certainly massacres, like that which ended the Pequot War of 1637–8 – but rather a slower process of settlement and pacification. The colonial period was marked by a series of wars between the newcomers, often allied with some tribes against other tribes, who in turn were usually aligned with the French. The culminating episode in this phase of conflict with the indigenous population was the 'French and Indian Wars', the North American theatre of the Seven Years' War (1756–63). The accounts of these struggles furnish us with a loose counterpart to Spanish sixteenth-century Conquest narratives in the sense that they provided a military subject to authors for whom war ran a close second to religion as the natural matter of history. A relatively early conflict, King Philip's War (named for the native chief who led it) was among the topics covered in Jeremy Belknap's (1774–98) *History of New Hampshire* (1784), which adopted the Enlightenment position against slavery and was critical of the colonists' harsh conduct against the Indians. The New Yorker Cadwallader Colden (1688–1776), who was born in the year of one British revolution and died at the opening of another, ventured an account of the Iroquois in his *History of the Five Indian Nations Depending on the Province of New-York in America*. Another historian who saw in the Indians a modern reflection of ancient European barbarians, Colden was convinced that the Iroquois needed to be cultivated as allies against French expansionism from Quebec.

Like the Spanish, the earliest historians in the future United States looked to Europe for their historiographic models as well as for the conceptual glasses through which they viewed their world. Older forms such as the chronicle and the providential narrative lingered across the Atlantic much longer than at home. Towards the end of the period, the great Enlightenment historians of Europe would be read, influencing revolutionary ideology. History played an enormous role in the creation and consolidation of the colonies' sense of identity, and then in the establishment and growth of the new republic. As with other modern nations that originated as settler offshoots of European powers, historical writing in the North American colonies had begun as a variant of travel literature, designed less to narrate the past than to describe for readers in the mother country the flora and fauna of the new territories and to provide some sense of the customs of their peoples; this drew on the chorographic model then emerging in England. The first writer to compose a 'history' in the sense of a more-or-less true story about the recent past was the explorer John Smith (1579–1631), in his *A True Relation* (1608) and later in his *General History of Virginia, New England, and the Summer Isles* (1624), a work modelled on contemporary English accounts of Near Eastern peoples such as the Turks.

In the very different religious climate of New England, history rapidly developed a providential strain, characteristic of early modern Protestant societies, that has never entirely disappeared from America's account of its own past. It is not hard to plot a direct trajectory beginning with the New Israel founded by refugees from English religious persecution, through the crystallization of a 'Redeemer

Nation' myth, to nineteenth- and twentieth-century beliefs in American 'exceptionalism' and manifest destiny, and ultimately to the United States' post-Cold War appropriation of the role of world's policeman and disseminator of liberal democracy. In New England, early historians were influenced by such English books as John Foxe's *Acts and Monuments* and Sir Walter Ralegh's *History of the World* (1614), both of which conveyed a strong sense of God's active role in human affairs. Colonists composed histories recounting the settlement of these rugged territories, interpreting the near-miraculous deliverance of the *Mayflower* migrants from hunger and cold as proof that God had willed a godly community to be established and to thrive. Biblical typology animates many of the narratives as new versions of Moses opened up a promised land for God's chosen and new Isaiahs and Jeremiahs kept its occupants pure. The separation of the wicked from the worthy and the redemption of sin, mirroring the transformation of the untamed wilderness into a fruitful land of milk and honey, runs through most of this material, sometimes linked with millennial expectations of Christ's imminent return. Antinomians and apostates are cast out into the wilderness, as in Old Testament times. A select list of the notable works in this genre illustrates its themes, for instance Edward Johnson's (1599?–1672) *The Wonder-Working Providence of Sion's Savior in New England* (1654), William Bradford's (1590–1657) *History of Plymouth Plantation* (1856) and William Hubbard's (1621–1704) *General History of New England to 1630* (1815). In 1676, Increase Mather (1639–1723) authored a *Brief History of the War with the Indians in New England*, perhaps the first example of American military history-writing, although cast like most other histories in providential terms.

Much more history was produced in New England than in the southern colonies, and of this, a great deal came from Massachusetts Bay, whose historians tended to view their colony as a synecdoche for all New England. Thus the Boston physician William Douglass (1691–1752) contributed a broad survey of the colonial experiments as seen from a Bay colony perspective in his *Summary View, Historical and Political, of the British Settlements in North America* (1747–50). Easily the most influential history of the early eighteenth century was the work of Increase Mather's son, Cotton (1663–1728). The *Magnalia Christi Americana; or the Ecclesiastical History of New England*, which the younger Mather began to write in 1693, was published in 1702. Its seven books' have a composite structure that is strangely reminiscent of Chinese official history, though of course Mather himself knew nothing of this. Beginning with an account of the establishment of New England's colonies in Book I, Mather then provides two books' worth of biographical accounts of important public figures, clerical and secular, and, in Book IV, a narrative of the history of Harvard College. These appealed to the growing public appetite for exemplary biography, offering accounts of the godly lives of Puritan colonists. The last three books turn to ecclesiastical history proper, with Book V – clearly influenced by Foxe – entitled 'Acts and Monuments of the Faith and Order in the Churches of New England'; the final two books chronicle instances of God's providence and 'the Wars of the Lord' respectively.

The last major history to be written in the colonial period was, perhaps appropriately, the work of the last civil governor of Massachusetts before the Revolution, Thomas Hutchinson (1711–80), who completed his multivolume history of the Bay Colony while in exile. Hutchinson, a native Bostonian, is a sympathetic figure, a political moderate who attempted in vain to mediate between angry colonists and an intransigent British government, earning the thanks of neither. A cosmopolitan in his view of American history, he corresponded with British historians like Robertson, who sent him a questionnaire on life in the New World. The first volume of his *History of the Colony of Massachusetts Bay*, impressively documented from manuscripts in the library of Samuel Mather (son of Cotton), appeared late in 1764. The history recounts the progress of the colony from a small Puritan settlement into a prosperous and contributing part of a British commercial empire. Further progress was retarded by Hutchinson's political career and by the Stamp Act riots of 1765, during which his library was stormed and much of its contents tossed into the street below. Though many of his manuscripts were lost, he was able to recover the draft of volume II of his history and publish it in 1767, his earlier optimism now rather dampened by a sense of regression and corruption among the colonists. Hutchinson quit the colony and the continent forever in 1774, as the crisis was entering its final phase. He would finish his history abroad during the Revolutionary War, ending it with the termination of his own governorship, and the last part would not reach print for half a century, when tempers had cooled.

Hutchinson was both historically and historiographically on the 'losing' side. Not so Mercy Otis Warren (1728–1814). A counterpart (and correspondent of) England's 'republican virago' Catharine Macaulay, Warren was, like Macaulay herself, unusual as a female historian. Her political sympathies were thoroughly revolutionary and, following independence, Jeffersonian. In an odd twist of fate, she would write her *History of the Rise, Progress, and Termination of the American Revolution* (comp. c. 1791 but unpublished till 1805) in the former home of Governor Hutchinson. Encouraged to write by another prominent woman, Abigail Adams, Warren's ability to combine eyewitness recollection from major political figures along with material derived from documents into a narrative forcefully told has made her history the best known of the Revolutionary era, quite apart from her sex. Holding views that differed strongly from those of Abigail Adams' husband John, of whom she was publicly critical, Warren drew from the United

Extract 23: Mercy Otis Warren on History

History, the deposite [*sic*] of crimes, and the record of every thing disgraceful or honorary to mankind, requires a just knowledge of character, to investigate the sources of action; a clear comprehension, to review the combination of causes; and precision of language, to detail the events that have produced the most remarkable revolutions.

To analyze the secret springs that have effected the progressive changes in society; to trace the origin of the various modes of government, the consequent improvements in science, in morality, or the national tincture that marks the manners of the people under despotic or more liberal forms, is a bold and adventurous work ....

The love of domination and an uncontrolled lust of arbitrary power have prevailed among all nations, and perhaps in proportion to the degrees of civilization. They have been equally conspicuous in the decline of Roman virtue, and in the dark pages of British story [*sic*]. It was these principles that overturned that ancient republic. It was these principles that frequently involved England in civil feuds. It was the resistance to them that brought one of their monarchs to the block, and struck another from his throne. It was the prevalence of them that drove the first settlers of America from elegant habitations and affluent circumstances, to seek an asylum in the cold and uncultivated regions of the western world. Oppressed in Britain by despotic kings, and persecuted by prelatic fury, they fled to a distant country, where the desires of men were bounded by the wants of nature; where civilization had not created those artificial cravings which too frequently break over every moral and religious tie for their gratification.

Mercy Otis Warren, 'Introductory Observations', in her *History of the Rise, Progress, and Termination of the American Revolution*, ed. Lester H. Cohen, 2 vols. (Indianapolis: Liberty Classics, 1988), vol. I, 3–5.

States' second president the now notorious retort that 'History is not the Province of the Ladies', another irony given that Adams himself, like his wife, had encouraged Warren's historiographical interests in the first place (Extract 23).

By the end of the century, a post-independence historiography was taking shape, most though not all of it improvising on the exceptionalist melodies of the seventeenth century. The concerns that had marked the histories of the pre-Revolutionary period did not disappear, but they were now supplemented by newer issues which required appeal to history as much as to abstract and inalienable rights. What sort of republic would this be – Federalist, commercial and oligarchic or democratic and agrarian? What was the relation of the parts to the whole? How far and fast should expansion west occur and (an ominous question) how should the Indians be dealt with? Where did slavery, soon to be abolished in the rest of the British Empire, fit into the picture? David Ramsay (1749–1815) captured these matters in his historical works. A Pennsylvania-born physician of Scottish descent, Ramsay migrated to South Carolina shortly before the Revolution, where he became both a congressman (until his anti-slavery views cost him reelection) and historian; in 1785 he published *The History of the Revolution of South-Carolina*. His major historical writing, the *History of the American Revolution*, was published in 1789 in the flush of success following the conclusion of the war and the revised constitutional settlement of 1788: having once trumpeted the simple agrarian republicanism of his adopted state, Ramsay would soon after evolve into a strong Federalist.

Like Jeremy Belknap, Ramsay had absorbed something of Scottish Enlightenment ideas and cosmopolitan opinions; though patriotic, his work is significantly less exceptionalist than that of some of his contemporaries. Ramsay's *American Revolution* begins with a brief account of the establishment of the colonies before jumping into a narrative of their deteriorating relations with Britain, starting in 1764. Two years after he died at the hands of a crazed assassin, Ramsay's three-volume *History of the United States* appeared, a revision of the earlier work in a more conservative direction. This valediction to the new republic, notably less sympathetic to the Indians than Ramsay's previous history, now saw them as the opposite of virtuous settlers and urged on an American form of conquest, virtually an inversion of his earlier views which had been heavily critical of the colonists' treatment of the natives. Ramsay had also backed away from his earlier critique of slavery, offering instead a defence of its place in southern culture.

CONCLUSION

David Ramsay's philosophic history places him in a very different historiographic space from his early colonial precursors; we need now to explore in greater detail the 'enlightened' thinking that lay behind it, and which constitutes both a bridge from the early modern world to the nineteenth century and a gap between both. This chapter has been concerned with the impact of Europe's historical culture on areas of the Americas that by geography or circumstance fell within its orbit from the late fifteenth to the eighteenth centuries. It has also illustrated many instances of the colonizers making use, often against strong intellectual prejudices, of indigenous writings, and a few examples of hybridity, innovative types of history being written by European, native and mestizo authors, from Sahagún to Garcilaso and Guaman Poma. We will return to the themes of both conquest and exchange in a future chapter, when we trace the spread of the Western practice of history across the rest of the world. What would be disseminated in the nineteenth century, however, was a very different conception of the past and how it should be studied than the early modern world had possessed. Fundamental changes in the understanding of history had occurred throughout the world during the intervening hundred or so years, and we must first examine these.

Notes

1 T. D. Goodrich, *The Ottoman Turks and the New World: A Study of Tarih-i Hind-i Garbi and Sixteenth-Century Ottoman Americana* (Wiesbaden, 1990).

2 Manuel de Almeida, *The History of High Ethiopia or Abassia*, in *Some Records of Ethiopia, 1593–1646*, trans. and ed. C. F. Beckingham and G. W. B. Huntingford (London, 1954), 3.

3 D. A. Brading, *The First America: The Spanish Monarchy, Creole Patriots, and the Liberal State 1492–1867* (Cambridge, 1991), 18.

4 Quoted in Edgar Prestage, *The Chronicles of Fernão Lopes and Gomes Eannes de Zurara* (Watford, 1928), 6.

5 Fernão Lopes de Castanheda, *The first booke of the historie of the discouerie and conquest of the East Indias, enterprised by the Portingales, in their daungerous nauigations, in the time of King Don Iohn, the second of that name*, trans. N. L. (London, 1582), dedication, sig. Aiiiv.

6 A selection in English has been published as *The Three Voyages of Vasco da Gama and his Viceroyalty, from the Lendas da India of Gaspar Correa*, trans. H. E. J. Stanley (London, 1869).

7 Aubrey F. G. Bell, *Gaspar Corrêa* (Oxford, 1924), 23.

8 *A Treatise on the Moluccas* (c. 1544), ed. and trans. H. T. T. M. Jacobs, S.J. (St Louis, MO, 1971), 83.

9 Joan-Pau Rubiés, *Travel and Ethnology in the Renaissance: South India through European Eyes, 1250–1625* (Cambridge, 2000), 264, 278.

10 *Chronicle of Fernão Nuniz*, included in R. Sewell, *A Forgotten Empire: Vijayanagar* (1900; London, 1962).

11 *Hans Staden's True History: An Account of Cannibal Captivity in Brazil*, ed. and trans. N. L. Whitehead and M. Harbsmeier (Durham, NC and London, 2008). All of these works merit modern attention. However, for reasons of space, the balance of this section will focus regionally on Mesoamerica and South America and discussion will be limited to Spanish historians, while the next section will deal with indigenous and mestizo writings in the same regions.

12 Bernal Díaz del Castillo, *The Discovery and Conquest of Mexico*, ed. G. García and trans. A. P. Maudslay (New York, 1956), author's preface.

13 Enrique Florescano, *Memory, Myth and Time in Mexico: From the Aztecs to Independence*, trans. Albert G. Bork and Kathryn R. Bork (Austin, TX, 1994), 91ff., 96.

14 Pedro Sarmiento de Gamboa, *History of the Incas*, trans. C. Markham (1907; Mineola, NY, 1999), 14.

15 Anthony Pagden, *European Encounters with the New World: From Renaissance to Romanticism* (New Haven, CT, 1993), 63.

16 Sarmiento de Gamboa, *History of the Incas*, 27–8.

17 Bernabé Cobo, *History of the Inca Empire*, trans. Roland Hamilton (Austin, TX, 1979), 98–9.

18 Thomas A. Abercrombie, *Pathways of Memory and Power: Ethnography and History among an Andean People* (Madison, WI, 1998), 188, 260.

19 José de Acosta, *Natural and Moral History of the Indies*, ed. Jane E. Mangan, trans. Frances López-Morillas (Durham, NC and London, 2002).

20 Ibid., 379.

21 James Lockhart (ed. and trans.), *We People Here: Nahuatl Accounts of the Conquest of Mexico* (Eugene, OR, 1993), 49.

22 Florescano, *Memory, Myth and Time in Mexico*, 123.

23 Elizabeth Hill Boone, *Stories in Red and Black: Pictorial Histories of the Aztecs and Mixtecs* (Austin, TX, 2000), 29.

24 Acosta, *Natural and Moral History*, 334–5.

25 John Bierhorst, 'Introduction', in *History and Mythology of the Aztecs: The Codex Chimalpopoca*, trans. Bierhorst (Tuscon, AZ and London, 1992), 7.

26 Alfonso de Zorita, *Life and Labor in Ancient Mexico: The Brief and Summary Relation of the Lords of New Spain*, trans. Benjamin Keen (New Brunswick, NJ, 1963), 272.

27 Fray Diego Durán, *The History of the Indies of New Spain*, trans. and ed. Doris Heyden (Norman, OK and London, 1994), 4, 213–14.

28 Florescano, *Memory, Myth and Time in Mexico*, 61–2.

29 Quoted in Joyce Marcus, *Mesoamerican Writing Systems: Propaganda, Myth, and History in Four Ancient Civilizations* (Princeton, NJ, 1992), 271.

30 D. Tedlock, 'Introduction', in *Popol Vuh: The Definitive Edition of the Mayan Book of the Dawn of Life and the Glories of Gods and Kings*, trans. Tedlock (New York, 1985); Joanne Rappaport, *The Politics of Memory: Native Historical Interpretation in the Colombian Andes*, rev. edn (Durham, NC, 1998); and Susan Niles, *The Shape of Inca History: Narrative and Architecture in an Andean Empire* (Iowa City, 1999).

31 Georges Baudot, *Utopia and History in Mexico: The First Chroniclers of Mexican Civilization (1520–1569)*, trans. Bernard R. Ortiz de Montellano and Thelma Ortiz de Montellano (Niwot, CO, 1995), 52.

32 Marcus, *Mesoamerican Writing Systems*, 52; H. B. Nicholson, 'Pre-Hispanic Central Mexican Historiography', in *Investigaciones contemporaráneas sobre Historia de México* (Mexico City, 1971), 38–81; Elizabeth Hill Boone, 'Aztec Pictorial Histories: Records without Words', in Elizabeth Hill Boone and Walter D. Mignolo (eds.), *Writing without Words: Alternative Literacies in Mesoamerica and the Andes* (Durham, NC and London, 1994), 50–76. For Nahua cartographic histories (relaying pre-Conquest events) see Dana Leibsohn, 'Primers for Memory: Cartographic Histories and Nahua Identity', in Boone and Mignolo (eds.), *Writing without Words*, 161–87.

33 Don Domingo de San Antón Muñón Chimalpahín Quauhtlehuanitzin, *Annals of his Time*, ed. and trans. James Lockhart, Susan Schroeder and Doris Namala (Stanford, 2006), 27.

34 *Historia de la Nacion Chichimeca*, in *Obras historicas*, ed. Alfredo Chavero, 2 vols. (1891–2; Mexico, 1965), vol. II. Most of Alva Ixtlilxóchitl's works have not been translated into

English, except Relación Thirteen of his *Sumaria Relación. De todas las cosas que han sucedidio en la Nueva España*, in *Obras historicas*, vol. I, 335–446, his defence of his ancestor Ixtlilxóchitl, published as *Ally of Cortés*, trans. Douglass K. Ballentine (El Paso, TX, 1969).

35 Florescano, *Memory, Myth and Time in Mexico*, 35.

36 Brading, *The First America*, 140.

37 Sarmiento de Gamboa, *History of the Incas*, 41.

38 Ralph Bauer, 'Introduction', in Titu Cusi, *An Inca Account of the Conquest of Peru*, trans. and ed. Bauer (Boulder, CO, 2005), 18.

39 Juan de Betanzos, *Narrative of the Incas*, trans. Roland Hamilton and Dana Buchanan (Austin, TX, 1996).

40 Acosta, *Natural and Moral History*, 331–3.

41 *Motolinía's History of the Indians of New Spain*, trans. and ed. Elizabeth Andros Foster (Berkeley, CA, 1950), 25.

42 Jorge Cañizares-Esguerra, *How to Write a History of the New World: Histories, Epistemologies and Identities in the Eighteenth-Century Atlantic World* (Stanford, CA, 2001), 101.

43 Garcilaso de la Vega, El Inca, *Royal Commentaries of the Incas and General History of Peru*, part one, trans. Harold V. Livermore (Austin, TX, 1966), 41–2.

44 Ibid., 615–16.

45 Ibid., 4, 40–1, 50.

46 Jean-François Lafitau, *Customs of the American Indians Compared with the Customs of Primitive Times*, ed. and trans. W. N. Fenton and E. L. Moore, 2 vols. (Toronto, 1974), vol. I, 27.

47 Lafitau, *Customs of the American Indians*, vol. I, 225; vol. II, 128–9.

6 | Progress and History in the Eurasian Enlightenments

Introduction

Two features of the eighteenth century are the principal subjects of this chapter. The first, continuing a theme opened up in Chapter 5, is the increasing consciousness in different parts of the world, first developed by the explorations and conquests of the previous two centuries, of alternative modes of historicity and, on occasion, actual interaction between them. This certainly carried on trends initiated in the sixteenth and seventeenth centuries, but it pushed them further, allying them to a world 'metahistory' or master-narrative recounting the march of civilization. The latter provides the chapter's second theme: the emergence of the idea of 'progress', building on early modern thought about change, but now clearly linked to 'History' defined as the cumulative past, and explained as a continual process with a forward motion, rather than a case-by-case set of accidents. An enveloping notion of civilization's progress, of a single path for mankind, now conflicted with the inescapable fact that different peoples (including both primitive and 'barbarian' ones in the Americas and Africa, and more advanced ones in Asia) were at different stages of development, some apparently stalled in their tracks. Identifying this universal path and speculating as to the reasons why some peoples were further along it than others would preoccupy many European thinkers through this and the next century, and most did not pause to consider the possibility that there were in fact multiple paths to modernity, much less different imaginable modernities.

A number of celebrated names feature prominently in this chapter, including major figures of Europe's literary and philosophical, as well as historiographical elite, from Vico, Voltaire and Montesquieu to Herder and Kant; they are juxtaposed with others less familiar to European readers such as Tokugawa Japan's Motoori Norinaga and Qing China's Zhao Yi. Geographically, we will confine ourselves to somewhat fewer countries than in the last two chapters. The itinerary will include return visits to China, where Qing evidentiary research achieved a critical attitude to sources comparable to that in seventeenth-century Europe, and to Japan, which itself experienced a period of historiographical ambivalence as Chinese-style criticism came into conflict with a newer, Japan-centred scholarship embracing the country's remote past. Finally, several continuing themes reappear here. We may begin with one of these, the evolving attitude of historians and their readers to the relative merits of writing and orality with respect to the memory and recovery of the past.

The Repudiation of the Oral

Historiographically, the eighteenth century has had a mixed press. Nineteenth-century critics recoiled against its universalizing tendencies and reversed its perceived hostility to periods such as the Middle Ages. Our own time has attributed to the several Enlightenments (the plural is significant) in different parts of the continent all manner of Eurocentric sins and condemned their civilizing agenda. For many postcolonial critics, Western modernity with all its exclusionary, imperialist and racist aspects grew up in the nineteenth century but was born in the eighteenth. The Caribbean poet and cultural critic Edouard Glissant has commented that it is from this moment that 'History is written with a capital H' simultaneously becoming 'a totality that excludes other histories that do not fit into that of the West'.[1] And, prominent among Western modernity's supposed sins, it created its own self-authorizing epistemology, including the historiographic notion 'the past is discovered objectively and factually by our being accurate about it'. A corollary of this, writes ethnohistorian Greg Dening, is the belief that '"primitive" societies have no history when in fact they are only missing the systematic conventionalities – rules of inquiry and evidence – that allow them to historicise in ways recognisable and persuasive to us'.[2]

The confrontation with other modes of historicity in the age of global circumnavigation forced Europeans to think carefully, and in more categorical terms than previously, about the essential elements needed in and for history. Writing was one of these, and it was in the eighteenth century that the process initiated in the previous 200 years, of denying oral societies a capacity to memorialize the human past, reached its apogee. The ambivalence of the sixteenth and early seventeenth centuries towards alternative forms, both oral and pictographic, had largely disappeared by the early decades of the eighteenth. The later seventeenth century had also supplied the eighteenth with a philosophical justification for the marginalization of oral tradition in nascent 'probability theory', which evaluated the reasonableness of testimony and the likelihood of its distortion. Via French works on historical criticism and, eventually, philosopher-historians such as David Hume, this attitude combined with social and religious biases against tradition to turn any past undocumented in writing into non-history. On the whole, eighteenth-century critics of oral tradition and pictographic work alike would prove even more hard-line in their alphabetic preferences than any Counter-Reformation missionary.

The very concept of 'oral tradition', a phrase that first occurs in the late seventeenth century, is largely an Enlightenment creation, the ability of voice to transmit knowledge without the inevitable accretion of fable being well articulated by the long-lived Bernard de Fontenelle (1657–1756) among others. The hue and cry that greeted the poet James Macpherson's publication (1760–5) of the epic *Fingal* as the genuine work of an ancient Celtic bard named Ossian went beyond the old philological objection to forgeries like the pseudo-Berossus or the Donation of Constantine. Hume denied outright the reliability of memory and oral tradition. Reacting to Ossian, he thought that the rules of probability and the evidence of experience made it unlikely that a history could survive orally from bardic times. In *The Natural History of Religion* Hume asserted (by way of defining a difference between 'historical facts' and 'speculative opinions') that

An historical fact, while it passes by oral tradition from eye-witnesses and contemporaries, is disguised in every successive narration, and may at last retain but very small, if any, resemblance of the original truth, on which it was founded. The frail memories of men, their love of exaggeration, their supine carelessness; these principles, if not corrected by books and writing, soon pervert the account of historical events; where argument or reasoning has little or no place, nor can ever recall the truth, which has once escaped those narrations.[3]

The English historian Edward Gibbon similarly subscribed to the view that letters divided the civilized and the more advanced barbarian from the outright savage, and thus the historical from the unhistorical. On the continent, the German historian August Ludwig Schlözer (1735–1809) proposed a sharp distinction between 'metahistory' (what we would call prehistory), which rested on non-literary evidence and folklore, and history proper, which must be built from written materials, though he allowed for their supplementing with non-literary sources. Herder saw the significant contribution of the Israelites to civilization as their writing of 'annals', and their derivation of these from family chronicles and historical tales rather than hieroglyphics.[4] Eighteenth-century Swedes, who saw the printing press as a decisive improvement in the process of enlightenment, praised the ancient inventors of early written systems such as runic inscriptions, which had expanded the human capacity to remember the past. In oral cultures, histories had to be brief in order to be passed down, and thus a minimalist original story would be embellished in subsequent telling. Anders af Botin (1724–90) thought that stories handed down orally might preserve history in memory but ran the risk of 'degeneration through oblivion and additives'.[5]

Imaginative souls such as Macpherson aside, there were legitimate dissenting voices, open to non-alphabetic alternatives, and later in the century sceptics such as Jean-Jacques Rousseau and Adam Ferguson who worried about the limiting aspects of letters and their incapacity to grasp all the nuances of spoken language.[6] As we will see, the Neapolitan Giambattista Vico recognized both the interdependence of oral and literate culture, and saw value in oral tradition as not merely the vessel *for* but a defining characteristic *of* ancient wisdom, which was not properly understood if taken as an inferior form of writing; historically, an appreciation of orality was essential to the study of law. The Peruvian chronicler Bartolomé Arzáns de Orsúa y Vela (1676–1736) was confident that the Incas had reliably recorded the past events of their empire on quipus. Later in the century, the Jesuit Francisco Xavier de Clavijero (1731–87), a patriotic defender of American aboriginal achievement, authored a widely translated *Historia Antigua de México* ('The Ancient History of Mexico', 1780–1) which defended the trustworthiness of indigenous record-keeping. But the Dutch scholar Cornelius de Pauw (1739–99) took the opposite point of view. In his widely read *Recherches philosophiques sur les Américains* ('Philosophical Dissertations on the Americans', 1768), an extremist denunciation of New World learning, de Pauw dismissed Garcilaso's *Royal Commentaries* as the poor creation of an American living in a degenerate continent whose inferiority was climatologically and biologically overdetermined. Traces of his attitude can be found, tempered somewhat, in William Robertson and other historians of the day.

A side effect of all this was a gradual decline among reputable historians of pursuit of ancient chronology, especially in identifying the precise antiquity of the earth *après* James Ussher. Newton's interest in the subject came at the tail end of chronology's hey-day, though it would continue to have its popular practitioners for two centuries more and though, too, synchronistic tables would remain a standard feature in universal histories or histories of the Church. The eighteenth century, when it turned at all to remote antiquity, was much more interested in its customs and manners, and deriving light therefrom on human progress. As the French physiocrat Turgot (1727–81) remarked, the world is very old, but its exact age unknowable precisely because writing does not extend far enough back:

Historical times cannot be traced further back than the invention of writing; and when it was invented, men could at first make use of it only to record vague traditions, or a few leading events to which no dates were ascribed, and which were mixed up with myths to such an extent as to render discrimination impossible.

The pride of nations has led them to shift their origins far back into the depths of antiquity. But in relation to time, men, before the invention of numbers, could scarcely have extended their ideas beyond the few generations with which they were acquainted, that is, three or four. It is only within a century or a century and a half that tradition, unaided by history, can indicate the period of a known event. Thus no history can be traced much further back than the invention of writing, unless it be by means of a mythical chronology, which men took the trouble to create only when nations, revealed to one another through their commerce, had converted their pride into jealousy.[7]

The first histories were 'fables', and before writing 'men had no records other than songs and a few stones beside which the songs were repeated'. Even Herodotus was only a poet, and only after him was it felt necessary 'that history should tell the truth'.[8]

An Overview of Eighteenth–Century European Historical Culture

Understanding the eighteenth century historiographically, at least within Europe and its colonial offshoots, is complicated by what appears on the surface to be countervailing forces running both for and against the study of the past. On the one hand, this was the 'Age of Enlightenment', concerned with natural and philosophical universals, the period of post-Newtonian science, of the classifying activities of physical scientists such as Buffon and Linnaeus, and philosophical arguments on abstract concepts of natural rights and liberty. On the other hand, David Hume was not boasting idly when he declared his the 'historical age' (and his native Scotland the 'historical nation'). The quantitative evidence to support this characterization is compelling: the stream of published history produced in the previous two centuries swelled into a Noachic deluge, the very commonplaceness of history itself posing a problem for readers and critics, as publishers used subscription and serial publication to market their wares more effectively and to differentiate them from those of their competitors.[9] Popular print spread history geographically and socially, and the growth of public and circulating libraries increased the readership of even the most expensive books. Meanwhile, major research libraries such as the French Bibliothèque du Roi continued to expand their collections of manuscripts, now extending to material from the Americas, the Arabic world and East Asia, making possible a more detailed universal or world history. Large publishing projects by collaborative teams produced several such projects in the course of the century, beginning with the *Universal History* (1747–68), the creation of a team of authors under the direction of the Arabist George Sale. A wide-ranging work which included the Orient in its scope, it was quite unlike medieval and early modern universal histories, or even Bossuet's late seventeenth-century *Discourse*.

Figure 36 | J. B. Belley, deputy of Santo Domingo, next to a bust of Guillaume T. F. Raynal, philosopher and historian who criticized French policies in the colonies. Painting on canvas by Anne Louis Girodet de Roussy-Trioson, 1797.

More impressive still was the multivolume *Histoire ... des ... deux Indes* published in Amsterdam in 1770 by the Abbé Guillaume Thomas Raynal (1713–96). This multi-authored work was a virtually global history of the non-European world (the 'two Indies' of its title, East and West, covered a great deal of territory), and in particular of the growth of commerce, the consummate engine of social progress and favoured subject of the philosophic historian. The *Histoire* was astonishingly successful, with over thirty editions appearing from 1770 to 1787; Bonaparte would eventually take it with him to Egypt.[10] Like Las Casas two centuries earlier, Raynal himself proved a popular icon of liberal thinking in conquered territories. During Haiti's revolution (1791–1804), Enlightenment values were turned against the French colonizers (Fig. 36), a foreshadowing of developments in the nineteenth and twentieth centuries (see Chapters 8 and 9 below).

As for Clio herself (Fig. 37), the muse of history was out and about in public, a constant and welcome guest in the salons and drawing rooms of Europe's so-cial elites in town and country and, frequently, in the chambers of an aspiring

Figure 37 │ The Muse Clio. Studio of François Boucher (1703–70), 1750s. Oil on canvas.

bourgeoisie. The age of historians' dependence upon private patronage and of the prominence of court-sponsored or 'official' history was drawing to a close, despite the persistence of such offices in several European monarchies and the Ottoman Empire. Historians were becoming public figures, widely recognizable in polite society, their own portraits painted and often engraved within books (Fig. 38). The success of their works depended upon public tastes and patterns of consumption. While expensive, personally bound folios and quartos graced the libraries of the wealthy and the powerful, they did not suit the habits of an increasing number of readers of middling status. 'A book that I can put into my pocket, take on a trip, and whose size does not deter our young and fashionable gentlemen pays considerably better than a large quarto which without a lectern is unreadable in their eyes', said Carl Christoffer Gjörwell, a Swedish publisher and champion of small formats.[11] As examples, Gjörwell pointed to French and British publishers of historians like Hume, and to bestsellers such as the Jansenist Charles Rollin's thirteen-volume *Histoire ancienne* (1734–9) and the Jesuit Gabriel Daniel's *Histoire de France* (1713).

Women were among the beneficiaries of this publishing explosion. Female readership of history had increased modestly during the sixteenth and seventeenth

Figure 38 | David Hume (1711–76), Scottish philosopher and historian; engraved portrait from a book.

centuries and grew at a more rapid pace in the eighteenth. While the eighteenth century produced only a small number of women historians such as England's Catharine Macaulay and the United States' Mercy Otis Warren (see Chapter 5 above) and Hannah Adams, history assumed a privileged place in female libraries, its virtues trumpeted by a host of educational writers of both sexes, including women such as Hester Chapone and Mary Wollstonecraft. The personal library of Russia's Tsarina Elizabeth (r. 1740–61), principally in French, was dominated by history books from the ancients through Rollin's *Histoire ancienne*; her German-born successor, Catherine the Great (r. 1762–96) found the time to publish her own 'Notes' on Russian history. The Swedish noblewoman Charlotta Frölich anonymously published a history book in 1759 for poor people and peasants, while Madame Roland, guillotined during the Terror, wished in her last days that she might have lived to have become the Catharine Macaulay of the French Revolution. Apart from religious tracts and courtesy manuals, history's only credible rivals for educated women's literary attention proved to be the French romance and its cross-Channel cousin, the English novel. In an effort to ensure that their accounts appealed to both women and men (male readers, too, being increasingly drawn to sentimental matters), historians leavened their normal fare of battles and political events with human interest, personality and emotion. This was not opportunistic artifice: the historian was obliged not simply to *depict* virtuous behaviour in a moral history but to go one step beyond and actively arouse in the reader sympathetic reactions to the good and antipathy to the wicked. The Scottish philosopher and jurist Lord Kames, expressing the wish that his own *Sketches of the History of Man* become a popular work 'chiefly with the female sex', took pains to translate any foreign or classical quotations. Voltaire formulated his own thoughts on the proper writing of history partly in response to his sometime lover Emilie du Châtelet's complaints about untidy assemblages of facts, disconnected details and 'a thousand accounts of battles which have decided nothing'.[12] It is not exaggerating to say that the eighteenth-century prototype of the modern 'cultural turn' away from political and military history was hastened by historians' wish to seem more relevant to female readers.

Enlightenment historiography leaned heavily on many of the accomplishments of the previous two centuries and in particular on the enormous corpus of 'erudite' knowledge in the form of printed documents and texts, engravings of archaeological and architectural remains, and extensive studies of different legal systems. Two centuries of overseas travel also encouraged many of the historians of the late seventeenth and eighteenth centuries to undertake a comparative approach to the study of the past. In a sense, comparison of persons or episodes had always been a part of historical writing, but now they were being made synchronously across space as well as backwards in time, and between collective entities – societies, peoples, customs and manners. At the same time, there was emerging a healthy degree of scepticism towards Plutarchan analogies between individuals and events divorced from their contexts.

One reason for this shift is that eighteenth-century historians were rapidly breaking free from the shackles of exemplarity. Linear thinking about the present's relation to what came before it was elbowing into the literary margins – advice-books, religious texts and morality literature – the time-indifferent search for exempla and lessons wherever they could be found. By 1800, this grasp of collective human development, and of the need to trace the step-by-step birth, growth and development of institutions, had turned the past into a cumulative process – that is, into History. This is precisely the period, the late Reinhart Koselleck observed, that it also became common to talk of History in the singular, and as more than a collection of multiple histories.[13] *Res gestae* and *historia rerum gestarum* were beginning to merge, things done with the account of those things, an observation

borne out by Hegel's declaration in the early nineteenth century of the dual meaning of the German word *Geschichte*:

> In our language, the word 'history' combines both objective and subjective meanings, for
> it denotes the *historia rerum gestarum* as well as the *res gestae* themselves, the historical
> narrative and the actual happenings, deeds, and events – which in the strictest sense, are
> quite distinct from one another.

For Hegel, this would be no coincidence: the writing of history and History itself, subjective and objective, had appeared contemporaneously because they were
both products of a transcendent order, and each was instrumentally created by the
state, which is simultaneously the fundamental subject of history (the narrative) as
well as the maker and self-aware recorder of History (the pattern of events).[14]

Arnaldo Momigliano once suggested that by the eighteenth century the various
different forms of studying the past had shaken out into three grand traditions:
straightforward history-writing in a neoclassical style, concerned largely with
politics and events; 'erudite' scholarship (embracing both of the major antiquarian streams, archaeological and philological, as well as the emergent ancillary
or *Hilfswissenschaft* disciplines); and an emerging third category of 'philosophic
history'. A major goal of Enlightenment historiography may be described as the
search for a synthesis and balance between different pairs drawn from this triad:
how to take erudite knowledge and convert it with philosophy into a pleasing
literary work; how to take a narrative and impregnate it with current philosophic
and political thought; or how to convert ideas drawn from experience and crystal-
lized through philosophy into a narrative of the past. Some of the best examples
show a turn away from the narration and description of political events towards
the consideration of civilization, customs and especially *moeurs* (the French word
for 'manners' or 'customs'). Having said that, by no means every historian during
the eighteenth century can be characterized as an *Enlightenment* historian, much
less as a practitioner of the narrower category of 'enlightened narrative'. Rather,
the century saw multiple journeys along different routes to define the scope and
purpose of historiography, voyages which invariably required their sailors to tack
between fact and generalization, between erudition and literary style, between
'impartiality' and reforming zeal, and even between truth and fiction.

University appointments in history, rare thitherto, drew the major teaching institutions of the continent more closely into the historical enterprise, a foretaste
of the academic dominance of professional history in subsequent times. Oxford
and Cambridge both acquired 'Regius' (that is, royally nominated) professors of
modern history in 1724, Edinburgh its professorship in 'Universal History and
Greek and Roman Antiquities' five years earlier. The new university of Göttingen
(est. 1734) would become the intellectual centre of the German Enlightenment

24: Russian Historical Writing Westernizes: Karamzin on the Kiev and Mongol Periods

The present is a consequence of the past. To judge the former one must recollect the latter; each, so to say, completes the other, and viewed together, the two present themselves to the mind more clearly.

From the Caspian Sea to the Baltic, from the Black Sea to the Arctic, amid deserts known to the Greeks and Romans more from fairy tales than from the correct descriptions of eyewitnesses, there lived a thousand years ago peoples given to nomadism, hunting, and agriculture. From these diverse tribes it pleased Providence to create the most spacious state in the world.

Rome, once strong with valor, had weakened from luxury, and collapsed, shattered by the might of the northern barbarians. New epochs followed; new peoples, new customs appeared, and Europe acquired a new appearance, the principal features in which are still to be seen in her political system. In a word, upon the ruins of Roman dominion there established itself in Europe the dominion of the Germanic peoples.

Russia also joined this new, general system. Scandinavia, the lair of restless knights – *officina gentium, vagina nationum* – furnished our fatherland with its first sovereigns, whom the Slavic and Finnic tribes dwelling on the shores of Lake Ilmen, the White Lake, and the River Velikaia accepted of their free will. 'Come,' the Finns and the Slavs told them, having wearied of internecine wars, 'come to reign and rule over us. Our land is rich and great, but there is no order in it.' This took place in 862, and at the end of the tenth century European Russia was already as large as it is today; that is, she had matured from infancy into extraordinary greatness. The Russians, as hirelings of the Greeks, fought in 964 against the Arabs in Sicily and later in the environs of Babylon.

What caused such an unusual historical phenomenon? The fervent, romantic passion of our early princes for conquests, and monocracy, which they founded on the ruins of this multitude of weak, quarreling, democratic states of which Russia had previously been made up. Rurik, Oleg, Sviatoslav, Vladimir, gave the citizens no opportunity of recovering from the rapid succession of victories, from the constant din of military encampments, compensating them with glory and with booty for the loss of their previous liberty, which had brought them poverty and conflict.

In the eleventh century, the Russian state, resembling a sprightly, impassioned youth, could look forward to a long life and to glorious deeds ....

From N. M. Karamzin, *Karamzin's Memoir on Ancient and Modern Russia*, trans. Richard Pipes (1959; New York: Athenaeum, 1974), 103–4.

Box 18   Historical Writing in Russia

Historians would be among the major architects of Russia's Europeanization and of the simultaneous secularization of tsarist authority. Vasilii Nikitich Tatischev (1686–1750) was an expert in mining who wrote the thirty volumes of his *Russian History* at night and between assignments; even the court historiographer Prince Mikhail Shcherbatov (1733–90) admitted that his *Russian History from Ancient Times* had been written more for personal pleasure than duty. Beginning with the late seventeenth-century Westernization under Peter the Great (r. 1682–1725) a new Russian national historiography emerged, first with Tatischev's compilation from older chronicles into a history from earliest times to 1613 and then with two national histories respectively by the polymath chemist, linguist and poet Mikhail Vasilyevich Lomonosov (1711–65) on the earliest periods, and the seven-volume survey by Shcherbatov, an admirer of the Briton David Hume's historical writing. Eighteenth-century Russian historical writing reached its peak just after the Napoleonic struggles with Nikolai Mikhailovich Karamzin's (1766–1826) multivolume *Istoriia gosudarstva rossiskogo* ('History of the Russian State', 1818–29).

and a locus of special significance for historical education. The periodical became for the first time a significant medium for public discussions of history. Fin-de-siècle literary journals such as Bayle's *Nouvelles de la République des Lettres* (1684–7) were succeeded in the early eighteenth century by many other such periodicals like Britain's *History of the Works of the Learned* (1699–1712) and *Gentleman's Magazine* (1731–1907), which responded to the already noted welter of historical books by offering their readers reviews of new works and advertising their publication. Early academic historical journals such as the *Allgemeine historische Bibliothek* and *Historische Journal* also appeared, though they often suffered a premature demise. Informally, history was a frequent subject in the salons and coffee houses, while gentlemen's clubs, secretive orders such as the Freemasons (with whom both J. G. Herder and the Russian historian Karamzin (Extract 24 and Box 18) were affiliated) and more formal societies of *savants* on the model of the Académie française (est. 1635) and Académie royale des Inscriptions et Médailles (est 1663; renamed the Académie des Inscriptions et Belles-Lettres in 1716) continued to spring up in Europe's capitals and even its provincial towns.

The intellectual activities of such groups ranged more widely than their names suggest – the Académie des Inscriptions, producer of vast works of learning, was also the scene of Bayle-like debates and papers on the accuracy of early Roman history, on French history and on the nature of medieval society. Many urban publications provided what amounted to clearing-house gazettes of knowledge: Leipzig had its *Acta Eruditorum*, Frankfurt the *Frankfurter Gelehrte Anzeigen*, with regular sections devoted to learned societies. The academies also offered prizes and medals on various subjects. The conversations previously conducted privately by scholars across political boundaries increasingly veered into the public domain, and though the tone could be as sharp as in the era of Valla or Scaliger, new rules of social civility provided some deterrent to bad behaviour. While Latin remained for a time the elite language of international scholarship, vernacular tongues (Italian, German and especially French) were increasingly favoured. The journals and magazines seem now disorganized and chaotic, offering miscellanies on any number of topics (a hangover from the virtuoso culture of the seventeenth century). History had not quite yet been 'disciplined' into a separate category – that would be the nineteenth century's work – but the institutions and organs created in the Enlightenment provided an essential step along that path by putting history firmly into the public sphere.

'Philosophic' History in Italy and Scotland

The job of history-master to Europe, and the world, would increasingly fall to Germans in the nineteenth century, and we will circle back to Germany at the end of this chapter. But the story of eighteenth-century Europe's search for meaning in the past begins elsewhere, in the 'philosophic' histories of two Italians largely ignored in their own time. The younger of this pair, Pietro Giannone (1676–1748), was a Neapolitan jurist who authored a *Civil History of the Kingdom of Naples* (1723) (see Box 19). This blended detailed knowledge of documents (albeit often derived at secondhand from the erudite works of earlier generations) with a focus on social history and a reform-minded and specifically anti-ecclesiastical outlook that would characterize much later Enlightenment thinking.

Giannone's older contemporary Giambattista Vico (1668–1744), Professor of Latin Eloquence at Naples, has ultimately attracted far greater attention. It did not start out that way. Although Vico had a few early admirers, he was largely ignored for a century, until first taken up by Herder and then championed by the French romantic historian Jules Michelet. Vico did not appeal to eighteenth-century audiences and even today his impact has been selective rather than overwhelming. He is hard to read, often allusive or ambiguous in his references. It is not easy to say

Box 19   **Pietro Giannone's *Civil History of the Kingdom of Naples***

Giannone's 'civil history' was a new genre, quite different from that identified by Francis Bacon over a century before as a synonym for political narrative. On the contrary, Giannone expressed the wish to avoid 'deafening' the reader with accounts of battles, nor, in the mode of a travel writer and some of the chorographers, to extol a city's virtue, but rather to explain the laws, customs and politics practised in the entire kingdom of Naples. While his *Civil History* was recondite and learned, Giannone was not interested in erudition for its own sake but as the necessary content of a narrative that could generalize effectively, and build a case, in this instance an argument that the weakness of Naples lay in ecclesiastical privilege and control of wealth. Giannone's anticlericalism put him in harm's way, and in 1736, while visiting Piedmont, he was abducted and imprisoned in Turin for the last dozen years of his life. Although by the standards of the century's revolutionary end it was no ringing tocsin of liberty, the *Civil History* nonetheless set the tone for much that was innovative in the next several decades. Others such as Voltaire would soon attack the Church and other forms of authority with relative impunity. More important, the inclusiveness of the genre of civil history opened the possibility of narrating a past beyond the political and biographical.

what his masterpiece, the *Scienza Nuova* ('New Science') is 'about' since it veers between history, philology and what we would now call sociology, from recommendations for proper history-writing to speculations about the nature of early society, to discussions of the Homeric poems and Vico's theory (taken up by later scholarship) that they were the work of many different hands rather than a single bard endowed with 'sublime esoteric wisdom'.[15] Moreover, the content of the *New Science* would not have resonated with most readers. Despite Vico's admiration of Bacon, his distinction between the realm of man and the realm of nature ran against the current of Baconian experimental philosophy which saw the human as subject to the same forms of analysis and classification as the biological or astronomical. Finally, this was a century that embraced, albeit inconsistently and often cautiously, notions of progress and improvement, and which would largely abandon both the notion of continuous and inevitable decay and the concept of historical cycles. Vico's vision of history saw little prospect of escape from a recurring sequence of *corso e ricorso*: though there is 'progress' from one age to another, there is no cumulative and absolute progress, and anything with a human origin will have an end. In one way, this is a reworking (and extension of scope from the political to the mental and social spheres) of the Polybian *anacyclosis*. While the completeness of Vico's philosophy and the breadth of his knowledge are dazzling, he was very much a creature of the humanist rhetorical heritage. Words, language and writing were the fundamental elements separating man from beast, and though he was as sceptical as Bodin of the claims of different peoples to absurdly ancient beginnings, he adopted the vocabulary of descent, genealogy and *origo gentis*. The grist for this mill was provided by a combination of ancient authorities (Tacitus' *Germania*, for instance, on barbarian customs), Renaissance linguistic philology and the erudite jurisprudence and political thought of Bodin, Selden, Grotius and Pufendorf.

The *New Science* was first published in 1725 and substantially revised in later editions of 1735 and 1744. Vico himself thought it a counterpart to Newton's *Principia*, doing for the human past what Newton had done for the laws of the cosmos, though there is little of the order that Newton imposed on his own material. It begins with a critique of historical method, proposing several conceits or errors that commonly lead historians astray. Not unlike Bacon's earlier 'Idols of the Mind', these include the conceits of nations (the tendency to write history from a narrowly national perspective) and of scholars (the assumption that everything we now know has always been known). The first, Vico says, has vitiated the work of modern chronologers who fail to recognize the bias in their ancient sources. The second has induced a lack of historical sense, and the fallacious assumption that people in remote antiquity thought as we do: ancient fables and hieroglyphs were not, in his view, codes covering up esoteric eternal truths; rather, they were the substance of ancient thought itself. Vico's intent was not to undermine belief in history: to the contrary, in his opinion, historical knowledge was more comprehensible than knowledge of the world of nature.

In a pair of early works, *Of the Study Methods of our Time* (1709) and *On the Most Ancient Wisdom of the Italians* (1710), Vico had already started developing a theory of knowledge that addressed the very Cartesian dismissal of philology and rhetoric which as a younger man he had once embraced. His solution to Descartes' repudiation of non-formal truths rested on the thesis that men *can* understand with certainty, or at least a high degree of probability, the things that they make – which include nations and their history. For Vico, *verum* (truth) was equivalent to *factum* (that which is made or, historically, *done*).[16] Things we make are mental or conceptual as well as material: 'against the sceptics', he concluded that 'Those truths are, indeed, human whose elements we fashion for ourselves, contain within ourselves and, by means of postulates, extend indefinitely: when we arrange these elements we make the truths which we come to know through this arranging.'[17] The things that men make include laws, customs and human institutions. Indeed, precisely *because* these were of human creation, they could be known much more perfectly than the realm of nature, which was the direct creation of God alone. History in a sense is a form of collective self-knowledge: as one scholar has aptly commented, Descartes' *cogito* ('I think therefore I am') was answered in Vico by 'I make, therefore I know.'

Vico espoused his own erudite synthesis of human histories, including those from outside the West, though his knowledge of the latter was secondhand. He erected this edifice on a postulated series of cycles of progress and decline, dividing the past into a series of recurring ages: of gods, of heroes and of men (the historical age) – there had been two such cycles of *corso e ricorso* up to his own time. Each age, which occurred at variable times and over variable durations in different parts of the world, was characterized by distinctive modes of speech, thought, law and government, and all unfolded against the imagined horizon of an 'ideal eternal history' (*storia ideali eterna*) which is 'traversed in time by the history of all nations'.[18] Vico's insight allowed him to explain the transition from one era to another, and the emergence of civility from that pre-social state of nature that the earlier philosophers had postulated. He identified four major tropes (figures of speech) that characterized different modes of thought: metaphoric, metonymic, synecdochic and ironic,[19] the first three representing successive levels of sophistication in man's cognitive organization of the sensory world; the ironic mode itself denotes a decline into questioning and criticism – a 'second barbarism' of reflection – the very scepticism against which he had now set himself. The application by Vico of philology and jurisprudence to the study of the past echoes the Renaissance philologists and jurists, while anticipating the work of later anthropologists, linguists and comparative religion scholars. Familiar with the chronological writing of the previous century and with a number of the clerical histories of non-European peoples, Vico was also able to generalize beyond the usual geographic boundaries of his continent.

While there was certainly progress between and within Vico's cyclical eras, he was no believer in absolute human progress. In this important respect, Vico was unlike many other philosophic historians of the eighteenth century. Among these, no group contributed more to the recasting of history as the story of human progress, to its global scope, and to the analysis of its non-narrative forms than a number of Scots intellectuals. Adam Ferguson, John Millar, Adam Smith and Henry Home, Lord Kames, among others, wrote variants of what eventually became named 'conjectural' history, a label that has stuck.[20] This involved using reasoned speculation or 'conjecture' to fill in the blanks left by the historical record, especially as applied to the most remote periods of time.

It was comparative, it was generally erudite and it focused not on politics and war but on culture, society, government and law. This was not universal history in the mode of either Bossuet or the ancients, there is no *eschaton* and, though none of these thinkers was especially anticlerical, religion did not occupy centre stage.

The sources of this spectacular burst of intellectual energy from a relatively obscure and underpopulated corner of Europe were diverse. They include both seventeenth-century legal scholarship and prior rationalist and sceptical discussions about how history, for all its manifest flaws and imperfections, could nonetheless be retained as a meaningful form of knowledge and literature – Scottish conjecture is in some ways the direct beneficiary of the late seventeenth-century decision by Newton, Leibniz and others *not* to follow Descartes down an antihistorical path. The eighteenth-century Scots also owed a debt to the *fact* of a longer tradition of Scottish historical thought, though not much to its *substance*: now living in a united Britain, they went out of their way to efface the nationalist tendencies of their medieval and early modern predecessors and repudiate their country's rough and uncivilized past. 'Nations, as well as men', the narrative historian William Robertson remarked, 'arrive at maturity by degrees, and the events, which happened during their infancy or early youth ... deserve not to be remembered.'[21]

Like Robertson, the Scottish economic and social theorists knew their French historians, Voltaire included, but they learned much more from a subtler-minded Frenchman who wrote no narrative history, Charles-Louis de Secondat, baron de Montesquieu (1689–1755) (see Box 20), whose focus on civil society and analysis of manners and culture are all on display in the work of the Scots. A good example of this influence is the lawyer-turned-critic Lord Kames (1696–1782). Kames published very late in life the *Sketches of the History of Man* (1774), a work he claimed to have been working on for three decades. This was a topically arranged study that drew on historians but eschewed a chronological narrative. The *Sketches* lack the psychological insight of other Enlightenment authors, Rousseau and Condorcet among them, but it provided readers with a synoptic survey of human arts, manners, reason, morality, theology, forms of government, military organization and even social policy.[22] Kames's earlier *Essays upon Several Subjects concerning British Antiquities* (1747) and *Historical Law-Tracts* (1758) placed Scotland's political and social development into a British and, ultimately, European context.

Among the Scottish theorists, Ferguson especially saw his *Essay on the History of Civil Society* as a working out of Montesquieu's ideas. Like the economist Adam Smith, Ferguson's attitude to progress was ambivalent: the very peace and security that this North Briton prized had a cost, in the production of a second-rate

Box 20   Charles-Louis de Secondat, baron de Montesquieu

Apart from his *Considérations* on the reasons for the decline of Rome (a work which influenced Gibbon later in the century), Montesquieu authored two works which set the comparativist agenda whose most sophisticated Scottish expression would come from Adam Ferguson. Montesquieu's mature work of 1748, *De l'esprit des lois* (well known to English-speaking readers as *The Spirit of the Laws*), was an ambitious interpretation of the origins and development of human society. Montesquieu approached the past as a system, or a field, whence could be drawn principles that did not especially depend on the veracity of minutiae – the epistemological debates and factual critiques of the late seventeenth century were of no interest to him. (If the point of history was to provide guidance for the future and moral edification, what did it matter whether everything claimed by its authors had actually occurred?) Heir to a whole tradition of political thinking traceable back via Machiavelli to Polybius, *The Spirit of the Laws* is most famous for its articulation of the doctrine of the separation of powers, but its impact on historiography and social science has also been profound – it is sometimes regarded, perhaps with some exaggeration, as the originating text of the modern discipline of sociology. Montesquieu took up suggestions from Bodin, Ibn Khaldūn and, more remotely, Herodotus, with respect to the influence of climate on national character, concluding that temperate zones (within which lay France itself) were most likely to produce civilized society.

society and consumer culture dominated by mediocre men. This historicization of the ancient theory whereby luxury leads to indolence, corruption and the loss of liberty would be quoted approvingly by Marx in the next century, and it is not hard to see in it an anticipation of later cultural critics such as Nietzsche, Huizinga or Spengler. One finds also in Ferguson a sympathetic understanding of past societies which differs markedly from most French contemporary scholars and anticipates the early historicism of Germans such as Herder (see below). 'Every age hath its consolations, as well as its sufferings', he observed, and those living in modern comfort will tend to exaggerate the misery of 'barbarous times'. Like Vico, Ferguson thought of fable and myth as characteristic of early thought about the past, and thus paradoxically a better kind of evidence than early forms of historical writing:

When traditionary fables are rehearsed by the vulgar, they bear the marks of a national character; and though mixed with absurdities, often raise the imagination, and move the heart .... It is only in the management of mere antiquaries, or stript of the ornaments which the laws of history forbid them to wear, that they become even unfit to amuse the fancy, or to serve any purpose whatever.

The mistake made by antiquaries is to interpret myth literally, as if it were the equivalent of classical historiography (which, in the form of Caesar and Tacitus in particular represents the best source on the early stages of man). 'It were absurd to quote the fable of the Iliad or the Odyssey, the legends of Hercules, Theseus, or Oedipus, as authorities in matter of fact relating to the history of mankind; but they may, with great justice, be cited to ascertain what were the conceptions and sentiments of the age in which they were composed ....'[23]

In evaluating historical writing proper, Ferguson was as much a neoclassicist as any of his contemporaries, praising the 'sublime and intelligent' Greek and Roman historians who 'understood human nature, and could collect its features, and exhibit its characters in every situation'. Of medieval historiography Ferguson had a lower opinion, flogging anew that much-scarred whipping boy of the Renaissance humanists, the 'monkish chronicler', and his alleged incapacity to listen past the buzz of disconnected serial events:

They were ill succeeded in this task by the early historians of modern Europe; who, generally bred to the profession of monks, and confined to the monastic life, applied themselves to record what they were pleased to denominate facts, while they suffered the productions of genius to perish, and were unable, either by the matter they selected, or the style of their compositions, to give any representation of the active spirit of mankind in any condition. With them, a narration was supposed to constitute history, whilst it did not convey any knowledge of men; and history itself was allowed to be complete, while, amidst the events and the succession of princes that are recorded in the order of time, we are left to look in vain for those characteristics of the understanding and the heart, which alone, in every human transaction, render the story either engaging or useful.[24]

Much of the vocabulary of the Scottish writers was inherited from the ancients through Renaissance thinkers such as Machiavelli. The interest in customs and manners is of course traceable as far back as Herodotus and was more recently found in Conquest-era works such as Acosta's 'natural and moral' history. That said, the eighteenth-century Scots did not live in either antiquity or the Renaissance, and they had to factor a variety of evidence into their picture of the cumulative past, including 250 years of encounters with other worlds both 'savage' (the most primitive tribes of the Americas and parts of Africa) and 'barbarian' (semi-civilized peoples like the Incas, northern Laplanders and the nomads of central Eurasia), as well as the conversion of empires to the advancement of commerce rather than simple aristocratic or dynastic aggrandizement. Adding these ingredients into the mix allowed them – perhaps forced them – to take much of this material in innovative directions. It also freed them to jettison some of its earlier explanatory paraphernalia: euhemerist inventors, miracles and even the reliable old crutch of the supposititious 'lawgiver' such as Sparta's Lycurgus, Athens' Solon or even the Bible's Moses, men who could single-handedly invent and impose complex civil and legal codes. Vico had doubted whether such figures ever really existed; several of the Scottish thinkers, while regarding them as historical, denied the lawgivers their authoritative role, seeing the kinds of institutions once ascribed to their genius as merely the natural outcome of a particular stage of development; these followed one another not in great leaps but 'by degrees'.[25] States, said Ferguson, 'proceed from one form of government to another, by easy transitions, and frequently under old names adopt a new constitution', human nature containing the seeds that spring forth and ripen at particular times. 'We are therefore to receive, with caution, the traditional histories of ancient legislators, and founders of states.'[26]

The recurrent challenge of writing outsiders into European history, posed in previous centuries first by Germanic barbarians and then by American natives, continued in the eighteenth century, now embracing the Chinese, a fully civilized society but one that the West would slot (along with the Turks, Persians and most South Asian rulers) into the category of nations ruled by 'oriental despots'. The eighteenth century converted the old discourse of *origo gentis* into reasoned speculation about the transitions from one stage of civilization to another, and the impact of conflict between peoples at those different stages. While the Trojans and their litter of fictitious kings were now by and large written off, the Scythians, Goths, Israelites and even – for Joseph de Guignes, a comparativist student of nomadic societies – Noah's children could not be dispensed with entirely. They offered, along with the biblical confusion of tongues at Shinar, the readiest explanation of both the population of the world and the forgetting of much ancient knowledge by the far-travelled descendants of once-wise founders. Though many Enlightenment observers shared the earlier scepticism of a Bayle, they avoided the latter's heterogeneous erudition dispersed over hundreds of different topics in favour of a higher level of generalization. And while they had inherited the Hobbesian vision of a pre-social 'state of nature', they displaced this abstract and rather atemporal notion with a more concrete set of theories, empirically derived from natural history and travel literature; these described human development out of primitive states set in real periods in the past, though not always at the *same* times in different countries.

The most sophisticated formulations of this evolutionary scheme of social progress are now collectively called 'stadialism', and were not without precedent.

Greeks and Romans had speculated on the progress of mankind from one type of society to the next, and there are hints of a developmental or 'civilizing' theory in the twelfth-century chronicler William of Malmesbury. Certainly there had been Renaissance thinkers and historians, such as England's Samuel Daniel (1562–1619) or France's Loys Le Roy (d. 1577), who had painted a picture of cultural or legal change as a slow and gradual process. Selden had sketched out a gradualist approach in the development of legal and social institutions such as honorific titles. Pufendorf had asserted that the 'state of nature' beloved of philosophers and jurists needed to be viewed as a real historical phenomenon, part of a temporal process, rather than a Hobbesian theoretical abstraction, and that commercial sociability lay at the end of historical progress. Early in the eighteenth century another writer of conjectural history, Antoine-Yves Goguet (1716–58, a bridging figure between biblical geneticism and Scottish stadialism) had theorized that mankind had, in successive vagrant and sedentary steps, recovered its learning following the post-Babel dispersal, by reacquiring the lost arts of hunting, herding, farming and exchange of goods. And, building on Acosta's view that savages can have no narrative history and must therefore be studied as a branch of natural history, the Jesuit traveller Jean-François Lafitau (1681–1746) eventually provided an explicit comparison between the North American natives and the tribal societies documented by Caesar, Tacitus and other classical historians.[27] The direct linkage between the barbarians of antiquity and more recent writings about modern savages is expressed in the oft-quoted remark by John Locke that 'In the beginning all the world was America.'

The unique contribution of the eighteenth century was to systematize much of this thinking. Stadialism has become almost synonymous with Scottish writers, beginning with the jurist Dalrymple's 1757 *Essay towards a General History of Feudal Property in Great Britain* and continuing with works like John Millar's *Origin of the Distinction of Ranks* and the same author's *Historical View of the English Government*. In its mature form, as it appeared in Adam Smith's (1723–90) *Lectures on Jurisprudence*,[28] stadialism postulated four stages of human development, defined principally as modes of subsistence ranging from the savage through a pastoral/nomadic stage (sometimes distinguished into two stages) and then an agrarian stage, ending in that of commerce. The culminating mode of subsistence featuring money, trade and intercourse between peoples and commerce would eventually provide the subject of Smith's magnum opus, *An Inquiry into the Nature and Causes of the Wealth of Nations* (1776); its economic invisible hand quietly displaced an older Providence, much as in the natural realm Newton's *Principia* had turned God into an arms-length creator operating through mathematically discernible laws, and Vico had made him the 'divine architect' of creation rather than its actual artisan.

Not every Scottish writer made use of stadialism, one reason being that it was much better as a systematic model for describing and analysing different types of society than as a master-narrative to explain change – its ability to account for *why* a society moved from one stage to the next was limited, and inferior to the explanation offered by Vico. It was also possible to tell a linear, developmental and progressive story without reference to 'stages' at all. Hume did not use stadial ideas in any significant sense, though his works certainly acknowledge different periods like 'the infancy of society', concepts that have a much longer pedigree. Robertson subscribed loosely to stadial views, and he recognized the importance of modes of subsistence as determinative of social arrangements, a key concept of the stadialists. But even he found stadialism much too exclusive of direct human agency, and of the moral decisions that attend individual actions.

A key difference between eighteenth-century stadial theory and later ideas of human development (such as nineteenth-century positivism or the theories of Karl Marx) is this: the stadialists assumed no inevitability to progress. The failure of certain peoples to progress beyond a particular stage demonstrated this. Moreover, the stages could overlap, even within geographic proximity of one another. And human achievement occurred as a consequence of combined environmental and social factors, not simply as the direct consequence of either climate, as Bodin would have had it, or providence – though both could be allowed a place. And 'progress' was not yet the only metanarrative available, for histories still testified to many examples of social and political decline, as Ferguson chronicled in his account of the death of the Roman republic.[29] Rome was the great case study of imperial collapse, and it would be left to another Briton, Edward Gibbon, to chronicle the gradual steps in its demise in his *Decline and Fall of the Roman Empire*, to which we will return below.

Historical Thought in the French Enlightenment

Apart from Montesquieu and Rousseau, neither of whom actually wrote a narrative history, the eighteenth-century Frenchman who exerted the greatest influence on historical thought and writing outside his homeland was arguably Voltaire, though the nature of this influence was more dispersed and ultimately superficial. His own ideas were themselves largely derivative. Yet Voltaire (born François-Marie Arouet, 1694–1778) merits our attention both for his reputation and for the ambitious global scope of some of his works. His *Essai sur les moeurs et l'esprit des nations* ('An Essay on the Manners and Spirit of the Nations') was an overview and critique of institutions and customs as they had developed over several centuries. Voltaire included non-Western civilizations such as the Chinese, though his references outside European culture were spare and offered more as a contrarian antidote to the idea of Judeo-Christian superiority. Over the course of a lengthy career, Voltaire consistently praised features in other civilizations while still concluding that Western culture represented the apogee of human reason, though its beneficial influences were undercut by superstition and religious fanaticism. Disparaging towards ancient barbarism, Voltaire could nonetheless be sympathetic to contemporary North American aboriginal 'savagery', an even more primitive state. He contributed to public knowledge of alien societies, often employing contemporary travel accounts as sources, and scoffed at the kinds of etymological and genealogical tricks still used on occasion to fabricate false ancestries.

Voltaire arrived only gradually at this cosmopolitan perspective on the past, and its emphasis on culture and civilization. Indeed, his very commitment to history is in some ways surprising, as he had inherited a good deal of the scepticism of Descartes and Bayle, to the point of eventually writing his own essay on *le pyrrhonisme historique*. His initial offering as a historian was the dramatic and entertaining but thoroughly conventional *History of Charles XII* (1731), focusing on the great achievements (and ultimate failure) of its central figure, the Swedish king (r. 1697–1718), juxtaposed with his modernizing foil, Russia's Tsar Peter the Great. The great men dominate the account, Charles especially, to the exclusion of most else, including lesser campaigns fought by Charles' subordinates – this is no 'life and times', though Voltaire's geographic range was impressive, embracing the Turks and Tartars with whom the king had come into contact. In a Thucydidean flourish, though he himself was no historical participant, Voltaire boasted that in *Charles XII* he had 'not set down a single fact on which we have not consulted eye-witnesses of unimpeachable veracity'.[30]

Voltaire's inclinations, however, soon grew ill-disposed to detail, and by the time of the *Essai* he would regard the kind of factual disagreements between historians as matter for lists of errata, not histories. (This was a variant on the natural philosopher d'Alembert's public dismissal of dry erudition without moral purpose, and of the activities of the Académie des Inscriptions in particular.) Bacon's earlier categorization of annals, philology and antiquarian activity as the mere ingredients to be developed by lesser scholars and obscure collectors (Fig. 39) for subsequent use by the true historian is also echoed here, with the addition of Voltaire's suggestion that the role of the authentic *historien* be distinguished from that of the *historiographe*, an assembler of facts, documents and dates from whose materials historians can draw. Details were important only to the degree that one might learn from them something of real significance, otherwise they ought not clutter the historian's page. Yet Voltaire, unsympathetically critical of the errors and folly of past ages and hostile to 'pedantic' scholarship and 'useless obscurities', also fiercely defended himself when attacked for factual inaccuracy.[31] His comment

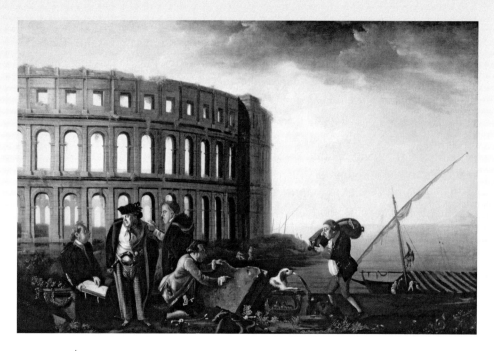

Figure 39 │ Antiquaries at Pola, Italy, by Thomas Patch (1725–82), illustrating eighteenth-century amateur archaeological activity.

on 'the necessity of doubt', written as an explanatory note to *Charles XII*, is a clear statement of the priority of common sense over even eyewitness testimony (Extract 25). Documents themselves are only believable if they were written during an enlightened time.

The shifts in Voltaire's interests are a sign of the eighteenth-century movement from the history of *men* towards a history of *man*. Twenty years after *Charles XII*, Voltaire would publish a very different type of history in *Le siècle de Louis XIV* ('The Age of Louis XIV', 1751). Though this praised that king, the book is not in any sense *about* Louis – despite its many entertaining courtly anecdotes – or even about France, but rather about the climax of civility and reason under a generally wise monarch. While more of it is concerned with battles and political life than its author might have liked to admit, Voltaire nonetheless included much on culture, science and the arts, finding in the first part of Louis' reign one of only four truly great eras in human history, comparable with Greece, Augustan Rome and the Renaissance. The reign provided Voltaire with a benchmark for reforms urgently needed in his own time. To this deist, such was the continued dark power of the Church that France and the world had declined since the early part of the century. Voltaire's optimism had limits, and never turned him into a living version of his

25: Voltaire on the Necessity of Doubt

Scepticism, let us remember, is the foundation of all wisdom, according to Aristotle. This is an excellent maxim for anyone who reads history, especially ancient history.

What absurd facts, what a conglomeration of fables that shock commonsense you find in it! Well then, do not believe them.

There were kings, consuls and decemvirs in Rome. The Romans destroyed Carthage; Caesar defeated Pompey; all that is true. But when you are told that Castor and Pollux fought for that nation; that a Vestal refloated a stranded ship with her girdle; that a chasm closed up when Curtius threw himself into it; do not believe a word of it. You will read everywhere of prodigies, fulfilled prophecies, miraculous cures wrought in the temple of Aesculapius; do not believe a word of them ....

I mistrust everything miraculous. But ought I to extend my incredulity to facts which belong to the natural order of human things, but are nevertheless highly improbable?

For example, Plutarch affirms that Caesar threw himself, fully armed, into the Mediterranean, holding aloft papers he did not want to get wet in one hand, and swimming with the other. Do not believe a word of this tale Plutarch tells you. Rather believe Caesar, who does not say a word of it in his Commentaries; and be quite certain that if one throws oneself into the sea holding papers in one's hand, they get wet ....

I do not even believe eye-witnesses when they tell me things that commonsense refuses to accept. It is no use the Sire de Joinville, or rather the person who has translated his memoirs of the crusades from the medieval French, affirming that the Egyptian Emirs, after having assassinated their soldan, offered the crown to their prisoner, St Louis: I would as lief be told that we offered the crown of France to a Turk ....

I say boldly to Mézerai, Père Daniel, and all the historians that I do not believe for a moment that a hailstorm made Edward III examine his conscience and procured peace for Philippe de Valois. Conquerors are not so pious and do not make peace because it rains.

Nothing is more certain than that crimes are committed, but they must be verified. In Mézerai's book you will find over sixty princes who were 'foully done to death'. But he says so without proof, and a popular rumour ought not to be reported except as a rumour ....

I should question the truth of Charles XII's fight at Bender, if I did not have the testimony of several eye-witnesses, and if the character of Charles XII did not make this heroic folly credible. This scepticism with which we ought to regard particular facts should be extended to the manners and customs of foreign nations. We should refuse to believe any historian, ancient or modern, who reports things contrary to nature and normal human feelings.

Selection from *The History of Charles XII King of Sweden*, trans. A. White (London: Folio Society, 1976), 272–5.

own fictional Professor Pangloss canting that all is for the best in the best of possible worlds, especially late in life when the horrors of the Lisbon earthquake of 1755 shook confidence as much as buildings.

The century's most optimistic views on human progress were espoused by Voltaire's Revolutionary-era successor, Marie-Jean-Antoine-Nicolas Caritat, marquis de Condorcet (1743–94). This aristocratic *philosophe* had been an intellectual *enfant terrible* in his youth, meeting Voltaire, whom he admired, in 1770 and eventually serving as his literary executor. Condorcet's own life ended in a Revolutionary prison, but he had completed a few months previously his *Esquisse* or *Sketch for a Historical Picture of the Progress of the Human Mind* (intended as the introduction to a larger *Tableau historique des progrès de l'esprit humain* that he never wrote). The *Esquisse* adumbrated a nine-stage history of humanity's development, with a climactic tenth stage of reason and achievement projected to follow the Revolution, the French republic marking a culmination in the joint progress of Virtue and Enlightenment. Published in a somewhat altered form in 1795, after the Terror had subsided, the *Esquisse* became a manifesto of progress and would influence a number of important nineteenth-century thinkers from the radical Henri de Saint-Simon to Auguste Comte.

Condorcet epitomizes some of the Enlightenment tendencies against which scholars of later eras have reacted, such as its supposed hostility to all things medieval, and its historical thinkers' willingness to hypothesize with boldly assertive generalizations based on an abstract homogenization of the histories of different periods and countries. Given the lack of information about remote, preliterate times, Condorcet adopted the by then standard 'conjectural' method of projecting the observed life of modern tribal societies on to an imputed prehistory. At the point where the historical record begins, generalization requires further hypothesis. 'Here the picture begins to depend in large part on a succession of facts transmitted to us in history, but it is necessary to select them from the history of different peoples, to compare them and combine them in order to extract the hypothetical history of a single people and to compose the picture of its progress.'[32]

Condorcet's explanation of progress allowed for both individual achievement and collective advances. Change could occur either in a sudden burst or more quietly over time; it was affected by environmental factors (echoes here of both Bodin and Montesquieu) as well as by custom, both of which can accelerate, retard or altogether halt progress, leaving some peoples spinning their cartwheels in the muck of the tribal and pastoral stages. Like most philosophic historians of the century, Condorcet saw unintended consequences as being quite as fruitful in the making of the world as the best-laid successful plans. So too were what had been called 'the heterogeneity of purposes', the interactions between myriad schemes of different men. Condorcet's general optimism and his faith in the capacity of the 'common man' admits the presence of countervailing, regressive aspects within any period: his eighth stage thus saw the shackles of priest-craft loosened by print but also witnessed the horrendous atrocities of the Conquests and the wars of religion. But of the general forward movement of consciousness and man's estate, there is in Condorcet no doubt. He is in that sense a figure more in tune with the positivism of the mid-nineteenth century than with the stadialism of the eighteenth.

While the clarity and forcefulness of his expression have made Condorcet a symbol of philosophe speculation at its most optimistic, the *Esquisse* is not especially original, except perhaps in its refinement of the stages of development into nine from the conventional four. Much of Condorcet's thought derived from earlier French writings, and while his stages of progress seem to resemble the work of Scottish writers across the channel, they lack the historical grounding and intellectual nuance of several of those authors, as well as their reservations about the inevitability of progress. The *Esquisse* is one of those magnificent summary speculations on the course of history that appear from time to time and which are quickly proved wrong by subsequent events: Condorcet's prediction on the basis of the past that 'the human race will never relapse into its former state of barbarism' seems somewhat over-optimistic two centuries further on.[33] The game of prophesying the triumph of this or that ideology, social arrangement or political system has proved popular, and the nineteenth and twentieth centuries would find new and ingenious ways to extrapolate from the past into the future.

The Triumvirate

In Britain, created in 1707 through the parliamentary union of England and Scotland, Enlightenment historical writing took a rather different turn. Neither the Scots nor the English had ever developed a French-style courtly tradition of historiography – only in the late seventeenth century had each kingdom even established the office of 'historiographer royal' – and in the early eighteenth century the uncomfortable rub of weighty erudition against literary grace was keenly felt. With the possible exception of Clarendon (see Chapter 4 above), no one, it was frequently asserted, had met the narrative gold standard of Thucydides. The English publishing market in particular was drowning in lesser works: a swelling number of epitomes, abridgements, reissues of older works, lives and letters of clerics and partisan histories of various kinds. The Tory politician Henry St John, Viscount Bolingbroke was highly critical of contemporary historiography and generalized memorably on the uses of history and its proper elegant style in his *Letters on the Study and Use of History*, first published posthumously in 1752 and widely read abroad (see Box 21).

Box 21   Henry St John, Viscount Bolingbroke

Bolingbroke (1678–1751) belongs to the same family tree of European writers on history that in recent centuries includes both Bodin in the sixteenth century and, near the end of the eighteenth century, the abbé Gabriel Bonnot de Mably (1709–85). He adapted the Renaissance *ars historica* to the modern world, and infused it with a modulated version of the scepticism he had found (and rejected) in late seventeenth-century French pyrrhonism, and in the critical scholarship of Bayle. Despite its relative unoriginality, his *Letters on the Study and Use of History* struck a chord with readers because of its apparently sensible balancing of doubt about particulars (including the reliability of chronology derived from the Old Testament) with continued faith in history's overall truth and its exemplary moral value; his foreign readers included Voltaire, Condorcet and a number of German historical thinkers.

The Briton who most clearly answered demands for an elegant national history was the eldest among a celebrated 'triumvirate' whose other two members were William Robertson and Edward Gibbon. David Hume (1711–76) is now recognized as one of the world's greatest philosophers, but in his own day he was better known as a historian. His two interests did overlap. Hume tried to apply his own sceptical theory of causation and his admiration of ancient historians, especially Thucydides, to England's past (and, more briefly, Scotland's). His *History of England from the Invasion of Julius Caesar to the Abdication of James II* (1754–62) was that Thucydidean narrative for which the English literati had been clamouring. It struck a chord with contemporary audiences, and Hume is also noteworthy for having developed in it a 'sentimental' approach to historical writing that he hoped would appeal to both male and female readers. In this aspiration he was wildly successful: seven full editions of the work appeared in his lifetime and 175 in the hundred years after his death. His efforts earned him over £3,000, roughly three-quarters of a million dollars in current prices. The *History* was published in three parts over eight years, and worked backwards beginning with the most recent period, the seventeenth century. The positive reception of this spurred him back in time to tackle first the Tudors and then the Middle Ages, now narrowing his scope to England alone.

Hume's historical reading had been reasonably broad long before he decided to write one for himself: the names of historians and allusions to historical episodes occur throughout his philosophical works. Though he was not impervious to scholarship, recognized the necessity of consulting documents and footnoted the work copiously, Hume's was a house built on the foundation of earlier historians, not on bricks he had made for himself through time spent in archives. He avoided the 'dark industry' of immersion in original printed sources: his purpose was to write a readable, accurate and persuasive history which fulfilled the canons of classical historiography, and which recounted the past in a sympathetic voice. He eschewed one characteristic component of classical historiography, the fictional speech. As with most historians of the century, he had difficulty melding a straightforward narrative with a more philosophic and topical consideration of customs, laws and *moeurs*: thus his own treatment of Anglo-Saxon civilization finds no place in his brisk account of events before the Norman Conquest, and is presented as an appendix. But his formula worked, and Hume's *History* became the closest thing to a bestseller on British history before the nineteenth century.

William Robertson (1721–93), Hume's junior by a decade, is now the least well-known member of the triumvirate, though in his time he was regarded by many as the greatest historian of the day, and one of his works, *The History of America* (the last parts of which appeared posthumously), was to exercise a formidable influence on Latin American countries' writing of their own past well into the next century. A Presbyterian minister ordained in 1743, for the next half century Robertson enjoyed a prosperous clerical and academic career, culminating in his appointment as Principal of the University of Edinburgh in 1762, a post he held for the rest of his life, soon adding the title of Historiographer Royal of Scotland. He was de facto leader of the 'Moderates' within the Presbyterian Church, a group which advocated clerical sociability and politeness and a degree of deference to lay influence, in contrast to the more traditional lines of Scottish Calvinism. He was, in short, a cleric who embodied Enlightenment principles not far removed from Voltaire, yet left room for an active providence involved in human history. This places him intellectually much closer to the tone of the German Enlightenment (see below) on both the Protestant and moderate Catholic sides of the Christian divide.

Robertson produced a number of historical works, including his speculative sermon on the state of the world at the time of Christ (1755). His first narrative history was a retelling of the reigns of Mary Queen of Scots and James VI under the title *The History of Scotland 1542–1603* (1759), part of a longer story, merely hinted at, of the country's development from a rough antiquity through the economic, religious and political difficulties of the sixteenth and seventeenth centuries, towards its happy union with England.[34] Politically, it repudiated Scotland's ancient and medieval pasts, the one obscure and not really narratable, the other a time of bigotry and feudal warfare: there is much here of that strand in the Enlightenment which supported strong central monarchy against aristocratic institutions in the name of progress.

Robertson's next work, his *History of the Reign of the Emperor Charles the Fifth* (1769), is a sweeping survey of Europe at the time of the Reformation and much more a philosophic history than his earlier Scottish study. Robertson's turn towards a French-style enlightened narrative is marked here by an opening 'View of the Progress of Society' covering the thousand years from the late fifth to the early sixteenth centuries, and followed by a dozen books of narrative ending in 1559. Effectively marketed by its publishers, this second history was translated into multiple languages, including French and Russian; it spread Robertson's fame across Europe and earned him a great deal of money. His final major work, and the one for which Robertson is best remembered today, is the *History of America* (1777), which picks up one thread of the story of Charles V's Europe, that of Spain's overseas empires and the contact of European with American native. The politician Edmund Burke regarded it as a masterpiece of 'gradation' since it depicted different indigenous tribes in a wide variety of stages of development. Robertson was guided here principally by the sixteenth- and seventeenth-century Spanish writers, above all Herrera and Acosta, and his original ambitions for the work were scuppered first by the publication of Raynal's juggernaut, the *Deux Indes*, in 1770, and then by the American Revolution, which forced the abandonment of his section on British North America, eventually published by Robertson's son after his death. The *History of America* remained an unfinished masterpiece, but enormously influential abroad.

Robertson wrote one more work shortly before his death, a work which aptly marks the British imperial reorientation to India in the aftermath of losing the wealthier and more populous part of its North American colonies. *An Historical Disquisition Concerning the Knowledge which the Ancients had of India* (1791), like his other works, begins in an earlier age before tracing its theme, familiarity with India, up to the 1500s. Unsympathetic to the American Revolutionary cause, and no admirer of North American natives, he now stressed the natural evolution of India to a present state which in his view far surpassed North America and which, left to its own devices, would continue to develop without coercion from Britain, or futile attempts at its religious conversion. He had a moderately sympathetic view even of the caste system, and Akbar, the sixteenth-century Mughal emperor, seemed a model Enlightened prince, who treated his Hindu subjects with, for the Muslims, uncharacteristic fairness. All the achievements that Robertson notes are measured by European standards, and there is a Eurocentrist theme here, as in the *History of America*, which will concern us more directly in our return to India in the nineteenth century. Yet the work also contains an utterance which could be a mantra for the next century, an injunction against evaluating the past by the standards of the present, made in the context of explaining why antiquity had failed to discover a sea passage to India: 'but judging with respect to the conduct of nations in remote times, we never err more widely than when we decide with regard to it, not according to the ideas and views of their age, but of our own'.[35]

While the general quality of Scottish thought and writing about the past during the eighteenth century was extremely impressive, the same could not be said of England to the south. Bolingbroke's indictment of English history-writing was not entirely misplaced, as England's overall historical output was to prove weighty in quantity but light in actual achievement: as Bolingbroke had feared, few works written by his countrymen achieved a high standard and even fewer would retain a readership even into the next century; Hume had written a brilliant history of England but was himself a Scot. Edward Gibbon (1737–94) is the major exception to this general picture, his luminosity enhanced by the relative dullness of the background. Gibbon was an avid reader and selective admirer of the work of his Scottish and French predecessors, though he committed himself to narrative rather than conjectural history, subordinating the philosopher to the erudite historian – theory informed his story but did not drive it forward, much less determine its selection of evidence. Gibbon was heir to several centuries' worth of conceptual vocabulary, including the very notions of 'decline', 'barbarism' and 'empire', and to eighteenth-century discussions of the role of economics in social and political change. He also reaped the benefit of a hundred recent years of erudition and enlightened history in the different modes of Tillemont (Gibbon's 'patient and sure-footed mule'), and Muratori or Giannone, Voltaire and Robertson. Telling the story of Rome's engagement with barbarians both east and west (the difference between the two is important to his story) required him to become a comparativist, though the *Decline and Fall* is in no sense a *histoire des moeurs*. And though he acknowledges the role that the barbarian had played in the emergence of the modern world, there is none of Rousseau's admiration of the noble savage (in his *Discourse on Inequality*, 1755) or the philosophe's sense of the primitive stage as that most naturally suited to man. Like many of the Scots, Gibbon was ambivalent with respect to the notion of progress, and there is some optimism but rather more doubt in his remark that if the modern commercial town of Glasgow once had cannibals as its citizens, perhaps there was hope 'that New Zealand may produce, in some future age, the Hume of the Southern Hemisphere'.[36]

Gibbon authored a few unpublished essays, principally the work of his youth, and the *Memoirs*, and his letters and journals are also in print.[37] While entertaining in their own right, none of these would be especially noteworthy but for the light they shed on his magnum opus. This was *The History of the Decline and Fall of the Roman Empire* (1776–88), a towering literary monument synthesizing enormous erudition in literary, numismatic and other antiquarian sources (albeit mainly at secondhand through the works of Tillemont and the Académie des Inscriptions) with a philosophical and critical outlook. Having flirted with several other topics ranging from British history to that of the Swiss or the Florentines, he alighted instead on late antiquity. He tells us (in a story that may be literary fabrication on his part but which nonetheless captures both his ironic style and his acute sense of historical distance) that it was at Rome in 1764 'as I sat musing amidst the ruins of the Capitol, while the bare-footed friars were singing vespers in the temple of Jupiter, that the idea of writing the decline and fall of the city first started to my mind'. The 'city' proved too narrow a compass and he soon aspired to recount the story of the tribulations of the whole empire, initially as far as the end of the western empire, and ultimately to 1453. Several years of more systematic reading and note-taking followed and at length, in 1773, he finally began to write. The first volume of the *Decline and Fall* appeared, after several years' labour, in February 1776, to instant acclaim. The booksellers could not keep sufficient copies in stock, and pirated editions appeared in Ireland. 'My book was on every table, and almost on every toilette', since it appealed to female as well as male readers.[38] Hume (one of his 'masters'),[39] who would die a few months later, praised it, as did most of literary London. The second and third volumes appeared in 1781, and the fourth, fifth and sixth were published on 8 May 1788, Gibbon's fifty-first birthday.

We have a very clear picture of the reception of the *Decline and Fall* among contemporaries, including both admirers and religious opponents who found Gibbon's take on Christianity dangerously irreverent. In particular, he aroused the antagonism of churchmen and the pious laity for disparaging the early Church, especially in the notorious fifteenth and sixteenth chapters of his first volume; his favourable portrait in volume II of an antichristian arch-villain, Julian the Apostate, would similarly raise eyebrows. On the whole, though, reaction was favourable and the *Decline and Fall* was successful enough to ensure that the last few years of its author's life were spent in both prosperity and literary celebrity.

It is no longer fashionable to regard the *Decline and Fall* as an updatable and still usable authority on Rome, nor, taken as a classic text, can it be seen in its entirety as a thoroughly consistent and seamless whole, a 'well wrought urn'. There are too many inconsistencies and shifts from its beginning to end, which is hardly surprising given the two decades of its composition. We know Gibbon's primary sources – noted and evaluated in some 8,000 often-discursive footnotes. These form a kind of paratext to his main narrative and range in subject from simple citations or engagements with contemporary authors, to disquisitions on the rarity of the giraffe. A master of the ironic outlook – a sense of distance and of detachment that allowed reflection from outside the whole story, and a matching style that carried weight through understatement – Gibbon could swing from warm endorsement of particular emperors (Julian the Apostate most controversially) to restrained but unambiguous invective heaped on others. He also dealt out judgment to his fellow historians: Voltaire he came to despise as 'an intolerable bigot', while he regarded Raynal as an entertaining writer but found the lack of quotations in the *Deux Indes* an unpardonable offence against scholarship. The ancients did not escape his scorn when wrong, not even Tacitus, 'the first of historians who applied the science of philosophy to the study of facts'.[40] Momigliano suggested that Gibbon's major contribution was to reconcile erudition and narrative, thereby bridging the old gap between antiquary and historian.[41] In fact, he executed a three-way merger, with philosophy making up the third, though Gibbon was neither antiquary nor philosophe.

West and East

As we saw in an earlier chapter, European historical writing had begun to become self-aware both of its own competing genres and, gradually, of the relationship of these to other modes of capturing the past including myth and fiction. Historians who evaluated the record-keeping, calendar-writing and tradition-telling of the Americas and India recognized that these practices were unlike those of the West to a greater degree than the historiographic traditions of that nearest of non-Christian neighbours, Islamic historiography, whose best-known representative, Ibn Khaldūn, was by now reasonably familiar among European historians. The development of comparative linguistics by scholars such as the philologist William Jones opened up consideration of India's Hindu epics as history (see Box 22). The capacity to grasp the essential differences between European genres of history-writing and, say, an Inca quipu remained limited, and alien forms of recollection and representation alike were slotted into Western categories, even Western literary genres, that were often a poor fit. But that a deeper awareness of the distinctiveness of European historiography (and eventually European History) was developing, and in ways it could not have during either antiquity or the Christian Middle Ages, there can be no doubt.

This consciousness extended to China, thanks to the writings of the Jesuit missionaries, whose works were generally well regarded through much of the eighteenth century, even in Protestant countries like Britain. Various aspects of Chinese history and culture proved popular, including the study of Confucianism (Fig. 40). Chinese historiography, it was conceded, was not to be placed in the same category as those native societies without alphabetic writings. But neither was it simply a parallel tradition. By the mid-eighteenth century, when

Box 22   William Jones, Language and Indian Historicity

Building on the work of seventeenth-century Arabists, European familiarity with Islam had improved considerably in the eighteenth century through the work of philologists; Ibn Khaldūn was known in Europe from at least the seventeenth century. But Islam was a culture of the book and thus offered less obvious a contrast to the European privileging of writing. Hindu India was a different story. The European understanding of South Asian culture leapt forward with the work of Sir William Jones (1746–94), whose philological studies of Sanskrit's connections with Greek, Latin and the Celtic languages famously opened up the field of comparative linguistics. His and other early orientalists' writings provided access for European historians to Indian works such as the *Mahābhārata*; understanding of the interrelations of the languages would play a significant role in history beyond scholarship, helping formulate, for instance, nineteenth-century German self-perception and ultimately the 'Aryan' myth. Jones served as a judge in Bengal, and he was the beneficiary of Asian travel writing about Europe as much as that by Europeans on Asia. He was influenced in his views of the relations of oriental languages to each other and to Sanskrit by a historical narrative, the *Dabistan-i Mazahib*, to which he was introduced by a Persian visitor to Oxford. His greatest contribution may have been his strong insistence, conveyed in advice to other historians of India, on the use of original sources for the writing of Indian history, and his belief that grains of precious historical gold could be panned from the gravel of myth and legend in the epics and *purāṇas*. Nonetheless, the work of Jones and other scholars, however sympathetic to the subject of their study, contributed to the 'orientalizing' of India. In Jones's case, India was part of a larger Asia that was manifestly inferior, in both antiquity and modernity, to Europe.

comparison between cultures was especially in vogue, it was possible to generalize about the differences between Europe's historiography and that of others, beyond the type of internal audits that la Popelinière, Bodin and some of the Renaissance *trattatisti* had conducted. Voltaire, a Sinophile whose play *The Orphan of China* was set in the time of Ghengis Khan, was provocatively enthusiastic about Chinese historiography. 'If any annals carry with them the stamp of certainty', he wrote (the 'if' is important: he was never certain that any actually *did*), 'they are those of China', which had escaped the tyranny of allegories, myths and

Figure 40 | Confucius thanking the heavens for his being given the time to write his six books. An illustration of eighteenth-century Sinophilia. Isidore S. H. Helman (1743–1809), engraving from *Abrégé historique des principaux traits de la vie de Confucius, célèbre philosophe chinois, d'après des dessins originaux de la Chine envoyés à Paris par M. Amiot, missionnaire à Pékin*. Paris, 1788.

absurd descent legends. 'Here is a people who, for upwards of four thousand years, daily write their annals'[42] (Fig. 41). Gibbon, in the final chapter of the second (1781) volume of the *Decline and Fall*, attributes modern knowledge of ancient and medieval Tartar history to that illiterate people's interactions with various European nations, but also to the Chinese historians, several of whom he cites in translation. He was acquainted with many of them, and with 'Sematsien' (Sima Qian) in particular, through the earlier writings of the French historian Nicolas Fréret (who had studied Chinese), available to him in the *Mémoires de l'Académie des inscriptions*, and especially through the work of Gibbon's own contemporary, Joseph de Guignes.

A polyglot linguist fluent in Chinese, Joseph de Guignes (1721–1800) provided the eighteenth-century West with its most important window into the world of Eastern historians. His *Histoire générale des Huns, des Turcs, des Mogols, et des autres peuples Tartares occidentaux* ('General History of the Huns, Turks, Mongols

Figure 41 │ *A First Reading of 'The Orphan of China' by Voltaire*, 1755. Painting on canvas by Anicet Charles Gabriel Lemonnier (1743–1824).

and Other Western Tartar Peoples', 1756–8) was an ambitious attempt to compare the civilized cultures of Europe with the nomadic societies of central Eurasia. De Guignes is perhaps the first Westerner to have been able to face directly, and to compare, the profound differences between oriental and occidental histories – a different comparison from that made in the previous centuries between European and Latin American indigenous ones because the Chinese were seen as near equals rather than inferiors. In the preface to his book, De Guignes reflects on the relative value of his sources, and thus on alien historiography, both Chinese and Islamic:

Perhaps it will not be tedious if I make known here in a few words the character of these historians. In general, the Chinese writes to form the heart, to set forth the mutual duties of the sovereign and his subjects, and to instil the love of the fatherland. The Arab seems to have no other purpose but to report facts; with much vivacity, he loses direction and ceases to interest. Both are dry. The methodical spirit which reigns among the Chinese leads them to strip history of its principal adornments. The Emperor has his history, likewise the army commander, and likewise the man of letters. These divided histories, set apart from one another, become arid and boring, whereas they would be interesting were they told together; but the Chinese seeks to be useful, not to give pleasure. He has nothing of those splendid descriptions and instructive episodes which we find in the authors of Greece and Rome. He writes austerely, expresses himself in a few words, and is careful to mark the divisions of time. The Arab on the other hand is either no more than a chronicler, scrupulous in assigning each event to the year, the month and even the day of its occurrence, as is the rule with general histories; or he assumes the role of an orator, hardly content with two pages to recount what he could have told us in a few lines, and addicted to pompous expressions, elevated figures of speech, and elaborate cadences whose uniform closures must take the place of pauses and convey the sense of his prose. He abandons himself to his passions and gives us nothing but a satire or a eulogy; such is the besetting sin of his particular histories. This Byzantine style of panegyric and declamation is also that of most Greek historians, and of those of the Crusades, who are in addition ignorant, credulous and superstitious. The Chinese historian is reliable when writing of his own nation, biased as regards foreigners, whom he despises too much and knows too little.[43]

De Guignes' critique of Islamic historiography (he did not recognize Islamic and Arabic as different categories) renders it inferior in one of two ways, both significantly resembling modes of historicity that the Enlightenment was trying hard to jettison. Either it is too much like the medieval chronicling mode (not here specifically mentioned by De Guignes but clearly implied) *or* it is too much a display of oratory combined with falsity.[44] It is in short either too factual *or* too fictional. Rather than seeing oriental historiographies as an entirely different corpus of writing springing from different priorities, De Guignes chose both to domesticate and temporalize them as the product of less advanced civilizations, something analogous to the West's earlier and now obsolete ways of seeing the past. Islam and, to a lesser extent, China, are thus not civilizations without history; they have simply not escaped earlier stages in history's development that Enlightened Europeans have moved beyond. This was not, of course, how most eighteenth-century Chinese saw the world.

De Guignes' comments on oriental modes of history hint at but do not yet explicitly signal the expansionist ambitions of Western historiography which would appear more clearly in the nineteenth and early twentieth centuries. In that sense, they are emblematic of the way in which the Enlightenment provides the bridge between the more tentative, early-modern episode of cross-cultural historiographic contact, and Europe's much more successful hegemony up ahead. More immediately, De Guignes' inquiries fit into the larger, pressing question Europeans had been asking themselves, which was how civilization and learning had come to achieve higher levels in Europe than in what Robertson called 'the mild and fertile regions of the east' where humanity 'began its career of improvement'.[45] Knowledge of the past was simply one of those categories of learning, and China became one of the most-cited Enlightenment examples of arrested development, a river that had silted into a stagnant pond.

Chinese Historiography in the Early Qing Dynasty

For its part, China was also becoming better acquainted with Western culture. In the later eighteenth century, the Manchu official Qishiyi would write in his *Xiyu Wenjianlu* ('Record of Things Seen and Heard in the Western Regions', 1777) about a variety of neighbouring peoples from the Russians to the Turks. The Jesuits were a conduit of information from West to East as much as in the other direction, and they retained influence as advisors and administrators in Beijing well into the Qing era – Lang Shining, propagandist to the mid-eighteenth-century Qianlong Emperor, was actually the Italian Jesuit Giuseppe Castiglione (1688–1766). In portraying Qianlong, Castiglione and several fellow missionaries followed the lead of their French counterparts who had manufactured Louis XIV into the model universal monarch.

In spelling out differences between European and Asian histories, Joseph de Guignes had missed certain similarities, as a closer look at China suggests. By the later eighteenth century, the Qing Empire, as serious an enterprise in the East as that of the Ottomans, French or British further west, had absorbed not only China but adjoining regions like Tibet and Mongolia. Allowing for its very different circumstances, China under the Qing experienced many of the same historiographical developments as the West. This included a homogenizing tendency over minority historiographies: the revived Mongol historiography of the seventeenth century (see Chapter 3 above) was by the late eighteenth century either marginalized or rewritten from a Manchu point of view. A Qing version of history, supported by official history-writing, cartography and physical monuments, overwhelmed competing versions of the past in most of the conquered territories. Qing China also shares the eighteenth-century West's inclination to universalism, though in this instance a Sinocentric rather than European version – universalisms are rarely universal in their appeal. And, something of the classificatory tendency in contemporary European thought can be observed in the late Ming-Qing principle of *jingshi* or 'ordering the world' within which history occupied a central role.

Yet if there are similar historiographical developments in East and West, they did not unfold in the same order. This is most striking in the early Qing dynasty when there was a flight from the philosophical abstraction of the Ming era back to close textual study. It has been characterized as a transition 'from philosophy to philology', as the Zhu Xi version of neo-Confucianism, a rationalist system that had underpinned the previous half millennium of Chinese historical writing, was seriously challenged and a new emphasis placed on evidentiary research.[46] At the same time, the 'classics' lost something of their immutable quality as critics began to treat them like any other historical text. This trend culminated in the

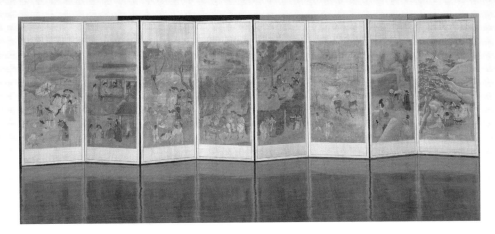

Figure 42 │ Scenes from the life of a *yangban*, by one of Korea's best-known painters, Kim Hong-do (c. 1745 to c. 1806). Eight-panel folding screen. Korean, Yi dynasty (1392–1910).

philosopher and literary historian Zhang Xuecheng's (1738–1801) declaration that 'the Six Classics are History' – meaning that they were the creation of the bureaucratic institutions of the ancient sage-kings, created for specific governmental purposes, rather than the wisdom of those sages deliberately committed to writing as timeless wisdom; a more thorough 'desacralization' awaited the late nineteenth century and the influence of German historicism. The process is visible in civil service examinations, always a good litmus test of the standing of historical knowledge in China: by 1800 they required students to reflect on the development of the classics as themselves historically created documents.

Some of these phenomena are visible elsewhere in East Asia. Korea had been a largely faithful satellite or tributary of China since as far back as the Tang, and the Yi family that ruled the Chosŏn kingdom were especially loyal to the Ming, who had expelled the invading Japanese in the 1590s. The Korean monarchy also depended heavily on its mandarin class, especially the *yangban* (Fig. 42), a hereditary caste of Confucian bureaucrats, and something analogous to the Chinese style of official history-writing had matured by the end of the sixteenth century. These ties began to loosen even as learning followed a similar trajectory, and moves to 'de-centre' China's place in the geographical and historical universe occurred, a foretaste of nineteenth-century nationalism. Yi Ik (1681–1773), an advocate of *sirhak* or 'practical learning' was a former politician-turned-historical thinker, who called for the study of Korean history in its own right. In the next generation Yi's pupil An Chŏng-Bok (1712–91) authored the first general history of Korea, *Tongsa*

Kangmok ('An Outline History of the East', 1778), and similarly advocated the use of the past as a reformist tool. Such concern for utility did not make truth, in a strict sense, the highest goal: morals would invariably trump evidence. As An Chŏng-Bok notes in his own preface:

Generally, the task of history writing is to make clear the succession of rule, to be stern on rebellion, to straighten out right and wrong, to praise loyalty and chastity, to detail the legal regulations. In this respect, the extant histories leave much room for debate. Therefore I have abbreviated and added things, have cleansed and excised. Of those items where errors and misinformation reach an extreme, I have made a special record attached at the end in two volumes.[47]

In a sense, the very shift taking place in eighteenth-century Europe from narrowly focused humanist philological erudition to rationalist and conjectural speculation about the past was, in both China and Korea, unfolding precisely in reverse. The focus of much of this learning was, as in Europe, the solution to social and political problems; and, also as in Europe, many of the most original thinkers counted themselves primarily as scholars in other areas than history. Huang Zongxi (1610–95), for example, used his extensive collections of Ming documents for a work, now lost, called *Case Studies of Ming History*; his *Mingru xue'an* ('Intellectual Lineages of Ming Confucians'), completed in 1676, amounts to an intellectual history of the previous three centuries. But Huang was not content with merely studying the past. In his *Mingyi daifang lu* ('Waiting for the Dawn: a Plan for the Prince') he commented on the entire span of Chinese history since the Qin, a stretch of nearly two millennia that Huang saw as a continuous degeneration into disorder, with China's progress impeded by ever-increasing centralization and bureaucracy, during which the masses had been oppressed. This was no forward projection of a future utopia: Huang's point was precisely the opposite – that a golden era of the sages had been lost and needed to be restored.

Huang was one of a number of scholars during the Ming-Qing transitional period who refused to serve the new rulers. So did his student, Wan Sitong (1638–1702), author of a chronologically broader history of Chinese thought since Confucius. Commenting on the current dynastic change was politically dangerous, so Wan used the device of relating instead two earlier dynastic shifts, that from the Song to the Yuan and, more remotely, the ancient transition from the Shang to the Zhou. His intent was to rehabilitate an entire category of persons, 'surviving subjects', who were generally treated by new regimes as obdurate resistors, and indirectly to counsel scholars in his own time both to avoid service to the Qing and to keep their heads down while doing so. This is a literature of prudence, not unlike the European neostoic works of sixteenth-century Taciteans. Both Huang and Wan also represent a move away from strict adherence to form towards an emphasis on evidence. Huang saw obsequious adherence to the compositional rules of the Standard Histories as a significant obstacle to historical knowledge. Wan took a similar view, and his self-declared methods called for verifying information from both official and (less trustworthy) private histories and writing in an appealing style, as well as being both impartial and attentive to the causes of events. This is not so very different from the ambitions of enlightened European historiography.

Strictures and quotas on civil service careers were imposed by the ethnically Manchu Qing, who by and large adopted the language and cultural practices of the conquered people they called 'Nikan' (a word derived from the Chinese 'Han'). Perhaps as a direct consequence of this tightening up, a higher degree of professionalism developed in the eighteenth century. Philology and ancillary disciplines such as epigraphy, palaeography, manuscript collation and phonology were practised against the background of an argument within Confucianism between Qing advocates of 'Han Learning' and their neo-Confucian 'Song Learning' opponents – an interesting if inexact analogue to the slightly earlier European *querelle* of ancients and moderns. During this period, official academies supplanted the private schools that had expanded considerably under the Ming. The bibliophilic tendencies that had followed the sixteenth-century expansion of woodblock printing continued as collections sprouted up in cities throughout China, with an inter-library network of seven collections actually emerging in Hangzhou in the later eighteenth century. The Manchu leaders had been reading Chinese history well before the completion of their conquest, seeking legitimizing precedents and instructive analogies in earlier dynasties, and constructing their own imperial ideology out of the collective history of former regimes. They continued the imperial practice of supporting scholarship. The first Qing emperors ordered the expansion and reorganization of the imperial library, some holdings of which had been damaged in recent assaults on Beijing; the Hanlin Academy was charged with developing a system for collecting and preserving books; this bibliographical research culminated in the imperially sponsored *Complete Works of the Four Treasuries*, a weighty attempt at a comprehensive bibliography of Chinese texts.

Ming-era survivors such as Gu Yanwu (1613–82) epitomized the careful attention to research among a wide range of sources, material as well as textual, especially in his *Rizhilu* ('Record of Daily Knowledge'). Gu likened histories that relied on secondary materials to coins that had been melted down and re-minted from the same metal. Like his predecessors over many centuries, he saw history as a mirror to provide lessons for the present, but he carried this beyond the traditional inculcation of moral lessons and models of virtuous behaviour to some concrete suggestions for institutional reform. The real lesson of history was that all things change and no custom should be viewed as unalterable if it fails to conform with a general principle which he called 'benevolence'.

A fourth member of this transitional generation, Wang Fuzhi (1619–92), in some ways embodies both the didactic tendencies of Renaissance historians and the later social thought of a European stadialist. In a commentary on Sima Guang's *Comprehensive Mirror* Wang suggested that the 'mirror' image itself needed to be taken not simply as meaning that a historical text reflected reality but rather that it should promote *self*-reflection in its readers so as to promote replication of past successes and avoidance of failures. But unlike his contemporaries, and like many of the European historical thinkers of the next century, Wang sought no restoration of a lost past. His sense of change was such that it presumed social progress from an ancient barbaric stage, with 'barbarian' defined as a matter of differing morals or manners. The ancient sages could not possibly have foreseen the changes in China, and thus neither they nor their principles could be taken as providing timeless and immutable wisdom. Wang Fuzhi also de-coupled the process of political change from its traditional heavenly engine: there was no necessary connection between cosmological forces and the vicissitudes of dynastic rises and falls. This carried with it the implication that there was no such thing as a 'legitimate' succession (*zhengtong*), merely retroactive justification by the winners. And if dynasties themselves lacked this intrinsic link to the ordered universe, how could they be taken as the natural unit of historical analysis? For Wang, a series of epochs detached from dynastic shifts provided a more meaningful way to organize the past.

Contemporary issues continued to provide a powerful stimulus for detailed and accurate research that could transcend polemical positions. A century after Huang and Gu, with the Qing now firmly established, Wang Mingsheng (1722–98) would assert the responsibility of the historian to examine all available evidence, observing that the same methods used to study the classics could be applied to history:

I began to understand that there are more similarities than differences in the ways we study history and the classics. How is this so? [It is because] the study of the classics is aimed at clarifying the Dao. Yet in doing so, one cannot indulge in empty discussions on principles and meanings. Instead, one must unravel the etymology, distinguish the pronunciation, analyze the paleography, comprehend the commentaries and glosses, so that the meanings and principles can reveal themselves; as does the Dao in this revelation. ... To study history, one should not seek laws and lessons through speculative discussions and regard passing moral judgment as its sole purpose. Rather, one should examine the veracity of regulations and institutions and ensure the factuality of events and records in order to see the truth. Thus, the two subjects are similar.[48]

If Britain had its triumvirate of Hume, Robertson and Gibbon, eighteenth-century China could answer back with its own distinguished trio, including Wang Mingsheng, known for his critical studies of the Standard Histories. Another was the respected teacher and lover of antiquity Qian Daxin (1728–1804), who rewrote the

Yuan History. In his *Ershi'ershi kaoyi* ('Critical Notes on the Twenty-two Histories'), Qian offered an expulsion of errors and inaccuracies comparable in its technical proficiency to the works of European textual scholars of the early eighteenth century. A master of *jinshi xue* (the collection and study of bronze and stone inscriptions, corresponding with European epigraphy), Qian's comment on the priority of evidence over rhetoric is striking. 'When the records are made squarely with the facts, the right and the wrong will then reveal themselves. If the historian, in order to blame or praise, tempers his records, it destroys the raison d'être of his work.'[49] Perhaps most original of all among the late eighteenth-century Qing scholars was Zhao Yi (1727–1814), who saw the task of the historian as not simply moral adjudication but the establishment of patterns of development and change that could be used to correct specific political problems. He composed works on Qing military achievements using both personal notes from his participation in campaigns against Burma and Taiwan and unpublished archival sources.

While Western influences were undeniably felt during this period of China's history, there are parallels with Renaissance and Enlightenment historiography which have little to do with mimicking Europe, including the considerable expansion of woodblock printing that began late in the Ming era, the frequent exchange of semi-public correspondence among scholars and the particularly high valuation of ancient learning. A consequence of this was that certain venerable texts were held up to the kind of critical scrutiny that Renaissance philologists had applied to forgeries like the Donation of Constantine. And, as the humanism of the Renaissance had preceded the rationalist scepticism of the Enlightenment, so the Han Learning revival eventually produced a decline in the dominance of neo-Confucianism. Methodologically, the 'School of Evidentiary Research' (*kaozheng* or *k'ao-cheng* – literally 'research and correct') is exemplified in works such as Yan Ruoqu's (1636–1704) exposure, in an unpublished but widely circulated work, of selected 'Old Text' chapters of the *Shujing* (the 'Book of Documents' or 'Classic of History') as a piece of later, post-Confucian authorship.

This iconoclastic pursuit of truth had effected momentous changes in scholarship before the School itself declined in the nineteenth century. It would clear the way by the end of the Qing era for more explicitly Western-influenced calls for a 'new historiography'. The Chinese stress on erudition continued to develop to the end of the eighteenth century, and the mounting attention given to collection and analysis of inscriptions on bronze and stone (the discovery of bones, urns and bamboo as epigraphical sources had yet to occur) as supplements of or correctives to venerable texts, neatly parallels the activities of the Académie des inscriptions. The *kaozheng* opinion that learning was best done as a collective endeavour, with the findings of one scholar followed up by others, led its practitioners to consider their own and older works not merely as stand-alone texts but as research tools. The effort to make the Standard Histories more usable in this regard through the addition of visual finding aids such as tables of major events replicates the use of tables and charts in seventeenth- and eighteenth-century European works, part of the wider shift to a graphic and visual culture that followed the introduction of printing.

Amid all this historical criticism, the business of maintaining the formal genres of Chinese historiography continued. The Qing ordered the compilation of a Ming History within a year of their accession, but in contrast to the precipitate speed at which the early Ming historians had produced an inferior *Yuanshi*, the Qing historians took their time about it. Apart from a brief chronicle of Ming events, drawn from the Veritable Records and delivered to the Shunzhi emperor in 1653, the compilation process was delayed several times, to be revived in the 1660s; an interim draft *History of the Ming* was completed early in the eighteenth century by Wang Hongxu (1645–1723) reputedly plagiarized from his assistant, Wan Sitong. There were controversies about the interpretation of particular reigns, such as the Yongle emperor's (r. 1402–24) displacement of his nephew Emperor Jianwen (see Chapter 4 above), an episode which Wang Hongxu whitewashed in a partisan application of what his opponents called the 'crooked brush' approach to history.

The Ming History would only be completed and presented to the court in 1739 during the Qianlong reign, a period of especially vigorous literary output. The problem was not a lack of enthusiasm on the part of the Manchu rulers for maintaining the historical forms that they had inherited. To the contrary, the Qing emperors were intensely interested in history, and in particular in bending it to reflect favourably on themselves and badly on their enemies: the destruction of the Mongol Zunghars as a people, for instance, was closely followed by the collection (1763) of all their genealogies and then their destruction, once a sanitized history had been written. The Shunzhi emperor (r. 1644–61) read the 1653 chronicle personally, and much of the delay in the *Mingshi* was occasioned by the regime's determination to produce a history of the early, pre-Conquest years of their own dynasty after the establishment of the Jurchen khanate in 1616.

In the 1660s, further problems resulted from the new emperor's unwillingness to keep his fingers out of the compilation process, though with the dynasty now secure there was less sensitivity to pro-Ming views. (This is just about exactly the same time that the Mughal emperor, Shah Jahan, was interfering in the work of his own hired historians.) But the long-lived Kangxi Emperor (r. 1661–1722) saw himself as a scholar, personally responsible for the final result, and he 'revised the historical record as he created it'. Kangxi wrote prefaces to the various campaign histories that he had ordered to be written, in both Manchu and Chinese, late in the seventeenth century, thereby inventing a genre, the *Fanglue*, that had little Ming precedent.[50] He also published his own version of Zhu Xi's commentary on Sima Guang, complete with his personal, throne-centred reinterpretations of events.

This heavy-handedness, and an insistence on commenting on every successive draft, held up the writing and poisoned the atmosphere in the History Bureau, appointment to which was in any case fast deteriorating into a sinecure. The pattern of interference continued under Kangxi's successors Yongzheng (r. 1723–35) and Qianlong (r. 1735–96; d. 1799); the latter even believed it an imperial prerogative to comment on drafts.

Yet in spite of this creeping imperial micromanagement, history prospered. A number of earlier histories were revised in the light of two centuries of bibliographical and philological research: thus Shao Jinhan (1743–96) used his association with the Four Treasuries bibliography project to collect materials with which he could purge the Song Standard History of mistakes. Moreover, a number of other important genres of historical writing appeared during the period. Histories of institutions (*Zhi guan*), previously annexed to the Standard Histories and other works, were now presented as independent reference books. The *fangzhi*, a pre-existing local 'gazetteer' dating back to the Song dynasty, continued to proliferate. Nearly 1,000 Ming and 5,000 Qing-era *fangzhi* survive; although they have no exact counterpart in other countries, their local focus and emphasis on multiple sources bears comparison with the natural histories and county 'surveys' of seventeenth-century and early eighteenth-century Europe.

The work of Zhang Xuecheng, who died at the beginning of the nineteenth century, provides a good place to close this section. Zhang wrote a great deal on many different topics, including the proper way to do local history, on family history, on the need for readable style and brevity in historical writing, on the topic of 'Virtue in the Historian', and on the very meaning of the word 'historian'. To Liu Zhiji's trio of qualities that the historian must possess, literary skill, erudition and insight, Zhang would add a fourth, moral integrity. Several of his projects were stillborn, such as a proposed revision of the Song History. Other works were completed hurriedly or in adverse circumstances: his general history of Hubei aroused criticism for its discussion of local persons and he complained that his informants were not forthcoming, the district clerks were slow to produce necessary documents and his assistants were incompetent. Most of what Zhang wrote languished unpublished till well after his death, and of that a good deal was lost during the Taiping Rebellion of the 1850s. What survives, however, includes some of the most interesting historical thought produced during the dynasty, including Zhang's proposal for a 'Critique of Historical Writings', a taxonomical bibliography that would embrace more than works narrowly considered historiographic. 'As I see it,' he wrote, 'anything in the world that has to do with writing is historical scholarship.'[51] Most bibliographical work made the mistake of assuming that history could be confined to one category or another, and such fixation on formal nomenclature was arid and unproductive. Zhang's investigations of the history of history firmly distinguish it from record-keeping, the one having the virtue of the 'circle', the other of the 'square'. Only a man of genius and perception, oriented to the future, can be a true historian; the record-keeper is a workmanlike memorialist, a useful preserver of facts, oriented to the past. We hear in this something like Voltaire's distinction between *historien* and *historiographe*. But, says Zhang – rather more Gibbon than Voltaire – all histories have something in them of both square and circle.

Zhang once confided to a friend that he thought it would take a century before his works were fully appreciated; this turned out to be astute, as late nineteenth-century conservatives would use his work to defend Confucianism and the classics against more radical reformist scholarship. Zhang's influence was even more profound on republican-era historians in the 1920s who warmed to his comprehensive views on *tongshi* (general history) and to his theoretical utterances on history. In some ways, Zhang resembles an earlier eighteenth-century figure, similarly academic, poor and neglected till long after his death. In Zhang's theory of the origins of ancient writing and the transition from orality, of the movement of man from an age of sages and poetic rites to one of philosophers and more prosaic expression, and of the passing of ancient wisdom as an esoteric art, we have an Asian answer to Giambattista Vico. And in Zhang's systematic philosophizing about human wisdom evolving as the *Dao* taking form through the agency of successive sages such as the twelfth-century BC Duke of Zhou – Zhang's equivalent of 'world historical individuals' – there are shadows of a slightly later Westerner, Hegel, and of the march of History towards Reason's awareness of itself.

Early Tokugawa Japan

Following several centuries of imperial decline and conflict among rival warlords, one of them, Tokugawa Ieyasu, emerged as victor in 1600. Three years later he accepted the title of shogun from the emperor and the Tokugawa bakufu (1603–1868) was established. As in the earlier Kamakura and Muromachi bakufus, appointed shoguns ruled the country on behalf of a figurehead emperor through regional *daimyo* or warlords, a system sometimes classed as 'feudal' using a Western model for medieval military governance. Since the shogunate acknowledged that all authority ultimately derived from the emperor, it was possible at least in theory to support the bakufu and cling to imperial loyalism. A relative of the shogun named Tokugawa Mitsukuni (1628–1700), *daimyo* in the domain of Mito, personally oversaw a pro-imperial history, the *Dai Nihon Shi* which had nearly 130 scholars working on it by the time Mitsukuni died; the work would be presented in draft to the bakufu in 1720 though it was not completed till the early twentieth century.

During much of this era, Japan was secluded from outside influences, and Christian missionaries were either persecuted or driven out. In the early Tokugawa, neo-Confucianism dominated Japanese intellectual life (at just the time that it was being challenged in China), initially in the 'orthodox' Zhu Xi variety that had in China been closely linked to the cult of imperial power; to some degree, this marked a return to Nara-era values and a retreat from the Buddhism that had so heavily influenced late medieval Japanese culture. With its validation of strict hierarchic principles in heaven and on earth, Zhu Xi neo-Confucianism was protected and promoted in Japan by the bakufu. The use of Chinese for historical writing resumed after Japan's medieval experiments with vernacular works such as the *Rekishi*. The *Dai Nihon Shi* was based on Sima Qian's *Shiji*, leading off with annals of the emperors, and allotting the shoguns a special section of biographies. The Mito scholars who succeeded Mitsukuni in compiling it went to great lengths to secure new documents, bringing them back to a central office called the Shōkan (est. 1657) and comparing different texts of old sources like the *Kojiki*. The Chinese historiographic practice of writing critical assessments of emperors, and recording the fall of dynasties as the unfolding Mandate of Heaven, continued to be a poor fit with a foreign culture that could not conceive of a breach in dynastic succession; even making assessments of the emperors seemed inappropriate and they would be purged during the eighteenth century from the *Dai Nihon Shi*. Furthermore, a nationalistic sentiment that rejected a notion of Chinese superiority, a thread picked up in the next century, is already detectable in some of this work. Yet Chinese-style evidentiary research proved profoundly influential: the Chinese term *kaozhengxue* had an equivalent in *kōshōgaku*.

Hayashi Razan (1583–1657), a former Buddhist monk with the ear of the shogun, was a leading figure in scholarship who established the bakufu's official academy. Though his interests were not at first historical, history was a core element of neo-Confucianism, and the shogunate saw the value of both. Razan was especially impressed by the *Spring and Autumn Annals* (still then believed to be the work of Confucius himself) and by Zhu Xi's commentary on Sima Guang's *Comprehensive Mirror*. In 1644 Razan began to write a new history of Japan, in classical Chinese, initially called *Honchō Hennen Roku* ('Annalistic Record of Japan'), at the request of the shogun. He died with the work incomplete, but it was continued by his son Hayashi Gahō (1618–80), assisted by Gahō's own sons, students and a number of clerks, under the title *Honchō Tsugan* ('General Mirror of Japan'). Razan's high opinion of the original Six National Histories and their Chinese models carried over into his own work, which repeats the old accounts and renders Japanese texts into Chinese. But he also took the trouble to compare the Six National Histories with some of their Chinese sources and endeavoured to reconcile anachronisms or errors he found in both. And he demonstrated a scepticism towards the ancient

myths of the gods and Emperor Jinmu since these, in his view, did not conform
with strict neo-Confucianism. According to Razan, the imperial line had been
founded by humans and not by the gods. He was willing to consider the old legend
of the Chinese immigrant Wu Taibo as a plausible, non-divine alternative to divine foundation, but he eventually rejected this, too, in his major published work.
Razan was among those historians who were quite capable of holding sceptical
views privately while conforming with orthodoxy in their public writings – not an
uncommon occurrence in Japanese historiography.

In the early eighteenth century historical thinking achieved higher intellectual
prominence to the extent that Ogyū Sorai (1666–1728) could confidently proclaim
history the highest form of scholarly knowledge. Among his contemporaries, Arai
Hakuseki (1657–1725) stands out for his *Tokushi yoron* ('Essays on History'), a set
of lectures on the past intended as exemplary instruction for the shogun which
made use of a wide variety of sources. Hakuseki was a *rōnin* or masterless samurai
owing to his father's disgrace, but he was also a child prodigy who mastered the
Chinese classics while very young and embarked on a scholarly career which saw
him progress from employer to employer, rising to the post of tutor to the future
shogun Ienobu (r. 1709–12). Hakuseki met his new disciple in 1693 when both
men were in their thirties, and by the time Ienobu died nineteen years later, the
master had completed 1,299 lectures. In the last three years of his pupil's life, when
Ienobu had finally succeeded to the shogunate, Hakuseki was able to apply his
knowledge of history to practical statecraft. *Tokushi yoron* is modelled on a Song
Chinese precursor, Sima Guang's *Comprehensive Mirror*. Considered a textbook in
'benevolent despotism', it compares in that regard with near-contemporary works
by the likes of Bossuet and Bolingbroke, and the many European histories written
for the benefit of enlightened absolutists.[52] Though an orthodox neo-Confucian,
Hakuseki was deeply suspicious of errors in the early history of Japan. He resolved
the issue of Jinmu and the gods largely by sidestepping it: he began his history
in the ninth century AD. Where he did have to refer to more ancient times, he
employed euhemerism, a tactic by now losing fashion in the West, according to
which the supposed acts of the gods could be interpreted not as myth but as the
real deeds of living men who had been understood in later times as gods largely
owing to spelling errors and misunderstandings of ancient sources.

Yamagata Bantō (1748–1821), a member of the merchant classes near the bot-
tom of the social hierarchy, was even tougher on the legends of early Japanese
history. Having served as a financial advisor to the Sendai domain, he was forced
to retire because of blindness and spent the last years of his life authoring *Yume
no Shiro* ('Instead of Dreaming'). Yamagata, who had been exposed to Western scientific writings, was profoundly sceptical of religion and may even have been an
atheist. He accepted Confucianism as a set of moral and political principles while

rejecting its spiritual aspects, and the third chapter of *Yume no Shiro* is a sustained critique of the historicity of the age of the gods. Some of his arguments rest on common sense or the apparent absurdity of chronology: how can one accept as fact life-spans of nearly a million years? While Arai Hakuseki had at least accommodated the gods through euhemerism, Yamagata swept them aside. In a striking parallel with contemporary Western critiques of prehistory, Yamagata believed the earliest histories had derived from an oral, illiterate society and were therefore worthless as evidence. The commonplace view was that Chinese script had arrived in Japan in the third century AD, after which written records became possible, and that earlier stories had simply been preserved by tradition until committed to writing. But, wrote Yamagata, expressing reservations we have seen before, 'since writing did not exist from Emperor Jinmu until Empress Regent Jingū [r. 201–69], those events cannot be known ... Even at the present day there are countries without writing systems. In such countries, events of two or three reigns previous are transmitted orally, but before that they cannot be known.'[53]

Yamagata was a voice in the wilderness for over a century, easily drowned out by that of one of his principal targets, Motoori Norinaga (1730–1801), who subscribed to a literal interpretation of the age of the gods, and believed that *Kojiki* was the product of an uninterrupted and accurate oral tradition. Norinaga was an exponent of the emerging 'National Learning' (*kokugaku*) school. This rejected Chinese-influenced accounts of the past in favour of the earlier record of *Kojiki*, which now regained a status it had not enjoyed for a millennium (Extract 26). Yet Norinaga was neither fool nor unscholarly. Though he sprang from a Buddhist family, his education had included the Confucian classics, and by nineteen he had read the Classic of History, the Classic of Changes and the Confucian *Analects*. He was trained for a career in commerce but continually found himself drawn to the world of learning, though without any particular inclination. This changed when the aimless young man was sent to Kyoto to study medicine, against his will. While in Kyoto in the early 1750s he changed his name to Motoori (the family name was Ozu), thereby abandoning a mercantile heritage for one associated with the samurai. He also rejected the neo-Confucianism of scholars such as Arai Hakuseki and their allegorical readings of early myths. 'It is a great misconception for one to believe that, if something does not exist in the present, then it did not exist in the past', he wrote about 1757, hearkening back to the eighth-century author Imibe Hironari (see Chapter 2 above).[54] At about the same time Norinaga is known to have acquired copies of *Nihon Shoki*, *Kojiki* and other early Japanese works. Though he completed his training in medicine over the next few years, he was still devoted to scholarship and for a time found himself as both a practising physician and a public lecturer on medieval Japanese literature: he would routinely interrupt a lecture to attend a sick patient, after which he would return to his audience.

26: Motoori Norinaga's Critique of *Nihon Shoki*

Now, to say that I will explain the *Kojiki,* why do I discuss the *Nihonshoki*? Since antiquity, people have for the most part valued and taken up the *Nihonshoki* only, and scholars through the ages have devoted their energies to this text. Although there are so many commentaries on the books on the 'Age of the Gods' to the point of being irksome, response to the *Kojiki* has been half-hearted and people have not found it to be a text which merited devotion of their energy. To ask why this should be so, it is simply because people of the world have been attracted to nothing but the spirit of Chinese writing, and have completely forgotten the spirit of antiquity of our great country. Therefore, the clearing away of the confusion caused by the Chinese spirit, and establishment of justification for reverence of the *Kojiki* should constitute a sign-post for the study of native things .... Since people do not realize that the *Nihonshoki* is full of embellishments and do not fully understand the circumstances of its compilation, it is difficult to dispel the deep illness of the Chinese spirit. Accordingly, if this illness is not dispelled, it is difficult to express the good points of the *Kojiki*. Unless people realize the good points of the *Kojiki,* they will not be able to understand the true path to the study of antiquity.

Our discussion should begin with the fact that the very title itself of the *Nihonshoki* is unacceptable. In the naming of this text, we have followed the names of Chinese histories, such as the *Han shu* (*History of the Former Han Dynasty*) and *Jin shu* (*History of the Jin Dynasty*) and added the name of our country. In China, since the name of the country changes from generation to generation, if the name of the age is not included in the title, it will be difficult to understand. In our imperial country, however, the imperial throne has continued along with the universe throughout the ages, and since there is no change in the throne, there is no need to divide it into ages and speak of things in that way. To put the name of our country on such a work is an act which is a type of comparison, but to just what is it that this title corresponds? It seems to be nothing more than a contrast to China ..., and is a title created in deference to China. ... Indeed, why was it that later generations praised this type of title as a noble thing? To my mind, it is quite unsatisfactory, and seems to be a title which is quite peripheral as well. Some persons have suggested that the title of *Nihonshoki* was given with the intent of showing it to China, but such was by no means the case ....

As for the style of what is written in the *Nihonshoki,* by virtue of the fact that efforts were made to have it conform completely to the Chinese [histories], it is full of nothing but ornamentation of both meaning ... and form ... and there are many parts which differ from the speech and essential facts of ancient times. ....

The legends of Chinese writings, including the accounts of the beginnings of heaven and earth, are all things which an ordinary individual created in his own mind through conjecture that established an arbitrary logic for things. Our legends transmitted from ancient times, however, are not of this sort; they are not words which someone suggested, but exactly those very words which have been transmitted from very ancient times. In a comparison of the two, it is the Chinese writings which sound quite logical, and lead one to assume that, indeed, things must have been as described. The Japanese legends transmitted from ancient times sound insignificant and simple. It is for this reason that all have been attracted solely to Chinese writings, and there is no one, from Prince Toneri through successive generations of scholars up until the present time, who has not been quite captivated by them.

The reason why everyone has been so attracted to Chinese writings is because the clever people of ancient times, in thinking deeply about all kinds of things and seeking a reason for them, created the legends in such a way that all would assume that, indeed, things must have been so. With clever brushes, they skillfully wrote these things down. Human knowledge, however, has limitations, and as the true underlying principle does not lie in something that can be measured and known, how can we know that such things as the beginning of heaven and earth should have been due to some purported principle of logic? Such guesswork is grossly in error much of the time even for things that are proximate. To think that with the application of principles of logic, there is nothing that cannot be known with regard to both the beginning and the end of heaven and earth, simply results in the inability to realize that there are limitations to human knowledge, and that the true principle is difficult to fathom. To accept things in the belief that everything corresponds to an underlying principle is simply a mistake.

Selection from Motoori Norinaga, *Kojiki-den: Book 1*, ed. and trans. Ann Wehmeyer (Ithaca, NY: East Asian Program Cornell University, 1997), 33–7. Translated with permission of Ann Wehmeyer and Cornell East Asia Series. Wehmeyer's notes omitted, and some Japanese phrases and editorial interpolations have been elided in this selection. Alternative spelling *Nihonshoki* has been retained in the extract.

Norinaga's *Kojiki-den* was the work of a lifetime, completed in 1798, when he was sixty-eight years old, but the result was a thorough philological analysis of the old text. Norinaga may have endorsed the myths of Japan's origins *in toto*, but this did not prevent him from correcting misreadings of *Kojiki*. We should not be surprised at this – after all, the great philologists of Europe's Renaissance had been quite able to practise critical scholarship while accepting the biblical account of Creation, or defend the existence of mythical figures like Brutus the Trojan. Ultimately, Norinaga's views of ancient history would be rejected, but in his time he had ably defended them using the most sophisticated methods.

Early in his career Norinaga developed a concept to explain one phenomenon of human emotion. *Mono no aware* translates rather crudely as 'the sadness of things', but it is more accurate to say that it is a theory of empathy, combining regret at the impermanence of things with an aesthetic appreciation for even short-lived beauty or joy, a sentiment that dates back to medieval works such as the *Heike Monogatari*.[55] This interestingly developed at almost the same time that

Europeans were attempting to understand this side of human psychology, and to infuse it into their writing – Norinaga is an older contemporary of Schiller, Herder and Goethe. Artistically, *mono no aware* provided Norinaga with a tool for understanding the appeal of medieval works like the *Genji Monogatari*: the emphasis on love in these works appealed to the strongest human sentiments, the heart being essentially feminine in men and women, even when superficially covered by manly virtues. He used the example of a loyal samurai, prepared to defend his lord to the death: however faithful such a servant, would not the same man, when dying, regret in his final hour the loss of his wife and children, or sorrow at never seeing his parents again? 'These feelings in the last moments are natural human feelings, shared by thousands and millions of people, without distinction between sages and ordinary men.'[56] The concept of *mono no aware*, which is a thorough departure from both the strict emotional control of Confucianism and the renunciation of the world in Buddhism, was more reconcilable with Shinto, and eventually led Norinaga to belief in an 'Ancient Way' (*inishie no michi*) or 'Way of Kami'. By the end of his life, when a series of economic and social problems had intruded on Japan (as well as a volcanic explosion comparable in its impact to the Lisbon earthquake), Norinaga's thinking had evolved into the view that ancient Japanese culture represented his country's peak, from which it had declined under Chinese influence. This conservative nationalism would continue to grow in the next century and a half, and survive the reintroduction of Western culture in the later nineteenth century, principally from the nation that by that time led the historiographical world, Germany.

The German Aufklärung

Germany in the eighteenth century was still a collection of independent states, with Prussia beginning to emerge as its dominant power. While there was no single intellectual centre for historical activity, and many authors continued to work without academic appointments, historical thought and writing was increasingly identified with the universities, rather earlier than this phenomenon occurred elsewhere in Europe. By the end of the century, a number of new universities had been established, either Catholic or Protestant, many of which had professorships in history; by the last third of the century history had successfully moved from the status of an ancillary or preparatory discipline and become an autonomous subject in its own right. Göttingen in particular was a hive of activity, with an influence disproportionate to its political stature or size.

Just how much Germany's Enlightenment differed in its impact on historiography from other countries' Enlightenments is a matter of interpretation. To some

Box 23   Justus Möser

Local history was by now well established in the world (see Chapter 4 above), but Möser's eventual multivolume *History of Osnabrück* (1768) has acquired a special place in the story of Western historiography, and has been seen as a harbinger of that German contribution to historical thought and writing which may, in the end, have had the most profound and lasting effects on the next century. The most remarkable aspect of Möser's book was its stress on particularity: the character of local political, legal and administrative institutions in the development of a community over time, and his insistence on the role of the irrational. It brought the soaring speculation and broad generalization of the first phases of the Enlightenment back down to earth. Although Möser's subject was a single city, his explanatory framework was geopolitical: the city was part of a whole, and the whole existed in a particular age which had a recognizable character or 'style' (*Zeitstil*). The development of the estates and of the militia provided the 'powerful thread' linking together the pieces of the history, which Möser sketched through four 'ages' of the loss and recovery of liberty. The resemblance to Scottish stadialism, and especially to Millar's later *Historical View of English Government*, is largely coincidental; that to Renaissance civic humanism, with its notion of free citizens exercising liberty in a republic, is more immediate, since Möser was a thorough student of Renaissance and seventeenth-century histories. His history also signals the anti-absolutist theme of much Aufklärung thought, though in the end Möser, no radical, spent his last years in vigorous opposition to the French Revolution. In terms of the late Enlightenment's values and its sense of the past, he was much more a Burke than a Rousseau.

degree the differentiation is an optical illusion created by the highly persuasive early twentieth-century scholar Friedrich Meinecke, for whom Germany played the leading role in the displacement of Enlightenment universalism with historicist particularism: Justus Möser's (1720–94) multivolume history of a single city, Osnabrück (1768), provides one such example (see Box 23). That the differences may have been magnified in the telling should not obscure the fact that they are actually there. In part this was because Enlightenment came slightly later to Germany and thus could draw eclectically on strands of thinking developed elsewhere, and even define itself in opposition to some of these; in part it was because despite an antipathy to dogmatism inherited from the time of Gottfried

Arnold, Germany remained a Lutheran and Pietist stronghold fundamentally un-receptive to Voltaire and his anticlericalism. Influenced, too, by the philosophy of the mathematician and historian Leibniz and his view of the universe as a series of 'monads' within which any aspect is a self-contained reflection of the whole, German thinkers also managed to accommodate Christian views of the past more easily within their belief systems. This included the framework of universal history and chronology to which the Germans had an especially strong scholarly commit-ment. Aesthetically, where many across Europe still saw Rome as the zenith of an-tiquity's achievements, the German taste ran preferentially to the *Kultur* of Greece and especially fifth-century Athens. On the philological side, Friedrich August Wolf (1759–1824) would lay the groundwork for an interdisciplinary approach to the study of antiquity in his *Prolegomena to Homer*. His blunt statement that 'The Homer that we hold in our hands now is not the one who flourished in the mouths of the Greeks of his own day, but one variously altered, interpolated, corrected, and emended' was built not just on the many previous 'learned and clever men' who had examined the epics using 'various scattered bits of evidence' but on a systematic arrangement of all this evidence together, so that 'history speaks'.[57] His reconstruction of the stages by which the *Iliad* and *Odyssey* had been composed in antiquity and how they had migrated from orality to writing would also help set the stage for a revival of interest in oral culture early in the next century.

All of this had implications for German historical thought. Where a conserva-tive like Johann Christoph Gatterer (1727–99) clung to a literal reading of the Old Testament and a conventional Christian chronology, others (including a group somewhat derisively known as 'Neologists') kept their faith while jettisoning strict adherence to biblical time. Sceptical of scripturally derived chronology, they read the Old Testament as sacred poetry, a prophetic and moral rather than historical text, written by different authors at different times and not to be understood as a literal record of events, but with its very contradictions providing evidence of its historicity, that is, its sequential authorship over a long duration. Unable to dispense with the biblical story entirely, some Neologists expanded the boundaries of Old Testament chronology, lengthening the period of time between Adam and Christ to account for evolutionary social change. In eighteenth-century Germany, theology, ethics and what was called 'pragmatic philosophy' were more highly esteemed than classical scholarship, and they had as significant an impact as philology on thinking about both history and History. The long tradition of bib-lical hermeneutics – the theory of interpretation as applied to the scriptures – would evolve in German hands into a potent tool for the criticism of all sorts of texts. It is the Aufklärers who developed a philosophy of the movement of human History towards perfectability, while retaining the belief that each individual peri-od was a valuable part of the whole, both hallmarks of nineteenth-century German historical thought. The classic antithesis, once beloved by intellectual historians, that paints the nineteenth century's historical thought as reacting sharply against a naively ahistorical eighteenth, seems nowhere less convincing than in the Aufklärung.[58]

Faced with three equally unattractive options, a 'secular' humanism that assigned the causes of all events to human intention, a cynical ascription of great events to random chance, or even a providence that blanketed every occurrence, miraculous or routine, the Aufklärers chose a fourth way. This made room for both providence and an overarching plan, as well as allowing for environmental factors derived from Montesquieu, an author who appealed to Aufklärers on ideological grounds as an advocate of moderate reform and limited monarchy. They assumed both individual and collective human agency and indeed began to work out by the end of the century a kind of classification of 'great historical figures'. But they did not fall into the trap, pointed out by Johann Lorenz von Mosheim (1694?–1755), of overrating the connection between intentions and their consequences or imputing unlikely prescience to individual foresight.

Among the other Enlightenments, Britain had more influence on German thinkers than France (Montesquieu notwithstanding), and within Britain, the Scots more than the English, the appeal of the former accentuated by the warmer reception in Germany of Macpherson's Ossianic poems. Hume and Robertson were quickly translated into German, and Ferguson's histories seem to have enjoyed exceptional popularity, earning him the rare honour of election to the Royal Prussian Academy of Sciences and Arts. Influenced by Adam Smith, a number of Aufklärers ventured into economic thought, trade, technological change and the study of statistics. Comparison strongly attracted them, complete with the use of parallels between societies at different stages of development: Schlözer, the Göttingen-based pioneer of Russian history, opened a published letter on historical methods with an explicit comparison of various ancient, medieval and modern peoples, and called for a global approach to the study of the past.[59] The Aufklärers also attributed influence, apart from environmental factors, to more ineffable notions such as 'national character' and what has come to be called *Zeitgeist* (the spirit of the age), impersonal forces that could – though this was not their intention – ultimately displace providence altogether as supra-human causal agents.

Already frequent contributors to the *ars historica* literature since the late sixteenth century, Germans had now become authors of numerous companions, introductions and handbooks. But many went beyond this to think more deeply about the past, about the mechanics of change and human agency in it, and about the 'science' (*Wissenschaft*) of history. Gatterer, a formidable force, was critical of history arranged as serial national accounts which missed the connection of part to whole. In its place he championed a revival of biblically rooted universal history, which was a major strand of early Aufklärung thought. His *Handbuch der Universalhistorie* ('Handbook of Universal History', 1761) and *Einleitung in die synchronistische Universalhistorie* ('Introduction to Synchronistic Universal History', 1769), early entries in his prolific output of handbooks to genealogy, chronology, heraldry and diplomatic, exploited the observations of natural history to explain problems in the biblical account of early history, such as the great longevity of prediluvian man. He would eventually modify his conventional Christian periodization of history, overlaying it with a quadripartite division of time according to degrees of social organization, forms of knowledge, including history, and major events in the Christian and non-Christian worlds.

The growing unease of the German Enlightenment with a rationalist universalism unable adequately to explain, or even offer comfort, in the face of uncontrollable revolutionary change, is well displayed in the fecund mind of Johann Gottfried Herder (or von Herder, 1744–1803). A schoolmaster and clerical official, Herder was a rolling stone in both career and intellect, a man who would change his mind abruptly on issues and people, falling out with former friends such as Kant and Goethe; in temperament he resembles that mercurial figure of the later French Enlightenment, Jean-Jacques Rousseau. A sardonic critic of abstract speculation in his polemical *Also a Philosophy of History* (1774) Herder proved just as capable of making philosophic generalizations. This work is sometimes seen as the earliest articulation, Vico aside, of a core principle of nineteenth-century historicism, that every age must be judged on its own terms and according to its own values. Widely translated, Herder probably more than any other eighteenth-century European also set the stage for the nationalism of the next century, together with its repudiation of the particular variant of universalism it associated with the Enlightenment – though not *all* versions of universalism. In Herder's view, all nations were not the same, nor did they follow a common developmental path; he was fond of organic metaphors which allowed him to see change and variety in biological terms. Each nation was part of nature, but germinated from different seeds; each would grow according to its own proclivities, the shape of the future being immanent in the past. Rejecting the French version of progress seen as the forward movement of the human mind, Herder drew attention to the role of irrational elements, including chance: he is among the very first to speculate using historical counterfactuals, the 'what-if?' game which ponders how things might have turned out if, for instance, Rome 'had been founded on a different spot' or 'how Caesar would have ruled in the place of Augustus', a variant of Pascal's question about the length of Cleopatra's nose.[60] Herder's stress on the role of individual achievement, especially that of exceptional men, raises them to a level above that of the ordinary and absolves them from normal rules and standards, sounding a theme that would be developed in the nineteenth century by Thomas Carlyle and, more ominously, by Friedrich Nietzsche.

Herder suggests that, although successive civilizations pass the torch of global leadership one to the next, none can ever truly die since it will be contained in the final story of *Humanität*, the essence of humanity progressing towards the fulfilment of universally shared goals. 'The whole history of mankind is a pure natural history of human powers, actions, and propensities, modified by time and place.'[61] Culture underlies events, rather than the other way around, and 'Chivalry arose not from the croisades [sic], but the croisades from chivalry.'[62] The bearer of culture and thus the vessel of *Humanität*'s history is the *Volk*, or people, a human monad which exhibited observable and differentiable cultural characteristics; it was the product of its language (itself variable and historically conditioned), social customs, manners, climate and experience, and the commonality of these transcended both political borders and the periods of political history. States may come and go, subdued by external conquerors, 'but the nation remains'.[63] *Völker* were not strictly comparable with one another, and they developed at different rates, not on the single accelerating scale measured out by Condorcet; and where Condorcet was ambivalent towards the humanity of savages, Herder is clear that they are contributors to the larger human story and not to be judged inferior: they all own shares in *Humanität* while maintaining a distinct identity. Yet the march of progress is obvious, and the mere flow of time ensures that humanity moves forward, learning from the past but also outdoing it.

Even disasters such as the slavery of the world under once-virtuous Rome can produce new civilization, rising phoenix-like from the ashes of the vanished nations. The medieval Catholic Church, which Herder condemned, did at least preserve order in barbarian western Europe; and a 'mad enterprise' like the Crusades could occasion unforeseen beneficial consequences such as the growth of commerce and the birth of modern Europe.[64] Herder directed attention away from political and military history towards the 'inner life' of humans discernible from art, music and literature, an approach that would ultimately evolve into the nineteenth-century idea of *Kulturgeschichte*. Like Voltaire but with less condescension, Herder included alien peoples such as the Chinese, Africans, Eskimos and American Indians in his sampling of *Humanität* while remaining fundamentally a Eurocentrist.

Voltaire's simplistic universalism, however, was odious to Herder, and he similarly rejected its more subtle formulations which had admitted regional variation. Instead, Herder looked to Rousseau for an authorizing myth that could displace cosmopolitanism, substituting for the latter's praise of Sparta and the Roman republic an older, Tacitean idealization of the simplicity and independence,

extract

27: Herder on the Succession of Cultures

It is undeniable, too, that this progress of time has influenced the mode of thinking of the human species. Bid a man now invent, now sing an Iliad; bid him write like Aeschylus, like Sophocles, like Plato: it is impossible. The childish simplicity, the unprejudiced mode of seeing things, in short the youthful period of the Greeks, is gone by. It is the same with the Hebrews, and the Romans; while on the other hand we are acquainted with a number of things, of which both the Romans and the Hebrews were ignorant. One day teaches another, one century instructs another century: tradition is enriched: the muse of Time, History, herself sings with a hundred voices, speaks with a hundred tongues. Be there as much filth, as much confusion, as there will, in the vast snowball rolled up by Time; yet this very confusion is the offspring of ages, which could have arisen only from the unwearied rolling on of one and the same thing. Thus every return to the ancient times, even the celebrated year of Plato, is a fiction, is, from the ideas of the World and of Time, an impossibility. We float onward: but the stream that has once flowed, returns no more to its source.

Selection from J. G. Herder, *Reflections on the Philosophy of the History of Mankind*, trans. T. O. Churchill, ed. Frank E. Manuel (University of Chicago Press, 1968), 106–7.

unspoiled by modern luxury, of early German tribes. Yet we can still place Herder in the tradition of Enlightenment cosmopolitanism. Notoriously inconsistent from work to work, Herder's mature writing on history, the *Ideen zur Philosophie der Geschichte der Menschheit* ('Reflections on the Philosophy of the History of Mankind', 1784–91), is both a synthesis of the previous century's discussions as well as a retreat from some of his earlier views, since it offers a kind of universal vision of history that the younger Herder would have found more problematic. It nonetheless remains apart from the standard early Enlightenment rationalist view of an unchanging nature common to all humans at all times. In short, Herder had swung back to the centre, settling on a middle ground not unlike that taken by Vico, with whom he shared both a sense of empathy with former ages and a vision of the whole as contained within the particular (Extract 27).

Amid all this ferment, the most celebrated thinker of the late Enlightenment was Immanuel Kant (1724–1804), Herder's teacher and eventual critic. Unlike his former pupil, Kant hit his stride in late-middle age, publishing within a few years of each other the *Critique of Pure Reason* (1781) and *Critique of Practical Reason* (1788), both of which would have a profound influence on the epistemology and ethics of the next century. Book-ended between these two monoliths lay Kant's shorter essay, 'Idea for a Universal History from a Cosmopolitan Point of View', published in 1784, the same year as Herder's *Ideen*, and a review by Kant of the *Ideen* published in the following year. Kant's major objection to Herder was not his modified universalism. Rather, it was the manner in which Herder had reached his conclusions, speculating on weak empirical evidence and dubious logic about the natural harmony between individual behaviour and social progress.

Kant was doubtful. Humans he thought flawed and selfish beings with short lives and conflicting desires. Individual desires pursued on their own would produce chaos (there is no Smithian 'guiding hand' here), but collectively antagonism and conflict produce progress and subdue another human failing, laziness. The worst consequences of unbridled human nature are overcome by obeying the dictates of Kant's 'categorical imperative', the choice of the free will not to do anything that one could not will as a universal principle. Collectively, humans might as a species tread a path towards the realization of reason and the fulfilment of the potential bestowed by nature. This would be achievable only in the context of society: men are like trees, with those that live in close proximity forced to grow upwards towards sunlight, and those that live in isolation putting out uncontrolled, crooked branches. The end result, in theory, is the 'moral whole' of an Enlightened society, one best governed on republican principles. Kant saw the most unworthy aspects of human nature as containing within themselves the kernel of their own resolution, and of human achievement. War produces the desire for safe cohabitation and eventually peace, while 'All culture, art which adorns mankind, and the finest social order are fruits of unsociableness, which forces itself to discipline itself and so, by a contrived art, to develop the natural seeds to perfection.'[65]

CONCLUSION

History in the eighteenth century continued its connection with the scholarship practised by philologists and antiquaries. In the West this occurred in parallel with a much closer connection to philosophy, and to the study of nature, than had been the case previously, as thinkers from Vico to Herder speculated about the course of the human story. Although the theological aspects of historical interpretation were preserved more strongly in Germany than other parts of Europe, by the time of Kant, Nature had largely wrested from Providence the responsibility for creating a plan for the human race. That plan could be only partly visible to the historian but, like a Cartesian curve, its trajectory could be plotted, some thought, from the cumulative tendencies of past events. In East Asia, during much the same period, critical scholarship moved to a higher level, verging sometimes on iconoclastic conclusions; the later nineteenth century would import to Japan and China (among other parts of the world) a further wave of methodological and conceptual change derived from Europe.

Within Europe itself, History had now truly arrived in that 'capital-H' form which the great speculators of the next century could develop further. Eighteenth-century theorists such as the stadialists had empowered History to move forward but admitted it could also stop (and sometimes doubted the benefits of progress). The nineteenth century would be less willing to give History much choice in the matter, bestowing on it at times an almost mechanical and unstoppable momentum. At the same time, 'small-h' history, a literary genre soon to become a professional discipline, was changing too. These two sets of changes, and their interrelationship to one another, are the concern of our next chapter.

Notes

1 Edouard Glissant, *Caribbean Discourse: Selected Essays*, trans. J. Michael Dash (Charlottesville, 1989), 64, 75.

2 Greg Dening, 'A Poetic for Histories', in his *Performances* (Chicago, 1996), 40.

3 David Hume, *A Dissertation on the Passions/The Natural History of Religion*, ed. T. L. Beauchamp (Oxford, 2007), 36.

4 J. G. Herder, *Reflections on the Philosophy of the History of Mankind*, trans. T. O. Churchill (1800), ed. Frank E. Manuel (Chicago, 1968), 135–6.

5 Peter Hallberg, *Ages of Liberty: Social Upheaval, History Writing, and the New Public Sphere in Sweden, 1740–1792* (Stockholm, 2002), 86.

6 Nicholas Hudson, 'Constructing Oral Tradition: The Origins of the Concept in Enlightenment Intellectual Culture', in A. Fox and D. Woolf (eds.), *The Spoken Word: Oral Culture in Britain 1500–1850* (Manchester, 2002), 24–55.

7 Anne-Robert-Jacques Turgot, 'On Universal History', in *Turgot on Progress, Sociology and Economics*, trans. and ed. Ronald L. Meek (Cambridge, 1973), 64–5.

8 Ibid., 92–3.

9 Mark Salber Phillips, *Society and Sentiment: Genres of Historical Writing in Britain, 1740–1820* (Princeton, NJ, 2000); D. R. Woolf, *Reading History in Early Modern England* (Cambridge, 2000).

10 Its full title is *L'Histoire philosophique et politique des établissements et du commerce des Européens dans les deux Indes*, 2nd edn, 4 vols. (1770; Amsterdam, 1774). Parts of the work are attributed to other authors, notably the philosophe Denis Diderot.

11 Quoted in Hallberg, *Ages of Liberty*, 96–7.

12 Henry Home, Lord Kames, *Sketches of the History of Man*, ed. James A. Harris, 3 vols. (1774; Indianapolis, 2007), vol. I, 5 ('To the Reader').

13 Reinhart Koselleck, *Futures Past: On the Semantics of Historical Time*, trans. Keith Tribe (Cambridge, 1985), 92–3.

14 From the second draft (1830) of Hegel's lecture on the course of world history, in G. W. F. Hegel, *Lectures on the Philosophy of World History*, trans. H. B. Nisbet (Cambridge, 1975), 135.

15 *The New Science of Giambattista Vico*, Book III: sec. i, trans. T. G. Bergin and M. H. Fisch (Ithaca and London, 1984), 301, para. 780.

16 Giambattista Vico, 'On the Ancient Wisdom of the Italians', in *Vico: Selected Writings*, ed. and trans. Leon Pompa (Cambridge, 1982), 50–2.

17 Ibid., 59–60.

18 Giambattista Vico, 'First New Science', in *Vico: Selected Writings*, ed. and trans. Pompa, 127; Vico, *New Science*, Book I: sec. lxiv, trans. Bergin and Fisch, 78, para. 240.

19 Giambattista Vico, *New Science*, Book II: sec. i–v, trans. Bergin and Fisch, 129–31, paras. 404–09.

20 The phrase 'conjectural facts' and the word 'conjectures' was used by Kames, for instance, in *Historical Law-Tracts* (1758) to describe the process of piecing together from very disparate and incomplete evidence, a 'historical chain' about the early development of law. On the more general term 'conjectural history', see H. M. Höpfl, 'From Savage to Scotsman: Conjectural History in the Scottish Enlightenment', *Journal of British Studies* 17 (1978): 19–40, a generally useful essay which however seems to me to establish a false contrast between 'narrative, document-based history' and conjectural history. This is to mix generic apples and methodological oranges since narrative is the *form* in which a history is cast (usually chronological but not necessarily) and can be document-based or not; conjectural history can be both narrative and non-narrative.

21 Murray Pittock, 'History and the Teleology of Civility in the Scottish Enlightenment', in Peter France and Susan Manning (eds.), *Enlightenment and Emancipation* (Lewisburg, PA, 2006), 90.

22 Kames, *Sketches*, ed. Harris.

23 A. Ferguson, *An Essay on the History of Civil Society*, ed. D. Forbes (Edinburgh, 1966), 7, 76–7.

24 Ibid., 78–9.

25 Höpfl, 'From Savage to Scotsman', 30.

26 Ferguson, *Essay*, ed. Forbes, 123.

27 In Lafitau's 1724 opus, *Moeurs des Sauvages Amériquains, comparés aux moeurs de premiers temps*. See ch. 5 above for Lafitau.

28 Adam Smith, *Lectures on Jurisprudence*, ed. R. L. Meek, D. D. Raphael and P. G. Stein (Indianapolis, 1982), 14–16, 107, 201ff., 459.

29 *History of the Progress and Termination of the Roman Republic* (1783).

30 Voltaire, *The History of Charles XII, King of Sweden*, trans. A. White (London, 1976), 29.

31 Ibid., 244–71.

32 Condorcet, *Sketch for a Historical Picture of the Progress of the Human Mind*, trans. June Barraclough (London, 1955), 8–9.

33 Ibid., 169.

34 William Robertson, *The History of Scotland during the Reigns of Queen Mary and of King James VI* (New York, [1844]), 271–2.

35 William Robertson, *An Historical Disquisition Concerning the Knowledge which the Ancients had of India; and the Progress of Trade with that Country, Prior to the Discovery of the Passage to it by the Cape of Good Hope* (New York, 1844; a separately paginated appendix to the *History of Scotland*), 62–3.

36 Edward Gibbon, *The History of the Decline and Fall of the Roman Empire*, ed. D. Womersley, 3 vols. (London, 1994), vol. I, 104 note 122 (for the reference to Tillemont); vol. I, 1001 (for New Zealand).

37 *The English Essays of Edward Gibbon*, ed. Patricia B. Craddock (Oxford, 1972); *The Letters of Edward Gibbon*, ed. J. E. Norton, 3 vols. (New York, 1956).

38 Edward Gibbon, *Memoirs of My Life*, ed. B. Radice (London, 1991), 165.

39 For Hume's influence on Gibbon see David Womersley, *The Transformation of the Decline and Fall of the Roman Empire* (Cambridge, 1988), ch. 2; J. G. A. Pocock, *Barbarism and Religion*, 5 vols. to date (Cambridge, 1999–), vol. II, 177–257. The fifth volume in Pocock's magisterial study of the *Decline and Fall* and its intellectual contexts was scheduled to appear in November 2010, regrettably too late for me to consult in writing this chapter.

40 Ibid., vol. I, 230.

41 Arnaldo Momigliano, *Studies in Historiography* (New York, 1966), 40–55.

42 Voltaire, *The Philosophy of History* (London, 1766), ed. Thomas Kiernan (New York, 1965), 82–4.

43 Joseph de Guignes, *Histoire générale des Huns, des Turcs, des Mogols, et des autres peuples Tartares occidentaux* (Paris, 1756–8), vol. I, xix–xx, quoted and translated in Pocock, *Barbarism and Religion*, vol. IV, 112–13.

44 Bernard de Fontenelle, thirty years earlier, had simply allowed the former charge (the analogy to medieval chronicling), wherein 'Even today, the Arabs fill their histories with prodigies and miracles, most often ridiculous and grotesque.' Fontenelle, *Of the Origin of Fables*, in B. Feldman and R. D. Richardson (eds.), *The Rise of Modern Mythology, 1680–1860* (Bloomington, IN, 1972), 14.

45 Robertson, *Historical Disquisition ... of India*, 5. For the problem of the movement of culture from East to West see also Anthony Pagden, 'The Immobility of China: Orientalism and Occidentalism in the Enlightenment', in Larry Wolff and Marco Cipollini (eds.), *The Anthropology of the Enlightenment* (Stanford, CA, 2007), 50–64.

46 Benjamin A. Elman, *From Philosophy to Philology: Intellectual and Social Aspects of Change in Late Imperial China* (Cambridge, MA, 1984).

47 Quoted in Marion Eggert, 'Ideology and Truth Claims in Korean Historiography of the "Empiricist School"', in Helwig Schmidt-Glintzer, Achim Mittag and Jörn Rüsen (eds.), *Historical Truth, Historical Criticism, and Ideology: Chinese Historiography and Historical Culture from a Comparative Perspective* (Leiden, 2005), 415.

48 Wang Mingsheng, quoted in an unpublished paper by Q. Edward Wang; I am indebted to Professor Wang for the reference and the translation.

49 For this quotation from Qian Daxin I once again thank Edward Wang.

50 Peter C. Perdue, *China Marches West: The Qing Conquest of Central Eurasia* (Cambridge, MA, 2005), 463.

51 David S. Nivison, *The Life and Thought of Chang Hsüeh-ch'eng (1738–1801)* (Stanford, 1966), 99.

52 For instance the state-sponsored *Svea rikes historia* ('History of Sweden', 1757–64) by that country's *historiographus regni*, Olof Dalin (1708–63), for whom there was no task more important than teaching – his principal pupil was the future king Gustavus III (r. 1771–92).

53 John S. Brownlee, *Japanese Historians and the National Myths, 1600–1945: The Age of the Gods and Emperor Jinmu* (Vancouver and Tokyo, 1997), 52.

54 Norinaga quoted in Peter Nosco, *Remembering Paradise: Nativism and Nostalgia in Eighteenth-Century Japan* (Cambridge, MA, 1990), 160–233, at 171.

55 I owe this point to Professor Donald Baker.

56 Shigeru Matsumoto, *Motoori Norinaga 1730–1801* (Cambridge, MA, 1970), 40.

57 F. A. Wolf, *Prolegomena to Homer 1795*, ed. and trans. Anthony Grafton, Glenn W. Most and James E. G. Zetzel (Princeton, NJ, 1985), 209.

58 Ernst Cassirer, *The Philosophy of the Enlightenment*, trans. Fritz C. A. Koelln and James P. Pettegrove (Boston, 1955), 197. See also Peter Hans Reill, *The German Enlightenment and the Rise of Historicism* (Berkeley, CA, 1975).

59 August Ludwig Schlözer, 'On Historiography [1783]', *History and Theory* 18:1 (1979): 41–51, at 41.

60 Herder, *Reflections on the Philosophy of the History of Mankind*, trans. T. O. Churchill (1800), ed. Frank E. Manuel, 264.

61 Ibid., 214.

62 Ibid., 378.

63 Ibid., 162.

64 Ibid., 119, 357.

65 Immanuel Kant, 'Idea for a Universal History from a Cosmopolitan Point of View', in *Peaceable Kingdoms: An Anthology of Utopian Writings*, ed. Robert L. Chianese (New York, 1971), 197–210, at 202.

The Broken Mirror

7

Nationalism, romanticism and professionalization in the nineteenth-century West

Rulers, statesmen and nations are often advised to learn the lesson of historical experience. But what experience and history teach is this – that nations and governments have never learned anything from history or acted upon any lessons they might have drawn from it. Each age and each nation finds itself in such peculiar circumstances, in such a unique situation, that it can and must make decisions with reference to itself alone (and only the great individual can decide what the right course is) .... (The instruction to be gained from history is not to be found in any reflections we may base on it. No two instances are exactly alike; they are never sufficiently identical for us to say that what was best on one occasion will also be best on another.) In this respect, there is nothing so insipid as the constant appeals to Greek and Roman precedents we hear so often, as for example during the French Revolution. Nothing could be more different than the character of those nations and that of our times.

G. W. F. Hegel[1]

Introduction

The nineteenth century is the great reservoir in the modern history of history, the watershed at which a number of the streams of thought we have been tracing over several centuries come together. Out of their confluence would emerge twentieth-century historical writing, its origins and its many contradictions still clearly traceable to the other side of the reservoir, but incomparably changed by the pooling of Eastern and Western traditions – or perhaps more accurately, the spread of Western historicity to most of the rest of the world, sometimes by force, but often by invitation. In the present chapter, we will concentrate on the Western experience, specifically Europe and its major autonomous offshoot, the United States. In the following chapter, we will peer further abroad to include some of Europe's other colonies, including Latin America and the Caribbean, India, Southeast Asia, the Islamic world in the age of Ottoman decline and, once again, East Asia.

More than most periods, the nineteenth century is riddled with Dickensian contradictions. It was a time of democratic liberalism and of conservative reaction; it was a time of vigorous return to religion and scientific or materialist rejection of the supernatural. It was a time of mass-distributed popular literary history and a time of professional elitism; it was a time of revolutionary nationalism and imperial domination. It was a time that emphasized the utility of history in the training of public servants and colonial administrators, but which increasingly rejected the lessons of history in favour of the study of the past for its own sake. It was a time that witnessed calls such as Augustin Thierry's for historians to embrace the common man, the beginnings of social history and the emergence of economic history as virtually a parallel discipline. But it also saw a cult of the 'heroic' in history, starting with Hegel's 'world-historical individuals', continuing with the Scottish Germanophile Thomas Carlyle and ending in the troubling figure of Friedrich Nietzsche; this was matched by a vast public appetite for biographies and collected letters of great men and women. And it was a time both of bold speculative theories on the past and future course of History and of the most cautious scholarly and vehemently anti-theoretical empiricism.

The nineteenth was also the century in which the influence of history and historians on public policy peaked. Historians in antiquity had often been politicians or soldiers first and turned to the past once their sway over the present had waned. In the early modern period and again in the Enlightenment, historians from Bacon, Clarendon and Pufendorf to Poland's Adam Naruszewicz and Sweden's Olof Dalin had been advisors to princes and educators of kings. But in the nineteenth century, Euro-American historians would be intimately involved not only with writing the past of their countries but with their present public business. Prominent historians served as: diplomats (Brazil's Francisco Adolfo de Varnhagen; Chile's José Victorino Lastarria, Benjamín Vicuña Mackenna and Diego Barros Arrana; America's George Bancroft); government ministers (Alexis de Tocqueville, Alphonse de Lamartine, Victor Duruy, the Egyptian 'Ali Mubārak and the Ottoman imperial historian Aḥmed Cevdet Pasha); senior civil servants (Francesco Lanzani); cabinet secretaries (Bancroft again) and prime ministers (François Guizot and Adolphe Thiers); leading legislators (T. B. Macaulay, Joachim Lelewel, Heinrich von Sybel, Theodor Mommsen, Heinrich von Treitschke, Giuseppe Ferrari and František Palacký); and even presidents (Theodore Roosevelt, Argentina's Bartolomé Mitre and his successor Domingo Faustino Sarmiento, and Honduras' Marco Aurelio Soto). A significant expansion of history at British and American universities had to do not with the promotion of research in the first instance, but with the education of the nation's future public servants, and in France, for similar reasons, history reaped much of the benefit of late nineteenth-century reforms, its share of professorial chairs in French arts faculties growing from 20 per cent in 1865 (when such posts still routinely included the teaching of geography) to 32.6 per cent in 1910.[2] This connection between history, politics and social reform would prove a major catalyst for Western historiography's adoption in other parts of the world.

Intellectual and Political Background

Europe in 1815 was recovering from the unsettling experiences of the French Revolution and Napoleonic wars. The almost inevitable consequence in the first decades of the century, though one that would not last, was a cultural revolt against the political and intellectual rationalism of the late Enlightenment, and a challenge to the eighteenth century's dominant neoclassical aesthetic. Nor were later eighteenth-century figures such as Rousseau, Robespierre or America's Tom Paine alone discredited for unleashing the Revolutionary Furies. A sizeable segment of the educated classes looked further back, to more moderate and even monarchist philosophes such as Voltaire, in assigning blame for what seemed now a horrendous wrong turn. The Jacobin-era critiques of radicalism associated with Edmund Burke were taken up with enthusiasm during the Napoleonic and post-Napoleonic period by conservatives fondly recalling the *ancien régime*, including Joseph de Maistre (1753–1821) and François-René, vicomte de Chateaubriand (1768–1848). One of the greatest European historians of the early twentieth century, Johan Huizinga (1872–1945) captured the mood of nostalgia for the past beautifully and with only mild hyperbole: 'The entire attitude to the past was transformed: the past no longer served as a model, as an example, as an oratorical arsenal, or a lumber room crammed with curios, but it now filled the mind with a longing for distant and foreign things, with a longing to relive what had been. The historical sense was replete with nostalgia and haunting memories.'[3]

Part and parcel of this new perspective was the emergence of what we now call medievalism, a reappraisal of the centuries between the fall of Rome and the Renaissance. When the future Emperor Napoleon III was imprisoned in 1840 following a failed coup, he initially spent his time contemplating a history of Charlemagne and his influence. For the romantic writer Chateaubriand, rethinking the Middle Ages was intimately tied up with the recovery of its spirituality. He described the experience of entering a Gothic church with the phrase: 'ancient France seemed to revive altogether'.[4] Thus the Gothic subculture of the eighteenth century now percolated to the top, bubbling over into the realms of art, architecture, literature and even historiography. Novelists such as Sir Walter Scott (1771–1832) mixed

Figure 43 | *The Princes in the Tower.* An episode from England's late medieval past as subsequently described by Shakespeare and others, whereby the sons of King Edward IV were murdered in the Tower by their uncle, King Richard III, who then usurped the throne. By the German painter Theodor Hildebrandt (1804–74).

history and fiction in their tales of heroism and martial struggle to great public acclaim, frequently selecting medieval settings (so successful were Scott's works that the American writer Mark Twain would famously blame him for the Confederate States' fighting of the civil war). Artists turned historical episodes into paintings, reimagining famous scenes from the past, with medieval subjects proving especially popular (Figs. 43 and 44). The Venetian Francesco Hayez's painting *Pietro Rossi*, which virtually launched Italian romanticism, was inspired by the artist's reading of older chronicles and recent histories, in particular the Swiss historian Jean Charles Léonard de Sismondi's (1773–1842) *L'histoire des républiques italiennes du moyenne âge* ('History of the Medieval Italian Republics'). Nor was medievalism exclusively the property of conservatives. Carlyle (1795–1881), not yet the

Figure 44 | *The Death of the Venerable Bede in Jarrow Priory,* by William Bell Scott (1811–90). From a set of murals illustrating Anglo-Scottish border history, designed in 1856, now found in the Central Hall at Wallington Hall.

reactionary he would become in later life, would make a rewriting of Jocelyn of Brakelond's (d. 1211) *Chronicle* the centrepiece of his influential social commentary entitled *Past and Present* (1843). The failed moderate politician Prosper de Barante wrote a highly successful history of the Dukes of Burgundy (1824–6) stylistically modelled on Froissart, while the liberal Thierry, an enthusiastic antiquarian and champion of 'new scholarship', introduced his history of the Norman Conquest of England, by declaring that his retention of the original spelling of eleventh-century names was a matter of historical truth. England's historians throughout the century, keen to stress a surviving Germanic heritage, paid renewed attention to their Anglo-Saxon past, and revived seventeenth-century attempts to find continuity in English institutions across the divide of the Norman Conquest.[5]

Against the post-Napoleonic conservatism that manifested itself most strongly in France, a more moderate current of liberalism was also taking shape. This was critical of the excesses of the Terror and the degeneration of the republic first into chaos and then into empire, and it steered a middle course between radicalism and 'ultra' reaction. Its adherents included liberal Catholics attempting to restore the clergy's reputation through historical research and teaching, and to make use of the latest developments in philology. Those on all parts of the ideological spectrum were deeply aware of the need for present-day power in order to implement or to resist change. The tensions between conservatism and liberalism would peak in the revolutions of 1830 in France and the Spanish Netherlands (leading to the creation of Belgium) and then again in the outbreaks of 1848, once again with France at the epicentre but extending out to the Habsburg domains in Central and southern Europe.

At the same time, nationalistic currents were stirring, unlocked in the Revolutionary years after 1789, fanned in resistance to Napoleonic centralization, and then barely contained by the 'Concert of Europe' which attempted to put the genie back in its bottle. This occurred at the very time that the major empires were approaching their peak of power and sway, and one story of the nineteenth century, stretching unhappily into the twentieth, is of the conflict between these opposing dynamics. By the century's end, the map of the world would look quite different. The 'second' British Empire was at its apogee, but with an ascendant rival in one of the new states born of nationalism, a Prussian-dominated imperial Germany. New nation-states such as Belgium and older ones like the Netherlands were either grasping at or seeking to hang on to holdings in Africa and South Asia; Spain, itself rocked by a military mutiny and liberal revolution in 1820, and Portugal, shaken by civil war from 1828 to 1834, were both beating a retreat from Central and South America, the site of some of the most vigorous nationalist movements (see Chapter 8 below). The three other empires of Europe and central Eurasia, Austria-Hungary (the newly reconfigured Habsburg Empire), the Russian Tsardom and the Ottomans, were soon to be on the ropes themselves, once-great monarchies in serious decline.

In the wake of a further revolution, an industrial and economic one experienced most acutely in Britain and America, the century would see huge strides in science and technology and enormous optimism in human ability to improve the world. Industrialization and mechanization too had their opponents, both conservatives who disliked the dissolution of long-standing community and agrarian values, and radical social critics such as Marx, who espoused a materialist view of History both to explain the rise and internal contradictions of capitalism and to prophesy its ultimate downfall. For the religious, the move from seventeenth-century pyrrhonism through Enlightenment rationalism to nineteenth-century criticism was something like a shift from frying pan through fire and ending in Hell. While there was a return to the values of Christianity in reaction to philosophe worship of Reason's golden calf, this resurgent spirituality now had new enemies, first in the kind of biblical criticism (in some ways leapfrogging backwards over the eighteenth century to the time of Richard Simon) to be found in David Friedrich Strauss's (1808–74) controversial *Life of Jesus* (1835), which demystified Christ and challenged his divinity. Anticlericalism remained attractive to some historians – the French historians Michelet and Quinet joined in with liberal critics of the Church in the 1830s and 1840s, targeting the Jesuits as an especially malign influence; and Marx thought religion the 'opiate of the masses'. To make matters worse for the faithful, the biblical scheme of chronology, including the Creation story, under stress for at least two centuries, was now approaching demolition thanks to Charles Lyell's *Principles of Geology* (1830–3) and later Charles Darwin's *Origin of Species* (1859). The House of Archbishop Ussher, subsiding for over a century, had finally fallen.

Yet it should also be stressed that the age was not irreligious, nor was its scholarship intractably opposed to metaphysical forces. Historians, no more than scientists (a term coined by the English natural philosopher and polymath William Whewell in 1833), found irreconcilable contradictions between their research and their faith, or even between a mechanical view of History and belief in a higher power. One of the century's most outstanding historical novelists, Tolstoy – a notably devout Christian and a critic of 'great man' history – could by the 1860s slip into the mechanical metaphor of a timepiece in describing the processes that produced Russia's great defeat at Austerlitz, 'the complex movement of numberless wheels and pulleys ... that is, a slow movement of the world-historical hand on the clock face of human history'; indeed, half of the epilogue to *War and Peace* is an extended disquisition on history and religion.[6] As had happened during the Reformation, religious fissures between and among Catholics and Protestants would exercise considerable influence over the direction of historiography, and the setting of research agendas, well into the twentieth century.

On a personal level, many historians took their faiths very seriously. Ranke, the great German scholar who will figure prominently throughout this and the next chapter, was a devout Protestant who believed that his documentary research into the past could provide insight into the divine plan for humanity; he counted Luther among his most important intellectual inspirations and the theologian Friedrich Schleiermacher among his close friends. Several of Victorian England's most celebrated historians, Sir John Seeley (1834–95), J. A. Froude (1818–94) and

Samuel Rawson Gardiner (1829–1902), were similarly religiously minded, while the social historian John Richard Green (1837–83) was an ordained cleric, and both Mandell Creighton (1843–1901) and William Stubbs (1825–1901) abandoned professorial chairs in Cambridge and Oxford respectively to take up bishoprics. The French historian Ernest Renan (1823–92) survived a youthful crisis of faith to become an outstanding historian of religion and, like Strauss in Germany, author of a life of Jesus. The French clerical tradition of advanced erudition, interrupted by the Revolution's abolition of the orders and the royal academies, was revived as early as 1795–6, when the old academies were recreated as l'Institut de France, and the Benedictine, *Recueil des historiens des Gaules et de la France* ('Collection of the Historians of the Gauls and of France') was revived.

Historicism, Romanticism and Nationalism

This is a chapter with a great many 'isms': romanticism, liberalism, conservatism and nationalism; we shall also run into positivism and Marxism further on. One 'ism' that is less commonly used in ordinary parlance, but which is crucial to an understanding of historiography in the nineteenth and early twentieth centuries, is 'historism' or its better-known variant, 'historicism'.[7] An Anglicization of a German term, *Historismus*, it has acquired nearly as many meanings as 'history' itself. Friedrich Meinecke (1862–1954) did not coin the term but it acquired currency through his book, *Die Entstehung des Historismus* (1936). Meinecke denoted in 'historism' a particularly Germanic historical outlook, though he paid attention to the non-German precursors of that *Weltanschauung* and, like many of his generation, tended to view the German approach as universally applicable in modern Western scholarship. At the other end of the spectrum, philosophers such as Karl Popper (1902–94) have focused on the metaphysical, political and speculative aspects of historicism, often unhelpfully conflating it with Comtean positivism (see below), and taking the word to mean *any* understanding of a forward-moving drive in History. Historicism on this view is a juggernaut, a merciless tank grinding resistors and stragglers alike under its unstoppable treads. For our purposes, however, historicism is best understood as an outlook on the past that builds on certain aspects of Enlightenment thought while rejecting others.

What were its hallmarks? There are several, and they do not all appear at once, or equally in any given author, but in general the following features apply. German historism tended to eschew mechanistic explanations of change for organicist ones, often using naturalistic analogies but with a strong undercurrent of both theology and idealism. In its mature form, the broader outlook that we now call 'historicism' insists on the value and agency of the individual (which can mean an individual society, state or culture, not just individual persons) and the contribution of each to the 'bigger picture' of human history. It accepted the notion of human progress, but not at the cost of demonizing some periods and celebrating others. Historicism grasped that while history shared some common features with the natural sciences, it was not a science *in the same way* that biology or chemistry were sciences; and it continued to draw analogies from nature for historical description, not least of all in accounting for the development through time of a social or political entity such as the state or the nation.

This developmental view of History, and of particular entities within it, has been taxed, not altogether unfairly, with having ultimately given rise to dangerous forms of exceptionalist nationalism, most notoriously Germany's *Sonderweg* (or 'separate path') theory. In that sense, historicism supplied the nationalism of the nineteenth century with a new historical underpinning to replace the old discredited legends of the past. Historical arguments about national origins depended rather less upon Trojans, Scythians and mythical or pseudo-biblical heroes such as Spain's Tubal, grandson of Noah, even as figures of exemplary virtue, since the entire course of a nation's past could be conceived as an organic process, as natural and predictable as the blooming of a plant. From the spirit and character of a nation, opined the Czech historian František Palacký, 'a nation's history is born, as a flower from a seed and a fruit from a flower'.[8] At the same time, historicism facilitated the appropriation of indisputably historical figures around whom could be woven a whole new set of myths. Certain venerable tropes – the Tacitean image of the free and virtuous Germanic warrior and his various national counterparts, Czech, Slovak, Dane and so on – remained very much in play. At the same time, the past *in toto* was shaping new, national states and citizenries whose primary loyalty was to their nation. This is the period at which recent historians have suggested 'modern' nationalism emerged, complete with public celebrations of past heroism, the construction of statuary and other *lieux de mémoires*, and even the outright 'invention of tradition'. In its most zealous form, it can be seen in the writings of conservative nationalists such as Britain's Edward Augustus Freeman (1823–92), or the Berlin professor Heinrich von Treitschke (1834–96), the 'herald of the Reich' (Fig. 45), whose multivolume history of early nineteenth-century Germany (1879–94) provided an adulatory narrative of the making of the Bismarckian state which would serve as a script for fin-de-siècle German imperialism. Justus Möser's *Osnabrückische Geschichte* (see Chapter 6 above) was singled out by Meinecke for its sensitivity to the uniqueness of the local community. When combined with Herder's understanding of the cultural differences among various peoples and the integrity of the *Volk*, and with the enormous influence of a cultural icon such as Johann Wolfgang von Goethe, late-Enlightenment Germans had anticipated a number of coming trends in European historical thought. In fact,

Figure 45 | Heinrich Gothard von Treitschke, German historian and political theorist. Anonymous photograph, c. 1865.

though it is customary to draw a sharp line between the Enlightenment and its romantic antiphony, this is once again a boundary created for our benefit by heeding too easily the characterizations of contemporary writers determined to reject their predecessors. One could equally well distinguish the 'romantic' historiography of the first half of the nineteenth century and the 'professional' or 'scientific' historiography of the latter half. Conversely, there are strong continuities between the late Enlightenment and romanticism, especially in Germany, where the entire century from 1750 to 1850 has been dubbed a *Sattelzeit* or bridging period.

Nevertheless, there is a noticeable change of intellectual tone throughout most of Europe in the aftermath of the Napoleonic wars, and amid the cultural wake of the romantic reaction to Enlightenment rationalism. Exceptions such as Hegel, Comte, Marx and Britain's Henry Thomas Buckle aside, the direction of nineteenth-century thought was away from grand theories and speculative world histories, and towards the narration of the heroic individual and the nation – something of the same narrowing of scope we saw towards the end of the Middle Ages. National champions of either recent or remote vintage (Switzerland's William Tell, England's King Alfred and Romania's Michael the Brave) were popular historical subjects. This was entirely reconcilable with a conception of history that

Figure 46 | Jules Michelet, by Thomas Couture (1815–79).

also emphasized the collective agency of the nation as a whole, since the heroic individual almost by definition embodied national characteristics and virtues. Mid-nineteenth-century French historians such as François Guizot (1787–1874) and Adolphe Thiers (1797–1877) postulated a unified past for their country, while their more radical contemporary, Jules Michelet (1798–1874) directed readers to the history of *Le peuple* ('the common people') in a ground-breaking work by that title published in 1845.

Michelet (Fig. 46) was a complex and multifaceted man of letters and part-time naturalist. A brilliant literary stylist, he maintained a safe distance from fiction, and often used scientific vocabulary, describing historical study as a kind of chemical process working upon the historian's consciousness. His historical masterpieces included a mammoth history of France completed in 1867 after thirty years of toil, and a seven-volume history of the French Revolution. A national icon in his time, his reputation declined in the latter part of the century in the face of the cult of objectivity and historical method, only to be revived in the twentieth when those attitudes, in turn, fell under attack. Michelet is not often read today outside his homeland except by specialists – rather a pity in view of his forceful and energetic style, and the endearing habit of inserting himself into the narration of his works as the personal spokesman for his country's past. His 'feel' for the immediacy of the past resembled his contemporary Carlyle's efforts to place his own readers into scenes that he described – in the present tense. Both would be at odds with the 'objective' inclination of historians for much of the next century or so. Among the liberal romantics of his day Michelet had a far-reaching influence, but rather like Vico, whom he introduced to nineteenth-century audiences, his greatest impact was long in coming. In his own day he was a respected literary historian, known for his passion for his topics, and his affection for the tangible experience of old documents, with which he had daily contact as an employee of the Archives from 1830 till the Bonapartist coup of 1852 deprived him of both this and his chair at the Collège de France. But modernity has profound debts to him: Marc Bloch, a founder of the Annales School (see Chapter 9 below) embodied many of Michelet's values as a historian, while Bloch's colleague Lucien Febvre openly acknowledged a debt to their long-dead predecessor. A great many historiographical trends of the second half of the twentieth century can also trace at least part of their lineage from him. For example, Michelet reaffirmed the value of oral sources, thereby be-coming a father of modern oral history (see Box 24). Michelet's populist approach would be taken up by later nineteenth-century students of what is now called so-cial history, such as England's John Richard Green and Denmark's Troels Frederik Troels-Lund (1840–1921). In more recent times, neither 'history from below' nor some of its variants, such as Subaltern studies (see Chapter 9 below), are conceiv-able without the stress Michelet had placed a century and a half earlier not only on *le peuple* as a collective, conceptual entity, but on the lives and livelihoods of 'the obscure masses', especially artisans.

However, romanticism had outcomes more immediate than Michelet's legacy to the twentieth century. Initially a culturally elitist or even reactionary movement that privileged nature over reason and revalued neglected periods such as the Mid-dle Ages, it proved adaptable by the next generations into a creed for the advance-ment of liberty and for the promotion of various nationalist causes. Nationalist sentiments had been stirring for some time, and paradigmatic wars of independ-ence such as the sixteenth-century Dutch revolt against Spain were celebrated even by the likes of Friedrich von Schiller, no admirer of fanaticism or extremism, in a history published in 1788. The American Revolution provided a more recent model of emancipation. It was thus possible for subject peoples to look for inspira-tions to struggle elsewhere than a French Revolution which had veered off course first into Terror and then into a centralizing, antinationalist empire. Herder's ar-ticulation of the *Volk* and of the critical role of language provided an intellectual

Box 24   Nationalism and the Oral Past

While Michelet used contemporary oral sources, that is, living people, it was clear that they could also reach much further back in time to help give shape to subjects that were without documentary traces. Indeed, even though the archives and their champions would dominate the historical writing of the second half of the nineteenth century, oral tradition would recover something of its earlier standing, particularly in the first half of the century. An interest in the Gaelic past runs through Sir Walter Scott's immensely popular historical novels at the beginning of the century; ballad collections such as Percy's *Reliques of Ancient English Poetry* appeared. The great philologist and folklorist Jakob Grimm's interest in the literature and fairy stories of Germany awakened while turning over pages in his mentor Friedrich Carl von Savigny's library. It is important to understand, as well, that oral sources could be utilized for decidedly nationalist ends as it was precisely the absence of written records sufficient to support the kind of continuous past which many early nationalist historians wished to create that turned them back to ethnographic material including folksongs, ballads, rituals and place-names. In this regard, romantic nationalist historians, allied with local antiquaries and folklorists, played an important role in showing that oral tradition facilitated a continuity of nationhood. Histories spoken or sung tied new states back to glorious founders, and bridged the chasm of centuries often winding their way through a newly fascinating Middle Ages.

basis for further rearrangement of the borders of Europe along ethno-linguistic lines over the next century and a half. New national states would appear such as 'Romania' (the former Dacia), a polity whose name reflected remote ties to the Roman Empire, created to encompass a region inhabited by people of perceived common ethnic origin and language yet embracing linguistic minorities.

No more than romanticism, nationalism per se was neither essentially liberal nor conservative though it has often been associated with both: in Germany it would be most closely linked to conservatism, but even there it had liberal adherents. Moreover, the vectors of historiography after 1800 were not always from post-Napoleonic reaction towards mid-century liberal recovery. In some cases it was quite the opposite. In Spain, for instance, Guizot had been an admired model historian during the 1820s and 1830s, amid the nationalist fervour that followed

Napoleonic occupation. But an increasingly conservative generation of Spanish historians in the 1840s and 1850s turned away from Guizot's early-career liberalism and instead looked to Vico whose pessimistic vision of historical *corsi e ricorsi* was more palatable than the liberal narrative of progress. The impact of nationalist historical consciousness was magnified, following the revolutions of 1848 and the return of progressive ideas in liberal or even radical political clothing, by national unification movements such as the Italian Risorgimento, in the emerging independence of former satellites in Europe from foreign rule, and the new freedom of former colonies in North and South America. Yet even then it had a conservative side: the Austrian historian Josef Alexander von Helfert (1820–1910), advisor to the minister of education, thought that a nationalism defined by cohabitation within the same boundaries and loyalty to the same government needed protection: an 'Austrian' history had to be invented and promoted, ideally through a new *Nationalgeschichte* which would head off any repetition of 1848.[9]

There had certainly been eminent historians in newly established kingdoms such as Belgium prior to their political birth. Nonetheless, autonomy provided an urgent need to establish both the shape of a national past and the capacity to articulate it in written or monumental form: recent struggles for independence were grafted on to a longer master-narrative that included much earlier, medieval conflicts with external oppressors. Even those regions such as Bohemia that did not achieve political autonomy during the period still celebrated their separate identity and marked out a distinctive past. The siren of nationalism was hard to resist even among those such as the archivist-turned-historian František Palacký (1798–1876) who believed that history could not simultaneously be both a servant and a whore. Palacký's five-volume account of the Czech nation from earliest times to the Habsburg union of 1526 espoused a highly romantic and nationalist view of the Czech heritage. He quipped that the Czechs had existed as a people prior to the Austrians and would still be around after them; and he celebrated the Hussites of the fifteenth century as champions of Bohemian liberty against Germanic authoritarianism rather than strictly religious reformers. European Jews, after centuries of rabbinically dominated treatments of their past, acquired a modern national history for the first time in the successive works of Isaac Marcus Jost (1793–1860) and Heinrich Graetz (1817–91). The pattern is similar elsewhere, including nations with complex multilingual and polyethnic populations such as Belgium and, among older states, Switzerland. Swiss historians stressed the continuity of their republic back to the age of legendary medieval hero William Tell, a more legitimate antiquity, in their eyes, than post-unification German claims to connections with the Ottonian Empire.

Not infrequently, people's own sense of their historical identity was fashioned in response or reaction to the perceptions of outsiders. Venetians, whose ancient,

serene republic had finally ended in 1797, found a new historical sense in re-
sponding, furiously, to the popular *Histoire de la République de Venise* by a former
associate of Napoleon, Pierre Antoine Noël Daru (1767–1829). To the southeast,
the Greek attempt to reject the more immediate Ottoman and Byzantine pasts and
position their new state in direct kinship with the classical Hellenes was manifested
in the substitution of classical Greek names for children in lieu of traditional Christian baptismal names. The Greeks marshalled their new historical consciousness
to beat off a Daruesque challenge to their historical continuity from an outsider,
the German ethnographer and historian Jakob Phillip Fallmerayer (1790–1861). In
1830, Fallmerayer published a history of the Peloponnese that purported to show
that the modern Greek population had been predominantly Slavic since the early
Middle Ages and Albanian since the fourteenth century. The first national history
written in reply to this by Spirídon Zambélios (1815–91) in 1852 began as a 600-
page introduction to a collection of folksongs; this was soon followed by a work
that would become the foundation of modern Greek historiography, Konstantinos
Papparigopoulos' (1815–91) *History of the Greek Nation from the Most Ancient
Times until the Present.*

Nationalism was not necessarily a good thing for history under all circumstances. Although nationalist-minded historians like Palacký saw no contradiction
between their promotion of a political agenda and their duty to the emergent 'profession', there were inevitably points of conflict – signalled in Palacký's warning
about making Clio a whore – between strict devotion to the evidence and the impulse to tell a coherent narrative that affirmed a continuous national identity. The
case of Hungary is apposite, and illustrates the tensions between nation-building
and history-writing, which were most acute in the first half of the century. As one
historian has noted, Magyar nationalism had the effect in Hungary of distract-
ing some of the best minds away from history and into political activism,[10] while
romantic tendencies subverted the development of a critical attitude to and sense
of distance from the past. Romantic historians such as István Horvat (1784–1846)
similarly created a popular if highly fictionalized remote past for the Hungarian
people. Nationalist history could be extraordinarily blinkered in gaze and aristocratic in voice – were not the great heroes of the past overwhelmingly nobles
and monarchs rather than the common man? As recently as 1884 the politician
and historian Kálmán Thaly (1839–1909), answering the charge that Hungarian
historians were woefully insular, declared that world history and democracy were
values and subjects alien to the Hungarian historiographical tradition. 'We do not
concern ourselves with the history of the world, but that of our own dear country, and we follow the aristocratic point of view ... we extol the Hunyadis, the
Zápolyas ... Rákóczis and other proud oligarchs – without them the Hungarian
nation would not even exist!'[11]

Only in the second half of the century did nationalism begin to produce a more lasting historiographical legacy. This was often though not always centred in national academies and especially in the universities, whose academic historiography would gradually marginalize the kind of history-writing associated both with gentlemen of leisure, and with increasingly suspect foundational myth and undocumentable falsehood. Hungary's unsuccessful revolt of 1848–9 was followed by nationalist histories (often authored by exiled liberals such as Mihály Horváth, 1809–78) and by the foundation of the Historical Commission of the Hungarian Academy of Sciences (1854) and the Hungarian Historical Association (1867), as well as by the extensive publication of source material in the *Monumenta Hungariae Historica* ('Historical Records of Hungary', initiated 1857). Romania, which achieved independence in 1877, established a national academy shortly thereafter, and history was introduced at its newly founded universities. Polish aspirations for independence and political reform are likewise reflected in the great quantity of sources published in the early nineteenth century, and in the liberal, pro-peasant multivolume history of Poland by Joachim Lelewel (1786–1861), a fierce nationalist who spent the last three decades of his life in exile in France or Belgium.

Some of the nationalist-inspired histories still clung to the racial myths and fictitious founders of an earlier age. The proto-Romantic nationalism of the historian Father Paisiy of Hilendar (1722–73), for instance, had set his native Bulgaria on a century of historical nation-building leading up to independence in 1878, at first affirming in an uncritical manner the nation's Slavic affiliations and its descent from ancient nomadic progenitors like the Scythians. Folklorists like the Norwegian Peter Andreas Munch (1810–63) used their countries' ancient pasts to construct heroic national histories where none had previously existed. Swedish Historiographer Royal Eric Gustave Geijer (1783–1847), a romantic nationalist who became a professor at Uppsala in 1817, penned *Svenska folkets historia* ('A History of the Swedes') which praised the country's preservation of liberty and independence during its medieval period (Extract 28). In Finland, autonomous from 1809, the nationalist impulse ensured that vernacular-language works eventually overtook in volume those written in Swedish; the first full-length Finnish-language history of Finland would be produced by Yrjö Sakari Yrjö-Koskinen (1830–1903). Historical consciousness was further stimulated by authors such as the journalist, educator and novelist Zacharias Topelius (1818–98), a Finnish counterpart to Sir Walter Scott. Unlike other ethnic groups, Lithuanians had little by way of historiographical tradition prior to the romantic historian Simonas Daukantas (1793–1864), who wrote in the vernacular and created a dubious pedigree for his people in a remote barbarian tribe. Earlier histories were rare. The 'Bychovko chronicle', the long version of a pro-Lithuanian sixteenth-century text generally known as the *Lithuanian Chronicle*, was not available till 1846, when it was published by Daukantas'

28: Geijer on Swedish Medieval History

Sweden's middle age is full of confusion, and destitute of that splendour which fascinates the eye. Whatever of pomp and grandeur the hierarchy, feudalism, powerful and flourishing cities, exhibited in the rest of Europe during those times, extended but in a small degree to this region; and if we put faith in common assertions, many admirable qualities, which distinguished our Pagan ancestors, must have perished with heathenism, and have been replaced in great part by new vices and errors of belief. To us, neither the old excellence nor the new corruptions are fairly apparent. In the gloom of Paganism there is ample scope for the play of imagination, if we refuse to hear, in the complaints of a desolated world, the witness of the reality. From the so-called energy of the Northmen, Europe suffered severely; and of the calamities which its own excesses brought upon themselves, after they were reduced to seek their fields of battle in civil wars at home, the annals of the northern middle age furnish abundant proof. But no one can deny that the people of Sweden best withstood that trial in which Norway lost its political independence, and Denmark the freedom of its people. In Sweden both were securely established, and this issue is sufficient to awaken interest for an age which had not laboured in vain, when such was to be its result. This struggle of our middle age we will here attempt to comprehend and to appreciate.

Selection from Eric Gustave Geijer, *The History of the Swedes*, trans. J. H. Turner (London, Whitaker and Co., n.d. [1845?]), 80.

contemporary, Teodor Narbutt (1784–1864). Unsurprisingly, the peoples of several of these territories were often considered as falling outside the main stream of History in accounts written by Russian, Polish and German historians, or they were awkwardly shoehorned into the national narratives of the larger states, as were many of Russia's subordinated populations, most notably Ukrainians. In the next chapter we will take up more explicitly the relations of empires to peripheries, and of dominant to subordinate histories, but it is important to note here that the same dynamic which can be observed *between* the West and the rest of the world had already emerged in the major European powers' treatments of their own ethnic and religious minorities within their national narratives.

A good illustration of the eastward spread of western European tendencies is provided by Russian historical writing. This continued to be influenced by other national histories (in particular French and German) in the late eighteenth and nineteenth centuries as it had in the time of Schlözer and Karamzin. As elsewhere, considerable activity was devoted in the post-Napoleonic era to the collection and publication of source materials, especially government documents, under the leadership of the Chancellor Nikolai P. Rumiantsev (1754–1826). An 'Archeographic Commission' undertook a nationwide survey of archives and repositories analogous to Victorian Britain's Historical Manuscripts Commission. Influenced by the German classicist B. G. Niebuhr (see below), M. T. Kachenovskii (1775–1842) adopted a highly sceptical approach to the early, Kievan period of Russian history. While Hegel's philosophy of history was widely read among the intelligentsia of the 1830s and 1840s, influencing a 'slavophilic' school of historians, the general trend was towards Europeanizing of practical historical methodology in a 'scientific' vein. Pavel (Paul) Nikolaevich Miliukov (1859–1943), for instance, the first Russian to teach a course on historiography at Moscow University, would proclaim to his students in 1892 that the proper subject of scientific history was the 'internal, fundamental processes of a people's development'.[12] Thus western European methodology became the key to establishing, on evidentiary grounds, the genius of the Russian people.

The two outstanding Russian historians of the second half of the nineteenth century were S. M. Solov'ev (or Soloviev, 1820–79) and V. O. Kliuchevskii (1841–1911). Solov'ev had travelled in the West and heard lectures by Guizot and Michelet; he was personally acquainted with the great Czech historian Palacký. Solov'ev's prodigious *Istoriia Rossiis drevneĭshikh vremen* ('History of Russia since Ancient Times') appeared in twenty-nine annual volumes beginning in 1851, accompanied by numerous monographs. A committed historicist, he envisaged history as a unified and continuous story of organic development. In the following generation Kliuchevskii, Solov'ev's pupil and successor, assigned a new prominence to the analysis of economic and social history, which would establish the groundwork for post-Revolutionary Marxist historiography, despite Kliuchevskii's own dismissal of Marx's ideas. Ironically, while a number of his one-time pupils, notably Miliukov, shared his constitutionalist views, others embraced Marxism and Bolshevism, becoming successful communist historians after the Revolution of 1917; one of these, Mikhail Pokrovskii, would almost single-handedly lay the foundations of Soviet historiography (see Chapter 9 below).

The redrawing of maps often led, as in the case of Scandinavia and the Low Countries, to divergent paths in the interpretation of the past. In British North America, the colonies separated historiographically as well as politically following the American Revolution. The northern colonies – what eventually became Canada – remained firmly within the British imperial orbit (despite the existence of a distinctive Francophone Catholic majority within the future province of Quebec). A consciousness of Canada as a nation with its own unique past did not mature until Confederation (1867) brought political unity and semi-autonomous status, and even then Francophone historiography remained apart from its Anglophone-imperial counterpart, with recurrent separatist movements building, even today, on the belief in a historically separate Quebecois nation awaiting its rightful sovereignty. To the south, the experience was very different. In the United

Figure 47 | Portrait of Washington Irving and his literary friends at Sunnyside, Irving's Tarrytown, New York home, by Christian Schussele (1824–79), 1864. The painting is a 'Who's Who' of the antebellum American literary elite which included popular historians: W. H. Prescott is seated centrally in profile, George Bancroft at far right. Irving is seated centrally, facing the viewer, to the right of Prescott; James Fenimore Cooper, the historical novelist, sits to the left of Bancroft.

States, a prototype for a nationalist historiography had already been established in colonial-era writings that acknowledged the colonies' place in the empire but also celebrated aspects of their New World distinctiveness. A nationalist American historiography had emerged quite quickly following independence from Britain, as early-republic historians such as Mercy Otis Warren and David Ramsay (see Chapter 5 above) narrated the United States' emergence as a free nation built on democratic values; the biographers of major figures such as George Washington helped establish a pantheon of national heroes analogous to those being created or resuscitated in Europe. James Fenimore Cooper (1789–1851) and other historical novelists imitated Sir Walter Scott. Both American and world history were enormously popular among readers during the first half of the nineteenth century, but their writing remained the domain of gentlemen of leisure (and the occasional woman like Warren) or of journalists. Famous examples (both severely sight-impaired through most of their careers) include William Hickling Prescott

(1796–1859), narrator of the Spanish conquests, and Francis Parkman (1823–93), historian of the western frontier. Both were members of a northeastern intellectual elite (the centres of which were Boston and New York) that also included the Göttingen-trained John Lothrop Motley (1814–77), historian of the Dutch Republic and US minister to Austria, and literary figures such as Cooper and Washington Irving (Fig. 47). Internationally, the most widely recognized American historian was yet another 'Boston Brahmin', George Bancroft (1800–91), a former Harvard professor-turned-diplomat and one of the first of his country to earn a Ph.D. from a German university, a trend that would increase in the second half of the century.

Ranke and the 'Professionalization' of History

If the first half of the West's nineteenth century is characterized by literary historical writing in a romantic and nationalist vein, the second half may be noted for a rapid growth in what may be loosely called 'professionalization'. Although this too has nationalist aspects, it is associated less with the 'nation' in any ethnic, linguistic or cultural sense than with the political 'nation-state' and its bureaucratic apparatus, whether in a new state or an older one that had reorganized or reconstituted itself. In France, for instance, the nascent Third Republic, established in 1870, promoted its version of French nationhood through semi-official historians like Ernest Lavisse (1842–1922), author of an influential school textbook. Italy provides an example of the evolving relationship between nationalism and professionalization in a newly unified monarchy. The new regime encouraged historical writing and promoted pedagogy, just as popular historians had themselves, earlier in the century, prepared the way for the Risorgimento. Prior to this, history had enjoyed at best a peripheral role in Italian universities, with chairs of history existing only at a select few such as Pavia and Turin. This changed in the 1860s as professorial posts were created and their occupants appointed directly by the Minister of Public Education. But for many of the most influential historians of the latter part of the century, the militant patriotism of the previous decades now needed to take a back seat to a more methodologically 'scientific' approach, embodied in important scholars like Pasquale Villari (1827–1917). They stressed the importance of research into the facts of the Italian past; for them, the main agenda of historiography was no longer a political one, though history could still contribute to civic education.

During the middle and later decades of the century, the romantic liberalism of national independence and unification movements refashioned itself in much of Europe back into an institutional conservatism dedicated once more to preservation, consolidation and social stability. Changes were signalled by a number of

Figure 48 | *Teaching.* A nineteenth-century fresco in the Sorbonne featuring some of France's greatest historians, including Renan, Quinet and Guizot. Michelet is standing, holding papers.

developments, many of them external to the emerging academic 'discipline' of history, such as a significant growth in the professional classes which created a market for history, a cadre of professors and schoolteachers to teach it (Fig. 48), a ready supply of textbooks for them to use, sometimes enlivened by pictures (Fig. 49), and civil servants to apply its lessons and sometimes even to write more of it themselves in their spare time. Technological changes such as mechanized printing made books much more affordable to a mass audience previously reliant on devices like serialization or on public libraries. Among the most significant changes specifically affecting the historical profession – for such it had become by 1900 – one should note in particular these: state support for historical activity, including particular publications, such as England's 'Rolls Series' publication of medieval chronicles (initiated in 1857) or the Second French Empire's creation of the *quatrième section* of the École pratique des hautes études; the regularization of academic life and (in France and Germany) the placing of university teaching positions on a civil service salary scale; the expansion of university systems and

Figure 49 | How the Danes came up the Channel a thousand years ago, 1925. An example of pictorial illustrations in history textbooks from a frequently reprinted early twentieth-century series, Highroads of History. This scene comes from Book II: *Stories from British History*, published by Thomas Nelson and Sons (London, Edinburgh, New York, 1925).

the turning of many of them by the century's end to formal training in historical scholarship; the introduction of earned doctorates and, in the German system, the higher level of 'habilitation' required for a permanent professorial rank; the systematization of public record systems in many countries; the advent of several new professional associations, frequently accompanied by a new style of high-standard and increasingly peer-reviewed periodical or journal; a continuation of the long-standing trend to publish archival documents, now often under government sponsorship and with a considerably higher standard of accuracy than previously applied; and, finally, the systematic convergence of the erudite skills that had matured over the previous three centuries (palaeography, diplomatic, numismatics and epigraphy) within an overarching historical science (*Geschichts-wissenschaft*).

Any account of nineteenth-century professionalization must begin at the new University of Berlin established in 1810, and focus on the imposing figure of Leopold von Ranke (1795–1886). Initially a student of ancient history and philology, at first he had little time for modern history, deeming it an inferior form of writing to the classics. This beginning as a classicist was anything but a false start, and to understand Ranke we must first appreciate the influence of two more senior scholars of antiquity, Barthold Georg Niebuhr and Friedrich Carl (or Karl) von Savigny. Research into the ancient past was a priority of early nineteenth-century German scholarship, and it was headed in a very different direction from the literary or philosophical writings of a Gibbon or Ferguson. Picking up on the Homeric scholarship of F. A. Wolf, the Danish-born Niebuhr (1776–1831) pioneered a holistic, source-driven and integrated study of antiquity in all its aspects, a kind of problem-based scholarship which would utilize the techniques of the philologist, the historian, the epigrapher and the literary critic, in a unified study of antiquity, or *Altertumswissenschaft*. His *Römische Geschichte* ('Roman History') would be the dominant text on Roman history until supplanted later in the century by Theodor Mommsen. Ranke would eventually name Niebuhr, along with Martin Luther, Thucydides and (despite his dislike of speculation) the philosopher Fichte, as his answer to Vico's 'four authors'.

Niebuhr's identification of an entire period as an object to be studied through a methodology with a distinctive set of rules and standards would be complemented and reinforced by a student of Roman law, Savigny (1779–1861), who at the age of twenty-four had already published a major book and arrived in Berlin at virtually the same time as Niebuhr. Savigny belongs to a long line of jurist-historians reaching back through the great seventeenth-century polymaths, Selden, Grotius, Pufendorf, to the era of Cujas, Hotman and the Renaissance *mos gallicus*, and ultimately to late medieval commentators like Bartolus of Sassoferato. What Savigny added to this impressive pedigree was a strong argument for treating law as the product of particular times and circumstances. It was not an absolute unchanging reflection of an idealized 'right' but a historically changing set of rules and customs. As a practising jurist, Savigny resisted the codification of laws in his own time – a prominent feature of the hated Napoleonic tyranny – and he took a dim view of the absolutism immanent in slavish deference to 'natural law'. Law was man-made and 'positive' – it was what Vico had called a *factum*. As such, individual laws could not be understood apart from the society that had created them. And if laws characterized civilization at a particular period, then it followed that the periods themselves were both distinctive and not strictly comparable, and that they needed to be studied independently, as organic entities. Savigny also demonstrated that Roman law, far from being an outdated ancient system merely of antiquarian interest, had survived through the Middle Ages; its traces could be found in local customs and ecclesiastical law. One could therefore not understand modern jurisprudence without decoding the different strata or layers of earlier laws that had developed in the fourteen centuries since the end of the western empire.

In some ways, Ranke's eventual achievement would be to merge the cutting-edge philological methods of Niebuhr with Savigny's sense of period and apply them to the study of post-1500 political history. In part because of an awakening interest in contemporary issues, he abandoned the ancient for the modern history of the world, beginning with *Geschichten der romanischen und germanischen Völker von 1494 bis 1514* ('The Histories of the Latin and Germanic Peoples from 1494 to 1514', 1824), a book roughly covering the same period tackled by Francesco Guicciardini three centuries earlier in his history of Italy (see Chapter 4 above), a country which in turn held a particular fascination for Ranke early in his career. Ranke appended to this work one of his first theoretical pronouncements, *Zur Kritik neuerer Geschichtsschreiber* ('A Critique of Modern Historians'), republished separately in the same year, a bold step from a historian still very young. In this essay Ranke took to task a number of his predecessors in the writing of early modern history, but none so fiercely as Guicciardini, whose vaunted use of original documents had in Ranke's eyes been grossly overestimated (Extract 29).

The *Latin and Germanic Peoples* earned Ranke his post at Berlin. There, he and Savigny (Niebuhr had quit Berlin in 1816 for a diplomatic posting) were soon joined by G. W. F. Hegel (see below), an unwelcome intruder thrust upon them by the Prussian government. Hegel took up the chair of philosophy in 1818 and soon came into conflict with the other two. Ranke, the junior member of this group, placed himself decisively in Savigny's camp during a dispute about the differing characteristics of historical periods. He would soon come to see these academic quarrels as symptomatic of a larger struggle between history and philosophy, and between the particular and the abstract. Ranke's discovery of the potential of an underused source, the manuscript reports of Venetian diplomats, for early modern history led to further works, including the history of *Die osmanen und die spanische Monarchie* ('The Ottoman and the Spanish Empires in the Sixteenth and Seventeenth Centuries', 1827). The Venetian reports were of particular interest not only because, in Ranke's eyes, they were accurate, but because of their comprehensive view of Europe. This ought to have enabled him to move from his earlier plural *Geschichten* to a singular *Geschichte*, but he was disappointed in the end because the work did not live up to this integrative goal. Ranke could not solve the problem of the different organization of the Turkish and Spanish states, leading him, again, to handle them separately and with different emphases: he had yet to find any 'large-scale historical process' to tie together his pieces. In the 1830s, Ranke moved on to write *Die Geschichte der Päpste* ('A History of the Popes') based

29: Ranke on Guicciardini's *History of Italy*

In its frequent interruptions and resumptions, Guicciardini's history is comparable to the poem of Ariosto. But an historian's work requires a stricter rule. Let us search for it.

In Book IV, Guicciardini retells the campaign of Cesare Borgia against Imola and Forlì, the state of the countess Caterina Sforza. Imola was conquered in December 1499; Forlì, in January 1500. The undertaking itself was carried on without interruption. Nonetheless, after Guicciardini speaks of Imola, he breaks off. The end of the year reminds him of an event which he then recounts: the attack of the Turks on Friuli, which had taken place in July, and might perhaps have had something to do with the war of Ludovico, but had not the least to do with Cesare's campaign. After he discusses this, he also recalls that 1500 had been a Jubilee Year – he then returns to the subject of Forlì.

He is even more rigid in observing the form of a yearbook. Alexander and Cesare Borgia made a joint attack against the Orsini. The son succeeded on December 31, 1502; the father, on January 3, 1503. This was sufficient motivation for Guicciardini to interject the story about a clash at Mirandola, which he himself admits has little significance, into the middle of his narrative ....

[Ranke then continues, changing from criticism of the *Storia*'s form to its reliability as a piece of contemporary history and source for future historians.]

The first question to be asked regarding those documentary histories, which we generally regard as sources, is whether they are written by participants or eyewitnesses or merely by contemporaries. In the year 1492, where Guicciardini begins, he was only ten years old. One could easily think that for the next two decades while he was studying and completing his legal training his observations must be incomplete. He himself, even after he was sent as ambassador to Spain, could have had only an inadequate knowledge of Italian affairs. But thereafter, when he was President of the Romagna, commander in Reggio and Parma, and Lieutenant of the Pope with the allied army, he participated in affairs himself and witnessed many remarkable events with his own eyes.

As a result, his history falls into two parts: one which contains the events in which he played a role, and the other in which this was not the case. It is obvious that for the latter, as extensive as they were, he must have based his work on documents and research. Therefore before we make any use of his book, we must ask if his information was original, or if borrowed, in what manner it was borrowed and what kind of research was employed to compile it.

It would be reasonable to assume that the second part of the *History*, that dealing with the period in which the historian often held high offices and had the best opportunity to ascertain the facts correctly, would be the most original, most instructive, and best researched account. But it is precisely here that his work shows itself to be unoriginal and dependent upon the work of another [Ranke then demonstrates Guicciardini's borrowings from the *Commentarii* by Galeazzo Capra or Capella, private secretary to the Milanese minister Jerome Morone].

Selection from 'Critique of Guicciardini' (originally included in *Zur Kritik neuerer Geschichtsschreiber* [1824], *Sämmtliche Werke* 33/34). The present selection comes from Leopold von Ranke, *The Secret of World History: Selected Writings on the Art and Science of History*, ed. and trans. Roger Wines (New York: Fordham University Press, 1981), 82.

on private Roman archives (access to the Vatican Library was denied him as a Protestant), which earned itself a place on the Index of Prohibited Books. Even today it remains admired for its scrupulous impartiality; indeed, some Protestants found it insufficiently hostile to Rome.

It was during the same decade that Ranke began to put together the views on universal history that would guide the remainder of his career. By the end of the 1830s the first part of one of his greatest books, *Deutsche Geschichte im Zeitalter der Reformation* ('History of the Reformation in Germany'), had appeared, in which he finally found a connecting theme in the struggle between universal religion and particular nationality. Ranke's subsequent works traced the emergence of the European state system that this good German public servant much admired as the source of modern civilization and individual freedom; and with a gaze wandering steadily outward in expanding circles, his career closed with an unfinished multivolume *Weltgeschichte*.[13] Commenced in Ranke's eighties, this world history had reached the twelfth century when its author died at the age of ninety-one; it was left to his students to bring it forward to the fall of Constantinople.

Throughout his long working life, Ranke reputedly saw no contradiction between his attendance to the particularity of history, displayed through the most meticulous and painstaking attention to a single document, and the interrelations between men and nations, among nations, and between all of the above and God. The state, the fundamental political unit of his narratives (encompassing more than simply the government), was pre-eminently worthy of study – not on its own but as the channel through which one accessed the past of the wider 'nation'. Nations in turn are the windows through which one sees the cumulative History of humanity. The close studies of modern historiographers have revealed that there are, in fact, tensions in Ranke's thought. The historian famous for valuing the God-given individuality (*Eigentümlichkeit*) and particularity of each era still believed in something like progress, and he also affirmed that there are timeless, transcendent ideas, especially in ethics. What he did not accept was the union of these two things in the way a philosopher like Hegel had put them together.

Individual actions, not reified ideas, powered the movement of the human race through time.

The edition of Ranke's collected works published between 1868 and 1890 runs to fifty-four volumes.[14] Staggeringly prolific as he was, however, Ranke is less important for any of his individual histories than for what he came to symbolize. Though he in fact wrote no book on method, in the modern historical profession's own account of its rise to its current position as guardian of the past, Ranke casts a longer shadow than anyone else, perhaps Thucydides alone excepted. He has been made into one of those 'lawgivers' that the eighteenth century rejected; through sheer volume of work, force of personality and the influence of an impressive number of intellectual progeny, he is widely believed to have prescribed the future goals and best practices for the nascent historical discipline. Cracks have begun to appear both in the figurative statue of this lawgiver and his rules, which were themselves the creation of a particular period and have not always been easily adjusted to accommodate newer forms of scholarship and subjects of interest during the twentieth century. Moreover, Georg Iggers is surely correct to argue that the methodological and critical aspects of Ranke's reputation – that part most enthusiastically adopted by eager admirers outside Germany – were neither wholly original to Ranke nor in the longer run the most important aspect of his œuvre.[15] But there is no denying his impact as scholar, teacher and icon (see Box 25). Over his long career at the University of Berlin, he thoroughly transformed the training of young historians (many of them foreigners) by focusing his research seminars on primary sources and their criticism. A devotee of such sources, he would eventually predict their dominance in research. 'I see the time approaching when we shall base modern history, no longer on the reports even of contemporary historians, except insofar as they were in the possession of personal and immediate knowledge of facts; and still less on work yet more remote from the source; but rather on the narratives of eyewitnesses, and on genuine and original documents.'[16]

Willingness to subject to criticism revered documents and texts, and the received notions that derive from them, has often been taken as a sign of secularism or impiety by contemporary opponents and later admirers alike: one recalls John Selden's experience in seventeenth-century England and the reaction to the Han Learning scholars of early Qing China, discussed above. Yet with Ranke we find a devoutly religious man, seeking God's handiwork in history, as had so many historians before him, but with a focus on the mechanics of human action on the earthly stage to the degree that these could be recovered through careful examination of sources. Allowing for God's plan, however, Ranke also upheld the distinctive value and contribution to the great human story of each historical era and people, all 'equal before God', a phrase he seems first to have used in a series of lectures. 'If one wants to know historical humanity one must attend both to the

Box 25   Ranke's Disciples

Among Ranke's pupils, he could include many of the great names of the later nineteenth century, such as Georg Waitz (1813–86) and Heinrich von Sybel (1817–95); colleagues and associates included Johann Gustav Droysen, the most important philosopher of history of his generation. These men deserve much of the credit for having converted Ranke's ideas into institutional form throughout Prussia and then Germany as a whole. Some of Ranke's students, to be sure, departed from the master's model. Sybel thought Ranke too aloof from the issues of the day, and Droysen, more theoretically minded, worried that Ranke had in the end done little more than collect facts. The Swiss historian Jacob Burckhardt (1818–97), in particular, was an unusual apprentice whose great *Kulturgeschichte, The Civilization of the Renaissance in Italy* (1860), remains today one of the most oft-read historical works of the nineteenth century and is a forerunner of modern cultural history.

infinite variety of life which fills the centuries and the course of the great changes in which it moves', he wrote. 'Let us regard both the life of each epoch and the connection of them all.'[17] He promoted a historiography that as far as possible could tell the story of the past *wie es eigentlich gewesen.*

This famous phrase is often the only thing many students know about Ranke. Uttered early in his career, it was neither a lightning bolt of methodological insight nor even entirely original to him: Thucydides had made a similar observation in antiquity, while the linguist and educational reformer Wilhelm von Humboldt (1767–1835) had begun an address to the Prussian Academy (1821) with the declaration that 'The historian's task is to present what actually happened.' Ranke's particular formulation of this idea appears in the introduction to his first major book, the 1824 *Latin and Germanic Peoples*, in the specific context of the author's extensive use of the Venetian archives, rather than as a philosophic generalization. It carries with it – though this was probably a secondary issue for Ranke – an abdication of the historian's judicial–didactic role. 'History has had assigned to it the office of judging the past and of instructing the present for the benefit of the future ages. To such high offices the present work does not presume: it seeks only to show what actually happened.' Apart from the fact that this disavowal may be a rhetorical feint, a standard apology that historians provide in their prefaces, issued to rule out-of-scope the things we find less interesting, this may not in fact be the most accurate translation of *wie es eigentlich gewesen*, which is rendered more accurately as 'the past as it essentially was'. For our purposes *what* he meant is of less consequence than *how* it came to be interpreted by some later admirers, especially in the United States. Many of them wrongly believed that the master had intended the complete avoidance of anything not based on a specific fact and the repudiation of conjecture or interpretation, thereby ignoring the moral and philosophical side of Ranke's writings, which is so obvious in later works as to make nonsense of his purported early utterances against didacticism.

Thanks to Ranke, his immediate disciples and the celebrated university seminar environment, German scholarship loomed large over European intellectual life in the second half of the nineteenth century and beyond. The Sorbonne historian Ernest Lavisse was initially so taken with Ranke's successes that he introduced the historical seminar into French higher education. There is no doubt that German scholarship also captured the imagination of many of Britain's leading historians, in Stubbs and especially E. A. Freeman's case not easily separable from their enthusiasm for ancient Saxon liberty. F. W. Maitland (1850–1906) modelled his legal scholarship on Savigny, one of whose works he translated. Lord Acton (1834–1902) trained with the German Catholic scholar Johann Joseph Ignaz von Döllinger (1799–1890). Stubbs emulated Rankean source criticism and his own pupils or disciples would in turn 'modernize' the British historical profession in the decades leading up to the First World War. J. R. Seeley similarly admired Ranke and repudiated the literary aspects of historiography; but in the end he took history education in a different direction than Stubbs, forging a closer tie with politics and 'practical' matters, demonstrable in his establishment of the history 'tripos' or degree study at Cambridge in 1873. By the end of the century, history at the British universities had arguably become the ultimate indoctrination programme for young men in undertaking the duties of empire together with the privileges and entitlements of class.

Yet the full-dress Germanic academic system was slow to catch on across the Channel. Unlike their French and American colleagues, Oxford and Cambridge both resisted the seminar, maintaining the undergraduate tutorial system combined with public lectures. It would fall to the upstart University of Manchester to develop something closer to Rankean training, with Stubbs-influenced scholars such as T. F. Tout (1855–1929) turning Manchester at the start of the twentieth century into Britain's leading institution of medieval history. The English universities did not adopt the doctorate as the essential 'union card' for a faculty position until well into the twentieth century; as late as the post-war era, many distinguished British historians earned their tutorial fellowships on the basis of brilliant performance as undergraduates. Against that, one has to admit the considerable impact of historians like the seventeenth-century specialist Sir Charles Firth (1857–1936), committed to the notion that the job of teaching young men history involved actually teaching them to become historians. By the first years of the twentieth century he was among those pushing for a research component in the undergraduate degree.

   The post-Rankean German influence was stronger outside western Europe than within. To the east, for instance, several generations of early twentieth-century Romanian historians derived inspiration from Germany, including the archaeologist Vasile Pârvan (1882–1927) and the methodologist Alexandru Xenopol (1847–1920). To the north, the Dane Kristian Erslev (1852–1930) and the Norwegian Gustav Storm (1845–1903) both spent extended periods in German seminars. The Japanese, in particular, would adopt Germanic methods with alacrity in the 1880s (see Chapter 8 below). American students flocked most frequently to Germany, returning home to run seminars and new graduate schools of history at United States' universities such as Johns Hopkins and Michigan. Of those historians working at American universities in the 1880s and 1890s, roughly half had spent some time studying in Germany, though frequently of too short a duration to permit them really to absorb German historical method – much less the whole philosophy behind it – quite thoroughly. The 'objectivity' mantra chanted in American historiography for many decades may be ascribed in large measure to the importation of a naive version of Rankeanism which upheld Ranke himself as an idol while largely misunderstanding the more subtle aspects of his thought. Indeed, the myth of Ranke was far more powerful in America than his methods. Nor did every American student enjoy his time in Germany. Bancroft as a very young man had been scandalized by the loose morals and drinking he observed in Göttingen. The prominent black historian and educator, W. E. B. Du Bois (1868–1963) suffered through one of Heinrich von Treitschke's racist rants in 1890, though he generally had a positive opinion of his teachers in Berlin. Some American scholars, such as Henry Adams, who introduced a seminar at Harvard, even held the entire German university system in low esteem. However, it was the aura of 'professionalism' radiating from the ambition of objective, value-free scholarship that was most appealing, and Germany appeared to provide the most advanced model of both. Professional standards which outlined a creed of 'scientific history' were upheld by the newly founded American Historical Association (1884) and policed by influential academics like the Johns Hopkins-trained J. Franklin Jameson (1859–1937), the first editor of the *American Historical Review* (*AHR*).

Journals and Handbooks

The *AHR* was North America's premier example of another major development of the nineteenth century, also emanating from Germany: the professional historical journal. History had appeared prominently in periodicals before this time, in literary reviews and the publications of learned academies (see Chapter 6 above). Local history societies, principally with an antiquarian focus, had sprung up in the late eighteenth and early nineteenth centuries. National associations for the study of history similarly appeared, such as the Swiss *Allgemeine geschichtsforschende Gesellschaft* established by a Zurich merchant in 1841. But the free-standing, edited academic journal to which new historical research could be submitted for peer review and publication is a creation of mid-nineteenth-century Germany. Ranke's pupil Heinrich von Sybel (1817–95), a professor at Munich, became in 1859 the founding editor of the *Historische Zeitschrift* (*HZ*). Previous journals such as the *Zeitschrift für Geschichtswissenschaft* (1844–8) had been short-lived, and the *HZ*'s beginning was not all that promising, since most of the leading historians were initially reluctant to publish in it, preferring to concentrate on monographs (a prejudice among humanities disciplines maintained to this day, in contrast to the natural and social sciences). But by its survival and longevity, its devotion exclusively to history and its insistence on a common standard of scholarship, it lit the way for other journals elsewhere. The German-trained reformer of French historical scholarship, Gabriel Monod (1844–1912) created his own version of *HZ* in the *Revue historique* (*RH*, 1876). The *Rivista Storica Italiana* (1884) and *English Historical Review* (*EHR*, 1886) followed; and in 1895 the *AHR* was created as the official publication of the American Historical Association. Interestingly, in each case the journals were started by relative outsiders seeking to alter the practice of historical scholarship in their country; and in each case, the innovators would soon evolve into insiders, conservative guardians of historiographic orthodoxy, 'objectivity' and 'sound' methods; new rebels would then spawn breakaway or rival venues to publish work on excluded topics. That pattern has continued through to the early twenty-first century.

There were some noteworthy differences among these early historical journals: the founders of the *HZ* and *RH* both saw history as still having a social role to play, and did not eschew a political agenda; the *EHR* explicitly disavowed these. Content also varied: the Americans followed the English in largely avoiding theoretical issues until the foundation of *History and Theory* in the early 1960s. The *AHR*, unlike its older European cousins, was created in an already mature institutional environment, its parent organization having been in existence for eleven years, which made it almost instantly a professional organizer and regulator rather than an innovator. In the beginning, there was also some scope for participation in each of these publications from schoolteachers, archivists and librarians, especially in the *EHR*, which in its early years was the least academically dominated of the major journals; its first editor, Mandell Creighton, was only just returned from a country vicarage to a chair at Cambridge. Those not employed at universities were, however, soon squeezed out, leading to further outlets being created: those disenfranchised by the *AHR*, for instance, established other journals like the *Mississippi Valley Historical Review* (1914; since 1964 known as *The Journal of American History*). Roman Catholics, largely excluded by Sybel from publication in *HZ*, set up the *Historisches Jahrbuch*. The most famous rebellion against an orthodox periodical, the *Revue historique*, would come in the 1920s with the establishment of the *Annales* (see Chapter 9 below) as a venue for social and economic history. There was also a tendency to give primacy to the national past: the *HZ* was dominated by German subjects, the *EHR* by English ones, and so on, though there were attempts to improve balance, for instance in Creighton's efforts to obtain foreign books for review in the *EHR*.

If new journals represented the vanguard of historical research, historical pedagogy, bringing up the rear, was assisted by handbooks. Some, such as the much-published epitomes of Carl Ploetz (1819–91), kept to the older format inherited from the eighteenth century, summarizing world historical events; others outlined the elements of historical method. Just as the historiographic ferment of the sixteenth and seventeenth centuries and its arguments over genre had been boiled down into the *ars historica* literature, and eighteenth-century successors like Gatterer and Mably had provided general guidebooks to the study of the past, so the methodological discussions and disciplinary refinements of the nineteenth century were digested and disseminated to students through a series of these manuals, beginning with Johann Gustav Droysen (1808–84) and continuing with Ottokar Lorenz (1832–1904) and Ernst Bernheim (1850–1942). Bernheim's massive *Lehrbuch der historischen methode* ('Textbook on Historical Method', 1889), which by its 1908 edition had swollen to over 800 pages, proved influential as far afield as Japan (see Chapter 8 below). Bernheim confidently avowed that many facts of history could be known with certainty, though he conceived that others could only be surmised as 'probable'.

This trend towards a rather narrow preoccupation with method was also observable in fin-de-siècle France. Earlier French historians such as Michelet and Edgar Quinet (1803–75) had indeed been affected by speculative history, the former by Vico and the latter by Herder; the Hebraist and religious scholar Ernest Renan, who developed his own Herderian theory of nationhood as a 'spirit', also flirted with philosophic materialism as a substitute for his shaken faith. But as in Germany, this was increasingly a minority position. The apparatus of modern French historiography was established with the founding of the famous graduate research centre, the École pratique des hautes études, in 1868 and of the *Revue historique*. Perhaps the most innocent expression of the evidentiary confidence at the root of scientific history – a belief in the rock-solid documentary foundation and continuous advancement through source criticism of historical knowledge, without reducing all human knowledge to the natural sciences – can be found in a more concise French counterpart to Ernst Bernheim. A hugely successful manual on method, based on a set of Sorbonne lectures, the *Introduction aux études historiques* ('Introduction to Historical Studies', 1897) by the medievalist Charles Victor Langlois (1863–1929), later Director of the *Archives Nationales*, and the historian of nineteenth-century politics Charles Seignobos (1854–1942), was soon translated or adapted into several other languages.[18] F. York Powell, Regius Professor of Modern History at Oxford, pronounced the work indispensable as the manual of a 'scientific' method in history, in his preface to the 1898 English edition. The prominent Greek historian, Spyridon Lambros (1851–1919), who translated the *Introduction* in 1902 and adapted it for his country's particular context, thought that the book would help prepare those doing research in Greek archives, many of whom were doing so without any prior training; it provided him with external validation for his championing of ancillary disciplines such as *graphognossia*, his term for palaeography.

This early enthusiasm for the *Introduction* has, understandably, waned, and not only because of its age. It is a book that has become, somewhat undeservedly, the symbol *par excellence* of the naive confidence of late nineteenth-century scholarship, with its step-by-step delineation of the preparatory, analytical and synthetic operations required in the writing of history. This came with some riskily bold assertions of what was (and was not) proper method, and a ringing declaration of the dependence of history on writing. Book III, on 'synthetic operations' opens with the following passage:

Let us begin by considering the materials of history. What is their form and their nature? How do they differ from the materials of other sciences?

Historical facts are derived from the critical analysis of documents. They issue from this process in the form to which analysis has reduced them, chopped small into individual statements; for a single sentence contains several statements: we have often accepted some and rejected others; each of these statements represents a fact.

Historical facts have the common characteristic of having been taken from documents ...[19]

The act of assembling the disparate facts from multiple documents into a coherent history, say Langlois and Seignobos, is akin to the scientific construction of a building. One has to choose one's materials carefully, since the wrong ones will prevent any design from being executed. It would be, said the learned authors, 'like proposing to construct an Eiffel Tower with building-stones'.[20]

History, Science and Determinism

One of the many paradoxes of the nineteenth century is that it is the great age of history as literary masterpiece and simultaneously of the argument by some that it was a 'science'. The contradiction is more apparent to us than it was to contemporaries, since science then was a broader term that still retained something of its Renaissance meaning of *scientia*, or knowledge in general; and it is less an issue in languages like French and German, both of which used terms (*science, Wissenschaft*) that are more inclusive and less tied than the English word has become to the experimental and mathematical spheres. Moreover, in the nineteenth century intellectuals could still occasionally travel between science and letters (though less often than in previous periods), and nature provided a common source of inspiration for both. Indeed, history seemed to be the quintessential amphibious activity that could straddle the boundary between the natural and social worlds. Clio had expanded her reach, and a much more comprehensive 'historicization' of outlook developed both in popular and learned culture, touching on nearly every domain of intellectual activity. It is not going too far to say that history became the 'master discipline' of the century, simultaneously the source of material for literary fiction, the Baconian–Herodotean catch-all term for the collection and display of nature, the basis of comparative philology and the foundation of disciplines such as sociology. The French anarcho-socialist Pierre-Joseph Proudhon (1809–65) expressed this faith in history's bountiful plenitude succinctly, declaring that 'all truth is in history' and that, like nature, history need but be interrogated to surrender the laws of human society. When the French jurist F. F. Poncelet declared in 1820 that 'History is the source of all human science',[21] he intended what we would now call social science, a term just then emerging. Ernest Renan included both philology and history within his definition of science. By about 1900, when science had begun to move off in its more specialized and technological direction, it was still not unreasonable for the Byzantinist and historian of progress John Bagnell Bury (1861–1927) to declare history a science, 'no less and no more'.

It is also true, however, that by the early decades of the nineteenth century sides were already being drawn between those who continued to see history as a moral resource, its individuals and episodes – even when understood within a longer narrative context – retaining something of their old didactic role, and those for whom the progress of History ever-forward was not merely an intellectual problem to be solved but a machine whose workings could be analysed and even reverse-engineered so as to increase its forward motion. For some the two views were not incompatible. Joachim Lelewel, the Polish nationalist and republican whose academic career would be cut short in 1824 by tsarist-imposed exile, certainly saw a liberal progressive pattern in his country's past, especially its medieval period. But he retained a didactic view that would not have been entirely out of place in the Renaissance, telling his students in 1815:

30: History as a Sentimental Observer: Carlyle on the Struggles of the Girondins and Montagnards

But, for the rest, let no man ask History to explain by cause and effect how the business proceeded henceforth. This battle of Mountain and Gironde, and what follows, is the battle of Fanaticisms and Miracles; unsuitable for cause and effect. The sound of it, to the mind, is as a hubbub of voices in distraction; little of articulate is to be gathered by long listening and studying; only battle-tumult, shouts of triumph, shrieks of despair .... So soon as History can philosophically delineate the conflagration of a kindled Fireship, she may try this other task. Here lay the bitumen-stratum, there the brimstone one; so ran the vein of gunpowder, of nitre, terebinth and foul grease: this, were she inquisitive enough, History might partly know. But how they acted and reacted below decks, one fire-stratum playing into the other, by its nature and the art of man, now when all hands ran raging, and the flames lashed high over shrouds and topmast: this let not History attempt.

The Fireship is old France, the old French Form of Life; her crew a Generation of men. Wild are their cries and their ragings there, like spirits tormented in that flame. But, on the whole, are they not *gone*, O Reader? Their Fireship and they, frightening the world, have sailed away; its flames and its thunders quite away, into the Deep of Time. One thing therefore History will do: pity them all; for it went hard with them all.

From Thomas Carlyle, *The French Revolution: A History*, ed. K. J. Fielding and D. Sorensen, 2 vols. in 1 (Oxford University Press, 1989), vol. II, 244–5.

History provides beneficial advice for state and national governments; in administering governments for common advantage, assuring security and internal peace and order for the general welfare. It revives a spirit of industry and progressive thought ... History also inspires society to great deeds ... [and] awakens a social consciousness.[22]

For some nineteenth-century thinkers, capital-H History – a recurrent character in a work like Carlyle's *French Revolution* where the personification is appealed to with frequency – was above all a progressive force demanding that its own story be told (Extract 30).[23] Although the general thrust of nineteenth-century historiography was towards critical scholarship and away from philosophical speculation, the period nevertheless spawned a number of schemes for the comprehensive explanation of the totality of the human past, often the creation of non-historians. The revelation of the ultimate direction of History would eventually be known as historical 'determinism', and while it had several celebrated practitioners (the English historian Henry Thomas Buckle (1821–62) for instance, see Extract 31), it was articulated most famously by Auguste Comte, G. W. F. Hegel and Karl Marx. The intellectual systems associated with these names were very different but they shared a belief in the inexorably forward momentum of human affairs.

31: Positivism and History: Buckle on Historiography

Of all the great branches of human knowledge, history is that upon which most has been written, and which has always been most popular. And it seems to be the general opinion that the success of historians has, on the whole, been equal to their industry; and that if on this subject much has been studied much also is understood ....

But if, on the other hand, we are to describe the use that has been made of these materials, we must draw a very different picture. The unfortunate peculiarity of the history of man is, that although its separate parts have been examined with considerable ability, hardly any one has attempted to combine them into a whole, and ascertain the way in which they are connected with each other. In all the other great fields of inquiry, the necessity of generalization is universally admitted, and noble efforts are being made to rise from particular facts in order to discover the laws by which those facts are governed. So far, however, is this from being the usual course of historians, that among them a strange idea prevails, that their business is merely to relate events, which they may occasionally enliven by such moral and political reflections as seem likely to be useful. ...

The establishment of this narrow standard has led to results very prejudicial to the progress of our knowledge .... [For] all the higher purposes of human thought history is still miserably deficient, and presents that confused and anarchical appearance natural to a subject of which the laws are unknown, and even the foundation unsettled ....

Whoever is at all acquainted with what has been done during the last two centuries, must be aware that every generation demonstrates some events to be regular and predictable, which the preceding generation had declared to be irregular and unpredictable .... This expectation of discovering regularity in the midst of confusion is so familiar to scientific men, that among the most eminent of them it becomes an article of faith: and if the same expectation is not generally found among historians, it must be ascribed partly to their being of inferior ability to the investigators of nature, and partly to the greater complexity of those social phenomena with which their studies are concerned.

Both these causes have retarded the creation of the science of history.

From H. T. Buckle, *History of Civilization in England,* 3 vols. (London: Longmans, Green and Co., 1872), vol. I, 1–9.

Comte, an estranged former disciple of Henri de Saint-Simon (see Box 26), developed a philosophy called 'positivism', the essential features of which are straightforward. Positivism assumes that progress is not only possible but inevitable; it ascribes such progress to forces other than providence; and it believes that human behaviour, hence History, operates according to 'laws' akin to the laws of the natural world. Comte had a training in mathematics that gave him a higher

Box 26   Henri de Saint-Simon

Both Marx and Comte were influenced by the early socialist thinker Henri de Saint-Simon (1760–1825), who had developed a theory of history as a kind of oscillating cycle between successive 'critical' and 'organic' periods. The first kind principally demolished the assumptions of earlier times – post-Socratic Greece, the Renaissance and the Enlightenment, for instance. 'Organic' periods were those of creative activity, such as the pre-Socratic period (later admired by Friedrich Nietzsche) and the Middle Ages, which would develop new philosophies and ways of living. Saint-Simon also asserted that there was a 'law' of progress governing the forward movement of History.

level of confidence in natural laws than those from a humanities background. Yet he had much in common with early nineteenth-century historical thought, especially romanticism. For Comte the key to understanding a current phenomenon (and its future development) lay in looking to its historical origins. His ideal 'positivist library' even included a section on history with a selection of authors from Herodotus to his own day. Comte's multivolume work known in English as the *Course in Positive Philosophy* (1830–42) outlined the entire history of human thought through three phases, a theological, a metaphysical and a positive age. There are smatterings here of Vico's eras of gods, heroes and men, of stadialism's changing modes of subsistence and of Condorcet's nine phases of History; looking further back, one can even glimpse the medieval mystic Joachim of Fiore's ages of Father, Son and Spirit.

The positive age, an era in which people would recognize the governing power of laws on human behaviour, lay ahead, and every mode of knowledge, every discipline, was following a parallel path through successive stages to wind up at this common destination. Aside from its socially deterministic metaphysics, Comte's theory carried with it an epistemology that viewed all forms of science (history among them) as progressive and cumulative. This has led to the application of the term 'positivist' to *any* historical thinking which assumes steady improvements in knowledge, akin to experimental progress in the natural sciences. The entire nineteenth-century Rankean approach to scholarship is thus sometimes referred to as 'positivist', a profoundly unhelpful expansion of its original meaning. It is somewhat more justly applied to the 'cumulative and steady improvement' model of historical scholarship, but even this analogy is problematic. To some degree, 'positivism' in the study of history has become in our own time a kind of scapegoat on to which the sins of all former 'naive' views of historical scholarship, especially evidentiary empiricism, can be heaped and then driven out into the intellectual desert of discredited ideas. Moreover, the vulgar use of the term unintentionally magnifies positivism's actual influence. Despite their impact on certain philosophical schools such as utilitarianism, and despite, too, their natural appeal to an age that took progress almost as an article of faith, Comtean ideas acquired relatively less purchase among western European and American historians in the nineteenth century than one might think, exceptions such as the English historian Buckle, the social Darwinist Herbert Spencer (1820–1903) and France's Hippolyte Taine (1828–93) aside, and even then only selectively. Asia and Latin America, we will see further on, provided rather more fertile ground. So would eastern Europe, where Comte offered an alternative to Marx: Russia's Miliukov, for instance, was an enthusiastic Comtean.

Positivism was one school of thought about the direction of History, German idealism another, beginning with Kant and Fichte and reaching its apogee with Hegel's philosophy of world history. History for that professor was the gradual self-realization of mind in time through a process of 'dialectic', the continuous conflict between thesis and antithesis and their resolution in synthesis. His views had roots in earlier Enlightenment thinkers, but Hegel decisively rejected – as Herder had earlier questioned – the long-standing classical notion that history was 'philosophy teaching by examples'. Instead, he substituted a different relation between history and philosophy, whereby the history *of* philosophy became in itself a story of progressions in human understanding as intellectual systems gave way to superior successors, marking the movement to self-consciousness of the World Spirit. History was not a teacher, or at least not a very good one. Rather, it was both a process and simultaneously a coherent narrative of that process. Moreover, though human history was universal, Hegel believed that attempts at universal history were problematic – ironically, what he called 'specialized history' (an approach to the whole through a particular subject such as art or law) was more likely to be fruitful. And it was the philosopher, not the historian, who had to work out History's meaning. Knowledge of this could not be complete until the end of History: the 'owl of Minerva', as he put it, spreads its wings only at dusk.[24]

In retrospect, Hegel seems now to have been to the early nineteenth century what Vico had been to the early eighteenth, a complex and often opaque academic who cannot be pigeonholed: he was neither a historian in the mode of Ranke, nor philosophically did his 'absolute idealism' become the dominant thread of philosophical metaphysics. But unlike Vico, Hegel did not toil away in obscurity, to be rescued by later generations. He was famous in his own time and attracted

Figure 50 | Berlin savants. Georg Wilhelm Friedrich Hegel (top centre) depicted with several stars of the early nineteenth-century Berlin intellectual firmament, including Wilhelm and Alexander von Humboldt. Lithograph, c. 1810, by Julius Schoppe.

prominent pupils or admiring disciples who became stars in their own right often by formulating views in reaction to their master. Despite his reputation as a conservative, he had a significant number of leftward-leaning associates. Foreign admirers included the French liberal philosopher Victor Cousin (1792–1867), a formative influence on the French historians Quinet and Michelet, and the principal conduit of Hegel's philosophy into Italy. Nearer home there were the 'Young Hegelians', a group that under Ludwig Feuerbach's (1804–72) influence inverted Hegel's idealist philosophy into a human-centred 'materialism'.

Hegel had been received coldly by his Berlin colleagues in 1818 (Fig. 50), and his ideas were controversial. A whole century's worth of foes would use him as the satanic symbol against which their own philosophies were formulated, from Søren Kierkegaard and Arthur Schopenhauer to Martin Heidegger and Bertrand Russell. And it is Hegel, more than any other nineteenth-century figure, who summarized two centuries' worth of European dismissal of non-Western cultures and especially of their lack of historicity, in the dual senses of having neither a sense of the past nor a place in the main plot of the human narrative: Africans and certain European peoples (the Slavs in particular) were thus both without *history* and of little significance to *History*. Only Asia (selectively) and Europe counted, and the latter lay at the more advanced end of History's road. Not surprisingly, this position too has been a lightning-rod for modern and postmodern criticisms of Eurocentrism and Orientalism, but in fairness to Hegel it should be pointed out that his reasons for adopting it were quite different from the conventional early modern and eighteenth-century ones – lack of alphabetic writing and overdependence on orality. For Hegel the key criterion of 'statehood' can alone confer status *in* History and generate the writing *of* history. 'It is the state which first supplies a content which not only lends itself to the prose of history but actually helps to produce it ... [and] thereby creates a record of its own development.'[25]

The most significant spinoff from Hegel's philosophy of history and its dialectical engine, if evaluated by sheer popular influence, must surely be its adaptation by the socialist and one-time Young Hegelian, Karl Marx (1818–83) into a materialist theory of economic and social change leading from primitive times, through feudal and capitalist phases, to communism and the triumph of the proletariat. With less obvious debts to the philosophy of Feuerbach (whose inconsistencies he severely criticized), the positivism of Comte (whom he viewed with contempt) and more remotely to Vico, Marx developed his philosophy of history piecemeal through early theoretical works such as *The German Ideology* (1846). He wrote at least one work that can be considered a political history, the *18th Brumaire of Louis Bonaparte* (1852) (the source of his famous remark, also derived from Hegel, that historical events occur twice, the first time as tragedy, the second time as farce). Without exception, no theory of history in modern times has had more sway, in terms of sheer numbers of adherents, especially among Marx's Russian, eastern European and Chinese admirers.

Marx either alone or with his associate Friedrich Engels (1820–95) was both prolific and complex, and no attempt at a full summary of his historical thought will be made here. His theories were never actually presented as a coherent system within a single work but are scattered across his vast œuvre. Generations of Marxist and non-Marxist scholars and ideologues have spilt copious amounts of ink, and more than a little blood, sorting it out. Concisely stated, the Marxian theory of History runs as follows. Mankind has passed or will pass through a series of social stages beginning with a primitive state in which the first form of association is the family, through the development of property and its exploitation, then to feudalism and eventually to capitalism before ending in a socialist state which marks the commencement of 'true' History. More specifically, Marx characterizes four epochs, the Asiatic (here borrowing the well-established concept of 'oriental despotism'), ancient, feudal and bourgeois, each defined by economic and social arrangements; only with the future fifth stage, after capitalism has collapsed, will a classless society emerge and will the engine of historical change be, as it were, turned off.

The movement from stage to stage or epoch to epoch is not unlike that proposed by the stadialists in the previous century, but any providential or supernatural element is completely removed, and it is less modes of *subsistence* than those of *production* that simultaneously constrain social arrangements and drive History forward. Transitions from one stage to another (that aspect which stadialism had never adequately explained) do not occur everywhere at the same time, nor at the same rate. They are not even absolutely inevitable in the strict sense, since in the Asiatic epoch there is little stimulus for development. Changes will sometimes occur because of external forces. More often, however, they happen due to interior contradictions and conflicts, especially class conflicts, which for Marx produce such phenomena as alienation, class-consciousness and ultimately revolution, the hammer striking home on the cocked pistol of change: Hegel's 'dialectic' is transposed from the realm of ideas down to that of economic and material life. The culmination of every stage of human existence is the resolution of the dialectic of conflict, and the acquisition of power by a previously subordinate class. The resulting new synthesis – the next stage – is however but a temporary stability as the dialectic will begin anew. All the more visible aspects of human life – political, religious, ideological – are like the one-tenth of an iceberg floating above the surface. They are but a 'superstructure' whose composition is predetermined by the material and economic 'base' on which it rests. In the course of outlining this theory, Marx articulated a number of essential concepts that have now influenced social, economic and historical analysis for well over a century, some of which have survived the collapse of European communism in the 1990s: the labour theory of value, primitive accumulation, class struggle and dictatorship of the proletariat, to name but a few.

Germany also produced other important theories concerning versions of thought about the unfolding of history, and about the nature of the historical discipline. The historian of Prussia and sometime theoretician J. G. Droysen (Fig. 51), though a believer in the possibility of improved historical knowledge, argued in his *Historik* (and its short and widely circulated summary, the *Grundriss der Historik*, 'Outline of the Principles of History') for a less naive view of the historian's relationship to sources.[26] A moderate critic of his former mentor, Ranke, Droysen thought that the cult of objectivity, along with its focus on source criticism, had taken history down the wrong path; his 'Historics' were intended to fill the role for the historical past occupied by Poetics in the imagined world of fiction. Droysen placed particular emphasis on the creative role of interpretation as guided by present-day circumstances and values and the need for firm and consistent methodological

Figure 51 | Johann Gustav Droysen. Anonymous photograph, c. 1870. A product of the University of Berlin, where Ranke presided, Droysen authored works of both history and the philosophy of history, including his influential *Outline of the Principles of History.*

rules. He was just as critical of historical positivists such as Britain's H. T. Buckle for their reduction of human actions and institutions to mere categories of the natural world.

Droysen had one foot in Rankean political history and another in philosophy. He is a member of the 'hermeneutic' tradition stretching back to the German theological schools of the eighteenth century and forward to our own time. A key element of hermeneutics is the belief that the situation or vantage point of the observer or interpreter of the past is critical to how he or she interprets evidence; different standpoints can reveal different truths, truth being unitary but multifaceted like one of Leibniz's monads. Wilhelm Dilthey (1833–1911) provided the definitive link within hermeneutics from the nineteenth to the twentieth century, and an equally important revision to the concept of historical knowledge. A turning away from the post-Rankean fetish of the document can be seen in Dilthey's assertion that history is a mental act of understanding (*Verstehen*) whereby the meaning of events must be intuited from our own inner experience; it cannot be lifted directly from the sources. As with Droysen's distinction between the world of nature, where there could only be endless recurrence, and that of history, where progress was possible, Dilthey's position was antipositivist, but more sharply so. Droysen had assumed that *Verstehen*, 'the most perfect form of cognition' available to humans, could still get at an objective reality. Dilthey, a generation younger, was less certain. On the one hand, he accepted something like the positivist view of the progress of man and the liberation over the centuries of learning from religion and metaphysics. On the other hand, he believed that the Rankeans had too easily rejected abstraction and had left themselves with an inadequate theory of knowledge incapable of offering a reasonable alternative to positivism. Moreover, Dilthey assumed that past events could be apprehended in a way that did not apply to the world of science, owing to our humanity shared with historical figures: history belonged to *Geisteswissenschaften*, the spiritual or moral sciences, not to *Naturwissenschaften*. In his *Introduction to the Human Sciences* (1883) Dilthey identified a problematic preoccupation, in place since the Renaissance, with the application to historical phenomena of principles of analysis derived from the study of nature; this had led to an under-recognition of their difference from natural phenomena, and thus to a poverty of historical theory.

In one way, Dilthey was reviving some of the premises of the classical didactic view of history, but taking them in an entirely different direction. Yes, there are fundamental common features among all people, but the utility of this fact lies in understanding the course of the past through human motives, not in deriving practical lessons from it. It was left to Wilhelm Windelband (1848–1915) to call down a heavy rain on the parade of historians who saw their discipline as a 'science'. In his rectorial address at the University of Strasbourg in 1894, Windelband rearticulated Aristotle's ancient principle that history deals in singularities, having the status of an 'ideographic' practice (representative of the unique and singular) rather than a 'nomothetic' or law-generating one. The distinction applied only to the 'modes of investigation' not to 'the contents of knowledge itself' since both history and natural science belonged under the larger umbrella of 'empirical sciences'. The ultimate aim of history 'is always to extract and reconstruct from the raw material of history the true shape of the past in robust and vital clarity. History produces images of men and human life in the total wealth and profusion of their uniquely peculiar forms and with their full and vital individuality preserved intact.'[27]

Not everyone was quite prepared to jettison the positivistic or 'scientistic' aspects of history, especially if they could broaden horizons beyond the state and politics. Or, indeed, if they could help to advance a nationalist agenda: the Greek Spyridon Lambros spoke in 1905 about the historian's duty being both scientific *and* national:

It is only the historian's pen that can compete with weapons. Therefore those nations which have not yet accomplished their high mission and achieved national unification should tie their potential national grandeur to two anchors: military organization and the development of historical studies .... [I]ndeed there is no greater companionship than the one between the historian's desk and the military camp.[28]

The fervent Romanian nationalist Alexandru Xenopol (1847–1920), who authored the first modern full-length history of his country, was determined to develop a science of history drawing from philosophy and the social sciences, though the one he ended up constructing, a mishmash of Dilthey and Windelband, was largely a retrospective attempt to describe his own work as 'scientific' in the face of its rejection by younger historians.

The Cultural and Social Alternatives to Ranke

What, one wonders, had become of the eighteenth century's approach to the history of man, to Voltaire's cultural perspective on the reign of Louis XIV and to the stadialist analysis of past societies? The nineteenth century's renewed focus on the political and the biographical appeared to have cast these aside along with its antithesis to systematic speculation in the mode of Hegel. This is not an altogether accurate picture, for the century did present some alternatives to Ranke, to European state-focused historiography and to the methodological limitations of both. These alternatives provide a route for the concerns of the Enlightenment into the twentieth century.

The first major challenge to the Rankean model had appeared in the work of a Swiss historian who had once attended Ranke's lectures at Berlin but who spent most of his life in Basel and Zurich. Jacob Burckhardt's (1818–97) most famous book, *The Civilization of the Renaissance in Italy*, was a brilliant study of the art and culture of the Renaissance, of the relationship of aesthetic to political life – he treated the 'state' as a 'work of art'– and of the rise of 'individualism'. The book remains one of those rare nineteenth-century histories still in print and regularly prescribed in courses on the Renaissance. In it Burckhardt practised, if he did not quite invent, a form of historical inquiry known as *Kulturgeschichte*, and it defied the conventions of the emerging discipline by eschewing narrative for a series of reflective essays on different aspects of the Renaissance. Though well received (Burckhardt was later offered, and declined, Ranke's chair in Berlin), his masterpiece remained *sui generis* for several decades.

The great French ancient historian of the mid-nineteenth century, Numa Denis Fustel de Coulanges (1830–89) offered another alternative. An impressive scholar, he falls into a sociological tradition of history that stretches from Comte to Max Weber. A moderate positivist, in the epistemological sense of the word, Fustel de Coulanges truly believed that history, through documents, could speak for itself and was an 'observational science'. He was far from averse to theory and generalization – his pupil Charles Seignobos was among those who thought his former master too devoted to systematic ideas – at the same time that he was a learned and erudite researcher, well known for his 1864 study of Greek and Roman religion, law and institutions, *La Cité antique* ('The Ancient City'). Yet both the theorizing and the erudition were home-grown: Fustel de Coulanges remained to the end of his days quite impervious to Rankean narrative or even to Niebuhrian *Altertumswissenschaft*. Others would eventually join him: near the end of the century, after the disaster of the Franco-Prussian war, German influences became increasingly suspect, and the First World War would magnify this trend. The erstwhile proponent of the Rankean seminar, Ernest Lavisse, a specialist in German history, even saw the development of proper training for French historians as an alternative means of 'fighting the Germans', though younger scholars like the medievalist Ferdinand Lot (1866–1952) still chafed at the inferiority of their nation's educational apparatus compared with the German universities.

A somewhat different challenge to the Rankean version of Germanic historiography came a generation later, and this time from within Germany itself. The notorious *Methodenstreit* or 'dispute about method' of the 1890s, set off by Karl Lamprecht (1856–1915), presaged some of the debates that have continued down to our own time. Critical of the neo-Rankeans of his own time, but more sympathetic to positivism than Droysen or Dilthey, Lamprecht proclaimed the need for a 'new' history. He cast doubt on the usefulness of history conceived as the account of leaders and particular events, as opposed to larger groups, and invoked the need for an alliance with the incipient social sciences, including psychology; he also argued that culture was the external expression of a people's collective soul (*Volksseele*). Lamprecht was a renegade in a number of senses. In 1895, he made an unsuccessful play for the vacant editorship of *Historische Zeitschrift*, proposing to amalgamate it with two other journals with which he was involved; he was outmanoeuvred by one of his fiercest critics, the future historian of *Historismus*, Meinecke, who contrived to put Treitschke into the position. Though marginalized by the German historiographic establishment during his career, Lamprecht was admired abroad: late nineteenth-century Scandinavian historians such as Troels-Lund could look to him as the father of their version of *Kulturgeschichte*, a less aesthetic and more populist pursuit than Burckhardt's a few decades previously. Lamprecht's own pupils would include the leading Romanian historian of the next generation, Nicolae Iorga (1871–1940), and following the Second World War a number of East German historians saw him as having provided an 'alternative to Ranke'. Lamprecht had other admirers in northern Europe, in particular two medievalists, the Belgian economic historian Henri Pirenne (1862–1935) and the Dutch cultural historian

Huizinga. They, in turn, provide important bridges from the turn of the century to later developments such as the Annales School and modern cultural history (see Chapter 9 below).

Lamprecht's ideas, and the hostile response to them, were a product of tensions, left unresolved at the end of the eighteenth century, between history and several neighbouring branches of knowledge, including psychology, economics, anthropology and sociology – the modern social sciences. The full consequences of this are still being worked out today on the borders between these subjects. Historically minded contemporaries, the philosopher Georg Simmel (1858–1918), the political economist Max Weber (1864–1920) and Émile Durkheim (1858–1917), a French former pupil of Fustel de Coulanges, were merging the study of the past with sociology, which has enjoyed a steady if rocky relationship with its parent discipline ever since. Economic historians were similarly turning (without the assistance of Karl Marx) to the history of material culture, industry and even labour; the economist Gustav von Schmoller (1838–1917) spoke for a German school of economics that saw historical data as the cornerstone of his own discipline. In America, Lamprechtian ideas found an audience in a generation of historians discontented with the agenda of American historiography. The brief assault on the supremacy of political history by Columbia University's James Harvey Robinson (1863–1936) and the 'New Historians' before and after the First World War, the critiques of nationalism and American exceptionalism by other New Historians such as Harry Elmer Barnes (1889–1968), and the work of Progressive Historians such as Carl Becker (1873–1945) and Charles Beard (1874–1948) would open the door to North American social history in the 1960s and 1970s.

Fin-de-siècle Uncertainties: Nietzsche

German historical thought was under duress from other sources than Lamprecht in the years leading up to the First World War. Windelband and Dilthey had, in different ways, drawn attention to the irrational aspects of human behaviour, though they had stopped short of challenging the belief that an objective, external, historical truth was attainable, a position which separates them quite firmly from superficially similar twentieth-century currents such as relativism and, later, postmodernism. For now, the epistemological moorings of historical writing were shaken but secure. On the metaphysical side it was a different story. The historical agency of 'spirit', 'providence', 'mind' and even God, so important for Hegel's or Ranke's predecessors and contemporaries, was fading fast in an era that included

Marxism, the rise of modern science and – at its close – the iconoclastic philosopher Friedrich Nietzsche.

Though he died on its very cusp, following a decade of debilitating mental illness, Nietzsche (1844–1900) is a figure more of the twentieth century than the nineteenth because his impact was overwhelmingly posthumous. Nietzsche's perspectives on history, culture and learning were the product of his philological training but took him to a position that largely repudiated four centuries of humanism. His 'genealogical' approach to the past, looking backwards through time for the origins of such things as modern morality or of reason have deeply affected late twentieth-century figures such as Michel Foucault. A friend of Richard Wagner the composer, and much influenced by Burckhardt, his views have become associated with totalitarian regimes and Nazism, a link the validity of which cannot detain us here. Although Nietzsche was arguably hostile to the entire nineteenth-century historiographical agenda (and was thus a major source for some of the late twentieth-century trends we will discuss nearer the end of this book), he was not indifferent to the past. As Hayden White comments, Nietzsche's views on history left professional historians as cold as did Hegel's, but for different reasons. Where Hegel's musings were often difficult to interpret as well as highly speculative, Nietzsche's were abundantly and menacingly clear. His purpose was 'to destroy belief in a historical past from which men might learn any single, substantial truth'.[29]

Nietzsche's opinions on History and history developed over the course of several major works, the English titles of which will be familiar to many readers, including *The Birth of Tragedy*, *The Genealogy of Morals* and especially the *Use and Abuse of History* or, to give the work its full name, 'On the Uses and Disadvantages of History for Life'.[30] History has witnessed cycles of progress and decay, beginning in a primitive barbarism, proceeding through the genius of pre-Socratic thought and especially Aeschylean tragedy, followed by a decline into the twin tyrannies of religion and science that have stifled creativity. Like Vico some 150 years earlier, Nietzsche saw his own age as part of a downward trajectory towards a future barbarism. The man-made world itself springs from the competition of two principles, the Dionysian force of chaotic, creative energy and the Apollonian force of order: both are necessary to the human condition and a superabundance of either is harmful. As far as historical knowledge is concerned, it is both a tool and a burden: a tool because it allows awareness of our debt to the past and a sense that there is a future superior state that can be struggled towards; a burden because it can prohibit us from living in the present and achieving great things in our time. Against the traditional equation of history with remembrance, and memory as an essential feature of humanity,

Nietzsche urges *forgetfulness* as a necessity, without which we cannot escape the endless process of becoming. In order to live, we must selectively forget, rather like putting on headphones to eliminate ambient noise.

History (the practice or the discipline) in turn can be found in three different forms, respectively reflecting man's tripartite existence as a being 'who acts and strives', 'who preserves and reveres' and 'who suffers and seeks deliverance': Nietzsche calls them respectively the Monumental, Antiquarian and Critical. The Monumental is the usual history of 'great men'. It teaches us that grand things were achievable in the past, and may be so again but its utility as a provider of relevant examples is limited because no two instances of greatness are the same, even if historians bludgeon them into the appearance of similarity. The Antiquarian form recovers the details of the past indiscriminately, seeking value in everything, and connections between everything. It occasions ossification or mummification if allowed to rule over the other two forms of history: it degenerates 'from the moment it is no longer animated and inspired by the fresh life of the present'. One can see in the description of these first two types of history Nietzsche's debt to earlier sceptical thought, both the Guicciardinian rejection of the comparability of historical events and the eighteenth-century rejection of erudition without social purpose, though Nietzsche takes these arguments further towards their logical extremes than his predecessors.

The third form, Critical history, brings the past before the tribunal of the present, 'scrupulously examining it and finally condemning it', not according to any principle of morality or justice but out of the sheer force of life, that 'dark, driving power that insatiably thirsts for itself'. Critical history necessarily dissolves any pre-existing story or process and takes the past as a pool of elements (or to use his preferred analogy, musical notes) that can be pieced together as needed to serve immediate moral and aesthetic goals, and as such, it is not necessary that history contain any factual truth at all. 'A historiography could be imagined which had in it not a drop of common empirical truth and yet could lay claim to the highest degree of objectivity.' Objectivity in history is in any case a chimera, because each individual must be free to extract what he needs from history in order to confront life, which is experienced only by subjective individuals. The ordinary historian protesting objectivity is thus little more than a hypocrite, whether 'the disguised egoists and party-men who employ an air of objectivity in pursuit of their crooked game' or simply 'those wholly thoughtless people who when they write history do so in the naive belief that all the popular views of precisely their own age are the right and just views .... [They] call all historiography "subjective" that does not accept these popular standards as canonical.'[31]

Too much or too little of any of these forms is harmful, as is a surfeit of history as a whole: the 'oversaturation' of an age with history is 'hostile and dangerous

32: Nietzsche on the Characteristics of the Historian

If you are to venture to interpret the past you can do so only out of the fullest exertion of the vigour of the present: only when you put forth your noblest qualities in all their strength will you divine what is worth knowing and preserving in the past. Like to like! Otherwise you will draw the past down to you. Do not believe historiography that does not spring from the head of the rarest minds; and you will know the quality of a mind when it is obliged to express something universal or to repeat something universally known: the genuine historian must possess the power to remint the universally known into something never heard of before, and to express the universal so simply and profoundly that the simplicity is lost in the profundity and the profundity in the simplicity. No one can be a great historian, an artist and a shallowpate at the same time: on the other hand, one should not underrate the workmen who sift and carry merely because they can certainly never become great historians; but even less should one confuse them with them, but regard them rather as the necessary apprentices and handymen in the service of the master .... These workmen are gradually to become great scholars, but cannot for that reason ever be masters. A great scholar and a great shallowpate – these two go rather better under one hat.

From Nietzsche, 'On the Uses and Disadvantages of History for Life', in his *Untimely Meditations*, trans. R. J. Hollingdale (Cambridge University Press, 1983), 94. Italics in original.

to life'. Yet we cannot live without history: some of it is necessary to human existence, and distinguishes us from the animal who lives in an endless moment (though with a 'degree of happiness' and without boredom or dissimulation). History is not for the weak, for it 'can be borne only by strong personalities' while lesser beings will be overwhelmed by it. History should also not be attempted by just anyone but by the 'experienced and superior man' – here Nietzsche is just as elitist as the historical establishment he purports to criticize (Extract 32). As to the derivation of 'laws' from history, it is a foolish pursuit that can generate only the most banal truths about the masses:

What, can statistics prove that there are laws in history? Laws? They certainly prove how vulgar and nauseatingly uniform the masses are: but are the effects of inertia, stupidity, mimicry, love and hunger to be called laws? Well, let us suppose they are: that, however, only goes to confirm the proposition that so far as there are laws in history the laws are worthless and the history is also worthless.[32]

Nietzsche's stress on the irrational, and his repudiation of much of the edifice of professional historiography, suggests that not all was well in Clio's European temple at the close of the nineteenth century.

CONCLUSION

But in her web she still delights
To weave the mirror's magic sights, …

Out flew the web and floated wide;
The mirror crack'd from side to side;
'The curse is come upon me,' cried
The Lady of Shalott.

Langlois and Seignobos' above-mentioned choice of the Eiffel Tower (1889), a triumph of nineteenth-century engineering, as a metaphor for the construction of history is unsurprising, given the frequency of the tower in Western culture as a symbol of human aspiration. But it is also an image of confinement. Alfred, Lord Tennyson would refer to another, fictional, tower in his Arthurian poem, first published in 1833, *The Lady of Shalott*. Tennyson was interested in the past, especially the medieval, though he was no historian. *The Lady of Shalott* unintentionally captures what was happening to history in the nineteenth century, and links the idea of the tower usefully with the present book's other recurring image, that of the mirror. In the poem, the imprisoned Lady, unable to peer directly at an inaccessible external reality beyond her room, on pain of a deadly curse, gazes at the outside world indirectly through her mirror, and records what she sees in her weaving. Succumbing to temptation, an impulsive decision to look directly through the window spells the Lady's doom.

Historians prior to the nineteenth century, like Tennyson's tower-bound Lady, had no direct view to an inaccessible past. The past was seen not only *as* an analogical mirror on to the present but, in a way, was itself observed *through* the present: past events could not be understood except by reference to modern ones, just as those modern ones were in turn viewed as reflections of the past; hermeneutic scholars recognized this with special clarity. In the nineteenth century, professional European historians began to gaze directly at the past – or so they convinced themselves – without the use of the mirror, having largely rejected the notion of an analogical connection between past and present events and with it the notion that the principal function and utility of history is in its provision of lessons for the present (even if the training of civil servants, officers and statesmen remained a useful benefit). They soon ceased to use the mirror at all and found in documentary sources that seemingly transparent window on to the past previously denied them – Ranke's *wie es eigentlich gewesen*. Unlike the Lady, they would continue to weave their web of narratives, representing what they saw. Having abandoned the mirror, they were unaware that the very disciplinary tower which they had constructed was in jeopardy, its foundations much less reliable than they had reckoned.

The title of this chapter refers to this broken mirror of the didactic view of history. While popular concepts of history occasionally allude to this belief in our own time, it has not had much allegiance in a historical profession that since the late nineteenth century has dominated the study of the past in a way that the most ardent Tang Mandarin could not have imagined possible. We seem now, Hayden White has observed, almost permanently stuck in an 'ironic' attitude to the past, a version of Vico's barbarism of reflection – or our version of the Lady of Shalott's curse. In the course of the twentieth century, doubt has shifted from the Lady's mirror to her web – the literary representation of 'observed' past reality, which has now floated wide, detached from its authors. At the same time that discarded mirror, once merely cracked, has been well and truly shattered. Paradoxically, its individual fragments would be pressed into service in the later twentieth century by the emerging sub-specializations of historical writing, each individual, jagged piece reflecting something different depending on the angle from which one gazes – a further extension, *in extremis*, of the hermeneutic stance. But we run here ahead of our own horse-drawn carriage, for our business with the nineteenth century is not yet concluded. It is time, first, to see how these confident Western developments played out in the rest of the world.

Notes

1 G. W. F. Hegel, *Lectures on the Philosophy of World History*, trans. H. B. Nisbet (Cambridge, 1975), 21.

2 Pim den Boer, *History as a Profession: The Study of History in France, 1818–1914*, trans. Arnold J. Pomarans (Princeton, NJ, 1998), 201.

3 Ibid., 124.

4 François-René de Chateaubriand, *The Genius of Christianity*, trans. C. I. White (Baltimore, 1856), Part Three, Book I, ch. 8, 385.

5 J. W. Burrow, *A Liberal Descent: Victorian Historians and the English Past* (Cambridge, 1981).

6 Leo Tolstoy, *War and Peace*, trans. R. Pevear and L. Volokhonsky (New York, 2007), vol. I, iii, xi, 258.

7 Not to be confused with the same-named artistic movement of the nineteenth century, which stressed a return to ancient style in architecture and painting.

8 Maciej Janowski, 'Mirrors for the Nation: Imagining the National Past among the Poles and Czechs in the Nineteenth and Twentieth Centuries', in Stefan Berger and Chris Lorenz (eds.), *The Contested Nation: Ethnicity, Class, Religion and Gender in National Histories* (Basingstoke, 2008), 455–6.

9 Walter Leitsch, 'East Europeans Studying History in Vienna (1855–1918)', in D. Deletant and H. Hanak (eds.), *Historians as Nation-Builders: Central and South-East Europe*

(London, 1988), 139–56, at 140–1. In the end Helfert got his wish for the study of *vaterländische Geschichte*, realized in the Institut für Österreichische Geschichtsforschung, established in 1854, while Vienna itself became the centre of gravity for apprentice historians from most of the empire.

10 Steven Bela Vardy, *Clio's Art in Hungary and in Hungarian-America* (Boulder, CO, 1985), 17.

11 Quoted in Irene Raab Epstein, *Gyula Szekfü: A Study in the Political Basis of Hungarian Historiography* (New York, 1987), 45.

12 Melissa K. Stockdale, 'The Idea of Development in Miliukov's Historical Thought', in Thomas D. Sanders (ed.), *Historiography of Imperial Russia: The Profession and Writing of History in a Multinational State* (London, 1999), 262.

13 Although Ranke's 'world' was largely confined to Europe, he was not uninterested in the rest of the planet; early in his career he expressed the view that Arabic was the most important language for world history apart from Latin, a view he abandoned in later life. I owe this point to Georg Iggers.

14 Ranke, *Sämmtliche Werke*, 54 vols. in 24 parts (Leipzig, 1868–90).

15 Georg G. Iggers, *The German Conception of History: The National Tradition of Historical Thought from Herder to the Present*, rev. edn (1968; Middletown, CT, 1983).

16 Leopold von Ranke, *History of the Reformation in Germany* (1905; reprinted London, 1972), xi.

17 Quoted in Leonard F. Krieger, *Ranke: The Meaning of History* (Chicago, 1977), 244.

18 On Seignobos, an aggressive advocate of the importance of history to public life and the democratic spirit, see den Boer, *History as a Profession*, 195ff., 247, 295–300; on Langlois, ibid., 301–4.

19 C. V. Langlois and C. Seignobos, *Introduction to the Study of History*, trans. G. G. Berry (New York, 1903), 211–12.

20 Ibid.

21 Proudhon quoted in Aaron Noland, 'History and Humanity: The Proudhonian Vision', in Hayden White (ed.), *The Uses of History: Essays in Intellectual and Social History Presented to William J. Bossenbrook* (Detroit, 1968), 63; and Poncelet quoted in Donald R. Kelley, *Historians and the Law in Postrevolutionary France* (Princeton, NJ, 1984), 56.

22 Joan S. Skurnowicz, *Romantic Nationalism and Liberalism: Joachim Lelewel and the Polish National Idea* (Boulder, CO, 1981), 24.

23 Though Carlyle's version of the Revolution was very nearly not told at all: on 6 March 1835 John Stuart Mill showed up at Carlyle's house and confessed that the whole first volume of the book, which Mill had been reading in manuscript, had been accidentally incinerated: John D. Rosenberg, *Carlyle and the Burden of History* (Oxford, 1985), 15.

24 Hegel, *Lectures*, trans. Nisbet, 23–4.

25 From the second draft (1830) of Hegel's lecture on the course of world history, in *Lectures*, trans. Nisbet, 136.

26 J. G. Droysen, *Outline of the Principles of History (Grundriss der Historik)*, trans. E. B. Andrews (Boston, 1893). The full work has been edited in a modern German edition,

Historik: historisch-kritische Ausgabe, ed. P. Leyh and H. W. Blanke, 3 vols. (Stuttgart-Bad Cannstatt, 1977–2008).

27 W. Windelband, 'History and Natural Science', trans. G. Oakes, *History and Theory* 19 (1980): 169–85, at 175, 177, 179.

28 Effi Gazi, *Scientific National History: The Greek Case in Comparative Perspective (1850–1920)* (Frankfurt, 2000), 84.

29 Hayden White, *Metahistory: The Historical Imagination in Nineteenth-Century Europe* (Baltimore, 1973), 332.

30 *Vom Nutzen und Nachteil der Historie für das Leben* (1874).

31 Nietzsche, 'On the Uses and Disadvantages of History for Life', in his *Untimely Meditations*, trans. R. J. Hollingdale (Cambridge, 1983), 75–6, 90–1.

32 Ibid., 83, 86, 113.

1749	Lê Quý Đôn's multivolume *Đại Việt thông sử* ('Complete History of Dai Viet') is published
c. 1801	'Abd al-Raḥmān al-Jabartī completes his *Maẓhar al-Taqdīs bi-Dhahāb Dawlat al-Faransis* ('The Demonstration of Piety in the Destruction of the French State')
1817	James Mill's *The History of British India* is published
1818	*Nong Chronicle* completed
1821–7	Carlos María de Bustamante's *Cuadro histórico de la revolución de la América Mexicana* ('A Historical Description of the Mexican Revolution') is published
1825	Date of earliest extant manuscript of *The Babad Dipanagara* ('Autobiographical History of Dipanagara')
1842	Wei Yuan completed his *Haiguo tuzhi* ('Illustrated Gazetteer of Maritime Nations')
1859	Bartolomé Mitre's *Historia de Belgrano y de la independence argentina* ('A History of [Manuel] Belgrano and Argentinian Independence') is published
1887	Ludwig Riess is appointed the first Professor of History in Tokyo Imperial University
1897	Samuel Johnson composes *The History of the Yorubas: From the Earliest Times to the Beginning of the British Protectorate*
1902	Liang Qichao's *Xin shixue* ('New Historiography') is published
1919	India establishes the Historical Records Commission
1928	He Bingsong's *Tongshi xinyi* ('New Principles of General History') is published; Shafīq Ghurbāl's *The Beginnings of the Egyptian Question and the Rise of Mehemet Ali* is published
1935	Mehmet Fuat Köprülü's *The Origins of the Ottoman Empire* is published
1942	Jawaharlal Nehru's *Glimpses of World History* is published

8

Clio's Empire
European historiography in Asia, the Americas and Africa

Introduction

European historical culture, the professionalization of which we have just recounted, reached the zenith of its influence over the rest of the world in the years between 1800 and 1945, at precisely the time that the countries which had developed disciplinary codes and institutions were also exercising political and intellectual sway over the rest of the globe. The tone was set at the very beginning of the nineteenth century with the Napoleonic empire. Short-lived though that regime proved, it spread French influence well beyond Europe, across the Mediterranean into Africa. The image on the present book's cover of Clio, the Greek muse of history, conversing with the nations of the world, signals that Europe's dominance of the globe would include sovereignty over perceptions of the past, and over the organization of its study. The conversion of history into a 'discipline' occurred at the very same time that the European metropolis was itself attempting to impose another kind of discipline on its periphery. From the peak of Napoleon's regime, through the convulsions of two World Wars, the history of the planet is one of large empires, some expanding and others in decline, exporting not only their own views of History but also their forms of historical writing and scholarship. This was the age of Clio's empire.

While the colonizers imposed their own 'regime of historicity' on directly subject territories – the use of history in schools and colonial colleges in Africa and India is the classic example – and on independent nations over whom they asserted various forms of economic or political influence, this was often a Conquest by invitation. As formidable as the collective Western imperial apparatus was, it could not have converted long-standing East Asian historiographies to 'modern' methods had there not been both an inclination on the part of reformers within those countries to adopt European practices, and a flexibility in, and variety among, those practices which made them adaptable to very different soil. Intellectuals such as China's Liang Qichao, who saw their countries outdistanced by the West on all fronts, thought traditional ways of doing history part of the problem, a prison-house of the past that neither narrated a story of social, political and economic advancement nor promoted a progressive future. In some parts of the world, the Enlightenment story of progress was embraced with enthusiasm, and even given either a Hegelian dialectic or Comtean positivist spin long discredited in its own homeland. Thus Puerto Rico's official historian Salvador Brau (1842–1912) commented in 1896 on the historian's purpose – to use the modern tools of historical understanding as a means of preserving national identity in a Brave New World:

Yes! We have a history and we must understand it in order to march ... with a firm and measured step to the future. We must make everyone understand this history so our regional character will distinguish itself ..., so no one will confuse us with any other people.[1]

From the point of view of the twentieth century, there is a certain inevitability to all this: of course, one instinctively thinks, Western methods and European genres triumphed, because the most progressive elements in African and oriental societies recognized their inherent superiority. There is plenty of evidence for this interpretation in the writings of non-Europeans themselves, who (at least at first) enthusiastically jumped aboard the steaming train of Western historical methods. Legend, myth and error should be uprooted and excised from accounts of the past, and rigorous criticism applied to evidence as a precursor to narrating a forward-marching story. Where surveys of the history of historical writing have paid any attention to histories outside Europe and the United States, the spread of Clio's empire looks to have been quite unstoppable. Europe, after centuries of debate on how best to do history, seemed at last to have put its house in order – imposed 'discipline' on the study of the past – with the advent of Rankean scholarly practices, the secularization of historical learning and its institutionalization in universities, journals, textbooks, learned societies and book reviews. If Europe was still hopelessly divided politically, it at least seemed to speak increasingly with one voice historiographically – an optical illusion of concord created by distance and by language. Who could resist such a juggernaut? Who, being shown the light, would want to?

A comprehensive survey of the spread of Western historiography to Asia, Africa, Australia and Latin America in this period would require a book on its own. We must settle here for a selective analysis, using a few regions to illustrate the differing ways in which Clio extended her dominions. A good place to begin is a part of the world, British India, where the imperial power found itself in need of displacing not one but several pre-existing modes of historicity.

A Case Study of Historical Imperialism: British India

The transformation of historiography in India through to independence in 1947 illustrates both a successful process of Westernization and its ultimate deployment against the colonizer. By 1800, the last remnants of the Mughal Empire had been gone for decades, and British colonial rule had been established over most of the subcontinent, in some instances mediated through local potentates. One of the first of the colonial commentators to write on Indian history – without ever setting foot in South Asia – was James Mill (1773–1836). A product of the Scottish educational system bequeathed by Robertson, Millar and Smith, Mill was also a close associate of the English utilitarian Jeremy Bentham, and father to the more famous John Stuart Mill. In 1817 Mill *père* published the work for which he is best remembered, *The History of British India*. It is a work of interest for many reasons. It departed from the Orientalism of the late eighteenth century, as expressed by the philologist Sir William Jones (see Chapter 6 above), in abandoning the treatment of India as quaint, different and incomparable, if inferior. Instead, it articulated a different, Robertsonian vision which viewed India through the lens of world history as a backward land with great potential but in need of reform along utilitarian lines. A critic of the British interventions in India to date, Mill saw the subcontinent as a great laboratory for Benthamite social experiments; India's recent past also permitted him an opportunity to comment on the present mores and values of his own country. His lack of direct experience, or of any of Jones's philological knowledge, was to Mill a great strength since it would permit a more dispassionate, objective analysis of the subject than could be made by those who had lived in India or spoke its languages.

The History of British India both spawned a century of imperial historiography and itself influenced colonial policy quite directly; its very lack of depth and original research paradoxically made it the ideal explanatory tool of colonialism in India. It also presented the most infamous dismissal of indigenous Hindu historicity, compared with that of Islam.

Compare the Mahabharata, the great narrative poem of the Hindus, with the Shah Nama, the great narrative poem of the Persians; the departure from nature and probability is less wild and extravagant; the incidents are less foolish; the fictions are more ingenious; all to a great degree, in the work of the Mahomedan author, than in that of the Hindu. But the grand article in which the superiority of the Mahomedans appears is history. As all our knowledge is built upon experience, the recordation of the past for the guidance of the future is one of the effects in which the utility of the art of writing principally consists. Of this most important branch of literature the Hindus were totally destitute. Among the Mahomedans of India the art of composing history has been carried to greater perfection than in any other part of Asia.[2]

Mill went well beyond Jones, who despite his empiricism and insistence on the differences between history and myth, had believed that 'some rays of historical truth' could be gleaned from puranic sources. But Mill's harder line with such materials would not be unique. The most respected British historian of the first half of the century, Thomas Babington Macaulay (1800–59), who thought Mill's book the finest history since Gibbon, reiterated the familiar notion that measured oriental cultural inferiority by its historiographic failures, for instance claiming in 1834 that 'all the historical information which has been collected from all the books written in the Sanskrit language is less valuable than what may be found in the paltry abridgements used at preparatory schools in England'.[3]

Many of the colonial writers on India's past were historians by accident, company employees or civil servants whose careers had given them purview of India, whether or not they actually spent any time there. Mill himself was a functionary at the East India Company's London office; Henry Beveridge (1799–1863), a failed Edinburgh lawyer-turned-professional writer, was engaged by the publishers Blackie and Sons to write a *Comprehensive History of India*, which he produced in three volumes (1858–63), also without leaving British shores. Among those who actually visited India, Mountstuart Elphinstone (1779–1859) authored a *History of India: The Hindu and Mahometan Periods* (1841) widely used in Indian education (and much more sympathetic to India's past than Mill's account). Elphinstone was governor of Bombay for eight years; his assistant Grant Duff (1789–1858), who had dealings with the Marathas and access to official documents, would write an extensive history of that people (1826). At the end of the century, Sir Alfred Lyall (1835–1911) resident in Rajputana and then secretary to the government in India, used his knowledge to narrate *The Rise and Expansion of British Dominion in India* (1893). In the early twentieth century, the pattern would continue with Vincent Arthur Smith (1848–1920), a Dubliner who spent thirty years in the Indian civil service. His *Early History of India* (1904) and *Oxford History of India* (1918) show the influence of a century of scholarly change in Europe, while still maintaining a firm conviction that an understanding of the past could help to solve present problems. By the time the Raj ended in 1947, several more such works could be added, including H. G. Rawlinson's (1880–1957) *British Achievement in India* (1948).

Smith's *Oxford History* would be especially influential as a school textbook. However, a Westernized Indian historical writing was not the exclusive property of the occupier. Indians themselves were encouraged to write their own history according to European models. Perhaps the first Western-style history of India to be published in a native language was *Rājā Pratāpāditya-Charit* ('Life of Raja Pratapaditya', 1802), written in Bangla by one Ramram Basu (c. 1751–1813) at the request of the missionary William Carey, who needed textbooks for the newly established Fort William College. Basu deliberately distanced himself from both the Hindu and Persian-Mughal historians who had preceded him, signifying his assent to the colonizers' preferred ways of representing the past, though he could not personally read English. His honorary membership in the 'club' of historians was acknowledged in Carey's own declaration of the work as a real history. As Ranajit Guha has observed, some years before Hegel's pronouncement that India lay beyond the frontier of world history, one of its own had 'sneaked across the border' into the historiographical pale.[4]

In the course of the century, many other Indians were co-opted by imperial institutions and took up the charge of writing their own history. Some did it in order to promote Indian identity and to criticize the Raj, including the novelists Bankim Chandra Chatterjee (or Chattopadhyay, 1838–94) and Rabindranath Tagore (1861–1941). Chatterjee was among a number of authors for whom fictional narratives based upon historical materials provided an opportunity to present the past in ways that appealed to embryonic national sentiment. Elsewhere, however, he would lament the apparent absence of Indian history. This deficiency had retarded India's political regeneration, and he urged a collective effort to fill the gap, and especially to create histories that stressed past heroic achievements by Indians. Others agreed that there was a deplorable absence of national history but, convinced of history's necessity to civilization, could not accept that this had always been the case. Surendranath Banerjea (1848–1925) posited that in very remote times, Indians, especially ancient Aryans, had indeed recorded the glories of their times in histories. It was the cumulative effect of centuries of subjugation to different empires, above all that of the Mughals, that had sadly resulted in the destruction of these books.

The language of these Western-style histories varied, with some like Gauri Shankar Hirachand Ojha (1863–1947) writing substantive works in Hindi or other Indian tongues. As Chatterjee's patriotic call suggests, some used their historical writings as vessels for an emergent Indian national consciousness, especially near the end of the nineteenth century and into the early twentieth, turning history into a form of resistance. The Hindu nationalist Vinayak Damodar Savarkar (1883–1966), for instance, represented the Indian Mutiny of 1857 as *The Indian War of Independence* (1909). Unsurprisingly, it was banned by British authorities. He was also among the earliest to assert, against the tide, that the ancient Hindus had indeed produced histories (other than supposititious ones destroyed by Muslims), echoing Jones's validation of the great historical epics. Muslim historians resented the manner in which their previously dominant culture and religion had been sidelined by British colonial scholars who, since Jones's day, had been much more interested in

Hindu India. They, too, looked to the past for reminders of their past greatness, which included Islamic historical writing. In the longer run, this trend
deepened the tensions between Hindu and Muslim that have plagued the subcontinent since 1947.

Regardless of their political leanings, Indian historians mainly looked westward
for models and methods. They adopted both the practices of European historians
and the civilizing agenda of the British, with the former being closely linked to
the promotion of the latter. English historical works were translated into Indian
vernaculars; Raja Shiva Prasad (1823–90), among the translators, also wrote his
own *Itihas Timirnasak* (1864, a title that literally means 'History as Destroyer of
Darkness'; the work itself is a Hindi history of India), intended to highlight both
the fact of historical change and the certainty, linked to British influence, of India's future progress. His disciple Harishchandra of Benares (1850–85) accepted
the need for progress, and saw historical study as one of its agents, though he
envisaged India's ultimate emancipation from the British who were despoiling the
country of its wealth. The essential point is this: it was neither necessary to endorse the colonial agenda nor even to support the Raj in order to see both history
and History in Western terms. As an orientalizer, Mill had a successor of whom he
might have been proud in Bankim Chatterjee's call in 1874 for an 'Indian historiography of India'. In fact, the very adoption of British historical methods and the
spread of historical textbooks played a not insignificant part during the nineteenth
century in manufacturing precisely that nationalist sense of India, transcending
regional or linguistic variations, and no longer dependent on myths of common
descent, that would ultimately bring down the colonial edifice. The British had
introduced to India the notion that there is a modern, correct way of telling the
past, derived from European models, and empowered Indian national consciousness in the process.

Late Victorian notions of 'scientific history' migrated into India during the first
third of the twentieth century through British-trained Indian historians returning
home to teach. In part owing to the influence of technically proficient scholars
such as the Sanskrit philologist Sir R. G. Bhandarkar (1837–1925), his son, D. R.
Bhandarkar (1875–1950), an epigrapher and numismatist, and the Mughal-period
scholar Sir Jadunath Sarkar (1870–1958), the institutional apparatus of Western
historiography gradually emerged, beginning with the Historical Records Commission of 1919 and the Indian History Congress established in 1937–8. Historiographical trends in Europe were replicated abroad: the success of economic
history in establishing itself as virtually a parallel discipline in late nineteenth-
century Britain was echoed in India by the retired Indian civil service officer
Romesh Chunder (or Chandra) Dutt's (1845 or 1848–1909) *Economic History of
India* (1902–4).

33: Europe and the Awakening of Indian National Self-Consciousness: K. M. Panikkar

This cult of the nation required in many cases a new historical background, for without a common history a nation cannot exist. In many Asian countries, especially India, such a history with a national purpose seemed hardly to exist. India had an undoubted geographical, cultural, social and even religious unity in the sense that all through its history ran the main thread of Hindu religious development. But political history was practically unknown except as myths and legends. From the identification of Sandrocottus as Chandragupta Maurya to the excavations of Mohenjodaro and Harappa, from the deciphering of the inscriptions of Asoka to the comprehensive survey of epigraphic records all over India, the material for the writing of Indian history was provided by the work of European scholars. Even more striking is the case of Indonesia, where a few European scholars, mostly Dutch, reconstructed from inscriptions the history of the great empires of Java and Sumatra which provided Indonesian nationalism with a solid historical basis. In this sense it cannot be denied that European scholars and thinkers, by their labours in the interests of knowledge, enabled India, Ceylon and Indonesia to think in terms of historic continuity.

From K. M. Panikkar, *Asia and Western Dominance* (London: Allen and Unwin, 1953), 492.

Many of these works were written from a nationalist, even moderately anti-colonial perspective, which would flourish in the 1930s and 1940s and achieve greater prominence after 1947. India's first post-independence president, Rajendra Prasad, publicly called for a history that covered the heroic ancient past as well as the more recent struggles; the country's first prime minister, Jawaharlal Nehru had personally written his *Glimpses of World History* (published in 1942) while imprisoned a decade earlier. The production of critical editions of original texts in India also played its part in the nationalization of the past, as it had done in nineteenth-century Europe. Several attempts at multivolume histories of India proved abortive, but advocates such as the novelist Kanaiyalal Maneklal Munshi promoted a Hindu rediscovery of their ancestral, pre-Islamic past. Following independence in 1947, Munshi called for a new history of India which, on this occasion, under the direction of Ramesh Chandra Majumdar (1888–1975), resulted in *The History and Culture of the Indian People* (11 vols., 1951–69). History, the tool of the colonizer, had become an instrument of liberation for India's political elites, though not as yet for the massive 'subaltern' population beneath them. A British-educated Indian lawyer, journalist and diplomat, Kavalam Madhava Panikkar (1894–1963), would make this point in 1953, incidentally anticipating the postcolonial scholarship of a later generation, in a book entitled *Asia and Western Dominance* (Extract 33).

History and Nation-Formation in Latin America

Nineteenth-century Latin America represents a very different case than India. Colonization there was much more advanced, and a European population had by the late eighteenth century intermixed and intermarried with a native one to produce a distinctive Creole society. By 1799, when Alexander von Humboldt arrived in what is now Venezuela to begin the travels and observations that would make him famous, Central and South America were very different places than Cortés and Pizarro had found 300 years previously. A multitude of provinces now existed where there had once been only New Spain and Peru. Cities with large populations had emerged as commercial powers or major ports, from Lima to Buenos Aires to Havana. In the Caribbean, where Spain shared influence with Britain and France, indigenous populations had been virtually wiped out long before but a large black slave population had taken their place. In the course of the 1810s and 1820s the colonies one by one left Spain's imperial orbit, in the process reconfiguring themselves into more or less the modern nations of South America. To the north, Mexico achieved her independence, following twelve years of civil war, in 1821; Central America followed suit, initially as a united federal republic, in 1823. Brazil declared independence in 1822, a fact recognized in 1825 by Portugal. The often bloody political changes that followed as various imperial and constitutional experiments unfolded cannot concern us here, but with few exceptions (Canada, British Honduras (now Belize) and significant parts of the Caribbean), the American hemisphere was now politically detached from its European masters.

New regimes, as we have seen on other occasions in this book, feel an urgent need to rewrite their history into forms that legitimize their power through stories fashioned to make their triumph seem inevitable, while trivializing or demoting to the footnotes other events, countervailing tendencies or rival factions. Where not only the government but the whole country is newly minted, that urgency is doubled: a history must be constructed that will cement the bonds between citizens and their new state and nurture nationalist loyalties and patriotism. Traditions must be revived, rediscovered, or even invented outright.[5] The enthusiasm for history, for document collection and for the establishment of private libraries that followed the struggles for independence in parts of Latin America would be invoked by politicians of various stripes throughout the nineteenth century, much as it had in the nationalist movements within Europe at about the same time. History, Argentina's former president Bartolomé Mitre told a constitutional convention in 1871, 'always ought to be open before our eyes, as a living lesson which teaches us to govern our conduct and our laws'.[6]

In this environment, military and political heroes, whether successful rebels or brave martyrs, a George Washington, a Simon Bolívar, a Juan Facundo Quiroga, were often transformed from real historical figures into legendary icons. At the same time, old grievances and recent atrocities needed to be publicly confessed in order that they could then be forgotten or at least set aside (a pattern that continues today with 'truth and reconciliation commissions'). The ghosts of the past were often hard to lay, and in the non-Anglophone Americas, old episodes such as the Conquests continued to dominate popular consciousness. The Mexican politician–historian Carlos María de Bustamante (1774–1848) would devote himself to the republication of older histories by Alva Ixtlilxóchitl, Gómara and Sahagún, and his own *Cuadro histórico de la revolución de la América Mexicana* ('A Historical Description of the Mexican Revolution', 1821–7) is haunted by the conquistadors and their victims.

Throughout Latin America, there had been a steady flow of historical writing in both Spanish and Portuguese areas since the Conquests of the sixteenth century, a good deal of it by expatriate Spaniards such as the Jesuit historian of Paraguay, Pedro Lozano (1697–1752). The liberal values of the late Enlightenment continued to inform the writing of history during the nineteenth century, first in the work of constitutionalist historians who focused on the European-inherited legal institutions underlying independence, and later in a more autonomous and romantic kind of writing that, following Herder and Michelet, emphasized instead the importance of the spirit of the people in establishing well-functioning new societies in a postcolonial era. The biographer of Argentina's Facundo, Domingo Faustino Sarmiento (1811–88), himself a future Argentine president, was well versed in French liberal historians and in Enlightenment thought. Explaining the process of nation-formation, Sarmiento positioned the violent recent history of his country (and by extension of much of the rest of the continent) as a conflict between *civilización y barbarie* (civilization and barbarism) – incidentally associating the latter with a heroic oral history recounted by *gaucho* 'cantors' (Extract 34). The Chilean Literary Society of the 1830s held regular meetings in which selections from Herder and other eighteenth-century historians were read. European historians were heavily utilized in the highly politicized task of writing books for schoolchildren. The liberal and anticlerical Chilean historian Diego Barros Arana (1830–1907), deliberating on textbook choices in the 1850s, criticized one because it had plagiarized whole paragraphs from Robertson. The committee of which Barros Arana was a member eventually settled on the safe choice of a French work, Victor Duruy's (1811–94) *L'abregé d'histoire universelle* ('Course of Universal History'), to supply the role of a general textbook, supplemented by Barros Arana's own two-volume *Compendio de historia de América* ('Compendium of the History of America', 1865). A third and later group emulated the positivism of Comte,

34: Barbarism and Civilization: Domingo Faustino Sarmiento

And now we have the idealization of this life of resistance, civilization, barbarism, and danger. The gaucho Cantor corresponds to the singer, bard, or troubadour of the Middle Ages, and moves in the same scenes, amidst the struggles of the cities with provincial feudalism, between the life which is passing away and the new life gradually arising ....

The Cantor is performing in his simple way the same labor of recording customs, history, and biography, which was performed by the medieval bard, and his verses would hereafter be collected as documents and authorities for the future historian, but that there [sic] stands beside him another more cultivated form of society with a knowledge of events superior to that displayed by this less favored chronicler in his artless rhapsodies. Two distinct forms of civilization meet upon a common ground in the Argentine Republic: one, still in its infancy, which, ignorant of that so far above it, goes on repeating the crude efforts of the Middle Ages; the other, disregarding what lies at its feet, while it strives to realize in itself the latest results of European civilization; the nineteenth and twelfth centuries dwell together – one inside the cities, the other without them.

From Sarmiento, *Life in the Argentine Republic in the Days of the Tyrants; Or, Civilization and Barbarism*, trans. Mary Mann (1868); (repr. New York: Hafner Press [1972]), 41–2. In this passage, Sarmiento associates the rural, romantic and heroic (but barbarous and violent) life of the *gaucho* or mestizo with the itinerant minstrelsy of the *Cantor* which he contextualized within the eighteenth-century stadial system as representing the 'shepherd state'. This he juxtaposed against the civilization represented by cities, industry and commerce of which he was a passionate advocate. He thus both continues the earlier European bias against oral sources, though in the end is not completely unsympathetic to them. Ironically, Sarmiento resorted frequently to anecdote, report and undocumented tradition as well as to written sources in recounting herein the life of the *caudillo* hero-martyr Juan Facundo Quiroga (d. 1835).

Buckle and Spencer in promoting a history that demonstrated the economic and scientific progress of the region along European industrial lines – knowledge of the past, said Vicente Fidel López in the 1840s, would allow planning for the future. The Chilean José Victorino Lastarria (1817–88) found in Comte an endorsement of his own ideas. The Brazilian historian João Capistrano de Abreu (1853–1927), influenced as a young man by Buckle and Taine, pursued a positivist line in his early work, only to be convinced, once he had spent time in the Biblioteca Nacional, that German *Historismus* offered a more attractive approach.

Journalism and fiction played a part in the popularization of history in Latin America. The novels of Walter Scott and Victor Hugo were read early in the century, and home-grown novelists such as Salomé Jil (pen-name of José Milla y Vidaurre, 1822–82, official historian of the republic of Guatemala from 1776 till his death) wrote their own historical fiction while at the same time championing

35: The Boundaries of History and Fiction: José Milla (1822–82)

In writing this novel, my principal objective has been to make known some personalities and certain historical events of which the majority of the readers to whom these lines are dedicated have no more than a very scant knowledge. I have adhered to the truth up to that point where the need to give some dramatic interest to the novel seemed indicated .... In our ancient Chronicles the characters of the people and the references to the events are found described in the most summary manner. Respecting this or that chronicle wherever possible, I have let my pen run freely in everything that did not involve anachronisms (which I consider unpardonable, even in this class of works), and in that which was not directly opposed to historical truth. Thus, the personalities that figure in this relation all really did exist, but the characters and the deeds attributed to some of them correspond to the fictional part of the work. In order not to be too diffuse, not to distract the reader with notes, I have not cited the passages to prove the accuracy of many of the events related.

From Milla's foreword to his first historical novel, *La Hija del Adelantado* ('The Daughter of Adelantado'), published in instalments in 1866 in the journal *Semana*. The novel concerns the daughter of a real-life figure, Pedro de Alvarado (1495–1541), governor of Guatemala. The selection (in English) is quoted in Walter A. Payne, *A Central American Historian: José Milla (1822–1882)* (Gainesville, FL: University of Florida Press, 1957), 40. Reprinted with permission of the University Press of Florida.

the publication of documents and the writing of national history (Extract 35). 'Professional' history in a Germanic key was slower to arrive, and not always popular. Gabriel René-Moreno (1836–1908), credited with introducing archival research techniques to Bolivia, had few imitators for half a century after his death, and as late as 1962 was less well known in his country than the world historian Arnold J. Toynbee. That being said, Latin American universities – many of them dating back to the early post-Conquest era – became centres of historiographical activity far earlier than their counterparts in Asia or Africa.[7]

Elsewhere in South America an intense debate concerning the proper method of history-writing followed the publication of Claude Gay's (1800–73) political history of Chile. Gay, a French botanist, was commissioned by the Chilean government to write this work, and despite its endorsement by the respected Venezuelan man of letters Andrés Bello (1781–1865), younger writers (including Bello's Chilean pupil, Lastarria) found unsatisfactory its recitation of facts without a unifying interpretation; Bello's pleas for objective history in the 1840s were ultimately ground under the wheels of polemical and ideological needs. Finally, there were those who sought meaning and instruction in the patriots of the South American past, drawing literary inspiration from across the Atlantic and, increasingly, from the United States. America, with a head start in both independence and the establishment of its own imperial ambitions throughout the hemisphere, exercised a potent influence on the writing of Latin American history, beginning with the novelist Washington Irving's *Life and Voyages of Christopher Columbus* (1828) and continuing with William Hickling Prescott's heroic retelling of the conquests of Mexico and Peru. The Francophile Argentine historian Bartolomé Mitre (1821–1906, president of his country 1862–8) was so taken with Prescott that he translated the latter's *History of Peru* into Spanish. Initially enamoured of positivism, and especially Buckle, Mitre also admired Voltaire and Michelet. In the end, though, Mitre gravitated towards Thomas Carlyle's 'great man' interpretation of history. His own account of Argentine independence focused on the careers of its leaders, the revolutionary heroes Manuel Belgrano and José de San Martín. Chile's Benjamín Vicuña Mackenna, similarly influenced by Carlyle, became a prolific biographer whose approach frequently got him into trouble with relations or descendants of the lesser mortals who were eclipsed in the aura of his heroes. In short, while the extent of European and North American influence on Latin American historiography was considerable, no single model or approach, including German practices, would achieve dominance, and history remained very much the domain of journalists and public intellectuals as much as academics. In part this may be attributed to Latin American attitudes to their European connections. Despite independence, they continued to view themselves as offspring of a European family tree. The historical practices and methods they imported from Europe were not those of an alien imperial presence but rather those of cousins. Consequently, they had an 'inside' view of European historiography, complete with all its variations and nuances, and were disinclined to privilege one model to the exclusion of others.

The Multiplicity of Historical Forms in Southeast Asia: Cambodia, Burma and Indonesia

The same could not be said of observers in other parts of the world, where Western historiography seemed rather more monolithically alien, even to its local admirers. Over the course of 150 years, from the late eighteenth to the early twentieth centuries, modern European genres displaced or marginalized, sometimes almost to the point of extinction, indigenous forms of history. This replicated on a grander scale the process we saw earlier in the early modern Americas, a process which also unfolded in the 'settler' societies of South Africa, Canada and Australasia, at the expense of the aboriginal populations' property and their pasts (see Box 27).

Box 27   Settler Historiographies

An overlooked category of national historiography produced in this period that displaced indigenous forms is that created in 'settler societies'. These are socie-ties in which a significant European immigrant population cultivated and cleared a new land, in the process seizing territory from and asserting superiority over an indigenous population which it then reduced in size. Nineteenth-century Canada, Australasia and South Africa are good examples of these societies because (unlike the different colonial experience of Asia or other parts of Africa) their so-called settler populations constructed a history for themselves that differed from that of the indigenous populations and while also marking out a separate path from that of the mother country. In South Africa, to give just one example, the indigenous black African oral tradition, a subset of which dealt specifically with historical events and genealogical details, was entirely ignored by the 'Settler School' of white historians in favour of an Afrikaner nationalist tradition of history-writing focused on the emergence of the Cape Colony into an independent Anglo-Boer nation. This tradition became consolidated in the historical writings of the Canadian-born George McCall Theal (1837–1919) whose major aim was to provide a narrative that would unite Boer and British settlers into a single nation. The indigenous African populations were not entirely excluded from his histories but rather deemed major beneficiaries of European intrusions, which had rescued them from millennia of savagery and despotism during which they had achieved virtually nothing. Theal's work in particular and much settler historiography in general was the product of a long-standing line of thought, dating from sixteenth-century conquests but culmi-nating in the 'White Man's Burden' of the nineteenth century.

Southeast Asia was slower to experience this culling of historiographical genres. Because the region has been hitherto unexplored in this book, some chronologi-cal backtracking to take account of its early history is necessary, as is immediate recognition of its linguistic and ethnic complexity. In Burma (now Myanmar), for instance, proximity to both China and India ensured exposure to the liter-ary, religious and historical cultures of both, as well as, from about 1200, Islam, which between the twelfth and fourteenth centuries had also pushed aside Bud-dhism and Hinduism in the southern Malay peninsula, parts of Java and the

Philippines. In comparison with Islam and the older religions, Christianity would be a latecomer to the region, arriving in the sixteenth century, initially with little widespread success; Western historicity would be even tardier in its appearance. Throughout the eighteenth and the first half of the nineteenth centuries, European administrators in parts of Southeast Asia introduced audiences at home to histories of the new colonies, while also quietly beginning the process that exploited, and eventually marginalized, the indigenous histories that they were required to use. As in India, local elites were eventually co-opted into the usage of Western genres. Among the early imperial powers, the Dutch gave the history of their 'East Indies' especially close attention. Beginning with encyclopedists such as François Valentijn (1656–1727), Dutch East India Company merchants had published historical information on the archipelago. In 1800, the Company ceased to exist and the short-lived Batavian Republic (that had succeeded the old Republic of the United Netherlands in 1795) took over direct administration of overseas possessions. Within a generation the Dutch had lost the last vestiges of their empire on the continental mainland of Asia, focusing colonial historians' attention largely on the archipelago.

Throughout Southeast Asia, historical writing had developed patchily prior to the early modern period. Despite over a millennium of literacy among its elite, Cambodia developed rather little that could be called historiography prior to 1700. The situation improved somewhat thereafter with the writing of *pangsavatar* (sometimes rendered *bangsavatar*), which can loosely be described as chronicles, though their factual veracity for early periods has been challenged. There are a few specimens from the nineteenth century such as the *Nong Chronicle* (comp. 1818),[8] which covers the years 1414–1800 and refers to an earlier chronicle that had by then been lost. Late exemplars of this form survive from the end of the colonial regime, under King Sisowath Monivong (r. 1927–41) and his grandson Norodom Sihanouk (b. 1922). Such histories or palace chronicles (*rajabangsava-tar*) as did exist were generally deemed unpublishable regalia (a feature of some Laotian and Javanese works of similar vintage), sometimes composed as part of royal restorations; strict crown control discouraged scholarship prior to the country's independence. The major Cambodian work from the early twentieth century is the *Tiounn Chronicle* (so-named for Tiounn or Thiounn, a powerful pro-French minister who directed its compilation) composed first from 1903 to 1907 and then from 1928 to 1934; this was based on a range of earlier materials. Under the French, European methods were gradually introduced, but Cambodian history was given low curricular priority. French scholars such as George Cœdès (1886–1969) devoted far more attention to the country's history than did its own inhabitants; foreign history was ignored altogether. *Pangsavatar*, which were never intended for performance or to entertain, did not circulate widely, nor were they read by historians outside the palace; the *Tiounn Chronicle* itself remained unpublished till 1969, on the eve of the civil war period.

A well-known Burmese history which became something of an object of ridicule to colonial historians, the *Hman-nan Raza-windaw-gyi* ('Royal Chronicle of the Glass Palace') lay at the end of a long tradition of historiography in that country (see Extract 36). Its precursors include a number of earlier histories which, one scholar has suggested, resemble Elizabethan English chronicles.[9] The inspiration for these works lay in Buddhism, and the first extant history, the *Maha Thamada Wuntha* or *Yazawinkyaw* ('Celebrated Chronicle'), was the work of a monk. Thila Wuntha or Shin Thilawuntha narrated the history of Buddhism in India, with a list of Burmese kings almost thrown in as an afterthought, its intent being to link current religion and the monarchy back to their South Asian roots. Much of it is drawn from the tenth-century Buddhist *Mahāvaṃsa*. Although Buddhist monks were forbidden to chatter about secular matters concerning kings, generals and ministers, which were not suitable to spiritual growth, they were permitted to use such tales to illustrate the impermanence of all things, and the mortality of even mighty kings. The laity, while not bound by this stricture, nonetheless made moral edification the focus of their histories. The very uncertainty of the future induced attention to the past, and explanations for unusual events could be ascribed to the karmic principle whereby past deeds or misdeeds are rewarded or punished in subsequent lives. A usurper's puzzling victory over a legitimate king was explicable through 'retroactive karma' – not, as a Renaissance human-ist might have put it, because of fortune, prudence or virtue, but because of the deficit or credit run up at the cosmic bank by the usurper and his victim during their previous lives.

Though they lacked a term for 'history' (as distinct from 'literature'), the pre-colonial Burmese had two traditional genres that we would recognize as historical: the *yazawin* (really a royal genealogy) and the *thamaing* – a term that originally denoted accounts of local events and religious sites, but which has come to de-note 'history' in modern Burmese.[10] Apart from some earlier works not really considered to be chronicles, such as the *Yaza Mu Haung* ('Ancient Actions of Kings'), by a royal tutor named Zambu Kungya, the earliest known extant Bur-mese chronicle was Thilawuntha's above-mentioned *Yazawinkyaw*, completed in 1520. In the former Shan-area state Jengtung or Kengtung, near the borders with China, Laos and Thailand, nineteenth-century compilations which reached back several hundred years include a 'state chronicle' and a chronicle of the monastery of Vat Pāḍaeng. The former, which was continued through British rule down to the 1930s, opens with a section of intermixed history and legend before launching into a genuine chronicle (with dates that are mainly verifiable from inscriptions) in its ninety-ninth verse:

extract

36: Burmese History: the Glass Palace Chronicle

Here endeth the second part. And we shall presently relate the full history of the kings of Burma, originally descended from the noble Sun dynasty of the Sakiyans. We shall begin with the founding of Tagaung, their first city, and add, moreover, the record of the sacred relics, the establishment of the religion, and the lineage of divers founders and rulers of cities.

102. *Of the first founding of the great kingdom of Tagaung by the Sakiyan Abhiraja of the Middle Country.*

[*The founding of Tagaung by Abhiraja.*] Tagaung was known as Thantharapura in the time of Kakusandha the Buddha, as Ratthapura in the time of Konagamana the Buddha, as Thintwè in the time of Kassapa the Buddha, and as Tagaung in the time of our Buddha Gotama. Abhiraja the Sakya Sakiyan was its first ruler. And this is the story of Abhiraja.

Once upon a time, long ago, before our Lord the Buddha unfolded the Four Truths under the Wisdom Tree at the Place of Conquest, the king of Panchala, lord of the two kingdoms of Kosala and Panchala, desired to ally himself by marriage with the king of Koliya, and sent ministers to ask the hand of a Koliyan princess. But the king of Koliya in his pride of birth answered him ill; so that a great war broke out between the two kingdoms. The king of Panchala was victorious, and the Sakiyan princes of the three kingdoms, Koliya, Devadaha, and Kapilavatthu, were isolated each from each and their empire wrecked. Later the Sakiyan princes of the three kingdoms arose again into prosperity; but when first their power was wrecked, Abhiraja, the Sakya Sakiyan king of Kapilavatthu, took all his army and left the Middle Country and ruled in the Tagaung country, called Sangassarattha, which he founded ....

[*Kanrazagyi and Kanrazangè.*] On the death of Abhiraja his two sons, Kanrazagyi and Kanrazangè, quarrelled over the throne. But a wise minister said, 'If ye princes fight a great fight, ye bring ruin on all beings in the country. Wage not therefore a war of enmity but wage a war of merit'. Then the princes asked, 'How may this be?' And the minister made answer, 'Princes! let each of you build in the course of one night an alms-hall on a large scale. And whoever first completeth the work, let him take his father's place and be king'. So the princes agreed, and each chose a hill and began to build an alms-hall on a large scale. Kanrazagyi completed not his hall, for he built it of massive timber and bamboo. But Kanrazangè completed his, for he built it of small timber and bamboo and covered it with white cloth and whitewashed it. And at dawn when the elder brother beheld the white hall put up by the younger brother he gathered his army and went down the Irrawaddy. Thence he passed up the Thallawadi, and having given the name of Rajagaha to the hill Kaletaung-nyo he held court there for six months. When the Pyus, Kanyans, and Theks of the Western Country desired a prince to reign over them, he made his son Muducitta king of the Pyus. And he founded the city of Kyauppadaung to the east of the river Kacchapa and reigned for seventy-four years. And moving thence he took possession of the old city of Dhaññavati, first built by king Marayu, and reigned there, building a new palace and fortifications. As for the younger brother, he ruled in Tagaung in his father's stead.

[*The kings of Tagaung.*] Thus in Tagaung, called Sangassarattha, thirty-three kings reigned in unbroken succession, beginning with Abhiraja the Sakya Sakiyan; his son Kanrazangè: his son Jambudiparaja: his son Sangassaraja: his son Vippannaraja: his son Devataraja: his son Munikaraja: his uncle Nagaraja: his younger brother Indaraja: his son Samutiraja: his son Devaraja: his son Mahindaraja: his son Vimalaraja: his son Sihanuruja: his son Manganaraja: his son Kamsaraja: his son Kalingaraja: his son Thintwèraja: his son Sihalaraja: his younger brother Hamsaraja: his son Vararaja: his son Alaungraja: his son Kolakaraja: his son Suriyaraja: his son Thingyiraja: his son Tainggyitraja: his son Maduraja: his son Minhlagyiraja: his son Samsnsiharaja: his son Dhanangaraja: his son Hindaraja: his son Moriyaraja: his son Bhinnakaraja.

[*The fall of Tagaung.*] In the time of the last of these kings, Bhinnakaraja, the kingdom of Tagaung, called Sangassarattha, perished under the oppression of the Tarops and Tareks from the Sein country in the kingdom of Gandhala. And Bhinnaka, mustering what follow-ers he might, entered the Mali stream and abode there. When he died his followers split into three divisions. One division founded the nineteen Shan States of the East and were known thenceforth as the descendants of Bhinnakaraja. Another division moved down the Irrawaddy and entered the Western Country, where dwelt Muducitta and other Sakiyan princes among the Pyus, Kanyans, and Theks. The third division abode in Mali with the chief queen Nagahsein.

From *The Glass Palace Chronicle of the Kings of Burma*, trans. Pe Maung Tin and G. H. Luce (London: Oxford University Press; Humphrey Milford, 1923), 1–3. The selection comes from the opening of the translation, with part III of the Chronicle, the first two parts having related the story of Buddhism and the Buddhist kings of India.

99. Here will be told the chronicle of Jengtung state from the time when the gourds burst and gave birth to the Lvas who inhabited the state when the Sakkarāja was 496. In Sakkarāja 591 Brayā Mangrāy chased the golden stag into Jengtung state. In 592 Brayā Mangrāy deputed Khun Gong and Khun Lang to fight the Lvas but did not defeat them. In Sakkarāja 605, Prince Mangrāy deputed Māngghūm to rule Jengtung state for four years, and [he] died.[11]

The first fully comprehensive Burmese chronicle did not appear till the early eight-eenth century, when one Maung Kala or U Kala (*fl.* 1714–33) – a name that means 'Mr Indian', suggesting his possible foreign ethnicity – composed the *Mahayza-wingyi* or *Maha Razawindaw-gyi* ('The Great Chronicle of Kings'). This included genealogies of the kings and lists of their accomplishments, and followed a chron-ological narrative.

The pattern set by U Kala would be imitated in the late eighteenth century, under the new Konbaung dynasty, when Twinthin Maha Sithu, a minister of King

Bodawpaya (r. 1782–1819), updated his predecessor's work into *Myanma Yazawin-thit* ('New Chronicle of Myanmar'), the first truly 'national' history of Burma since it comprehended the several ethnic groups living within Burmese territory. Though he shared the purpose of earlier writers to legitimize the dynasty, Maha Sithu, a learned polymath, introduced a hitherto-absent dimension to historical writing in the region through the study of inscriptions. The king himself was interested in reading history and commanded the collection of inscriptions from throughout the kingdom. As the interior minister, Maha Sithu was responsible for verifying claims to religious property in Burma, giving him privileged access to the inscriptions, a position which he exploited, using the information on these, including dates, to correct U Kala's chronicle.[12] Epigraphy, which we usually associate with the *érudits* of late seventeenth- and eighteenth-century Europe, was thus being practised in Southeast Asia at about the same time, even if it had not evolved into a formal method. We should not overstate the 'scientific' character of these works, since much Burmese historiography was – as elsewhere in the world – written with didactic intentions. The *Maniyadanabon* by the late eighteenth-century monk Shin Sandalinka, for example, is a repository of historical examples illustrating pragmatic political principles worthy of Machiavelli.

Though it shares a form of Malay with modern Malaysia and Singapore as its official language, the history of history in what is now Indonesia is especially complicated, because of its many constituent ethnicities. Javanese historical writings date back at least as far as the fourteenth-century *Deśawarṇana* (also known as the *Nāgarakṛtāgama*), and by the nineteenth century include the *babad*s, historical poems relating various episodes in Javanese history including wars. These *babad*s, which also feature in the literature of Java's neighbour Bali, were often composed by court poets and intended for oral recitation. They are generally of recent (post-1700) origin, and scholars differ on the degree to which they may be relied upon for factual accuracy – though it has been argued that the Western dichotomy between fact and fiction is simply irrelevant since the concept of fiction does not exist, only a notion of degrees of veracity (see Box 28). Examples include the *Babad Tanah Jawi* ('Chronicle of the Land of Java'), sometimes known as the 'Javanese State Chronicles'. This is a group of texts in modern Javanese covering the era from mythical times to the late eighteenth century, first partially translated into Dutch in 1779. Another is the *Babad ing Sangkala* ('Chronicle of the Chronograms'), a 2,000-line chronicle running from 1478 to 1720 (written *c.* 1738) (Extract 37): this is a specimen of a genre of verse historical writing, the *babad sangkala*, in which events are related with their dates provided through chronograms (sets of words with a numerical value). A third example is the *Babad Jaka Tingkir* ('The History of Jaka Tingkir'). The latter is a mid-nineteenth-century account, some of it drawn from Dutch sources, of the early life of a sixteenth-century ruler of the

Box 28   **Truth and Fiction in the *Babad*s**

The writers of *babad*s could use the same subject for different purposes. They could also provide conflicting information. Among the three different *babad*s relating the life of the late seventeenth-century hero Surapati (d. 1706), one was written for didactic or moralizing purposes and a second to justify a particular political situation; a third appears to have been intended as an epic. None was written as 'history' in a European sense and to fault their authors for inaccuracy or, conversely, to praise them for adhering to ideals of historical truth to which they would not have subscribed is to misunderstand the purpose for which the *babad*s were written. For instance, when the author of the *Babad Buleleη* refers to the Dutch only at the mid-nineteenth century (though they had been in Bali since the seventeenth), it is not because he is oblivious to their earlier presence but because until then they were of no significance to his subject, which is a genealogical narrative; it is only after that point that the foreigners began to intervene in Balinese succession questions.

Javanese sultanate of Pajang. War appears to have been the major stimulus behind the writing of *babad*s through the eighteenth and nineteenth centuries. The *Babad Dipanagara*, one of the most famous, relates the outbreak of the Java War of 1825 to 1830 against the Javanese prince Dipanagara (or Diponegoro, the supposed author of the *babad*), whom the Dutch defeated and exiled to Makassar on the island of Sulawesi.[13]

A well-known early history from the sub-region, and one which more closely resembles Western genres such as genealogy and chronicle, is the *Sĕjarah Mĕlayu* (usually rendered somewhat misleadingly as the 'Malay Annals').[14] Once believed to have been composed about the end of the fifteenth century, it has more recently been placed as late as 1612, the date of its longest extant manuscript version. *Sĕjarah Mĕlayu* was written at the command of the sultan of Malacca (now part of Malaysia), who ordered his Treasury 'to make a chronicle setting forth the genealogy of the Malay Rajas and the ceremonial of their courts, for the information of my descendants who come after me, that they may be conversant with the history and derive profit therefrom'. A *sĕjarah* is literally a genealogical tree, but only a few pages in some versions are properly genealogy, and these were principally written by later authors down to 1832. The author of the 1612 manuscript, having heard the sultan's wishes, 'wrote this chronicle as he received it from his fathers and forebears, assembling in it all the stories of the men of bygone days, for the

37: A Javanese *Babad*: *Babad ing Sangkala*

31. The great square at Karta was given a Siti Inggil,

in the same year when in Surabaya

the Adipati left the city;

also in the same year

the Sultan went to Samanggi [Sala],

when 'the horse looked like a demon;

   and in the same month' [Ś 1547/Mar. 1625–Feb. 1626]

was the move to Kĕmbangan

and there were great epidemics, indeed;

many people were caught.

32. 'The poet outstanding arranged the world' [Ś I548/Mar. 1626–Feb. 1627]

when Madurarĕja departed

from Mataram. The beginning of

the destruction of Pathi was calculated

when 'nine described the ways of the courageous' [Ś1549/Mar. 1627–Feb. 1628].

Pangeran Surabaya

appeared

to pay obeisance in Mataram;

'without sleep, he lay upon the ground' [Ś1550/Mar. 1628–Feb. 1629];

at the same time was the affair of Jakarta.

33. After the attack on Jakarta, for a second time

all the *mantris* of Mataram were called up;

the Adipatis all marched out,

taking with them the great guns

Subrastha and Satomi, 'the people were all arranged;

the same' [Ś1551/Mar. 1629–Feb. 1630] year

in Girilaya was constructed

and embellished the grave of the queen;

the mausoleum was embellished.

34. After the Dutch had landed at Samarang,

after landing they went to Mataram;

the Dutch were two in number,

with four sailors,

'forcing their way, evil and defiant' [Ś1552/Mar. 1630–Feb. 1631].

Not a year later,

after the destruction,

many people suffering adversities,

the people to the south of Wĕdhi all became

disciples of Shaikh Bungas.

35. After the arrival of Captain Joharsih [Jorge d'Acunha?],

the Portuguese landed at Japara,

presenting a tapir to His Majesty,

with its saddle

and all the appurtenances for riding upon it,

'made to look like a demon by

men' [Ś1553/Mar. 1631–Feb. 1632]. When

the Portuguese were received

it was made known that all must appear in *bathik* court attire

who paid obeisance to the Sultan.

From the *Babad ing Sangkala*, transcribed in M. C. Ricklefs, *Modern Javanese Historical Tradition: A Study of an Original Kartasura Chronicle and Related Materials* (London: School of Oriental and African Studies, University of London, 1978), Canto I, stanzas 31–5, pp. 35–7. The entire work is four cantos long. Ricklefs (introduction, p. x) dates the manuscript of this work to 1738 CE, though the events it records occurred in the seventeenth century. The passages in quotation marks are chronograms; these have been converted by the text's editor to Javanese and then Christian calendar dates, which are given in square brackets.

greater pleasure of his lord the King'.[15] As with other such 'palace' chronicles, its function is not to establish accurate dates in the modern Western style but to argue a case, in this instance for the descent of the fifteenth-century Malaccan sultanate, predecessor of the Johor Empire, from Iskandar Zulkarnain (Alexander the Great). This was a Southeast Asian version of medieval Christendom's *translatio imperii* (Extract 38).

A feature that many of these indigenous forms of history hold in common is their emphasis not on relating 'facts' or 'events' as people in the West understand them but on other ends entirely, which are as variable as the verification of *perceived* rather than *literal* truth, the upholding of social values or the legitimation of current political arrangements. Their relation with writing is also complex since they were often intended for performance rather than reading. In

38: *Sĕjarah Mĕlayu*: the 'Malay Annals'

And when Sultan Mansur Shah had reigned for seventy-three years, then in the process of time he fell sick. And summoning his children, the Bendahara and the chiefs, he said to them, 'Be it known to all of you, this world I feel to be slipping from my grasp and all that I now yearn for is the City of Eternity. To Bendahara Paduka Raja and all the chiefs we commit our son Raja Radin here; he shall take my place with you all and if he does aught that is wrong, you must forgive him, for he is but a boy, ignorant of our customs ....' .... Sultan Mansur Shah then died, and he was buried with all the traditional ceremonies accorded to princes. And he was succeeded on the throne by Raja Radin, who was installed by Bendahara Paduka Raja with the title of Sultan Ala'u'd-din Ri'ayat Shah. Now Sultan Ala'u'd-din was a man of such strength that he had no rival in those days.

[The Sultan grows ill from diarrhoea and his death is coveted by his grandmother who wishes her favourite son to rule instead; the plot is suppressed by his advisers]. And Bendahara Paduka Raja, the Treasurer and the Laksamana tended Sultan Ala'u'd-din diligently and he was preserved by God Almighty: his allotted span in the Book of Life was not yet rubbed out.

From *Malay Annals*, trans. C. C. Brown from MS Raffles No 18 (repr. Perpustakaan Negara, Malaysia, 2009), 111. First published as *Sĕjarah Mĕlayu or Malay Annals*, trans. C. C. Brown (Kuala Lumpur, Singapore and London: Oxford University Press, 1970), itself a reprint of Brown's translation in the *Journal of the Malaysian Branch of the Royal Asiatic Society* 25 (1952): 2–3.

northern Sumatra, historical narratives imported from Malay and other languages circulated orally before being written down in verse forms, and continued to be recited from memory even where a written copy was present. One example, the eighteenth-century Acehnese-language epic *Hikajat Pòtjoet Moehamat* ('The Epic of Prince Moehamat', Extract 39), describes an earlier civil war in a manner quite different from the official versions generated by successive Dutch and Indonesian rulers. Oral traditional historical narratives, or *tutui teteek* ('true tales'), circulated widely on the southeast Indonesian island of Roti, as did oral dynastic genealogies of the Rotinese lord or *manek*; many of these traditions have been independently verified by reference to Dutch colonial documents. On Sulawesi (formerly Celebes), Bugis and Makasar historical works date from the seventeenth century and include chronicles or narratives called *attoriolong* which use a chronology based on lengths of reigns and elapsed times between events rather than absolute dates. An example is provided by the *Attoriolonna Bone* ('Chronicle of Bone') which covers events in the state of Bone from the arrival of a *tomanurung*

39: A Sumatran *Hikayat*

In the name of God, the merciful and compassionate,
Oh wondrous things! Listen as I tell of kings;
Listen as I tell of a new turn in the course of things, as they sat in the gate of the great mosque.
It was there that Pòtjoet Moehamat, son of a king, had first arranged a meeting.
It was there that the *oelëëbelang*, all of them ministers of the king, gathered.
They had been deliberating for three days when he wished to see a secret revealed by a dream ....
(lines 1–6)
Now here is another story of Pòtjoet Moehamat, son of a king.
He was the son of Alaédin, who was a firm believer in our Lord.
He went to Salasari, and from that time a chronicle has been handed down in the stronghold.
'Salasari' was the old name; it is not certain if there was a ruler there.
'Salasari' was the name in earlier times; there the foundations of religion were first laid.
Later it was given the name of 'Pasè', a peculiar, vile name.
From that time to this day it is called by this senseless name.
It was called 'Pasè' after a dog who hunted deer.
From the time they gave it this name until now it has had the name continuously.
(lines 1250–9)

From *Hikajat Pòtjoet Moehamat*, trans. James Siegel, in his *Shadow and Sound: The Historical Thought of a Sumatran People* (University of Chicago Press, 1979), 36, 99. Siegel's notes have been omitted. Line 1250, repeated in the original, is omitted by Siegel, leaving only nine lines between 1250 and 1259. *Oelëëbelang* refers to rulers of territories within Aceh; Pòtjoet is a title for princes and princesses (ibid., glossary, 283–4). *Hikayat* (or *hikajat*) are historical accounts, in prose or verse, in the Malay language, often characterized by a mixture of past and future tenses such that events from the past appear to be 'prophesied'. Another genre intended to be performed publicly, *hikayat* are often self-referential, recording within them other examples of the recitation of a *hikayat*.

or 'descended one', probably in the fourteenth century, up to more firmly dated events in the late seventeenth, concluding in 1667. In contrast to Javanese works like the *Babad Tanah Jawi*, these chronicles are remarkable for their conciseness, their frequent adherence to a clear chronology and the relative dearth of non-historical content such as prophecies. Authorial scepticism to certain episodes is signified, in the Chronicle of Bone, by the use of phrases meaning 'so the story goes' or 'it is said'.

The construction of a national sense of the past in the face of multiple ethnicities proved no less daunting than the establishment of the Indonesian state itself. In the first half of the twentieth century, Dutch-trained Indonesian historians concentrated on providing a narrative framework to support aspirations for Indonesian national independence. With the backing of Japanese occupiers at war with Western colonial powers, a nationalist-anticolonial historiography was introduced during the early 1940s. As in many decolonizing societies following the Second World War, Indonesian historians faced the challenge of rejecting the agenda of Dutch-centred historiography while retaining its Western methodology, which was required to establish the factuality of key episodes and personalities in the Indonesian past.[16]

Construction of a comprehensive vision of the past for the entire archipelago was largely the work of the nationalist leader and future president Sukarno (1901–70), the textbook writer Sanusi Pane (1905–68, author of a key textbook written during the Japanese occupation) and especially the lawyer Muhammad Yamin (1903–62). Sukarno was especially sympathetic to Marxist views of the past. Yamin, an admirer of the *Sĕjarah Mĕlayu* and a reader of the French historian Ernest Renan, popularized a romantic and Java-centred vision of the country's history. In the late 1950s and early 1960s a number of academics criticized the nationalist bent in historiography, but it acquired new teeth with the advent of the Suharto 'New Order' regime after 1965, the very year in which a collection of essays on Indonesian historiography had been published by the Western-influenced scholar Soedjatmoko.

Two Cases of Colonial Appropriation: Vietnam and the Philippines

The enforced Europeanization of Southeast Asian histories is better illustrated by the slightly differing experiences of Vietnam and the Philippines. David Marr suggests that the 'Vietnamese take history very seriously, possibly more so than anyone else in Southeast Asia'.[17] Unlike their Cambodian neighbours, the Vietnamese had practised historical writing in some form for eight or more centuries; a great deal of genealogical activity occurred at the family level from the fifteenth century on, by which time the Vietnamese had embraced Confucianism. A satellite of China through much of its history, Vietnam's early historical writing was also Chinese-influenced (either Confucian or Buddhist) and written in now-archaic Sino-Vietnamese characters. Although successive Chinese invasions and domestic struggles are thought to have destroyed many older sources, an interest in the past extended down to local communities and clans that scrupulously maintained genealogical and biographical information (*gia pha*). The *chanhsu*, Chinese-style dynastic histories or imperial annals, record major events reign by reign and were intended to celebrate the current ruling house, often at the expense of its predecessor. Vietnamese kings, who had inherited the Chinese emperors' interest in the application of history to public policy, strenuously enforced an 'authentic history' during the pre-colonial period. The most noteworthy distinctive historical texts include the *Đại Việt sử lược* ('Historical Annals of Viet') from the fourteenth century, itself abridged from a now-lost thirteenth-century text by Lê Văn Hưu, and the 1479 *Đại Việt sử ký toàn thư* ('Complete Historical Annals of Great Viet') by Ngô Sĩ Liên, which also includes a version of Lê Văn Hưu's lost history. Hưu, a Tran-dynasty (1225–1400) civil servant and scholar, was commissioned to edit Vietnamese records; he presented his thirty-chapter *Đại Việt sư Ký* to the throne in 1272, a work covering Vietnamese history from the third century BC to the ascension of the Tran. Writing at a time when Vietnam was straining against its tributary relationship with Yuan China, and when its indigenous 'ancient learning' was revered at court, Hưu's history adopted the form of a Chinese history but the perspective of a Vietnamese patriot.

During the eighteenth and nineteenth centuries Vietnamese scholars were able to build on several centuries of historical writing, including the *gia pha*, and produced major works such as Lê Quý Đôn's (c. 1726–84) multivolume *Đại Việt thông sử* ('Complete History of Dai Viet', also known as the 'Complete History of the Lê Dynasty'). By the 1860s, official historians of the Nguyen dynasty had completed half of the 500-book *Đại Nam thuc luc* ('Veritable Records of Đại Nam'). Traditional Vietnamese historiography, which retained the Chinese-influenced Confucianism of previous centuries, would survive the arrival of Europeans, especially the French, although it was subject to official censorship. *Việt Nam Sử Lược* (1929–30) was a popular general history by Trần Trọng Kim (1883–1953), prime minister of the brief Empire of Vietnam set up by the Japanese in 1945.

French scholars working in Vietnam (and French-educated Vietnamese returning home) gradually succeeded in introducing Western models of historiography during the 1900s, along with potent concepts such as nationalism and Marxism, with formidable effects on the country's subsequent development. Phan Bội Châu (1867–1940), an anticolonial activist sometimes regarded as his country's first 'modern' historian, was among those who abandoned dynastic history and adopted Western historical categories, together with a concept of progress and social development derived from Sino-Japanese interpreters of Darwin and Spencer. By the 1920s, Zhu Xi-style neo-Confucianism, with its emphasis on virtue and heroism, and an exemplary approach to the past, was having to share space with the study of History as cumulative process, as writers seeking independence from colonial rule attempted to locate Vietnam's

present and future along a continuous historical path. The advent of the printing press in turn gave history a much wider public currency. Patriotic and anti-
French historians like Phan Bội Châu were either jailed or exiled from 1908 till
the 1920s. The flurry of publishing in the 1920s, 1930s and 1940s included a
significant proportion of historical and biographical books and pamphlets, and
Ho Chi Minh himself, after his 1941 return to Vietnam, authored a poetic history
of his country.

The Philippines represents a slightly different process of Westernization, but
with the same result. Long under Spanish and then American rule, the peoples of
the Philippines, rather like Latin American populations, had adapted early to the
historical interests of their conquerors (a further testament to the extraordinary
early effectiveness of Hispanic historians and missionaries), to the great detriment
of pre-existing historical memory. The first example of post-Conquest historical
writing is the *Sucesos de las Islas Filipinas* by the Spanish official Antonio de
Morga (1559–1636), published in Mexico in 1609; this was to be the only early
history to be written by a layman. Throughout the seventeenth and eighteenth
centuries, the various resident religious orders produced chronicles largely focused
on their own missionary activities. However, as they had also done in the Americas, the Spanish appropriated native forms selectively in order to establish their
authority: having largely eradicated other pre-colonial forms of literature, Spanish
missionaries found in the *awits* or metrical poems a ready-made tool of colonization, in essence a box into which heroic Spanish historiography could be packaged
for native consumption. Written in the indigenous Tagalog language, *awits* include the early nineteenth-century *Historia famosa ni Bernardo Carpio*, a romance
derived from stories of medieval Spanish–Moorish conflict. These stories had become so familiar in both written and oral form that the average Filipino 'knew
more about Emperor Charlemagne, the Seven Peers of France and the destruction
of Troy than of pre-Spanish Philippine rajahs and the destruction of Manila by the
conquistadores'.[18] Ironically, the chivalric and heroic figures in the *awits* would
prove inspirational to Tagalogs dreaming of emancipation from Spanish rule at
the end of the nineteenth century: the Bernardo Carpio of Spanish legend was easily domesticated into a Filipino figure, becoming a superhuman champion of the
downtrodden whose messianic return would deliver the Filipinos from the yoke of
foreign oppression.

As with the *awits*, Western histories proved useful tools of incipient nationalism,
especially in the hands of young Filipino secular priests sent back to Europe for
higher education in the 1860s. Published work on Filipino folklore and customs
began to appear soon thereafter, along with previously unpublished chronicles
issued in the *Biblioteca Historica Filipina* series (1892). A Europeanized approach
to history would emerge with José Rizal (1861–96), who had visited Germany

and became aware of Western historical methods. During an exile in London in 1887–8, Rizal provided a carefully annotated edition of Morga's work, stressing the achievements of pre-Spanish Filipinos and their moral decline under foreign rule. In this form, Rizal's views would both contribute to revolutionary sentiment following his execution, and ultimately to the continuation of indigenous historical study through the ensuing decades of American rule.

Historicity by Royal Proclamation in Thailand

Perhaps the best example of a regime imposing European-style historiographical practices on itself, and in the process departing from a long-standing but different tradition of historicity, is provided by Thailand, once known as Siam. Theravada Buddhism had arrived there from Sri Lanka in the thirteenth and fourteenth centuries, bringing with it the *vaṃsa*s (see Chapter 1 above). This proved an encouragement to historical writing in the next two to three centuries: the Siamese elite valued knowledge of the past, producing historical poetry (for example, the fifteenth-century *Yuan Pâi* or 'Defeat of the Yuan'), and generating an extensive series of chronicles in various forms. The Buddhist-oriented *tamnan* (stories or legends), variously inscribed on palm leaves in a number of different scripts and languages (including Pāli), were composed from the fifteenth to the nineteenth century. Annalistically organized chronicles, *tamnan*, record the histories of the several kingdoms of medieval and early modern Thailand, often beginning with the time of the Buddha, or earlier, and dealing with a wide variety of localities and peoples and their origin myths. Some, written in Thai or Pāli, amount to 'universal histories' while others deal with the distant past or with the relics and monuments of particular Buddhist institutions. The *tamnan* have in modern times been distinguished from another annalistic genre, the *phongsāwadān* (dynastic chronicles) which superseded them in central Thailand during the seventeenth century. The differences are often ones of emphasis since both are chronologically arranged, and some works contain examples of each. The major differences are that the *phongsāwadān* take as their subject not Buddhist history as such, but the histories of particular dynasties, for instance the rulers of the kingdom of Ayudhyā (or Ayutthaya, 1351–1767); and whereas *tamnan* were written by monks, these dynastic chronicles are the products of court secretaries or officials. Perhaps the best-known example of this genre is the family of works collectively known as the *Phongsāwadān Krun Si Ayutthaya*, the Ayudhyā chronicles, the name of which derives from the Siamese capital (and associated dynasty) destroyed by the Burmese twice in the mid-sixteenth century and again in 1767. At least seven major versions of this text exist, each associated with a particular author, and written from the late seventeenth to the mid-twentieth century, with a peak period falling during the prolonged period of struggles with neighbours, especially Burma, from 1760 to 1828. Excluding earlier fragments, the earliest and briefest version, which differs in some important respects from the rest, is the *Luang Prasert* or *Prasoet* chronicle (discovered in 1907 and named for its manuscript owner). Covering Thai history back to the fourth century, it was written about 1680, probably by a court scribe named Luang Horathibòdi;[19] apart from Jeremias van Vliet's 1640 chronicle in Dutch, which used then-extant sources,[20] it is our earliest account of Ayudhyā. Subsequent recensions of the chronicles of Ayudhyā, written in the late eighteenth century, extend its history to that time.

The kings of the Chakri dynasty (1782 to the present) continued to support historical writing during the nineteenth century, and used history as a political tool both internally and internationally: Siamese officials at one point presented French diplomats with a chronicle to substantiate a claim to Cambodia.[21] King Rama I (r. 1782–1809) commanded the revision of a number of *phongsāwadān*, and his famous later successor, the Westernizing monk-turned-monarch Mongkut (Rama IV, r. 1851–68), authorized the definitive Royal Autograph edition of the chronicles of Ayutthaya. Keenly interested in history, Mongkut also pursued the study of epigraphy. He and his heir, Chulalongkorn (Rama V, r. 1868–1910), commissioned the last work in this tradition, a series of chronicles of his four Chakri predecessors by their long-serving administrator Chaophraya Thiphakorawong (1813–70). Outside Bangkok, a particularly vigorous tradition of local chronicle-writing developed in northern Thai communities and subsidiary kingdoms. That of the northern city of Chiang Mai (capital of the old kingdom of Lan Na), the work of an anonymous author who borrowed selectively and carefully from earlier sources, recounts its history from its foundation in the late thirteenth century down to the nineteenth century. Over a hundred different versions of this chronicle are extant. Usually written, as with most Thai literature before the late nineteenth century, on palm-leaf manuscripts or *samutthai* (bark folded into pleats), these chronicles peaked in the early nineteenth century, although there are well-known later examples such as the *Nan Chronicle*, compiled in 1894 by Saenluang Ratchasomphan, a servant of the Nan king.[22] Similar chronicles were written in Tai-language regions of Burma and what is now Laos.

Western-style modern histories and school textbooks first began to appear in the late 1920s. At the same time, the introduction of printing expanded the circulation of historical works, including many from abroad, among the Thai learned classes. As in Europe during the sixteenth and seventeenth centuries, opportunistic authors took advantage of this growing public interest in history – an enterprising ex-monk-turned-publisher named Kulap found himself in trouble with the government at the end of the century for creative fabrication and emendation of royal manuscripts, and the foisting of invented historical episodes upon his readers.[23] History-teaching at a university level also commenced in the 1920s, at which time a Westernized Thai historiography (*prawatsat*) emerged. A tradition of royalist-nationalist historiography was established by Mongkut's younger son Prince Damrong Rajanubhab or Rachanuphap (1862–1943). A successful minister of the interior under his brother Chulalongkorn, Damrong was himself a prolific author and educational reformer who turned to history following his retirement from office. An admirer of Ranke and Western scholarship in general, his historical work embodied a use of source criticism while retaining the dynastic focus of the older *phongsāwadān*; it is he who was responsible for the publication of an extensive series of histories, the *Prachum phongsāwadān* ('Collected Histories') – a Thai equivalent to the *Monumenta Germaniae Historica* ('Historical Records of Germany') or Britain's 'Rolls Series'. Damrong also helped to establish an accepted chronology for Thai history, and he encouraged historians to venture beyond the recitation of kings' deeds and provide an account of the nation and people.

In this modernized scholarly environment, and with the monarchy being challenged from both the political right and left, alternative views were not long in developing. The long-serving Luang Wichit Wathakan (1898–1962), propagandist for the Thai People's Party, developed an ultra-nationalist and militaristic view of the past (borrowing from European-imported racial theory) in a twelve-volume history, *Prawattisat Sakon*, which appeared opportunely in 1931, just before his party overthrew the absolute monarchy. This martially oriented work veered away from dynastic history in favour of an account of the Thai nation as a whole. At the other end of the ideological spectrum, left-wing historiography was launched by Phra Sarasas' *My Country Thailand*, first published by its author, then living in exile in Tokyo, which in the 1870s and 1880s had become the entry point for European historiography into East Asia.

History, Historiography and Modernization in Japan

We must here reverse our past practice of treating the island empire of Japan after its larger Chinese neighbour, for Japan turned to modernization, and to Western influences, a good two or three decades before China, and unlike China did not require the overthrow of its empire in order to achieve this. Long closed to the West during the Tokugawa era, Japan opened up to international influence in the years running up to and following the Meiji Restoration of 1868, which brought an end to nearly seven centuries of rule by successive bakufus. The Meiji Restoration marked a sharp break with what went before and was perceived as such by many observers. In 1876 the German physician Erwin Baelz observed that 'the Japanese have their eyes fixed exclusively on the future, and are impatient when a word is said of their past. "That was in the days of barbarism" said one of them in my hearing. Another, when I asked him about Japanese history, bluntly rejoined, "We have no history. Our history begins today."[24]

This was of course nonsense – we have seen plenty of evidence of Japanese historiographic activity dating back well over a millennium. Yet it illustrates the alacrity with which some Japanese repudiated the recent, feudal past, which soon meant rejecting the histories inscribed with its record. At first they looked to their own antiquity, rather than abroad for the reform of historiography. Within a year of the Restoration, an Imperial Rescript or declaration called for the creation of a *shikyoku*, or Office of Historiography, in order that the 'good custom of our ancestors be resumed and that knowledge and education be spread throughout the land'.[25] In other words, historiography would be tied closely to an ideological programme and to the implementation of a new political and social agenda built on the administrative arrangements associated with the heyday of imperial power in the Nara and Heian eras. The new regime quickly established an official Department of History (*rekishika*) within the government's highest ministry, the Central Chamber (1872), and then, in 1875, an expanded Office of Historiography, quickly followed within two years by a College of Historiography. The initial purpose of each of these institutions was to organize the compilation of the *Dai Nihon hennenshi* ('Chronological History of Great Japan'), a new history along the lines of the Six National Histories, to be written from a pro-imperial perspective. It was also charged with completing the *Fukkoki* ('Chronicle of the Restoration', not published till 1930), and with devising national histories that could be displayed abroad in venues such as the world exhibitions in Philadelphia in 1876 and Paris in 1878. Finally, it inaugurated the regime's policy of closely controlling what would be taught in public schools, producing a series of textbooks, published by the Ministry of Education, beginning with *Shiryaku* ('Outline of History', 1872), 130,000 copies of which were sold in its first five years.

By the 1880s little of this ambitious agenda had been completed, and the *Dai Nihon hennenshi* was abandoned altogether in 1893. While some of this failure was due to internecine squabbles, under-resourcing and recurrent reorganization, there were also deeper intellectual obstacles. Language was one: Japan's adaptation of its native language to Chinese script had put its written and spoken tongues increasingly out of step, and by the later nineteenth century the dominance of traditional Sino-Japanese or *kanbun* as the 'literary' or 'official' script was coming to an end as, again under Western influence, attempts were made to bring speech and writing into closer alignment.[26] This was not an esoteric point so far as history-writing was concerned, since the choice of language in turn indicated a position either respectful towards or pushing against traditional Chinese influences, and the History Office, electing to stick with *kanbun*, put itself behind the curve before it even began to produce. Moreover, it was not possible simply to revive older forms of historical writing, or to model institutions after ancient predecessors, not least because a principal goal of the Restoration's architects was to accomplish what the shoguns had failed to do: deal with the now inescapable presence of the West on a not merely equal but manifestly superior footing, and to learn from Europeans and Americans without sacrificing Japanese identity. Japan in many ways followed, during a much more compressed period, the same trajectory of rapid change experienced by Europe in the second half of the nineteenth century, with pressure to modernize counterbalanced by an equally strong attachment to tradition and the past. Moreover, centralized sponsorship of official history was itself an outdated practice in much of the rest of the world, no longer much respected in the very European countries which were supposed to provide a model for reformed historiography. There, the universities had come to the fore. After a further series of renamings and reorganizations in and after 1881, the Office of Historiography was finally transferred to Tokyo Imperial University in 1888, and a department of Japanese history founded there in 1889, during which year the new national constitution that had been promised for two decades was finally proclaimed. In 1893 the government disapproved of the Historiographical Institute's research agenda, and briefly closed it down.

Any residual Chinese traditional influences on historiography were soon overwhelmed by Western scholarship. As early as 1878 a young official (and in later life, influential politician) named Suematsu Kenchō (1855–1920) was dispatched to London and asked by the History Office to report back on French and British historiography, several examples of which were already available in Japanese. His letters home indicate a strong admiration for the classical tradition of political history from Thucydides through Clarendon to Guizot, but also a respect for the positivist approach of Buckle. Within a few months, however, Suematsu had decided that the Japanese needed a custom-written history of Europe, by a European, and commissioned one from a Hungarian ex-revolutionary named George Gustavus Zerffi (1820–92). Zerffi's hastily written *The Science of History* (1879), notable for its praise of German historical methods, would have only a glancing impact on Japanese historiography. However, by this time Westerners were also beginning to take up academic appointments in Japan, and in 1887 the director of the Office of Historiography, Shigeno Yasutsugu (1827–1910), arranged for one of Ranke's more remote disciples, the German Jew Ludwig Riess (1861–1928), to come to Japan as the first professor of history in Tokyo Imperial University. Riess retained this position till 1902, by which time he had trained a substantial number of the next generation of Japanese history professors. The transfer of the History Office to the university, as a subsidiary research institute, and the formal appointment of Kume Kunitake, Shigeno and other historians as professors followed soon thereafter. Japanese history became the subject of a separate department (1889) and acquired its own chair in 1904. At the same time, the Historical Society, a rough equivalent to the American Historical Association, was also established and began to publish a journal, *Shigaku zasshi*, modelled on the European periodicals of Riess's experience, especially the *Historische Zeitschrift*. The *Dainihon shiryō* ('Chronological Sourcebook of Japanese History'), one of two major Meiji-era collections of historical texts, was nominally modelled on the *Monumenta Germaniae Historica*, the grandparent of such projects, though in substance there is little resemblance between the two, since the Japanese version follows a more conventional Confucian format of chronologically arranged events with accompanying extracts. More broadly, visiting Japanese dignitaries in Germany during the 1880s were impressed by the connection between nationalism, history and a growing military capacity. Germany became the admired model in more than one sense, with ominous consequences up the road.

As in Europe, however, not everyone accepted the value of academic historiography. Yamaji Aizan (1864–1917) was an outsider and popular historian highly critical of the sterility of scholarship at Tokyo Imperial, and – echoes of Nietzsche? – of 'dead history'. He advocated the writing of narratives covering a wide range of subjects, as opposed to the government-sponsored focus on document criticism and factual verification. Yamaji coined the term *minkan shigaku* or 'private historical scholarship' to distinguish his sort of history from that generated through state sponsorship. Moreover, the scholarship generated by the source criticism that Riess's Japanese friends espoused was by no means always welcome, especially among conservative nationalists determined to maintain the tradition of a social and moral function in historiography. Shigeno (who was also president of the Historical Society established in 1889) was himself reviled as 'Dr Obliterator' for his attacks on traditional verities such as the reliability of the *Taiheiki*, one of the most revered of medieval histories, and the historicity of some of its figures. His colleague, Kume Kunitake (1839–1931) (see Box 29) was forced to resign from his position in 1892 for using scholarly methods to undermine the historicity of one of Japan's foundational myths.

Meanwhile, reform-minded and generally pro-Western scholars such as Fukuzawa Yukichi (1835–1901), a reader of Alexis de Tocqueville, Buckle, Spencer and Guizot, formulated a theory of civilization espousing the superiority of the West and the need for Japan to catch up with the rest of the world after centuries of isolation. Others practised the equivalent of British 'Whig history', describing the Meiji Restoration as a major milestone on the road to modernization. By the end of the nineteenth century, Japanese historians had divided themselves into three formal fields: national (Japanese) history (*kokushi* or *Nihonshi*), oriental history (*Tōyōshi*) and Western history (*Seiyōshi*). Stefan Tanaka has explored the process whereby

Box 29   **The Kume Affair**

The article that got Kume Kunitake into so much trouble was published on
25 January 1892 in the popular history magazine *Shikai*. Its title was 'Shintō wa
Saiten no Kozoku' ('Shinto is an Outdated Custom of Heaven Worship'). Kume
argued that Shinto was not a religion but a primitive cult, which he analysed
historically and critically through comparisons with other world religions. Shinto,
according to Kume, represented an early stage of religious development, one that
was long surpassed by other religious traditions. Shintoists were particularly ap-
palled and some even demonstrated in front of his house. Conservative critics
charged Kume with irreverence towards the emperor and Japan itself, focusing
attention on the moral implications of his analysis rather than its scientific merits.
Complaints were made to the Ministry of Home Affairs, the Imperial Household
Ministry and the Ministry of Education, the latter of which suspended and later
forced Kume to resign. A year later, the Historiographical Institute was closed and
other iconoclasts, including Shigeno Yasutsugu, were dismissed.

Japan used the idea of *Tōyō* – conceived by Tsuda Sōkichi (1873–1961) as 'that
which was not the Occident' – to construct a past for themselves which inserted
Japan into world history as an entity separate from China but also distinct from
and equal to the West. *Tōyōshi* was initially the handiwork of one of Riess's former
pupils, Shiratori Kurakichi (1865–1942), professor of history at Tokyo Imperial
University from 1904 to 1925 and, along with Kyoto University's Naitō Kōnan
(1866–1934), one of the most distinguished Sinologists of the age. The challenge
to a Japanese Rankean such as Shiratori was to reconcile a historicist sense of
unique phenomena with a supposedly 'timeless' institution like the position of emperor. To solve the problem Shiratori crossed Hegel with Ranke, elevating 'spirit' as
a global norm, while denying that this 'universal' attribute could actually be found
in all cultures. Japan could thus be both part of the world as a whole while remaining free to follow its own version of the 'separate path' constructions of late nineteenth-century nationalist history-writing, comparable to American exceptionalism. Shiratori was himself critical of historians who conceived of world history as
'the history of Europe with a part of Asian history appended', a practice his own

Japanese colleagues had fallen into during the Meiji years by too easily embracing a Western agenda. Yet the ultimate result of *Tōyōshi* was to create in the object of its study, *Tōyō*, a Japanese version of European Orientalism, with the rest of Asia caught in between Western and Japanese developmental paths.

As the Kume affair and the attacks on Shigeno illustrate, there was also an uneasy tension in the application of what the Japanese themselves called 'scientific history' to the construction of a national and imperial-focused account of the past. In the decade leading up to the Second World War, a view of history centred on the *Tennō* (emperor), combined with legal penalties for offences against *kokutai* (literally, the nation's 'body' or 'essence', that is, the traditional belief in the emperor's personification of national sovereignty), constricted freedom of interpretation: to historicize an institution such as the structure of Japanese government, widely seen as unchanging and divine, was to undermine a strongly held orthodoxy. Though actual incidents of government interference were not numerous, they have become well known. The textbook controversy of 1911 turned on an especially sensitive period of medieval history, that of the Northern and Southern Courts at the time of Emperor Go-Daigo, and the implications of this for the legitimate descent of the modern emperors. Shigeno, by now a private citizen but still not averse to debate, proposed that this was *une question mal posée* since the whole concept of dynasties was borrowed from China. The official position of the government, never really openly articulated, was to endorse the fourteenth-century position of Kitabatake Chikafusa (see Chapter 3 above) that the Southern Court was indeed the sole legitimate one, but most historians avoided trouble by referring to both courts.

The situation exploded in 1911, during a period of political instability and treason trials, when a school textbook author named Kita Sadakichi publicly took the position that both courts had been legitimate. When the dust settled, several historians had lost their positions, and academic and school-level history ('applied' history to use an older category) diverged along separate tracks that have continued to the present day. In 1942, the historian Tsuda Sōkichi was condemned for undermining the still-revered national mythology of the *Kojiki* in a work he had published nearly three decades earlier on the ancient imperial court. His doubts about the historicity of Emperor Jimmu and his immediate successors were entirely unacceptable in an aggressively militaristic state that had marked the founding emperor's 2,600th anniversary in 1940 with national celebrations. The degree to which these were heavy-handed acts of censorship should not be overstated, nor should they be viewed from a Western liberal perspective. There is little evidence that Tsuda Sōkichi's contemporaries, even among the scholars, regarded this as an infringement of what we call academic freedom; rather, they saw it as an issue of needing to represent the past in such a way that public beliefs and traditional values were not offended. Moreover, such episodes of reaction were often relatively brief and alternated with periods of rather more permissive temperament.

Modernization in Korea and China

Japanese experimentation would provide Western historiography with a port of entry into the rest of East Asia. Though it had experienced European influences for at least two centuries, especially through the Catholic Church, Korea was exposed to modern historiography in the first instance through its island neighbour. Japanese scholarship would dominate the study of Korea during the period of occupation (1910–45) that followed the end of the Chosŏn era. One of the early consequences was a rewriting of early Korean history on liberal, progressivist and nationalist rather than dynastic lines by historians such as Sin Ch'aeho (1880–1936) and Ch'oe Nam-sŏn (1890–1957). Introduced into common parlance about 1890, the concept of *minjok* (a rough equivalent of the German *Volk*), a Korean nation defined ethnically rather than territorially, proved crucial in the formulation of this historical outlook: for the first time, Koreans conceived of themselves as a people constituted by more than allegiance to a shared monarch. For Sin Ch'aeho, the *minjok* would provide the essential unifying concept to his new history. It also provided a kind of antidote to contemporary Japanese historiography, similarly defined. Where some Japanese historians such as Kume Kunitake began to conceive of a wider empire whose past boundaries had once enclosed Korea, so Koreans like Sin used the reverse argument as justification for Korean resistance. Where other Japanese, most notably Shiratori Kurakichi, cast doubt on accounts of the early history of Korea and its legendary founder Tan'gun, Sin came to the rescue of both the historical figure himself and of Korean arguments for a remote and heroic antiquity earlier than and independent of either Japanese or Chinese influence.

The most dramatic changes to East Asian historiography, however, would be felt in the very home of Confucianism, coincidental with the final decades of the Qing dynasty and of the empire itself. As noted in Chapter 6, the late seventeenth and eighteenth centuries had seen significant developments in the methods of historical research, in particular the highly empirical investigations of philologically oriented scholars such as Qian Daxin. By the early nineteenth century, moreover, Chinese historians were warming to the notion that the organization of the past primarily along dynastic lines could be abandoned or at least departed from; in fact, they knew that alternatives to the model of the Standard Histories had existed for centuries in a variety of different genres of both private and official history-writing. Some such as Zhuang Cunyu (1719–88) picked up on the Han-era scholar He Xiu's (129–182) notion that the 'Three Systems' articulated by Confucius could be historically located in antiquity, and that dynastic successions could actually represent not merely a shift in the mandate of heaven but a progressive change from an age of disorder to one of 'approaching peace' and ending in one of 'universal peace'. Zhuang's grandson Liu Fenglu (1776–1829) would push this further, dividing past time into large chunks, first the three ancient dynasties (Xia, Shang, Zhou), then the period of Confucius and the *Chunqiu* and finally that of posterity. Wei Yuan (1794–1856), an ex-pupil of Liu, postulated a cycle of alternating Simplicity and Refinement, unfolding during a succession of the Three Systems; his *Mingdai bingshi erzheng lu* ('A Record of the Two Administrations of the Military and Economy in the Ming Period') was a series of essays analysing the cause of Ming decline. Wei's point of view took him outside the closed system of Chinese history: in his *Haiguo tuzhi* ('Illustrated Gazetteer of Maritime Nations') he offered the first full-length Chinese investigation into the history and geography of Europe.

All of these authors envisaged change as natural, inevitable and at least sometimes benign, while not abandoning the essential Confucian belief in a stable order underlying the surface of events. But by the early nineteenth century, the fabric of the Qing Empire was beginning to unravel. Wei's contemporaries had already witnessed rebellions, wars and economic crises, which doubtless informed their sense of historical ages of disorder. Scholars in the south nursed an especially acute dislike of the Manchu rulers, their part of China having been more brutally subdued than the north. Dissatisfaction with the civil service examination system also played a role. Despite rigid penalties for cheating, serious corruption was unearthed in 1858 by the Xianfeng emperor (r. 1850–61). A purge followed in which corrupt examiners were beheaded or banished and cheaters on any exam lost all credit for their previous achievements, but the confidence in the system had been irrevocably shaken. It would lead directly to the Taiping Rebellion (1851–66), whose leader was a disappointed candidate. The rebellion was a blow from which the empire never fully recovered, foreshadowing its final collapse in 1911. In 1904, following the failed 'Hundred Days of Reform' (1898), the examination system itself was terminated and with it one of the crucial structures that had bound official historiography to the imperial service for many centuries.

Meanwhile, commercial conflict with Western powers was mounting: trade disputes with Britain led to the First Opium War in 1839–42 (by which Britain acquired Hong Kong); attempts to continue the policy of limiting international contact, including the confinement of 'foreign devils' to particular locations such as Macao and Guangzhou, were met with resistance. By the end of the century, three decades after Japan had opened itself to foreign influence, the Qing clung to the xenophobic isolationism that culminated violently in the Boxer Rebellion. Economic disaster also loomed as the population of the empire doubled between the dynasty's foundation and the mid-nineteenth century, but without any parallel technological development, industrialization being seen as another subversive influence from the West. Finally, quite apart from the loss of territory to Britain and France, nearer neighbours like Russia and Japan were carving pieces out of the empire, and thereby chipping away at the Sinocentric worldview held as an article of faith by most Chinese.

Understanding the circumstances of the relatively sudden collapse of a twenty-three-centuries-old empire is essential to grasping why China, perhaps the most self-contained of all world cultures (its importation of foreign religions such as Buddhism excepted), suddenly began to absorb Western historiographical practices at the close of the nineteenth century. It is doubly important because historians such as Kang Youwei (1858–1927), Hu Shi (1891–1962), Gu Jiegang (1893–1980) and the philologist Fu Sinian (1896–1950), as well as historically inclined social theorists such as Liang Qichao (1873–1929), were at the forefront of movements for either reform or revolution. Kang, whom Liang dubbed the 'Martin Luther of Confucianism', was a conservative reformer who saw social change as inevitable even within a Confucian context; he turned Confucius himself into a prophet of progress. His proposal for a constitutional monarchy was an option foreclosed by the dowager Empress Ci Xi's reactionary rule, and by the death in 1908 of her own son, the figurehead Guangxu emperor, shortly before she herself died. This left the country in a political vacuum for four years, and by the time that the child emperor Puyi finally abdicated in 1912, China had become a republic. Over three decades of political instability, armed conflict and occupation by Japan followed before the foundation of the communist leader Mao Zedong's People's Republic in 1949.

Western works had been trickling into China in greater numbers through the nineteenth century, and a translation bureau was established at Guangzhou in 1839. Consequently, key texts in European political philosophy and history were becoming available, and even traditionalists such as the journalist and translator Wang Tao (1828–97), no believer in Chinese inferiority, were beginning to devote themselves to the study of Western history. In the first instance, however, Western historiography was derived not immediately from Europe but at second-hand, via Japan. China's eastern neighbour had a significant head start on the road to modernization, and its recent successes were far more frightening to the Chinese than those of the European powers. In 1894–5 Japan overwhelmed China in the Sino-Japanese war, largely fought over control of Korea; and in 1905 the Japanese

modelled oriental success-through-modernization (*gendaika*) even more spectacularly by defeating Russia. Chinese historical thought had long been inclined to
cyclical views of history as a series of alternating periods of order and disorder,
throughout which individual dynasties rose and fell. In the face of rapid political
change and a sense of crisis, historians would turn instead to an explanation of
the past as linear development over a series of periods, and to an understanding
of their country no longer as *tianxia* (all under heaven) but as a temporally finite,
geographically circumscribed nation-state (*guojia*).

During this period, historians can be broadly divided into three groups: traditional Confucians, liberal-nationalists and, developing somewhat later, Marxists.
In the last years of the Qing, a group of nationalists including Zhang Taiyan (1869–
1935) and Liu Shipei (1884–1919) had founded the 'National Essence' movement,
publishing historical essays and promoting the writing of a new Chinese history.
More importantly, the liberal-nationalist reformer Liang Qichao was exiled in Japan and elsewhere for twelve years (1899–1911), and while in Japan he quickly
acquired the language and came into contact with the views of Meiji reformers
such as Fukuzawa Yukichi. As a result, Liang became the major importer of recent
Japanese cultural and political developments into China, and a virtual personification of the Chinese abandonment of the long-standing apparatus that had guided
historiography at least since the Tang.

Liang read no Western languages, but numerous European works were by now
available in either Japanese or Chinese. It was through Fukuzawa and lesser Japanese authors such as the journalist and geographer Shiga Shigetaka that Liang
encountered the theories of H.T. Buckle, which played well in East Asia long
after they had been resoundingly rejected by Buckle's fellow Britons. While in
Japan, Liang authored his own articles on European thinkers such as Rousseau,
Bentham, Darwin and Kant. In 1902 he would publish a guide to Japanese books
which included a bibliography of Japanese histories then in use, a list that features
Michelet and Guizot as well as various Japanese historians. Liang also looked to
the West, rather than to older Chinese alternatives, for a non-dynastic periodization; he noted the commonplace division of time into ancient, medieval, modern
and contemporary, which he then applied to China, though stressing that its epochs were not precisely synchronous with their counterparts in the West. Liang
rejected the annalistic model of Chinese historical writing and deplored the lack of
a cumulative national history. China had been a major contributor to the world's
culture for thousands of years, but its story had 'never been narrated historically',
having been obscured in the chopping up of the country's past along dynastic
lines.[27] He, too, believed that there could be no modern understanding of history
while China continued to see itself as a world unto itself rather than a nation, and

he drew an explicit comparison, derived from his reading of Gibbon, with ancient Rome: in both places, he argued, a lack of appreciation of the polity's status as a 'nation' within a wider world, compounded by a complacent sense of superiority over other peoples, had destroyed true patriotism.

Interested in History as well as history, Liang came to the conclusion that it was still not too late for China to modernize itself and catch up with the world. Liang had discovered in Descartes and Bacon two complementary prophets of rationalism and progress in an earlier century; among more recent figures he admired Voltaire and Tolstoy. Where Europe and Japan had gone, China could now follow, shaking off two millennia of stagnation. Liang joined with the nationalist Zhang Taiyan in advocating a general history (*tongshi*) based on Western methodology, and in the six instalments of his *Xin shixue* ('New Historiography', 1902) he was highly critical of the current status of history in China, a practice that he argued was still fixated on the court, individuals and defunct dynasties, rather than with more relevant historical subjects such as the nation as a whole and various collectives within it.

In 1922, near the end of his career, Liang assembled a set of lecture notes into a book called *Zhongguo li shi yan jiu fa* ('Research Methods for Chinese History'). This made a plea for a shift from narrative forms towards a reorganization of history along subject lines (history of music, history of science, philosophy, etc.). There is less of the high tide of Rankean historicism in this endorsement of collective and subject-based history than there is of Enlightenment historical thought, embodied in Gibbon and Voltaire or, looking ahead, to the French scholars who were about to found the Annales (see Chapter 9 below). His influential essay on *Intellectual Trends in the Qing Period*, written in two weeks originally as a preface for a friend, Jiang Fangzhen's (1882–1938) history of Europe's Renaissance, has the flavour of Burckhardtian *Kulturgeschichte*.[28] Liang himself was not insensitive to the role of the individual: he dabbled in biography and used heroic figures frequently to illustrate his arguments in the manner of Carlyle, whom he quotes explicitly in an unfinished life of England's Oliver Cromwell. Although Liang defended the autonomy of history from propaganda or service to political utility, he was no devotee of historical scholarship for its own sake since accurate understanding of the past was to be a tool in China's breaking of her shackles. If there are Germanic notes sounded here, they are Lamprechtian rather than Rankean ones, which Liang probably derived from Fukuzawa and which resembled contemporary American movements such as the New History. And if there is nationalism, it is not of the Treitschkean sort, since the Anglophile Liang saw China within a global and cosmopolitan context, albeit one now modified by a century of racial and evolutionary theory in which Teutonic peoples had come to the top of the heap. It is as if Kant had been glossed by Herbert Spencer, Houston Stewart Chamberlain and E. A. Freeman, and then translated into Chinese.

Liang Qichao opened a door into China through which other Western influences would soon pass, and through which Chinese scholars began to write more frequently about the history of other parts of the world. As in parts of Southeast Asia, distance altered perspective on alien others: Chinese readers tended to lump European methods together and diminish differences that, to Europeans themselves, would have seemed very large, such as that between positivism and idealism, or between Rankean methodology and its Lamprechtian departures. A few years further on, in the wake of the 'May Fourth' New Culture movement that began in 1919, American-style academic history arrived with the translation of the Columbia University historian James Harvey Robinson's *The New History* into Chinese by one of his admirers, He Bingsong (1890–1946). He, who had studied at Wisconsin and Princeton, also adapted, rather than translated, the much more conventional text by Langlois and Seignobos into Chinese as a work on the writing of general history, *Tongshi xinyi* ('New Principles of General History', 1928). Chen Yinke (1890–1969), a brilliant linguist who became a distinguished authority on the Tang and the Sui, was educated at Harvard and Berlin. A Columbia-trained historian (who would eventually return to the United States as his country's ambassador) and admirer of the philosopher John Dewey, Hu Shi authored a history of Chinese philosophy, borrowing from such disparate European sources as Wilhelm Windelband and Langlois and Seignobos. Hu's pupil Gu Jiegang was perhaps the most formidable mind of the group. A relentless debunker of bogus ancient texts in the great international philological tradition that includes Lorenzo Valla and Isaac Casaubon, Gu published a popular school textbook situating China in world history. Fiercely sceptical towards early Chinese history before the Zhou dynasty in the eleventh century BC, he became the central figure of a 'Doubting Antiquity School', a position itself soon undermined, however, by the discovery of Shang oracle bone inscriptions, a new source which put the early dynasties back into historical time.

At the same time, German-trained Chinese scholars were introducing the very Rankean type of historical writing of which Robinson's New Historians had been critical, a fine distinction that, again, seems to have been lost on the Chinese readers of both. Among the younger members of this generation, Fu Sinian, a student leader during the May Fourth reform movement which followed the First World War and another disciple of Hu Shi, saw in Western theories of history the solution to China's problems. As a historian, he is especially well known first for embracing with a positivist fervour Germanic philological methods (though he probably owed as much to Ming-Qing *kaozheng* as to Niebuhr), and second for rejecting dynastic history in favour of an analysis based on ethnicity, in particular the conflicts between Han and non-Han peoples within China, and for pointing out the contributions of the latter throughout China's past. Fu's friend and schoolmate, Yao Congwu (1894–1970), studied in Germany during the 1920s and early 1930s. He was as great a Germanophile as Fu and, Edward Wang suggests, the most 'Rankean' historian of his generation, expounding German historical methods and philosophy for a Chinese audience and offering an alternative of sorts to the New History embraced by the Columbiaphiles. There was, of course, another German alternative at hand in Karl Marx, but we must defer discussion of his Chinese followers to our next chapter.

Africa: Written History and Oral Tradition Revisited

Africa, which has not featured prominently in this book so far, brings us back to the recurrent theme of relations between speech, written texts and history. African oral tradition and oral literature have been closely studied for some time; while there is no space here to recapitulate these discussions, a brief overview of some examples of African oral epic, taking us back several centuries, is in order. Many of these have only recently been transcribed, such as the epic of the fifteenth-century Songhay ruler Askia Mohammed (r. 1493–1528); previously referred to in sixteenth-century Muslim histories, it was recorded as recently as the early 1980s from the mouth of a griot (a West African bard or poet) in Niger. There are many variants of these by different names, such as the Wolof *woy jallore* or *cosaan*, a song of great exploits or of genealogy. The Songhay term for a long narrative about the past with genealogical detail is *deeda*. Some of these words have clear ties to others denoting written historical genres: the *tariko* of the Gambia and the *tariku* of Upper Guinea appear to derive from the Arabic *ta'rīkh*. A few such epics refer to events from a very long time ago: the 'Epic of Musadu' from the Mande people of southwestern Guinea purports to tell the story of a slave named Zo Musa who founded the town of Musadu some time between the thirteenth and fifteenth centuries, and of a warrior, Foningama, who took over the town, probably in the sixteenth century. What is not known is how far back these epics originate and how they may have been altered over the passage of years.

Examining oral traditions for historicity, much less for precise chronological information, is often not very productive. We are better off considering them for what they can tell us about contemporary values. Sympathetic experts have pointed to complicating factors such as 'telescoping' (the truncation or expansion of dynastic lines to fill chronological gaps), 'feedback' (the effect of writing on spoken testimony, and specifically the risk that a tradition has been contaminated by, and is simply repeating, facts gleaned from colonial or external literary sources) and 'structural amnesia' (the collective forgetting of details of the past, and figures of history, that no longer fit with present political circumstances). On the other hand, it has also been argued that these distorting influences can be filtered out. The techniques of oral traditionalists have been applied outside Africa, in the study of Southeast Asian, Latin American and Caribbean cultures, as well as to indigenous cultures in North America and Australasia. For all its potential weaknesses as a source, there is no doubt that oral tradition has reopened a road to the past once closed off by the bias of historiography towards writing which commenced with the early modern contacts and was consolidated during the Enlightenment. Yet we need not rely on oral traditions to find evidence of history in Africa, before the white man appeared. Contrary to popular belief, the continent was not devoid of written history, nor is all 'darkness' prior to the arrival of the colonial powers.

By the time the Portuguese were rounding the Cape of Good Hope, Islam had been present in the northern parts of the continent for some centuries, and had gradually extended its cultural reach past the Maghreb (the northwest region including Tunisia, Morocco and Algeria) and south of Sudan, below the Sahara. Many indigenous African tongues were represented with Arabic script (a practice known as *adjami*), for instance those of the Hausa of Sudan and the nomadic Fulani who would conquer much Hausa territory in the nineteenth century. Historiographically, the Hausa were especially influenced by the *Ta'rikh al-khulafa* ('History of the Caliphs') by the prolific Jalal al-Din al-Suyuti (1445–1505); as late as the early twentieth century, for instance, Abubakar dan Atiku's *Chronicle of Sokoto* imitated al-Suyuti's form and style. The Hausa also evolved a courtly tradition of contemporary historical writing, exemplified by the earliest known Sudanese historical writing; this dates from the 1570s, when a Chief Imam, Aḥmad b. Fartuwa (or Aḥmad ibn Fartua) composed a chronicle of the first twelve years of the reign of King Idrīs Alōma of Bornu (r. 1570–1602). By the early eighteenth century a West African coastal kingdom, Gonja, was transferring its oral traditions into Arabic-language annals such as the *Kitāb Ghanjā* and *Amr Ajdādinā* ('The Departure from Mali'). Elsewhere in East Africa, *Kitāb al-Sulwa fi-akhbar Kilwa*, a history of the town of Kilwa in modern Tanzania, was recounted in an anonymous early sixteenth-century work commissioned by the Sultan Muhammad b. al-Husayn and later used by the Portuguese historian João de Barros.

Ethiopia has perhaps the richest and most long-standing tradition of historical writing in sub-Saharan Africa. Ethiopian monarchs authorized inscribed steles as early as the fourth century, when Ezana of Aksum (r. c. 320–60) made Christianity

Figure 52 | Solomon grasping the hand of the Queen of Sheba. Illuminated page from *The History of the Queen of Sheba*. Ethiopia, late nineteenth century, text in Ge'ez and Amharic.

the state religion. Royal chronicles written by court scribes, in an alphabet derived from the archaic Ethiopian Ge'ez tongue, first appear in the thirteenth century. This was coterminous with the 'Solomonic Restoration', a dynastic change ushered in by Prince Yekuno Amlak (r. 1270–85), who claimed descent from Menelik I, legendary son of King Solomon by the Queen of Sheba. The next two centuries would see a number of chronicles of successive Ethiopian kings, and a famous work known as the *Kebra Nagast* ('Glory of Kings') telling the story of the birth of Menelik (Fig. 52). The chronicles would continue in both Ge'ez and Amharic (the country's modern language of government) down to the twentieth century.

40: Early Historical Writing in Ethiopia

He was not yet fourteen years old ... Until he had completely reached the age of reason he entrusted his power to the hands of his mother and his mother's sister. He did nothing without them until he was grown up; in this he was like our Saviour Jesus who obeyed his mother ... until he was baptized at the age of twenty by the hand of John .... Having followed this example during his youth he later devoted himself to war because the governors of that time had revolted against him, and among them were to be found many of his relatives, of high families, whom his ancestors had raised to high position; some of these [rebels] perished by the spear and the sword, some fled, repented and made their submission ....

[In the course of his reign Sartsa Dengel carried out a campaign against the Falashas in the mountains of Semien, of which the chronicler writes, with some admiration for the enemy, as follows:]²⁹

A very strange thing happened that day to a [Falasha] woman who had been reduced to slavery. A man was leading her behind him and had tied her hand to his; when during the march she saw herself near the precipice ... she threw herself into it, dragging with her the man who had attached her hand to his. The energy of this woman who preferred death to joining the Christian community is a surprising thing! She was not the only one to do this remarkable thing; many men imitated her action, but she was the first.

Selection from the chronicle of Sartsa Dengel (r. 1563–97), king of Ethiopia, in *The Ethiopian Royal Chronicles*, ed. Richard P. Pankhurst (Addis Ababa and Oxford: Oxford University Press, 1967), 82, 86–7. Pankhurst's italicized interpolations have been omitted, and capitalization modified. Sartsa Dengel, who inherited the throne as a child, ruled under the name Malak Sagad, contemporary with Elizabeth I of England, Philip II of Spain and Ivan the Terrible of Muscovy.

Other Ethiopian historical literature in Ge'ez or Amharic appears in the sixteenth century, such as the *History of the Galla*, composed in the 1590s by Bahrey, a monk who may also have authored the contemporary chronicle of Emperor Sartsa Dengel (Extract 40).³⁰ Further south, Swahili literature includes a number of narrative poems (*utendi*), of which the earliest written example, *Utendi wa Tambuka* ('The Story of Tambuka', 1728), is a historical epic set during the life of Muhammad. At the other end of the Sahara, West African kingdoms developed an Arabic-language historical literature, such as the *Ta'rīkh al-sūdān* ('Chronicle of the Blacks') by 'Abd al-Raḥmān al-Sa'dī (*fl.* 1596–1656).³¹

Modern Western-style historical writing appears first in nineteenth-century colonial times – not a great deal later than its establishment in Europe. Initially, it was overwhelmingly the preserve of the colonizers, especially missionaries, who were concerned to integrate African schoolchildren into the Christian and

European past. There were some notable indigenous exceptions, largely unnoticed at the time, such as Samuel Johnson (1846–1901), the Yoruba son of a Sierra Leone freedman who returned to his parents' home in Nigeria as a missionary. Johnson, strongly affected by classical historians such as Xenophon, authored a *History of the Yorubas: From the Earliest Times to the Beginning of the British Protectorate* (comp. 1897, published posthumously in 1921). This was based largely on Yorubaland oral historical narratives (*itàn*) and eyewitness accounts, in addition to colonial documents; Johnson's purpose, as he announced at the start of his book, was to ensure 'that the history of our fatherland might not be lost in oblivion, especially as our old sires are fast dying out'. Carl Christian Reindorf (1834–1917), another African cleric, used both oral and written evidence for his 1895 *History of the Gold Coast and Asante*, and the Buganda (part of Uganda) politician, Sir Apolo Kagwa (*c.* 1869–1927) provided an oral-source-based history of *The Kings of Buganda* (1901).[32] In the west central African territory of the Bamum (modern Cameroon), its local sultan, Njoya (*c.* 1880–1933) first created his own ideographic script, modelled on European writing, and then commissioned the writing of a 548-page manuscript on the history and customs of his people.

The process of Westernizing African history-writing is well illustrated in the lengthy career of Uwadiae Jacob Egharevba (1893–1991) of Benin, in modern Nigeria. Educated in Yoruba territory while travelling with his trader parents, Egharevba soon abandoned commerce for a full-time literary career. In his *A Short History of Benin*, the most well known of his over thirty historical and literary works, Egharevba exploited his connections with Benin chiefs and 'court historians', including those responsible for the Benin king list, and became convinced that the future survival of his people's traditions depended on their being recorded and documented. He published the *Short History* first as *Ekhere Vb 'Itan Edo* (1934) in the Edo language, of which he was a zealous advocate, but he concluded that a wider readership necessitated an English translation. The work proved so popular that several subsequent editions were published in ensuing decades. Though Egharevba never lost his devotion to oral sources, he made increasing use of written European materials; he appears to have been less interested, a recent analysis suggests, in reproducing traditions as he heard them than in homogenizing and reconciling them into 'a story that appears real'.[33] The English version also tones down certain anti-British views of the *Ekhere*, deleting entire passages that British administrators would have found objectionable. In the 1953 edition of the *Short History* he abandoned some of the traditional origin stories he had previously accepted in favour of the so-called Hamitic hypothesis (see Box 30) to trace the origins of the Edo back to the ancient Egyptians.

Box 30   The Hamitic Hypothesis

Much early indigenous African historical writing was devoted to countering racist assumptions about the inferiority of Africans. These in turn were often derived from the 'Hamitic hypothesis' – essentially the nineteenth century's pseudo-scientific and ethnographic spin (encouraged by linguistic research) on an older, Bible-derived view that Africans were descended from Ham, son of Noah, or alternatively that the 'civilized' cultures of Egypt and North Africa derived from 'European' peoples such as the Phoenicians. In its modern form, the hypothesis drew on eighteenth-century sta-dialism with its distinction between agricultural and pastoral societies. The hypothesis continued to be used by early twentieth-century racial theorists, for whom a distinctive Hamitic race had intermarried with more primitive Negroid peoples, and who attributed the progress of civilization in Africa to the positive Hamitic influence on a more agrarian and tribal black African population. Arguably the most famous exposition of these views in the early twentieth century was the British ethnologist Charles Gabriel Seligman's (1873–1940) book, *The Races of Africa* (1930).

All of these works were ethnically focused, that is, devoted to recovering and telling the past of a particular tribe. The clerical careers of most of these historians ensured a strong Christian influence, and most were heavily reliant on European sources, as was the somewhat later work of the Xhosa missionary John Henderson Soga (1860–1941), *The Southeastern Bantu* (1930). In areas colonized by Germans such as Tanganyika (part of modern Tanzania), Swahili historical works in Roman script and verse chronicles in *adjami* appeared in the early twentieth century, be-ginning with Abdallah bin Hemedi 'l Ajjemy's (*c.* 1835–1912) *Habari za Wakilindi* ('Chronicles of the Kilindi', completed in 1906);[34] this was an extensive record of the Kilindi dynasty that ruled the area in the nineteenth century, derived from oral traditions of the Shambala, a non–Swahili-speaking tribe, and from the author's own memories of recent events. A reminder that the traffic between spoken tra-dition and written history can run in both directions, and that both can flourish simultaneously within the same environment, is provided by *The Chronicle of the Kings of Pate*. The original manuscript of this work covered the kingdom's history

(Pate is in modern Kenya) from the thirteenth to the late nineteenth century. The manuscript was destroyed or lost during the British assault on Witu, the capital of Pate, in 1890, but knowledge of its contents was so vivid that several writers were able to produce new written versions in the decades thereafter, largely thanks to the memories of a member of the royal family, Bwana Kitini (d. 1931), who in turn relied on the testimony of his grandfather, Bwana Simba, 'keeper of the royal tradition'.[35]

It was not until after the Second World War, however, that African history as an academic subject began to make its way, slowly, on to mainstream history curricula within and outside Africa. Beginning in the late 1940s with the retreat of the European colonial powers and the establishment of independent nations in ensuing decades, a deeper interest in exploring their own past quickly emerged among African populations, stimulated by reaction to decades of education in an alien imperial historiography. With this came an urgent need to recast the historical record and to recover evidence of many overlooked pre-colonial civilizations. One consequence of the decolonization of Africa was that at first, a European-style master-narrative of progress was simply imported and converted to local purposes. The political withdrawal of Europe occurred just at the point when very new academic institutions were created, principally as overseas extensions of European models. These were highly dependent on European academic staff or affiliated universities abroad – Britain created universities in its colonies starting in the late 1940s, and the French and Belgians quickly followed. A triumphal nationalist narrative of the advance of this or that former colony into a free and full member of the international community marked much of the new African historical writing up to about 1970. It came with most of the trappings of pre-war 'whig' historiography, such as the steady development in the past of political institutions, the centralization of power and the improvement of administration – all the features of the modern Western state.

At the same time, European intellectuals' own discomfort with the Eurocentrism of previous scholarship provided a significant stimulus for the intensive academic study of African history, an innovation that had spread to North America by the late 1960s. Foundational research was done at the School of Oriental and African Studies (SOAS) in London by scholars such as Roland Oliver (b. 1923, co-founder in 1960 of the *Journal of African History*) and by the Belgian Jan Vansina (b. 1929), an authority on oral tradition. Francophone scholars have been equally influential. But African historiography has not been the sole creation of interested Europeans. African universities have, despite the instabilities of politics and civil war in many areas, trained their own scholars and sent many others overseas for doctoral training. They have also attracted

European scholars into their teaching ranks: the 'Ibadan' school of historians (initiated in the 1950s at the University of Ibadan in Nigeria and influential into the 1970s) included both native Nigerians and transplanted Britons. The pioneering Nigerian historian Kenneth Onwuka Dike (1917–83) studied at Durham, Aberdeen and London, and SOAS alone has educated several leading African-born scholars, including the Ghanaian Albert Adu Boahen (1932–2006). Boahen in turn participated in the important early summary work of postcolonial historical writing, the UNESCO *General History of Africa*, directed by a 'scientific committee,' two-thirds of whom were Africans, and written by over 300 authors including the Kenyans Ali Mazrui (b. 1933) and Bethwell Allan Ogot (b. 1933), Joseph Ki-Zerbo (1922–2006) of Burkina Faso (formerly Upper Volta) and the Nigerian J. F. Ade Ajayi (b. 1929). The development of European historiography in Africa over the past century is thus rather reminiscent of Indian historical writing of the same period: the tools and concepts of the colonial powers were adopted by the colonized first to embrace and later to push against those powers in support of a nationalist (and more recently, a Marxian, class-oriented) goal.

Religion, Nation and History in the Islamic World

In the second half of the nineteenth century, intellectuals in both the Arabic and non-Arabic parts of the Islamic world began to write histories devoted to establishing national pasts, which now also included the pre-Islamic periods. Older pan-Islamic cultural and religious impulses remained as important as newer Arab nationalism: Middle Eastern peoples of various religions had to face the dilemma of coexistence with Western powers. Modern Islamic thought, influenced by Western science and technology, was also beginning to take shape in the hands of activist-reformers like Sayyid Jamal al-Din Afghani (1838–97), the author of a history of Afghanistan. The social origins and interests of historians were also quite different than in previous ages. With the European presence had come the collapse of the '*ulema*', or learned religious men who had dominated historical writing in the Muslim world for centuries, many of them polymaths and scientific thinkers rather than exclusively historians. Their place would be occupied by a 'bourgeois' class (doctors, lawyers, journalists), often very Western-oriented, and seeing history as *adab* or a branch of *belles-lettres*.[36] During this period, efforts were made to print historical sources, and several learned societies with historical interests were founded.

The Egyptian 'Abd al-Raḥmān al-Jabartī (1753–1825) anticipated this revival of historiography with his anti-French account of the Napoleonic occupation of Egypt

41: Napoleon in Egypt: al-Jabartī's *Chronicle*

On Thursday the sixteenth it was [proclaimed] that if anyone had a quarrel with a Christian or a Jew, or vice versa, one antagonist could testify against the other, and demand for him to be brought to the house of the Ṣārī 'Askar.

On that day they killed two persons and walked around with their heads, calling out 'This is the punishment of all who deliver letters from the Mamlūks or bring letters to them.'

On that day they told the people to desist from burying the dead in cemeteries close to dwellings, such as the cemeteries of al-Azbakiyya and al-Ruway'ī and to bury them only in graveyards far (from the populated areas). Those who had no vaults in the cemetery should bury their dead in the vaults of the Mamlūks. And when they buried someone they were required to increase the depth of the graves. They further ordered people to hang out their clothing, furnishings, and bedding on their roofs for several days and to fumigate their houses with fumes which would remove the putrescence. All this was out of fear, as they claimed, of the smell and contagion of the plague ...

As for the French it is their custom not to bury their dead but to toss them on garbage heaps like the corpses of dogs and beasts, or to throw them into the sea. Among the other things which they said is that when someone becomes sick they must inform the French who then send an authorized representative to examine him and to find out whether he has the plague or not. Then they decide what to do with him.

From *Napoleon in Egypt: al-Jabartī's Chronicle of the French Occupation*, trans. Shmuel Moreh (1975; Princeton and New York: Markus Wiener, 1983), 71. The selection comes from the section of the chronicle covering daily events on 16 Rabī el-Thānī 1213 AH (= 9 September 1798 AD).

(1798–1801), *Maẓhar al-Taqdīs bi-Dhahāb Dawlat al-Faransis* ('The Demonstration of Piety in the Destruction of the French State', comp. *c.* 1801) (Extract 41) and a longer historical account of events from the late seventeenth to early nineteenth century, *'Ajā'ib al-Āthār fi'l-Tarājim wa'l-Akhbār* ('Wondrous Accounts Regarding Biographies and Historical Reports'), which is markedly less critical of the recent European invaders. Jabartī's work came at the end of a long fallow period, historical writing in Ottoman-ruled Egypt having been relatively scant and generally of poor quality, but other historians soon appeared, such as Muḥammad b. 'Umar al-Tūnisī (1789–1857), who wrote a record of his travels in the Sudan which included historical material, and two associates of Jabartī, 'Abdullāh al-Sharqāwi (d. 1812) and Ismā'īl al Khashshāb (d. 1814).

Most of these works, Jabartī's included, can still be viewed as late examples of traditional Islamic historiography. The political circumstances underpinning that historiography were, however, disappearing rapidly in the early nineteenth century, a period that would see rising Arab nationalism chafe against Muslim unity, notionally represented by a declining Ottoman Empire. Jabartī wrote much of his work during the opening years of the lengthy reign in Egypt of the pasha Muḥammad ʿAlī (1805–49), a reader of history and an admirer of Alexander the Great and Caesar. While Jabartī was no supporter of the pasha, whom he deemed both a tyrant and a heretic, another Egyptian, Rifāʾa Rāfiʿ al-Tahṭāwī (1801–73), took the opposite view, becoming one of Muḥammad ʿAlī's most favoured intellectuals and flourishing under him and his successors. Tahṭāwī had spent five years in Paris, and he became a major channel through which modern European historiography began to enter the Arabic-speaking world. He translated into Arabic or oversaw translations of several Enlightenment works, including Voltaire's *Charles XII* and Robertson's *Charles V*; a translation of Georges-Bernard Depping's (1784–1853) *Aperçu historique sur les moeurs et coutumes des nations* ('Historical Summary of the Manners and Customs of Nations') would prove especially popular among Tunisian readers. A vigorous 'translation movement' may for a time have deterred new historical writing, but under Muḥammad ʿAlī's successors, especially the Westernizing Khedive Ismāʿīl (1863–79), Tahṭāwī also narrated the history of ancient Egypt in a work (1868–9) that is a hybrid of modern and classical Islamic historical forms. It continues to stress some of the long-standing values of Islamic historiography as outlined in authors like Ibn Khaldūn (whose *Muqaddimah* Tahṭāwī had shepherded into print in 1857) and in the *hadith*s. Islam plays a crucial role in Tahṭāwī's narrative, giving Egypt its modern identity as Tahṭāwī tells it. However, the work departs from Islamic history-writing in treating Egypt, for the first time, as a distinctive unit, that had existed continuously from antiquity to modern times, celebrating the country as a seat of world civilization and learning; this built on contemporary fascination with Egypt elsewhere in the world following recent advances in the understanding of hieroglyphics. The division of history by Tahṭāwī into human and sacred spheres, and periodization of the former into ancient and modern (with subject matter further arranged as either 'universal' or 'particular'), shows signs of Western influence.

Tahṭāwī was instrumental in reforming the Egyptian school curriculum, which by the 1870s routinely included history. Universities were established early in the twentieth century, and with them the academic training of scholars in history and other arts and sciences. During this period, the era of British rule in Egypt (1882–1922), the influential politician Muṣṭafà Kāmil (1874–1908), himself the author of a number of historical works, further encouraged nationalist views of his country's past; his protégé Muḥammad Farīd (1868–1919) composed a history of Egypt under Muḥammad ʿAlī (1891) and another on the Ottoman Empire (1894). Ideologically, Kāmil's and Farīd's works marked a new, more intensely nationalist and anti-Western trend that cut across and often contradicted the Islamic values of most historical writing during the previous millennium. This trend was aided by the rapid transition in literary and intellectual life away from Turkish towards expression in Arabic.

Syria was occupied by Egypt in the 1830s, introducing it, too, to Western reforms, which the Ottomans continued to pursue after the Egyptians eventually withdrew. The study of history was encouraged in Syria by the father and son Buṭrus and Salīm al-Bustānī, publishers of *al-Jinān*, a literary magazine, and in the development of new schools. The Bustānīs had a more secular outlook on the past than Tahṭāwī, stressing Arabic unity and downplaying the role of Islam; the elder of the two compiled an Arabic dictionary and began work on an encyclopedia of Arabic. Most Arabic historians in this period tended to be non-academics, and not all were Muslims: the Syrian Christian Ilyās Maṭar (1857–1910) was an Ottoman official, physician and lawyer, and his compatriot Jurjī Yannī (1856–1941) an ethnically Greek and religiously Greek Orthodox journalist and intellectual. The Western-educated Maṭar decided while still a student to embark on a history of Syria. The *Tārikh al-mamlaka al-Sūriyya* ('History of the Province of Syria'), published at Beirut in 1874 during the period of Ottoman reforms, conveys its author's disappointment at the dearth of histories of his land, and once again privileges issues of national identity over religion.

Not all this nationalism was linked to particular states or territories, and it is possible to identify an emerging 'pan-Arab' historiography that, rather like German history of the same era, promoted ethnic solidarity against foreign influences, whether Ottoman or European. The Lebanese-Egyptian Jurjī Zaydān (1861–1914) epitomizes this strand of historical writing at the beginning of the last century. Himself a Christian, Zaydān was a journalist and author of several historical novels in addition to his multivolume history of Islamic civilization (1902–6).[37] But as with other pan-Arab nationalist writers, he saw religion as a second-order affiliation, and pushed his historical writing back beyond the arrival of Islam into the very remote past; his study of the pre-Islamic Arabs took this to extremes, arguing that the ancient Babylonians had been Arabs.

Academic historiography began slowly in the post-Ottoman era starting in the 1920s, initially in the hands of North American- and European-trained scholars, thus extending the dominance of Western-style academic history over the Islamic world's long-distinct historiographic traditions. Perhaps the earliest work to practise modern archival scholarship – its author used British and French manuscript materials – was Shafīq Ghurbāl's (1894–1961) English-language *The Beginnings of the Egyptian Question and the Rise of Mehemet Ali* (1928). Ghurbāl was among a group of Egyptian historians, including Muḥammad Rifʿat Bey and the Sorbonne-trained Muḥammad Ṣabrī (1890–1978), each of whom had studied in Europe. Ghurbāl had been sent to Liverpool in 1915, where he studied history, and after a brief period as a schoolteacher in Alexandria, he returned to England (1922) to study at London's Institute for Historical Research, where he submitted parts of his future book for the MA degree, supervised by a young Arnold J. Toynbee.[38] The rest of Ghurbāl's career was spent in Egypt as an influential professor and administrator in both university and government. His various histories, which turn Muḥammad ʿAlī into a nationalist hero and modernizer, established what ultimately became a 'national' school of Egyptian historians. Western methodological texts were also catching on, with a lag-effect that disseminated ideas already dated in their European home: Asad Rustum (1897–1965), a historian of Syria, published an Arabic-language manual on Western historical method in 1939, largely drawn from Langlois and Seignobos' famous textbook, which was by then fast losing ground in France to the emerging *Annaliste* historical revolution (see Chapter 9 below).

Nationalist and secular tendencies were, however, also being felt in non-Arabic Islam, and nowhere more strongly than in Turkey itself, where the longer traditions of Ottoman historical writing had survived through the eighteenth into the nineteenth century. Official historians were still being appointed through this period, and the spread of both printing and literacy stoked a public appetite for historical works. Until at least the mid-1800s, court-appointed annalists (*vakʾanüvis*) or others (*müverrih*) who either had court connections or were fishing for such rewards, continued to dominate, and truly independent historiography was rare. The outstanding historian of the period, Aḥmed Jevdet (Cevdet) Pasha (1822–95), spent three decades preparing a twelve-volume history of imperial events from 1774 to 1826, the early instalments of which earned him his appointment as official historiographer. As in the rest of the Ottoman world, this was a period of transition during which interest in western European culture and its history-writing grew along with knowledge of Western languages and literatures; new genres were developed, including memoirs and local histories that were more than mere biographies of local worthies. The 'ancillary disciplines' of history, such as sigillography, epigraphy and numismatics, began to appear in the second part of the century, and Western-style academic training followed when the University of Istanbul was established in close to its modern form soon after the turn of the century. The production of textbooks after 1880 were more closely controlled by government, and reflected a more secular understanding of the Ottoman past which emphasized its territorial gains; stories about deposed or deranged sultans, which had featured prominently in histories from earlier periods, were increasingly deemed dangerous to the state. This was precisely the time when the Young Ottomans, a mid-century group determined to maintain the empire's unity through a cohesive 'Ottomanism' (leavened by certain Enlightenment ideas derived from Montesquieu and Rousseau), were at the peak of their influence.

The conversion of Ottomanism to Turkism, a less ethnically inclusive, more nationalistic vision of the state, was under way by the end of the century, and a new generation of politicized intellectuals, the Young Turks, led a revolution in 1908 that also advanced the process of constitutional reform. This would culminate, following the disaster of the First World War and the loss of most of the empire's satellites, in the establishment of Turkey as a republic in 1923. The new state's leader, Mustafa Kemal Atatürk (1881–1938), was well read in European histories, and under his initiative the former Ottoman Historical Society was refounded in 1931 as the Turkish Historical Society. In 1935 Atatürk established a Faculty of Geography, History and Language in Ankara explicitly to provide a Western-style academic institution in which young scholars could train. He aggressively supported historical writing from a nationalist perspective in an effort to displace older images of the despotic, weak, oriental Ottomans with a 'Turkish Historical Thesis' (*Türk Tarih Tezi*) which glorified the Turkish nation and its past; this was firmly linked to Turkish territorial occupation of Anatolia since Atatürk wished to discourage any 'pan-Turkic' imperial adventures outside these borders, and it linked the Turks with 'white' Europe and Central Asia (whence all civilization was held to originate) rather than with 'yellow' East Asia. A Turkish Historical Research Committee was established in 1931 and in the following year the *Türk Tarih Tezi* was declared to be the official doctrine of the Turkish state.

These developments provided a backdrop to the writings of the first generation of republican historians. Unsympathetic to the struggling empire of the previous 200 years, the republicans nevertheless embraced the successes of the Ottoman glory days between the thirteenth and the seventeenth centuries. The academic founder of modern Turkish historiography, Mehmet Fuat Köprülü (1890–1966) began to articulate this vision in the 1930s in a series of lectures at the Sorbonne, soon published as *The Origins of the Ottoman Empire* in French and Turkish (English edition, 1992). The task of his generation of Turkish historians, sorting out legend from fact and balancing ethnicity, religion and other influences, is reminiscent of the romantic nationalist historiographies of the early nineteenth century and, more remotely, of Renaissance debates about national origins, albeit now approached with the tools of modern scholarship. The opening of Ottoman archives in the 1940s redirected scholarship towards social and economic history, and since the mid-twentieth century, Turkey has continued to produce prominent scholars such as the left-leaning economic historian Mustafa Akdağ (1913–72) and his critic Halil Inalcik (b. 1916), a student of Köprülü.

CONCLUSION

Writing from a prison cell in 1933, Jawaharlal Nehru (1889–1964) recorded, in the epistolary history he addressed to his teenaged daughter (the future Indira Gandhi), the following sentiments, which at the end of these two long chapters seem apropos:

The nineteenth century! What a long time we have been held up by these 100 years! For four months I have written to you about this period, and I am a little weary of it, and so perhaps will you be when you read these letters. I began by telling you it was a fascinating period, but even fascination palls after a while.[39]

Nehru had lived through the First World War, which he regarded as 'the close of one epoch and the beginning of another', so there was already some distance between him and the end of the previous century. A historian surveying the world at the end of that century, from a library in France, a teacher's college in India or a study in Tokyo, might with reason feel giddy enthusiasm for what Clio – the symbolic female embodiment of historiography in the Western 'mother countries' – and her acolytes had accomplished in the past hundred years. Not only had history established a set of academic codes and disciplinary procedures, still largely in use today; it had also achieved a global hegemony for those codes, a pre-eminence now extending to parts of the world which until the nineteenth century had practised modes of historicity quite different from the West's. Either through literal colonization or through other forms of influence (and sometimes with the willing collaboration of locals), European historiography had swaggered through the world, overwhelming opposition with its methodological canons in ways that real, metal cannons could not. It was easy to overlook the fact that in order to thrive in different climates Western historiography had been obliged to adjust syncretically to local cultural and institutional realities, and that in doing so it had not entirely escaped transformation – and appropriation – by the very peoples its apostles and missionaries had supposedly converted.

A certain confidence and buoyancy was only natural at the end of the nineteenth century, but even as the West drew the extra-European world into its cultural embrace, trouble was brewing at home, and with it serious challenges to the nineteenth century's historiographical edifice. Within a few decades this would look less like Langlois and Seignobos' Eiffel Tower, or even the Lady of Shalott's, than like that much earlier tower erected at Babel, its progress halted amid a confusion of tongues from which we have yet entirely to escape. We turn now to the twentieth century.

Notes

1 Quoted in Allen Woll, *Puerto Rican Historiography* (New York, 1978), 53.

2 James Mill, *History of British India*, 3 vols. (London, 1817), vol. I, 648.

3 Quoted in Eric Williams, *British Historians in the West Indies* (New York, 1966), 53.

4 Ranajit Guha, *History at the Limit of World-History* (New York, 2002), 11.

5 See ch. 7 above for parallel nationalist experiences in Europe. The 'invention of tradition' associated with modern nationalism in its colonial context has been extensively treated. See in particular Eric Hobsbawm and Terence Ranger (eds.), *The Invention of Tradition* (Cambridge, 1983) and Benedict Anderson, *Imagined Communities: Reflections on the Origin and Spread of Nationalism* (London, 1983).

6 Quoted in John L. Robinson, *Bartolomé Mitre: Historian of the Americas* (Washington, DC, 1982), 41.

7 Though at different times: Chile was one of the earliest to develop university-based historiographical institutions (1840s to1920s), a process that did not occur in Mexico till the early decades of the twentieth century. I owe this point to Juan Maiguashca.

8 Much of the material in Cambodian histories written before the later nineteenth century may in fact have been copied wholesale from Thai chronicles.

9 U Tet Htoot, 'The Nature of the Burmese Chronicles', in C. H. Philips (ed.), *Historians of India, Pakistan, and Ceylon* (London, 1961), 50.

10 To confuse matters further, histories tended to be based on *yazawin*, not on *thamaing*, despite the application of the latter rather than the former term to 'history': Michael Aung-Thwin, 'Mranma Pran: When Context Encounters Notion', *Journal of Southeast Asian Studies* 39 (2008): 193–217.

11 *The Pāḍaeng Chronicle and the Jengtung State Chronicle Translated*, trans. Sao Sāimöng Mangrāi (Ann Arbor, MI, 2002), 234, verse 99.

12 Twinthin Maha Sithu also introduced an innovation that set the pattern for much subsequent Burmese historical writing. By organizing his kings into dynasties named for their capital cities – sacred locations in receipt of the Buddha's prophecies – rather than their founding rulers, he created the dynastic names (Pagan, Ava, Toungoo and Konbaung) still in use by historians today. Thilawuntha's earlier *Yazawinkyaw* is also organized the same way, but since its original manuscript is not extant it is not known whether this was added by its editor when the manuscript was published. I owe this information to Michael Aung-Thwin.

13 *Babad Dipanagara: An Account of the Outbreak of the Java War (1825–1830)*, trans. P. B. R. Carey (Kuala Lumpur, 1981).

14 *Sĕjarah Mĕlayu* is the name assigned to one recension of a work called *Sulalat'us-Salatin* ('Genealogy of Kings'). Its authorship is ascribed, not altogether convincingly, to one Tun Seri Lanang, a prime minister of Johor, and covers the early centuries of the Islamic Malay sultanates. U. Kratz, 'Malay Historical Writing', in D. R. Woolf (ed.), *A Global Encyclopedia of Historical Writing*, 2 vols. (New York, 1998), vol. II, 587.

15 *Malay Annals*, trans. C. C. Brown (Kuala Lumpur, Singapore and London, 1970; repr. Perpustakaan Negara, Malaysia, 2009), intro. and 12–13. The work was first translated by the English colonial administrator Sir Thomas Stamford Raffles (1781–1826).

16 I owe this point to Ann Kumar.

17 David G. Marr, 'Vietnamese Historical Reassessment, 1900–1914', in Anthony Reid and David Marr (eds.), *Perceptions of the Past in Southeast Asia* (Singapore, 1979), 313.

18 R. C. Ileto, 'Tagalog Poetry and the Image of the Past during the War against Spain', in Reid and Marr (eds.), *Perceptions of the Past*, 381.

19 The chronicles are edited and compared in *The Royal Chronicles of Ayutthaya*, trans. Richard D. Cushman and ed. David K. Wyatt (Bangkok, 1995).

20 Jeremias van Vliet, *The Short History of the Kings of Siam*, ed. David K. Wyatt, trans. Leonard Andaya (Bangkok, 1975).

21 Craig J. Reynolds, *Seditious Histories: Contesting Thai and Southeast Asian Pasts* (Seattle and London, 2006), 55.

22 *The Chiang Mai Chronicle*, ed. D. K. Wyatt and Aroonrut Wichienkoo, 2nd edn (Chiang Mai, 1998).

23 Reynolds, *Seditious Histories*, 67–73.

24 Erwin Baelz, *Awakening Japan: The Diary of a German Doctor*, ed. Toku Baelz (Bloomington, IN, 1974), 17.

25 Margaret Mehl, *History and the State in Nineteenth-Century Japan* (Basingstoke, 1998), 1.

26 Ibid., 68–71.

27 Xiaobing Tang, *Global Space and the Nationalist Discourse of Modernity: The Historical Thinking of Liang Qichao* (Stanford, 1996), 36.

28 Liang Qichao, *Intellectual Trends in the Ch'ing Period*, trans. Immanuel C. Y. Hsü (Cambridge, MA, 1959). By this time in his life, disillusioned by the First World War and the peace process at Versailles (which he observed as part of the Chinese delegation), and turning towards Buddhism, his passion for modernization had been dampened.

29 My interpolation; other interpolations are the translator's.

30 Bahrey, *History of the Galla*, included in *Some Records of Ethiopia, 1593–1646*, trans. and ed. C. F. Beckingham and G. W. B. Huntingford (London, 1954), 111–29.

31 *Timbuktu and the Songhay Empire: Al Sa'dī's Ta'rīkh al-sūdān*, ed. and trans. J. O. Hunwick (Leiden, 1999).

32 Samuel Johnson, *The History of the Yorubas: From the Earliest Times to the Beginning of the British Protectorate* (1921; Lagos, 2001), viii; C. C. Reindorf, *The History of the Gold Coast and Asante, Based on Traditions and Historical Facts Comprising a Period of More than Three Centuries from about 1500 to 1860*, 2nd edn (Basel, [1951]); A. Kagwa, *Basekabaka be Buganda*, translated as *The Kings of Buganda*, trans. and ed. M. S. M. Kiwanuka (Nairobi, 1971); Kagwa, *The Customs of the Baganda*, trans. E. B. Kalibala and ed. May Mandelbaum Edel (New York, 1934).

33 Uyilawa Usuanlele and Toyin Falola, 'A Comparison of Jacob Egharevba's "Ekhere Vb Itan Edo" and the Four Editions of its English Translation,"A Short History of Benin"', *History in Africa* 25 (1998): 370.

34 Abdallah bin Hemedi 'l Ajjemy, *The Kilindi*, ed. J. W. T. Allen and William Kimweri bin Mbago bin Kibwana bin Maiwe wa Kwekalo (Mlungui) bin Kimweri Zanyumbai (Nairobi and Boston, 1963).

35 *The Pate Chronicle*, ed. and trans. Marina Tolmacheva (East Lansing, MI, 1993), 16–17.

36 Tarif Khalidi, *Arabic Historical Thought in the Classical Period* (Cambridge, 1994), 233–4.

37 Partially translated as *Umayyads and 'Abbasids: Being the Fourth Part of Jurjí Zaydán's History of Islamic Civilization*, trans. D. S. Margoliouth (Leiden, 1907).

38 Shafik Ghorbal [*sic*], *The Beginnings of the Egyptian Question and the Rise of Mehemet Ali* (London, 1928).

39 J. Nehru, *Glimpses of World History: Being Further Letters to his Daughter Written in Prison, and Containing a Rambling Account of History for Young People* (New York, 1942), letter 145, 22 March 1933, 607.

9 | Babel's Tower? History in the Twentieth Century

Introduction

> ... wherefore God, to confound the said pride, suddenly sent confu-
> sion upon all mankind, which were at work upon the said tower; and
> where all were speaking one language ..., it was changed into seventy-
> two divers languages, so that they could not understand one another's
> speech. And by reason of this, the work of the said tower had of neces-
> sity to be abandoned .... And afterwards this tower remained for the
> walls of the great city of Babylon ... and the name Babylon is as much
> as to say 'confusion'.

So reads an early twentieth-century English translation of the late medieval Florentine chronicler Giovanni Villani, who in turn was paraphrasing Genesis 11:4. God did
not destroy the unfinished tower at Babel, but He confounded the languages ensur-
ing that the proud architects and their descendants could no longer communicate
in a common tongue. Villani's paraphrase is eerily prophetic of the fate of history in
the hundred years just finished. Following the apparent triumph of Western historical methods chronicled in our last two chapters – indeed while it was still occurring
in many parts of the world – the historical profession would grow steadily more
divided, unfocused and conflicted not only about *what* should be studied but about
whether even accurate versions of the past are possible.

None of this seemed very likely in 1911 when Eduard Fueter published his famous
history of modern historiography since the Renaissance.[1] Fueter ably summarized
European historiographical developments over the previous half millennium. Asia
and Africa merited incidental mention as the subjects of European historical writing;

the Americas appear briefly through a handful of 'greats' such as Bancroft. Fueter's Eurocentrism was entirely consistent with his time and is a perfect example of the sense that history, after its long travels, had finally arrived at its destination. And, although Fueter was reasonably inclusive in his treatment of history's many genres and sub-genres, of its unity he had little doubt. Fueter could not possibly have anticipated the developments of the next century, which will be the subject of this final chapter: social history; the Annales School; new variants of totalitarian historiography on right and left; feminism and women's (gender) history; psychohistory; 'cliometrics'; and postmodernism. The place of the nation-state at the centre of history's research programme would come into question (or perhaps it is more accurate to say that the countervailing discourses of class, race and even gender, present but largely subdued in the nineteenth century, would seep through the cracks in the foundation). Of fundamental questions of history's status as a branch of knowledge and its capacity to make true statements concerning the past, Fueter had little to say. Nietzsche rated no more than an incidental reference in one of Fueter's footnotes; there was no reason to suppose that his work would have much impact on historical study, much less that within seventy years the obscure philosopher would become a pillar of the postmodern assault on history's privileges.

A Crisis of Historicism?

The consensus achieved by the nineteenth century on history's status, social function, epistemological superiority and methodology was both loose and fragile. Even within German historical thought, so often associated with a prescriptive role for both Europe and the rest of the world, there were already significant theoretical and methodological fissures. We should thus not view the twentieth century as a sharp break with the nineteenth so much as a working out of the contradictions inherent in the earlier age's construction of history as a 'master discipline', a methodological and programmatic code, self-regulated and autonomous, but also guiding and informing intellectual activities in other spheres. Within a few decades three things had happened: first, within the academic profession the priority of political history and the centrality of the nation-state had been challenged; second, the door was thrown open to a seemingly endless multiplication of historical specializations and ideological interest groups; third, the status of history as a unifying discipline among the humanities and social sciences had been decisively rejected, along with any remaining illusion that knowledge of the past could ever be perfectable, or, for some – in an apparent return to sixteenth-century pyrrhonism – more than a fiction.

In the final chapter of a book such as this, we must content ourselves with an overview of twentieth-century history-writing and consider above all how history descended from the lofty position of public authority it had held barely a century ago. In many ways the course of world 'History' over the past century has been reflected in the evolution of 'history' the discipline across the world. The ardour of history's practitioners across much of the planet in 1900 was already beginning to cool. For some, it had lost its explanatory capacity: the American essayist, novelist and sometime historian Henry Adams (1838–1918) resigned from Harvard after realizing that his lengthy history of the early nineteenth-century United States had failed to generate a definitive explanation for the war of 1812. The First World War (1914–18, the 'Great War' to its contemporaries) alone did not cause these doubts to emerge, and one must consider essential contemporary intellectual and cultural developments such as the theory of relativity, the indeterminacy principle, cubism, expressionism and atonality. But the war certainly undermined the confidence of many historians in both the possibility and the point of their enterprise. The long tradition of German historicism did not perish in the trenches, but it was maimed; by 1932, at the end of Germany's Weimar Republic, the ecclesiastical historian Karl Heussi (1877–1961) was already pronouncing it mortally wounded. It seemed as if history had failed the world, and as the French essayist and poet Paul Valéry (1871–1945) would comment, its very claim to usefulness had even made it a danger to humanity. 'History will justify anything. It teaches precisely nothing, for it contains everything, and furnishes examples of everything.'[2]

The First World War also profoundly ruptured international ties among historians as, with few exceptions, nationally based scholars closed ranks with their governments. The great love affair with German scholarship was chilled in western Europe and, to a lesser degree, in North America. The cost to international historical cooperation is illustrated in the broken relationship of Karl Lamprecht and the Belgian historian Henri Pirenne. After Germany invaded Belgium, Lamprecht attempted to visit his old friend, who had recently lost a son in battle. Pirenne refused to receive him, and went on to veto the invitation of German historians to international conferences well into the 1920s. These rifts had not healed when the Nazis came to power in 1933, and the isolation of German scholars continued through the Second World War, though with some important differences, including the flight of significant numbers of German and other European historians, many of them Jewish, to Britain and America, where they would become influential doctoral supervisors in the post-war era (few would return). Following Germany's second defeat, its scholarly community was split together with the country into western liberal-democratic and eastern communist halves (1949–90).

Notwithstanding the suspicion of some intellectuals, demand for history books and historical fiction nevertheless increased after the war. At universities such as Cambridge, the war changed very little in the curriculum and history enrolments actually dominated the humanities, though more students began to focus

Box 31   Relativism

The First World War had a lasting influence on the writing of history, particularly the mental aspects of the sense of the past. Although it was not only an American phenomenon, 'relativism' in history became associated in particular with the 'Progressives' Carl Becker (1873–1945) and his contemporary Charles A. Beard (1874–1948). Becker, the milder of the two major commentators, was part of the generation of historians for whom historiography was of particular interest in its own right. His 1932 essay 'Everyman his own Historian' did not set out to show that there were no reliable historical facts; rather, it demonstrated that 'history' is made by the perceiving mind, recollecting events; that any individual can think histori-cally about past occurrences, ordering them into a meaningful sequence; and that any such story is thus potentially history. Although Becker thought historians unable to escape the boundaries of their own subjectivity, he remained loyal to the notion that there was an objective past reality to be described. Beard's view was less subtle, more immediately objectionable and ultimately more dangerous to the discipline. In an essay entitled 'That Noble Dream', published, like Becker's 'Everyman', in the *American Historical Review* in 1935, Beard took on the cult of 'objectivity' directly, asserting it to be a will o' the wisp, at best an unachievable goal, however much his-torians fooled themselves into believing that a dispassionate and completely neutral inquiry into the past might be possible. Though it was scarcely a 'movement' and did not long endure, relativism opened the door to later and more extensive doubts about the possibility of historical knowledge, beginning in the 1970s.

on modern history. For many, the past offered a refuge from contemporary prob-lems. Broadly speaking, the trends outlined for the nineteenth century contin-ued into the first half of the twentieth, though the Einstein–Planck challenges to Newtonian physics, closely followed by the horrors of the trenches and the end of the old empires, shook faith in progress, science and even objectivity (see Box 31). Nationalism, too, loosened its grip somewhat in the wake of the war, and some of the most ambitious works of post-1918 historiography, including the great speculative ventures into world history, were devoted to moving away from the state as the fundamental unit of historical analysis. The pessimism which followed the war's unprecedented mayhem produced some gems of cultural history, built on the themes of civilization's decline, such as the Dutch historian Huizinga's brilliant Burckhardtian study of late medieval art, religion and literature, *Herfsttij der Middeleeuwen* (trans. *The Autumn of the Middle Ages*) (1919), which can be read today as an allegory for pre-war aesthetic and cultural decadence. A Sanskrit scholar-turned-historian of the Netherlands, Huizinga was unimpressed by the social sciences, but much enamoured of *Kulturgeschichte*, now reconceived as *Geisteswissenschaft*. A striking feature of his perspective on the past is a longing to reconnect with its very 'pastness' through its artistic and literary traces, an instinct largely suppressed for the previous hundred years (Burckhardt aside), since the days of Michelet and Carlyle.

Philosophies of 'History' and 'history'

Among the works about which Huizinga was himself ambivalent (though he shared some of its sentiments) one finds a considerably longer example of *Kulturpessimismus*, a speculative analysis of distinctive cultures through history. The best-known work of a sometime schoolmaster, Oswald Spengler (1880–1936), *Der Untergang des Abendlandes* (1918–22), has become better known by its catchy English title, *The Decline of the West*. Spengler's views as contained in his magnum opus are, like Nietzsche's, superficially anticipatory of Nazism, but Spengler himself eventually rejected Hitler's vulgar racialism. *The Decline of the West* was a work of reactionary generalization and extreme intellectual relativism, building on then-recent revivals of cyclical theory to postulate alternating periods of growth and decay, with each culture having its own learning and forms of reason, and thus little in common with other cultures: both cumulative progress and the finding of any common ground became impossible in this scheme. Spengler begins his account in the mid-fourth millennium BC, but dispenses with the 'ancient-medieval-modern' periodization that in his opinion had outlived its usefulness, and calls for the elimination of arbitrary geographic terms like 'Europe'. Instead, he examines eight civilizations in all, West European and American, Graeco-Roman, Arabian, Indian, Babylonian, Mexican, Chinese and Egyptian, but placing most of his emphasis on the first three in this list. He speculated that Russia would eventually form a ninth. Though they share little in common, each civilization has traversed a cycle of rise and fall, Spengler's answer to Vico's 'course the nations run' (see Chapter 6 above), and their development is more or less independent of each other, with the sole exception that one can intrude on or suppress the development of another. Largely completed before the beginning of the First World War, the first volume of Spengler's book was published to great fanfare in September 1918, a few weeks before the armistice. His challenge to the European master-narrative of progress has been echoed on the left side of the ideological spectrum in more recent decades, especially in postcolonial studies; his Nietzschean doubts about the existence of an absolute truth independent of its cultural context are echoed in postmodernism. More immediately, *The Decline of the West* would inspire the very different (if equally speculative) British take on comparative civilizations, Arnold J. Toynbee's (1889–1975) *A Study of History* which its author began in earnest in 1920.

Spengler, a morose loner, came from a lower middle-class background and, while university-educated, never held an academic post. Toynbee on the other hand was as academic and sociable as one can get. His uncle, also named Arnold Toynbee (1852–83), had been a short-lived but well-regarded economic historian and social reformer, and the younger Toynbee's childhood inspiration was the Oxford historian, E. A. Freeman. There are significant similarities between Toynbee's *Study of History* and Spengler's *Decline*, including its worldwide scope and its rejection of the centrality of the nation-state in history. But Toynbee was not simply Spengler with an Oxbridge accent and a smile. For one thing, though an agnostic in youth, the mature Toynbee was a committed Christian while he composed most of his *Study*. He saw the world in religious terms, as would his contemporary, Christopher Dawson (1889–1970) and another, slightly younger historian of comparable range but greater subtlety, Herbert Butterfield (1900–79). Yet even when back in the Christian fold in the 1930s, Toynbee dismissed various forms of determinism, whether Calvinist, Marxist or Islamic. Unlike Spengler, Toynbee saw nothing inevitable in the process of decline, providing more space for contingency and accident. When Toynbee's civilizations died, this historiographic coroner pronounced 'a verdict of suicide', not murder. The causes of collapse were not 'cosmic forces outside human control' nor racial decline, but various other factors including schism in the 'body social', failures of will or self-determination and (one that looks rather prescient amid twenty-first-century ecological preoccupations) loss of command over the environment. If Toynbee had an earlier intellectual exemplar as a world historian, it may well have been Ibn Khaldūn, for whom he expressed admiration. Perhaps most importantly, Toynbee rejected Spengler's explicit relativism. While Toynbee would agree that there was no such thing as a 'unity of civilization', comparison between cultures remained possible; and there are, too, some transcendent ideals and ethics.[3]

A Study of History grew in popularity among a general readership in the aftermath of the Second World War, and may be one of the better examples of the gap, widening since the early twentieth century, between academic historiography and a broader public readership. The academic critics of Toynbee, including the Dutch historian Pieter Geyl (1887–1966), were less exasperated by his global ambitions than by his subordination of evidence to theory. Western historians for the past two hundred years have been on the whole deeply sceptical of 'grand theory', and nowhere more so than with respect to capital-H History. This is somewhat less true with respect to small-h history as a genre of writing, a mode of explanation, a mental act, a type of narrative or, to use the most recent terms, a 'linguistic construct' or form of 'discourse'. Academic reactions to strict scientific history in the more narrow, positivist sense, echoing Dilthey's earlier qualifications, can be seen first in an approach that has been called 'idealism' but which should not be confused with the German idealism of Kant's and Hegel's time. The most distinguished and influential representative of this tendency was the Italian philosopher and historian, Benedetto Croce (1866–1952).

Croce wrote histories of Europe and his native Naples, and was interested in historiography, but he is more often read today as a philosopher of history. In many ways a creature of nineteenth-century historicism who had to adapt it to fit a twentieth-century world, he was also a throwback to a liberal tradition of progressive history, complete with its rather limiting fixation on the political. Croce eventually called his historical outlook 'absolute historicism', to distinguish it from the German variety. Rather than agree with the historicist critique of Enlightenment universalism (which, however, Croce also rejected), he bypassed this oppositional pairing in favour of a more radical view. History was not *part* of reality, manifested synecdochically in every past nation or culture. It *was* reality, all of it, a total process whereby the world as a whole develops, though not according to any transcendent force like providence, and without any fixed resolution, whether a Christian or Hegelian ending. Only the present actually survives, but everything that has occurred in the past has gone into the making of the current reality, bad things as well as good, just as our own present, too (and the efforts we make in determining its contents), will become an ingredient of future people's presents.

Like Dilthey earlier, Croce rejected positivism, arguing instead for the autonomy of history from science, and the inseparability of history and lived experience. Records and documents, said Croce, only have significance insofar as living humans can reflect upon them and, indeed, relive them; conversely, we only make sense of life by thinking historically. The dead have another life to live in us. This is why the erection of monuments and tombs is a moral act. And so are the modes of historical activity that Nietzsche had dismissed as monumental and antiquarian:

Although dead, they live in our memory and will continue to live in the memory of times to come. And that collecting of dead documents and writing down of empty histories is an act of life which serves life. The moment will come when they will serve to reproduce past history, enriched and made present to our spirit.[4]

In his celebrated remark that 'all history is contemporary history' Croce meant not that all past events are really present and coeval, but rather that every generation must select and order its past on the basis of the context and circumstances in which it finds itself – the questions the historian asks will be determined by his or her own world's requirements. Without a question or pressing problem, no understanding of the past is possible, only a replication and rearrangement of its documentary materials. Among other things, Croce's notion offers a solution to the challenge that Nietzsche had issued in urging suppression of the superfluous past. The burden of history need not be so crushing if it can be regularly lightened, superfluous aspects discarded, and only that which is of contemporary interest carried forward for the moment.

While Croce's views appealed to many western Europeans of the first half of the century, enamoured by neither Marxism nor positivism, his vision of history was perhaps nowhere more influential than with his younger British contemporary, the archaeologist-turned-philosopher R. G. Collingwood. Collingwood's posthumously published *The Idea of History* (1946) advanced the notion that 'all history ... is the history of thought' and suggested that the historian must empathize with his or her subjects, enter into the 'interior' of a historical event (the thought of the agent behind the event) and mentally 're-enact' it in order to retell it. This was not a new notion – the resemblance to Dilthey's *Verstehen* is obvious – but it has become most familiar to the English-speaking world in the Collingwoodian itera- tion. Despite its explicit Eurocentrism, which ignores all history apart from the Western variety, *The Idea of History* remains very widely read, and its concept of historical imagination has come back into vogue in the past twenty years with the advent of a postmodernism Collingwood himself would not have understood. He has had an international influence through figures like the Brazilian-born Spanish literary scholar and historian, Américo Castro (1885–1972), who echoed Colling- wood in his assertion that 'To write history demands a historian willing (and able) to enter into the living consciousness of others through the door of his own life and consciousness.'[5]

The Rise of the Annales

Perhaps the most significant historiographic creation of the inter-war period was what has become known as the Annales 'School'. Arising in France, the Annales is so called after the journal *Annales* that began publication in 1929 at the University of Strasbourg under the guidance of Marc Bloch and Lucien Febvre. Both men were scholars much influenced by the earlier work of the sociologist Durkheim and the philosopher–geographer Henri Berr (1863–1954) (Extract 42), editor of a journal called *Revue de synthèse historique* and an early exponent of the need for a more comprehensive approach to the study of the past. Bloch and Febvre also had close connections with the Belgian medieval- ist Henri Pirenne. Both the journal and the practices of those associated with

42: The Relations of Geography and History: Henri Berr

The purely 'geographical geographer' does not trouble himself about history, or is even disposed to absorb it in geography. The treatment of this complex problem needs a geographical historian, or a historical geographer, who is also more or less a sociologist. The present
volume will undoubtedly prove that an historian who has a wide and, at the same time, a
profound conception of his work, who seeks to disentangle all the threads, external and
internal, of human conduct, who, whilst specializing his studies, refuses to neglect anything
which will contribute to their effectiveness – that such an historian, and there are very few
such, is especially fitted to take up the important and delicate question of the relations
between man and his natural environment ....

Selection from Henri Berr, 'Foreword' to Lucien Febvre and Lionel Bataillon, *A Geographical
Introduction to History*, trans. E. G. Mountford and J. H. Paxton (1924; London: Routledge and Kegan
Paul, 1949), v–vii.

it have evolved through successive generations but they remain an influential
force in France and are much admired elsewhere. The Annalistes' repudiation of
political history in favour of an *histoire totale* that examined geography, climate,
economy and agricultural and trade patterns, as well as manners, still seems
fresh after seventy-five years. It is also a reminder of the recurrent pendulum
swings in European historiographical taste between the social and the political,
the general and the particular, the expansive and the selective, dating back to
Herodotus and Thucydides.

Bloch (1886–1944) has become the nearest thing to a historiographical folk hero
in the decades since his execution by the Nazis for resistance activities. Virtually
all of his works remain in print in several languages, including *The Historian's
Craft*, a collection of essays and ruminations on history assembled posthumously.
Bloch served with distinction in the First World War and then took up a post at
Strasbourg before assuming a chair in economic history at the Sorbonne. His first
major book, *Les rois thaumaturges* (1924) (English version, *The Royal Touch*), about
the medieval practice of touching for the 'king's evil' or scrofula, has become a
foundational text in the cultural history of ritual. Bloch's later works, written after
he had collaborated with Febvre to found the journal *Annales*, include *Les carac-
tères originaux de l'histoire rurale française* (1931; English version, *French Rural
History*), famous for its evocative treatment of the countryside over a long period
of time, and *La société féodale* (1939; English version, *Feudal Society*), which again
took an anthropological and sociological approach to feudalism as not merely a
military but a social and cultural system, and to the *mentalités* ('mentalities') that
underlay it.

Febvre's (1878–1956) works have not had the same long-lasting impact as have Bloch's but they were no less important in their day. His doctoral thesis on Spain's King Philip II and the Franche-Comté, completed in 1911, provided an intensive description of the social and material structures of life in that region during the sixteenth century. His interest in historical geography soon shifted to the subject of *mentalités*. In his most famous work, *Le problème de l'incroyance au XVI siècle* (1942; trans. *The Problem of Unbelief in the Sixteenth Century*), Febvre, a religious sceptic, explored the concept of atheism, in connection with the Renaissance writer Rabelais, trying to demonstrate that the mental habits of a sixteenth-century European did not allow for true atheism, however irreligious or heterodox a writer may appear to have been. Febvre also became interested in print culture, and that third string to his bow has been taken up with great success by French *historiens du livre* such as Roger Chartier (b. 1945) and by North American scholars such as Robert Darnton (b. 1939). Unlike Bloch, Febvre survived the Second World War and lived into the 1950s, and this made him the principal architect of the Annales 'farm system' for the longer-term production of historians trained to study topics outside a still-dominant political history. In 1947 he helped to found in Paris the famous *Sixième section* of the École pratique des hautes études, established in 1868. The École was an institution for postgraduate training only, intended to complement rather than duplicate the universities' curricula. The new section was devoted specifically to advanced research in the social sciences, and by 1975 had established itself as an independent institution in its own right, the École des Hautes Études en Sciences Sociales (EHESS). The section and EHESS have provided the Annales with a base in the heart of Paris for over six decades.

The Annales approach to scholarship has changed its orientation several times in the past eight decades and is more appropriately regarded as an evolving tradition rather than a 'school'. In fact, its capacity to reinvent itself in response to new trends, symbolically reflected in several changes to the journal *Annales*' subtitle, has been a mark of its strength and a reason for its continued importance.[6] The first major shift came almost immediately after the Second World War, driven in part by wider experimentation with the social sciences (see below). It was engineered by the 'second generation' Annalistes, a distinguished group at the head of which stood Febvre's student Fernand Braudel (1902–85). A product of the interests of both Bloch and Febvre, especially their devotion to geography, Braudel aggressively pushed the idea of the earth and the sea as agents of change. Braudel called for the subjugation of *histoire événementielle* (short-term human actions, for instance in the political world) to the study of mid-length periods of social, material and economic *conjonctures*, and to the much slower geographical and climatological changes that occurred over the *longue durée* of centuries. This last was the sphere in which natural forces ruled, providing the constraints and the *structures* within which the secondary and tertiary realms of change, and the individual event, could occur. The notion of climatological influence has a long history, going back through Montesquieu to Bodin and Ibn Khaldūn, though the older link between climate and 'national character' was eschewed by Braudel in favour of a more complex, dynamic relationship which permitted scope for human agency. The classic expression of this layered periodization is Braudel's own study of *La Méditerranée et le monde méditerranéen à l'époque de Philippe II* (1949; English version, *The Mediterranean and the Mediterranean World in the Age of Philip II*), the first draft of which he wrote from memory during his years in a German prisoner-of-war camp. The degree to which the approach is in fact applicable to different subjects remains unclear. Critics of *The Mediterranean* have pointed out that Braudel was not successful in integrating the three levels of time, nor were subsequent works like his multivolume study of *Civilisation matérielle, économie et capitalisme, XVe–XVIIIe siècle* (1967–79; English version, *Capitalism and Material Life*) able to make full use of the deep time of the *longue durée*.

The quantitative tendencies of this stage of Annales historiography, also evident in the work of Braudel's non-Annaliste older contemporary, Ernest Labrousse (1895–1988), were elaborated by historians usually considered part of Braudel's 'generation' though actually a decade or two his junior, such as Pierre Chaunu (1923–2009). Intellectual historians such as Robert Mandrou (1921–84) and François Furet (1927–97) also employed a quantitative approach to the history of *mentalités*, opening up what has since evolved into *histoire du livre* ('history of the book'). In more recent decades, however, a further shift in the tradition has occurred. Many Annales historians, and others abroad who self-identify as their admirers or associates, have veered away from quantification back to the study of *mentalités* in Bloch and Febvre's mode, placing considerably more emphasis on individual and collective beliefs, and on life experienced in local settings. Some have worked on a deliberately smaller scale, for instance the German proponents of *Alltagsgeschichte* – literally the history of everyday life – during the 1980s, in a parallel reaction against the abstraction of German 'historical social science' (see below). The 'microhistory' or *microstoria* (its Italian name) genre of the late 1970s, 1980s and 1990s, including works like Emmanuel Le Roy Ladurie's (b. 1929) *Montaillou: The Promised Land of Error* (a study of a medieval Cathar village) and Carlo Ginzburg's (b. 1939) *The Cheese and the Worms: The Cosmos of a Sixteenth-Century Miller*, has proved highly saleable in the academic and even popular book market and has spawned numerous additional examples around the globe. Japanese practitioners of *seikatsushi* and *seishinshi*, roughly corresponding with *Alltagsgeschichte* and *histoire des mentalités* respectively, similarly drew inspiration from both German and French models.

History and the Social Sciences

The Annales and microhistory are themselves both products of history's hot-and-cold flirtation with the social sciences, a phenomenon with pre-modern origins. Theoretically inclined minds during the Enlightenment had experimented with the past: the mathematician and physicist Jean d'Alembert (1717–83) thought that pyrrhonist doubts about knowledge of the past might be solved through a scientific approach to its study. The Scottish stadialists closely linked the study of the past to the study of society. We have also seen a number of non-European examples, among whom Ibn Khaldūn is the most famous. Nineteenth-century historians had been mainly suspicious of the emerging social sciences, due to the dominance of Rankeanism and its emphasis on political history, to the more general historicist attention to the individual rather than society, and to the popularity of heroic biography and history among the reading public. By the end of the century, however, this began to change. In the midst of the debate over history's relation to the natural sciences, the 'human' sciences seemed to offer a compromise. Economic history had emerged by the century's end as a powerful sub-discipline. Marx had already outlined a particular version of the tie of history to economics, Comte to sociology. Both the German *Methodenstreit* and the work of the American 'New Historians' involved the nature of history's connection to these and other disciplines, especially anthropology, geography and psychology.

Among the founders of social science-driven history, two other early sociologists stand out: the Frenchman Émile Durkheim (1858–1917) and the German Max Weber (1864–1920). Both were enormously interested in the past. Durkheim saw history as falling short of a science itself, but nonetheless a useful source of material for social science. He described collective phenomena that exist independently of individual instances of them, and encouraged an impartial, almost clinical detachment in their study, exemplified in his classic *The Elementary Forms of Religious Life* (1912), a work notable also for the global span of its reference group. Weber, who self-identified more as a historian than a sociologist till near the end of his life, represents a somewhat different tendency. Equally ill-disposed to mainstream German historical scholarship of the late nineteenth century and to positivist critiques of it, he had joined with the denunciators of Lamprecht's *Deutsche Geschichte*. Weber's sociological thought was influenced by Dilthey's clarification of the distinctions between the natural and human sciences. While Weber insisted on the rationality of the latter and their need for clear concepts and practices, he also stressed the subjective element to inquiry and the gap between actual lived reality and systematic representations of it such as 'ideal types'. Weber was also a strong comparativist, interested among other issues in explaining the differences between oriental and occidental cultures, and in exploring the connections between the economic and ideological – for instance in a famous book on *The Protestant Ethic and the Spirit of Capitalism* (1904–5).

The essential elements of social science-based history were already evident as early as the outbreak of the First World War: a rejection of the particular and incidental except insofar as it forms part of a whole; the use of the past as a data mine for generalizations about society and human nature; the appropriation of key concepts from other disciplines in order to make sense of the past and to provide structure for it; and a fondness for comparison across chronological, national and geographical boundaries. Even political historians adopted sociology's emphasis on collective behaviour in their attempt to analyse historical events through collective biography or 'prosopography'. This first seriously appeared in the late 1920s, when Lewis Namier (1888–1960) published his study of the state of British politics at the accession of King George III in 1760. Namier used the technique to relate the voting behaviour of members of parliament to their connections with networks of aristocratic patronage. Prosopography would subsequently be employed in a variety of other contexts: the New Zealand-born classicist Ronald Syme (1903–89), for instance, used it to explain the transition of Rome from republic to empire at the time of Augustus.[7]

Both sociology and especially economics are highly quantitative disciplines, and quantification has always been an important component of social science-oriented history. While it, too, has a long pedigree, it emerged most clearly as a potential 'silver bullet' for historians anxious to return their craft to the ranks of the 'hard' sciences after the Second World War. The Braudelian generation of Annalistes was, as we saw earlier, much taken with quantification, and as late as the 1970s one of Braudel's most illustrious pupils, Emmanuel Le Roy Ladurie, was prophesying that within a decade all historians would have to become computer programmers. Despite the ubiquity of personal computers on current historians' desks, this has proved a gross overestimate, though many historians have used quantitative methods as a supplement to their normal toolkit. Public attention has focused on a relatively small subset of quantifiers, principally those drawn to and often trained in advanced statistics and econometric theory. 'New economic history' or 'cliometrics' first arose in the 1960s. It often generates not only the large datasets and broad conclusions of which quantitative historians are fond, but also something additional, the use of the 'counterfactual' or 'what-if?' questions. This involves setting up a model of how various elements within a past system interact, removing one or more of them, and seeing what, if anything, changes. Thus Robert William Fogel (b. 1926) investigated the role of railroads in America (1964) and, by eliminating them from his model of the economy, showed that other forms of transportation would have been developed or extended with very little long-term effect on prosperity. Even more controversial, because it hit on the rawest nerve in the American body politic, race and slavery, was his subsequent book, *Time on the Cross* (1974; co-authored with Stanley Engerman). This used plantation records to suggest that far from being a backward, economically unproductive system, southern slavery was in fact relatively efficient; unfree blacks, far from being the lazy, shiftless characters of a century of post-emancipation racism, were in fact industrious and accomplished. Leaving aside the objections that non-historians might have to any defence of the 'peculiar institution' of slavery (and the authors had been careful to declare their personal moral objections to it), the book was criticized for a range of methodological flaws and false assumptions. However, a number of mainstream historians began making public arguments against the use of quantification, often lumping all of it with cliometrics. As early as 1962, two years before Fogel's book on railroads appeared, Carl Bridenbaugh (1903–92), a historian of colonial America, had issued perhaps the most memorable philippic against 'the bitch goddess, quantification' in his presidential address to the American Historical Association. Jacques Barzun (b. 1907), of Columbia University, attacked cliometricians in a book called *Clio and the Doctors* in 1974. And the German-born Cambridge historian of Tudor England, Geoffrey Elton (1928–94), no admirer of social science-influenced quantification, debated its merits with Fogel in a jointly published book.[8]

In the 1970s, the stock of both sociology and economics began to fall among historians. Some looked for an alternative to anthropology, and in the first instance the 'structuralist' variety epitomized by Claude Lévi-Strauss (1908–2009). The Oxford historian Keith Thomas (b. 1933), who had written a celebrated essay on 'History and Anthropology' in 1963, used insights derived from anthropology in a magisterial, and enormously influential, 1971 study of early modern witchcraft and other aspects of English popular beliefs.[9] This was just at the same time that European historiography was beginning to retreat from a focus on large patterns and systems and instead turn to the examination of particular, local, sometimes typical and sometimes quite atypical cases. The often exotic Asian, Latin American or African settings of anthropological investigations offered a compelling comparative dimension to Europeanists looking to generalize beyond their own immediate experience. Cultural anthropologists such as Clifford Geertz (1926–2006), Marshall Sahlins (b. 1930) and Victor Turner (1920–83) offered a reliable touchstone for the shift from the large-scale and structural to the local and particular (and thereby provided a theoretical dimension to microhistory, discussed above). Sahlins' study of the death of Captain Cook in the Sandwich Islands (Hawaii), for instance, provided a concrete instance of a single historical event which could be read on many levels from the ritual to the symbolic to the linguistic.[10] Geertz's much-used term 'thick description' and his analysis of popular events such as a

Balinese cock-fight, have become references *de rigueur* for many cultural historians and for literary scholars.[11]

The continuing dialogue between history and the social sciences is a direct outgrowth of that late nineteenth-century conversation about history and the *natural* sciences, a debate that survived the interventions of Windelband and Croce. It would spin off into two other areas, philosophy of history and sociology of science, and from there double back into the discipline of history itself. In the former case, a critical contribution was that of the German-émigré philosopher Carl Hempel (1905–97). In 1942 Hempel published an article arguing that a core function of historical inquiry was to offer explanation in terms of 'covering' or 'general' laws, and that explanations which did not adduce or develop such laws were unsatisfactory. The article helped touch off a generation of debates in what is usually called the 'analytic' philosophy of history. In these exchanges, which focused on questions such as the nature and proper form of historical explanation, Hempel's views were largely rejected not only by most historians but by many members of his own discipline, including the Canadian William H. Dray (1921–2009), the American Arthur Danto (b. 1924) and Oxford's Patrick Gardiner (1922–97).

The other development also involved science – specifically its history and sociology. In 1962 Thomas Kuhn (1922–96), a physicist-turned-historian, published an unassuming little book called *The Structure of Scientific Revolutions*. Instead of trying to maintain the highly positivist notion of science's steady progress, Kuhn suggested that science was conducted in two distinct modes: routinely as 'normal science', in which scientists operating under shared assumptions and rules incrementally augmented data and knowledge; and occasionally in a 'crisis' mode during which those old assumptions broke down – principally from the weight of data which now contradicted them – and new ones entirely incommensurable with the previous had to be generated. Kuhn called the collection of assumptions and practices a 'paradigm', and thus bestowed that word on the social sciences forever more. In his account, paradigms determine the agenda of experiments and even of whole scientific programmes.

The impact of Kuhn's explanation of scientific change has been significant, though more so outside the scientific community than within. With respect to historiography in general, the concepts of 'paradigm shifts' and 'normal science' have had two major effects. First, within the history of science itself (which in the course of the later twentieth century evolved into a free-standing discipline), the Kuhnian model helped bring about a different kind of history fixed less on the detailed explication of past scientific ideas and more so on their social and cultural contexts regardless of their normative status or internal consistency. The second way in which Kuhn's ideas have affected historiography goes well beyond history of science into other areas. For example, if his model helps explain scientific change, can it also be applied to our understanding of how history works? Should the history of history itself, the subject of the present book, be told as a series of paradigm shifts where a few of the key thinkers of the past are highlighted at the expense of the rest who are deemed mere 'problem solvers' working away at plugging the holes in the dominant paradigm and thereby doing the work of 'normal' history? Such an approach would certainly draw the historian's attention towards the external social and cultural factors that lead one to embrace one paradigm over the other, but it would necessarily minimize types of historical inquiry unable to achieve the status of a paradigm – including most non-Western ones. However, Kuhn's 'paradigm' has been employed with somewhat greater success to account for the rise and fall of historical interpretations *about* particular events or problems (for instance, the French Revolution or the origins of the First World War). It is a sufficiently elastic term that allows for a great deal of variation in use, and is thus rather less closed than the term 'school'.

History Under Dictatorships and Totalitarian Regimes

The Austrian-born philosopher Karl Popper (1902–94), a formidable figure in some of the same debates about science as Kuhn, also became famous as an outspoken critic of one strand of social science theory which he rather unhelpfully called 'historicism'.[12] By this usage, which has little or nothing to do with the Germanic *Historismus* we have previously encountered, Popper really intended any totalizing theory that could be used to subvert an 'open' society. If his choice of words was confusing, his misgivings were not without basis. The twentieth century has seen both History and history turned to the service of a number of dictatorships, juntas and totalitarian regimes on the right and left of the political spectrum, and a level of control and repression practised that made the state or crown interventions of earlier centuries seem almost amateurish and benign.

The most infamous of those regimes on the right were in the Axis powers, Fascist Italy, imperial Japan and Nazi Germany during the 1930s and 1940s. In Mussolini's Italy, right–left divisions in historiography were created which have never really disappeared. The anti-Fascist historian Gaetano Salvemini (1873–1957) fled the country in the 1920s, becoming an American citizen before he returned to Italy after the war. Others left for good, including the classicist and historiographer Arnaldo Momigliano, who lost his position following the Fascist imposition of anti-Jewish laws in 1938; he reestablished himself at Oxford and London, and later in Chicago. But the Fascists did not stop, like some regimes, at the elimination of perceived enemies: they co-opted historians such as Gioacchino Volpe (1876–1971) to write ideologically agreeable accounts. Japan followed a similar course in the 1930s, highlighting connections to a glorious imperial past and to more recent military successes against neighbouring powers such as Russia. Dissenting historians were persecuted, for instance like Noro Eitarō (1900–34), a Marxist economic historian and political activist who died in police custody. As in Italy, the military government was also directly supported by historians of a pro-imperial inclination. The post-war reaction would produce both a reaction to the militarism of the past and a turn in the direction of non-Marxian social and cultural or 'people's' history (*minshūshi*).[13]

In Germany, an aggressive and nostalgic nationalism provided the ideological backbone to Nazi historiography and justified the purging of the profession and wider intelligentsia. Jewish and left-wing historians fled Germany in large numbers during the 1930s, mainly landing in Britain and the United States, where they would have a profound impact on the post-war professions in both countries. Others from Nazi-conquered Europe, such as the prominent Russian-Lithuanian Jewish historian Simon Dubnow (1860–1941) or the Polish Jew Emanuel Ringelblum (1900–44), were less fortunate and eventually became victims of the Holocaust.[14] Under the Nazis, even conservative historians of the old style failed to prosper: Friedrich Meinecke, a monarchist-turned-Weimar Republic supporter, was eventually pushed out of his editorship of the *Historische Zeitschrift*. Gerhard Ritter (1888–1967), a devout Lutheran of conservative views, would end up involved in the bomb plot on Hitler, though he survived the subsequent reprisals. The historical writing of the Nazi period is exactly what one might expect, virulently anti-Semitic and anti-Bolshevik, conscious of the unfair deal that Germany received at Versailles in 1919, and imbued with the racialism that would produce the Final Solution. It need not detain us long, though one of its outputs, *Volksgeschichte*, is of passing interest: this brought to a rather pathetic end the long tradition of 'Teutonism' in historiography that began with Tacitus, and was then taken up by Reformation-era humanists, reformulated by Herder and Fichte at the end of the eighteenth century and adopted by many non-German historians in the nineteenth.

Of greater significance is the aftermath of Nazi historiography since 1945, the revision of German history, and the difficult, often painful process of reflection on its distinctive recent past. The major transition occurred after the war's end, as the profession's resistance to social science methods broke down. A few old guard historians such as Gerhard Ritter, and some rehabilitated former practitioners of *Volksgeschichte*, looked for the roots of Nazism in the failure of democracy and weakness of mass society. Others on the left, however, such as Hans-Ulrich Wehler (b. 1931) looked to the modernization of German political and social institutions in the nineteenth century. Wehler called for a new, 'historical social science', synthesizing aspects of American and British social science with ideas

Box 32   The Fischer Controversy and *Historikerstreit*

The course of German history has been a topic of continuous debate that on at least two occasions since 1945 has flared up into full-scale public controversy. The first of these episodes took place in the 1960s, ignited by the work of a reformed ex-Nazi named Fritz Fischer (1909–99), and surrounding his interpretation of the First World War. In *Griff nach der Weltmacht: Die Kriegzielpolitik des kaiserlichen Deutschland 1914–1918* (1961; English version, *Germany's Aims in the First World War*), Fischer asserted German responsibility not only for the Second World War, which was routinely accepted, but for the First, which was not. In his view, a direct line from the policies of late nineteenth-century German statesmen to the outbreak of the First World War could be drawn, and German leaders had clearly sought to become a world power well before the war erupted. Since it was also axiomatic that the Second World War was a more or less inevitable consequence of the settlement of the First, Fischer had, in effect, constructed an anti-*Sonderweg*, an evil twin of the old notion of Germany's 'special path' to greatness, beginning in the nineteenth-century Bismarckian state. Outrage was instantaneous. Fischer's publisher's office was fire-bombed, and a number of reputable historians attacked Fischer's methods and sources.

The second controversy erupted about twenty-five years later, on a separate but not unrelated topic, and ultimately on an even bigger stage. Whereas the Fischer affair was only indirectly concerned with the Second World War, the *Historikerstreit* focused on it directly, and especially on its single most morally defining episode, the Holocaust. The question here was whether the Holocaust was the anomalous act of a small group of criminals (the Nazi leadership) or rather something even more sinister – the appalling culmination of deep structural problems within German society. Accelerated by its rapid progress to modernization and statehood in the nineteenth century (again, along a 'separate path' from that of the western European democracies), these societal weaknesses had led to the First World War and the failure of democracy in the 1920s, and had then been exploited by the Nazis in their rise to power; it had thus, in the longer run, produced both the Second World War and, ultimately, the Final Solution. On this view, the nation as a whole continued to bear a profound burden of guilt. The controversy began when Ernst Nolte (b. 1923), a conservative historian, contended that the Holocaust was (within Germany) a one-off act of a small circle of fanatical anti-Semites and that Auschwitz, for instance, was not another inevitable consequence of Fischer's doppelgänger *Sonderweg*, but rather an answer to and imitation of Soviet gulags. The riposte to this issued principally from the left, beginning with the philosopher and social theorist Jürgen Habermas (b. 1929) in *Die Zeit* charging Nolte with attempting a 'settlement of damages', an exculpatory move to bury the unburiable. It was arguably Habermas' intervention in a matter which might have been dealt with more quietly within the historians' guild that transformed it from a disciplinary debate into a more widespread public spectacle.

drawn from Max Weber, Marx and the 'Critical Theory' of another group, just returned to Germany from exile, known as the Frankfurt School. The central problem addressed by several post-war generations of historians would be the emergence of Nazism, and their most prominent organ the journal *Geschichte und Gesellschaft* (est. 1975). In the past five decades, the debate over Germany's 'Special Path' or *Sonderweg* has touched off two major historiographical tempests, the Fischer controversy in the early 1960s and the '*Historikerstreit*' of the late 1980s (see Box 32).

Globally, the second half of the twentieth century has seen numerous neo-Fascist and authoritarian regimes assert control over historical writing and suppress dissent. As in the Italian and German examples, this has taken both active and reactive forms. The active consists in the energetic support by governments for ambitious, often multivolume national histories – the old tradition of official historiography, long marginalized in democratic Europe and the Americas, remains alive and well in East and Southeast Asia. The reactive side of this policing of the past is observable in those regimes, right or left, where blatant suppression and censorship occurs, the channels of publication are tightly controlled, opinion is monitored and dissent is punished with violent reprisals, exile or imprisonment. 'New Order' Indonesia of the Suharto regime (1967–98) offers an example of the two approaches combined. There, a militaristic 'official' history emerged under the direction of Nugroho Notosusanto (1931–85), a historian, soldier and minister of education. A virulently anticommunist and 'patriotic' multivolume history of Indonesia prepared in the 1970s, *Sejarah Nasional Indonesia* (1975; rev. 1984), was an uneasy amalgam of official history with the work of university-based historians. A rival historiographic school, influenced by the social sciences, and paying attention to the history of the wider population (in contravention to New Order policy), developed in the 1970s under the leadership of Sartono Kartodirdjo (1921–2007). A further alternative was provided by independent local histories, many of them oral traditions now making their way into writing for the first time. On the whole, however, during the New Order period a right-wing nationalist tradition was strictly enforced on schools, even in outlying and problematic territories such as East Timor. Since Suharto's resignation, nationalist historiography has been openly challenged by a number of competing visions of the past, including those representing different regions and minority ethnic groups such as the Acehnese. Despite the declaration of Indonesia's historians of their independence from state control, it remains unclear today whether the project for the 'rectification of history' (*pelurusan sejarah*) is simply going to displace one set of ideological orthodoxies with a new one. By 2007 a return to the anticommunism of the Suharto era was signalled with a confiscation of history textbooks by order of Indonesia's attorney-general.

On the communist left, the conditions for historiography during much of the twentieth century were remarkably similar. If irrationalism, scepticism and pessimism were the dominant chords struck in western Europe after 1918, leading to Fascism, the dissonant tones from further east came in the form of Marxism, the first major laboratory for which was Soviet Russia. The architects of Soviet Marxist historiography were in the first instance two men, one a professional historian, one not, both of whom had been at work formulating a Marxist historiography well before the October Revolution. The latter, Georgi Plekhanov (1856–1918), did not long survive the Revolution. A theoretician, Plekhanov had authored in 1891 a key text of Marxism, *The Materialist Conception of History*, followed in 1895 by *The Development of the Monist View of History*, which traced the origins of materialism in late eighteenth- and early nineteenth-century France, its initial intellectual weakness compared to German idealism, which could explain change and evolution more effectively, and the responses of Feuerbach and then Marx on which 'modern' materialism was based. Despite his siding with the unsuccessful Mensheviks, Plekhanov remained revered as a pioneer of Soviet Marxist thought. The other key figure, more immediately influential on academic historiography, was a former pupil of V. O. Kliuchevskii, Mikhail Nikolaevich Pokrovskii (1868–1932). Pokrovskii had been in exile after the failed 1905 Revolution, when he had got an early start on the first problem of revolutionary historiography, displacing the standard imperial account of the consolidation of Russia with a Marxist version. Pokrovskii's early take on Russian history appears in his five-volume study, endorsed by Lenin, *History of Russia from the Earliest Times to the Rise of Commercial Capitalism* (1910–14; English trans. 1931). Other works followed.

Politically astute, Pokrovskii tied his fortunes in the early 1920s to the ascendant Joseph Stalin (1878–1953), and by 1928 had become the dominant voice in Soviet historiography.

In the next few years, as Stalin solidified his authority, opinion narrowed further still. Pokrovskii's influence at first survived his own death. Moscow University was temporarily renamed in his honour, and in early 1934 the country's most distinguished female historian, Anna Mikhailovna Pankratova (1897–1957) defended his reputation. But by the end of the year, Pokrovskii's stock had started to sink sharply. Too orthodox a Marxist, he was now posthumously condemned by Stalin for his lack of nationalist sentiment and for too deterministic a depiction of the impact of economic forces on events. His portrayal of pre-Revolutionary Russia as the backward land of Marx's estimation did not fit with the Stalinist encouragement of Russian pride and belief that the country had not followed, exactly, the same course of History as western Europe. With the simultaneous weakening and then dissolution (1936) of the Society of Marxist Historians, previously the engine of much debate over the past, and the establishment of the Institute of History in the Communist Academy, the moderately tolerant atmosphere of the 1920s gave way to strict Party controls, and thenceforth the state would exercise an overbearing influence on history-writing. Historians would be among the victims of the purges in the 1930s. Apart from rival party ideologues like Leon Trotsky (1879–1940), nationalist historians of non-Russian ethnicity were also targeted: the leading Ukrainian professional historian, Mykhailo Hrushevsky (1866–1934), was exiled first to Moscow and then the Caucasus where he died suddenly under mysterious circumstances.

Rigid censorship peaked in the latter years of Stalin's rule, during which virtually any form of history in book, film or broadcast had to reflect the judgments contained in the Stalinist textbook, *History of the Communist Party of the Soviet Union (Bolsheviks): Short Course* (Extract 43), published in 1938, the very same year that the control of Soviet archives passed under the control of the state security agency, the NKVD. Following the death of Stalin, history remained under the oversight of the Party and the state, though not without producing a few dissenters from Marxist orthodoxy, for instance the medieval cultural historian Aaron Gurevich (1924–2006) and the literary critic and theorist Mikhail Bakhtin (1895–1975). The latter survived internal exile and the failure of his doctoral thesis to produce a study of popular culture in sixteenth-century France (*Rabelais and his World*, 1941), which remains widely cited after seven decades.

With the arrival of the Cold War, Party oversight soon spread beyond the borders of the USSR to include its Warsaw Pact 'allies' in Romania, Poland, Bulgaria, East Germany, Hungary and Czechoslovakia, all of which imposed varying degrees of constraint on historians. During the era of Soviet dominance, historiography in

43: Stalin on Historical Science

... [T]he history of development of society is above all the history of the development of production, the history of the modes of production which succeed each other in the course of centuries, the history of the development of productive forces and people's relations of production ....

Hence, if historical science is to be a real science, it can no longer reduce the history of social development to the actions of kings and generals, to the actions of 'conquerors' and 'subjugators' of states, but must above all devote itself to the history of the producers of material values, the history of the labouring masses, the history of peoples.

Hence the clue to the study of the laws of history of society must not be sought in men's minds, in the views and ideas of society, but in the mode of production practised by society in any given historical period; it must be sought in the economic life of society.

Hence the prime task of historical science is to study and disclose the laws of production, the laws of development of the productive forces and of the relations of production, the laws of economic development of society.

Selected from an anonymous American translation of Joseph Stalin, *Dialectical and Historical Materialism* (New York: International Publishers, 1940), 29–30. The work was originally included in *History of the Communist Party of the Soviet Union (Bolsheviks): Short Course* 1938, published under Stalin's oversight, and eventually mandatory reading for Party members in China. See also *The Essential Stalin: Major Theoretical Writings 1905–52*, ed. Bruce Franklin (London: Croom Helm, 1973), 300–1, 320.

its European satellites often mirrored, with variations of timing, the experience of the USSR itself. The various communist regimes kept a firm grip on the activities of historians, though its pressure was unevenly applied. Hungary, for instance, began to liberalize relatively soon after the failure of the 1956 Revolution. So did Poland, which had also experienced an aborted revolution in that year. Pre-war ties between Polish historians and the Annales were rekindled, works in French and Polish were mutually translated, and a number of Polish historians, such as the Braudel-influenced Witold Kula (1916–88) and the theorist Jerzy Topolski (1928–99) published work in *Annales*. Elsewhere such liberalization did not occur. In Bulgaria, a 1968 issue of the country's leading academic history journal announced that the Politburo had decided to commission a national history of the country, which would be assigned to scholars who enjoyed the Politburo's confidence. The planned series, in ten volumes, would be written according to strict Marxist–Leninist principles. The first volume of this 'people's history' appeared in 1979 in a print run of 50,000 copies – the authorities were clearly determined to give the work wide circulation.

The imposition of state Marxism on historiography in communism's other major bastion, mainland China (since 1949, the People's Republic), was complicated by the fact that Maoist dogma had to be superimposed on a society still in many ways organized on Confucian principles. The adaptation was not easy. Confucianism saw the world as a stable continuum punctuated by dynastic rises and falls, Marxism as the arena of linear progress; Confucianism was all about order and harmony; Marxism turned on class struggle and revolt. Yet China became the second major home for Marxist historiography during the twentieth century, and today remains the last superpower state to retain Marxism as official ideology despite recent economic liberalization. Although the ancient classics lost their scriptural aura rather quickly following the earlier, 1911 Revolution, neither republicans nor Marxists could easily jettison the whole apparatus of Confucianism. Many Marxists found it useful, as Joseph Levenson elegantly put it, to convert this old currency rather than cancel it.[15] They turned Confucius the conservative into an early theorist of progress, and his very associations with class and feudalism were perfectly acceptable because they were appropriate for his own age, which had now vanished, along with its social arrangements.

By the 1920s, in the wake of the Russian Revolution, explicitly Marxist and materialist ideas of history were beginning to have a greater impact on Chinese thought, though they were not yet explicitly linked to calls for revolutionary change or a commitment by intellectuals to the imposition of communism. Once again, Japan provided an essential conduit between the West and China, and several critical Marxist texts were first translated into Chinese from Japanese versions. Chinese Marxist historians, many of whom had been children at the fall of the Qing in 1911–12, soon emancipated themselves from dependence on Soviet interpretations, in particular the Stalinist view that China had never escaped the feudal stage and thus had not entered the bourgeois-capitalist stage which must precede a proletarian revolution. Most Chinese Marxists held that this transition had occurred earlier, while the feudal period itself had been ushered in as early as the Zhou dynasty, a period that received much more attention than the entire twenty-two centuries from early Qin to late Qing, though it was conceded that feudal traces remained in certain political and social superstructures. The poet, playwright and historian Guo Moruo (1892–1978) contributed a number of articles on the ancient past which, published in 1930 as *Zhongguo gu dai she hui yan jiu* ('Research on Ancient Chinese Society'), quickly became a relative bestseller, with over 7,000 copies in print. Guo offered a chronology of Chinese development in four stages, with primitive or asiatic society having characterized the age before the Zhou, followed by a slave society (a stage not always acknowledged in Marxism, and sometimes thought to follow feudalism) and then, in the aftermath of the Spring and Autumn period, a transition to feudal or medieval society. The penultimate transition, to capitalist society, had occurred only in the past century. Though he revised some of this chronology in response to criticism, Guo's study was significant in other ways: he was the first author within the Marxist context to make use of the newer, archaeological materials on antiquity that had been unearthed in recent decades, in this case to argue against claims that the Zhou had been a feudal period. The quarrels over periodization and other disputes among Chinese Marxists are emblematic of a larger problem within Marxism (and indeed all universalizing theories): its models are not easily transportable from one context to another.

Notwithstanding the internal contradictions and disagreements, the outcome of this 'Social History Controversy' was, eventually, the adaptation of the Chinese past into European historical categories such as 'feudalism', completing the process of Westernizing Chinese historiography begun in the 1890s. Even more than Liang Qichao or the republican May Fourth scholars (see Chapter 8 above), early Chinese Marxist historians set about engineering a permanent break with the Confucian didactic and moralizing practices that had dominated two-and-a-half millennia of history-writing. An important early adherent of Marxism was Fan Wenlan (1891–1969), whose *Zhongguo Tong shi jian bian* ('General History of China', 1941) is considered a landmark of Chinese Marxist historiography. With the founding of the People's Republic (PRC) after the chaotic period of the Japanese occupation and the ensuing Communist–Nationalist civil war, Marxist historiography became state-sponsored orthodoxy. Many former exponents of Marxism did not become communists: Tao Xisheng (1899?–1988), one of the most formidable of early Marxist Chinese historians, chose exile in Taiwan. Fan Wenlan (1893–1969), by contrast, had been a communist since the 1920s and was eventually appointed to head the Institute of Modern History – his close relationship with Mao Zedong probably saved his life during the Cultural Revolution.

Beginning in the early 1950s and continuing into the 1970s, the focus of Chinese scholarship turned to the history of the peasantry and of capitalism, with the triumph of communism depicted as inevitable. 'Party history' (*dangshi*) was a significant subject in its own right in university curricula from the beginning of the PRC, with some universities even creating departments dedicated to it. From 1949 till Mao's death in 1976, writings in this area showed an increasing preoccupation with discussion of the ruler's thought, treating him as a synonym for the whole Chinese Communist Party. The texts produced in connection with Party History continue to be carefully controlled and orchestrated from above in a manner that makes the bureaucrat-historians of the Tang era seem positively individualist by comparison. Since 1949, historians at various times have suffered persecution for heterodox statements, while within the Communist Party itself, different factions have sought historical support for contending political positions. The Great Leap

Forward (1959–61) opened a rift among older and younger Marxist scholars and pushed academic historians towards a militant repudiation of 'feudal' or 'bourgeois' dynastic history, along with the construction of general histories on Marxist principles, purged of reference to former dynasties, emperors and events. This was accompanied by directives to subordinate past to present, history to theory, in a simplistic manner resisted by moderate academics such as Beijing University's Jian Bozan (1898–1968).

The Cultural Revolution had an even more terrible impact a few years later. It began with an attack on a respected historian of the Ming era, Wu Han (1909–69), who would ultimately be beaten to death in prison. Wu had written a play several years previously entitled *The Dismissal of Hai Rui*, about a real-life Ming dynasty functionary famous for populist sympathies and opposition to corruption. This was first performed in 1961, and because of its alleged veiled criticism of the current regime and the Great Leap Forward, it quickly aroused the suspicion of Mao's wife Jiang Qing (1914–91). An attack on Wu in late 1965 by Jiang Qing's ally, Yao Wenyuan (1931–2005), inaugurated ten years of violent persecution during which China's intellectual and academic cohorts were imprisoned, tortured or sent into forced labour in the countryside. Wu was only one of many historians whose careers and lives were destroyed in these years, including Jian Bozan, who was hounded into suicide. Both Jian and Wu were later posthumously rehabilitated while, following Mao's death and the fall of the extremist Gang of Four (Jiang Qing, Yao Wenyuan and two associates), a degree of liberalization began. Since the 1980s, entire eras have been opened up for examination, though a Party resolution of 1981 attempted to cut off ongoing historical discussions of the Maoist period in the name of unity. In the last quarter of the twentieth century, Chinese historiography has also begun interacting once again with the West, Chinese academicians have been trained in Western graduate schools and many Western books have been translated into Chinese (though there has been less traffic of Chinese books in the other direction). This equivalent of Soviet Russian 'glasnost' has largely continued, despite brief setbacks such as the 1989 Tiananmen Square reaction.

The Chinese experience with Marxist historiography has been reflected on a smaller scale in that of its former satellite, Vietnam, where, since the American evacuation of the south in 1975, a communist regime has ruled. 'Historian cadres', working-class members given historical training while continuing their regular jobs, provided popular input into historical writing. The tension between nationalism and Marxism that early Soviet historians had encountered in the 1920s and 1930s was repeated in Vietnam: early impulses to do away with the dynastic histories of the 'feudal' past were quickly quashed, and the old works themselves rehabilitated into evidence of the country's lengthy and heroic past. Attempts were even made initially to establish contacts with historians in the non-communist south, though by the early 1960s these had been abandoned. The work of colonial-era historians and archaeologists, both French and Vietnamese, was more controversial and easily repudiated, though the quantity of it in comparison with the older histories meant that it simply could not be ignored.

Vietnamese 'New History' signalled a further turn in scholarly historiography while the country was partitioned. During the extended period of war between north and south prior to 1975, state-enforced Marxist interpretations in the north were met with equally fervent anticommunist historiography in the south, seriously constraining the range of topics that could be addressed. Since the introduction of a government policy of 'renovation' in the late 1980s, some liberalization has occurred, including better exchanges of information with the rest of the world. However, an official history, subordinate to political ends, is still conveyed in textbooks, and certain subjects remain proscribed. In Vietnam, as in other parts of East and Southeast Asia, control over what is read in schools has been close in recent decades, the state's assumption being that national identities are fashioned from the ground up and future citizens best shaped in their youth by exposure to historical orthodoxy.

This section has perhaps created an exaggerated impression of a sharp contrast between democratic and non-democratic states insofar as freedom of historical inquiry and interpretation is concerned. Unfortunately, political intolerance is not the exclusive preserve of totalitarian regimes, and limitations on historians' speech and publication occur even under democratic governments. In 1956, the young Australian historian Russel Ward had his appointment to a lectureship vetoed by the institution's chancellor because of his 'seditious' and communist associations, causing the department head (who by no means shared Ward's views) to resign in protest against the violation of academic freedom. The left-wing British historian George Rudé (1910–93), who did not complete his doctorate on the crowd in the French Revolution until he was forty, then found obstacles in the way of his employment in Britain; he spent most of his career in Australia and Canada. When one of Japan's most distinguished modern historians, Ienaga Saburō (1913–2002), was commissioned to write a history text in 1953, his manuscript was rejected by the authorities because it appeared to oppose the Tokugawa family system, treated peasant uprisings as legitimate and spent too many pages on the recent history of the Pacific region. On resubmitting the manuscript, without changing a word, it was passed, suggesting to him the arbitrariness of the system. Many examples of censorship and persecution have come from the United States, where left-wing historians or those suspected of communist affiliation were blacklisted in the 1950s. A number emigrated to Canada, Britain and other countries. The ancient historian Moses Finley (1912–86), a New York-born Jew, was fired from his position at Rutgers University in 1952, subsequently moving to Cambridge where he had a long and successful scholarly career culminating in a knighthood. A historian of early modern France, Natalie Zemon Davis (b. 1928), emigrated to Toronto in the early 1960s with her mathematician husband (a victim of political persecution) though she would eventually commute to the United States and teach at Berkeley and Princeton. During the 1960s activist historians such as Howard Zinn (1922–2010) and Staughton Lynd (b. 1929) were dismissed from academic posts, the latter for visiting Hanoi in protest against the Vietnam War.

History from Below

Without state authority to support it, academic Marxism never attained a monopoly position in the West, but it has had a significant influence, which has waned somewhat since the 1980s. Marxist, socialist or broadly left-leaning historiography began to appear in the Western democracies relatively early in the twentieth century. Part of the left's resilience has derived not from rigid orthodoxy but from its opposite, a rather broad ability to intermix with other agendas and to mutually cross-fertilize with other approaches to history. The French politician Jean Jaurès (1859–1914), assassinated on the eve of the First World War, provided in his *Socialist History of the French Revolution* an early example of a non-Marxist socialist history exemplified in a number of historians born in the last decades of the nineteenth century, such as the Polish economic historian and educational reformer Franciszek Bujak (1875–1953) and his English counterparts, R. H. Tawney (1880–1962) and John L. (1872–1949) and Barbara (1873–1961) Hammond. Others of that generation were more radical: the leading Norwegian historian Halvdan Koht (1873–1965), for instance, was an early self-avowed Marxist (albeit one critical of Marx's strict materialism) (Extract 44); the Greek historian Yannis Kordatos (1891–1961) narrated his country's revolution as a conflict of class rather than ethnicity. The attractions of Marxism increased in the aftermath of the Wall Street crash of 1929, which seemed to bear out Marx's prediction of the inevitable collapse of capitalism. Georges Lefebvre (1874–1959) would place the French Revolution into a Marxist historical scheme, whereby it became the necessary transition to the bourgeois state. His most famous book, *The Coming of the French Revolution*, was republished in 1939 on the eve of the Second World War, only to have the collaborationist Vichy government order all known copies of it to be burned following France's defeat in 1940. It would eventually become a favoured text of the British left.

The dalliance of many inter-war British and some American intellectuals with Marxism provided the earliest examples of historiography that, in the 1960s, would evolve into Labour history, 'radical history' and what is sometimes called

44: The Education of a Marxist Historian: Halvdan Koht

I joined the Labor Party through its branch at Baerum, where I had become domiciled upon my return from abroad in 1909. It was not long before I became active in the local politics of the community. Through that I came into more active contact with party work, and frequently I spoke before party meetings on cooperation between farmers and laborers as well as on national issues ....

[The question of] socialism as nationalistic politics, had been discussed by me as early as 1910, as soon as I had formed my conclusion about the underlying unity to be found here. Year by year I developed the topic more fully, gradually securing more support within the Labor Party ... I make bold to assert that my work in this field influenced the entire thinking of the Labor Party, so that it was no longer content merely to reject bourgeois conceptions of nationalism, but adopted nationalistic ideas to its own purposes .... Few things in my life have given me so much pleasure as having helped to bring about this intellectual transformation of the Norwegian Labor Party.

Psychological Research

It should be clear from all that I have written about historical research and practical work based on the idea of class struggle, that what was consistently uppermost in my reasoning was not the fact of economic life itself, but rather the temperament, the way of thinking, the type of intelligence which was fostered by the class struggle. I could call myself a Marxian well enough, and I made much of Marxism in my work on *The Norwegian Farm Uprising*. But I disliked the term 'materialistic historiography' which really had no basis other than Marx's having combined his view of history with his philosophy of materialism. No such doctrine of materialism was essential to my view of history.

I was thoroughly in agreement with the good Marxist historian, M. N. Pokrowski [*sic*], when he said to me at the historical congress in Oslo in 1928: 'We must always remember that Marxism is a *method*, not a doctrine or a formula into which all historical events can be squeezed.'

From Halvdan Koht, *Education of an Historian*, trans. E. Wahlgren (New York: Robert Speller & Sons, 1957), 214–16. Halvdan Koht, Norway's leading historian through much of the twentieth century, here recounts his early activism and involvement in Norwegian socialism; in the second passage he explains his reservations about strict materialism which in his view allowed little room for psychological and intellectual factors.

'history from below'. Several key Anglo-American examples of twentieth-century social history such as George Rudé's above-mentioned work on crowds, E. P. Thompson's (1924–93) *The Making of the English Working Class* (1963) and Herbert Gutman's (1928–85) *Work, Culture and Society in Industrializing America*

(1977) were products of an explicitly Marxist, but more humanistic and less rigidly deterministic, perspective; this emphasized the daily lives of history's downtrodden, and highlighted their own agency, an aspect undervalued in the determinism of mainstream Marxism. A similarly 'soft' approach to Marxism was adopted in other parts of the world, for example by the Dutch journalist-historian Jan Romein (1893–1962), who owed as much to Huizinga's brand of *Kulturgeschichte* as he did to Marx and was excluded from membership in the Dutch Communist Party because of his unorthodox opinions.[16] A further modification of Marxism was articulated by the Italian socialist, and victim of Fascism, Antonio Gramsci (1891–1937), whose 3,000-page *Prison Notebooks*, first published a decade after his death, has become one of the great political texts of the left. With his concept of cultural 'hegemony', the process whereby ruling powers or elites maintain authority with the willing cooperation of the subordinated, Gramsci's star has risen further since the 1960s, and his ideas continue to appear in much non-Marxist historical scholarship and literary history.

France and Italy aside, no democratic country has generated so vigorous a Marxist historiography as Britain, where virtually every period from the Middle Ages to the early twentieth century has been well covered, and where socialist historians have enjoyed a high public profile quite disproportionate to their relatively small numbers. They have also, by and large, escaped the political persecution (though not always the career disruption, as Rudé's example shows) meted out to left-leaning historians in the United States and Australia. Many British Marxists, such as Christopher Hill (1912–2003, a historian of radical ideas and beliefs in seventeenth-century England), were initially active Communist Party members, but left it after the Soviet invasion of Hungary in 1956, along with several of their French counterparts. Others such as Eric Hobsbawm (b. 1917), a historian of the industrial era, retained their party affiliation while nonetheless taking critical stands against the excesses of Soviet expansionism. Perhaps the most important collective contribution that many of them made was the establishment of the journal *Past and Present* in 1952. Quickly establishing itself as an alternative to the more mainstream political history journals, it has since then achieved the kind of international prominence that *Annales* had earlier acquired in France.[17] Soon jettisoning its initial subtitle 'a Journal of Scientific History' (now become merely 'a Journal of Historical Studies'), *Past and Present* had become sufficiently centrist by the mid-1970s that it eventually ceded the space on its left to newer organs like the *History Workshop Journal*.

The United States has similarly a long tradition of 'left history', dating back to the Progressive and New Historians of the early twentieth century. A post-1945 recommitment to the twin ideas of America's exceptionalism and the 'consensus' on which this was built – papering over the fissures of race, class and (yet to be heard from) gender – had the effect of cooling any radical impulses at the same time that the Cold War was getting started. Those with leftist affiliations often found themselves facing tough questions about their 'loyalty' during the late 1940s and 1950s. By the mid-1960s, however, with Vietnam and the civil rights movement dominating public discourse, radical history returned with a vengeance, and sometimes with polarizing violence: the liberal historian of France, Orest Ranum (b. 1933) had a year's worth of his notes destroyed by student protesters at Columbia in 1968, and soon found the attitude of his more radical colleagues so oppressive that he relocated to Johns Hopkins. While the radicalism of the late 1960s in America and western Europe dissipated within a few years, it left a formidable pedagogical legacy. History from below, along with Black history, women's history and native history, had by the early 1970s established a small but firm beachhead in university history departments. By the end of that decade, the curricular position of all of these was rather more secure – just in time to resist the resurgent conservatism of the 1980s in the United States and several of its Western allies.

Women's History and Gender from the Nineteenth Century to the Present

The nineteenth century had witnessed something else not seen before historiographically, namely the far greater involvement of women in historical writing in Europe and North America. Women had been readers of history for many centuries, and a handful of female historians have been mentioned in earlier chapters of this book. The number of women writing popular history and biography increased after 1800 and by 1900 women had begun to enter the emerging 'profession'. The resistance that they encountered there was formidable: the research seminar remained a male preserve in contrast to the more open-access undergraduate lecture – Treitschke actually declared that the admission of women to his classes at Berlin would be an insult to his male pupils. Outside the universities, women were making their mark in various ways, including the hosting of intellectual salons, as did the wives of both Ranke and Augustin Thierry. Women such as Ireland's Mary Agnes Hickson (1825–99) made a name editing sources for seventeenth-century Irish history. The lack of opportunities for academic careers inevitably caused some to abandon history for other pursuits: the Swiss historian Maria Waser (née Krebs, 1878–1939) earned a doctorate at Bern on fifteenth-century Swiss history, but soon left the discipline for a literary career.

With their admission to some universities women began to make even more significant contributions to scholarship. Within the universities, economic history, by now well established as a strong alternative to political history, would prove especially attractive to women. Lilian Knowles (1870–1926), a former student at Cambridge (which did not grant degrees to women till after the First World War) became a successful member of the London School of Economics (LSE). A mentor to many younger women, Knowles's pupils included Alice Clark (1874–1934). A prominent political activist and businesswoman, Clark never held an academic post, but her *Working Life of Women in the Seventeenth Century* (1919) has become a foundational text of women's history. Clark's younger contemporary, Eileen Power (1889–1940), one of the early twentieth century's outstanding medievalists, cracked the masculine bastion of European archival scholarship when she studied at the École des Chartes as a graduate student in 1910. Like Knowles before her, Power would become Professor of Economic History at the LSE (1931), and she was a pioneer in both comparative economic history and medieval women's history. A popular lecturer, Power also had the gift of bringing seemingly dry academic topics into the public sphere, in her case through early radio broadcasts on history.

Apart from economic history, family and social history provided an outlet for female historical interests. As Anne Wharton put it in 1893, 'to read of councils, congresses and battles is not enough: men and women wish to know something more intimate and personal of the life of the past'.[18] The American Lucy Maynard Salmon (1853–1927), who was influenced by classical archaeology, can be seen retrospectively as a pioneer in the history of material culture. The Japanese feminist Takamure Itsue (1894–1964) flirted with Marxism in her study of the matriarchal aspects of early Japanese culture; her antipathy to Confucianism and China, to which she ascribed the creation of Japanese patriarchy, would ironically turn her into a pro-war supporter of her government in the 1930s and 1940s.

The challenges facing early women academic historians were legion and examples of their mistreatment or exploitation equally so. In France, where the Annales School was charting new directions in social and economic history, women such as Suzanne Dognon (1897–1985) contributed to scholarship; at the same time, they struggled to maintain their identity and independence in association with powerful male academics such as Dognon's husband, two decades her elder, Lucien Febvre. The Jewish émigré Lucie Varga (1904–41), Febvre's sometime associate and briefly his mistress, provided a link between the world of the Annales and that of German scholarship. Recognition in their own right as academics was harder to achieve than close involvement in the work of a famous spouse. The widow of German historian Otto Hintze (1861–1940), Hedwig Hintze (1884–1942), herself an innovative specialist on the French Revolution, fled to the Netherlands because of her Jewish ancestry, committing suicide on the eve of deportation to Auschwitz. A less fatal but probably more typical case that illustrates the profession's 'glass ceiling' is that of the little known Jessie Webb (1880–1945), an Australian who taught at Melbourne for many years, carrying a higher teaching load than her male peers and never progressing beyond the rank of lecturer.

Prominent exceptions like Eileen Power aside, women historians on the whole lost ground and prominence in the years following the conclusion of the First World War, a trend that continued into the 1960s. Practising history on the margins was one thing; entering the profession as an academic historian another – a career goal denounced by Mary Ritter Beard (1876–1958), despite her own university connections, on the grounds that the rules of academe were entirely set by men. Alice Williams had complained in 1919 of the absence of women from the programme of the American Historical Association (AHA). While the situation improved somewhat in the following years, the AHA elected only one female president (1943), the medievalist Nellie Neilson, in its first hundred years of existence. Outside North America and western Europe the prominence of women historians has been even more uneven. In China, the profession remains today a largely masculine preserve. In Bulgaria, roughly a quarter of all its historians since the mid-nineteenth century have been female, a proportion that had improved considerably by the end of communism in 1989. In Finland, by contrast, very few women prior to the 1950s achieved Ph.D.s in history, though many more earned Masters degrees. The Finnish profession remained overwhelmingly male in the first decades after the Second World War, despite the activity of many women biographers and amateur historians.

The gendering of historical interests that occurred in the early modern period and continued in the early twentieth century also endures today. Women have continued to gravitate to social history in its various forms, to cultural studies and to women's and gender history. Among the many subfields to have emerged in the past forty years, women's history (itself equally a descendant of social and economic history) and its own recent offshoots, the histories of gender and of sexuality, have perhaps been the most successful in reshaping the agenda of the entire discipline. Women's history first began to make serious inroads within universities in the early 1970s though the prehistory of the subject goes back well over a century in many parts of the world: in the Arabic world, for instance, a number of Syrian and Egyptian women, principally from prosperous backgrounds, began to write history in the late nineteenth century, and one, Zaynab Fawwasi (c. 1860–1914), observed that 'History, which is the best of all sciences, is largely dominated by men. Not a single one of those male historians has dedicated a single chapter in which to discuss women who represent half of human-kind.'[19] In this Fawwasi anticipated by several decades Mary Ritter Beard's *Woman as Force in History* (1946), which suggested that historians, being predominantly male, had simply not 'seen' women's contributions in the past.

The problem by the 1960s was not really a lack of interest in women's history but rather its absence from university curricula and research agenda. In short, the study of women in the past remained an occasional subject within the main streams of military, political and social history, and most often written outside the universities. The initial solution to this seemed to lie in establishing women's history as a recognizable and distinct sub-discipline without detaching it from the professional mainstream wherein lay the academic rewards and honours of which women had been struggling to gain a share for half a century. The push for women's history in the 1970s followed the growth of the Women's Liberation movement and the development of feminist perspectives in philosophy and the social sciences, with intellectual inspiration coming from key texts of twentieth-century feminism such as Simone de Beauvoir's *The Second Sex* (1949) and Virginia Woolf's *A Room of One's Own* (1929). There had already been sporadic courses on women's history offered at American universities, the Viennese-born Gerda Lerner (b. 1920) having taught the subject at various American institutions since the middle of the 1960s. An important factor in establishing women's history on undergraduate curricula, and in making it a research topic in its own right, may have been the decision by a number of other well-established female historians to shift interests or expand the focus of their scholarship and teaching. Natalie Zemon Davis, whose early research was on French print workers, authored a pioneering essay on women and popular culture in early modern France in the 1970s. Gisela Bock (b. 1942), a prominent German feminist historian, had written her first book on the Renaissance philosopher Tommaso Campanella before her own political activities on behalf of pay equity for female workers moved her in the direction of women's history.

Meanwhile, arguments continued to occur on campus as to where and how the history of women fitted into 'history proper' or 'the main stream'. From the point of view of some male historians, women's history was the symbol *par excellence* of the continuing fragmentation of the discipline along 'interest group' lines. It was frequently discounted as of lesser importance, despite its obvious intersection with family history, and 'serious' graduate students (that is males, and any female who really wanted career advancement) were steered elsewhere. Nor were women practitioners entirely agreed on an agenda for their subject as the 1970s ended. Was women's history simply a 'supplement' to the main agendas of historians, an addition to the pool of knowledge of achievements previously and unjustly left out? Was it sufficient simply to attribute an agency to women that had previously been attached to men, or was this simply to fall into a historiographic analysis (and agenda) that had been established by males in the first place? In short, was it enough to write 'contribution history' or, as the saying went, to take conventional accounts of the past and 'add women and stir'?

The major shift came after 1986, in which year Joan Wallach Scott (b. 1941), an American scholar working in French history, published a seminal article, 'Gender: A Useful Category of Historical Analysis', urging a refocusing of attention away from women as biologically essentialized beings and towards the study of gender and its social (and linguistic) construction. The immediate effect of this was to enlarge considerably the areas of potential study for both feminist and non-feminist historians: instead of focusing on women's oppression, subordination or heroic agency, one could now focus on the way in which gender had an impact across the entire sphere of past human activity, including those areas such as political life in which women had been conspicuously rare. Scott, however, went further than simply advocating for gender's equivalency with race or class as a category. She questioned what 'gender' meant in particular contexts and how it acted as a determinant of other phenomena. Influenced by French cultural theorists such as Michel Foucault (1926–84), whose own later works focused on the history of sexuality, Scott asserted that the written discourses generated by a society are forms of power in their own right, and that they have created and constrained notions of male and female, and of masculine and feminine qualities across time. Though Scott herself has been criticized for too close an allegiance to postmodernism (see below) at the expense of more traditional feminist agendas, her article had an almost immediate impact. In the past two decades much Western scholarship has shifted gradually from women's history to gender history. The prior connections with social history and economics have been complemented by a linkage to more recent interdisciplinary approaches such as cultural studies. Gender history in turn has also overlapped with two other recent subfields, the history of sexuality and its spinoff, queer studies.

Intellectual History and Psychohistory

Historians have studied ideas as well as events for centuries, and both *Kulturgeschichte* and *Geistesgeschichte* attended to the impact of human thought in past times. Within the modern historical discipline, what is usually called intellectual history established itself by mid-century as a distinctive subfield under different names and in different styles: Meinecke's *Ideengeschichte* was the German variant; in France the study of *mentalités* emerged with the Annales. In the United States, the 'history of ideas' as a recognizable subject of study began with the foundation of the journal by that name in 1939 under the direction of Arthur O. Lovejoy (1873–1962). Lovejoy himself produced in *The Great Chain of Being* (1936) a book that epitomized his method: identify a key concept or 'unit idea' and trace it forward in time as it combined and recombined with other unit ideas. Allying themselves with philosophy as much as history – in the sense that sorting out a thinker's precise arguments and their afterlife became the priority – intellectual historians produced some remarkably fine work during this period but the Lovejoy approach began to attract criticism in the 1960s. The *Journal of the History of Ideas*, though it did not respond immediately to changes in historiographical fashion, nevertheless provides a good index of them: in the seventy years since its foundation it has gone through a relatively small number of editors, and in recent times it has complemented its traditional diet of 'high intellectual' history, concerned with elite thinkers, with broader 'cultural history' topics. It has also begun to abandon the almost exclusively Western focus which, along with an 'internalist' philosophical approach, had previously limited the appeal of this style of intellectual history in much of the wider world.

Intellectual history in the European and North American context peaked in popularity in the 1950s and fell out of fashion in the 1960s and 1970s (a victim of the rapid success of social history), reinventing itself as the less elitist-sounding 'cultural history' in the 1980s, since when it has regained a good deal of ground. Lovejoy's old 'history of ideas' has been expanded at one end to include newer fields like the history of the book (*histoire du livre*), and at the other into the pursuit of the meaning of terms and of texts in their linguistic and/or social contexts. The latter stream is in turn divisible into a so-called Cambridge School of the history of political thought, associated most often with Quentin Skinner (b. 1940) in Britain and the New Zealander J. G. A. Pocock (b. 1924) in the United States, and with the *Begriffsgeschichte* (history of political and social concepts) approach advocated by the German Reinhart Koselleck (1923–2006). Koselleck's method has somewhat more in common with Lovejoy's, though its focus is not on the 'unit idea' as a kind of free-floating entity, but on the semantic usage of particular words and their signification. A good example, relevant immediately to this book and already cited in Chapter 6, is the advent during the eighteenth century of 'Geschichte' in German (displacing the older term 'Historie'), along with the development of what we have been calling capital-H History. A former pupil of Herbert Butterfield, Pocock has examined ideas historically, within their sequential political and intellectual contexts, with major authors considered often by comparison with others now of less note but important at the time of writing. His mid-career masterpiece, *The Machiavellian Moment* (1975), demonstrates this method most fully, as it follows key political and historical concepts like 'civic humanism' and 'republicanism' backwards to ancient and early medieval thought, then examines their working out in the context of sixteenth-century Italy, before tracing them forward, via seventeenth-century English thinkers into a transatlantic, eighteenth-century Britanno-American world. Quentin Skinner's approach is very similar in insisting that great works be studied not simply to generate internally coherent meanings but within the context of other works of their time, though Skinner places a somewhat greater emphasis on particular leading thinkers such as the seventeenth-century philosopher Thomas Hobbes, and his own writing makes much more explicit use of linguistic theory.

The psychoanalytic theories of Sigmund Freud (1856–1939) inspired a very different form of inquiry into the influence of the mind in history, in this case of the irrational and subconscious. In his later works, especially *Moses and Monotheism* (1939), Freud applied his theories and clinical experience to the 'diagnosis' of history. Freud had dabbled in history earlier in his career, using psychoanalysis in a 1910 book on Leonardo da Vinci and more systematically in *Civilization and its Discontents* (1930). The process of civilization Freud envisaged as an endless struggle of love and hate, sex and death, arising from primal patricide, and carried forward by leader-figures such as Moses in conflict with the mobs whom they dominated – the similarity in this regard between the ideas of Freud, a Viennese Jew, and aspects of the thought of his contemporary Nietzsche is striking.

Psychohistory has probably aroused more passion among its most fervent devotees and contempt from its most outspoken critics than almost any other theoretical approach to the study of the past, even the 'linguistic turn' (see below). Its heyday came a generation after Freud's death, in the late 1950s, 1960s and early 1970s. In 1957, the president of the American Historical Association, William L. Langer, used the podium to call for historians to move on to 'the next assignment', which was the application of psychology to historical research. In the very next year, a German-born trained psychoanalyst and refugee from the Nazis, Erik H. Erikson (1902–94), published *Young Man Luther*, the first full-length attempt to psychoanalyse a particular historical figure. He would go on to write several further such works, though none as well regarded as the study of Luther. Though neither Erikson nor psychohistory has ever won wide acceptance beyond a core group of admirers, and while Freudian theories have been marginalized within psychology by modern neuroscience, a psychoanalytic approach has been championed by the occasional mainstream historian such as Peter Gay (b. 1923), who himself underwent psychoanalytic training and has written extensively about Freud. Indirectly, it has had a quiet but significant effect on aspects of postmodernism, though that approach has also challenged the possibility of understanding the psyche since the self in its own right may be simply a constructed feature of Western culture. At its best, in the work of a trained analyst like Erikson, psychohistory offers a plausible alternative set of explanations for individual actions. At its worst, it becomes as hopelessly deterministic and reductionist as the documentary positivism that it ostensibly opposes.

The Linguistic Turn, Postmodernism and Postcolonialism

In the late 1960s, with social history in the ascendant, few professional historians were thinking much about their millennia-old relationship to the world of literature. The overwhelming majority of readers and writers of history accepted that there was a fundamental difference between works of fiction and history, which recounted a true story. In the following decade, this began to change, at the very same time that, partly as a consequence of 1960s unrest and rapid decolonization across the world, renewed questioning was occurring of the rationalist, 'Enlightenment' agenda of the previous three centuries. In short, doubts about both history and History (and, increasingly, about the connection between the two), sounded in the early years of the century but largely suppressed during and immediately following the Second World War, began to re-emerge, now in a post-atomic world and within a discipline much more fractured than it had ever been.

A direct outgrowth of this is the so-called linguistic turn, often identified with the broader theoretical movement known as postmodernism or, with declining frequency, poststructuralism. This has roots in literary theory and in continental philosophy, especially works of the Frenchmen Michel Foucault and Jacques Derrida (1930–2004), the German Martin Heidegger (1889–1976), his one-time pupil the hermeneuticist Hans-Georg Gadamer (1900–2002) and, further back, Nietzsche. Other influences include the pre-war German intellectuals Walter Benjamin (1892–1940) and Theodor Lessing (1872–1933), and there are echoes of early twentieth-century antipositivism. Postmodernism also draws selectively from cultural anthropology. If one wants to trace the genealogy further, one can go back through the eighteenth-century and Renaissance debates about the merits of history vs imaginative literature, and end up back at Aristotle's *Poetics*. Although the linguistic turn has by no means exclusively been concerned with this issue, a major thrust of it has been seriously to challenge conventional boundaries between history and fiction, and to overturn the superiority history has assumed for a good two centuries based on its claim to portray real rather than imagined events. Leading exponents of this view include the Americans Hayden White (see Box 33), Hans Kellner (b. 1945) and Dominick LaCapra (b. 1939), and the British theorist Keith Jenkins (b. 1943). Although its origins are Western, it has in recent years spread into Asian historical discourse, aided by the somewhat freer transfer of ideas and peoples since the late 1980s; there, it has become associated less with epistemological critiques of history than with efforts to locate Asian pasts on a trajectory leading to alternative forms of modernity, distinctive from that which has characterized the West.

Box 33   Hayden White and *Metahistory*

Hayden White's (b. 1928) influential *Metahistory* (1973) purports to demonstrate, through close study of a series of nineteenth-century historians and philosophers from Ranke and Burckhardt through Nietzsche and Croce, that there is no fundamental difference between the writing of history, philosophy of history and fiction, arguing in effect that there is no 'real' past outside of our representation of it; every narration or description of the past involves the historian in a series of mental operations that require a poetic act of imagination which in turn predetermines the story that will be 'discovered'. Borrowing from Vico, White argued that historical narratives are constituted through four master tropes (metaphor, metonymy, synecdoche and irony) or figures of speech that create a meaningful past out of the raw materials that make up the unprocessed 'historical field'. These tropes in turn help determine the author's choices among three different strategies of explanation, whereby a mere *chronicle* is turned into a *story*: modes of emplotment (the kind of story that is being told), modes of formal argument (the way in which events and persons interact within the historical world leading to an end) and modes of ideological implication (the moral to be drawn from the story). *Metahistory* was influential on several levels, particularly for the theoretical scaffolding constructed by White in understanding historical narrative structures and for its readings of diverse nineteenth-century historical writers. He has expanded on his views, and taken them further, in a number of collections of essays published subsequently. Perhaps more influential (and controversial), however, was his conclusion that there is no essential difference between the writing of fiction and that of history in the sense that one depicts imaginary occurrences and the other 'real' events. White certainly does not say that history and fiction are the *same* thing, nor does he suggest that one can simply make up documents and historical figures in the same way a novelist creates characters, but his arguments do have the effect of dissolving some key assumptions that have sustained the history–fiction distinction for centuries. Because of this, his work has become a focal point in the postmodern debate insofar as it involves history, motivating both outspoken defenders (who often take his arguments to further extremes than White himself) and equally fierce critics such as Arthur Marwick (1936–2006) and Geoffrey Elton, the latter in a much fiercer attack than the one he had launched a few years earlier on cliometrics.

If history from below turned the world of the past upside down, postmodernism has arguably turned it inside out. Postmodernism is often explicitly political, and at times almost fundamentalist in its antagonism to orthodoxies, master-narratives and power structures. It is devoted to demolishing these orthodoxies, and the knowledge structures on which they rest, as well as to 'de-centring' those objects of learning previously deemed central, and to re-centring, at least temporarily, the previously marginal and peripheral. It is committed to dissolving essences and investigating the modes whereby objects of intellectual inquiry, analytical categories (gender, race, class) and even individuals are viewed as the product of social and even linguistic 'construction'. Rationalism is regarded with suspicion by many postmodernists, and in particular 'Enlightenment' rationalism. The latter is a convenient shorthand for much that postmodernism resists because of its tendency to universalism, essentialism, an assumption of transcendental, objectively exist-ing values, and faith in the direct and recoverable relationship between things and the words that signify them. 'Positivism' is to a postmodernist even more dubious and 'naive', its parallel messages of social and scientific improvement (as in Comte and Buckle) and epistemological progress being doubly suspect since they presup-pose both linear forward change and the veracity of the narrative underlying and endorsing it.

In their zeal to caricature all opponents as 'positivist', rationalist or simply naive, many adherents of postmodernism have ironically constructed their own convenient 'other', a fabricated knowledge-villain that in itself is an example of essentialization and generalization. They have also, with some exceptions, im-puted a ubiquitous and omnipotent blanket-like quality to post-Enlightenment narratives, homogenizing currents of thought from the eighteenth and nineteenth centuries that were much less harmonious and single-minded than they are repre-sented as being and which contained their own elements of resistance and coun-ter-argument. Opponents of postmodernism and the entire linguistic turn have come from the left as much as the right: some Marxist and labour historians have seen the fixation on language and discourse as a regrettable retreat from the main agenda of class analysis back into the airy regions of ideas and abstraction, and as a betrayal of the materialism and socioeconomic analysis on which progressive or radical histories are based.

One need not buy the entire postmodern stock of ideas to acknowledge that it has provided a salutary reminder to all historians that documents and texts never 'speak for themselves'; they are interpreted by historians, and even the most 'neutral' document is ultimately an artefact created by a human driven by the assumptions, social pressures and linguistic conventions of his or her own time. In other words, the sources themselves are already interpreting the past when the historian first confronts them, and few historians would now endorse Fustel de

Coulanges' optimistic admonition to a group of nineteenth-century students that it was not he who spoke to them but 'history, which speaks through me'. Yet while postmodernism has been highly influential in literature and language departments, it has remained at best a dissenting voice in most history departments; it has, however, found a receptive audience among historians of gender, and among new cultural historians for whom it has provided a set of categories to replace those once derived from Marx.

The postmodern agenda has also crossed into other areas, such as postcolonial studies, an equally broad term that includes some representatives of the Indian 'Subaltern studies' approach (in its early days, a South Asian answer to 'history from below') and the 'Orientalist' critique of Edward Said (1935–2003). Postcolonialism is, one of its exponents observes, less a theory than a critique of its own 'other' – often defined as a broad 'post-Enlightenment' agenda characterized by reason, progress, the unstoppable increase of Western cultural and economic dominance, and even the false notion of the stability of the nation-state.[20] Anticipated in mid-century by writers such as the Martinican Frantz Fanon (1925–61) and the Trinidadian C. L. R. James (1901–89), postcolonialism is now often associated with Said (whose 1978 book *Orientalism* is a key text), and with a number of prominent Indian-born authors such as Gayatri Chakravorty Spivak (b. 1942), Partha Chatterjee (b. 1947) and Homi K. Bhabha (b. 1949).

Postcolonialism as a critical tool has been deployed most widely in Indian or Middle Eastern studies, and has overlapped with postmodernism in having the common goal of destabilizing, subverting or de-centring existing master-narratives in favour of the local and previously marginalized, and reading texts and documents 'against the grain' to detect what they do not say as much as what they do. Postcolonialism has redirected scholarship concerned with former colonies such as India towards the subjected masses rather than on the imperial rulers and their Indian elite allies or political successors. The Subaltern Studies Group, a 'school' of Indian historiography founded by Ranajit Guha (b. 1922), is a prominent example of this latter trend, critical not only of pre-Independence historiography but also of the rewriting of history after 1947 into simply a counter-history with roles reversed, focused on indigenous political elites and omitting nine-tenths of the population. The Subaltern agenda prioritizes the subordinate and the voiceless, the local and regional rather than the national – 'subaltern' in this sense is a term derived from Gramsci. Spivak, a literary critic often associated with the group, has extended the Subaltern approach to feminist topics. In recent years, some early Subalternists such as the social historian Sumit Sarkar (b. 1939) have broken with the movement's increasing radicalism and its associations with postmodernism. A good many others, however, have shifted away from Marxist categories of analysis towards postmodern concerns with deconstructing the language of colonialism. In some cases, they reject Western historicity itself as a tool of imperial control, born of the Enlightenment's progressivist agenda, and enabling a 'dominance without hegemony' over India's (and, by extension, other colonized countries') true sense of the past, a sense that must be liberated from the seemingly inevitable Hegelian story of nationhood.

This repudiation of Western historicity by Indian postcolonial critics is not entirely new. A powerful early statement of the position, long before the current discussions, came from no less a figure than Mohandas K. Gandhi (1869–1948), who rejected not only British rule but ultimately much of Western culture, including history. The Mahatma saw European modernization as part of India's problem not its solution, and was of a view that Indians would be better off without history. 'It is my pet theory', he said, 'that our Hindu ancestors solved the question for us by ignoring history as understood today and by building on slight events their philosophical structure.' Ancient epics such as the *Mahābhārata* were not, *pace* Sir William Jones, remotely like a history: they were *better* than histories, since they contained eternal truths, portrayed allegorically. In fact, said Gandhi, not just India but the world might profit from a bit less history, because history is at best a pathology of things that have gone badly wrong. 'History, as we know it, is a record of the wars of the world ... How kings played, how they became enemies of one another, how they murdered one another, is found accurately recorded in history, and if this were all that had happened in the world, it would have ended long ago.' History cannot record harmony, peace and love because it must necessarily focus on rupture and discontinuity rather than on the non-violence that Gandhi championed. 'Hundreds of nations live in peace. History does not and cannot take note of this fact. History is really the record of every interruption of the even working of the force of love or of the soul.'[21] Gandhi's position thus diverged from that of his close associate Nehru or the earlier nationalist-novelist Bankim Chatterjee (see Chapter 8 above), for both of whom history was an essential ingredient in the construction of nationhood and achievement of emancipation.

Both Subaltern studies and Said's related concept of Orientalism have now spread to include other regions of the world than those that gave them birth, overlapping with slightly older, more economically focused anticolonial critiques such as 'dependency theory', a model adduced in the 1960s to explain the unequal relationship between developed and underdeveloped parts of the world. Later twentieth-century Latin American historians, for instance, have come to view Western historical scholarship as much more monolithic and alien than did their nineteenth-century precursors. However, fierce criticism of the imperial, Westernizing enterprise had rather older, and most often Marxist, origins, for instance in African and Caribbean 'diasporic' historiography. Parallels to the early twentieth-century Indian redeployment of European historical methods against British colonialism

45: An Early Postcolonial Critic of History: Eric Williams on British Historians and Imperialism

But what good came of it? little Perkin asked of the battle of Blenheim.

The historical prophecies have not been fulfilled. The passive races have become active. India is free and independent, and Gandhi's educational ideas, the philosophy of Radhakrishnan, and the poetry of Tagore are now part of the world's culture. The Suez Canal could not be maintained against Nasser. The Organization of African Unity symbolizes the independence of Africa, which has not in any way been due to the British inheritance of the tradition of Wilberforce or anyone else. Jamaica and Trinidad and Tobago are independent Caribbean states. Independence has not meant retrogression or peeling off of their clothes. Independence under a local governor-general and coloured prime ministers and cabinets has not meant a reversion to barbarism.

This is not to say that a century and a half of denigration of the West Indies in British universities have not left their mark on British attitudes to the West Indies. Britain's double standard, self-government for white colonies and crown colony status for black colonies, one attitude to a black rebellion in Jamaica and another to a white rebellion in England, cannot possibly be divorced from the attitude to colour and race which West Indians associate with the Commonwealth Immigration Act.

The British historians wrote almost as if Britain had introduced Negro slavery solely for the satisfaction of abolishing it. They have made such play of the compensation provided by Britain to the planters as wiping off the debt to the West Indians in respect of slavery that it is difficult not to see in this attitude, developed and propagated over a century and a quarter, the explanation of the British Government's attitude on economic aid to the West Indies and on preferential treatment of the West Indies sugar industry.

These are political conclusions. As such they are a legitimate reply to the political conclusions drawn by the British historians themselves. These men occupied important positions in British life as professors and even rectors of universities .... The historical field therefore provides the battleground on which imperialist politics struggle against nationalist politics ....

It is in this sense particularly that the West Indian historian of the future has a crucial role to play in the education of the West Indian people in their own history and in the merciless exposure of the shams, the inconsistencies, the prejudices of metropolitan historians.

Selected from the conclusion to Eric Eustace Williams, *British Historians and the West Indies* (New York: Scribner's, 1966), 233–4. The Oxford-educated Williams was Prime Minister of Trinidad and Tobago from 1956 till his death in 1981.

(see Chapter 8 above) can be found in the writings of the Trinidadian historian–politician Eric Williams (Extract 45) and in Williams' one-time teacher C. L. R. James. With an intellectual parentage going back to Michelet (whose sympathetic treatment of the French Revolution he much admired), James offered in *The Black Jacobins* (1938) a Marxist analysis of the Haitian slave revolt of the late eighteenth century and its interconnection with contemporary events in France. Revisiting his book in the early 1960s, in the wake of Fidel Castro's successful revolution in Cuba but despairing of much of the rest of the West Indies (still dominated by wealthy white minorities, American-backed dictators and cooperative black middle classes), James anticipated the Subaltern critique by nearly two decades, declaring that of 'Historical tradition, education in the sense of grappling with the national past, there is none. History as taught is what it always has been, propaganda for those, whoever they may be, who administer the old colonial system.'[22]

Revisionism and 'History Wars'

In its most extreme versions postmodernism hearkens back to Renaissance pyrrhonism in its radical denial of the fixity of any historical meaning, the existence of any external reality beyond language and the impossibility of making 'true' statements about the past. It is an extreme variant of what historians have for a very long time called 'revisionism', with one important difference: unlike mainstream revisionist historians, who debate particular interpretations of events but generally share a common vocabulary and set of reference points (usually key events, individuals or structures), postmodernists question the very parameters within which meaningful argument can occur. A conclusion derived from this – that any interpretation of history is no more or less valid than another – while seemingly liberal, also opens the door to the legitimation of morally repugnant positions such as Holocaust denial (positions that most postmodernists would presumably not wish to claim). This issue has come to the fore in recent years through a number of celebrated cases which had little to do with postmodern theorizing, perhaps most notoriously the 1990s libel suit brought by Holocaust denier David Irving (b. 1938), a prolific writer outside the academy, against the American historian Deborah Lipstadt (b. 1947). Lipstadt had accused Irving of gross fabrication and the distortion of evidence to support his theories. The ensuing civil trial involved the historian Richard Evans (b. 1947) and a team of graduate students scrutinizing Irving's research intensively, the results of which were the utter demolition of Irving's arguments and a resounding vindication for Lipstadt and her publisher.

Holocaust denial is an egregious, hot-button example of what is at issue when perceptions of the past, heavily freighted with moral views of right and wrong, come into conflict with historians' sense of their right to 'tell the truth as they see it' – something that has been a tension in historiography virtually as long as there have been historians. Irving, and Holocaust deniers generally, rarely appeal to post-modernism or relativism in formulating their arguments: it is not a matter, in such cases, that their view may be as valid as the next person's so much as asserting that the 'facts' as they see them support an alternative 'truth' that should displace publicly held orthodoxy. In the Irving–Lipstadt case, historical research was adduced to explode Irving's arguments, reveal their evidentiary flimsiness and methodological flaws, and thereby sink his claim to having been libelled. Irving claimed to be telling the truth and practising proper, document-based historical method; the defendants and their expert witness accused him of deliberate sins of distortion, omission and manipulation of evidence. Other cases of prominent historiographical conflict are less clear-cut. This can be because the issues themselves are more ambiguous and (marginally) less loaded, or because the evidence is more equivocal. These also involve conflicts between historians' statements about the past and public perceptions of what actually happened. The difference is that in these cases, the historians themselves, often in significant numbers, are either badly divided on the evidence and how to interpret it, or are ranged against powerful non-professional interests: government, veterans' groups and nationalist or religious movements.

Public disagreement over history education is not especially new, having been an issue in some of the nation-building debates of nineteenth-century Europe and Latin America. But the 1990s saw a growing number of such episodes. In Canada, a 1992 television series on the war, questioning the necessity of the Allies' intensive bombing campaign, enraged veterans, leading to the programme's producers and writers being condemned in Parliament. More recently, an exhibit at the new Canadian War Museum has inflamed passions once again, with veterans complaining about various aspects of its representation of the Second World War, such as the depiction of the bombing campaign, or the display of paintings showing Canadian soldiers engaged in atrocities. Museums, because of their wide accessibility to the public, many of whom will never read a history book, are especially vulnerable to popular criticism of the ways in which they present the past. They are highly visual, but their selection of exhibits, and the highly simplified, brief descriptions they must provide, can easily provoke reaction if the subject discussed has anything to do with a controversial past event. This can also be a remote episode: plans in various parts of the world to mark the five hundredth anniversary of Columbus' 1492 voyage were highly polarizing, with critics finding nothing to celebrate in the conquest and depopulation of the Americas. More often than not, however, the troublesome events are of more recent vintage, with living survivors leading the charge, as in the Canadian cases. These controversies fall into the grey zone between memory and history. A famous example occurred in the United States in

1994 around a planned Smithsonian Institution exhibit to mark the fiftieth anniversary of the dropping of the atomic bomb on Hiroshima. The suggestion in the
exhibit – that the decision to drop the bomb was morally complex and perhaps
even unnecessary – aroused the fury of US Air Force veterans and conservative
politicians. In vain its curators tried to tack between creating an exhibit that would
make veterans 'feel good' and one that could also discuss the long-term legacy of
the creation and use of atomic weapons. Unsuccessful attempts followed to rewrite
the historical script and by the time the affair was finished, advisory committee
members had quit in protest against the watering down of scholarly standards, and
the Director of the National Air and Space Museum had resigned. In the end, the
exhibit itself was cancelled in early 1995.

Such controversies are not limited to museums. Occasionally, academic historiography, most of the time safe within its academic cloister, finds itself in the public
spotlight, and in an uncomfortable position. The German *Historikerstreit* is one
such example. The Australian 'History Wars' are another. These began with that
country's 1988 bicentennial and still continue over two decades later. The Australian conflicts also had a museums aspect, but went well beyond this to include
a wider range of issues and historical media. The 'wars' pitted liberal and left-of-
centre historians against their ideological opponents both within the profession
and outside, the Liberal-Nationalist coalition government of Prime Minister John
Howard becoming an active participant. In the wake of his 1996 electoral victory,
Howard himself denounced what the nationalist historian Geoffrey Blainey (b.
1930) called 'Black Armband History', an 'insidious' development in Australian
political life that seeks 'to rewrite Australian history in the service of a partisan
political cause'. Various historians had for some time been painting a rather critical picture of the treatment of the aboriginals by nineteenth-century whites. The
fear that this was going to place Australia in the same league as other countries
with genocidal histories, and comparisons with the Holocaust, induced sharp reaction. Historians such as Keith Windschuttle (b. 1942, a one-time radical-turned-
conservative, and already a fierce critic of postmodernism and feminism) weighed
in with alternative explanations of depopulation such as disease and internecine
violence, purporting to demonstrate that the numbers of aboriginal dead at white
hands had been exaggerated by propaganda, and attacking opponents' apparent reliance on aboriginal oral tradition. One Australian journalist claimed that
the school history curriculum had been hijacked by left-wing, politically correct
ideologues. He wanted it back. 'Our history does not belong to an undistinguished
syllabus committee of pedants but to the community as a whole.'[23]

The Australian controversy involved a systematic attempt by a democratically
elected government and the conservative press to limit discussion, and to redress
the perceived leftist bias of the profession and the influence of special interests.

One may agree or disagree with the perspective, and also worry about the control of history textbooks as a worldwide issue which we have already seen in other jurisdictions such as Japan.[24] But the analogy of property is in itself not misplaced. What many of these disputes come down to is a variant of the questions 'Who owns the past?' or 'Whose history is it, anyway?' Do members of groups of different kinds have a stronger or even an exclusive claim to be the authentic historians of their common past? Why should the alternative views of outsiders be permitted to 'steal the voices' of the dead? Should even sympathetic outsiders be permitted to capitalize on past injustice and misery in order to sell books and achieve career advancement? Are some episodes – the Holocaust, for instance – so horrific and beyond the bounds of normal human experience that they are simply indescribable historically? And what of the conflict between the personal recollections of participants and the evidence used by historians: does Major Smith's right, as a decorated Falklands' War veteran, to his own and his peers' view of the war, trump Professor Jones's academic freedom to use evidence to construct an interpretation contrary to Smith's?

A further question applies to almost any history that is defined in terms of a particular group: to what degree must one be *of* that group in order to be able to study and render an opinion on its past? Can men legitimately do women's history, and can a white man research native or African-American history? Several white historians of slavery were attacked by black scholars in the 1960s and early 1970s: in a tragic incident, a sympathetic young white historian, Robert Starobin (d. 1971) was driven to suicide after being publicly humiliated by black speakers at a convention. The Haitian ethnohistorian Michel-Rolph Trouillot once recalled how some years earlier, when teaching a course on the Black Experience in the Americas, a young woman had asked why he made the class read 'all those white scholars. What can they know about slavery? Where were they when we were jumping off the boats?'[25] Fortunately, in recent years there appears to have developed a more inclusive and pluralist attitude towards 'outsiders' writing a group's history, perhaps a positive if indirect consequence of the rejection of essentialism espoused by postmodernism and postcolonial criticism.

The history wars in various countries have heightened awareness of the intimate connection between history and memory, which has emerged in recent years as a subject of inquiry in its own right. This has taken various forms, of which perhaps the most well known is the analysis of what might be called national 'memory cultures'. The work of the early sociologist and pupil of Durkheim, Maurice Halbwachs (1877–1945), who died in Buchenwald, has been fundamental in the development of concepts such as 'collective memory', 'social memory', 'shared memory' and so on. There is now a host of works on the subject, as well as a journal devoted to it, and memory has provided a new point of intersection for history with philosophy,

Box 34   **The New Oral History**

The most recent five or six decades prior to a historian's present have been of considerable interest at various times, and here 'oral history' has come into its own, especially in dealing with the large majority of persons, often of working-class background, who will never commit their experiences to paper. Although it shares some features in common, modern oral history is to be distinguished from the study of oral *tradition* that we have seen in earlier chapters (the two are sometimes grouped together as 'oral historiography'). Oral tradition deals with more remote periods beyond the memory of persons still living, and thus crossing multiple generations. Oral history, in contrast, is a set of methodologies, mainly refined in the 1960s and 1970s, for interviewing human subjects and extracting from them their personal recollections about particular events in history through which they lived, or simply recording their descriptions of their own past lives and experiences. Although open to some of the same objections as oral tradition, in particular the natural human tendency to see one's own past through the prism of intervening times, or simply to misremember, oral history now has a well-established set of standards or 'best practices' for methodologically and ethically correct collection of data. A number of important archives of oral interviews have been created around the world to preserve the testimony of particular groups – Holocaust survivors for example – before their voices are permanently silenced by death.

anthropology, psychology and sociology. In recent years, the study of memory has increasingly crossed agendas with postmodernism, particularly with respect to 'traumatic' episodes of the past such as the Holocaust, which signals not the continuity of History beloved since the eighteenth century but its discontinuities, ruptures and radical turns, emphasized alike in Michel Foucault's 'archaeologies' of knowledge and by contemporary interest in recapturing the 'sublime' aspect of historical experience, a direct, powerful, emotive and even overwhelming connection with the past which works against the cautious, objective 'distance' most historians have maintained since the end of romanticism.

The precise relation between memory and history is ambiguous, and consideration of it often circles back to other and older methodological issues such as the relative value of written and oral sources, or the usefulness of oral history as a methodology (see Box 34); there have been useful studies on the significance

Box 35   Indigenous Historicity

Among the justifiably aggrieved groups of the world, its indigenous peoples have a special claim on our historical consciences. Few subjugated populations have suffered the same degree of demographic devastation as have they, along with the purging or marginalization of their beliefs and traditions about the past – to say nothing of the general misunderstanding and mischaracterization of those beliefs. Indigenous populations, as we saw in Chapter 5, tended to rely much more heavily, if not entirely, on visual and oral sources, and their historical narratives appeared to text-obsessed white observers as more fantastic myth than concrete reality. Thankfully we have come a long way since the anthropologist Robert Lowie in 1915 argued that '[American] Indian tradition is historically worthless' though we should certainly avoid imposing European categories on indigenous records that superficially resemble, but are fundamentally different from, our own. An example of this fallacy occurred when a white scholar, Helen Blish, argued that Amos Bad Heart Bull's (c. 1868–1913) sketchbooks on the Oglala Sioux indicate that his purpose was clearly the same as Herodotus'– that he was 'attempting to preserve the record of the life of a people' and 'consequently *earns the name historian*'. Bad Heart Bull probably had several different intentions, some of which do resemble those of Herodotus. But it is doubtful that he was emulating the ancient Greek pattern, and equally that he would have seen the posthumous bestowal of 'the name historian' as a desirable honorific. In fact, Bad Heart Bull left his sketchbook to his sister and it was buried with her when she died, following Oglala custom, suggesting that the last thing its author had in mind was the creation of a permanent record. In more recent decades indigenous history has come into its own, especially in the hands of 'ethnohistorians' (usually working in anthropology departments), with greater sensitivity to its social functions, which are often of a religious or ritualistic rather than strictly commemorative or explanatory nature.

of the destruction or wholesale removal of archival material on 'community' memory. It might be assumed that every modern nation has a strong national memory, in the sense of shared beliefs about what happened in recent decades, and indeed in more remote times, and what it means. This does not, however, appear to be the case. In France, Pierre Nora (b. 1931) has emphasized the

46: The North American Indigenous Past: Anna Lee Walters

The histories of my tribes in ancient and historic times always enter into my view of the world, and therefore my writing. It is an element that is sometimes very alien and unfamiliar to some readers. The history of the United States, as told by mainstream society, and its omission of indigenous peoples, along with its consistently negative images, also deeply affects me. As a tribal person knowledgeable about my own tribal histories, my writing and perspective defy the cherished historical American myths about tribal peoples. We were not defeated and eradicated by the colonizers. We were seriously harmed by them, but we survived and we live!

Today, my occupation as a writer is related to what my grandfather and grandmother did when they repeated family history in the manner of their elders, leading the family all over this sacred land, this continent most recently called America in the last five hundred years, in their retelling of the Otoe journey from the dawn of time until they came to rest at Red Rock Creek a little over a century ago. In the same way, I repeat their words to my children and grandchildren. In tribal society, this is who history is for, after all, in a very personalized version of time. Receiving and passing on of history is the responsibility of each generation. We are its keepers.

Scholars or authorities from academia, from outside tribal societies, do not necessarily know tribal people best. There is an inherent right of tribal people to interpret events and time in their worlds according to their own aesthetics and values, as a component of American history, even when this interpretation is different from that of mainstream history.

Selected from Anna Lee Walters (b. 1946), *Talking Indian: Reflections on Survival and Writing* (Ithaca, NY: Firebrand Books, 1992), 86.

significance of *lieux de mémoires*, literally 'sites of memory', in promoting a robust sense of the past. These are locations scattered around the countryside, or in cities, marking particular events. They may be as localized as a war memorial, church or statue, or as national or global as a celebrated battlefield such as Waterloo or Gettysburg; and they can be man-made or natural. The key feature that these sites have in common is association with an event or chain of events in the past. Moreover, much of the remembered past is not nationally but regionally or locally based; North and South American indigenous history would be an obvious example (see Box 35 and Extract 46) but one could also recall the travellers of earlier centuries, such as the sixteenth-century antiquaries, who found and reported village and urban traditions about the history surrounding particular places or structures.

CONCLUSION: The Fragmentation of Historiography

Of the various words that characterize historiography since 1914, and especially since 1960, one would have to be *fragmentation*. A more optimistic descriptor might be *diversity*, or perhaps more neutrally, *specialization*. In some ways, a concern with fragmentation is bandied about most noisily in the United States; European and Asian historians seem rather less troubled by the prospect. Specialization has been a worry in some corners of the American profession for over a century, but not consistently so and never to every historian. Quite apart from any ideological differences they may have, historians now routinely self-identify as political, military, family, gender, women's, economic, social, environmental, intellectual or cultural. The expansion of university history departments throughout the world, especially in the 1960s, along with considerably greater pressure on academics to publish early and often has encouraged a high degree of sub-specialization, together with a proliferation of journals and book series (which the relatively recent advent of the internet shows no sign of slowing down given its capacity to offer a cheap alternative to conventional print). Although Marxism is much less prominent in most North American history departments, social history has been preserved, albeit now often dissolved into various components.

There have also been integrationist attempts to recapture a past for the whole planet, freed from the metaphysical trappings of a Toynbee or Spengler. The casual reader with little time but much curiosity instinctively gravitates to the 'big picture'. The popularity of world history during the 1960s and 1970s, in the wake of Braudel, produced an initial wave of global history introductory courses in university curricula, competing with the older 'Western Civ' or 'Plato to NATO'. This coincided with the beginnings of 'world systems theory', articulated by social scientists such as the American historical sociologist Immanuel Wallerstein (b. 1930), with the early emergence of modern medical history and an interest in biological and ecological transference, and an upward spike in the popularity of Latin American and African history among students. The resurgence in the past two decades of a reconfigured 'global history', with the earth divided in very different ways than during the Cold War, has lent those earlier efforts renewed relevance. In the long tradition of 'universal history' going back through eighteenth-century *Weltgeschichte* all the way to Polybius, our time has produced its fair share; in the current language of 'transnational' and 'entangled' histories, one can recognize a postmodern counterpart to the ancient Greek historian's concept of *symploke*. Yet global history seems itself at the moment no more than another, wider, window on to the past, rather than a house that can bring back under one roof all the prodigal, contentious children of Clio.

The degree of fragmentation is sufficiently extensive, and its further development so unpredictable, that this chapter's title of Babel's Tower may not actually
do it justice. For some observers, seeing the discipline as irreparably broken rather
than merely confused, Humpty Dumpty may be more appropriate. There are periodic attempts to put history together again, such as the establishment in the late
1990s in the United States of a new Historical Society by the one-time leftist-
turned-conservative Eugene Genovese (b. 1930) and others to redress the compart-
mentalization of history and its association with identity politics. The Canadian
historian J. L. Granatstein (b. 1939) has made similar pleas. The 1980s and 1990s
witnessed a number of reactions against the various perceived enemies of Clio
– interest group history, social theory, feminism and above all postmodernism;
this in turn was related to a wider campaign against 'political correctness' on and
off university campuses. As recently as 2009, Russia inaugurated a presidential
commission to counteract 'the falsification of history contrary to the interests of
Russia' and refurbish the battered Soviet image. The response of the political right
to perceived challenges has been just as sharp as that of the left in advocating its
interests. An ill-fated attempt in 1994 to create 'National History Standards' in
the United States and address a perceived decline in student knowledge of history
brought down the collective wrath of conservative talk-show hosts, former National Endowment for the Humanities' chairwoman Lynne Cheney and ultimately
the United States Senate. Similar experiments in national curricula elsewhere have
not been remarkably successful. The level of discourse in many of the exchanges
is often reminiscent of the meanest varieties of Reformation-era religious polemic.
Or it is absurdly simplistic: as the ultra-conservative commentator Rush Limbaugh
declaimed in the middle of the American curricular debate (blithely conflating
history the study with History its subject), 'History is real simple. You know what
history is? It's what happened ... and history ought to be nothing more than the
quest to find out what happened.'[26]

Notes

1 Eduard Fueter, *Geschichte der Neueren Historiographie* (Munich and Berlin, 1911). The
   epigraph from Villani at the head of the chapter is from *Villani's Chronicle*, trans. Rose E.
   Selfe and ed. Philip I. Wicksteed (London, 1906), 3.
2 Quoted in Hayden White, *Tropics of Discourse: Essays in Cultural Criticism* (Baltimore,
   1978), 36.
3 Arnold Toynbee, *A Study of History* (Oxford, 1934–61), vol. I, 255, 257, 275, 342.
4 Benedetto Croce, *Theory and History of Historiography*, trans. D. Ainslie (New York, 1921),
   24.
5 Américo Castro, *An Idea of History: Selected Essays by Américo Castro*, trans. and ed.
   Stephen Gilman and Edmund L. King (Columbus, 1977), 305.

6 Originally *Annales d'histoire économique et sociale* (1929–39), then *Annales d'histoire sociale* (1939–45), *Annales. Économies, sociétés, civilisations* (1946–94) and *Annales. Histoire, sciences sociales* (1994–).

7 L. B. Namier, *The Structure of Politics at the Accession of George III* (London, 1929); R. Syme, *The Roman Revolution* (Oxford, 1939).

8 Carl Bridenbaugh, 'The Great Mutation', *American Historical Review* 68:2 (1963): 315–31; R. W. Fogel and G. R. Elton, *Which Road to the Past? Two Views of History* (New Haven, CT, 1983).

9 Keith Thomas, 'History and Anthropology', *Past and Present* 24 (1963): 3–24; Keith Thomas, *Religion and the Decline of Magic* (London, 1971).

10 Marshall Sahlins, *Islands of History* (Chicago, 1985) and *How 'Natives' Think: About Captain Cook, for Example* (Chicago, 1995).

11 Clifford Geertz, *The Interpretation of Cultures: Selected Essays* (New York, 1973).

12 Karl Popper, *The Poverty of Historicism* (London, 1957).

13 Carol Gluck, 'The People in History: Recent Trends in Japanese Historiography', *Journal of Asian Studies* 38 (1978): 25–50.

14 Michael Marrus, *The Holocaust in History* (Hanover, NH, 1987), xiii.

15 Joseph R. Levenson, 'The Place of Confucius in Communist China', in A. Feuerwerker (ed.), *History in Communist China* (Cambridge, MA, 1968), 56–73.

16 A. R. Douglas, 'Marx and Huizinga: Jan Romein as Historian', *Virginia Quarterly Review* (Winter 1980): 152–61. Romein was also responsible, along with his wife, Anne Verschoor, for bringing to world attention the diary of Anne Frank after the Second World War.

17 Analogous Italian and German journals recognized for pioneering new departures are *Quaderni Storici* (1970–) and *Geschichte und Gesellschaft* (1975–).

18 Quoted in Julie Des Jardins, *Women and the Historical Profession in America: Gender, Race, and the Politics of Memory, 1800–1945* (Chapel Hill, NC, 2003), 17.

19 Quoted in Anthony Gorman, *Historians, State and Politics in Twentieth-Century Egypt: Contesting the Nation* (London, 2003), 104.

20 Prasenjit Duara, 'Postcolonial History', in Lloyd Kramer and Sarah Maza (eds.), *A Companion to Western Historical Thought* (Oxford, 2002), 417–31; Duara, *Rescuing History from the Nation: Questioning Narratives of Modern China* (Chicago, 1995).

21 Michael Gottlob (ed.), *Historical Thinking in South Asia: A Handbook of Sources from Colonial Times to the Present* (Oxford and New Delhi, 2003), 62, 215.

22 C. L. R. James, *The Black Jacobins: Toussaint l'Ouverture and the San Domingo Revolution*, 2nd edn (London, 1938; New York, 1963, repr. New York, 1989), 408.

23 Stuart Macintyre and Anna Clark, *The History Wars* (Carlton, Victoria, Australia, 2003), 178.

24 For instance, the Indian textbook controversy of the late 1970s (when a number of historians were criticized by the Janata government for being 'soft' on Islam's history in India and insufficiently pro-Hindu).

25 Michel-Rolph Trouillot, *Silencing the Past: Power and the Production of History* (Boston, 1995), 71.

26 Quoted in Gary B. Nash, Charlotte Crabtree and Ross E. Dunn, *History on Trial: Culture Wars and the Teaching of the Past* (New York, 1997), 6.

Epilogue

When I was an undergraduate studying history and classics in the 1970s I took a number of courses in ancient history. I recall seeing a cartoon on the office door of one of my professors. The cartoon had been drawn, affectionately, by a student, and gently lampooned the professor in question for his relentless insistence that students adduce, in class, the source of their statements, which in practice meant identifying the ancient historian who provided the information. In the cartoon, my professor was magically teleported back to late fifth-century Athens, and into a history class being taught by a rather stern looking Thucydides, who insisted that *his* students (including the chronologically displaced professor) produce *their* sources when speaking.

It is tempting to ask what would happen in reverse, if Thucydides *and* Sima Qian found themselves in a (post?)modern History Department. A great deal of the discussion they might hear would confuse them, as would its modern context. They would also (language aside) have some difficulty understanding each other's perspective on the past. But there is also a core of activity that they would share with each other, and with us: an understanding that history tells, or ought to tell, true stories about the past; a sense that whatever moral judgments the historian may intrude, he or she has an obligation to present evidence without distortion or fabrication; and a conviction that the best-written histories are not merely vessels for evidence of the past, but become themselves bequests to posterity, literary artefacts to be read in future ages.

This raises the question, asked with frequency in journal articles and at learned conferences, as to what the future of history may be. The present book, a history of history, has related something like a classical narrative of 'rise' and 'fall', wherein history in general as an organized approach to the recapturing and representation of the past evolved into a major aspect of the modern world's educational and cultural life, and a specific mode of historicity, that of the West, gradually displaced the alternatives, some of them (South Asian puranic; Latin American pictographic; African and indigenous oral traditional; Southeast Asian) radically different, others (East Asian and Islamic) somewhat less so. This story has been linked explicitly to the parallel 'conquest' by Europe (and its settler offshoots) of the rest of the world's broader cultural institutions and accompanied in many though not all cases by a political subjugation in the form of colonization. It is no coincidence that the key moments in the suzerainty of 'modern' or 'scientific' history occurred at points of ambitious imperial expansion, first in the sixteenth and seventeenth centuries, and then again in the nineteenth century. It is similarly no coincidence, and has been a central argument of this book, that Western historicity was itself affected deeply by its engagement with alternatives, not so much because it adopted those alternatives as because understanding and criticizing them obliged a level of self-consciousness about what made the Western approach to the past distinctive, and why – in the minds of Europeans, and their Asian and colonial admirers – it had a claim to superiority. And finally, it is no coincidence, again, that the nineteenth-century moment of Western historicity's apparent global triumph was a short one in the *longue durée* of this story, and that Clio's claim to an empire over knowledge of the past became, in the twentieth century, just as subject to internal dissension, rebellion, secession and threatened irrelevance as the literal empires that had enabled her hegemony in the first place, and which the master-narratives spun by her acolytes had both promoted and helped to sustain. If the last sixty years has seen a process of *literal* decolonization throughout the world, it has also begun to see a parallel process of *historiographical* decolonization, a breaking free from modern Western attitudes, methods and models. Certainly, the empire of Clio has not quite fallen, but it has evolved into something more like a loose federation. Most of us in the profession work away silently in classroom, library and archive, and only a small minority spend much time considering the discipline's own past and future prospects. In that unconscious quotidian 'practice' of our profession, are we perhaps like those 'bare-footed friars' whom Gibbon once spotted in the Capitoline, singing methodological vespers in the temple of our muse, blind to the changes of time that make our own activity an anachronistic obeisance to a decayed empire, now become a mere archaeological site, the ruined remains of nineteenth- and twentieth-century intellectual ambition?

I suggested in the introduction that the story told by this book, if one were to assign it to a classical dramatic genre, would be one of tragedy, with the central character of history first successfully beating the odds to supplant a number of rival claimants only to fall from grace. This fall can be attributed to not one but three fundamental flaws. The first of these is the hubris of assuming an unchallengeable and prescriptive authority over the world's pasts – both in the sense of enforcing a master-narrative of Progress in capital-H History, and in the related sense of legislating the methods and institutional arrangements not merely *sufficient* but *necessary* for the accurate narration of that or any other story about the past. The second lies in the conviction – which in the early twenty-first century now seems hopelessly naive – that there is, in fact, an ultimately true story to be told, and that incremental improvements to method, together with the independence of the historian from state or partisan control, will enable its telling; this is a modernist variant of the Renaissance European grail of 'perfect history'. The third flaw is a sense of entitlement to public regard – a belief that after having escaped its ancient place on the margins of knowledge, and a time when it was often no more than a mode of 'entertainment', history is critically important – and its principal practitioners (professional historians) deserve to be heeded. A steady stream of critics of 'factoid' history and its dullness from antiquity to the eighteenth century argued for a larger purpose and a more philosophical approach; Nietzsche warned both of the burden of the past and of the need for critical history. The Spanish philosopher José Ortega y Gasset (1883–1955), who thought that man had a history but no nature, captured the feeling of irrelevance in the first half of the twentieth century, which he blamed on historians' obsession with research into details. 'I firmly believe that God will not forgive the historians', Ortega wrote. 'Even the geologists have succeeded in awakening our interest in dead stones; but all that the historians, who have the most fascinating subject in their hands, have achieved is that less history is being read in Europe than before.'[1]

Yet Ortega was mistaken. Rumours of the death of history are greatly exaggerated, and an autopsy would be quite premature. We are not, quite yet, Gibbon's monks. There are at least two reasons to be hopeful for history's longevity. The first, already addressed at the end of our last chapter, is the considerably more profound internationalization or 'globalization' of the historical discipline that has been occurring for the past two decades since the end of the Cold War. The International Congress of the Historical Sciences, which meets at five-year intervals in different locations, routinely includes world history themes in its programmes and draws historians from around the globe. Academic journals are increasingly publishing articles devoted to transnational topics, and new journals such as the *Journal of World History* (1990) and *Journal of Global History* have appeared. The internet and the rapid spread of English as a common language of scholarship has facilitated contact with other academics at a long distance, and almost instantaneously. Major collaborative projects are occurring across borders and oceans at an impressive pace, suggesting both a new cosmopolitanism and an international commitment to large-scale initiatives. And, although many historians would not now share Leopold von Ranke's European focus, his conservatism or his insistence on the primacy of the state, it is interesting to note that some of the values of the new global history, in particular its insistence on treating other civilizations on their own merits and as of equal value, recall at least the spirit of the great German's thoughts about history, if not aspects of his actual practice.[2]

Secondly, history retains a social relevance and even a popularity in spite of two centuries of our best academic efforts to deprive it of both qualities. If historical thinking has never quite been universal, there lingers in the contemporary world an instinctual, perhaps even existential, interest in the past, whether autobiographical, genealogical or archaeological. While academic history has lost the privileged position it enjoyed in the nineteenth and early twentieth centuries (when it still retained at least a vestigial tie to literature), popular history has never been so evident, from television and movies through fiction. History occurs everywhere from family photographs and home videos to amateur genealogical research.[3] It is as much a hobby as a calling. Even apparent critics acknowledge the near ubiquity, if not of professional academic historiography, of the activity of pursuing the past. The Australian ethnohistorian whom we quoted in the introduction, Greg Dening (1931–2008), a critic of modern historicity, asserted, echoing Carl Becker's Everyman, 'We all make histories endlessly. It is our human condition to make histories. No sooner is the present gone in the blink of an eye than we make sense of it as past. We tell stories about it .... We make a narrative of the past in our mind, in our conversations. We record it in some way – in a diary, in a letter, on a certificate, in a tax return.' To Dening, history was less textual declaration of truth than it was – as it had been for many indigenous cultures and, at an earlier point, for the West – a kind of performance.[4] Michel-Rolph Trouillot, himself the nephew of a Haitian historian, has made a similar comment, in his case targeting historical pedagogy and history books as at best incomplete or superficial channels to the past. 'We all need histories that no history book can tell, but they are not in the classroom – not the history classrooms, anyway. They are in the lessons we learn at home, in poetry and childhood games, in what is left of history when we close the history books with their verifiable facts.'[5]

The summons back to relevance echoes the ancient Ciceronian notion of history's role as *magister vitae* while urging a greater sense of ethical responsibility on the part of historians, of the Crocean 'duties of the living to the dead',[6] and of an obligation to protect the past from interference and manipulation. It is also a call to put history into service anew to rectify the world's evils, which in a world of genocides, terrorist attacks and rampant commercial greed ought to be just as compelling a reason as it was for our ancestors. Others, however, have suggested that history needs to 'lighten up' and stop taking itself so seriously. Writing in the midst of the Australian history wars, Beverley Kingston comments that the risk factor of bad history is simply not high enough to justify some of the excited political rhetoric around its potential misuse. 'Bad history is not life threatening like a faulty bridge or a wrongly diagnosed illness. At worst we can deceive ourselves, defame the dead, or infuriate the living.'[7] Seemingly, there is still disagreement as to whether history is primarily an educator and potential force for good in the present, or a less pragmatic mode of entertainment, a toy rather than a tool.

It is not the purpose of this book, and of a historian approaching the tail end of his active career, to speculate very far about the long-term prospects of the activity of studying the past. There are other books available to prognosticate on the likely fate of our discipline, and there have been so many changes of direction, in the past hundred years alone, as to make this a not very useful exercise. Nothing dates faster than our vision of the future, and that includes the future of the activity of describing the past. Rather, I hope to have demonstrated that, if indeed there is a 'natural' inclination on the part of humans to recover pasts of some sort (an arguable point), then there is no necessary mode of its pursuit, no single purpose for so doing and no inevitable medium for its presentation. It is possible to imagine a counterfactual version of humanity's story in which the West did not achieve the dominance it has won (and is now at risk of losing), and thus just as possible to imagine an outcome in which the types of history practised by Sima Qian or Ibn Khaldūn or perhaps even the Mayans achieved hegemony over their rivals – for such has been the connection of history to power. The widely varying forms of history we have seen across the world over the several millennia covered here help us to understand that the emergence of modern historiography was a complex story involving many turns, multiple engagements between cultures, numerous back-and-forth revisitations of the *same* questions (for instance the relation of the particular to the universal or, now, global; or the boundaries between history and fiction) and experiments with genre and form. At the same time, the story of history's past has been intimately linked with humanity's broader past, and its successes and failures have been at least as much a function of social and political circumstances as they have of intellectual change. History and history, the cumulative past and the ways we have in different times and places related chunks of it, are not easily detachable from one another. Capital-H History has carried small-h history on its back, and the rider, for better or worse, has done more than sit facing backwards to glare at the ground covered. Indeed, the rider has played no small part in spurring on the sometimes uncontrollable, galloping horse.

Notes

1 Ortega, quoted in K. J. Weintraub, *Visions of Culture* (Chicago, 1966), 285.

2 For which reminder I thank Professor Peer Vries.

3 See, for instance, Roy Rosenzweig and David Thelen, *The Presence of the Past: Popular Uses of History in American Life* (New York, 1998); David Lowenthal, *The Past is a Foreign Country* (Cambridge, 1985).

4 Greg Dening, 'A Poetic for Histories', in his *Performances* (Chicago, 1996), 35.

5 Michel-Rolph Trouillot, *Silencing the Past: Power and the Production of History* (Boston, 1995), 71–2.

6 Antoon De Baets, *Responsible History* (New York and Oxford, 2009).

7 Beverley Kingston, 'A Plea from the Peripheries for Modesty', in Stuart Macintyre (ed.), *The Historian's Conscience: Australian Historians on the Ethics of History* (Carlton, Victoria, Australia, 2004), 75–83, at 83.

FURTHER READING

What follows is a series of recommendations for further reading, arranged according to the chapters of the present book and generally though not always subdivided according to the respective chapter's subsections (in some instances, subsections have been combined, especially where a significant number of the books or articles apply to multiple sections). This is not a comprehensive bibliography, nor even a list of all those works consulted in the preparation of this book, but rather a highly selective – and perhaps subjective – assortment of key books and articles that may be of particular interest to those wishing to pursue further the themes and topics discussed in the preceding pages. Given the predominantly English-reading audience for this book, I have disproportionately favoured works in English; on occasion I have included certain works in other languages. Citations for books or articles are cited in full once for each chapter's further reading list in which they occur, and by short title at subsequent occurrences within the same chapter.

The classic histories of history that follow the typical Western-centred model are Eduard Fueter, *Geschichte der neueren Historiographie* (Munich, 1911); James Thomson Shotwell, *An Introduction to the History of History* (New York, 1922); James Westfall Thompson, *A History of Historical Writing*, 2 vols. (New York, 1942); Harry Elmer Barnes, *A History of Historical Writing* (Norman, OK, 1937); Herbert Butterfield, *Man on his Past: The Study of Historical Scholarship* (Cambridge, 1955) and *The Origins of History* (New York, 1981); Ernst Breisach, *Historiography: Ancient, Medieval, and Modern*, 3rd edn (1983; Chicago, 2007); Benedetto Croce, *Theory and History of Historiography*, trans. D. Ainslie (New York, 1921); R. G. Collingwood, *The Idea of History* (1946; Oxford, 1961); Donald R. Kelley, *Faces of History: Historical Inquiry from Herodotus to Herder* (New Haven, CT, 1988), see also Kelley's *Fortunes of History: Historical Inquiry from Herder to Huizinga* (New Haven, CT, 2003) and *Frontiers of History: Historical Inquiry in the Twentieth Century* (New Haven, CT, 2006); and J. W. Burrow, *A History of Histories: Epics, Chronicles, Romances and Inquiries from Herodotus and Thucydides to the Twentieth Century* (London, 2007). Michael Bentley (ed.), *A Companion to Historiography* (London and New York, 1997) is a wide-ranging collection which includes some non-European chapters, but they are principally concerned with Western writings about Africa, Latin America and select Asian countries.

For some examples of a more sociological approach see Bernard Guenée, *Histoire et culture historique dans l'Occident médiéval* (Paris, 1980) (on the Middle Ages); Charles-Olivier Carbonell, *Histoire et historiens: un mutation idéologique des historiens français, 1865–1885* (Toulouse, 1976); Pim den Boer, *History as a Profession: The Study of History in France, 1818–1914*, trans. Arnold J. Pomarans (Princeton, NJ, 1998); and Reba N.

Soffer, *Discipline and Power: The University, History, and the Making of an English Elite, 1870–1930* (Stanford, CA, 1994). The 'linguistic turn', discussed in Chapter 9, has gone in the other direction, towards a much deeper analysis of the texts themselves; this has challenged the triumphalist account. Hayden White's enormously influential *Metahistory: The Historical Imagination in Nineteenth-Century Europe* (Baltimore, 1973), while it tells a narrative of sorts (in the form of a movement through his series of tropes), ends up in a very non-celebratory place, with the ironic mode of late twentieth-century historical thought. Gabrielle Spiegel's work on thirteenth-century French prose histories, *Romancing the Past: The Rise of Vernacular Prose Historiography in Thirteenth-Century France* (Berkeley, CA, 1993), has similarly placed these within a social and political context rather than examining them as proto-histories, evolutionary stages en route to the true history of modern times.

A few early efforts at a global history of history deserve note, such as the composite article on 'Historiography' in D. Sills (ed.), *International Encyclopedia of the Social Sciences*, 19 vols. (London and New York, 1968), vol. 5, 368–428, which includes brief sections on Islam, South and Southeast Asia, China and Japan. Geoffrey Barraclough, a medievalist who turned to world history, also ventured into the historical writing of the non-European world in a late work, *Main Trends in History* (New York, 1978). However, the major advances have come only in the past ten or fifteen years, most recently with Georg G. Iggers, Q. Edward Wang and S. Mukherjee, *A Global History of Modern Historiography* (Harlow, UK and New York, 2008). Comparison between different historical cultures is even rarer, though here too there have been useful efforts: in particular see the collections edited respectively by Jörn Rüsen, *Western Historical Thinking: An Intercultural Debate* (New York and Oxford, 2002) and Eckhardt Fuchs and Benedikt Stuchtey (eds.), *Across Cultural Borders: Historiography in Global Perspective* (Lanham, MD, 2002). For those able to read German, a concise single-authored global history of historical writing may be found in Markus Völkel, *Geschichtsschreibung* (Cologne, Weimar and Vienna, 2006). There are now a number of encyclopedic reference works with global coverage: D. R. Woolf (ed.), *A Global Encyclopedia of Historical Writing*, 2 vols. (New York, 1998; hereafter cited as *GEHW*) and K. Boyd (ed.), *Encyclopedia of Historians and Historical Writing*, 2 vols. (London, 1999). The five-volume *Oxford History of Historical Writing* (Oxford, 2010–, hereafter cited as *OHHW* by volume number) provides scholarly essays on most regions of the world from antiquity to the present. Some of the material in the present book has previously appeared (in a more concise form) in my essay, 'Historiography', in M. C. Horowitz (ed.), *New Dictionary of the History of Ideas*, 6 vols. (New York, 2005), vol. I, xxxv–lxxxviii.

Chapter 1

The ancient Near East

The earliest forms of historical writing have been studied mainly by philologists with a specialty in Near Eastern languages, and by archaeologists, historians of religion and theologians. An enormous amount of this work is in German. Of English works, very little, unfortunately, is easy for the beginner. The most accessible recent survey, though readers may not be interested in its polemical debates, is John Van Seters, *In Search of History: Historiography in the Ancient World and the Origins of Biblical History* (New Haven, CT and London, 1983). See also Mario Liverani, *Myth and Politics in Ancient Near Eastern Historiography* (London, 2004). Helpful anthologies of texts, complete with commentary are A. K. Grayson, *Assyrian and Babylonian Chronicles* (Locust Valley, NY, 1975) and Jean-Jacques Glassner, *Mesopotamian Chronicles*, ed. B. R. Foster (Atlanta, 2004). An older selection (late Babylonian only) is D. J. Wiseman (ed.), *Chronicles of the Chaldaean Kings (626–556 B.C.) in the British Museum* (London, 1961). The essays in R. Dentan (ed.), *The Idea of History in the Ancient Near East* (New Haven, CT, 1955) are easier to read though now very out of date. Although they presume some knowledge, the essays in Christina Shuttleworth Kraus (ed.), *The Limits of Historiography: Genre and Narrative in Ancient Historical Texts* (Leiden, 1999) are clear and concise, and cover much the same territory as this chapter. H. Butterfield, *The Origins of History*, ed. A. Watson (London, 1981), the last and posthumous work of a great historiographer, is very readable, but Eurocentric, though it does briefly consider Sima Qian. J. H. Plumb, *The Death of the Past*, rev. edn (1969; Basingstoke, 2004), ch. 1, offers a brief but readable assessment of ancient historical writing, including Mesopotamia.

The beginnings of Jewish historical thought

If Mesopotamian historiography is arcane, that on the ancient Israelites is even more challenging and also highly technical. This is partly a consequence of the sharp reaction in the past century against a rather laudatory approach to ancient Jewish history and historiography on the part of mainly Christian theologians for whom Old Testament history is a critical backdrop to Christianity. A good deal of the literature is highly polemical. Apart from older work such as Dentan (ed.), *The Idea of History in the Ancient Near East*, introductions may be had in Marc Zvi Brettler, *The Creation of History in Ancient Israel* (London and New York, 1995), Tomoo Ishida, *History and Historical Writing in Ancient Israel* (Leiden, 1999) and, again, Van Seters, *In Search of History*. For Hellenistic Judaism see Ida Fröhlich, *'Time and Times and Half a Time': Historical Consciousness in the Jewish Literature of the Persian and Hellenistic Eras* (Sheffield, 1996) and Carl R. Holladay (ed.), *Fragments from Hellenistic Jewish Authors*, vol. I: *Historians* (Chico, CA, 1983), which includes extracts.

Greek historiography

Studies of Greek and Roman historians are virtually innumerable, not least because they are, for classicists, much more important as sources than most long-dead historians are for modern historians of other areas and periods. The beginner may find the bibliography bewildering, but some very well-written and clear introductions are available: see in particular Arnaldo Momigliano's *Studies in Historiography* (New York and Evanston, IL, 1966) and 'Time in Ancient Historiography', in *Essays in Ancient and Modern Historiography* (Middletown, PA, 1977), 179–204. More recently, John Marincola's *Authority and*

Tradition in Ancient Historiography (Cambridge, 1997) and *Greek Historians* (Oxford, 2001) are excellent and readable; A. J. Woodman, *Rhetoric in Classical Historiography* (London, 1988) is especially good on literary style. Simon Hornblower (ed.), *Greek Historiography* (Oxford, 1993) is a useful collection of essays with an informative introduction. Felix Jacoby, *Atthis: The Local Chronicles of Ancient Athens* (Oxford, 1949) on local histories is difficult but a classic in its own right. Charles W. Fornara, *The Nature of History in Ancient Greece and Rome* (Berkeley, CA, 1983) is an exhaustive study of historiography in both Greece and Rome, and benefits from an arrangement by topic and genre rather than historian. Books on individual historians also abound. On Thucydides and Herodotus respectively see F. M. Cornford, *Thucydides Mythistoricus* (London, 1907), now a century old, and highly controversial, but worth a look; and François Hartog, *The Mirror of Herodotus: The Representation of the Other in the Writing of History*, trans. Janet Lloyd (Berkeley, CA, 1988), which is challenging but wide-ranging and suggestive, as are Hartog's later thoughts in 'The Invention of History: The Pre-History of a Concept from Homer to Herodotus', *History and Theory* 39 (2000): 384–95. On fourth-century Greek historians, especially Xenophon, see Frances Pownall, *Lessons from the Past: The Moral Use of History in Fourth-Century Prose* (Ann Arbor, MI, 2004). For Polybius see F. W. Walbank, *Polybius* (Berkeley, CA, 1972) and '*Symploke*: Its Role in Polybius' Histories', in Donald Kagan (ed.), *Studies in the Greek Historians in Memory of Adam Parry* (Cambridge, 1975), 197–212; and Kenneth S. Sacks, *Polybius on the Writing of History* (Berkeley, CA, 1981).

Roman historians to the second century AD

Works on Roman historians and historiography are nearly as thick on the ground as those on the Greeks. Apart from Fornara, *The Nature of History in Ancient Greece and Rome*, a superb recent survey of the major figures is Ronald Mellor, *The Roman Historians* (London, 1999). For Livy see Andrew Feldherr, *Spectacle and Society in Livy's History* (Berkeley, CA, 1998). Ronald Syme, *Tacitus*, 2 vols. (1958; Oxford, 1989) on Tacitus is an exhaustive classic. Early Roman historiography is summarized well in T. J. Cornell, 'The Formation of the Historical Tradition of Early Rome', in I. S. Moxon, J. D. Smart and A. J. Woodman (eds.), *Past Perspectives: Studies in Greek and Roman Historical Writing* (Cambridge, 1986), 67–86.

The pagan historians of late antiquity

For late antique historiography there are now serviceable surveys covering both pagan and early Christian historians in David Rohrbacher, *The Historians of Late Antiquity* (London and New York, 2002) and Warren Treadgold, *The Early Byzantine Historians* (Basingstoke, 2007). Graeme Clark et al. (eds.), *Reading the Past in Late Antiquity* (Rushcutters Bay, NSW, Australia, 1990) contains several specialist essays. The best studied (and most highly regarded) late antique historian is Ammianus Marcellinus, for recent studies of whom see John Matthews, 'Ammianus and the Eternity of Rome', in Christopher

Holdsworth and T. P. Wiseman (eds.), *The Inheritance of Historiography 350–900* (Exeter, 1986), 17–43, and the extensive bibliography in T. D. Barnes, 'Literary Convention, Nostalgia and Reality in Ammianus Marcellinus', in Clarke et al. (eds.), *Reading the Past in Late Antiquity*, 59–92.

Chinese historiography from earliest times to the Han dynasty

Chinese historiography has been well studied, and there is now much available in English, through translations of many of China's classic histories. The most recent survey, which covers virtually the whole period from pre-imperial to early twentieth century, is On-Cho Ng and Q. Edward Wang, *Mirroring the Past: The Writing and Use of History in Imperial China* (Honolulu, 2005). A now old but useful collection of essays is W. G. Beasley and E. G. Pulleyblank (eds.), *Historians of China and Japan* (London, 1961); Charles S. Gardiner, *Chinese Traditional Historiography* (Cambridge, MA, 1938) is even older but very accessible and clearly written. Somewhat more specialized but important are David Schaberg, *A Patterned Past: Form and Thought in Early Chinese Historiography* (Cambridge, MA, 2001) and, on the Han historian Sima Qian, Stephen W. Durrant, *The Cloudy Mirror: Tension and Conflict in the Writings of Sima Qian* (Albany, NY, 1995) and Grant Hardy, *Worlds of Bronze and Bamboo: Sima Qian's Conquest of History* (New York, 1999). G. E. R. Lloyd, *The Ambitions of Curiosity: Understanding the World in Ancient Greece and China* (Cambridge, 2002) offers suggestive comparison of Chinese and Greek mentalities, including historical thought.

Southern Asia from antiquity to the mid–first millennium

A brief single-volume survey covering ancient through Mughal-era Indian historiography, including many regional variants, is provided by A. K. Warder, *An Introduction to Indian Historiography* (Bombay, 1972). Most other works deal with shorter periods. The question as to whether ancient India had an idea of history or not has been highly contentious. Among recent students of the subject, Romila Thapar, 'Indian Historiography – Ancient', in *GEHW*, 455–8 and Thapar, 'Some Reflections on Early Indian Historical Thinking', in Jörn Rüsen (ed.), *Western Historical Thinking: An Intercultural Debate* (New York and Oxford, 2002) are clear and concise, favouring a middle-road position. This acknowledges that chronological history with identifiable dates and persons was slow to come in Hindu culture but ultimately argues that historical thinking and an interest in the past occurred nonetheless, with descriptions of the past often embedded in other non-historical genres of literature. D. K. Ganguly, *History and Historians in Ancient India* (New Delhi, 1984) tends to a more sceptical and rather European view of history that excludes most of ancient Indian literature. G. P. Singh, *Ancient Indian Historiography: Sources and Interpretations* (New Delhi, 2003) is comprehensive but argues in the opposite extreme for puranic historicity. Accessible English translations of puranic texts can be found in F. E. Pargiter (ed.), *The Purāṇa Text of the Kali Age* (London, 1913) (Pargiter was an early twentieth-century champion of puranic reliability as history) and R. Morton Smith, *Dates and Dynasties in Earliest India*, ed. J. L. Shastri (Delhi, 1973). A more recent treatment, Ludo Rocher, *Puranas* (*A History of Indian Literature*, vol. II, fasc. 3), trans. Jan Gonda (Wiesbaden, 1986), 115–31, also reviews the changing opinions on puranic historicity over the past two centuries. On Sri Lankan Buddhist historical literature and its spread to Southeast Asia see B. C. Law, *On the Chronicles of Ceylon* (Calcutta, 1947) and Kanai Lal Hazra, *The Buddhist Chronicles of Southeast Asia* (New Delhi, 1986); a useful recent essay is Roy W. Perrett, 'History, Time, and Knowledge in Ancient India', *History and Theory* 38 (1999): 307–21. For brief but insightful comparison of Vedic and Herodotean history see François Hartog, 'The Invention of History' listed above under readings for Greek historiography.

Chapter 2

Historical writing in Christian and barbarian Europe

This section once again covers a very wide terrain chronologically and geographically. Especially useful are David Rohrbacher, *The Historians of Late Antiquity* (London and New York, 2002); Warren Treadgold, *The Early Byzantine Historians* (Basingstoke, 2007) (which includes a chronology and a list of translations of early Byzantine historians); and Graeme Clarke et al. (eds.), *Reading the Past in Late Antiquity* (Rushcutters Bay, NSW, Australia, 1990). Glenn F. Chesnut, *The First Christian Histories: Eusebius, Socrates, Sozomen, Theodoret, and Evagrius*, 2nd edn (Macon, GA, 1986) is confined to a select number of Christian historians and is especially focused on Eusebius, but provides more analysis of the ideas in those historians. Averil Cameron's *Agathias* (Oxford, 1970) and *Procopius and the Sixth Century* (Berkeley, CA, 1985) are excellent case studies, by a leading authority on late antique culture. The essays in Yitzhak Hen and Matthew Innes (eds.), *The Uses of the Past in the Early Middle Ages* (Cambridge, 2000) examine attitudes to the past more broadly and thus range beyond historiography but are of interest. On the great 'barbarian' historians of the West, Walter A. Goffart, *The Narrators of Barbarian History (AD 550–800): Jordanes, Gregory of Tours, Bede, and Paul the Deacon* (Princeton, NJ, 1988), which concentrates on their literary and rhetorical qualities rather than adopting an older *Quellenforschung* approach, is indispensable. A readable survey, with the advantage of some well-chosen pictorial illustrations, is Beryl Smalley, *Historians and the Middle Ages* (London, 1974). For ecclesiastical historiography, the most comprehensive study of its beginnings to the modern era (in German) is Peter Meinhold, *Geschichte der Kirchlichen Historiographie*, 2 vols. (Munich, 1967).

The beginnings of Islamic historiography

Despite its neglect in most historiography surveys, Islamic historiography has been well studied, especially recently, with a large number of works having appeared in the past ten to fifteen years. Among studies available in English, the standard, still useful book, complete with lengthy translated extracts is Franz Rosenthal, *A History of Muslim Historiography*, 2nd edn (Leiden, 1968). Hamilton Gibb, 'Tarikh [*sic*],' in his *Studies on the Civilization of Islam*, ed. S. J. Shaw and W. R. Polk (Boston, 1962) provides a succinct overview. The most accessible introduction is Chase F. Robinson, *Islamic Historiography* (Cambridge, 2003), which de-emphasizes textual summary, focusing instead on the social context of Islamic history-writing. In addition, the student wishing further detail can consult Tarif Khalidi, *Arab Historical Thought in the Classical Period* (Cambridge, 1994); A. A. Duri, *The Rise of Historical Writing among the Arabs*, ed. and trans. Lawrence I. Conrad (Princeton, NJ, 1983); Marilyn Robinson Waldman, *Toward a Theory of Historical Narrative: A Case-Study in Perso-Islamicate Historiography* (Columbus, OH, 1980); and Julie Scott Meisami, *Persian Historiography to the End of the Twelfth Century* (Edinburgh, 1999). Albrecht Noth (with L. I. Conrad), *The Early Arabic Historical Tradition: A Source-Critical Study*, trans. M. Bonner, 2nd edn (Princeton 1994) is also worth reading though probably of greater interest to specialists.

Chinese historiography to the end of the Tang dynasty

On-cho Ng and Q. Edward Wang, *Mirroring the Past: The Writing and Use of History in Imperial China* (Honolulu, 2005), provide a concise summary, and there are a number of essays in W. G. Beasley and E. G. Pulleyblank (eds.), *Historians of China and Japan* (London, 1961), in particular Pulleyblank, 'Chinese Historical Criticism: Liu Chih-chi and Ssu-ma Kuang', 135–66, on the organization of official historiography from the Tang to the Ming. The wider scholarly environment and the development of Confucianism is dealt with by David McMullen, *State and Scholars in T'ang China* (Cambridge, 1988); see especially 159–205 on history. The most detailed account of Tang official history, and in particular of the History Bureau, is Denis Crispin Twitchett, *The Writing of Official History under the T'ang* (Cambridge, 1993).

Early Japanese histories to the end of the tenth century

The following are recommended for early Japanese historiography: Tarō Sakamoto, *The Six National Histories of Japan*, trans. J. S. Brownlee (Vancouver and Tokyo, 1991); John Harrison (ed. and trans.), *New Lights on Early Medieval Japanese Historiography: Two Translations and an Introduction* (Gainesville, FL, 1959); J. Ketelaar in *GEHW*, 481–5; John S. Brownlee (ed.), *History in the Service of the Japanese Nation* (Toronto, 1983), introduction; and G. W. Robinson, 'Early Japanese Chronicles: The Six National Histories', in Beasley and Pulleyblank (eds.), *Historians of China and Japan*, 213–28. John S. Brownlee, *Political Thought in Japanese Historical Writing: From Kojiki (712) to Tokushi Yoron (1712)* (Waterloo, Ontario, 1991), is a very readable survey of a thousand years of Japanese historical writing, focusing on its authors' political thought; John R. Bentley, *Historiographical Trends in Early Japan* (Lewiston, NY, 2002) includes translations of eleven shorter Nara- and Heian-era historical works.

Historiography in the Latin West during the ninth and tenth centuries

In addition to those works listed for earlier sections, the following, while rather more specialized, are of use: Felice Lifshitz, *The Norman Conquest of Pious Neustria: Historiographic Discourse and Saintly Relics 684–1090* (Toronto, 1995); the multilingual essays in Erik Kooper (ed.), *The Medieval Chronicle* (Amsterdam, 1999); Jason Glenn, *Politics and History in the Tenth Century: The Work and World of Richer of Rheims* (Cambridge, 2005); Antonia Gransden, *Historical Writing in England*, vol. 1 (Ithaca, NY, 1974); Jean Blacker, *The Faces of Time: Portrayal of the Past in Old French and Latin Historical Narrative of the Anglo-Norman Regnum* (Austin, TX, 1994); and Emily Albu, *The Normans in their Histories* (Woodbridge, 2001). For an analysis of the biographies of saints (usually known as 'hagiography', a term that does not really do it justice) see Patricia L. Cox, *Biography in Late Antiquity: A Quest for the Holy Man* (Berkeley, CA, 1983). For a brilliant exposition of the visible medieval line connecting the ancients to the humanists of the Renaissance see a series of essays by R. W. Southern collectively entitled, 'Aspects of the European Tradition of Historical Writing', reprinted in *History and Historians: Selected Papers of R. W. Southern*, ed. R. J. Bartlett (Oxford, 2004). The best concise treatment of the genre question (in French) is Bernard Guenée, 'Histoire, annales, chroniques: essai sur les genres historiques au Moyen Age', *Annales: ESC*, 28:4 (1973): 997–1016; see also the very old, and somewhat more simplistic survey by Reginald Lane Poole, *Chronicles and Annals: A Brief Outline of their Origin and Growth* (Oxford, 1926). For 'official history' at this time see Rosamond McKitterick, 'Constructing the Past in the Early Middle Ages: The Case of the Royal Frankish Annals', *Transactions of the Royal Historical Society*, 6th ser., 7 (1997): 101–29; Yitzhak Hen, 'The Annals of Metz and the Merovingian Past', in Hen and Innes (eds.), *The Uses of the Past in the Early Middle Ages*, 175–90; and M. Innes and R. McKitterick, 'The Writing of History', in R. McKitterick (ed.), *Carolingian Culture: Emulation and Innovation* (Cambridge, 1994), 193–220.

Chapter 3

Classical Islamic historiography to the fifteenth century

In addition to the titles listed for Islam in the previous chapter see Mohamed Taher (ed.), *Medieval Muslim Historiography* (New Delhi, 1997); Donald P. Little, *An Introduction to Mamlūk Historiography* (Montreal, 1970); and further essays in Bernard Lewis and P. M. Holt (eds.), *Historians of the Middle East* (London, 1962). An insightful brief overview of Islamic historiography is R. Stephen Humphreys, 'Turning Points in Islamic Historical Practice', in Q. Edward Wang and Georg G. Iggers (eds.), *Turning Points in Historiography: A Cross-Cultural Perspective* (Rochester, NY, 2002), 89–100. Ibn Khaldūn has been more often studied than most European historians of his time, with several books available in English: in particular see Muhsin Mahdi, *Ibn Khaldūn's Philosophy of History* (1957; Chicago, 1964); Nathaniel Schmidt's very brief, essay-length study, *Ibn Khaldun:*

Historian, Sociologist and Philosopher (New York, 1930); and Heinrich Simon, *Ibn Khaldun's Science of Human Culture*, trans. F. Baali (Lahore, 1978).

Europe from the Crusades to the early Renaissance

In addition to works cited in the European sections of the previous chapter see Leah Shopkow, *History and Community: Norman Historical Writing in the Eleventh and Twelfth Centuries* (Washington, DC, 1997) and Ian Wood and G. A. Loud (eds.), *Church and Chronicle in the Middle Ages* (London, 1991). On the Crusades see Aziz S. Atiyah, *The Crusade: Historiography and Bibliography* (Bloomington, IN, 1962). On the rhetoric, style and literary aspects of later medieval historical works see Gabrielle Spiegel's *Chronicle Tradition of Saint-Denis: A Survey* (Brookline, MA, 1978) and *The Past as Text: The Theory and Practice of Medieval Historiography* (Baltimore, MD, 1997); and Nancy Partner, *Serious Entertainments: The Writing of History in Twelfth-Century England* (Chicago, 1977). For England see Antonia Gransden, *Historical Writing in England*, 2 vols. (Ithaca, NY, 1974–82). On late medieval French and Burgundian chroniclers see Paul Archambault, *Seven French Chroniclers: Witnesses to History* (Syracuse, NY, 1974); Graeme Small, *George Chastellain and the Shaping of Valois Burgundy* (Woodbridge, 1997); and Frank Collard, *Un historien au travail à la fin du XVe siècle: Robert Gaguin* (Geneva, 1996). An application of the social-scientific and *histoire du livre* approach can be found in Bernard Guenée's *Histoire et culture historique dans l'Occident médiéval* (Paris, 1980). Medieval Spanish historiography is covered in an older study, Benito Sánchez-Alonso, *Historia de la Historiografía Española: Ensayo de un Examen Conjunto*, vol. II (Madrid, 1947), which is part of a longer survey on Spanish historiography; Peter Linehan, *History and Historians in Medieval Spain* (Oxford, 1993) is a more recent and exhaustive work on an under-studied area. Eastern and Central Europe have been less well served by historiographers writing in English or other western European tongues, but see Urszula Borkowska (ed.), *Uniwersalizm i Regionizm w kronikarstwie Europy Środkowo Wschodniej* (Lublin, 1996) (a collection of multilingual essays). For Russia a useful anthology of readings in English is G. Vernadsky et al. (eds.), *A Source Book for Russian History from Early Times to 1917*, vol. 1: *Early Times to the Late Seventeenth Century* (New Haven, CT, 1972). The only exhaustive survey of the Russian chronicles of which I am aware (and which I have not been able to read) is M. D. Priselkov, *Istoriia russkogo letopisaniia XI-XV vv.* (Leningrad, 1940). Two brief studies of relatively late fifteenth-century works are Jakov S. Luria, 'Fifteenth-Century Chronicles as a Source for the History of the Formation of the Muscovite State', in Michael S. Flier and Daniel Rowland (eds.), *Medieval Russian Culture* (Berkeley, CA, 1994), vol. II, 47–56; and Boris M. Kloss, 'Determining the Authorship of the Trinity Chronicle', ibid., 57–72.

Chinese historiography from Song to Yuan

There is no detailed English-language guide to Song official history to compare with D. C. Twitchett's book on the Tang (cited in the previous chapter), but see Thomas H. C. Lee (ed.), *The New and the Multiple: Sung Senses of the Past* (Hong Kong, 2004) for a useful set of essays on a variety of issues in Song historiography. On the Song, Jin and Yuan On-cho Ng and Q. Edward Wang's survey, *Mirroring the Past: The Writing and Use of History in Imperial China* (Honolulu, 2005) is helpful, as are the older essays in W. G. Beasley and E. G. Pulleyblank (eds.), *Historians of China and Japan* (London, 1961). On Sima Guang, the outstanding historian of the dynasty, see Ji Xiao-bin, *Politics and Conservatism in Northern Song China: The Career and Thought of Sima Guang (A.D. 1019–1086)* (Hong Kong, 2005), which is, however, more concerned with Sima Guang's career than with his historical thought. For the role of historical thought in public life and the educational system see Robert M. Hartwell, 'Historical Analogism, Public Policy and Social Science in Eleventh and Twelfth Century China', *American Historical Review* 76 (1971): 690–727. On Chinese Buddhist historical writing see Jan Yun-hua, 'Buddhist Historiography in Sung China', *Zeitschrift der Deutschen Morgenlandischen Gesellschaft* 114 (1964): 360–81.

Japan and Korea from the tenth to the fifteenth centuries

G. W. Robinson, 'Early Japanese Chronicles: The Six National Histories', in Beasley and Pulleyblank (eds.), *Historians of China and Japan*, 213–28; Beasley, 'Japanese Historical Writing in the Eleventh to Fourteenth Centuries', ibid., 229–44; and Delmer M. Brown, 'Pre-Gukanshō Historical Writing', in Brown and Ichirō Ishida (trans. and ed.), *The Future and the Past: A Translation and Study of the Gukanshō, an Interpretative History of Japan written in 1219* (Berkeley, CA and Los Angeles, 1979), 354–401, all summarize the period and its genres. In addition to these and to the works cited in the previous section on Japan (in Chapter 2), there are good accounts of eleventh- through to fifteenth-century historical writing, including the poems and chronicles, not least in a number of textual editions. See in particular *The Clear Mirror: A Chronicle of the Japanese Court during the Kamakura Period* (1185–1333), trans. and ed. George W. Perkins (Stanford, CA, 1998); Minoru Shinoda, *The Founding of the Kamakura Shogunate 1180–1185* (New York, 1960), which includes selections from the *Azuma Kagami*; and *The Taiheiki: A Chronicle of Medieval Japan*, trans. and ed. Helen Craig McCullough (1959; Rutland, VT and Tokyo, 1981). On the various Japanese 'mirrors' of this time see John S. Brownlee, *Political Thought in Japanese Historical Writing: From Kojiki (712) to Tokushi Yoron (1712)* (Waterloo, Ontario, 1991). In comparison with China and Japan, Korean historical writing has been less well studied. There is no secondary literature in English to compare with the essays in Beasley and Pulleyblank's collection on China and Japan (cited above). See, however, the survey in Ch'oe Yŏng-ho, 'An Outline History of Korean Historiography', *Korean Studies* 4 (1980): 1–28.

India and Tibet

Aside from the literature already cited in the section above for Chapter 1 see in particular Peter Hardy, *Historians of Medieval India: Studies in Indo-Muslim Historical Writing*, 2nd edn (New Delhi, 1997); Jagadish Narayan Sarkar, *History of History-Writing in*

*Medieval India: Contemporary Historians: An Introduction to Medieval Indian Historio-
graphy* (Calcutta, 1977); and Sudipta Sen, 'Imperial Orders of the Past: the Semantics of
History and Time in the Medieval Indo-Persianate Culture of North India', in Daud Ali
(ed.), *Invoking the Past: The Uses of History in South Asia* (New Delhi, 1999), 231–57.
On non-Chinese Buddhism see Kanai Lal Hazra, *The Buddhist Chronicles of Southeast
Asia* (New Delhi, 1986) and a few of the relevant essays in S. P. Sen (ed.), *Historians and
Historiography in Modern India* (Calcutta, 1999). On the history of the *Rājataraṅgiṇī* see
the introduction to *Bahāristān-i-Shāhī: A Chronicle of Mediaeval Kashmir*, trans. K. N.
Pandit (Calcutta, 1991).

Chapter 4

Renaissance and seventeenth–century Europe

Early modern European historiography has been well studied from a number of vantage points. The best brief general survey remains Peter Burke, *The Renaissance Sense
of the Past* (London, 1969); but see also Orest Ranum (ed.), *National Consciousness,
History, and Political Culture in Early-Modern Europe* (Baltimore, MD, 1975); and
Bruce Gordon (ed.), *Protestant History and Identity in Sixteenth-Century Europe*, 2
vols. (Aldershot, 1996). For the relation between law and history see especially Donald
R. Kelley, *Foundations of Modern Historical Scholarship: Language, Law, and History
in the French Renaissance* (New York, 1970) and J. G. A. Pocock, *The Ancient Constitution and the Feudal Law: A Study of English Historical Thought in the Seventeenth
Century: A Reissue with a Retrospect* (Cambridge, 1987). For philology see Anthony
Grafton, *Forgers and Critics: Creativity and Duplicity in Western Scholarship* (London,
1990) and *Defenders of the Text: Traditions of Scholarship in an Age of Science,
1450-1800* (Cambridge, MA, 1991). Joseph M. Levine, *The Battle of the Books: History
and Literature in the Augustan Age* (Ithaca, NY, 1991) offers a brilliant account of one
key philological struggle in the context of the broader European *querelle* between the
'ancients' and the 'moderns'.

For antiquarianism and history from the Renaissance through the eighteenth century,
Arnaldo Momigliano's 'Ancient History and the Antiquarian' reprinted in his *Studies in
Historiography* (New York and Evanston, IL, 1966) remains seminal, but see also Ann
E. Moyer, 'Historians and Antiquarians in Sixteenth-Century Florence', *Journal of the
History of Ideas* 64 (2003): 177–93.

For antiquarianism and its interrelations with art, science, archaeology and geologi-
cal thought see Michael Hunter, *John Aubrey and the Realm of Learning* (London, 1975);
Roberto Weiss, *The Renaissance Discovery of Classical Antiquity*, 2nd edn (Oxford,
1988); Francis Haskell, *History and its Images: Art and the Interpretation of the Past*
(New Haven, CT, 1993); Philip J. Jacks, *The Antiquarian and the Myth of Antiquity: The
Origins of Rome in Renaissance Thought* (Cambridge, 1993); Paula Findlen, *Possessing
Nature: Museums, Collecting, and Scientific Culture in Early Modern Italy* (Berkeley, CA,

1994); Leonard Barkan, *Unearthing the Past: Archaeology and Aesthetics in the Making of Renaissance Culture* (New Haven, CT, 1999); Peter N. Miller, *Peiresc's Europe: Learning and Virtue in the Seventeenth Century* (New Haven, CT, 2000); Daniel Woolf, *The Social Circulation of the Past: English Historical Culture 1500–1730* (Oxford, 2003); Joseph M. Levine, *Doctor Woodward's Shield: History, Science and Satire in Augustan England* (Berkeley, CA, 1977); and William Stenhouse, *Reading Inscriptions and Writing Ancient History: Historical Scholarship in the Late Renaissance* (London, 2005). The activities of the Bollandists and other major erudite undertakings of the late seventeenth and early eighteenth centuries are covered in David Knowles, *Great Historical Enterprises: Problems in Monastic History* (London and New York, 1963) and D. C. Douglas, *English Scholars, 1660–1730*, 2nd rev. edn (London, 1951).

There has been some attention of late to recovering the involvement of women in historical writing after the Renaissance: see especially Natalie Zemon Davis, 'Gender and Genre: Women as Historical Writers, 1400–1820', in Patricia H. Labalme (ed.), *Beyond their Sex: Learned Women of the European Past* (New York, 1980); K. J. P. Lowe, *Nuns' Chronicles and Convent Culture in Renaissance and Counter Reformation Italy* (Cambridge, 2003); Charlotte Woodford, *Nuns as Historians in Early Modern Germany* (Oxford, 2002); and D. R. Woolf, 'A Feminine Past? Gender, Genre, and Historical Knowledge in England, 1500–1800', *American Historical Review* 102 (1997): 645–79.

There are significant numbers of regional or national studies. For northern and central Europe (including Scandinavia and Germany but excluding France and Britain) see Gerald Strauss, *Historian in an Age of Crisis: The Life and Work of Johannes Aventinus 1477–1534* (Cambridge, MA, 1963); Peter G. Bietenholz, *Historia and Fabula: Myths and Legends in Historical Thought to the Golden Age* (Leiden, 1966); Kurt Johannesson, *The Renaissance of the Goths in Sixteenth-Century Sweden: Johannes and Olaus Magnus as Politicians and Historians*, trans. and ed. James Larson (Berkeley, CA and Los Angeles, 1991); Karen Skovgaard-Petersen, *Historiography at the Court of Christian IV (1588–1648)* (Copenhagen, 2002); and Irena Backus, *Historical Method and Confessional Identity in the Era of the Reformation (1378–1615)* (Leiden, 2003).

For the Italian Renaissance Eric Cochrane, *Historians and Historiography in the Italian Renaissance* (Chicago, 1981) remains the authoritative survey; see also the essays in S. Dale, A. W. Lewin and D. J. Osheim (eds.), *Chronicling History: Chroniclers and Historians in Medieval and Renaissance Italy* (University Park, PA, 2007). These can be supplemented by more specialized works such as Donald Wilcox, *The Development of Florentine Humanist Historiography in the Fifteenth Century* (Cambridge, MA, 1969); T. C. P. Zimmerman, *Paolo Giovio: The Historian and the Crisis of Sixteenth-Century Italy* (Princeton, NJ, 1995); Felix Gilbert, *Machiavelli and Guicciardini: Politics and History in Sixteenth-Century Florence* (Princeton, NJ, 1966); Gary Ianziti, *Humanistic Historiography under the Sforzas* (Oxford, 1988); and Simon Ditchfield, *Liturgy, Sanctity and History in Tridentine Italy* (Cambridge, 1995). Nancy Struever, *The Language of History in the Renaissance* (Princeton, NJ, 1970) is more difficult but worth the effort; and B. L. Ullman, *Studies in the Italian Renaissance* (Rome, 1973) includes a series of old but wonderfully entertaining essays, many on the recovery of the ancient historians and study of their manuscripts.

For France see Julian H. Franklin, *Jean Bodin and the Sixteenth-Century Revolution in the Methodology of Law and History* (New York, 1963); George Huppert, *The Idea of Perfect History: Historical Erudition and Historical Philosophy in Renaissance France* (Urbana, IL, 1970); Orest Ranum, *Artisans of Glory: Writers and Historical Thought in Seventeenth-Century France* (Chapel Hill, NC, 1980); and the magisterial four-volume survey by Blandine Barret-Kriegel, *Les historiens et la monarchie*, 4 vols. (Paris, 1988). For central Europe, especially Bohemia, see Howard Louthan, *Converting Bohemia: Force and Persuasion in the Catholic Reformation* (Cambridge, 2009), 115–45. For Spain, B. Sánchez-Alonso, *Historia de la Historiografía Española: Ensayo de un Examen Conjunto*, vols. II and III (Madrid, 1944, 1950) remains useful, but most treatments of Spain have focused on the historical literature of expansion and conquest, for which see the next chapter. England has been studied by F. J. Levy, *Tudor Historical Thought* (San Marino, CA, 1967); A. B. Ferguson, *Clio Unbound: Perception of the Social and Cultural Past in Renaissance England* (Durham, NC, 1979); Daniel Woolf, *The Idea of History in Early Stuart England* (Toronto, 1990) and *Reading History in Early Modern England* (Cambridge, 2000); Philip Hicks, *Neoclassical History and English Culture: From Clarendon to Hume* (New York, 1996); and a recent collection of essays, Pauline Kewes (ed.), *The Uses of History in Early Modern England* (San Marino, CA, 2006). Scotland has been less well covered but see David Allan, *Virtue, Learning and the Scottish Enlightenment* (Edinburgh, 1993) and Roger Mason, 'Scotching the Brut: Politics, History and National Myth in Sixteenth-Century Britain', in R. A. Mason (ed.), *Scotland and England 1286–1815* (Edinburgh, 1987), 60–84.

For the relationship between monarchs or princes and history see, in addition to above-listed works by O. Ranum and G. Ianziti the following: Chantal Grell and Catherine Volpihac-Auger (eds.), *Nicolas Fréret, légende et vérité* (Oxford, 1994) on France; Richard L. Kagan, *Clio and the Crown: The Politics of History in Medieval and Early Modern Spain* (Baltimore, 2009) on Spain; and Chantal Grell, Werner Paravicini and Jürgen Voss (eds.), *Les princes et l'histoire du XVIe au XVIIIe siècle* (Bonn, 1998) on Europe as a whole. On the *ars historica* Anthony Grafton, *What was History?* (Cambridge, MA, 2007) is both definitive and extremely readable; but Girolamo Cotroneo, *I trattatisti dell'Ars historica* (Naples, 1971) also contains valuable insights; as does the briefer (and now very old) treatment by Beatrice R. Reynolds, 'Shifting Currents of Historical Criticism', *Journal of the History of Ideas* 14 (1953): 471–92.

Chinese historical writing under the Ming

In addition to general works cited in previous chapters see On-cho Ng, 'Private Historiography of the Late Ming: Some Notes on 5 Works', *Ming Studies* 18 (1984): 46–68; Timothy Brook, *Geographical Sources of Ming-Qing History* (Ann Arbor, MI, 2002); Wolfgang Franke, 'The Veritable Records of the Ming Dynasty (1368–1644)', in W. G. Beasley and E. G. Pulleyblank (eds.), *Historians of China and Japan* (London, 1961), 60–77, Franke, *An Introduction to the Sources of Ming History* (Kuala Lumpur, 1968) and 'Historical Writing during the Ming', in F. W. Mote and D. C. Twitchett (eds.), *The Cambridge History of*

China, vol. 7, *The Ming Dynasty*, part I (Cambridge, 1988), 726–82; and Franklin Perkins, *Leibniz and China: A Commerce of Light* (Cambridge, 2004). For a recontextualization of Huang Zongxi's political tract *Mingyi daifang lu*, as well as his other works, see Lynn A. Struve, 'Huang Zongxi in Context: A Reappraisal of his Major Writings', *Journal of Asian Studies* 47 (1988): 474–502. On the political and military lessons of Luo Guanzhong's *Romance of the Three Kingdoms* (as consulted under the Ming) see Roger Des Forges, 'Toward Another Tang or Zhou? Views from the Central Plain in the Shunzhi Reign', in Lynn A. Struve (ed.), *Time, Temporality and Imperial Transition: East Asia from Ming to Qing* (Honolulu, 2005), 73–112.

Islamic historiography among the Safavids, Mughals and Ottomans

Perhaps reflecting the political divisions within Islam since the thirteenth century, there is no survey of early modern Islamic historiography comparable to the literature cited for chapters 2 and 3 on formative and classic Islamic historians. One has to approach the subject via works on the different regions and dynasties. Fortunately, such works are plentiful. For Persia, see especially Sholeh A. Quinn, *Historical Writing during the Reign of Shah 'Abbas: Ideology, Imitation and Legitimacy in Safavid Chronicles* (Salt Lake City, UT, 2000); the latter part of Bertold Spuler, *Persian Historiography and Geography*, trans. M. Ismail Marcinkowski (Singapore, 2003) (a translation of a much older work); R. M. Savory, '"Very Dull and Arduous Reading": A Reappraisal of the *History of Shāh 'Abbās the Great* by Iskandar Beg Munshi', *Hamdard Islamicus* 3 (1980): 19–37; and Felix Tauer, 'History and Biography', in Jan Rypka et al., *History of Iranian Literature*, ed. Karl Jahn (Dordrecht, 1968), 438–61.

India has perhaps the best coverage of its 'medieval' period (encompassing the Western late Middle Ages and the Mughal era) including translations of many of the major works such as the *Baburnama*, *Akbarnama*, *Shah Jahan Nama* and a rare instance of a female-authored history, the *Humayun-Nama* by the second Mughal emperor's sister, Gul-Badan Begum. Much of this is due to the activities of a number of nineteenth-century British officials and scholars, most famously Colonel James Tod (1782–1835) and Sir Henry Miers Elliot (1808–53). Tod, a member of the school of thought that sympathized with the Hindu while regarding Islamic India as a period of tyranny, assembled an enormous amount of information on the Rajputs, including transcriptions from some of his materials, and published these in two volumes as *Annals and Antiquities of Rajast'han* (London, 1829–32). Elliot published a *Bibliographical Index to the Historians of Muhammedan [sic] India*, 4 vols. (Calcutta, 1849), and edited a large number of Indo-Muslim texts from the ninth to eighteenth centuries. Many of these were included in the posthumously published eight-volume series entitled *The History of India, as told by its Own Historians: The Muhammadan Period*, ed. J. Dowson (London, 1867–77), a work that has been widely criticized on philological as well as ideological grounds. Secondary sources are similarly plentiful: apart from essays in C. H. Philips, *Historians of India, Pakistan, and Ceylon* (London, 1961), see Mohibbul Hasan and Muhammad Mujeeb (eds.), *Historians of Medieval India* (Meerut, 1968); Jagadish Narayan Sarkar, *History of History-Writing in*

Medieval India: Contemporary Historians: An Introduction to Medieval Indian Historiography (Calcutta, 1977); Peter Hardy, *Historians of Medieval India: Studies in Indo-Muslim Historical Writing*, 2nd edn (1960; New Delhi, 1997); and Harbans Mukhia, *Historians and Historiography during the Reign of Akbar* (New Delhi, 1976). Sanjay Subrahmanyam, 'Reflections on State-Making and History-Making in South India, 1500–1800', *Journal of the Economic and Social History of the Orient* 41 (1988): 382–416 is a perceptive essay on the relations between historiography and the state in South India during the period. Finally, Velcheru Narayana Rao, David Shulman and Sanjay Subrahmanyam, *Textures of Time: Writing History in South India 1600–1800* (New York, 2003) is a provocative and generally convincing exploration of several South Asian genres of historical writing in the sixteenth, seventeenth and eighteenth centuries, with important implications for the assessment of other non-European forms of history.

Although the Ottomans have suddenly become fashionable again in recent years, few of their historical works have been translated into English. Franz Babinger, *Die Geschichtsschreiber der Osmanen und ihre werke* (Leipzig, 1927) is a now-dated bio-bibliographical study; it is in the process of being superseded by a major research project at Harvard University, *Historians of the Ottoman Empire*, http://www.ottomanhistorians. com, which has at least tripled the list of historians in Babinger. Cemal Kafadar, *Between Two Worlds: The Construction of the Ottoman State* (Berkeley, CA, 1995) discusses both early sources and modern historiography. Useful brief general studies are Halil Inalcik, 'The Rise of Ottoman Historiography', in Bernard Lewis and P. M. Holt (eds.), *Historians of the Middle East* (London, 1962), 152–67; and Suraiya Faroqhi, *Approaching Ottoman History: An Introduction to the Sources* (Cambridge, 1999) (who reviews the historiography on the historiography); and more often by studies of individual historians, among which Cornell H. Fleischer, *Bureaucrat and Intellectual in the Ottoman Empire: The Historian Mustafa Âli* (Princeton, NJ, 1986) is both exemplary for its detail and clarity and includes a general overview of the subject; a more detailed study of the same material is Johannes Schmidt, *Pure Water for Thirsty Muslims: A Study of Muṣṭafa 'Alī of Gallipoli's Künhü l-Ahbār* (Leiden, 1991). Other studies of individuals are Lewis V. Thomas, *A Study of Naima*, ed. N. Itzkowitz (New York, 1972) (a posthumously published doctoral thesis on Naima, with lengthy English extracts from the historian); and V. L. Ménage, *Neshri's History of the Ottomans: The Sources and Development of the Text* (London, 1964). See also Machiel Kiel, 'Mevlana Neşri and the Towns of Medieval Bulgaria', in Colin Heywood and Colin Imber (eds.), *Studies in Ottoman History in Honour of Professor V. L. Ménage* (Istanbul, 1995), 165–86. Gabriel Piterberg, *An Ottoman Tragedy: History and Historiography at Play* (Berkeley, CA, 2003) is a fascinating, if theoretically challenging, case study from the early seventeenth century, dealing with progressive rewritings of events surrounding the assassination of Sultan Osman II in 1622. Baki Tezcan, 'The Politics of Early Modern Ottoman Historiography', in V. H. Aksan and D. Goffman (eds.), *The Early Modern Ottomans: Remapping the Empire* (Cambridge, 2007), 167–98; and Christine Woodhead, *Ta'līkī-zāde's Şehnāme-i hümāyūn: A History of the Ottoman Campaign into Hungary, 1593–94* (Berlin, 1983) and 'An Experiment in Official Historiography: The Post of Şehnāmeci in the Ottoman Empire c. 1555–1605', *Wiener*

Zeitschrift für die Kunde des Morgenlandes 75 (1983): 157–82 are helpful on court-sponsored and official historiography. Finally, on Western historians of the Ottomans see Margaret Meserve, *Empires of Islam in Renaissance Historical Thought* (Cambridge, MA, 2008).

Chapter 5

European historical writing about the Indies and Americas

For the impact of the discoveries on European historical thought see David Armitage, 'The New World and British Historical Thought from Richard Hakluyt to William Robertson', in Karen O. Kupperman (ed.), *America in European Consciousness, 1493–1750* (Chapel Hill, NC and London, 1995), 52–75; and Peter Burke, 'America and the Rewriting of World History', ibid., 33–51. Joan-Pau Rubiés, *Travel and Ethnology in the Renaissance: South India through European Eyes, 1250–1625* (Cambridge, 2000), ch. 8 deals with histories of eastward Spanish expansion to South Asia. On the Iberian histories and historians of the Americas, two now dated surveys are Francisco Esteve Barba, *Historiografía Indiana* (Madrid, 1964) and A. Curtis Wilgus, *The Historiography of Latin America: A Guide to Historical Writing, 1500–1800* (Metuchen, NJ, 1975); see also Jack Ray Thomas, *Biographical Dictionary of Latin American Historians and Historiography* (Westport, CT, 1984). Benjamin Keen, *The Aztec Image in Western Thought* (New Bunswick, NJ, 1971) is excellent on perceptions of the Aztecs in Europe and debates about their culture. D. A. Brading, *The First America: The Spanish Monarchy, Creole Patriots, and the Liberal State 1492–1867* (Cambridge, 1991) is a superb study of the fashioning of identity through history in the three or so centuries after contact. Angel Delgado-Gómez, *Spanish Historical Writing about the New World 1493–1700* (Providence, RI, 1994) is an item-by-item description of Spanish histories, with illustrations. Specialized books on individual historians such as Las Casas, Acosta, Sarmiento and Sahagún are too numerous to list here. The mid-nineteenth century collection (in Spanish) of the early historians published (from a late eighteenth-century edition) by Enrique de Vedia under the title *Historiadores primitivos de Indias*, 3 vols. (Madrid, 1852) was reissued in 1946. Nearly all the major Spanish historians of the New World have been translated into English, several of them multiple times.

Indigenous and mestizo histories from the Americas

In contrast to the rather short shrift given by Esteve Barba (cited above) to indigenous historians and their texts, there has been intense study of both named authors and of South and Mesoamerican historical thinking more generally, before and after European arrivals. The historical sources for pre- and early post-Columbian Central and South America have been well studied, and there are now very accessible editions of many of the most important Mesoamerican texts, many of which include extensive illustrations or facsimiles. See for instance M. Jansen and G. A. Pérez Jiménez (eds.), *Codex Bodley: A Painted Chronicle from the Mixtec Highlands, Mexico* (Oxford, 2005); *Historia Tolteca-Chichimeca*, ed. Paul Kirchhoff, Lina Odena Güemes and Luis Reyes Garcia (in Spanish and Nahuatl) (Mexico, 1976); Eloise Quiñones Keber (ed. and trans.), *Codex Telleriano-Remensis: Ritual, Divination, and History in a Pictorial Aztec Manuscript* (Austin, TX, 1995); and Elizabeth Hill Boone, *Stories in Red and Black: Pictorial Histories of the Aztecs and Mixtecs* (Austin, TX, 2000). H. B. Nicholson, 'Native Historical Traditions of Nuclear America and the Problem of their Archaeological Correlation', *American Anthropologist* 57 (1955): 594–613 provides an analysis and typology of the central Mexican examples. There are accessible editions of the major late sixteenth- and seventeenth-century authors, notably El Inca Garcilaso de la Vega, Guaman Poma and Alva Ixtlilxó-chitl. James Lockhart (ed. and trans.), *We People Here: Nahuatl Accounts of the Conquest of Mexico* (Eugene, OR, 1993) is a useful selection of Nahuatl texts with Spanish and English parallel translations. For secondary sources on the Incas see especially Susan Niles, *The Shape of Inca History: Narrative and Architecture in an Andean Empire* (Iowa City, 1999); Catherine Julien, *Reading Inca History* (Iowa City, 2000); and Gary Urton, 'From Knots to Narratives: Reconstructing the Art of Historical Record Keeping in the Andes from Spanish Transcriptions of the Inkha Khipus', *Ethnohistory* 45 (1998): 409–38. On the interactions between conquerors and conquered see Walter D. Mignolo, *The Darker Side of the Renaissance: Literacy, Territoriality, and Colonization*, 2nd edn (1995; Ann Arbor, MI, 2003) and Enrique Florescano, *Memory, Myth and Time in Mexico: From the Aztecs to Independence*, trans. Albert G. Bork and Kathryn R. Bork (Austin, TX, 1994). Both are provocative accounts, stressing the suppressive aspects of European historicity. They should be balanced with three works more attuned to the bidirectional nature of the influence: Georges Baudot, *Utopia and History in Mexico: The First Chroniclers of Mexican Civilization (1520–1569)*, trans. Bernard R. Ortiz (Niwot, CO, 1995) concerns the utopian and millenarian aspects of early historical writing in Mexico; José Rabasa, *Inventing America: Spanish Historiography and the Formation of Eurocentrism* (Norman, OK and London, 1993) traces the impact of the New World in forming Eurocentric attitudes at home; and Jorge Cañizares-Esguerra, *How to Write a History of the New World: Histories, Epistemologies and Identities in the Eighteenth-Century Atlantic World* (Stanford, CA, 2001) discusses the historians of the eighteenth century on both sides of the ocean.

History in colonial North America

Michael Kraus and Davis D. Joyce, *The Writing of American History*, rev. edn (Norman, OK, and London, 1985) is a serviceable update of work first published in 1937; its author-by-author approach makes it useful for reference purposes but rather dull reading. David D. Van Tassel, *Recording America's Past: An Interpretation of the Development of Historical Studies in America 1607–1884* (Chicago, 1960) is an interpretative and selective account running up to the 1880s, more readable but containing factual errors and tending to over-stress the distinctiveness of American historical writing from its European origins; Peter Gay, *A Loss of Mastery: Puritan Historians in Colonial America* (Berkeley, CA, 1966) is an elegant study of a select group of Puritan historians. Trevor Colbourn, *The Lamp of Experience: Whig History and the Intellectual Origins of the American Revolution* (Chapel Hill, NC, 1965) concerns not historians per se but connections between English and American Revolutionary historical thought, including in an appendix an early effort at documenting historical reading patterns. Stephen Carl Arch, *Authorizing the Past: The Rhetoric of History in Seventeenth-Century England* (De Kalb, IL, 1994) and David Read, *New World, Known World: Shaping Knowledge in Early Anglo-American Writing* (Columbia, SC and London, 2005) are literary studies, the former useful on Johnson, the Mathers and Winthrop, and the latter especially good on John Smith and William Bradford. Peter C. Messer, *Stories of Independence: Identity, Ideology, and History in Eighteenth-Century America* (De Kalb, IL, 2005) covers much the same ground and stresses Scottish Enlightenment influences (for readings on which see the next chapter); it contains a useful chronological list of American histories. Lawrence H. Leder (ed.), *The Colonial Legacies*, 2 vols. (New York, 1971) is an edited collection of essays on early American historians. Rosemarie Zagarri, *A Woman's Dilemma: Mercy Otis Warren and the American Revolution* (Wheeling, IL, 1995) and Kate Davies, *Catharine Macaulay and Mercy Otis Warren: The Revolutionary Atlantic and the Politics of Gender* (Oxford, 2005) handle Warren, an outstanding Revolutionary-era figure. Early American women's historical writing is anthologized in Sharon N. Harris (ed.), *Women's Early American Historical Narratives* (Harmondsworth, 2003). Indigenous historicity is the subject of an anthropological study, Amy E. Den Ouden, *Beyond Conquest: Native Peoples and the Struggle for History in New England* (Lincoln, NE, 2005).

Chapter 6

The repudiation of the oral

There is no single study of eighteenth-century discussions of orality, alphabetic writing and history. However, see Nicholas Hudson, *Writing and European Thought 1600–1830* (Cambridge, 1994) and the same author's 'Constructing Oral Tradition: The Origins of the Concept in Enlightenment Intellectual Culture', in A. Fox and D. Woolf (eds.), *The Spoken Word: Oral Culture in Britain 1500–1850* (Manchester, 2002), 24–55. See also the present author's essay, 'The "Common Voice": History, Folklore, and Oral Tradition in Early Modern England', *Past and Present* 120 (August 1988): 26–52.

An overview of eighteenth–century European historical culture

General works on Enlightenment historical thought in English are rare, though history and historians figure prominently as a subject in most cultural or intellectual surveys of the period. For a perceptive guide to the general historiographical environment and treatments of many of the authors mentioned here see J. G. A. Pocock's ongoing study of Gibbon's *Decline and Fall of the Roman Empire*, which ranges far beyond Gibbon himself to include historians such as Hume, Robertson, Voltaire, Mosheim and many others: *Barbarism and Religion*, 5 vols. to date (Cambridge, 1999–). Paul Hazard's *European Thought in the Eighteenth Century: From Montesquieu to Lessing* (Cleveland, OH, 1963) and *The European Mind 1680–1715*, trans J. Lewis May (Harmondsworth, 1973); and Ernst Cassirer's *The Philosophy of the Enlightenment*, trans. Fritz C. A. Koelln and James P. Pettegrove (Boston, 1955), while older, remain insightful. Friedrich Meinecke, *Historism: The Rise of a New Historical Outlook*, trans. J. E. Anderson, 2nd edn (translation revised by H. D. Schmidt) (London, 1972) is a classic account, somewhat idiosyncratic in its choice of iconic figures, and inclined to treat the eighteenth century as a curtain-raiser for the main attraction, nineteenth-century historicism; this is a weakness, too, of Herbert Butterfield's *Man on his Past: The Study of Historical Scholarship* (Cambridge, 1955). Anne Goldgar, *Impolite Learning: Conduct and Community in the Republic of Letters, 1680–1750* (New Haven, CT, 1995) surveys the intellectual atmosphere among the 'republic of letters'. There are also collections of essays such as Roy Porter and Mikuláš Teich (eds.), *The Enlightenment in National Context* (Cambridge, 1981); and Karl Hammer and Jürgen Voss (eds.), *Historische Forschung im 18. Jahrhundert* (Bonn, 1976) (the last of these containing essays in German and French). Though over a century old, Wilhelm Dilthey's 1901 essay, 'The Eighteenth Century and the Historical World', trans. P. Van Tuhl, in Dilthey, *Selected Works*, ed. Rudolf A. Makreel and Frithjof Rodi (Princeton, NJ, 1985–), vol. IV, 325–85, is a classic summary and evaluation by the leading philosopher of history of his time. On the whole, the historiographical activity of the period has been best served by accounts of individual figures and by national studies. For France, Italy, Britain and Germany see below. Under-studied northern countries such as Sweden and Russia are covered in Peter Hallberg, *Ages of Liberty: Social Upheaval, History Writing, and the New Public Sphere in Sweden, 1740–1792* (Stockholm, 2002); Max J. Okenfuss, *The Rise and Fall of Latin Humanism in Early-Modern Russia* (Leiden, 1995); and Rudolph L. Daniels, *V. N. Tatishchev, Guardian of the Petrine Revolution* (Philadelphia, 1973).

'Philosophic' history in Italy and Scotland

Italy between Renaissance and Risorgimento is somewhat neglected, a gap that includes its historical writing. Vico and (to a lesser extent) Giannone are notable exceptions. There is relatively little available in English on Giannone, but those who read Italian should consult Giuseppe Ricuperati, *L'esperienza civile e religiosa di Pietro Giannone* (Milan and Naples, 1970), especially ch. 3. B. Dooley, *The Social History of Skepticism* (Baltimore, 1999) and the same author's essay 'Snatching Victory from the Jaws of Defeat: History and Imagination in Baroque Italy', *Seventeenth Century* 15:1 (2000): 90–115 are helpful. Vico in contrast has been exhaustively studied in several languages: B. A. Haddock, *An Introduction to Historical Thought* (London, 1980) has a clear and readable chapter on his thought; fuller studies, with different emphases, are to be found in Leon Pompa, *Human Nature and Historical Knowledge: Hume, Hegel, and Vico* (Cambridge, 1990) and *Vico: A*

Study of the 'New Science', 2nd edn (Cambridge, 1990); and Donald Phillip Verene, *Vico's Science of Imagination* (Ithaca, NY, 1981). Giorgio Tagliacozzo and Hayden V. White (eds.), *Giambattista Vico: An International Symposium* (Baltimore, 1969) is a comprehensive collection of essays on different aspects of Vico's thought. General works on Scotland include Richard B. Sher, *Church and University in the Scottish Enlightenment: The Moderate Literati of Edinburgh* (Princeton, NJ, 1985) and *The Enlightenment and the Book* (Chicago, 2006); Colin Kidd, *Subverting Scotland's Past: Scottish Whig Historians and the Creation of an Anglo-British Identity* (Cambridge, 1993); and David Allan, *Virtue, Learning and the Scottish Enlightenment* (Edinburgh, 1993). A concise recent survey of historiography in the Scottish Enlightenment is Murray Pittock, 'Historiography', in Alexander Broadie (ed.), *The Cambridge Companion to the Scottish Enlightenment* (Cambridge, 2003), 258–79.

Historical thought in the French Enlightenment

France is so central to the Enlightenment that studies of the period as a whole almost invariably give it pride of place. For Voltaire see J. H. Brumfitt, *Voltaire, Historian* (Oxford, 1958); Bruce Mazlish, *The Riddle of History: The Great Speculators from Vico to Freud* (New York, 1966); and Karen O'Brien, *Narratives of Enlightenment: Cosmopolitan History from Voltaire to Gibbon* (Cambridge, 1997). On Montesquieu see Suzanne Gearhart, 'Reading *De l'Esprit des Lois*: Montesquieu and the Principles of History', *Yale French Studies* 59 (1980): 175–200. On Condorcet see Mazlish, *The Riddle of History* (again), a work that also covers Vico and is readable if judgmental. Robert Darnton, *The Business of Enlightenment: A Publishing History of the Encyclopédie, 1775–1800* (Cambridge, MA, 1979), while not about history per se, is essential reading on the dissemination of knowledge, by a leading authority on eighteenth-century culture. Lionel Gossman, *Medievalism and the Ideologies of the Enlightenment: The World and Work of La Curne de Sainte-Palaye* (Baltimore, 1968) offers a corrective to the conventional interpretation of the eighteenth century's anti-medievalism through the activities of one prominent scholar in the *érudit* tradition.

The triumvirate

On Hume see Nicholas Phillipson, *Hume* (London, 1989) and David Wootton, 'David Hume, "the historian"', in D. F. Norton (ed.), *The Cambridge Companion to Hume* (Cambridge, 1993), 281–312. Leo Braudy, *Narrative Form in History and Fiction* (Princeton, NJ, 1980) covers Hume and Gibbon in conjunction with Henry Fielding, the novelist. Victor Wexler, *David Hume and the History of England* (Philadelphia, 1979) is concise and readable but contains frequent factual errors and should be used with caution. Mark Salber Phillips, *Society and Sentiment: Genres of Historical Writing in Britain, 1740–1820* (Princeton, NJ, 2000) is a brilliant analysis of the emotive quality of eighteenth-century historiography (Hume included) and its relations to the novel. There is no full-length monograph on Robertson as a historian (a lamentable deficit), though various essays and articles exist, including Jeffrey R. Smitten, 'Impartiality in Robertson's *History of America*', *Eighteenth-Century*

Studies 19 (1985): 56–77 and 'Modernism and History: William Robertson's Unfinished History of British North America', in Richard B. Sher and Jeffrey R. Smitten (eds.), *Scotland and America in the Age of Enlightenment* (Chicago, 1990), 163–79; and the essay collection Stewart Brown (ed.), *William Robertson and the Expansion of Empire* (Cambridge, 1997), especially the essay by N. Phillipson. The bibliography of works on Edward Gibbon in the past thirty years alone is impressive, but see in particular Pocock, *Barbarism and Religion*, cited above; Lionel Gossman, *The Empire Unpossess'd: An Essay on Gibbon's Decline and Fall* (Cambridge, 1981); David Womersley, *The Transformation of the Decline and Fall of the Roman Empire* (Cambridge, 1988) and *Gibbon and the 'Watchmen of the Holy City': The Historian and his Reputation 1776–1815* (Oxford, 2002).

West and East

There is no sustained study of Western consciousness of Chinese and Islamic historical writing, but see Franklin Perkins, *Leibniz and China: A Commerce of Light* (Cambridge, 2004). Awareness of other cultures in general however is the subject of P. J. Marshall and G. Williams, *The Great Map of Mankind: British Perceptions of the World in the Age of Enlightenment* (London, Melbourne and Toronto, 1982). Pocock, *Barbarism and Religion* deals with awareness of both as it influenced Gibbon, especially through Joseph de Guignes, the subject of a lengthy treatment in volume IV. For a selection of contemporary writings about India, including Jones on Hindu chronology, see P. J. Marshall (ed.), *The British Discovery of Hinduism in the Eighteenth Century* (Cambridge, 1970).

Chinese historiography in the early Qing dynasty

The Qing are discussed in the final chapter of Ng and Wang, *Mirroring the Past*, cited in earlier chapters. The historical writing and historical scholarship of the early Qing, the period up to *c*. 1800 covered in the present chapter, can best be accessed through Benjamin A. Elman, *From Philosophy to Philology: Intellectual and Social Aspects of Change in Late Imperial China* (Cambridge, MA, 1984). Lynn A. Struve, 'Huang Zongxi in Context: A Reappraisal of his Major Writings', *Journal of Asian Studies* 47 (1988): 474–502; Struve (ed.), *Time, Temporality and Imperial Transition: East Asia from Ming to Qing* (Honolulu, 2005); Pamela Kyle Crossley, *A Translucent Mirror: History and Identity in Qing Imperial Ideology* (Berkeley, CA, 1999); and Peter C. Perdue, *China Marches West: The Qing Conquest of Central Eurasia* (Cambridge, MA, 2005) are all valuable and stress the Qing empire's inclusiveness (like the Ottoman or British empires) of countries and ethnicities beyond China; each includes aspects of historical thought in their purview. Finally, David S. Nivison, *The Life and Thought of Chang Hsüeh-ch'eng (1738–1801)* (Stanford, CA, 1966) offers an excellent portrait of a late eighteenth-century scholar, Zhang Xuecheng, who is also discussed more briefly by P. Demiéville, 'Chang Hsüeh-Ch'eng and his Historiography', in W. G. Beasley and E. G. Pulleyblank (eds.), *Historians of China and Japan* (London, 1961), 167–85.

Early Tokugawa Japan

Japanese studies of Tokugawa historiography in English are harder to come by than Chinese of Ming and Qing writing, but John S. Brownlee, *Japanese Historians and the National Myths, 1600–1945: The Age of the Gods and Emperor Jinmu* (Vancouver and Tokyo, 1997), offers a good introduction, as does W. G. Beasley and Carmen Blacker, 'Japanese Historical Writing in the Tokugawa Period (1603–1868)', in Beasley and E. G. Pulleyblank (eds.), *Historians of China and Japan* (London, 1961) (covering a period beyond that discussed in this chapter). Kate Wildman Nakai, *Shogunal Politics: Arai Hakuseki and the Premises of Tokugawa Rule* (Cambridge, 1988) is an illuminating study of an important early eighteenth-century figure, while Nakai, 'Tokugawa Confucian Historiography: The Hayashi, Early Mito School, and Arai Hakuseki', in Peter Nosco (ed.), *Confucianism and Tokugawa Culture* (Princeton, NJ, 1984), 62–91, provides a more general but concise summary; Shigeru Matsumoto, *Motoori Norinaga 1730–1801* (Cambridge, 1970) studies the pivotal figure in the 'National Learning' movement. Maruyama Masao, *Studies in the Intellectual History of Tokugawa Japan*, trans. Mikiso Hane (Princeton, NJ, 1974) is a classic survey of the intellectual scene, with an emphasis on philosophical aspects, by one of Japan's leading modern historians.

The German Aufklärung

The most thorough recent survey, which challenges conventional notions of the rupture between Enlightenment and nineteenth century, is Peter Hans Reill, *The German Enlightenment and the Rise of Historicism* (Berkeley, CA, 1975); a similar argument is made by Georg G. Iggers, 'The European Context of Eighteenth-Century German Enlightenment Historiography', in Hans Erich Bödeker et al. (eds.), *Aufklärung und Geschichte: Studien zur deutschen Geschichtswissenschaft im 18. Jahrhundert* (Göttingen, 1986), 225–45, while Leonard Krieger, 'The Philosophical Bases of German Historicism: The Eighteenth Century', ibid., 246–63 looks in the other direction, to the roots of eighteenth-century historical thought in the late seventeenth century. Friedrich Meinecke, *Historism: The Rise of a New Historical Outlook*, trans. J. E. Anderson, 2nd edn (translation revised by H. D. Schmidt) (London, 1972) is readable on Möser, Herder and Goethe. Georg G. Iggers, *The German Conception of History: The National Tradition of Historical Thought from Herder to the Present*, rev. edn (Middletown, CT, 1983), though mainly about the nineteenth century, provides useful background. On Gatterer see P. H. Reill, 'History and Hermeneutics in the Aufklärung: The Thought of Johann Christoph Gatterer', *Journal of Modern History* 45:1 (1973): 24–51, while Donald R. Kelley, *Faces of History: Historical Inquiry from Herodotus to Herder* (New Haven, CT, 1998) is excellent on German historical thought and hermeneutics. S. Mark Lewis, *Modes of Historical Discourse in J. G. Herder and N. M. Karamzin* (New York, 1995) compares Herder with his Russian contemporary. For Kant, see William A. Galston, *Kant and the Problem of History* (Chicago, 1975), and a concise survey by Harold

Mah, 'German Historical Thought in the Age of Herder, Kant, and Hegel', in Lloyd Kramer and Sarah Maza (eds.), *A Companion to Western Historical Thought* (Oxford, 2002), 143–65.

Chapter 7

In this chapter, further reading for multiple sections has been consolidated to conserve space and because the same work often relates to more than one subject. Given the importance of national historiographies, a separate addendum, arranged by country, is provided at the end.

Intellectual and political background / Historicism, romanticism and nationalism

For a general survey of nineteenth-century historiography G. P. Gooch, *History and Historians in the Nineteenth Century*, 2nd edn (London, 1952) is a reissue of a work first published in 1913 and thus now nearly a century old; it is principally useful as a retrospective on the period by Gooch (1873–1968), a historian educated at its tail end. Even more than that of earlier eras, the historical writing of the nineteenth century has been the subject of literary analysis and the focus of critics and theorists (operating out of history, English, comparative literature and philosophy departments). The controversial influence over the past three decades of Hayden White, *Metahistory: The Historical Imagination in Nineteenth-Century Europe* (Baltimore, 1973) (and particularly its complicated quadripartite scheme of tropes, modes of emplotment, ideological implication and explanation) on criticism, the history of ideas and general historiography, well beyond its nominal nineteenth-century subject, has – rather unfortunately – eclipsed the fact that it is also a fine analysis of several key historians and philosophers of history. Though not a work for beginners, it is now essential reading. Works in a similar vein include Hans Kellner, *Language and Historical Representation: Getting the Story Crooked* (Madison, WI, 1989).

Historismus or historicism has acquired nearly as many meanings as 'history' itself. Apart from Friedrich Meinecke's *Historism*, listed in the previous chapter, see Georg G. Iggers, *The German Conception of History: The National Tradition of Historical Thought from Herder to the Present*, rev. edn (1968; Middletown, CT, 1983) and Charles R. Bambach, *Heidegger, Dilthey, and the Crisis of Historicism* (Ithaca, NY, 1995); further titles are listed in the further reading section for Chapter 9. For romanticism see (in addition to titles cited in the section on national literatures below) Roy Porter and Mikuláš Teich (eds.), *Romanticism in National Context* (Cambridge, 1988); Stephen Bann, *The Clothing of Clio: A Study of the Representation of History in Nineteenth-Century Britain and France* (Cambridge, 1984) and the same author's *Romanticism and the Rise of History* (New York, 1995); and Ann Rigney, *Imperfect Histories: The Elusive Past and the Legacy of Romantic Historicism* (Ithaca, NY and London, 2001).

For nationalism, which has generated a great deal of interest in the past twenty years, especially as it relates to historiography, see the addendum below.

Ranke and the 'professionalization' of history/Journals and handbooks

If the first half of the West's nineteenth century is characterized by literary historical writing in a romantic and nationalist vein, the second half may be noted for a rapid growth in what may, with due caution, be loosely called 'professionalization'. The literature on nineteenth-century professionalization is enormous, and much of it is now quantitative, merging with 'history of the book'. Charles-Olivier Carbonell, *Histoire et historiens: un mutation idéologique des historiens français, 1865–1885* (Toulouse, 1976) is a pioneering work of quantitative historiography especially good on the publication of history books in France over two decades, though criticized for underestimating the influence of local history. Two more recent major studies on France map the contours of the profession: Pim den Boer, *History as a Profession: The Study of History in France, 1818–1914*, trans. Arnold J. Pomarans (Princeton, NJ, 1998) and Gabriele Lingelbach, *Klio macht Karriere: die Institutionalisierung der Geschichtswissenschaft in Frankreich und den USA in der zweiten Hälfte des 19. Jahrhunderts* (Gottingen, 2003); the latter, covering both France and the United States, is available only in German, but see the concise English-language summary in Lingelbach's 'The Historical Discipline in the United States: Following the German Model?', in Eckhardt Fuchs and Benedikt Stuchtey (eds.), *Across Cultural Borders: Historiography in Global Perspective* (Lanham, MD, 2002), 182–204. Peter Novick, *That Noble Dream: The 'Objectivity Question' and the American Historical Profession* (Cambridge, 1988) on the United States is indispensable, and a sobering corrective to the triumphalist accounts in older surveys like Harry Elmer Barnes, *A History of Historical Writing* (Norman, OK, 1937). A useful essay on the misunderstanding of Ranke in the United States is Georg Iggers, 'The Image of Ranke in American and German Historical Thought', *History and Theory* 2 (1962): 17–40; however, see Dorothy Ross, 'On the Misunderstanding of Ranke and the Origins of the Historical Profession in America', in Georg Iggers and James M. Powell (eds.), *Leopold von Ranke and the Shaping of the Historical Discipline* (Syracuse, 1990), 154–69; and Eileen Ka-May Cheng, 'Exceptional History? The Origins of Historiography in the United States', *History and Theory* 47 (2008): 200–28 for challenges to that position. The subsequent specialization of historians is matter for a subsequent chapter, but it should be noted that not all modern historiographers regard this as a positive development, particularly in its isolation of academic history from a wider public readership and impact on public policy: for a brief example see Theodore S. Hamerow, 'The Bureaucratization of History', *American Historical Review* 94 (1989): 654–60. For handbooks see Hans Schleier, 'Ranke in the Manuals on Historical Methods of Droysen, Lorenz, and Bernheim', in Iggers and Powell (eds.), *Leopold von Ranke*, 111–23. The involvement of women in historical writing and in the 'professionalization' of the discipline has also been studied closely in the past decade or so: see in particular Nina Baym, *American Women Writers and the Work of History, 1790–1960* (New Brunswick, NJ, 1995); Maxine Berg, *A Woman in History: Eileen Power, 1889–1940* (Cambridge, 1992);

Murriam E. Burstein, 'From Good Looks to Good Thoughts: Popular Women's History and the Invention of Modernity, ca. 1830–1870', *Modern Philology* 97 (1999): 46–75; Julie Des Jardins, *Women and the Historical Enterprise in America: Gender, Race, and the Politics of Memory, 1880–1945* (Chapel Hill, NC, 2003); Jacqueline Goggin, 'Challenging Sexual Discrimination in the Historical Profession: Women Historians and the American Historical Association, 1890–1940', *American Historical Review* 97 (1992): 769–802; Bonnie G. Smith, *The Gender of History: Men, Women, and Historical Practice* (Cambridge, MA, 1998); Devoney Looser, *British Women Writers and the Writing of History, 1670–1820* (Baltimore, 2000); Mary O'Dowd and Ilaria Porciani (eds.), *History Women*, Special Issue of *Storia della storiografia/History of Historiography* 46 (2004); Mary O'Dowd, 'From Morgan to MacCurtain: Women Historians in Ireland from the 1790s to the 1990s', in Maryann Gialanella Valiulis and O'Dowd (eds.), *Women in Irish History: Essays in Honour of Margaret MacCurtain* (Dublin, 1997); Jennifer Scanlon and Shaaron Cosner (eds.), *American Women Historians, 1700s–1900s: A Biographical Dictionary* (Westport, CT, 1996); and Mary Spongberg, *Writing Women's History since the Renaissance* (New York, 2002).

Ranke himself has been well studied: selections from his works are available in Leonard F. Krieger, *Ranke: the Meaning of History* (Chicago, 1977). A new edition of Ranke, *The Theory and Practice of History*, ed Georg G. Iggers, first published in 1973, will appear in 2011 with a revised introduction. On the historian himself see, in addition to Iggers, *The German Conception of History*, the following: White, *Metahistory*; the essays in Iggers and Powell (eds.), *Leopold von Ranke* and (for readers of German) Rudolf Vierhaus, *Ranke und die soziale Welt* (Munster, 1957). Further titles are listed below in the addendum on national historiographies.

History, science and determinism/The cultural and social alternatives to Ranke/Fin-de siècle uncertainties

Despite the hostility of many contemporary historians to speculation, history and philosophy of history are rather hard to disentangle in the nineteenth century; Hayden White's *Metahistory* shows how similar the structures of both were. Those wanting a clear introduction can find Hegel, Marx, Comte and many other major thinkers in Bruce Mazlish, *The Riddle of History: The Great Speculators from Vico to Freud* (New York, 1966), an idiosyncratically judgmental but well-written account. A more recent collection of essays on a variety of historical speculators from Sima Qian and Augustine through the twentieth century is Johan Galtung and Sohail Inayatullah (eds.), *Macrohistory and Macrohistorians: Perspectives on Individual, Social and Civilizational Change* (Westport, CT, 1997). Each of these authors, Marx most of all, has generated enormous secondary bibliographies few items of which can be listed here; see Eric Hobsbawm, 'Karl Marx's Contribution to Historiography', in R. Blackburn (ed.), *Ideology in Social Science: Readings in Critical Social Theory* ([London], 1972), 265–83; Paul Q. Hirst, *Marxism and Historical Writing* (London, 1985); Matt Perry, *Marxism and History* (Basingstoke, 2002) is a brief summary of key concepts and of major modern debates among Marxist historians. For Saint-Simon and the Saint-Simonians see Frank E. Manuel, *The World of Henri Saint-Simon* (Cambridge, MA, 1956). On 'idealist' philosophy of history see Michael Ermarth,

Wilhelm Dilthey: The Critique of Historical Reason (Chicago, 1978); Robert Southard, *Droysen and the Prussian School of History* (Lexington, KY, 1995); and Hayden White, 'Droysen's *Historik*: Historical Writing as Bourgeois Science', in his *The Content of the Form: Narrative Discourse and Historical Representation* (Baltimore, 1987), 83–103. On Lamprecht see Roger Chickering, *Karl Lamprecht: A German Academic Life (1856–1915)* (Atlantic Highlands, NJ, 1993); on Nietzsche see the chapter in White, *Metahistory* and Allan Megill, *Prophets of Extremity: Nietzsche, Heidegger, Foucault and Derrida* (Berkeley, CA, 1985). Burckhardt has been written about extensively, including a chapter in White, *Metahistory*. See also Felix Gilbert, 'Ranke as the Teacher of Jacob Burckhardt', in Iggers and Powell (eds.), *Leopold von Ranke*, 82–8; Gilbert, *History: Politics or Culture? Reflections on Ranke and Burckhardt* (Princeton, NJ, 1990); and John R. Hinde, *Jacob Burckhardt and the Crisis of Modernity* (Montreal and Kingston, 2000).

An addendum on national historical literatures

Brief summaries of most countries' historiographies can be found in *GEHW*, and lengthier chapters in volume IV of the *Oxford History of Historical Writing* (Oxford, forthcoming). More generally, the relations between nationalism and history-making in nineteenth-century Europe (and by extension its colonies) have recently been the subject of a major collaborative research endeavour, funded by the European Science Foundation, under the direction of Stefan Berger (Manchester). An excellent discussion of the place of the nation in European culture more broadly, reaching back beyond the nineteenth century, is provided in Joep Leerssen, *National Thought in Europe* (Amsterdam, 2006). The reader interested in pursuing the history of historical writing on a national basis in the nineteenth and twentieth centuries (including some countries not specifically mentioned in the chapter) will also find the following titles of use. The reader is once again cautioned that this is not remotely exhaustive of the secondary literature available on the topic.

Belgium: Hervé Hasquin (ed.), *Histoire et historiens depuis 1830 en Belgique* (Brussels, 1981) and Jo Tollebeek, 'Historical Representation and the Nation-State in Romantic Belgium (1830–1850)', *Journal of the History of Ideas* 59 (1998): 329–53. **Britain**: Michael Bentley, *Modernizing England's Past: English Historiography in the Age of Modernism 1870–1970* (Cambridge, 2005); J. W. Burrow, *A Liberal Descent: Victorian Historians and the English Past* (Cambridge, 1981); Duncan Forbes, *The Liberal Anglican Idea of History* (Cambridge, 1952); Rosemary Jann, *The Art and Science of Victorian History* (Columbus, OH, 1985); Christopher Parker, *The English Historical Tradition since 1850* (Edinburgh, 1990) and *The English Idea of History from Coleridge to Collingwood* (Aldershot, 2000); Peter R. H. Slee, *Learning and a Liberal Education: The Study of Modern History in the Universities of Oxford, Cambridge and Manchester 1800–1914* (Manchester, 1986); and Reba N. Soffer, *Discipline and Power: The University, History, and the Making of an English Elite, 1870–1930* (Stanford, CA, 1994). The Victorian debate about history 'as science' is well treated in Ian Hesketh, *The Science of History in Victorian Britain: Making the Past Speak* (in press, London, 2011);

I am indebted to Dr Hesketh for allowing me to read his book in manuscript. **Canada:** M. Brook Taylor, *Promoters, Patriots, and Partisans: Historiography in Nineteenth-Century English Canada* (Toronto, 1989) and Donald Wright, *The Professionalization of History in English Canada* (Toronto, 2005). **France:** Ceri Crossley, *French Historians and Romanticism: Thierry, Guizot, the Saint-Simonians, Quinet, Michelet* (London, 1993); den Boer, *History as a Profession*, cited above; Donald R. Kelley, *Historians and the Law in Postrevolutionary France* (Princeton, NJ, 1984); William R. Keylor, *Academy and Community: The Foundations of the French Historical Profession* (Cambridge, 1975); and Linda Orr, *Headless History: Nineteenth-Century French Historiography of the Revolution* (Ithaca, NY, 1990). **Germany** (see also above under Historicism, Ranke, etc.): Carlo Antoni, *From History to Sociology: The Transition in German Historical Thinking*, trans. Hayden White (London, 1962); Stefan Berger, *The Search for Normality: National Historical Consciousness in Germany since 1800* (London, 1997); Susan A. Crane, *Collecting and Historical Consciousness in Early Nineteenth-Century Germany* (Ithaca, NY, 2000); Harold Mah, 'German Historical Thought in the Age of Herder, Kant, and Hegel', in Lloyd Kramer and Sarah Maza (eds.), *A Companion to Western Historical Thought* (Oxford, 2002), 143–65; and Theodore Ziolkowski, *Clio the Romantic Muse: Historicizing the Faculties in Germany* (Ithaca, NY, 2004). **Greece:** Effi Gazi, *Scientific National History: The Greek Case in Comparative Perspective (1850–1920)* (Frankfurt, 2000). **Habsburg lands (non-German):** Joseph F. Zacek, *Palacký: The Historian as Scholar and Nationalist* (The Hague and Paris, 1970); Monika Baár, *Historians and Nationalism: East-Central Europe in the Nineteenth Century* (Oxford, 2010); Maciej Janowski, 'Mirrors for the Nation: Imagining the National Past among the Poles and Czechs in the Nineteenth and Twentieth Centuries', in Stefan Berger and Chris Lorenz (eds.), *The Contested Nation: Ethnicity, Class, Religion, and Gender in National Histories* (Basingstoke, 2008), 442–62. **Italy:** M. Moretti, 'The Search for a "National" History: Italian Historiographical Trends following Unification', in Stefan Berger, Mark Donovan and Kevin Passmore (eds.), *Writing National Histories: Western Europe since 1800* (London, 1999), 111–22; Ilaria Porciani, *'L'Archivio Storico Italiano': Organizzazione della ricerca ed egemonia moderata nel Risorgimento* (Florence, 1979); and Martin Thom, 'Unity and Confederation in the Italian Risorgimento', in Berger, Donovan and Passmore (eds.), *Writing National Histories*, 69–84. **Netherlands:** Nicholas A. Rupke, 'Romanticism in the Netherlands', in Porter and Teich (eds.), *Romanticism in National Context*, 191–216. **Poland:** Peter Brock, John D. Stanley and Piotr J. Wróbel (eds.), *Nation and History: Polish Historians from the Enlightenment to the Second World War* (Toronto, 2006); Anita Shelton, *The Democratic Idea in Polish History and Historiography: Franciszek Bujak (1875–1953)* (Boulder, CO, 1989); and Joan S. Skurnowicz, *Romantic Nationalism and Liberalism: Joachim Lelewel and the Polish National Idea* (Boulder, CO, 1981). **Romania:** Lucian Boia, *History and Myth in Romanian Consciousness* (1997; Bucharest, 2001); and Paul A. Hiemstra, *Alexandru D. Xenopol and the Development of Romanian Historiography* (New York, 1987); Baár, *Historians and Nationalism*, cited above. **Russia and Ukraine:** Anatole G. Mazour, *Modern Russian Historiography*, rev. edn (Westport, CT, 1975); Serhii Plokhy, *Unmaking Imperial Russia: Mykhailo Hrushevsky and the Writing of*

Ukrainian History (Toronto, 2005); Thomas D. Sanders (ed.), *Historiography of Imperial Russia: The Profession and Writing of History in a Multinational State* (London,
1999); and George Vernadsky, *Russian Historiography: A History*, ed. Sergei Pushkarev,
trans. Nickolas Lupinin (Belmont, MA, 1978). **Spain and Portugal:** Derek Flitter, *Spanish
Romanticism and the Uses of History: Ideology and the Historical Imagination* (London,
2006); and Sérgio Campos Matos and David Mota Álvarez, 'Portuguese and Spanish
Historiographies: Distance and Proximities', in Berger and Lorenz (eds.), *The Contested
Nation.* **Switzerland:** Guy P. Marchal, 'National Historiography and National Identity:
Switzerland in Comparative Perspective', in Berger and Lorenz (eds.), *The Contested
Nation*, 311–38; and Oliver Zimmer, *A Contested Nation: History, Memory, and Nation-
alism in Switzerland, 1761–1891* (Cambridge, 2003). **United States:** Ernst Breisach,
American Progressive History: An Experiment in Modernization (Chicago, 1993); Ellen
Fitzpatrick, *History's Memory: Writing America's Past 1880–1980* (Cambridge, 2002);
Jurgen Herbst, *The German Historical School in American Scholarship in the Transfer of
Culture* (Port Washington, NY, 1965); and Novick, *That Noble Dream*, cited above.

Chapter 8

British India

Vinay Lal, 'The History of Ahistoricity: The Indian Tradition, Colonialism, and the Advent
of Historical Thinking', in Lal, *The History of History: Politics and Scholarship in Modern
India* (Oxford and New Delhi, 2003), 35–9. On James Mill's *History of India* see in particular Javeed Majeed, *Ungoverned Imaginings: James Mill's* The History of British India *and
Orientalism* (Oxford, 1992); Indira Chowdhury, 'Excavating the Past: History and its Icons',
in her *The Frail Hero and Virile History: Gender and the Politics of Culture in Colonial
Bengal* (Delhi, 1998), 40–65; Ranajit Guha, *An Indian Historiography of India: A Nineteenth-Century Agenda and its Implications* (Calcutta and New Delhi, 1988); and Meenakshi Mukherjee, 'Rhetoric of Identity: History and Fiction in Nineteenth Century India',
in Alok Bhalla and Sudhir Chandra (eds.), *Indian Responses to Colonialism in the 19th
Century* (New Delhi, 1993), 34–47. See also Daud Ali (ed.), *Invoking the Past: the Uses of
History in South Asia* (New Delhi,1999), several chapters of which are relevant here.

Latin America and the Caribbean

John L. Robinson, *Bartolomé Mitre: Historian of the Americas* (Washington, DC, 1982);
Stuart Schwartz, 'Introduction', to João Capistrano de Abreu, *Chapters of Brazil's Colonial History 1500–1800*, trans. A. Barkel (New York, 1997); E. Bradford Burns (ed.),
Perspectives on Brazilian History (New York and London, 1967); the last portions of
D. A. Brading, *The First America: The Spanish Monarchy, Creole Patriots, and the Liberal State 1492–1867* (Cambridge, 1991) are also relevant. On the Caribbean countries
see Allen Woll, *Puerto Rican Historiography* (New York, 1978); Eric Williams, *British*

Historians in the West Indies (New York, 1966); and Elsa V. Goveia, *Historiography of the British West Indies to the End of the Nineteenth Century* (1956; Washington, DC, 1980). B. W. Higman (ed.), *General History of the Caribbean*, vol. VI: *Methodology and Historiography of the Caribbean* (London and Oxford, 1999) is indispensable; see especially the editor's introductory essay, 'The Development of Historical Disciplines in the Caribbean', ibid., 3–18.

Southeast Asia (all sections)

Apart from numerous essays and entries on individual historians in *GEHW* (to which the present writer is indebted), there are several edited collections on Southeast Asian history-writing relevant for the period covered in the three sections on Southeast Asia in this chapter, for instance Abu Talid Ahmad and Tan Liok Ee (eds.), *New Terrains in Southeast Asian History* (Athens, Ohio and Singapore, 2003) and Anthony Reid and David Marr (eds.), *Perceptions of the Past in Southeast Asia* (Singapore, 1979), which has a particularly useful appendix that lists extant writings by Southeast Asians about their own pasts with references to available editions as of 1979, a list that has, however, increased in the past thirty years. See in particular the chapters by David Chandler (on Cambodian palace chronicles), David G. Marr (on Vietnamese historiography), Charnvit Kasetsiri (on Thai historiography) and R. C. Ileto (on Philippine historiography). C. H. Philips (ed.), *Historians of India, Pakistan, and Ceylon* (London, 1961) includes a chapter by U Tet Htoot on Burmese chronicles. D. G. E. Hall (ed.), *Historians of South East Asia* (London, 1961) is a volume in the same Oxford University Press series on non-European historiography that appeared in the early 1960s and which includes Philips' book on South Asia. It has been largely superseded by subsequent work but C. C. Berg's paper on Javanese historiography among others is still useful. Modern Indonesia is mainly dealt with in the next chapter, but there are materials on this period in Soedjatmoko (ed.), *An Introduction to Indonesian Historiography* (Ithaca, NY, 1965). See also Nancy K. Florida, *Writing the Past, Inscribing the Future: History as Prophecy in Colonial Java* (Durham, NC, 1995) and Ann Kumar, *Surapati, Man and Legend: A Study of Three Babad Traditions* (Leiden, 1976). For Thai chronicle traditions see especially the chapter by David K. Wyatt in C. D. Cowan and O. W. Wolters (eds.), *Southeast Asian History and Historiography: Essays Presented to D. G. E. Hall* (Ithaca, NY, 1976) and Donald K. Swearer, 'Myth, Legend and History in the Northern Thai Chronicles', *Journal of the Siam Society* 62:1 (1974): 67–88. For Vietnam and Cambodia see the edited collections mentioned above and Alexander Woodside, 'Central Vietnam's Trading World in the Eighteenth Century as Seen in Lê Quý Đôn's Frontier Chronicles', in K. W. Taylor and J. K. Whitmore (eds.), *Essays into Vietnamese Pasts* (Ithaca, NY, 1995), 157–72; and Yu Insun, 'Lê Văn Hưu and Ngô Sĩ Liên: A Comparison of their Perception of Vietnamese History', in Nhung Tuyet Tran and A. J. S. Reid (eds.), *Viet Nam: Borderless Histories* (Madison, WI, 2006), 45–71. For the Philippines, see the above-cited edited collections and John A. Larkin (ed.), *Perspectives on Philippine Historiography: A Symposium* (New Haven, CT, 1979).

Japan

For an excellent study of historical writing in Japan during the long nineteenth century see Margaret Mehl, *History and the State in Nineteenth-Century Japan* (Basingstoke, 1998), and the latter portions of John S. Brownlee, *Japanese Historians and the National Myths, 1600–1945: The Age of the Gods and Emperor Jinmu* (Vancouver and Tokyo, 1997). Also particularly useful is Stefan Tanaka, *Japan's Orient: Rendering Pasts into History* (Berkeley, CA, 1993) and Peter Duus, 'Whig History, Japanese Style: The Min'yūsha Historians and the Meiji Restoration', *Journal of Asian Studies* 33 (1974): 415–36. For George Gustavus Zerffi see Tibor Frank, *From Habsburg Agent to Victorian Scholar: G. G. Zerffi 1820–1892* (Boulder, CO, 2000). On the Kume affair see Margaret Mehl, 'Scholarship and Ideology in Conflict: The Kume Affair, 1892', *Monumenta Nipponica* 48 (1993): 337–57. Christopher L. Hill, *National History and the World of Nations: Capital, State, and the Rhetoric of History in Japan, France, and the United States* (Durham, NC and London, 2009) studies Japan against the context of two Western countries; its focus inclines to non-canonical forms of history, including a Japanese short story.

China

Luke S. K. Kwong, 'The Rise of the Linear Perspective on History and Time in Late Qing China', *Past and Present* 173 (2001): 157–90, studies shifting views of time and history, and their connection with reform, in the late Qing. On the republican period see Q. Edward Wang, *Inventing China through History: The May Fourth Approach to Historiography* (Albany, NY, 2001). Several influential historians and other scholars of the late Qing and republican periods have received extensive treatments in English. On Liang Qichao see Joseph R. Levenson, *Liang Ch'i-ch'ao and the Mind of Modern China* (Cambridge, 1959); Hao Chang, *Liang Ch'i-ch'ao and Intellectual Transition in China, 1890–1907* (Cambridge, MA, 1971), a study of his early reformist career; and especially Xiaobing Tang, *Global Space and the Nationalist Discourse of Modernity: The Historical Thinking of Liang Qichao* (Stanford, CA, 1996), which focuses much more clearly on his historical thought. The contribution of Japan in westernizing China is the subject of Joshua A. Fogel (ed.), *The Role of Japan in Liang Qichao's Introduction of Modern Western Civilization to China* (Berkeley, CA, 2004). On Gu Jiegang see Laurence A. Schneider, *Ku Chieh-kang and China's New History: Nationalism and the Quest for Alternative Traditions* (Berkeley, CA, 1971). On Fu Sinian see Axel Schneider, 'Reconciling History with the Nation? Historicity, National Particularity, and the Question of Universals', *Historiography East and West* 1:1 (2003): 117–36; and Fan-sen Wang, *Fu Ssu-nien: A Life in Chinese History and Politics* (Cambridge, 2000).

Africa

On African oral tradition and oral literature see in particular the influential Jan Vansina, *Oral Tradition as History* (Madison, WI, 1985); see also Thomas A. Hale, *Scribe, Griot and Novelist: Narrative Interpreters of the Songhay Empire* (Gainesville, FL,1990); John William Johnson, Thomas A. Hale and Stephen Belcher (eds.), *Oral Epics from Africa* (Bloomington, IN, 1997); and R. S. O'Fahey et al. (eds.), *The Writings of Eastern Sudanic Africa to c. 1900* (Leiden, 1994). Specifically on the Kano Chronicle see John Hunwick et al., *The Writings of Central Sudanic Africa* (Leiden, 1995) and, in greater detail, Hunwick, 'A Historical Whodunit: The So-Called "Kano Chronicle" and its Place in the Historiography of Kano', *History in Africa* 21 (1994): 127–46. For a study of the Gonja Chronicles, including transcription and translation, see Ivor Wilks, Nehemia Levtzion and Bruce M. Haight, *Chronicles from Gonja: A Tradition of West African Muslim Historiography* (Cambridge, 1986). For overviews of the early development of African academic historiography, in Africa and elsewhere, see J. D. Fage, 'History', in Robert A. Lystad (ed.), *The African World: A Survey of Social Research* (New York, 1965) and Fage, 'The Development of African Historiography', in J. Ki-Zerbo (ed.), *General History of Africa*, vol. 1: *Methodology and African Prehistory* (Paris and London, 1981), 25–42; and essays in J. D. Fage (ed.), *Africa Discovers her Past* (London, 1970). For an interesting collection of essays studying both African and South Asian historiography, with a focus on local and regional writings, see Axel Harneit-Sievers (ed.), *A Place in the World: New Local Historiographies from Africa and South-Asia* (Leiden, 2002).

Islam including the Ottoman Empire

On al-Jabartī, David Ayalon, 'The Historian al-Jabartī', in Bernard Lewis and P. M. Holt (eds.), *Historians and the Middle East* (London, 1962), 391–402 is a useful essay, but must be read with caution, offering as it does a highly effusive encomium of al-Jabartī while mistakenly viewing his work as 'only a local history' (395). For a more restrained view see Jack A. Crabbs, Jr., *The Writing of History in Nineteenth-Century Egypt* (Detroit, 1984), who stresses the continuity of Jabartī's work with medieval Islamic precursors; Youssef M. Choueiri, *Modern Arab Historiography: Historical Discourse and the Nation-State* (London, 2003); Ulrike Freitag, 'Writing Arab History: The Search for the Nation', *British Journal of Middle Eastern Studies* 21 (1994): 19–37; and Israel Gershoni, Amy Singer and Y. Hakan Erdem (eds.), *Middle East Historiographies: Narrating the Twentieth Century* (Seattle, 2006). On Egypt see Michael Winter, 'Attitudes toward the Ottomans in Egyptian Historiography during Ottoman Rule', in Hugh Kennedy (ed.), *The Historiography of Islamic Egypt (c. 950–1800)* (Leiden, 2001), 195–210. For the more recent 'Arabization' of Egyptian history in the late 1950s see Thomas Mayer, *The Changing Past: Egyptian Historiography of the Urabi Revolt, 1882–1983* (Gainesville, FL, 1988). For the Ottomans and later Turkish historiography see Cemal Kafadar and Hakan T. Hareteke, 'Late Ottoman and Early Republican Turkish Historiography', in *OHHW*, vol. IV (Oxford, forthcoming), which provides a complete list of the imperial annalists of the nineteenth and early twentieth centuries, up to the end of the empire. See also Ercüment Kuran, 'Ottoman Historiography of the Tanzimat Period', in Lewis and Holt (eds.), *Historians and the Middle East*, 187–206; and Bernard Lewis, *From Babel to Dragomans: Interpreting the Middle East* (Oxford, 2004). Selçuk Akşin Somel, *The Modernization of Public Education in the Ottoman Empire 1839–1908: Islamization, Autocracy and Discipline* (Leiden, 2001) offers a critique of the 'steady Westernization' model of Ottoman modernization. For a revisionist account that takes issue with usual 'orientalist' views of Western dominance and implicates Persians themselves in orientalizing Persia/Iran (and 'occidentalizing' Europe) through the writing of history, see Mohamad Tavakoli-Targhi, *Refashioning Iran: Orientalism, Occidentalism, and Historiography* (Basingstoke, 2001).

Chapter 9

General reading: history–writing in the twentieth century

Single-author surveys of twentieth-century historiography are in fact rare (though see Georg G. Iggers, *Historiography in the Twentieth Century: From Scientific Objectivity to the Postmodern Challenge* (Hanover, NH, 1997) and Michael Bentley, *Modern Historiography: An Introduction* (London, 1999)), most works falling into various different categories arranged by nation, region, theoretical orientation or issue. Works covering the entire globe, as opposed to the West, are even more scarce; however, see now Georg G. Iggers, Q. Edward Wang and S. Mukherjee, *A Global History of Modern Historiography* (Harlow, UK and New York, 2008), which offers a much fuller and more detailed account of twentieth-century developments than I have been able to include in a single chapter of the present book. There are a number of recent surveys or edited collections, especially on the various theoretical approaches of the last hundred years: Rolf Torstendahl (ed.), *An Assessment of Twentieth-Century Historiography: Professionalism, Methodologies, Writings* (Stockholm, 2000); Stefan Berger, Heiko Feldner and Kevin Passmore (eds.), *Writing History: Theory and Practice* (London, 2003); and Donald R. Kelley, *Frontiers of History: Historical Inquiry in the Twentieth Century* (New Haven, CT, 2006).

A crisis of historicism?/philosophies of 'History' and 'history'

For Spengler see John Farrenkopf, *Prophet of Decline: Spengler on World History and Politics* (Baton Rouge, LA, 2001). For a concise study of Toynbee and the major criticisms levelled against him see Roland N. Stromberg, *Arnold J. Toynbee: Historian for an Age of Crisis* (Carbondale, IL, 1972). See also the essays in C. T. McIntire and Thomas Perry (eds.), *Toynbee: Reappraisals* (Toronto, 1989). For a survey of world historians, including Toynbee and Spengler as well as others, see Paul Costello, *World Historians and their Goals: Twentieth-Century Answers to Modernism* (De Kalb, IL, 1994). The discussion of Benedetto Croce in this chapter relies considerably on David D. Roberts, *Benedetto Croce and the Uses of Historicism* (Berkeley, CA, 1987) and the same author's *Historicism and Fascism in Modern Italy* (Toronto, 2007). See also A. Robert Caponigri, *History and Liberty: The Historical Writings of Benedetto Croce* (Chicago, 1955) and Edmund E. Jacobitti, *Revolutionary Humanism and Historicism in Modern Italy* (New Haven, CT, 1981). An excellent study of Collingwood is William H. Dray, *History as Re-enactment: R. G. Collingwood's Idea of History* (Oxford, 1995).

The rise of the Annales

No single 'school' or group of twentieth-century historians has been more discussed than the Annales, on whom several monographs and many articles are available. Traian Stoianovich, *French Historical Method: The Annales Paradigm* (Ithaca, NY, 1976) is somewhat over-celebratory and inclined to exaggerate the unity and coherence among the Annales scholars; Stuart Clark (ed.), *The Annales School* (London, 1999) and Peter Burke, *The French Historical Revolution: The Annales School, 1929–1989* (Stanford, CA, 1990) (the latter with a useful glossary of *Annaliste* terminology) provide more nuanced assessments. Philippe Carrard, *Poetics of the New History: French Historical Discourse from Braudel to Chartier* (Baltimore, 1992) takes a literary approach to the 'poetics' of French 'New History' (the term used in France for the work of the 'third' generation of Annalistes, especially in cultural history). Jean-Pierre Hérubel (ed.), *Annales Historiography and Theory: A Selective and Annotated Bibliography* (Westport, CT, 1994) is a useful bibliography, but like all such works quickly dated. The involvement of women in the movement is the subject of a brilliant article by Natalie Zemon Davis, 'Women and the World of the Annales', *History Workshop Journal* 33 (1992): 121–37; see also Peter Schöttler, 'Lucie Varga: A Central European Refugee in the Circle of the French "Annales", 1934–1941', *History Workshop Journal* 33 (1992): 100–20. Of the Annales' major early architects, Bloch's story has been well told in Carole Fink, *Marc Bloch: A Life in History* (Cambridge, 1989). For microhistory, see the titles cited in the text, and also E. Muir and G. Ruggiero (eds.), *Microhistory and the Lost Peoples of Europe*, trans. E. Branch (Baltimore, 1991).

History and the social sciences

The best overview of history's engagement with social theory is Peter Burke, *History and Social Theory*, 2nd edn (Ithaca, NY, 2005). Kevin Passmore presents a useful analytical summary in 'History and Social Science in the West', *OHHW*, vol. V (Oxford, forthcoming). There are many works describing Thomas Kuhn's transformative influence on the history of science but see in particular Jan Golinski, *Making Natural Knowledge: Constructivism and the History of Science* (Cambridge, 1998); for the history of science and technology in general see Seymour Mauskopf and Alex Roland, 'The Historiography of Science and Technology', *OHHW*, vol. V. For the debate on cliometrics see the works by Elton and Fogel, Barzun and Bridenbaugh cited in the text and notes. For counterfactuals, see Simon T. Kaye, 'Challenging Certainty: The Utility and History of Counterfactualism', *History and Theory* 49 (2010): 38–57 and Niall Ferguson, *Virtual History: Alternatives and Counterfactuals* (London, 1997).

History under dictatorships and totalitarian regimes

Antoon De Baets, *Censorship of Historical Thought: A World Guide, 1945–2000* (Westport, CT, 2002) is an exhaustive catalogue of instances of the censorship of historians since the end of the Second World War in places as geographically dispersed as Franco's Spain, the military juntas of Argentina and Chile, and contemporary Burma/ Myanmar and several African states. It makes for informative but depressing reading. For historians under Nazism see Winfried Schulze and Otto Gerhard Oexle (eds.), *Deutsche Historiker im Nationalsozialismus* (Frankfurt, 2000); for East Germany after the war see Andreas Dorpalen, *German History in Marxist Perspective: The East German Approach* (Detroit, 1985). For discussions of recent controversies see Stefan Berger, *The Search for Normality: National Historical Consciousness in Germany since 1800* (London, 1997); A. D. Low, *The Third Reich and the Holocaust in German Historiography: Toward the Historikerstreit of the Mid-1980s* (Boulder, CO, 1994). The Soviet Union has been well treated in English: Konstantin F. Shteppa, *Russian Historians and the Soviet State* (New Brunswick, NJ, 1962); George Vernadsky, *Russian Historiography: A History*, ed. Sergei Pushkarev, trans. Nickolas Lupinin (Belmont, MA, 1978) has useful biographical material but is misleadingly titled as it begins only in the mid-eighteenth century and its treatment of the Soviet period is selective. A classic early Soviet account of historiography, still unavailable in any Western language, is Nikolai Rubinshtein, *Russkaia Istoriografiia* (Moscow, 1941); I owe this last reference to Denis Kozlov. On Plekhanov see Samuel H. Baron, *Plekhanov in Russian History and Soviet Historiography* (Pittsburgh, PA, 1995); on Pokrovskii see George M. Enteen, *The Soviet-Scholar-Bureaucrat: M. N. Pokrovskii and the Society of Marxist Historians* (University Park, PA, 1978) and John Barber, *Soviet Historians in Crisis, 1928–1932* (Basingstoke, 1981). An insider's perspective is provided by Alter L. Litvin, *Writing History in Twentieth-Century Russia: A View from Within*, trans. and ed. John H. L. Keep (Basingstoke, 2001). For an excellent account of the process of displacing the standard imperial account of Russian history with a Marxist one see Serhii Plokhy, *Unmaking Imperial Russia: Mykhailo Hrushevsky and the Writing of Ukrainian History* (Toronto, 2005). See R. W. Davies, *Soviet History in the Gorbachev Revolution* (Basingstoke, 1989) and his *Soviet History in the Yeltsin Era* (Basingstoke, 1997) for Soviet historiography following Stalin. For history in the Soviet satellites before and after 1991 see Maciej Górny, 'Past in the Future: National Tradition and Czechoslovak Marxist Historiography', *European Review of History* 10 (2003): 103–14; and Ulf Brunnbauer (ed.), *(Re)Writing History: Historiography in Southeast Europe after Socialism* (Münster, 2004).

For the conversion of the Confucianism in communist China see Joseph R. Levenson, 'The Place of Confucius in Communist China', in Albert Feuerwerker (ed.), *History in Communist China* (Cambridge, MA, 1968), 56–73. On one victim of the Cultural Revolution see Clifford Edmunds, 'The Politics of Historiography: Jian Bozan's Historicism', in M. Goldman (ed.), *China's Intellectuals and the State: In Search of a New Relationship* (Cambridge, MA, 1987), 65–106. Arif Dirlik, *Revolution and History: The Origins of Marxist Historiography in China, 1919–1937* (Berkeley, CA, 1978) reviews the pre-1949 history of Marxist history-writing. For Japan see titles listed in Chapter 8 and in addition, Nozaki Yoshiko, *War Memory, Nationalism, and Education in Postwar Japan, 1945–2007: The Japanese Textbook Controversy and Ienaga Saburo's Court Challenge* (London, 2008). Ienaga Saburō recounts his misadventures with certification and subsequent legal challenges to it in *Japan's Past, Japan's Future: One Historian's*

Odyssey, trans. Richard H. Minear (Lanham, MD, 2001), 151–87. For recent developments in the relationship between history and public opinion in Japan see Sven Saaler, *Politics, Memory and Public Opinion: The History Textbook Controversy and Japanese Society* (Munich, 2005). For an overview of Indonesian historiography since the advent of Suharto, and especially the impact of military ideology, see Katharine E. McGregor, *History in Uniform: Military Ideology and the Construction of Indonesia's Past* (Honolulu, 2007). On Vietnam see Patricia M. Pelley, *Postcolonial Vietnam: New Histories of the National Past* (Durham, NC, 2002).

History from below

For a polemical account of the debates within English Marxist history-writing see Perry Anderson, *Arguments within English Marxism* (London, 1980). On the evolution of Marxist social history see Geoff Eley, *A Crooked Line: From Cultural History to the History of Society* (Ann Arbor, MI, 2005). On the origins of *Past and Present* see Christopher Hill, R. H. Hilton and E. J. Hobsbawm, '*Past and Present*: Origins and Early Years', *Past and Present* 100 (1983): 3–14; for British Marxism in general see Harvey J. Kaye, *The British Marxist Historians* (1984; New York, 1995). For Gramsci, see John Cammett, 'Antonio Gramsci: Marxism and the Italian Intellectual Tradition', in Hayden White (ed.), *The Uses of History: Essays in Intellectual and Social History Presented to William J. Bossenbrook* (Detroit, 1968), 175–86; and T. J. Jackson Lears, 'The Concept of Cultural Hegemony: Problems and Possibilities', *American Historical Review* 90 (1985): 567–93.

The literature on oral history, a frequent tool of those studying contemporary populations below the level of the elite, is voluminous; the most accessible introduction remains Paul Thompson, *The Voice of the Past: Oral History*, 3rd edn (Oxford, 2000).

Women's history and gender

On women and the profession of history in the West during the last two centuries see in particular Bonnie G. Smith, *The Gender of History: Men, Women, and Historical Practice* (Cambridge, MA, 1998) and Julie Des Jardins, *Women and the Historical Profession in America: Gender, Race, and the Politics of Memory, 1800–1945* (Chapel Hill, NC, 2003). A special issue of *Storia della Storiografia* 46 (2004) edited by Mary O'Dowd and Ilaria Porciani on 'History Women' is largely modern and exclusively European in focus, but with multilingual essays on under-studied regions such as the Baltic and the Balkans. For Ireland see Nadia Claire Smith, *A 'Manly Study'? Irish Women Historians, 1868–1949* (Basingstoke, 2006). Non-Western examples of women's history are also becoming more common, especially within the Muslim world and in Africa. See, for example, Leila Ahmed's *Women and Gender in Islam: Historical Roots of a Modern Debate* (New Haven, CT, 1992) and numerous works by the Moroccan sociologist Fatima Mernissi, such as *Women and Islam: An Historical and Theological Enquiry*, trans. Mary Jo Lakeland (Oxford, 1991). Recent collections of essays such as Guity Nashat and Lois Beck (eds.), *Women in Iran from the Rise of Islam to 1800* (Urbana, IL, 2003) and *Women in Iran from 1800 to the Islamic Republic* (Urbana, IL, 2004) have also explored the historical place of women in Islamic societies from very early times. See also Julia Clancy-Smith, 'Twentieth-Century Historians and Historiography of the Middle East: Women, Gender, and Empire', in Israel Gershoni, Amy Singer and Y. Hakan Erdem (eds.), *Middle East Historiographies: Narrating the Twentieth Century* (Seattle, WA, 2006), 70–100. On the gradual shift from women's history to gender history and the influence of Joan Scott in particular see Des Jardins, 'Women's and Gender History', *OHHW*, vol. V. Joan Wallach Scott's own early work in the area is included in her *Gender and the Politics of History* (New York, 1988).

Intellectual history and psychohistory

For surveys of the history of ideas, cultural history and similar approaches see Peter Burke, *What is Cultural History?* (Cambridge, 2004) and Donald R. Kelley, *The Descent of Ideas: The History of Intellectual History* (Burlington, VT, 2002). For the failure of intellectual history to catch on as a method in India see K. N. Panikkar, 'The Intellectual History of Colonial India: Some Historiographical and Conceptual Questions', in Sabyasachi Bhattachaya and Romila Thapar (eds.), *Situating Indian History* (Delhi, 1986), 403–33. On psychohistory see Lynn Hunt, 'Psychology, Psychoanalysis and Historical Thought', in Lloyd Kramer and Sarah Maza (eds.), *A Companion to Western Historical Thought* (Oxford, 2002), 337–56. A defence and critique respectively are offered by Peter Gay, *Freud for Historians* (New York, 1985) and David E. Stannard, *Shrinking History: On Freud and the Failure of Psychohistory* (New York, 1973).

The linguistic turn, postmodernism and postcolonialism

For an early consideration of the linguistic turn see Linda Orr, 'The Revenge of Literature: A History of History', *New Literary History* 18 (1986–7): 1–21. For an especially clear exposition of the links between poststructuralist thinkers and their predecessors see Allan Megill, *Prophets of Extremity: Nietzsche, Heidegger, Foucault and Derrida* (Berkeley, CA, 1985). On Hayden White, see Frank Ankersmit, Ewa Domańska and Hans Kellner (eds.), *Re-figuring Hayden White* (Stanford, CA, 2009). For a Marxist labour historian's critique of the poststructuralist turn see Bryan D. Palmer, *Descent into Discourse: The Reification of Language and the Writing of Social History* (Philadelphia, 1990). Conservative reactions include Keith Windschuttle, *The Killing of History: How Literary Critics and Social Theorists are Murdering our Past* (New York, 1997) and G. R. Elton, *Return to Essentials: Some Reflections on the Present State of Historical Study* (Cambridge, 1991). More positive reflections can be found in Mark Poster, *Cultural History and Postmodernity: Disciplinary Readings and Challenges* (New York, 1997) and Patrick Joyce, 'The Return of History: Postmodernism and the Politics of Academic History in Britain', *Past and Present* 158 (1998): 207–35. Among the more well-argued and moderate reactions to the perceived enemies of Clio see Joyce Appleby, Lynn Hunt and Margaret Jacob, *Telling the Truth about History* (New

York, 1994); the common-sense approach taken by Richard J. Evans, *In Defense of History* (London, 1997), while regarded by some of its critics as theoretically naive, is nonetheless a good introduction to the issues at stake, and points out that many of the epistemological issues raised by postmodernism have been considered by historians for a very long time. A collection of some of the key exchanges (edited by one of postmodern history's most extreme exponents) is Keith Jenkins, *The Postmodern History Reader* (London, 1997).

For postcolonialism and Subaltern studies, apart from Edward Said's *Orientalism* (London, 1978), there are several key monographs, articles and essay collections. Ranajit Guha's work is essential, including: *An Indian Historiography of India: A Nineteenth-Century Agenda and its Implications* (Calcutta and New Delhi, 1988) and 'On Some Aspects of the Historiography of Colonial India', in Ranajit Guha and Gayatri Chakravorty Spivak (eds.), *Selected Subaltern Studies* (New York and Oxford, 1988), 37–44 and Guha, *History at the Limit of World-History* (New York, 2002). A somewhat more extreme position on Western historicity is taken by Ashis Nandy, 'History's Forgotten Doubles', *History and Theory* 34:2 (1995): 44–66, and many of its views are extended in Vinay Lal, *The History of History: Politics and Scholarship in Modern India* (Oxford and New Delhi, 2003). See also Arif Dirlik, Vinay Bahl and Peter Gran (eds.), *History after the Three Worlds: Post-Eurocentric Historiographies* (Oxford, 2000); Dipesh Chakrabarty, *Provincializing Europe: Postcolonial Thought and Historical Difference* (Princeton, NJ, 2000); Axel Harneit-Sievers (ed.), *A Place in the World: New Local Historiographies from Africa and South-Asia* (Leiden, 2002); Arnold Temu and Bonaventure Swai, *Historians and Africanist History: A Critique. Post-Colonial Historiography Examined* (London, 1981); Sugata Bose, 'Post-Colonial Histories of South Asia: Some Reflections', *Journal of Contemporary History* 38 (2003): 133–46; Robert Young, *White Mythologies: Writing History and the West* (London, 1990); Harish Trivedi and Meenakshi Mukherjee (eds.), *Interrogating Post-Colonialism: Theory, Text and Context* (Rashtrapati Nivas, Shimla, 1996); and Michel-Rolph Trouillot, *Silencing the Past: Power and the Production of History* (Boston, 1995). For a challenge to the postcolonial indictment of the Enlightenment as relentlessly imperialistic see Sankar Muthu, *Enlightenment against Empire* (Princeton, NJ, 2003). '

Revisionism and history wars/The fragmentation of historiography

For episodes of controversy over historical pedagogy in the twentieth century see Gary B. Nash, Charlotte Crabtree and Ross E. Dunn, *History on Trial: Culture Wars and the Teaching of the Past* (New York, 1997). Peter Novick, *That Noble Dream: The 'Objectivity Question' and the American Historical Profession* (Cambridge, 1988), discusses post-war fragmentation within the discipline. Several other high-profile American cases of attacks on historians, many though not all ideologically motivated, are discussed in Jon Wiener, *Historians in Trouble* (New York, 2005). For the particular controversy of the atomic bomb display in the National Air and Space Museum see Richard H. Kohn, 'History at Risk: The Case of Enola Gay', in Edward T. Linenthal and Tom Engelhardt (eds.),

History Wars: The Enola Gay and Other Battles for the American Past (New York, 1996), 140–70; and Linenthal, 'Anatomy of a Controversy', ibid., 9–62. On Australian history wars see Stuart Macintyre and Anna Clark, *The History Wars* (Carlton, Australia, 2003); Keith Windschuttle, *The Fabrication of Aboriginal History*, vol. 1: *Van Diemen's Land, 1803–1847* (Sydney, 2002) and 'Doctored Evidence and Invented Incidents in Aboriginal Historiography', in Bain Attwood and S. G. Foster (eds.), *Frontier Conflict: The Australian Experience* (Canberra, 2003), 99–112. On memory and historical writing see Alon Confino, *Germany as a Culture of Remembrance: Promises and Limits of Writing History* (Chapel Hill, NC, 2006) and Jeffrey K. Olick (ed.), *States of Memory: Continuities, Conflicts, and Transformations in National Retrospection* (Durham, NC, 2003). On sites of memory see Pierre Nora, 'Between Memory and History: Les Lieux de Mémoire', *Representations* 26 (1989): 7–25. For the various 'textbook' controversies that have occurred globally in recent years see Edward Vickers and Alisa Jones (eds.), *History Education and National Identity in East Asia* (New York and London, 2005); Laura Hein and Mark Selden (eds.), *Censoring History: Citizenship and Memory in Japan, Germany, and the United States* (Armonk, NY and London, 2000); and Nozaki Yoshiko, *War Memory, Nationalism, and Education in Postwar Japan, 1945–2007: The Japanese Textbook Controversy and Ienaga Saburo's Court Challenge* (London, 2008).

On indigenous historicity in the Americas see Peter Nabokov, *A Forest of Time: American Indian Ways of History* (Cambridge, 2002); Penny Petrone, *Native Literature in Canada: From the Oral Tradition to the Present* (Toronto, 1990); Julie Cruikshank, *The Social Life of Stories: Narrative and Knowledge in the Yukon Territory* (Vancouver, 1998); Thomas A. Abercrombie, *Pathways of Memory and Power: Ethnography and History among an Andean People* (Madison, WI, 1988); David Carey, Jr., *Our Elders Teach Us: Maya-Kaqchikel Historical Perspectives* (Tuscaloosa, 2001); Joanne Rappaport, *The Politics of Memory: Native Historical Interpretation in the Colombian Andes*, rev. edn (Durham, NC, 1998); Jonathan D. Hill (ed.), *Rethinking History and Myth: Indigenous South American Perspectives on the Past* (Urbana, IL and Chicago, 1988); and Neil L. Whitehead (ed.), *Histories and Historicities in Amazonia* (Lincoln, NE and London, 2003).

For some prominent examples of global history and world history see I. Wallerstein, *The Modern World System*, 3 vols. (New York, 1974–89), a key work in the 'dependency' school; Janet L. Abu-Lughod, *Before European Hegemony* (New York, 1989); Philip D. Curtin, *Cross-Cultural Trade in World History* (New York, 1984); and Alfred W. Crosby, *The Columbian Exchange: Biological and Cultural Consequences of 1492* (Westport, CT, 1972). Global history as a trend in historical writing is treated in Patrick Manning, *Navigating World History: Historians Create a Global Past* (Houndmills, UK, 2003) and Pamela Kyle Crossley, *What is Global History?* (Cambridge, 2008). See also Jerry H. Bentley, 'World History', in *GEHW*, 968–71 and Bentley, 'The New World History', in Kramer and Maza (eds.), *A Companion to Western Historical Thought*, 393–416. For a comparative approach to the subject see Dominic Sachsenmaier, *Global Perspectives on Global History: Patterns in the United States, Germany and China* (Cambridge, 2011), which had not yet appeared as the present book went to press but which I had the opportunity to read in manuscript.

INDEX

Notes: For reasons of space persons mentioned only in passing are not indexed.
Page numbers in **bold** indicate principal subjects of extracts or boxed sections.